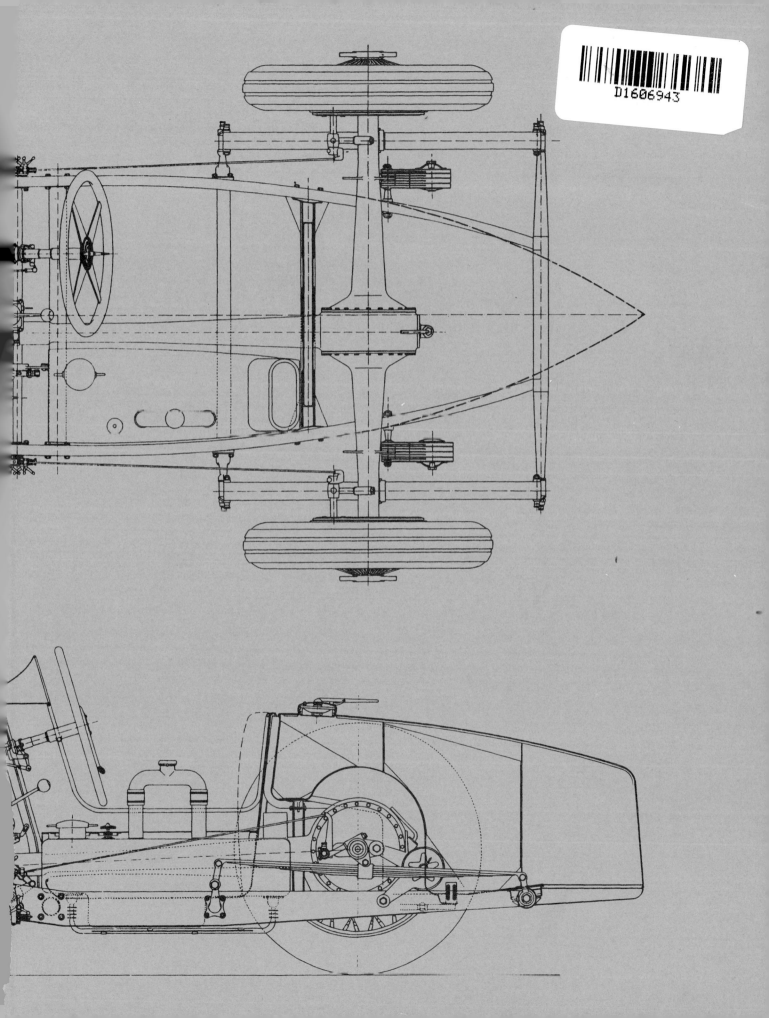

The V12 Engine

Other books by this author

ISBN 1 85960 649 0
£25.00

ISBN 1 85960 655 5
£25.00

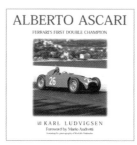

ISBN 1 85960 680 6
£25.00

ISBN 1 85960 824 8
£25.00

ISBN 1 85960 625 3
£25.00

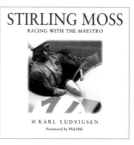

ISBN 1 85960 816 7
£25.00

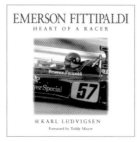

ISBN 1 85960 837 X
£25.00

ISBN 1 85960 436 6
£25.00

The V12 Engine

THE UNTOLD INSIDE STORY OF THE TECHNOLOGY, EVOLUTION, PERFORMANCE AND IMPACT OF ALL V12-ENGINED CARS

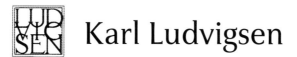 Karl Ludvigsen

Haynes Publishing

My brother Eric
In memoriam

First published in June 2005

A catalogue record for this book is available from the
British Library

ISBN 1 84425 004 0

Library of Congress catalog card no 2005921420

Haynes North America Inc., 861 Lawrence Drive,
Newbury Park, California 91320, USA.

Published by Haynes Publishing, Sparkford, Yeovil,
Somerset BA22 7JJ, UK.

Tel: 01963 442030 Fax: 01963 440001
Int. tel: +44 1963 442030 Int. fax: +44 1963 440001
E-mail: sales@haynes.co.uk
Website: www.haynes.co.uk

Printed and bound in Britain by J. H. Haynes & Co. Ltd,
Sparkford

Contents

Introduction   9

Chapter 1 ORIGINS   12

The early debate over the number of cylinders an auto engine should have – Daimler's vee-twin and its connecting-rod layout – side-by-side rods, link rods and fork-and-blade rods – developments in other fields, marine and aviation, with up to 24 cylinders – the first-ever V12 of 1904, made in Britain for marine racing – Sunbeam's Toodles V of 1913 is the first European V12 auto – Packard takes an interest – in 1908 George Schebler builds the first V12-powered car.

Chapter 2 AMERICAN TWIN SIXES   26

Duesenberg and Miller build V12 aero engines – Buick and Hudson assess twelves – Packard sets the pace, first with aero engines and then in 1915 with its spectacular and dramatic Twin Six – many others follow quickly: National, Enger, Haynes and Pathfinder, the last using the Weidely V12, as did HAL, Austin, Meyer, Kissel, Singer, Ambassador, Meteor and Heine-Velox.

Chapter 3 EUROPEAN TWELVES   50

Exploration of twelves by Lorraine-Dietrich, Lancia, Fiat and Voisin – Sunbeam's spectacular twelves – the 350 hp that Malcolm Campbell used to break the land speed record – 4-litre Tiger and Tigresse, LSR success for Segrave – Delage's 10.7-litre DH record-breaker – its magnificent Grand Prix 2-liter of 1925 – Cappa's bizarre design for Itala, the smallest V12 ever – Fiat's Type 806 U12 of 1927.

Chapter 4 AERO SPEED   74

Napier's W12 Lion from World War 1 powers Golden Arrow, Campbell's Blue Bird and Cobb's Railtons, one for his track car and two for his land-speed-record breaker – Australia's 'Wizard' Smith – America's Liberty V12 and successful LSR cars Babs and Triplex – the '1,000 horsepower' Sunbeam with its twin aero engines for Segrave – Sunbeam's disastrous Silver Bullet – R-Type Rolls-Royce used by Campbell in Blue Bird and (two of them) by Eyston's Thunderbolt – Rolls-Royce Kestrel in Eyston's Speed of the Wind – Curtiss Conqueror the choice of long-distance record-breaker Ab Jenkins – Porsche-designed Type 80 for Mercedes-Benz.

Chapter 5 CLASSIC-ERA AMERICANS   106

Late 1920s and early 1930s see explosion of twelves in America's classic-car era – Cadillac pioneers, followed by air-cooled Franklin – Packard returns to the fray with a race-bred V12 – Lincoln's KB and KA twelves – Buffalo's Pierce-Arrow builds America's biggest twelve of this era – extraordinary Cord E-1 provides the basis for Auburn's ultra-affordable Lycoming-built V12 – Howard Marmon and his HCM prototype.

Chapter 6 BRITISH AND FRENCH CLASSICS   128

Eminent European auto companies embrace the twelve – Laurence Pomeroy at Daimler produces no less than five different series, all with sleeve valves save the last – Rolls-Royce produces its most controversial model ever, the Phantom III – Walter Bentley designs a V12 for Lagonda and races it at Le Mans – Gabriel Voisin returns in 1929 with sleeve-valve twelves – Lorraine-Dietrich is heard from – Hispano-Suiza caps the era with by far the biggest twelve of the times.

Chapter 7 TEUTONIC TWELVES 150

Germanic nations were not left behind – Ledwink's T80 for Tatra – other Czech twelves by Walter and Gräf & Stift – Horch and its ambitious V12 patterned after American examples – Maybach builds one of Europe's most elaborate twelves without regard to cost – just before the war Mercedes-Benz launches V12 prototypes.

Chapter 8 RACERS IN AMERICA 170

Auburn's V12 Speedster sets records on the dry lakes – Ab Jenkins and Pierce Arrow get together to break speed records at Bonneville – evolution of the Ab Jenkins Special – Charles Voelker's V12 is launched at Indy in 1937 – Voelker engine competes at the Speedway twice and is still trying to qualify in 1953.

Chapter 9 GRAND PRIX GLORIES 180

V12s come into their own in racing in the 1930s – amazing record-breaker of Voisin – Alfa Romeo's Type A with two sixes side by side – Alfa Romeo's 12C-36 Grand Prix car and its successors through 1939 – creation of an unblown sports-car version, the 412, in 1939 – Alfa Romeo's S10 V12 road-car prototypes – 12-cylinder Mercedes record-breakers and Avus racers powered by the big DAB engine – successful 1938-39 Grand Prix twelves of both Auto Union and Mercedes-Benz – Auto Union's designs for a 1½-litre E-Type V12 – Lago Talbot's V12 plans by Walter Becchia – Louis Delage's V12 sports-racer of 1937 – Delahaye's Type 145 twelve and winning 'The Million' at Montlhéry – monoposto edition a flop – Delahaye Type 165 production version.

Chapter 10 POST-WAR POTENCY 216

Aero engines in cars again – Rolls-Royce Kestrel in Flying Triangle, Merlin in Swandean Spitfire Special, Meteor in 2003 Thunderbolt that broke British records at Millbrook – America's Allison V12 is taken up by many – Jim Lytle puts one in a BMW Isetta and four in a Fiat Topolino – Art Arfons starts a record-breaking career with Allisons – Athol Graham's 300+ mph at Bonneville – Enzo Ferrari builds twelves – Colombo's 125, 159, 166 and four-cam 125F1 engines – Mercedes-Benz plans a 1½-litre V12, its M195 – Auto Union engineers build the 2-liter 'Sokol' Type 650 – Ferrari's big twelves, the 375 and 340 America – Gordini and OSCA collaborate on the design of their Type G 4½-litre V12 – Lagonda's disappointing DP100 V12 – Ferrari's big twelves: 375MM, 375 America, 290MM and 315S through 1957 – smaller Ferrari series: 212, 250MM, 250GT, 250TR, GTO – 4-litre Ferrari Type 209, 400 Superamerica and 330P2 – Giulio Alfieri's Maserati V12 in Grand Prix cars in 1957-58, 350S sports-racer, mid-engined Type 63 & 64.

Chapter 11 COMPETITION AMBITIONS 244

Two V12s built for the 1½-litre Formula 1, one by Maserati and one, which races, Honda's RA271E – Ferrari's four-cam sports-racers from the 330 P4 – stillborn twelves: Abarth's Type 240 and Moteur Moderne's engine – with the 3-litre Formula 1 in 1966, an eruption of vee-twelves – Ferrari 312F1-66, V12s through 1969, 312P prototype – big-twelve Ferrari family with 612P, 512P and 512S – Cooooper-Maserati engines, Types 9 and 10 – BRM P101, P142, twelves through 1977 – AAR's Eagle-Weslake V12 – Harry Weslake's own WRP-190 twelve and its travails – BRM P351 sports-racer engine broadly derived from it – Matra's shrieking V12s in both GP cars and sports-racers, MS9, MS12 – Autodelta's V12 for Brabham, Alfa's own car and engines for Osella – Honda's RA273E Grand Prix engine and Nissan's sports-racing R382.

Chapter 12 ENGINES FOR THE ELITE 284

Lincoln's Zephyr V12 is a link between luxury cars pre-war and port-war – insights into its troubled reputation – it does well in Britain in Allard, Brough, Atalanta and Jensen models – Packard considers relaunching a V12 – Bugatti designs a V12, its Type 451, but the company folds before it can mature – GM's Cadillac develops a V12 in the early 1960s but decides against production – two dreamers, Franco Romanelli in Canada and Alejandro de Tomaso in Italy, show twelves but don't produce them – Ferrari's luxury models from 365GT to 275GTB/4, 365GTB/4 Daytona, 365GTC4, 400I and 412 – newcomer Lamborghini decides on a twelve – 350GT, Miura, Islero, Countach and four-valve version.

Chapter 13 CAT, ROUNDEL AND STAR   308

As early as the 1950s Jaguar starts planning a V12 – its four-cam racing version in the 1960s in the XJ13 – insights into the gestation of the great Jaguar V12 by Heynes, Hassan, Mundy et al – its use in racing in USA and Europe, leading to victory at Le Mans – BMW begins studying V12s as a marriage of two of its fine sixes – experimental M70, M73 and M66 prototypes – introduction of M70 V12 in 1987, improved as M73 in 1994 – BMW's activity spurred Mercedes-Benz engineers, who had been thinking of a V12, the M101, for their 600 – new 'KOMO' prototype of 1985 – using six-cylinder components to create the M120 of 1991 – employed in Pagani's Zonda – racing the M120 in AMG's CLK-GTR of 1997.

Chapter 14 FORMULA TWELVES   336

After the banning of turbos and the setting of a 3½-litre limit, Formula 1 exploded with 12-cylinder engines – designs for GM by Scott Russell – Motori Moderni's efforts – Austrian NeoTech engine for Walter Brun – designs from HKS, Nissan and Isuzu in Japan, their tests and problems – Paul Rosche's BMW studies including a six-cam 60-valve twelve – Porsche's catastrophic Type 3512 for Footwork Arrows – unraced twelves of Renault and Cosworth – the W12 idea is revived by Harry Mundy for his Trident, Guy Negré's MGN and Franco Rocchi's Life engine – Yamaha's entry, evolving into its OX99 road car, built in Britain – Honda's RA121E and successor RA122E/B – Lamborghini's 3512 V12 powers several teams including its own – Ferrari's Grand Prix V12s from 1989 through 1995 – derived from them, F50 and F333SP engines.

Chapter 15 AMERICAN AND GERMAN LUXURY   372

Comedian Jay Leno's 29,4 litre Patton tank V12-powered hot rod – Detroiter Cyril Batten's engines machined from scratch – Ryan Falconer's successful Chevrolet-derived V12s – their use in a prototype for a planned Packard revival – Cadillac's XV12 programme and its use in the mid-engined Cien – Mazda's V12 plans for its Amati range – Toyota introduces a V12 for its Japan-only Century prestige model – relationship between the new turbocharged Maybach V12 and the 3-valve Mercedes-Benz M137 twelve – AMG super-powered versions and an AMG engine for Chrysler's mid-engined ME Four-Twelve – BMW's twelves for the McLaren F1 and its P74 for a Le Mans winner – 2002 introduction of new N73 BMW twelve and its use as basis of engine for new Rolls-Royce Phantom – inside story of creation of VW's family of W12 engines – its use in record-breaking 'W12' sports car, Phaeton. Audi A8, Bentley Continental GT – Peugeot's '907' concept car of 2004.

Chapter 16 ULTIMATE SPORTS-CAR POWER   392

At Ford, engineer Jim Clark builds V12s – they power Ford's GT90 and Indigo concept cars – Aston Martin discovers them when looking for a new engine – creation of the Aston engines and their evolution to suit new models – TVR's Speed Twelve on a fabricated steel crankcase – Al Melling's engine design for a Lola GT car project – Monte Carlo's MCA Centenaire and its various twelves – Paolo Stanzani's amazing design for Bugatti's EB110 – new generation of big twelves for Lamborghini's cars, inspired by its sport-utility for Saudi Arabia – Ferrari's F116 and F133A evolution in its 456GT, 550 Maranello and 612 Scaglietti – new-generation F140 V12 introduced in Enzo in 2002 to be basis of future Ferrari twelves – F140 also powers Maserati's MC12, stunning new road and race car of 2004.

Appendix – V12 Firing Orders   410

Index   415

INTRODUCTION

No excuse is needed for tackling the topic of vee-twelve engines in cars. They've always woven a certain fascination, and for good reason. The twelve is a wonderfully well-balanced mechanism, sprightly and supple as well as strong. On driving a Hispano-Suiza twelve, car connoisseur Cecil Clutton wrote that "There is an indefinable magic about every V12 I have driven, whether it is this one, or the [Rolls-Royce] PIII, or the splendid Packard, or the one-and-only 10½-litre world-speed-record Delage."

"I don't know what it is about V12s," remarked Damon Hill, 1996 F1 World Champion, "but this arrangement delivers a peculiar pulse that is the sonic equivalent of strawberry mousse and cream." "When I hear your twelve cylinders," wrote famed conductor Herbert von Karajan to Enzo Ferrari, "I hear a burst of harmony that no conductor could ever re-create."

"I loved the early Ferrari V12s," said 1961 world-champion driver Phil Hill. "An important aspect of the Ferrari engine is its multiple stages of performance. They are beautifully flexible from way down in the revs where you have a nice little power band for any kind of pottering around. The more revs you use, the more torque and power are available." So wedded to his twelves was Enzo Ferrari, in fact, that in the mid-1980s he threatened to desert Formula 1 and race in CART instead if any lesser limit on numbers of cylinders was imposed. Fortunately he wasn't around to see Ferrari lop two cylinders from its Grand Prix cars in 1996.

A fallow period for vee-twelves came in the late 1950s, when Ferrari was the type's main advocate. "It is a great source of surprise to me that the type now survives solely by the championship of the Commendatore," wrote Laurence Pomeroy, Jnr at that time. "The V12 engine seems an excellent compromise between a lack of effective piston area in the 6-cylinder unit and over-complexity with a V16, and many of the great racing engines of the past have been of this configuration."

How right Pomeroy was. Among the great racing twelves during his time were those of Delage, Sunbeam, Alfa Romeo, Mercedes-Benz and Auto Union. Road twelves were legion as well, from the American explosion before and after World War I to a global eruption into and through the 1930s. Ferrari showed the way after Hitler's War and many followed. Vee-twelves for racing were much in favour in the 3-litre Grand Prix Formula 1 starting in 1966 and again when the limit became 3½ litres in 1987. In the modern era no major auto maker seemed satisfied unless he had a vee-twelve to call his own.

This isn't to say that the power race among car makers is viewed with unalloyed approval in this politically correct age. "Flashy 12-cylinder cars have no place on a planet increasingly beset by damaging greenhouse gases," wrote a correspondent to *Business Week* in 2004.

*Opposite: **Matra's magnificent 3.0-litre V12 of 1968 exemplifies the twelve-cylinder fever of the new 1966 Grand Prix Formula 1 that saw such engines on the grid from BRM, Ferrari, AAR Eagle, Maserati and Honda as well. The lure of the twelve has always been strong for racing-car engineers, who exploited its high-revving potential. Conversely, its silky, seamless smoothness has been the attraction for luxury-car designers. Both racing cars and road cars have kept the V12 alive and well in the 21st Century.***

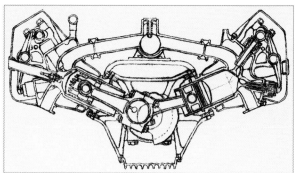

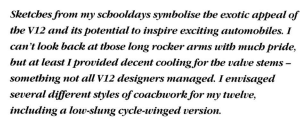

Sketches from my schooldays symbolise the exotic appeal of the V12 and its potential to inspire exciting automobiles. I can't look back at those long rocker arms with much pride, but at least I provided decent cooling for the valve stems – something not all V12 designers managed. I envisaged several different styles of coachwork for my twelve, including a low-slung cycle-winged version.

Road & Track correspondent Paul Frère, who won Le Mans in a V12 Ferrari in 1960, expressed concern about the 'power race' in 2002. "Is it really so important for a large sedan to accelerate to 60 mph in 5 rather than 7 or 7.5 seconds?" he asked.

"I am not talking about road safety," Frère continued. "What I am talking about is the waste of a non-renewable source of energy and an insult to reasonable ecologists and common sense." He pointed out that big-engined cars running at moderate speeds are far from what one engineer called the 'sweet spot' of best power with lowest fuel consumption. Paul Frère concluded that "the current power race is only an absurd matter of prestige among manufacturers," whom he urged to find a way to curb their excesses.

These minatory observations have had little braking effect on car makers' rush to power. As this book was written vee-twelve road cars boasting more than 500 horsepower were on offer from Aston Martin, Bentley, Ferrari, Lamborghini, Maserati, Maybach and Mercedes-Benz. Some indeed surpassed the 600-horse level. It's difficult to disagree with Paul Frère's view that this is excessive. When car makers see fit to engage in 'mine's bigger than yours' competitions, however, it's not easy to apply the stoppers. And when more power is required, the twelve-cylinder engine is often asked to oblige.

This volume makes the bold claim to cover all vee-twelve-engined cars since the very first, George Schebler's 1908 roadster. It even aims to describe engines and projects that were mooted or planned but for one reason or another didn't take to the road or enter production. The knowledgeable reader will test me by

looking for the most obscure twelve in his memory bank; I'm sure they're out there and I'll look forward to getting cards and letters that will allow me to update the next edition accordingly.

Definitely *not* included is the range of vee-twelve-engined cars that I sketched in high school. They were powered by a V12 engine of $4\frac{1}{2}$ litres with its banks set at a BRM-influenced 135° angle – not ideal for a twelve, as I know now. Roots-supercharged, my dry-sump engine had one-piece heads and cylinders and long rocker arms that opened its exhaust valves from a single overhead camshaft. I can see its many faults today but it did make a nice drawing.

I'd best confess at this point that other twelves not included are all flat-opposed engines. I ruled them out as a topic too far. Perhaps horizontal boxer-type engines deserve a book to themselves. Thus I apologise to fans of the Ferrari 312B and Porsche 917.[1] Among engines that *are* included, however, are all so-called W-type twelves that have three or more banks of cylinders. These range from the great Napier Lion of World War I to the less-than-great Life W12 of 1990. Also included are the remarkable W12 engines in the VW Group's inventory.

I apologise also to those younger readers for whom Watts and Newton-metres are as natural as breathing. By far the bulk of the engines described were born in the era of horsepower and pound-feet so I've used those units where applicable. I've also calculated all cylinder displacements against bore and stroke dimensions, often finding discrepancies or cases where rounding in the wrong direction has given a misleading impression of an engine's capacity. Thus while some of the values given will differ from those found elsewhere, I hope they're more accurate.

One topic that I haven't touched on in the text is the issue of firing order. Although I appreciate the importance of firing order to the efficient functioning of a twelve, it seemed an engineering step too far for this narrative. Fortunately, as a member of the Aviation Engine Historical Society I found that this topic had been

dealt with masterfully by Dan Whitney, who penetrated the codes of the producers to reveal the actual firing orders of a number of engines. To my surprise, Dan found nine different firing orders in the twelves he investigated. With his permission and that of the AEHS – for which many thanks – an abridgement of Dan's findings is an Appendix to this volume.

I must also apologise for the lack of a bibliography. It simply wasn't practicable to list all the thousands of sources, the books, periodicals and reports that were consulted in the writing of this history. I've tried to give credit where it's due in the text when quoting from various sources; I hope this will be judged satisfactory.

A key source, one that gave me the confidence to undertake this project, consisted of the Van Wyck Hewlett Papers in the Ludvigsen Library. An automotive engineer on New York's Long Island, Van was an indefatigable clipper and collector of technical periodicals from the turn of the last Century. Thanks to his files I was able to gain a good appreciation of the early evolution of the vee-twelve both in America and abroad.

Away from base I've pestered, annoyed and interviewed many experts and engineers to get their perspective on the evolution of the automotive vee-twelve. I am deeply in their debt. Among those who have assisted are Sabu Advani, Ian Arnold, Frank Barrett, Stephe Boddice, Ermanno Bonfiglioli, Michael Bowler, Terry Boyce, Barbara Brailey, Michael Bromley, Paul Bryant, Paul Buckett, David Burgess-Wise, Reeves Callaway, Marco Cassinelli, Bill Close, Leroy Cole, Eric Coyne, Trevor Crisp, Sean Danaher, Josh Davidson, Patrick Delage, Richard Divila, Brandy Elitch, Jessie Embry, James Fack, Nathalie Fiancette, Herb Fishel, Brian Fitzsimons, Katia Gamberini, Antonio Ghini, Geoff Goddard, John Grant, Guiseppe Greco, Karen Hall, Rick Hall, Peter Hofbauer, David Holland, Tim Jackson, Michael Kacsala and D. J. Kava.

I also express my thanks for the assistance provided by

Beverly Rae Kimes, David King, Gerd Langer, Richard Langworth, Sasha Lanz, David Lee, Robert Lenz, Mary Ellen Loscar, Robert Lutz, Jim Lytle, Josh Malks, Paul Marr, Alfieri Maserati, Ralph McKittrick, Ron McQueeney, Al Melling, William Morrison, Robert Neal, Peter Nicholson, Rory O'Curry, Graham Orme-Bannister, Harold Pace, Peter Panarisi, James Patterson, Stanislav Peschel, Tracy Powell, Barbara Prince, Günther Raupp, Eric Rosenau, Kate Samuelson, Kenichi Sasaki, Annette Schultz, Mamoru Shinshi, Kees Smit, Brian Smith, Eiji Taguchi, Dick Teeter, Greg Wallace, Tim Watson, Bernie Weis, Gordon White, Chris Willows, George Wingard, Anne Wittstamm, Peter Wright, Jack Yamaguchi and Tim Younes. As always, the author alone is responsible for all errors and omissions.

At home I've enjoyed the great support of my wife Annette and my stepson Sam Turner, who looked after the Ludvigsen Library. Thanks so much to you both. At Haynes, Mark Hughes and Steve Rendle are among those most involved with bringing home a project that expanded somewhat beyond both their expectations and those of the author. Many thanks indeed to you and your professional team at Sparkford.

I suppose we've taken a venturesome line in producing this book. It's not a marque history with a predictable audience. It's not focused on racing, or on sports cars, or on classic cars. It spreads its twelve-cylindrical wings widely over the whole world of cars, indeed since the first-ever V12 was built for marine racing in 1904. Whether it has merit will depend entirely on how interested you are in engines. If you are, I'm confident you'll find much to relish in the amazing saga of the vee-twelve-engined car.

Karl Ludvigsen
Scoles Gate
Hawkedon, Suffolk
January 2005

[1] Both are described in my book *Classic Racing Engines* (Haynes Publishing).

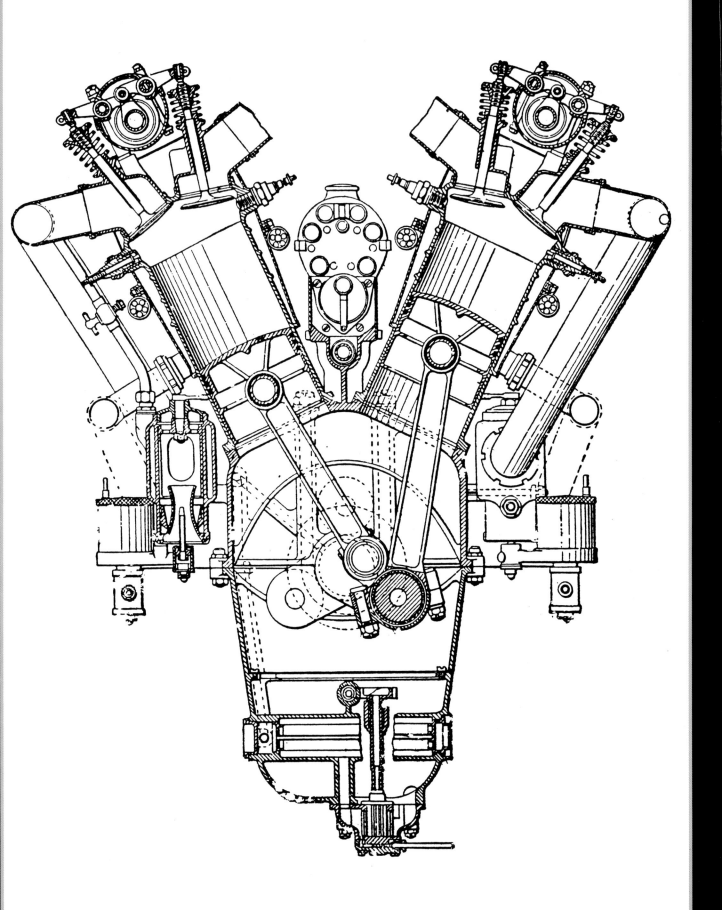

Chapter 1

ORIGINS

It may seem obvious that more cylinders produce more power, but how to use those cylinders and how to deploy them strained the best brains of the motor industry in the first years of the 20th Century. Power was not the only issue, of course. Other early engine-related concerns included smoothness of power application, vibration-related problems, durability, fuel economy and cost. Numbers of cylinders and their disposition would play an important role in automobile-engine design in the years leading up to World War I.

After the turn of the century the world's auto industry had effectively standardised its use of in-line four-cylinder engines. Their archetype was the 1901 Mercedes designed for the Daimler Motor Company by Wilhelm Maybach. It used mechanically operated rather than automatic inlet valves and placed its valves in the 'T-head' configuration, beside the cylinders and parallel to them with the inlet valves on one side and exhausts on the other, operated by two camshafts placed low in the block alongside the crankshaft. This obliged the use of a wide combustion chamber, extending across the engine from valve to valve above the piston, which was not too onerous at a time when compression ratios were still low, less than 4.0:1.

The in-line four had many advantages for early autos. It could easily be assembled from four individual cylinders on a common crankcase. During the first decade of the Century they'd be cast in pairs and finally as a single cylinder block, after machinists gained confidence that their techniques were good enough to produce four good bores – and the other necessary apertures – in a single casting. Machining errors in a single cylinder had less disastrous consequences.

Engineers still struggling with inlet-manifold design found the four-cylinder engine relatively easy to feed from their updraft carburettors. A simple Y-manifold from a single instrument to a pair of Siamesed inlet ports would give near-equality of distribution. Ignition too was straightforward. Cranking a four to start it wasn't difficult, aided by the massive flywheel that a four needed to smooth out its power delivery. The engine didn't require too much space and gave excellent access to all its parts for service. The four's fewer parts, most engineers reckoned, meant fewer likely to fail.

Fewer, that is, than a six-cylinder engine. America's first six was the Gasmobile, a lone prototype introduced at 1902's New York Show. Europe's first was the Dutch Spyker of 1903, though it too remained a prototype. Also, in 1903 Montague Napier and Selwyn F. Edge of Napiers introduced England's first series-production six, a type for which Edge would be an active and successful advocate. In 1904 both Napier and Sunbeam offered sixes. Two companies, Stevens-Duryea and National, introduced sixes to the American market in 1905, followed a year later by Ford. No sooner had Henry Ford introduced his six, however, than he abandoned it, saying, "A car should not have any more cylinders than a cow has teats." National, too, gave up its production of sixes in 1909.

Opposite: *Among the makers of twelve-cylinder engines for aircraft during World War I, Renault was a pioneer. It used master and link rods for a twelve produced toward the end of the war with liquid-cooled cylinders and a vee angle of 47.5°.*

"Most makers furnish the six-cylinder power plant on the larger models," reported Victor Pagé in 1911, "because it is an advantage to increase the number of cylinders rather than their cubical contents when more powerful motors are needed." The six was quieter too, Pagé averred, because "the lapping of the expulsion of spent gases means that the flow through the muffler is continuous, making for more uniform pressure in the silencer and tending to minimise the noise produced as the gas is discharged in the outer air."

With the state of the auto industry's early art, however, an in-line six posed engineering challenges. The most severe was twisting of its crankshaft. Big cylinder bores combined with small main and big-end bearings to create spindly and stretched-out crankshafts that contorted excessively. For this reason, wrote H. Davis, "the early versions possessed a fierce crankshaft vibration expressing itself in an abominable rattling noise." One pioneer motorist referred to "octaves of chatter from the quivering crankshaft" of his sixes. Overcoming this torsional flexing and resulting fractures was possible but only with bottom-end components that were more massive and thus heavier than the engine's power and torque levels mandated. A more superficial approach, said Davis, was adopted by Napier's arch-publicist Selwyn Edge, who "made the most of it by calling it a 'power rattle'."

Induction was another challenge. The simplicity of feeding four cylinders contrasted with the bizarre convolutions to which some designers resorted for six-cylinder carburation from a single instrument. In many early sixes equality of fuel/air-mixture distribution among the cylinders was more by chance than calculation. Starting was another bugbear, with a huge six anything but easy to crank. By 1911 the introduction of self-starting devices began to overcome this handicap. Finally, these engines were long as well as heavy, taking up valuable chassis space.

The moment of truth came for Wilfred Leland after a drive from Washington to New York in a new Hudson six. With his father Henry, Leland was a guiding light of Detroit's Cadillac, renowned in its early years for the precision of design, machining and assembly insisted upon – and implemented by – both Lelands. Cadillac's engineers were developing an in-line six, but Wilfred harboured severe reservations about its potential smoothness. "Noisy sixes, even though more powerful than fours, could not be allowed to walk away with a competitor's prize," recalled Wilfred's widow. "Wilfred's mind was occupied with these vibrations and how to overcome them."

After his Hudson drives the younger Leland turned over the problem in his mind, including a sleepless night on the trail from New York back to Detroit. His solution was novel, albeit not unique: "putting two fours together at an angle," his wife remembered. He dictated his concept to her: "eight smaller cylinders would produce lighter impulses, more frequent impulses and smoother action." Accepting his idea, Cadillac stopped work on its six and built an influential V8 instead. It was introduced in September 1914 as a 1915 model.

Here was a solution that perfectly suited the needs of the time. A V8 could draw on all the knowledge already invested in in-line fours, including their induction and ignition. Its short crankshaft would present few torsional-vibration problems. By setting its banks at a 90° included angle, a V8 could be made to generate power impulses at regular intervals. With a much lighter crankcase and crankshaft, the V8 could also weigh less than a six of comparable output.

Such was Cadillac's reputation – as the two-time winner of Britain's prestigious Dewar Trophy – that its introduction of a V8 was the strongest vote yet in favour of a vee-type engine for cars. Its predecessors were many. Composed of the tandem mounting of two V4s, the first V8 to be used in a car powered three of Clément-Agnès Ader's entries in the Paris-Madrid Race of 1903. Also in France, Léon Levavasseur was designing and building ultra-light water-cooled V8s for use in racing boats and aircraft. Made by the Société Antoinette, named in honour of its chairman's daughter, from 1905 these engines powered the successful early years of French aviation.

It was noteworthy that Levavasseur did not attempt a V12. Instead, he added power by adding V8 modules. For boat racing he built an Antoinette V16 this way, and then a V24 with its clusters of four individual opposing cylinders all on a single crankcase. With what Ettore Bugatti called "delicatessen engineering, manipulating cylinders like strings of sausages," Levavasseur even essayed a V32 and then a V48 but, as Griff Borgeson wrote, "this was beyond the point of diminishing returns". 'Delicatessen engineering' was inadequate to keep the rapid pace of the growing aero industry and Antoinette engines – and even a short-lived Antoinette V8 automobile – were soon obsolete.

With lightness and simplicity a major virtue of the Antoinettes, we should spare a moment to consider how they tackled the problem of two facing cylinders sharing a common big-end journal, on the crankshaft. Here was one of the toughest challenges facing the early engineers. Some of them argued that with two pistons and connecting rods driven by and driving a journal the loads

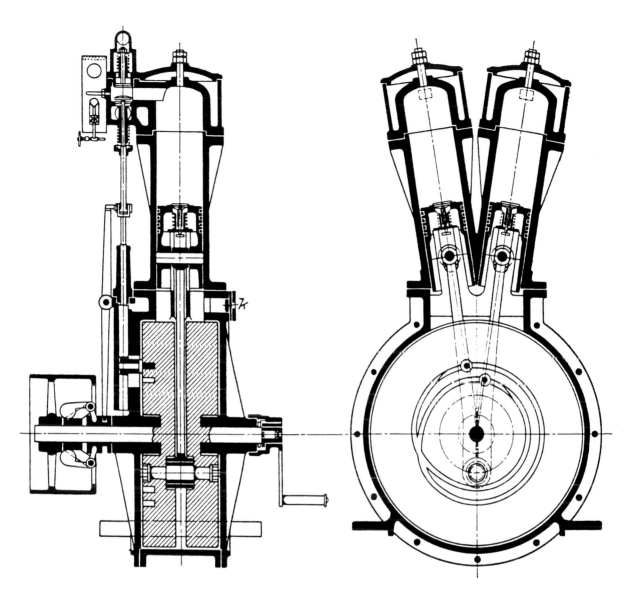

to which it was subjected were much higher, while others maintained that the loads came at different times from different directions so the journal's burden wasn't that much greater. Either way, a means of attaching two connecting rods to one journal had to be found.

Léon Levavasseur's solution was to offset one bank of cylinders longitudinally from the other – the right-hand bank being shifted forward in this case – so that facing con-rod big ends could sit side-by-side on the same crankshaft journal. Although some critics felt that this would make the engine too long, with the wide bearings that were then customary, this was not a disadvantage of the Antoinettes, which also enjoyed five main bearings that took up additional room along their crankshafts. The French engines ran reliably albeit at speeds of little more than 1,100rpm.

All vee-type engines trace their origins to the 1889 Daimler vee-twin designed by Wilhelm Maybach. Maybach arranged for the two connecting rods of the engine, with its 17° vee, to share a common crankpin with what became known as the fork-and-blade big-end bearing system.

Cadillac chose a different solution. It elected to use fork-and-blade big ends. These had been a feature of the first-ever vee-type Otto-cycle engine for cars, the 565cc twin, introduced in 1889 by Germany's Daimler.[1] Designed by Wilhelm Maybach, the 17° V2 powered Daimler's *Stahlradwagen* and the Panhards and Peugeots that competed in 1894's Paris-Rouen Trials. Maybach's fork-and-blade concept allowed the facing cylinders to be directly opposite each other by having one conventional-looking rod – the 'blade' – embraced

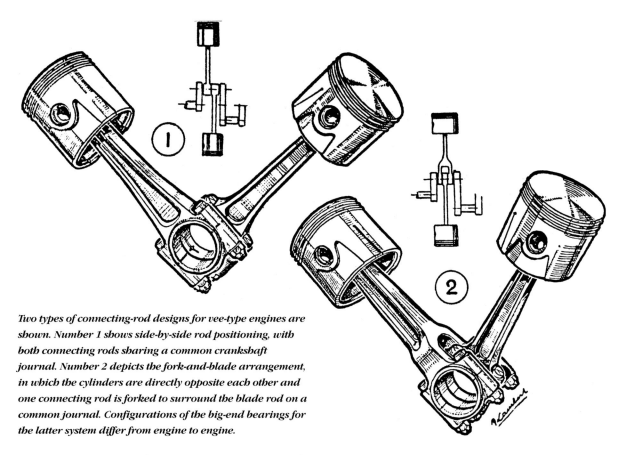

Two types of connecting-rod designs for vee-type engines are shown. Number 1 shows side-by-side rod positioning, with both connecting rods sharing a common crankshaft journal. Number 2 depicts the fork-and-blade arrangement, in which the cylinders are directly opposite each other and one connecting rod is forked to surround the blade rod on a common journal. Configurations of the big-end bearings for the latter system differ from engine to engine.

by a sister rod that was forked – hence its name – to fit around the blade rod and be held by two big-end bearings instead of one. Although several configurations were devised, this generally required the forked rod to have a separate journal inside its big end on which the blade rod's bearing ran.

Compared to side-by-side rods, the fork-and-blade design achieved a shorter engine because it didn't require the blocks to be offset. A slight improvement in dynamic balance resulted because the facing cylinders and pistons were in the same lateral plane. It was clearly more costly, with the need to make two different kinds of connecting rods, one with a more elaborate big-end design. This was not an obstacle in aero engines, built in smaller numbers under less cost constraints, so fork-and-blade rods were often used there. Examples were an experimental aero V12 made by Harry Miller in 1917 and the Liberty V12, America's most-produced aero engine of the First World War.

A third method of accommodating con-rod pairs in a vee engine was the use of a master rod and articulated

A third method of accommodating the rods and pistons of a vee-type engine, like the fork-and-blade system allowing the cylinders to oppose each other directly, employs a master connecting rod and a link rod joined to it by a pin analogous to a gudgeon pin. While keeping reciprocating masses light, this introduces an elliptical rather than circular motion for the pin to the link rod.

link. Like the fork-and-blade pairing, this allowed cylinders to face each other directly to create a light and compact engine. One rod looked conventional, with a big end that occupied the full crank journal. It differed, however, in having a pivot point near its big end. From this pivot a link rod extended to the facing piston. Master and link rods were joined by a pin not unlike a wrist or gudgeon pin.

Although not very elegant-looking, the articulated link was in fact a valid and often-used mechanism for vee-type engines. Its reciprocating masses were the lightest of all three solutions. A peculiarity was that the motion of the link pin as the crank rotated was not circular but elliptical, and in a manner that tended to give the linked piston a longer stroke than its master-rodded neighbour. In large engines with lower compression ratios running at moderate speeds this was not a matter for concern. Thus like fork-and-blade rods the link-rod system was widely used in aero engines, such as the first Rolls-Royce V12s produced in 1915.

Both aviation and marine engines played their part in the early evolution of vee engines with twelve cylinders. Nautical impetus came from the annual motor-boating carnival in the sea off Monaco and the races that were their highlight. Mention has already been made of the Antoinette vee-type engines that competed there. In 1904 London's Putney Motor Works completed a new marine racing engine: the first vee-twelve ever made for any purpose. Like the cars the company also produced, it was known as the Craig-Dörwald engine after Putney's founding partners.

The Putney artisans mounted pairs of L-head cylinders at a 90° included angle on an aluminium crankcase, using the same cylinder pairs that powered the company's standard two-cylinder car.[2] The Craig-Dörwald twelve had a single camshaft running down its central vee to open its valves directly. As in many marine engines the camshaft could be slid in its bearings to give timing that reversed the engine's rotation. Tubular connecting rods sat side-by-side on the rod journals, with the cylinder banks offset. To cope with the problem of the long crankshaft, the twelve's main bearings increased in diameter as they approached the flywheel. Its crankshaft was described as having 'fluted webs'.

Induction arrangements were exemplary with three carburettors each feeding four cylinders, nestling underneath a cylindrical collector that carried exhaust gases away. Trembler-coil ignition was used to start the twelve after its cylinders had been suffused with a fresh charge. Displacing 18,345cc (123.8 x 127mm), the Craig-Dörwald V12 weighed 950lb and developed 155bhp at

The first vee-type twelve-cylinder engine was produced in 1904 by the Putney Motor Works in London. Commissioned for a racing boat, the Craig-Dörwald V12 was impressively light at 950lb for its 18.3 litres. Its vee angle was 90°.

1,000rpm. Little is known of the engine's achievements in the 40-foot hull for which it was intended, while a plan to power heavy freight vehicles with it never came to fruition.[3] Nevertheless the Craig-Dörwald engine marked a significant and historic breakthrough in engine thinking toward twelve cylinders in a vee formation.

Motorboat racing of 1909–10 saw two more V12s in action, one of them big and the other of veritably Brobdignagian dimensions. Side-by-side rods and offset blocks were used in the 25,560cc (133.4 x 152.4mm) V12 built by Clinton Iowa's Lamb Boat & Engine Company for the company's 32-foot *Lamb IV*. Its weight was massive at 2,114lb.

Weight wasn't quoted for the V12 built by the Orleans Motor Company but in view of its capacity of 56,758cc (177.8 x 190.5mm) it must have been substantial. Output was quoted as "nearly 400bhp" for a twelve of 'F-head' design, this having side exhaust valves and overhead inlets both operated from a single central camshaft. Two such huge engines were installed in a Canadian boat, *Maple Leaf IV*. By 1914, when Panhard built two 38,611cc (127 x 254mm) V12s with four-valve cylinder heads to power a single racer at Monaco, the V12 was well established in motorboat competition.

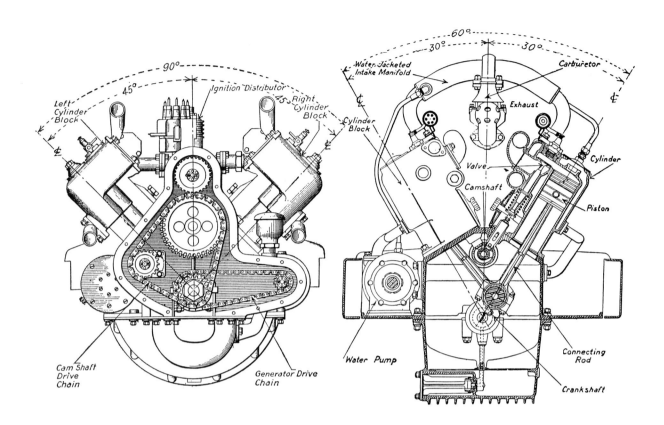

An illustration prepared before World War I compared the configurations of a 60° V12, right, with a 90° V8. Although the pioneering Craig-Dörwald V12 was a 90° engine, engineers were quick to appreciate the evenly spaced power impulses provided by a vee-twelve featuring a 60° bank angle.

Though weight wasn't a primary concern in these marine engines, it certainly was in power units for cars and aircraft. Here, as noted earlier, the early in-line six was disadvantaged if the torsional vibration of its long and spindly crankshaft were to be suppressed. When in-line sixes became better established however, in the air as well as on water, the idea of doubling them up to make V12s grew apace. A pioneer here was Renault, which had cast its lot with air-cooled vee engines for aviation use. Its individual finned cylinders were of F-head design with overhead exhausts and side inlets opened by a camshaft in the crankcase.

Soon after building a 90° V8 with side-by-side rods in 1909, Renault introduced a 60° V12 with articulated rods. A first version, measuring 90 x 140mm, was followed by one with a larger bore of 96mm (12,160cc). With a 4.0:1 compression ratio it produced 138bhp at 1,800rpm from a weight of 772lb. An ingenious feature was the driving of its propeller from the nose of the camshaft in the central vee, which gave an automatic half-speed reduction to the prop, improving efficiency. Later World War I Renault twelves had overhead camshafts, liquid cooling and the narrower vee angle of 47.5°.

Renault designs were followed closely in Britain by the Royal Aircraft Factory. Although established in 1909 to build better balloons, the Factory was moved by its new director Mervyn O'Gorman into heavier-than-air craft and their engines. Like its Renault counterpart the Factory's V12 had articulated rods, but all valves were overhead with their carburation on the engine's flanks. In RAF-4 form the engine displaced 13,195cc (100 x 140mm) and produced 140bhp at 1,800rpm from 637lb. Its RAF-4A derivative was produced in substantial numbers during the war.

Early-bird British V12 aero engines were also produced by London's ABC Motors Ltd., where Granville Bradshaw was chief engineer. By 1912 ABC was offering a water-cooled V12 of 17,375cc (127 x 114.3mm) claimed to produce 170bhp at 1,400rpm and to weigh only 390lb – 520lb with its radiator and coolant. This sounded good, but late in the war ABC submitted to the government its air-cooled nine-cylinder radial engine, the Dragonfly, with a promised 340 horsepower. This was so appealing that a

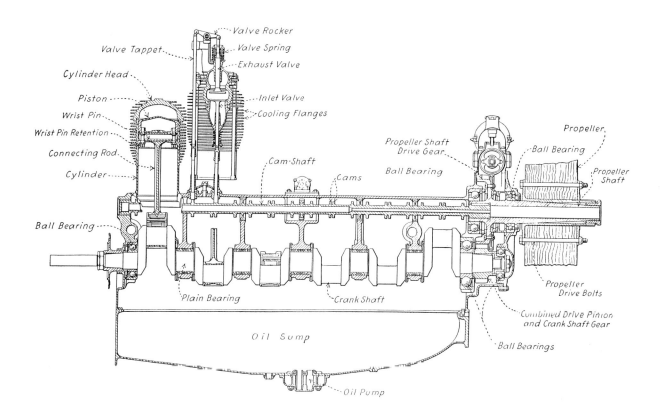

Labels on diagram: Valve Rocker, Valve Tappet, Valve Spring, Cylinder Head, Exhaust Valve, Piston, Inlet Valve, Wrist Pin, Cooling Flanges, Wrist Pin Retention, Connecting Rod, Cylinder, Cam-Shaft, Propeller Shaft Drive Gear, Propeller, Cams, Ball Bearing, Ball Bearing, Propeller Shaft, Ball Bearing, Plain Bearing, Crank Shaft, Propeller Drive Bolts, Oil Sump, Combined Drive Pinion and Crank Shaft Gear, Ball Bearings, Oil Pump

substantial order was placed, well over 1,000 being built, but the radial Dragonfly proved a lamentable failure.

Another British V12 made its official bow in 1914's Aero Show at the Olympia exhibition halls. This was the Mohawk, built by Wolverhampton's Sunbeam Motor Car Company. Sunbeam traced its origins to 1887, when it was founded by John Marston as the Sunbeamland Cycle Factory to build bicycles of quality. In 1899 it built its first automobile, and in 1909 it gained a new chief engineer who was to transform its fortunes. Wrote W.F. Bradley, "He brought the company to a high commercial, technical and sporting level."

The new man was Louis Hervé Coatalen, then just 30 years old. Born in Brittany, after three years at the École des Arts et Métiers in Brest young Coatalen tried his hand at Panhard, Clement and De Dion Bouton before concluding, at the age of 21, that he'd do better in England where the motor industry was not overburdened with qualified engineers. He soon settled at Humber, where Coatalen designed that company's first successful cars. Having already shown at Humber what he could do in the way of fast autos, the confident Coatalen soon involved Sunbeam in racing and record-breaking, taking full advantage of Surrey's high-banked

Carrying its crankshaft in seven main bearings, with an outrigger bearing at the propeller end, Renault's air-cooled V12 of World War I drove its propeller through a half-speed reduction gear which also turned the camshaft that operated its F-head valve arrangement with side-mounted inlets and overhead exhausts.

Brooklands track. Taking part in racing, he said, "crushes out the conservatism which is always apt to prevail in a works, bucking up the designers and constructors and putting everyone on his mettle."

While advancing Sunbeam's production cars, Louis Coatalen warmed up the company's competition side with a series of record cars named 'Toodles' after his wife Olive's nickname. He added a triumphant sweep of the 3-litre category in the 1912 Coupe de l'Auto at Dieppe that astonished his countrymen.

At the end of 1912 Coatalen began testing his first aero engine, a V8 based on a side-valve six-cylinder Grand Prix engine being developed in parallel. And on 4 October 1913 at Brooklands a new single-seat racer, Toodles V, was entered in the 100mph Short and Long Handicap races. With its steel artillery wheels and shrouded radiator Coatalen's latest Toodles was a mélange of automotive ideas old and new. Under its strapped-down bonnet was

Europe's first V12-powered car made its debut on 4 October 1913 at Brooklands. Built by Sunbeam, it carried the charming nickname 'Toodles V' which belied its considerable capacity for speed. Jean Chassagne was the first chauffeur of a car that showed a distinct penchant for record-breaking.

something entirely novel: Europe's first V12 engine to be installed in a car.

The car's chassis was that of the Sunbeam 25/30, a Coatalen six-cylinder design that had been introduced in 1911. In single-seater form it had already shown its record-breaking form as Toodles IV. Its wheelbase was 126in, suspension was by semi-elliptic leaf springs with Houdaille shock absorbers, and the rearmost two feet of both sides of its frame were filled with lead to shift more of its weight to the rear. The tail also carried an oil reservoir for the engine's dry-sump oiling system, pipes to and from it running outside the car on the left to cool the oil.

Mounted at three points in the front of the racer's chassis was a subframe which carried its V12 engine. With the same bore and stroke as Coatalen's V8 (80 x 150mm) the twelve displaced 9,048cc. Its cylinder banks were at an included angle of 60°, which with the V12 configuration gave evenly spaced power impulses. An aluminium crankcase carried two blocks of three cylinders along each side, cast of iron with integral cylinder heads.

The Sunbeam's combustion-chamber design was L-head, with inlet and exhaust valves in rows down the central vee and driven from a central camshaft. Valve clearance was set by grinding the relevant parts, the engine lacking any easy means of adjustment. This pointed to Coatalen's ultimate aim of using his new V12

in aircraft, where any adjustment method that could go wrong in flight was to be avoided.

The left-hand bank of the Sunbeam's cylinders was shifted forward enough to permit side-by-side connecting-rod big ends on a crankshaft that was supported by seven main bearings, those at the centre and drive end being wider than their sisters. Long, slim connecting rods controlled steel pistons. A gear train at the front of the V12 – as it was installed in the car – turned its camshaft and its accessories: the two oil pumps and a water pump. Two Bosch HL6 six-cylinder magnetos – one for each bank – were mounted transversely and driven from the camshaft nose by a skew-geared shaft. Thanks to its dry-sump oiling, a novelty at the time, the finned copper sump was shallow, which aided the engine's installation in Toodles V.[4] Operating oil pressure was 40psi.

The racer's twelve exhaust ports vented into the central vee, from which piping took the exhaust down and away beneath the chassis. Each block of three cylinders had two inlet ports on its outer surface, whence the mixture found its way to the block's three inlet valves through cast-in passages. At first these ports were fed by long pipes from a pair of carburettors under the scuttle, but this gave way to a water-warmed updraft Y-type manifold and Claudel-Hobson carburettor for each block – the same layout that the V12's airborne version would use.

As initially built the V12 was rated at 200bhp at 2,400rpm and would have scaled much the same as its aero engine version at 725lb. Shorn of the reduction gear needed for aerial use, its crankshaft drove a cone clutch directly and then a four-speed transmission. The rear axle dispensed with a differential and had a ratio of 2.0:1, giving 100mph at 2,000rpm. Torque reactions were taken by a pressed-steel arm from the axle forward to the frame, alongside the propeller shaft. Braking, as was then customary, was on the rear wheels only.

Although not excessively weighty at 2,800lb, this was heavy metal indeed. Disappointment was great when problems with its cone clutch – never the car's strong point – forced it to non-start in an August 1913 meeting at Brooklands, but by October it was fit and ready. Although Louis Coatalen had driven his previous Toodles creations, and well, he tapped talented countryman Jean Chassagne to pilot number five.

In the Short Handicap the Sunbeam started from scratch alongside the Talbot of Percy Lambert, a combination that earlier in 1913 had set a world one-hour record at better than 100mph, the first time the magic figure had been broken. Chassagne defeated Lambert (but not two earlier starters) and clocked a fastest lap of 114.49mph. In the subsequent Long Handicap the Sunbeam was the winner at an average of 110mph, the first Brooklands race to be won at such a speed. Its fastest lap was a dizzying 118.58mph, tantalisingly close to two miles a minute.

Jean Chassagne stayed in England to back Coatalen's bid to seize the coveted world one-hour speed record, which then stood at 106.2 miles. After one try was aborted by tyre failure another attempt was launched on 11 October 1913. With Chassagne treading lightly to save his tyres and the Sunbeam "emitting a steady, continuous growl" the record was taken with 107.95 miles covered. Coatalen waved Toodles V onward and managed a 53-second change of tyres that let her continue to the 250-kilometre distance, just over 150 miles, and thus claim a total of nine outright world records, most of which were not surpassed until 1924.

During the 1914 season Italian Dario Resta was nominated to handle Toodles V, shod with Rudge wire wheels with knock-off hubs. She performed well both at Brooklands and on Saltburn Sands and set short-distance Class H records at Brooklands including a one-mile speed of 120.73mph.

The other relevant event of 1914 was, of course, the showing of the airborne version of Toodles V's engine at Olympia in March with its aviation designation of 'Mohawk'. Racing it in 1913 had helped prove its design and details and encouraged a 10mm increase in its bore to 90mm, its rated output now being 225bhp at 2,000rpm.[5] Significant differences from the car engine included wet-sump oiling and water jackets

Designed by Louis Coatalen, Sunbeam's Toodles V had side-valve cylinders with exhausts in the central vee and carburettors on the outside of each block of three cylinders. It was credited with 200bhp at 2,400rpm.

At Brooklands in October 1913 Jean Chassagne set a new world record for one hour, covering 107.95 miles. Then and into 1914 Toodles V ran on Rudge wire wheels and proved capable of two miles a minute.

electrolytically deposited of copper, lightening the cylinders. The most powerful engine available to British aviation at the start of the war, Sunbeam's Mohawk was taken up by the British Navy for its seaplanes and served with distinction in Short's 827 and 184.[6] Further enlargement to 100 x 150mm created a 240-horsepower V12, the Gurkha.

Meanwhile the Mohawk's test bed, Toodles V, had a new lease of life in the New World. In 1915 she was shipped to America, where she won two match races on the two-mile Sheepshead Bay board track against Bob Burman's powerful Blitzen Benz, driven by Ralph DePalma. They were four-mile and six-mile races on 2 November, called "the most exciting of the afternoon, the finishes being so close that one car was alongside of the other." Her best winning speed was 113.86mph.

The Sunbeam's later career in America was less distinguished. Fitted with a two-seat body she non-finished at Corona in 1916 and placed seventh at Ascot, driven by Hughie Hughes. Toodles V led from the start of a 100-mile dirt-track race at Kalamazoo, Michigan but

then skidded and collected its pursuers in a terrible crash. "Within a few minutes," said a witness, "there were ten dead, all piled in a heap of wrecked cars." Thereafter there's no record of the Sunbeam's survival.

Overlooked by many then and later was that Toodles V had crossed the Atlantic because she'd been purchased by Detroit's Packard Motor Company.[7] Packard's chief engineer, Jesse Gurney Vincent, was not averse to acquiring interesting cars if he felt they could be of value to his company, and the speedy Toodles V caught his fancy.[8] The fact that it was powered by Europe's first V12 auto engine was naturally of interest, for by 1915 Packard had launched production of the world's first passenger car to be V12-powered – its Twin Six. That Ralph DePalma had driven the Sunbeam at New York's Sheepshead Bay was not a chance assignment, for the handsome Italian was a close associate of Packard. After the board-track races Packard's most senior executives – clearly bitten by the speed bug – stayed on to try the Sunbeam and their own stripped V12 at speeds of better than 100mph.

Without naming Packard, Sunbeam's Louis Coatalen – whose jug ears were matched by Jesse Vincent's – went on record as stating that the American company had robbed Sunbeam of its rightful patrimony. In December 1916, at his company's annual meeting, Coatalen made a statement that included the following:

At the outbreak of war the Sunbeam Company had something quite new in cars, notably the twelve-cylinder machine, with which they established many World's Records something like twelve months before the commencement of the campaign. This was the first car in the world of such a type, and it would have been marketed but for the war. As it was, they sent it to America where it performed notably and was bought by a motor manufacturing firm of perhaps the highest reputation in that continent. In consequent that firm studied the engine and standardised the twelve-cylinder car from the Sunbeam Company's machine with a degree of success that had compelled it to more than double its works, to increase its capital two-fold and it had, moreover, enabled the Company to pay a dividend of 50 per cent on that doubled capital for its financial year just concluded.

Thus, wrote Anthony Heal, Coatalen "wished to draw attention to the fact that the war had robbed the Sunbeam Company of the credit and the profit of being the first in the world to market a twelve cylinder car."

This was strong stuff, obviously referring to Packard. Had Coatalen's accusation any basis in fact? If we are to attribute Sunbeam's influence to Packard's purchase of Toodles V, this would seem unlikely. She first competed in England toward the end of the 1913 season, and the Packard Twin Six was revealed in all its detail in May 1915. Even if Packard had acquired the racer during the 1914–15 winter – and it is likely to have been bought later – that would hardly have given enough time for its detailed design to influence the Twin Six.[9]

Not excluded is the possibility that Packard's engineers saw the V12 Sunbeam at Brooklands as early as the end of 1913. In the 1906–1910 period Packard engineers spent 'many months' in Europe each year looking at the latest in-line sixes before they built their own, a habit they were not likely to have broken. Seeing a new engine, however, and perhaps being inspired by it, is not the same as studying the actual artefact in the manner suggested by Coatalen. The evidence thus suggests that the Sunbeam engineer's accusation was unjustified.

Louis Coatalen could, of course, have proposed that Sunbeam build a V12 road car. He would go on to build aviation engines in wild profusion and – as we will see – record-breaking cars with V12 engines, but never a road-going twelve. "Louis Coatalen gives the impression of being very mercurial," wrote Alec Brew, "easily bored with whatever project he was working on, and anxious to move on to the next." He had clearly declared in 1913 that

the engine in Toodles V was intended for aviation use, as its design features indicated, and was only being tested in a car. Only in retrospect, it seems, did Coatalen appreciate what he might have achieved with a V12 in a car, then seeking to justify his actions by calling Packard a copyist.

The two engines were not without similarities. Both had aluminium crankcases with cast-iron blocks whose heads were integral, and a single central camshaft operating L-head valve gear. Both had their left-hand cylinder banks offset forward to allow side-by-side connecting rods. Where the Sunbeam had two blocks for each bank, however, the Packard had but one. Induction was through the tops of the Packard cylinder heads instead of through the sides, and the American engine's pistons were aluminium instead of steel. Packard made do with three main bearings rather than seven, and placed its spark plugs above the exhaust valves instead of in the centre of the combustion chambers. In short, at worst the Americans could be accused of being inept copiers.

We are obliged to look elsewhere for inspiration for Packard's path-breaking Twin Six. By 1913, when its decision to build a V12 had to be taken, both marine and aviation examples of twelves were active and well publicised, especially in Europe. The type was gaining a credible track record. In August of that year Sunbeam's V12 racer first broke cover at Brooklands, although it didn't race. Interestingly, however, there was a role model closer to home for Detroit-based Packard.

Although the Packard Motor Car Company gave the impression of being a conservative auto maker, it was run by a man whose name betrayed his pleasure in life. Scion of a wealthy Detroit family, Henry Joy became active in Packard in 1902 after discovering the car's merits. He put both cash and his great enthusiasm into the company, which moved from its original home in Ohio to Detroit's West Grand Boulevard at the end of 1903. In 1910 Joy hired Alvan Macauley as general manager. The ying to Joy's yang, Macauley became the conservative and meticulous soul of Packard.

Macauley oversaw the 1912 launch of Packard's new range of six-cylinder cars. First to make its bow was a big six of 8.6 litres, followed in 1913 by a smaller six of 6.8 litres. Both had T-head valve gear, blocks cast as three pairs and seven main bearings – indicative of the challenge that engineers faced in coping with the six's crankshaft oscillations. Starting problems were solved by the use of Delco's electrical system. New though these engines were, by 1914 they were replaced by similarly sized L-head sixes with pairs of three-cylinder blocks.

Contributions to the design of the new 1914 sixes were made by a former colleague of Alvan Macauley's at the

America No Stranger to the Twelve

Schebler's Car, 7 Years Old, Also Can Be Six

WITH fours, sixes and eights occupying the attention of the motoring public at the present time, it may come as a surprise to some to know that for the last 7 years George Schebler, inventor of the carbureter bearing his name, has been driving a twelve over the country roads of Indiana. But such is the case and the odometer shows that the car already has covered something like 30,000 miles.

It is a most remarkable twelve at that, it being of the V type, with the valves in the head and with the cylinders set at 45 degrees. That is not uncommon practice, but Mr. Schebler, who directed the construction of the big motor, which was built by Philip Schmoll, of the company's engineering staff, has made it ambidexterous, if one can apply this term to a motor car engine, by being able to run it either as a six or a twelve. He can use either set of six cylinders, or he can use the entire dozen, depending on the character of the road over which the car is running.

Two Carbureters

Accomplishment of this is simple. Two carbureters — Scheblers, of course — are used, and these may be controlled independently or together. Mr. Schebler employs six cylinders when the roads are good and no difficulties are met with, and twelve when a sand pit is encountered or the car required to pull through deep mud.

In these days when the eight-cylinder motor is attracting a great deal of attention, some of the mechanical details of the Schebler twelve should command the consideration of the motor enthusiasts. This will be especially true in the matter of connecting-rod design since the engine is of the V type. In our present eights two types of rods are used, the yoked and the side-by-side. The Schebler twelve uses neither. Instead, one long rod is employed and a shorter one attached to it on the bearing cap, by means of a steel pin as shown in the illustration herewith. This means that the large rod is almost the same as the conventional type only on one side and slightly near the I-beam section there is provision for coupling a forked

rod by means of a steel pin, which forms the bearing for the small rod. The present motor uses rods made of bronze, the larger 9 7/16 inches long and the smaller 7 1/2 inches.

The crankshaft is not startling in design, being similar to that of a six-cylinder shaft using seven main bearings. These are 2 inches long and 1.75 inch in diameter. The crank-pin bearings, plain like the main ones, are 1.5 inch in diameter and 2 1/2 inches long. This shaft is set between the cylinder blocks and directly above it is a cam shaft with twenty-four cams, each operating a roller push rod directly. These pushrods are extended angularly to operate rocker arms. However, between the valve tappet and the valve stem is a finger, such as is used on a few valve-in-the-head motors, to allow the valve stem to take a

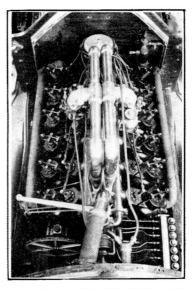

TOP VIEW OF SCHEBLER TWELVE-CYLINDER ENGINE, SHOWING DOUBLE INTAKES AND OVERHEAD VALVES

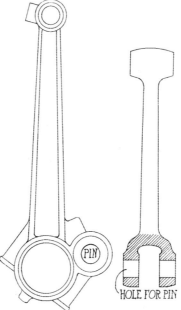

UNUSUAL CONSTRUCTION OF CONNECTING RODS, ONE OF A PAIR BEARING ON CRANKSHAFT AND THE OTHER YOKED TO PIN ON FIRST

direct thrust instead of one at an angle.

During the early stages of the development of this motor 45-degree valves were used. This is the conventional type. But because of excessive valve trouble due to warpage, the designer turned to flat-seated valves and while a little valve trouble was encountered for a while, it has been slight recently.

Road Speed Not Known

The Schebler twelve has a bore and stroke of 3 1/4 by 5 and up to this time no dynamometer test has been made of its power output. On the road exceptional power and speed is shown and according to Mr. Schmoll, no one has had the courage to keep both throttles wide open for any length of time.

Ignition of this motor is by a Mea magneto of the six-cylinder type fitted with a Schebler-made twelve-contact distributer. The armature, of course, is operated at three times the crankshaft speed.

There is nothing unusual in the timing, it being just like a six-cylinder motor firing 1, 4, 3, 6, 2, 5. But a cylinder on the left side fires and this is followed by an explosion from one on the right just as explosions are balanced in an eight.

There is a slight deviation from common practice in the oiling system. A large plunger pump operated from an auxiliary shaft forces oil through pipes, to the main bearings and directly to the cylinder wall which is drilled for the purpose. This hole is drilled low enough so that it never is uncovered by the piston. Besides the force feed, splash is used for the rod bearings, etc., there being six troughs the overflow from which falls to a sump from which it is again picked up by the pump and recirculated.

GEORGE SCHEBLER'S 7-YEAR-OLD TWELVE-CYLINDER ROADSTER

Opposite: As illustrated in this historic article about George Schebler's twelve-cylinder roadster, his pioneering design used master and link connecting rods. The first-ever V12 to power an automobile, the Indianapolis-built Schebler was clear inspiration for Packard's subsequent creation of a vee-twelve-powered production car.

Burroughs Adding Machine Company, Jesse Vincent. Born in Arkansas, Vincent made up for scant brushes with higher education with a distinct knack for mechanical problem-solving. His passion for cars led him to leave Burroughs to become Hudson's chief engineer at the end of 1910. He was plucked from Hudson by Macauley to join Packard at the end of July 1912. The team was now in place that would lead Packard for decades to come. In February 1915 Jesse Vincent became Packard's engineering vice-president, a post he would hold to 1948.

While Packard – like most makers in those days – had no proving ground of its own, it did enjoy privileged access to one of America's newest and finest high-speed tracks. The Indianapolis Motor Speedway had been open for business since 1909, and one of its leading lights was Carl G. Fisher, Packard dealer in that Indiana city. June 1914 saw two standard Packard sixes making one-hour speed runs on the 2½-mile oval, the bigger averaging 70.447mph. The runs served both for research and for the positive publicity that Jesse Vincent relished.

Another partner in the Speedway was Frank H. Wheeler, proprietor of carburettor maker Wheeler-Schebler. Inventor of the carburettor and chief engineer was George Schebler. Such was Schebler's creativity that, not satisfied with his carburettor work, in 1907 he decided to build a car with the help of one of the company's engineers, Philip Schmoll. By 1908 it was complete and running: a raceabout-style roadster which

was the world's first V12-powered car.[10] Schebler and Schmoll installed their engine in a chassis made by another Indianapolis company, Marion.[11]

Schebler's twelve had individual cylinders set at an included angle of 45°. Each monobloc cylinder was of F-head design, with side inlets and overhead exhausts operated by pushrods and rockers from a single central camshaft. Bore and stroke were 82.6 x 127mm for a capacity of 8,157cc in cylinders that were directly opposite each other, thanks to the use of articulated connecting rods. Unusually the rods were made of bronze. No chances were taken with the crankshaft, which ran in seven main bearings.

Twin updraft Schebler carburettors hovered above the engine's centre to feed a pair of manifolds that curved down to feed the inlet ports. Each carburettor was separately controlled, which allowed the engine to be run either as a six or a twelve. "Mr. Schebler employs six cylinders when the roads are good and no difficulties are met with," reported *Motor Age*, "and twelve when a sand pit is encountered or the car required to pull through deep mud." Schebler and Schmoll adapted a twelve-contact distributor to a Mea six-cylinder magneto, which ran at triple crankshaft speed.

Here was a remarkable car which vividly demonstrated the practicability of the V12 engine for automobiles. The Indianapolis connections to Packard were so intimate that it is inconceivable that Schebler's roadster didn't come to the attention of Jesse Vincent, an ardent admirer of fast cars. Packard's V12 of 1915 bore no resemblance to this Indianapolis one-off; it could only have served as inspiration. But it would have been quite some inspiration. "According to Mr. Schmoll," *Motor Age* related, "no one has had the courage to keep both throttles wide open for any length of time." Here was an attribute many future twelves would share.

Chapter 1 Footnotes

[1] The very first such engine, delivered in December 1888, was destined not for cars but for a Spohn locomotive. Credited as it was with six horsepower, it must have been considerably bigger than the car version, which produced 1.5bhp at 600rpm.

[2] Griff Borgeson wrote that its vee angle was 120°, but this seems to be a misreading of a not-very-clear description of the engine's design. A photo shows a 90° vee to be more likely.

[3] In the 1970s the engine was said still to be running in a Hong Kong junk.

[4] Anthony Heal reported that the sump's scavenge pump was too small, requiring the engine's sump to be emptied before it started a race or record run at Brooklands lest it overflow during the contest.

[5] At the end of 1913 Sunbeam released a concept drawing of a car with this larger engine whose dual rear tyres were intended to help it attack speed records on French roads, but no such Sunbeam was ever built.

[6] Post-WWI a Mohawk was installed in a Napier chassis which Cyril Bone acquired and stripped of its four-seat body to race at Brooklands. Fitted with 'B' hubcaps, the awesome Bone Sunbeam-Napier first failed and then crashed in its two 1925 attempts at the Surrey track and was not seen again.

[7] The author is indebted to Robert J. Neal's magnificent book, *Packards at Speed*, for this information.

[8] In 1925 Vincent bought a supercharged 2-litre front-drive Miller Indy car and in 1926 a supercharged Mercedes while on a trip to Europe.

[9] At the time of the Sheepshead Bay races in November 1915 Packard was said to have purchased the Sunbeam "some months ago".

[10] Griff Borgeson hypothesised that Schebler was inspired by the V4, V6 and V8 engines built earlier in the decade by Indianapolis's Howard Marmon, but these were air-cooled engines.

[11] This has given rise to erroneous reports that Marion produced a V12-powered car.

THE V12 ENGINE

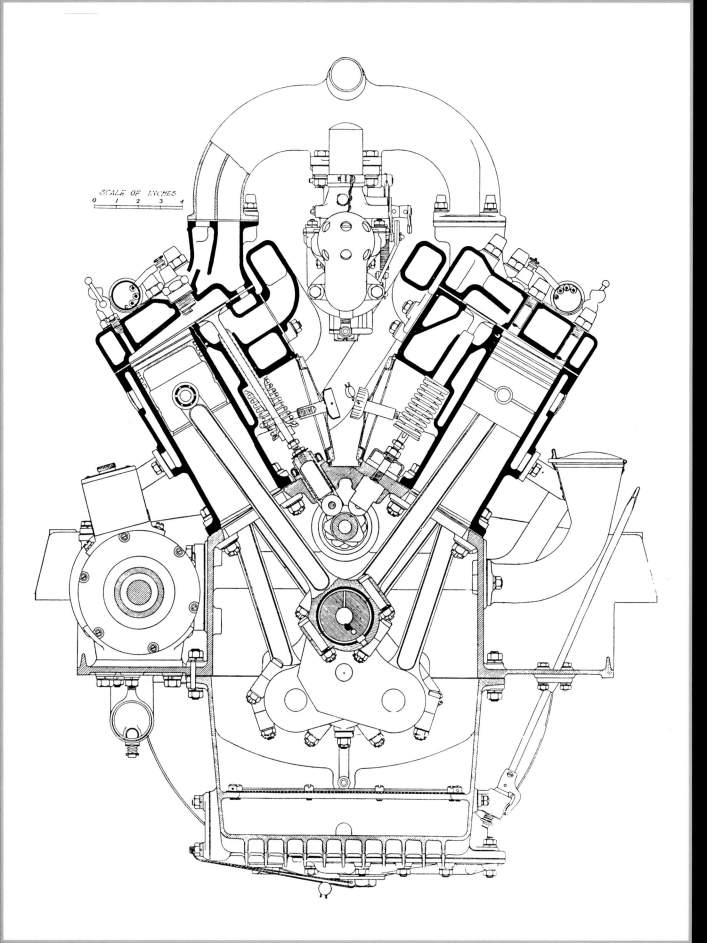

SCALE OF INCHES
0   1   2   3   4

Chapter 2

AMERICAN
TWIN SIXES

The automotive age unleashed America's awesome inventive potential. Fascinated by the concept of powered transport, frontier tinkerers from Phoenix to Portsmouth equipped their barns with tools to create their own cars and engines. The way forward was already paved by the wave of enthusiasm for the bicycle, whose construction and maintenance demanded mechanical skills. Remarkable talents emerged. Packard's Jesse Vincent was one such. Aviation spurred still more creativity. And when it seemed self-evident that aviation would play an important role in the war that began ravaging Europe in 1914, America's emerging automotive experts turned their attention to aero engines.

The Duesenberg brothers, Fred and Augie, were archetypal prairie pioneers of high-performance power. From their first workshop in Rockford, Iowa emerged engines and cars that startled the racing world with their power and endurance. With a war on, in 1917 the Duesenbergs moved to Elizabeth, New Jersey, where the government commissioned them to build a sixteen-cylinder Bugatti engine – composed of conjoined straight eights – under licence. The brothers also tried out some ideas of their own, one of them a V12.[1]

To achieve a narrow engine that would minimise aeroplane frontal area, the brothers set their engine's banks at a 45° included angle, accepting that this would produce uneven spacing of its power impulses. Offsetting its left cylinder bank forward made room for side-by-side tubular connecting rods with four-bolt big ends. Compactness was also aided by relatively small bores with dimensions of 123.8 x 177.8mm for a capacity of 25,683cc. Each bank comprised three two-cylinder blocks on an aluminium crankcase containing four main bearings.

Carried over from successful racing Duesenbergs was a vertical combustion chamber from which the valves protruded horizontally, in this case toward the central vee where they were opened by a single camshaft operating long roller-tipped rocker arms. Pistons were aluminium, still relatively rare, shaped to protrude up into the combustion chamber in a manner which would have provoked a welcome turbulence in the fresh charge. Paired cylinders were thin-wall iron castings with integral heads, closed at their sides by aluminium access plates. Water was circulated through them by a tandem pump that served each bank independently.

Dual ignition was provided by two twelve-cylinder magnetos, mounted laterally at the rear of the V12. Several induction systems were tried, one with carburettors in the vee and another placing them at the engine's flanks and feeding upward through log manifolds to the siamesed inlet ports of each block. With an electric starter and generator the Duesenberg V12 weighed 1,040lb, from which it produced 300bhp at 1,400rpm.

While the Duesenbergs' aero engine proposal presented a distinctly antiquated aspect with its six paired cylinder blocks, the same couldn't be said of the aviation offering

Opposite: *Roller-tipped tappets were a feature of the Packard twelve's valve gear in the 1918 model, which saw pistons reverting to thin-wall iron instead of aluminium, in search of quieter running. Packard's Twin Six was produced in this final configuration until mid-1923.*

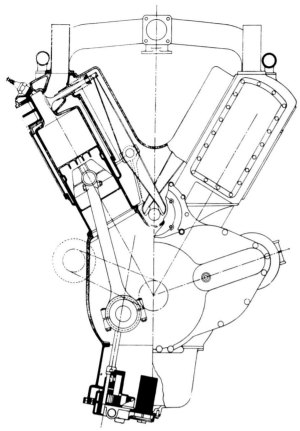

Akin to their earlier auto-racing engines, the V12 built for aircraft use by the Duesenberg brothers in 1917 used very long rocker arms to operate its valves from a single central camshaft. Its designed output from 25.7 litres was 300bhp at 1,400rpm.

Viewed from its anti-drive end, the 60° vee-twelve built for aviation use by Harry Miller in 1917 flaunted the designer's flair for style and integration. A large water pump was driven directly by the crankshaft and large vertical ports served the exit of the exhaust gases.

of another protean American creative force, California's Harry Miller. Born in Menominee, Wisconsin in 1875, by 1894 Miller was in Los Angeles, where he became involved in the budding automotive world. His fine carburettors brought Miller into contact with the racing crowd, and soon he was making engines as well. Reportedly bankrolled to the handsome tune of $50,000 by an ambitious aviator, Miller produced a V12 of surpassing novelty. Although its capacity was akin to that of the Duesenberg twelve at 23,167cc, its dimensions were more nearly square at 127 x 152.4mm.[2] The Miller's bank angle was 60° and fork-and-blade tubular connecting rods, 304.8mm long, allowed opposing cylinders to be directly in line.

This alignment was important because Miller arranged for a single central cam lobe to operate the valves on both sides of the vee. Geared from both ends of the crankshaft in an attempt to ensure that its timing was consistent in spite of its length, the camshaft ran in ball bearings and had individual lobes keyed to its shaft. Valve gear was

unique. A forked rocker arm with rollers on both sides embraced an oddly-shaped cam lobe that operated first the valve on one side, then the valve on the other. Almost horizontal, like the Duesenberg's, the valves opened on a vertical combustion chamber that had one spark plug at its top, while the other was at the bore's outer periphery. Two twelve-cylinder Dixie magnetos were along the engine's flanks and driven from the gear train at the rear, as was the single large water pump.

Also gear-driven were two scavenge pumps and one pressure pump for the Miller V12's dry-sump lubrication system. Seven main bearings carried its crankshaft in one of the most extraordinary cylinder blocks of 1917. It was a one-piece aluminium casting from sump to detachable cylinder heads, so big, wrote Miller expert Mark Dees, that it was "the largest object cast in aluminium in the western hemisphere up to that time". Inserted into the block were wet steel cylinder sleeves, held in place by the head. While exhaust gases were released upward, the inlet passages were cast as part of the block and fed by

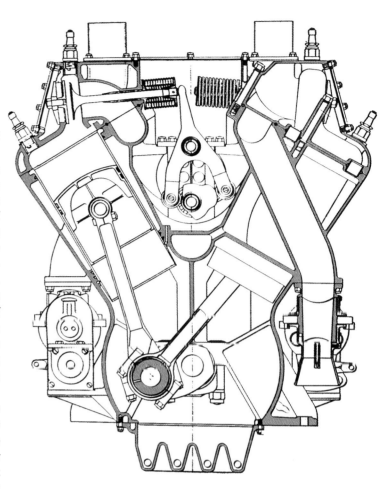

four updraft Miller carburettors, two along each side of the engine.

Although the big twelve was said to have spun a propeller for 100 hours at the Miller workshops, we have only sketchy information on its performance. The figure of 300bhp at 1,600rpm sounds right, as does a weight of only 600lb, thanks to its ultra-light construction. When it was tested by the Government at Dayton, Ohio in January 1918, the big twelve suffered from leaks through the O-rings that sealed the bottoms of its steel cylinder liners. Far in advance of its time, we can be sure that its massive one-piece block posed insuperable problems of porosity and consistency. According to aircraft historian Bill Gunston, "it was to be about 1930 before the aluminium casting industry could guarantee perfect products." The Miller's unique valve gear may also have been a durability nightmare.

Most remarkable, in retrospect, is that these two towering figures of the American high-performance automotive world failed to follow up their V12 aero engines with similar power units for cars, racing or otherwise.[3] Famed racer Barney Oldfield had in fact announced plans to install one of the Miller aero V12s in a sister to his sensational enclosed 'Golden Submarine' Miller racer, to attack straight-line speed records, but regrettably this marriage was never consummated. After its 1918 tests Harry Miller abandoned further work on his 23-litre twelve.

Fred Duesenberg had something in common with Sunbeam's Louis Coatalen in his eschewing of V12s for his road cars. Harry Miller resembled Coatalen in another respect, said Mark Dees, in his "vexing propensity to drop the pursuit of promising projects," adding that "Miller had a tendency to jump onto a new bandwagon once he had satisfied his own curiosity on the old." Thanks to both his creativity and his unquenchable optimism, Harry Miller seldom lacked for angels to fund his automotive flights of fancy. None, however, asked for vee-twelves.

Duesenberg's case was different. In both racing and road cars – and with its Model A – Duesenberg was one of the pioneers of the straight-eight engine that swept the upper echelons of the world motor industry in the 1920s and 1930s. Closely followed by Miller, Duesenberg concentrated on in-line eights for its championship racing cars, and when they were commissioned by E.L.

Below: *Harry Miller challenged the foundry practice of 1917 with the massive aluminium casting of the cylinder block of his 23.2-litre aviation engine. Two of Miller's own-design carburettors fed each side of the engine, which never reached a stage of development suitable for installation in an aircraft.*

In parallel with its work on V12 production cars, America's Packard built a special racing car, named the 299 after its capacity in cubic inches. It was first tested in April 1916 at Sheepshead Bay, New York and was destined to have a lengthy racing career. (Robert J. Neal)

Cord to build their ultimate auto, the Model J, the brothers made it a straight-eight rather than the V12s with which many luxury-car makers greeted the 1930s. It would be up to another company in Cord's group, Auburn, to launch a twelve.

Another American auto maker was even faster out of the blocks in the design and production of a V12 aero engine – of a sort. Not unlike Louis Coatalen at Sunbeam, when

Behind the traditional notched Packard radiator the 299's 4.9-litre vee-twelve was an impressive piece of machinery with its central induction manifold and side-mounted exhausts. (Robert J. Neal)

Jesse Vincent was asked by Packard's Henry Joy to produce an aviation engine, he came up with a V12 that was initially installed in a racing car. Unlike Coatalen's engine, however, which went on to become the Mohawk, Vincent's first high-performance twelve was never even offered up to an aeroplane.

In fact his twelve was too small to be a viable aero engine, as Jesse Vincent certainly knew. Instead, he designed it to conform to the then-current size limit for much of America's organised auto racing, 300 cubic inches. At 4,902cc (67.5 x 114.3mm) it was a pygmy alongside the later Miller and Duesenberg twelves and almost half the size of Sunbeam's nine-litre Mohawk. Its displacement in cubic inches caused it to be known as the '299', as was the car in which it was installed.

With Packard also coping with the launch of its roadgoing V12s, creation of the 299 was relatively leisurely. From Joy's request in the autumn of 1914 its design was not completed until November 1915. It first ran in February 1916 and was tested on the road on 26 April of that year at Sheepshead Bay, where Packard had established a garage as a base for its trials. The new 299 was installed in a special chassis with a 112-inch wheelbase, weighing 2,580lb. Fronted by the classic Packard radiator, its aluminium body had a long pointed tail and a two-seater cockpit with the driver on the right. Its bonnet was handsomely louvered with bulges to clear the valve gear above twin exhaust pipes.

Although Packard's statements at the time implied that the 299 was close cousin to the Twin Six, the two were completely different. They shared a 60° vee angle and an aluminium crankcase but otherwise their architecture couldn't have differed more. Cast-iron cylinder blocks were triple-bore units with integral heads, two to each side, with hemispherical combustion chambers and vee-inclined overhead valves – the latest in high-performance engine design. Two valves per cylinder were operated by a single overhead camshaft through rocker arms.[4]

AMERICAN TWIN SIXES

One strong indication that the 299 was never intended for aviation use – contrary to Packard's statements then and later – was its geared drive to its overhead cams at the back or drive end of the engine. In addition to gears being heavy for airborne use, the 299's protruding gear towers would have made it impossible to achieve a clean profile behind the propeller. Another sign that the engine was designed to power a car, not an aeroplane, was the integration with its crankcase casting of the four big bearers that united it with the car's frame rails.

The 299's cylinder blocks faced each other thanks to the use of fork-and-blade connecting rods, running on a three-bearing crankshaft. Pistons were by Lynite and spark plugs – two per cylinder – from Rajah. They were fired by coil-and-battery ignition through a Delco distributor driven at the rear of the engine. Induction was through a log manifold, fed by a central updraft carburettor, from which remarkably modern-looking individual ram pipes sloped down to the inlet ports. A bevel-driven water pump, sitting horizontally at the V12's nose, had separate outlets for each cylinder bank.

The 299 was developed to produce 130bhp at 3,300rpm, a good albeit not remarkable result in view of its advanced specification. Nevertheless it proved lively enough between the frame rails of Packard's 299 racer. In a test run on the Indianapolis Speedway on 2 August 1916, with Packard man Bill Rader at the wheel, it became the first 300-cubic-inch car to lap the track at better than 100mph – 100.76 to be exact. By then two 299s had been built. One had very little running before its chassis was commandeered to be powered by Packard's first true aviation V12. The other, acquired by Ralph DePalma late in 1916, embarked on a remarkable and ultimately influential racing career.

Early races in 1917 saw reliability problems with DePalma's 299, including defective battery ignition. It did better in shorter match races against such rivals as Barney Oldfield in his 'Golden Submarine,' a Harry Miller creation. In these events at Detroit, Providence and St Louis the 299 had more than her share of wins. At Sheepshead Bay in August, DePalma defeated Oldfield and Louis Chevrolet in match races of 20, 30 and 50 miles and took home a handsome $15,000 – certainly more than paying for the 299. They won 20- and 50-mile races at Chicago in September. Back at Sheepshead Bay in November, after two false starts, DePalma and 299 set American closed-circuit records from 10 to 600 miles and from one to six hours with a best speed of 109.5mph.

Although a suspension was mooted at the end of 1917, racing continued in the USA throughout the war. The 299 and DePalma had one of their best wins on 30 May 1918 at Sheepshead Bay, winning the 100-mile race against

Although Packard liked to depict the 299 as an early stage of its aviation-engine development, the chassis bearers cast integrally with its aluminium crankcase clearly showed that the engine was planned and designed for automobile use. A gear train at the clutch end of the engine drove its single overhead camshaft along each bank. **(Robert J. Neal)**

strong opposition at a speed of 102.8mph to take the trophy offered by the board track's owner, Harry Harkness. On 4 July another 100-miler fell to the pairing at the even higher rate of 105.2mph. At the end of July they won three shorter events on the Chicago Speedway that netted DePalma $17,000 in prizes. He duplicated this

During the development of the 299 Packard its inlet manifold was raised, lengthening the individual ram pipes to each cylinder. Placed horizontally, a single water pump served both banks. **(Robert J. Neal)**

Italian-born Ralph DePalma, here at the wheel of Packard's 299 at Sheepshead Bay in 1919, enjoyed many racing successes with the twelve. In 1917 it held most American closed-circuit speed records. (Robert J. Neal)

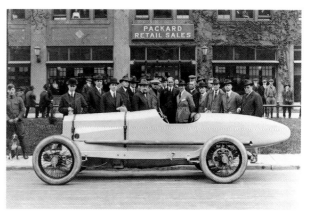

Ralph DePalma, in fedora, and hatless Jesse Vincent stand behind the cockpit of the Packard 299 as it was revised to race at Indianapolis in 1919. Front-wheel braking was not yet considered essential. (Robert J. Neal)

prize haul at Sheepshead Bay in August where his times set new American closed-circuit records at distances of up to 50 miles. That the best timing at 10 miles was 111.1mph showed that the five-litre Packard was gaining speed as DePalma mastered her tuning and as tyre quality – always a limiting factor – improved.

In 1919 the Indianapolis 500-mile race was reinstated, still with a 300-cubic-inch limit, and Packard entered its

In 1919's 500-mile race at Indianapolis the 299 raced without its bonnet sides in place for better cooling. Slowed by valve and bearing problems, DePalma was placed sixth after holding the lead at half distance. It remains the only twelve-cylinder car to have completed the race. (Robert J. Neal)

299 for DePalma. Its preparation included a new body with plain instead of louvered bonnet sides[5], straight exhaust pipes and a taller inlet manifold with longer downpipes that would have improved mid-range torque. After qualifying at 98.20mph, DePalma held the race lead at half-distance only to pit with a failed exhaust valve. He recovered from its replacement to climb to third, then to have the highly stressed right-front-wheel bearing fail. With this repaired he finished in sixth place. Although other twelve-cylinder cars have started the 500-mile race, none but the Packard 299 has ever finished it.

The rest of the 1919 season – the last before a new 3-litre limit was imposed for American racing – brought only one major success for the 299; a 50-mile victory at Sheepshead Bay at 113.8mph. No longer eligible for US racing, the 299 was acquired by a dealer in Milan, Italy, Adalberto Chiesa, who in turn sold it for 280,000 lire to the Baroness Maria Antonietta Avanzo, whom Enzo Ferrari called "the first courageous woman driver of the post-war era". In her stewardship the big Packard was given magneto instead of coil ignition, downdraft instead of updraft carburation and elegant side mounts for spare wheels.

With Europe's Grand Prix racing also governed by a 3-litre limit, the 299 was only useful for sprint and Formule Libre[6] events. The Baroness engaged a driver, Eugenio Silvani, to race her powerful Packard in some of these. Piston trouble stopped him in the Susa-Moncenisio hill climb in August of 1920, but on November 14 he set the fastest time in the Gallarate speed trials with a timing of 97.26mph over the flying kilometre. Nineteen twenty-one began well with Silvani's victory in the 15 January Vermicino-Rocca di Papa hill climb at a speed of 42.17mph. The Baroness herself took the wheel for Denmark's speed trials on the beach at Fanoe, near

No stranger to speed, the Italian Baronessa Maria Antonietta Avanzo acquired Packard's 299 in time for the 1920 racing season. It competed in numerous racing events in Italy before fading from the scene after 1922.

Copenhagen, where she had to drive it into the sea to extinguish an engine-room blaze.[7]

The last known racing appearance of the Packard 299 was at Monza, north of Milan, where the baptism of that town's new permanent racing circuit was being celebrated. Its 249-mile Autumnal Grand Prix on 22 October 1922 was open to all comers without regard to displacement. In a rainy contest Franco Caiselli piloted the much-raced six-year-old Packard to a ninth-place finish. By then it was no longer in the hands of the Baronessa. She had given up on it after the Fanoe disaster, swapping it to dealer-racer Antonio Ascari for a scarlet Fiat 501.[8]

Though the ultimate fate of this unique Packard is unknown, we can be confident that in one or more of its Italian appearances it was witnessed and indeed admired by a man in his early twenties from Modena, a disciple of Antonio Ascari, who had ambitions in the race-driving line. When a quarter-century later he would think of building a car of his own, he would not have forgotten the stimulating twin-pipe roar of the Baronessa's twelve-cylinder Packard.

In the meantime the sister chassis to this 299 had been allocated to another project at Packard: the testing in a car of Jesse Vincent's first V12 with the potential to be an aero engine. Substantially larger than the 299 at 14,827cc (101.6 x 152.4mm), its vee angle was only 40° to keep its frontal aspect narrow to suit possible aeroplane installations. Its capacity in cubic inches provided its designation, 905. Its valve gear was akin to that of the 299 and also driven by a gear train, but in this instance at the engine's anti-drive end. As in the 299 the blocks faced each other through the use of forged fork-and-blade connecting rods, linked to aluminium pistons. Its drive to the propeller was through a spur-type reduction gear,

which Vincent credited with reducing crankshaft breakages caused by out-of-balance propellers.

The 905's development progressed through three prototypes, aided by the addition to Packard's team of an experimental engineer, Vincent's younger brother Charles. Like Jesse he was a refugee from Hudson. Prototype 905-1 had each cylinder bank cast as one block, like the Twin Six, but this was a step too far for the foundry practice of the time, if lightness were to be achieved through thin wall sections. Its output was 248bhp.

Engine 905-2 marked a sharp change to the construction method used by Mercedes and – following their example – by Rolls-Royce: individual forged steel cylinders surrounded by welded-on water jackets of sheet steel, united in groups of three.[9] This reduced weight by some 100lb from 905-1 in an engine that produced 275bhp at 2,000rpm. The final 905 iteration used the same construction method but in two-cylinder groupings, compatible with its four instead of three main bearings. With dual carburation Packard's 905-3 produced 285bhp, also at 2,000rpm.

Prototype 905-2, completed in April 1917 and bench-tested in May, is the engine that interests us here. Minus its reduction gear, in the summer of '17 it was installed in the other 299 chassis, said *Motor Age*: "It is a complete aviation engine with the propeller removed and an electric starter installed because no man could crank it by hand." Its bodywork remained that of the 299, albeit with bonnet sides that bulged outward to suit the bigger engine. In its final form the racy two-seater weighed 3,230lb. This was a

Designed for aviation use, Packard's 905-2 twelve had a narrow 40° vee-angle and cylinders in groups of three. After removal of the propeller drive and reduction gear shown at the right, this 905-2 engine was installed in a second 299 chassis. **(Robert J. Neal)**

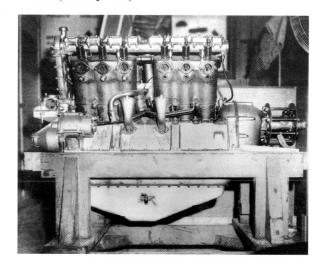

Packard test driver William Rader was at the wheel of the 905, as the bigger-engined car was known, for speed-record attempts at Sheepshead Bay on 27 July 1917. It set new circular-track marks at speeds of up to 130mph. (Robert J. Neal)

car whose only destiny could be sheer speed, because it fitted no known racing formula. And Packard lost no time in establishing that the 905 – as the racer was also known – was, in fact, the fastest car in the world.

After a preliminary sortie in July at Sheepshead Bay,

In February of 1919 Ralph DePalma took the wheel of Packard's 905 to make some officially timed high-speed runs at Florida's Daytona Beach. Although not internationally recognised, his speed of 150mph over the kilometre established the 905 as the world's fastest vehicle of any kind.

which had now become established as America's counterpart to Brooklands, Packard tester Bill Rader with mechanic Fred Farber boarded the 905 on 27 July 1917 to make major speed. That day and the next they set official circular-track records at all distances from the quarter-mile to ten miles at speeds from 130.43 to 123.76mph. Their timings were faster than those of the awesome front-drive Christie in America and those set by the 200-horsepower Benz in the USA and at Brooklands.

This was the 905's last hurrah before its creator, Jesse Vincent, accepted an Army commission and began his work on what became the Liberty aero engine. Returning from the service as a Lieutenant Colonel (he would henceforth be 'Colonel Vincent'), he directed the immediate overhaul of the 905 as a pure record-breaker. A new front axle was fitted and its bonnet sides were smoothed, front dumb irons faired and driving position converted to a single seat for Ralph DePalma, who was added to the Packard salary rolls "for special racing work for the Advertising Department".

Between 12 and 17 February 1919 the big Packard wintered at Florida's Daytona Beach, where it took some exercise. There it was officially timed at 149.88mph for the flying mile and an even 150mph for the kilometre – good margins over Bob Burman's 1911 record of 141.73mph in the Blitzen Benz. Distances up to 20 miles were also tackled on the hard Florida sand, achieving speeds of better than 132mph, and the standing-start mile was covered at an average of 92.74mph. These timings for one-way runs were not internationally recognised, but there was no reason to doubt their authenticity. Packard's 905 had surpassed the Blitzen Benz as the world's fastest automobile – indeed, it was then officially the fastest vehicle of any kind.[10]

The rest of 1919 saw the 905 shipped from coast to coast to road and track venues where DePalma could demonstrate that Packard's proud radiator stood for speed as well as luxury. It was on display and turned some exhibition laps at Indy in May and made a final appearance at Toronto, Canada in September. Sadly, no glamorous Italian baroness came forward to rescue the 905 and prolong its career. Although in 1921 Colonel Vincent minuted that the 905 had been sold "for $10,000.00 less war tax,"[11] the big speed machine remained in Packard's hands at least until 1923. While apart from a few chassis components the car has vanished, its engine is preserved in the Smithsonian's collection in Washington.

After the war Packard's racers may well have outlived their usefulness, for although Packard would continue to make its Twin Six until 1925, a six-cylinder car was under development after the war and a straight eight would soon follow.[12] Publicising the merits of the twelve-cylinder engine by racing and record breaking was no longer a dominant objective for Packard. In fact the post-war years saw the waning of the astonishing craze for twelve-cylinder engines that swept America in mid-decade.

The first New York Automobile Show to be graced by V12-powered cars was that of 1916, when five were on display. The year 1917 marked the mania's apogee with no fewer than 16 twelve-cylinder models. By 1918 the numbers had reduced to nine, then eight in 1919 and seven in 1920. The final dwindling took place in 1921 to three, then to two the following year and one in 1923: Packard on its own. The pioneer was the sole survivor as well.

Thought must be spared for those companies that tested the vee-twelve waters but decided not to take the plunge. One of these was Flint, Michigan's Buick. A founding member of Billy Durant's General Motors, Buick rivalled Ford in annual output at the end of the 20th Century's first decade. Ford then accelerated ahead as Buick moved out of the low-price field to make a planned shift upmarket. Even so, in 1914 only Ford and Willys Overland were outselling Buick. In that year Buick launched its first six and adopted the new Delco electrical/starting system.

Buick was not short of talent, with Charles Nash its president, Walter Chrysler its works manager and Walter Marr its chief engineer. The brilliant, demanding Marr was credited with introducing the pushrod-operated overhead-valve system that became a Buick hallmark as early as 1901. That Walter Marr brooked no compromises

The mechanically savvy Ralph DePalma checked the engine of his Packard 905, with its single overhead camshaft on each cylinder bank operating inclined overhead valves. DePalma would be retained as a driver and consultant by Packard well into the 1920s. (Robert J. Neal)

was shown by his decision to uproot his family from Detroit to a cottage on Signal Mountain near Chattanooga, Tennessee, a mere 663 miles due south of Flint, at the beginning of 1915. He slept better there, and that was reason enough for Marr.

Film star Douglas Fairbanks joined Ralph DePalma next to Packard's 905 at Santa Monica in 1919. Although the Packard did not compete officially, DePalma drove it at high speeds in demonstration laps. (Robert J. Neal)

Buick's standard D55 chassis of 1916, with a touring-car body, was used to test the new V12 designed for Buick by Walter Marr and Leo Goossen. The twelve took up less space than the D55's usual in-line six. (Paul Marr)

A look inside the central vee of the 1916 Buick vee-twelve showed its two-throat updraft carburettor serving an inlet manifold that arched between the two cylinder heads. The twelve's vee angle was 60°. (Paul Marr)

Marr, then 49, brought with him a fellow Michigander, 22-year-old Leo Goossen. Marr plucked Goossen from the Flint drafting pool to work closely with him on his more innovative projects. Joined later by several more draftsmen, the talented and conscientious Goossen initially lived and worked in the Marr family cottage. As part of Buick's upmarket thrust, the remotely located team was assigned the task of designing a vee-twelve for future Buicks. By the autumn of 1915 Goossen, under Marr's direction, was well along on his drawings for the new model.

To carry his new twelve Marr relied on a lightly modified version of the 1916-model D55 chassis, with seven-passenger touring-car body, powered by Buick's then-biggest engine, a 5.4-litre in-line six. A sign of the new unit's compactness was that the twelve's bonnet could be 41mm shorter than the six's. With its 60° vee angle the V12 just squeezed within the existing bonnet's confines. It was a long-stroke design – more so than Buick's other engines – with dimensions of 76.2 x 149.2mm (8,166cc). Within each cylinder block the bore centre distance was 95.3mm for the front and rear trios, with a longer spacing at the centre of the block to suit the single centre bearing of the engine's three-bearing crankshaft.

Walter Marr had enough confidence in Buick's foundry to specify a single iron casting for the block on each bank. In fact, in the interest of economy of scale he and Goossen contrived to make one design of casting serve for both banks of the twelve.[13] Heads were integral, with vertical valves carried in cages, complete with their valve seats, which screwed into the top of the block. Inserted at a 45° angle to the cylinder centreline on the inside of the vee, the spark plugs were accessible and well placed between the valves. The inlet valves were those closest to the centre of each block, to minimise the distance the mixture had to travel. Bolted to the tops of the blocks, the inlet manifolds were fed from a single central updraft carburettor by a cross tube. During the twelve's development engine-water warming was added to the cross tube.

Designed in Tennessee to be symmetrical with a central takeoff, the exhaust manifolds were reconfigured in Flint to clear the steering gear on the left and the engine accessories on the right. Ingeniously, the new asymmetrical manifold design was common to both sides of the engine. An encased chain at the front of the Buick twelve drove its central camshaft and, on the right, the generator, behind which was a single water pump serving both sides of the engine. A vertical shaft at the front drove a Delco ignition, with separate distributors for each six-cylinder bank. Coils were cowl-mounted, together with the vacuum tank that encouraged petrol flow to the carburettor.

Also cowl-mounted, on the left, was a perch for an oilcan to encourage frequent lubrication of the exposed rocker-arm pivots with their lubricant reservoirs. Offering no mechanical advantage, the rocker arms opened the vertical valves, which were closed by single coil springs. Valve-clearance adjustment was provided at the top end of each pushrod. Camshaft and crankshaft were carried in an aluminium crankcase, where a pump provided pressure oiling. Side-by-side placement of the connecting rods on their journals was facilitated by the forward offset of the left-hand cylinder bank.

Drawings created on Signal Mountain were rushed to Flint, where two V12 prototypes were built in 1916. We don't know how much power they produced, but based on the Buick sixes their output wouldn't have fallen far short of 100bhp. They underwent testing in Michigan, where Walter Chrysler took a close interest in the design – so much so that one of them eventually became his property. After some delay – and a decision by Chrysler not to produce the twelve, with the sales of Buick's sixes booming – the other came to Chattanooga and Walter Marr.[14] An offshoot of the project was the design and construction of a prototype V6 based on the twelve's design, but this too remained an experiment.

Almost as prominent among those who decided not to embrace the V12 was Hudson, a solid mid-range

With the technology at their disposal, Marr and Goossen were to be commended for the compact layout of their Buick twelves, two of which were built as prototypes. With the sales of its sixes remaining strong, however, Buick decided against producing the twelve. **(Paul Marr)**

Walter Marr provided individual lubricant reservoirs for the rocker-arm pivots of his 8.2-litre Buick V12. As was customary in the earliest twelves, the rocker gear was exposed. **(Paul Marr)**

performer that was just breaking into five-figure annual sales and rising. Returning to Hudson to head a new engine programme under chief engineer Howard Coffin was Charles Vincent, after his brief sojourn with Packard. Coffin and Vincent developed a palette of possible power units including several sixes, a sleeve-valve V8 and a V12.

Stephen Fekete was credited with the design of Hudson's V12, which was sensationally novel apart from its 60° bank angle. An aluminium crankcase carried its crankshaft in three bearings and extended upward to form central buttresses into which an iron six-cylinder block was inserted along each side. The long-stroke engine's spindly connecting rods were of fork-and-blade design. Valves were virtually horizontal at the very top of the engine, driven by a single central camshaft turned by chains in two stages, the first at the front of the engine to a layshaft running at more than engine speed, and from there by a less-than-halfspeed chain at the centre of the block. The layshaft also drove a dynamotor at the rear. Each cam lobe operated valves on both sides of the engine through flat tappets attached to their stems.

Fekete's design created a combustion chamber of triangular cross-section with the addition of two three-cylinder heads along each block. Exhaust ports curved upward to the tops of the blocks while an inlet manifold was cast as part of each block and fed by a single carburettor on each side. Although Fekete's concept was likely to have produced a light engine with a minimum of components, its valve gear may have carried simplicity too far.

In the summer of 1917 Hudson declared its intentions in an advertisement. "We have built every type of motor – from one to twelve cylinders," it stated. "The result of this research convinced us more firmly than ever before of the

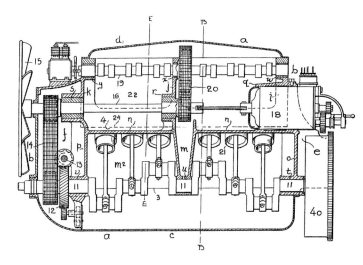

Under Howard Coffin and Charles Vincent, Stephen Fekete designed a remarkable V12 prototype for Hudson in 1916. Three main bearings supported its crankshaft, which drove a single overhead camshaft through two stages of chains. Built into the central vee was a dynamotor for both starting and generating.

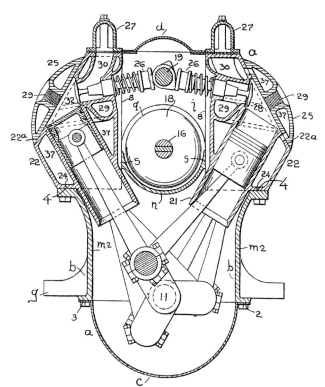

A cross-section of Stephen Fekete's prototype vee-twelve for Hudson showed its 60° vee angle, long-stroke configuration and ultra-simple valve gear. Hudson decided not to proceed with Fekete's ingenious design.

absolute supremacy of the Hudson six-cylinder motor." Henceforth, the advertisement declared, "The Hudson car will use a six-cylinder motor in all future models planned by this Company." Thus Hudson took full advantage of the debate that still raged in the industry over the right number of cylinders for an auto engine. The issue of a magazine in which the ad appeared carried a lively discussion of the relative merits of the V8 and the V12.

Meanwhile, Packard was creating and producing its passenger-car twelve. The previous chapter gave us insights into the thought process that led Jesse Vincent to conceive a vee-twelve engine as a successor to Packard's sixes. Twelve-cylinder antecedents, from Sunbeam to Schebler, gave him valuable ammunition to convince Henry Joy, Alvan Macauley and others on West Grand Boulevard that such an unusual engine would be viable.

Packard's sixes, Vincent pointed out, already possessed perfect inherent balance. This was an attractive feature of the in-line six, but one which could only be realised in practice at that time by excessively heavy components to keep its long crankshaft under control. "We want not only the present ability," Vincent told his colleagues, "but we want a greater range of ability. So the only way out is to have more pistons." By building what was in effect a double six, the advantages of superb balance were retained in combination with the potential for much lighter components that could further minimise vibration in a luxury automobile.

Jesse Vincent had an important ally in his V12's creation in Ormand E. Hunt, effectively his assistant and his successor in 1915 as chief engineer when Vincent stepped up to his vice presidency. Together they explored various engine layouts using wooden models made by Packard's expert patternmakers, a technique for visualisation of design alternatives that was also used by Vincent's *Doppelgänger*, Henry Ford. In 1913 the new engine's design was well along, enough so for Packard's management to be mulling likely production volumes. In December 1914 it foresaw making 5,000 in the first year, "with the privilege of stopping off at three thousand". In fact, such was the demand for its new twelve that Packard made 7,746 in its first full model year.

Vincent backed up his claim of high efficiency and performance for his V12 by making it only slightly larger than the smaller of the two sixes it would replace: instead of the six's 6.8 litres, it displaced 6,950cc (76.2 x 127mm). One reporter, expecting to find a monster under the new Packard's bonnet, lifted it, looked around and assured his readers that "the twelve cylinders are there all right". In every aspect its design showed close attention to compactness and simplicity, starting with its three-bearing crankshaft and side-by-side connecting rods permitted by shifting the left-hand cylinder block forward by 32mm. Both main and rod journals were 57.2mm in diameter. Main bearings were embraced by the crankcase, above, and 2.1-gallon oil pan below, both being aluminium castings that united at the rear to form the clutch housing. The three-speed transmission was now in unit with the engine instead of in the rear axle, as in Packard's sixes.

As well as optimum balance, even firing was achieved with a 60° vee angle. An impressive feature of the new twelve was the casting of each iron cylinder block in one unit at a time when three-cylinder blocks were still common. Showing high confidence in Packard's foundry practice, together with the small cylinder bore, this was one of the key decisions that helped keep the engine short and compact. Its aluminium pistons – novel at that time – carried Burd rings while its connecting rods, machined all over for lightness and consistency, piped oil to the gudgeon pins.

Cylinder heads were integral with the blocks, topped by a long access plate that helped the foundrymen keep their sand cores in place. Cored into the block was the inlet manifolding, fed from a central inlet by a water-heated pipe arching above both blocks with an updraft Packard carburettor at its centre. Spark plugs, in the removable caps above the exhaust valves, were fired by a single set of breaker points and two six-cylinder

An elegant and effective job of engineering in its day, Packard's V12 was introduced in 1915. Iron cylinder blocks with integral heads were bolted to a two-piece aluminium crankcase. Clutch and transmission were integral with the 7.0-litre engine. **(Robert J. Neal)**

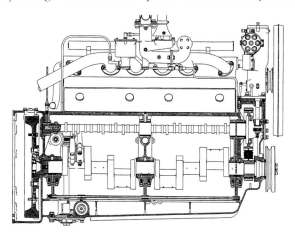

Above: *A longitudinal section of Packard's V12 of 1915 showed its three-bearing crankshaft and camshaft as well as its passages for pressure lubrication. At the top both inlet and exhaust manifolding were visible within the engine's central vee.*

Right: *A single central camshaft operated the valves for both banks of Packard's 1915 vee-twelve. The water pump was mounted at the side, and the bottom of the aluminium sump was finned for cooling.* **(Robert J. Neal)**

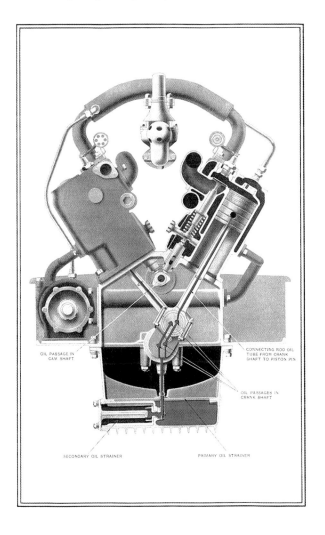

OIL PASSAGE IN CAM SHAFT

CONNECTING ROD OIL TUBE FROM CRANK SHAFT TO PISTON PIN

OIL PASSAGES IN CRANK SHAFT

SECONDARY OIL STRAINER

PRIMARY OIL STRAINER

Delco distributors, skew-gear-driven high at the front of the twelve.

In their L-head configuration the stems of the valves were angled fractionally away from the axis of the cylinders to tilt their 38.1mm heads enough to make the combustion chamber slightly more compact. The valves were in the central vee, opened by roller tappets from a single camshaft that was driven by a Morse chain from the crank nose. The chain made a detour to the right side of the engine to turn a sprocket which drove the generator and, behind it, the tandem water pump. Under thermostatic control, one impeller delivered water directly to the right bank and, through a cast passage in the crankcase, the other supplied the left bank. Starting and lighting, by Bijur, drew an accolade from *The Automobile*: "Owing to the even torque of the twelve cylinders the starting motor cranks at a steady speed and very quietly; there is none of the rising and falling wail of gearing found with the four-cylinder."

Integral with the crankcase were the four bearers that tied Packard's V12 rigidly into its frame. Weighing 900lb, some 400lb less than the bigger predecessor six, the twelve produced 88bhp at 2,600rpm and could run smoothly to 3,000. "At a road speed of well over 60 miles per hour," reported *The Automobile*, "the motor is hardly audible even at full revolutions. It is possible to exceed 50 miles an hour on second gear and to run on high at 3 miles an hour…there is no sense of effort whatever in opening up from 3 miles on high gear." When journalist Hi Sibley was given Packard's hospitality during the American military's chase of Mexican revolutionary

Aptly dubbed the Twin Six, Packard's new twelve was the sole model offered by the company from 1915. The carriage trade was quick to embrace such models as the 61-25 coupé with its rakish rear fender lines and twin spare wheels. (Robert J. Neal)

Pancho Villa in 1916, he wrote that "it was like riding on velvet when those big Packards laid back their ears and breezed along as though their only ambition was to catch up with the horizon."

"Never before have the principles of high-speed motor design been applied to a touring car engine of so large a size as this new Packard," said *Motor Age*, "and it needs but a little handling of the car to realize that the result is not merely encouraging, but in excess of all possible expectations." "A very short experience of the twelve on the road is enough to prove that there is much more in the system than anyone would have imagined," echoed *The Automobile*. "It is the most noteworthy combination of racing motor power with the quietness of the highly developed six that has yet been produced in any part of the world." A correspondent to the *Illustrated London News* wrote, "It is not enough to say that the car is silent, or that it runs smoothly; when we are talking about the Twin Six we have to find some other manner of describing these essential qualities."

Announced in May 1915, the Twin Six was offered as a 1916 model in two wheelbase lengths. It was priced in the range of $2,600 to $4,600, strikingly less than the $3,350 to $6,150 of its predecessor sixes. Owed to the new engine's ingenious design, concentration on a single model and investment in manufacturing equipment, this brought the sales success referred to earlier. Louis Coatalen wasn't exaggerating when he told his shareholders that Packard had made good with an idea that he thought was his own.

Vincent and Hunt found time in their busy schedules to make substantial changes in their 1917-model Twin Six. That they were not *entirely* satisfied with its smoothness was shown by their purchase of a licence to use the Lanchester flywheel-type torsional-vibration damper to suppress unwanted crankshaft resonance. A major change was to detachable cylinder heads with combustion chambers that were fully machined to equalise compression ratios. Easing both assembly and service with their attachment by 25 studs and nuts, they moved the V12 toward the modern era and allowed the spark plugs to be placed more centrally in the chamber. New too was the combining of the V12's water off-take with the central arcuate – bow-shaped – manifold that held its carburettor, so the water inherently warmed the incoming charge (see page 26).

For 1918 the Packard's pistons were changed from aluminium to iron, in search of quieter running. Detail changes, including revisions to the inlet manifolding, now supported a horsepower rating of 90. This remained the engine's specification through the rest of its life. The 1917 model year had seen the excellent assembly of 8,999

Twin Sixes, and the 1918–1923 period found 14,176 built and sold, the last in June of '23. Total production of this pioneering V12 was 35,102.

"If any single model of a distinguished line could be said to have most greatly affected the standing of Packard," wrote Richard Langworth, "it would probably have to be the Twin Six. It was in production longer, with greater quantities built, than any other Packard to date. It introduced a radical and successful new V12 that eclipsed in its time the rival V8s from America and abroad." "It was the most sought after, the most sold and the most successful of all cars in the so-called 'Gentleman's Car' class," said Menno Duerksen. In 1921 it also had the honour of being the first automobile to carry an American president, Warren G. Harding, to his inauguration. That Harding proved less than a success as president was not the Packard's fault.

The Twin Six wasn't exempt from the passion for speed that gripped Jesse Vincent and his colleagues; quite the contrary. No sooner had the Twin Six been launched than Vincent had a skimpy racing body fitted to an open-wheeled short-wheelbase chassis. He hotted up its engine with a more extreme camshaft, taller pistons for a higher compression ratio and new inlet manifold to hold a Zenith double-throat carburettor. Its ability to shift the

New features of Packard's twelve for 1917 included detachable cylinder heads, fitting of a Lanchester-patent vibration damper and warming of its inlet manifold by water exiting the cylinder head. (Robert J. Neal)

With headlamp surrounds that mimicked its radiator shape, this 1922 Packard Twin Six was the height of smooth, elegant transportation in its day. The twelve played a major role in establishing Packard's reputation as a car at the top of its market. (Robert J. Neal)

Mad for speed, Jesse Vincent lost no time in building a hot-rodded version of the Twin Six. Dubbed the 'Twin Six Typhoon' by Packard's publicists, this easily lapped Sheepshead Bay at better than 100mph with Vincent at the wheel, shown, with Packard's Henry Joy.

car's 3,780lb suggested that the tuned V12 produced at least 120bhp at 3,000rpm.

Packard publicists dubbed Vincent's hot rod the 'Twin Six Typhoon'. In November 1915 he took its wheel to turn a lap of Sheepshead Bay at 102.25mph. Works driver Bill Rader covered 32 laps – 64 miles – at better than 100mph. Though this rough and ready racer was quickly supplanted by the 299 and then the 905, it served to show what the Twin Six was made of.

The new vee-twelve was proof-tested in other ways. Henry Joy took one overland for his annual summer break as a quasi-cowboy in the far west. We have to believe, as well, that Packard's close relationship with the Indianapolis Motor Speedway meant that disguised Twin Six prototypes were hammered over its bricks to check performance and durability. With no secrets safe in that city of speed, we also have to believe that Packard's plans did not remain secret long. It can be no coincidence that those of Packard's rivals who were quickest off the mark

in building rival vee-twelves were based in Indianapolis or nearby in Ohio.

Arthur Newby was president of Indianapolis's National Motor Car and Vehicle Company, where W. Guy Wall and A.J. Paige were on the engineering strength. National, they decided, would build its own vee-twelve for its Highway series, for which they'd buy a six from Continental. "While the Packard had been developed for maximum smoothness and tractability," wrote Jan Norbye, "the National V12 was created for high performance. It has smaller displacement and higher specific output. Its Indianapolis heritage clearly shone through in its exhaust note as well as in its throttle response."

Knowingly or not, National's engineers took a diametrically opposite approach to Packard's in placing their valve gear. The two engines were similar in having six-cylinder cast-iron fixed-head blocks with L-head valves at a 60° vee on an aluminium crankcase. Both also had side-by-side connecting rods, with this engine's left block shifted forward 25mm, and initially aluminium pistons. The difference lay in National's decision to put the valves on the outside of the blocks instead of in the central vee. The latter position used by Packard had more than a few mechanics with bruised knuckles cursing the

West Grand Boulevard engineers. The National's valve clearances were easily adjusted through aperture plates on the sides of its blocks.

This required two camshafts along the sides of the crankcase, driven from the crank nose by helical gears. They opened the valves through mushroom tappets. From the right-hand camshaft a silent chain drove the cooling fan and, in the central vee, a Splitdorf magneto that was a sign of the National's racy origins. A Westinghouse starter motor was in the rear of the vee. Gear-driven along the engine's right flank were its generator and its water pump, the latter having a divided volute to supply both cylinder banks. Exhaust manifolds were conveniently along the sides of the blocks, while induction manifolding was cast into the blocks and supplied centrally as in the Twin Six, using a Rayfield carburettor.

Introduced in the summer of 1915 as a 1916 model, the National Highway Twelve displaced 5,550cc (69 x 120.7mm) and developed on the order of 70bhp at 2,800rpm. Priced at a moderate $1,990, it accounted for a production of around 1,000 cars before a new Series AK version was introduced in May 1917 for 1918 that was given a remarkable makeover. The blocks were aligned on the crankcase to permit the use of fork-and-blade connecting rods in place of the previous side-by-side type and, as in the Packard, pistons retrogressed from aluminium to iron. They were larger in diameter for the National V12's new bore of 73mm, bringing displacement to 6,067cc.

The 1918-model engine's cylinder heads were now detachable, the opportunity being taken to revise the block design to give more inlet-manifold hot-spotting that helped the engine burn wartime fuels of lower volatility. Exhaust manifolding was given a more flowing central takeoff. Replacing the magneto was a Delco ignition system like Cadillac's. A pulley was now arranged from its drive shaft in the central vee to allow the belt-driven fan to be sited higher. Experiments with counterbalancing led to the use of four scimitar-shaped weights welded to the crankshaft, two at the centre and two at the ends.

Combustion-chamber clearance with the National's new heads was closer to the pistons to give a compression ratio of 5.0:1. The Series AK developed 81bhp at 2,800rpm and peak torque of 164lb-ft at only 800rpm. In the National's relatively light chassis this gave lively performance for its day. Like so many pioneer auto companies, however, National was underfunded, and the cost of the engine overhaul couldn't have helped its finances. The New York group that took National over continued the V12 in its line until 1920, after which it was dropped. National itself succumbed in 1924.

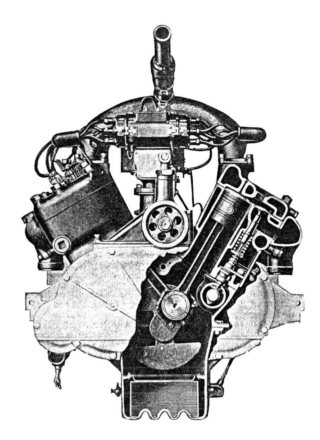

Indianapolis-based National took a racy approach to its 60° V12 introduced in the summer of 1915. Shown in its 1918 version, which had detachable cylinder heads, the National twelve had two camshafts flanking its crankshaft so that its valves could be at the sides of its blocks instead of in the central vee. (Robert J. Neal)

The 1918 National V12 was a lively performer with 81bhp from its 6.1 litres. Fork-and-blade connecting rods had replaced the previous side-by-side design. National produced its V12 throughout the 1920 model year. (Robert J. Neal)

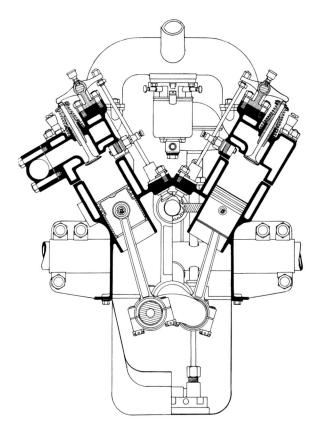

Remarkably small in displacement by American standards at only 3.7 litres, the twelve introduced by Cincinnati's Enger in September 1915 sold for a modest $1,095.

Over in Cincinnati, Ohio, 103 miles south-east of Indianapolis, another auto maker was quick off the mark with its vcc-twelve. The Enger Motor Car Company's proposition was distinctly different from the large, heavy 'Gentleman's Car' entries of the other American 'dozens'. Its wheelbase was a mere 115in, its weight 2,685lb and its price a stunningly low $1,095 – virtually half that of the next costly twelve. Frank J. Enger announced his new twelve in September 1915, when he said his demonstrators were already en route to dealers.

Enger's twelve was of all-iron construction, including its pistons, with a 60° vee angle and side-by-side connecting rods with its left cylinder bank more forward. Its displacement was a modest (for America) 3,725cc (66.7 x 88.9mm).[15] Cylinder heads were detachable, with generous water passages, although failure to surround the valve guides with water could be considered a flaw.[16] The guides were in the head, for Enger's was an overhead-valve engine, its vertical valves operated by rocker arms and pushrods from a chain-driven camshaft in the central vee. Like the crankshaft, the cam was carried in three bearings. Single-coil valve springs were conical in shape.

Log manifolds carried exhaust to the rear through twin pipes, while a central arched pipe supplied mixture from the single updraft Stromberg carburettor to inlet passages cast into the heads. A vertical shaft skew-gear-driven from the cam turned the oil pump in the pressed-steel sump, and the ignition breaker points. A distributor for the Remy ignition was mounted at the rear of the engine, while Westinghouse supplied starter and generator. Cooling was by thermosyphon,[17] with two pipes from the bottom of the radiator to both sides of the block.

An under-bonnet view of the Enger was anything but tidy, for its valve gear was entirely exposed, including the grease cups that lubricated its rocker-arm shafts. Nevertheless for its price the Enger V12 was an appealing proposition, with 55bhp at 3,000rpm, and some 1,000 cars were sold in 1916. Late that year Frank Enger revealed a much-improved 1917 model, his 'Twin-Unit Twelve'. He had worked out a way to enclose its valve

For 1917 Frank J. Enger enclosed the valve gear of his twelve and introduced a new feature: a means of deactivating the left-hand bank of six cylinders to gain improved fuel economy. Enger's suicide the same year brought an end to this promising line of development.

gear, albeit not its pushrods, which helped justify an increase in price to $1,295. It had a more striking innovation as well.

Moving a lever on the steering column of the Enger turned a set of six cams that held open the intake valves on the engine's left bank. At the same time a butterfly valve closed the inlet passage to that bank, which was thus deactivated. The butterfly was similar to the throttle closing used in George Schebler's car, but by holding the valves open as well Frank Enger made a proper job of an engine that could run on either six or twelve cylinders. "Just a touch of the little lever on the steering column does it all – cuts out six of your twelve cylinders and cuts them in again – in an instant," boasted his advertising. "This Enger invention makes possible the supreme motor car combination – luxury and economy."

Enger's company was well poised to capitalise on his ingenuity but this was not to be. "On January 4, 1917," wrote Beverly Rae Kimes, "Frank Enger, in ill health, shot himself. Despite leaving a note giving full instructions for his vice-president to continue, his widow elected to bail out to protect her investment." Cincinnati lost her last motor car maker when Enger's equipment was auctioned in July of that year.

Another Ohio-based enterprise, Cleveland's Ferro Machine and Foundry Company, deserves mention although its V12 never found a home in a production car. Designed by Alanson P. Brush, Ferro's proprietary engines, a V8 and V12, were impressively advanced. Their cylinder blocks and crankcases were cast in iron as a single unit, something that Frank Enger achieved but was seen only seldom in vee-type engines until the late 1920s.

Common to both Ferro types were detachable iron cylinder heads with overhead valves set into a flat surface, the chamber being formed by the top of the bore. From a central helical-gear-driven camshaft pushrod valve gear, with roller tappets, opened each valve through a rocker arm. The latter, exceptionally light, rocked against a spherical pivot which extended downward from a rigid rocker cover. In the spherical pivot was a genial concept which would not surface again until the Chevrolet and Pontiac V8s of the mid-1950s.

Although Ferro's V8 gained customers, Jackson cars and others, its V12 didn't. It differed from the eight, which had fork-and-blade rods, in having offset cylinder banks and side-by-side rods on its three-bearing crankshaft. A weight of 716lb was quoted for the twelve, albeit without such essentials as starter, generator, ignition and carburettor. It was a reasonable figure for an engine of 5,741cc (73 x 114.3mm). No power figure was quoted by Ferro, but at the same specific power as its V8

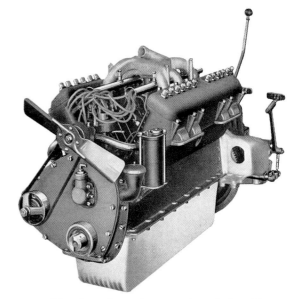

A successful maker of proprietary engines designed by Alanson Brush, Ferro of Cleveland, Ohio introduced a 5.7-litre V12 for 1916. Ferro failed to find customers for it, however.

the twelve would have delivered 80bhp at 2,250rpm on a compression ratio of 4.0:1.

Cleveland was also home to two refugees from that city's Peerless Motor Car company, executive Frank Harding and engineer Nathan Wyeth. In 1914 – ranking them among America's earlier advocates of V12s – they decided to put the Harding Twelve on wheels. Its engine, which followed conventional lines with two iron blocks on a separate crankcase and side-mounted valves, displaced 5,840cc. On a 132-inch wheelbase, the Harding was tested in 1915 and announced in 1916 with a price tag of $2,000. Balked by growing wartime shortages of materials, however, the Harding venture stalled. Its sole prototype became the property of engineer Wyeth.

In Indiana two Indianapolis companies, Weidely and Pathfinder, teamed up to put another twelve-cylinder car on the road surprisingly quickly after the launch of Packard's Twin Six. In August of 1915 the Weidely Motor Company, already the producer of a six, announced that it had readied a V12 engine for the customer market. The following February, Pathfinder revealed a new model powered by it – "The car that makes the imported car unnecessary".

Weidely's moving spirit was George Weidely, who had made his reputation with the road and racing models of Premier in Indianapolis.[18] He made a good fist of his own overhead-valve vee-twelve effort, producing a tidy-looking engine that won patronage. Its capacity was akin to that of the Packard less one-eighth of an inch in the bore for 6,379cc (73 x 127mm) and its bank angle was 60°

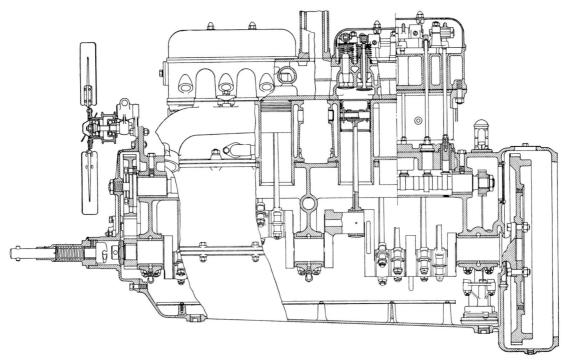

Above: *In 1915 George Weidely of Indianapolis was quick to place on the market a 6.4-litre V12 that he made available to his automotive customers. Weidely chose three wide main bearings and four blocks of three cylinders apiece for his handsome twelve, fitting a single cylinder head above all six cylinders on each bank.*

as well. Shifting the right-hand bank 32mm forward allowed the connecting rods – forged with elliptical-section shanks – to be side-by-side on 54mm journals. An aluminium crankcase carried the crankshaft in three main bearings, also of 54mm. Although the crank initially lacked counterbalancing, in the developed version curved sickle-shaped counterbalances were attached.

George Weidely's unique approach to the iron blocks and detachable heads of his V12 was to make the blocks very simple three-cylinder units, spigoted deeply into the crankcase, and to cap them with a six-cylinder head. There seems every likelihood that Weidely designed both the blocks and the heads so that only a single casting sufficed for both, bringing production economies. Vertical overhead valves 38mm in diameter opened onto a combustion chamber contained entirely in the head, into which all the inlet passages were cored and fed from a central inlet. Unusually the exhaust ports curved out and down to exhaust manifolds that were bolted to the underside of the head face.

Flat-faced tappets, driven by a single central camshaft, had provision for clearance adjustment at the pushrod abutments, Weidely eschewing the opportunity – taken by Enger – to put the adjusting screw at the end of the rocker arm. The rocker was highly leveraged – arms differing in length to magnify the lift given by the cam lobe – and had

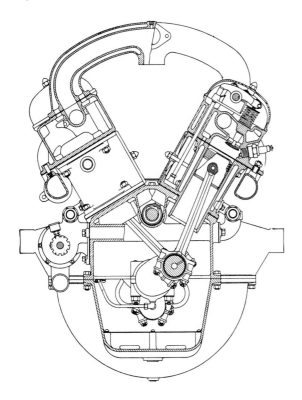

Left: *George Weidely chose a single central camshaft operating overhead valves through pushrods for his proprietary vee-twelve. It produced 87bhp at 3,000rpm.*

a roller where it contacted the valve stem. Initially aluminium, pistons were soon changed to iron, while the long connecting rods carried oil to their gudgeon pins. Racing experience was shown by the use of a baffle below the crankshaft to reduce power-robbing oil splashing.

At the crank nose a train of wide helical gears drove the Weidely's forged camshaft and, along the right side, the generator and then the water pump, whose position and water-flow ducting were akin to those of Packard. Like the latter the inverted-U inlet manifold to the two banks also carried warm water away from the engine, while holding an updraft Stromberg carburettor. The engine's central vee was designed to allow any excess of petrol to flow freely away lest it present a fire hazard. A skew-gear drive at the rear of the camshaft drove the oil pump below and the ignition timing apparatus above. Less the latter and its carburettor the Weidely V12 weighed 750lb. On the modest compression ratio of 3.6:1 it developed 70bhp at 2,000rpm, rising to 87bhp approaching 3,000rpm.

Seeing no reason to hide its light under a bushel, Weidely's home-town customer dubbed its car 'Pathfinder the Great'. Among its body-style offerings were Pathfinder's 'La Salle' touring car and its 'Cloverleaf' roadster. "The cloverleaf design fuses completely into the *tout ensemble*," boasted the catalogue, "producing a magnificent effect. A high-powered, flexible, twelve-cylinder Cloverleaf Pathfinder roadster is its own recommendation. It represents an ideal fostered by every true motor-loving devotee." Priced at $2,900, the Cloverleaf and its other Pathfinder variants failed to find enough devotees, for after the 1917 model year – in which its Twelve was the company's sole model – Pathfinder was no more.

As early as June 1915 another Weidely customer, the H. A. Lozier Company of Cleveland, Ohio, announced its plan to

Pathfinder of Indianapolis was the first to use the Weidely V12, enjoying bespoke rocker covers. As was customary with many of the early twelves the inlet manifold also served to draw off warm coolant from the cylinder heads.

produce a V12-powered auto. While the Lozier name was well respected in the American industry for the production of cars of quality under that brand, the founder's son, Harry A. Lozier, was eased out of the company in 1912 by its financial backers. He set up on his own account in Cleveland as the producer of the H.A.L. With a car scaling 3,555lb on a 135in wheelbase, Lozier claimed a high power-to-weight ratio for his creation, which was at the January 1916 New York Show with a $2,100 price tag. An initial production of 50 cars per week was claimed, and the H.A.L. Twelve did remain on the market until 1918 – then with a price of $3,600 – but that was its last year of availability. When the company folded in February 1918 future president Warren G. Harding bought one of its unsold Twelves at the liquidation auction.

Realistic pricing for the 'Gentleman's Car' market was a feature of the Weidely-powered Highway Twelve

A depiction of the Weidely vee-twelve in the catalogue of Cleveland's H.A.L. showed the features of the engine fitted by the Ohio company set up by Harry A Lozier.

The handsome Weidely-built engine was an important asset of the H.A.L. Twelve, which was produced into early 1918.

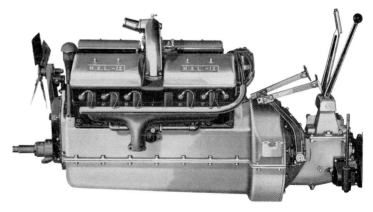

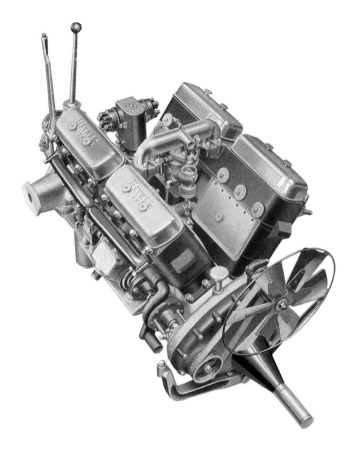

America's oldest auto producer, Haynes of Kokomo, Indiana, introduced a twelve-cylinder model in the autumn of 1916. Called a 'Light Twelve' by Haynes, it developed more than 70bhp from 5.8 litres.

produced from 1917 by the Austin Automobile Company of Grand Rapids, Michigan. Its roadster was $3,750 and its limousine $5,250 on the generous wheelbase of 142in. Distinctly majestic, these American Austin vee-twelves used two-speed rear axles. Offering its V12 through the 1920 model year, Austin is credited with the production of at least 1,861 twelves.

Other Weidely engine customers were more ephemeral. The well-known Wisconsin firm of Kissel opportunistically offered its vee-twelve in the 1917–1918 period at prices of $2,250 to $2,650. By 1920, when Mount Vernon, New York's Singer Motor Company began marketing its Weidely-powered Series 20, the engine was rated at 90bhp at 3,000rpm. With prices for the chassis alone of $4,500 and from $6,500 to $8,800 in bodied form, Singers were in the stratosphere. The company did not see out the end of 1920.

In 1921 Chicago's Ambassador showed a Weidely-powered prototype, but didn't proceed to production. Another Chicago producer, Meyer, offered a vee-twelve at $7,000 and may – or may not – have used a Weidely engine. A former furniture factory in Piqua, Ohio was the home of Maurice Wolfe's Meteor, which showed a Weidely-engined twelve in 1916. Few, however, were produced.

If Reno's Bill Harrah hadn't added a 1921 Heine-Velox to his famous collection, we could be entitled to doubt the existence of this legendary early auto on a 148in wheelbase with a cockpit like that of a speedboat behind a sloped windscreen. With headlamps mounted on its wings in the Pierce-Arrow manner, the huge San Francisco-built Heine-Velox featured early hydraulic brakes behind its big artillery wheels and was powered by a modified Weidely twelve.

One of America's largest cars, at least until the 1930s, the Heine-Velox was initially laid down in five chassis priced between $17,000 and $25,000, depending upon the body design. The dream car of piano maker Gustav Otto Heine, the Heine-Velox turned into a nightmare with nary a buyer stepping forward. By 1923 he had dissolved his car-making enterprise.

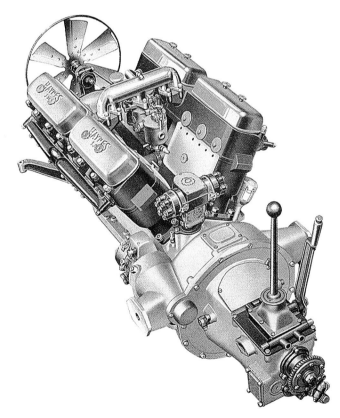

Overhead valves operated by a central camshaft were a feature of the Haynes Twelve. Although the engine itself was well styled, Haynes failed to match this with sufficiently attractive designs for its cars. Its final Twelve was offered in 1922.

A relatively late but respectable entry in America's dozen-cylinder derby was made by that country's first automobile producer, Haynes of Kokomo, Indiana. Although production of its Light Twelve only began in the autumn of 1916, Haynes first showed samples of its new model in New York at the beginning of the year. Sharing its chassis with a six, Haynes's twelve offered modest wheelbases of 121in and 127in, with its twelve priced modestly at $2,225 for its seven-passenger touring car. By the 1922 model year, penultimate for the Haynes Light Twelve, that model would cost $3,635.

The V12 from Kokomo was distinctive, yet much in the mould of the other American twelves. It was amongst them with its capacity of 5,840cc (69.9 x 127mm) and its output of "over 70 horsepower". It was based on an aluminium crankcase with a three-bearing, fully pressure-lubricated crankshaft. Pistons were aluminium and connecting rods were side-by-side, with the right-hand cylinder block staggered forward. Disposed in a 60° vee, the iron blocks contained six cylinders each and were topped by six-cylinder heads with overhead valves. The central camshaft operated the valves through pushrods, with clearance adjustment at the rocker arms.

The Haynes twelve was a clean, handsome job, looking more European than American with its sheer lines. Initially it had rocker covers for each trio of cylinders, but in its final version it had full-length covers. Its earlier simple log exhaust manifolds were replaced by a more flowing pattern. As in the Packard a chain at the engine's front drove both the camshaft and accessories along its right flank; first the water pump and then the generator. Initially at the rear of the Haynes V12, its Delco ignition was later moved to the front. In the usual manner its updraft carburettor fed a bridge manifold between the two banks, with the final manifolding cast into the heads.

Short of styling with the flair to reflect the effort invested in their engines, the Haynes twelves were not swift sellers. According to serial numbers, between 1917 and 1921 only 646 were made. After the 1922 model year Haynes no longer offered a vee-twelve and by 1925 the company was defunct.

Haynes and Packard thus shared the honour of being the final representatives of the incredible explosion of twelve-cylinder engines that swept America before and during the war in Europe. Briefly sustained by a post-war boom fuelled by Liberty bonds, car sales turned sour with the bust of 1920. Tightening credit terms sent car sales south, crippling not only the luxury-car market but also many auto makers.

The straight-eight was the engine of survival. Well suited to the long bonnets of luxury cars, exploiting the charisma of an association with Millers and 'Dueseys' at Indy, it displaced the vee-twelve – for the time being. Not for long would America's dozens be denied. And twelves were alive and well in Europe.

Chapter 2 Footnotes

[1] This was not their first twelve. They had previously (in 1914) built one for marine racing – an in-line twelve-cylinder engine. Two of them in *Disturber IV* made her the first to surpass a mile a minute on water.

[2] A 'square' engine has equal bore and stroke dimensions. An oversquare engine has a larger bore than stroke, while an engine that's under-square has a longer stroke than bore.

[3] Both did build V12 engines for marine-racing installations.

[4] Many reports credit the 299 with four valves per cylinder, but it did not have this feature.

[5] For better cooling it raced at Indy without its bonnet sides in place.

[6] Free-for-all races in which no restrictions on car specifications apply.

[7] Information on the 299's adventures in Italy was researched by Brad Skinner and Jim Dillon and related by Robert J. Neal.

[8] This is the Baronessa's own testimony in a 1969 interview with Valerio Moretti.

[9] Packard was familiar with this concept, having prepared for Ralph DePalma the 1914 Mercedes Grand Prix car that won the Indianapolis 500-mile race in 1915.

[10] On 7 February 1920 its speed was officially surpassed by an aeroplane for the first time: Sadi Lecointe's new record of 171.04 mph in a Nieuport-Delage 29.

[11] This was a drop in the bucket of $400,000 that Packard said it had spent on all its aviation-engine development to 1917.

[12] Its introduction of a six may well have influenced Packard's decision to give six-cylinder engines to its bespoke 1923 Indianapolis racers. It certainly had no mandate to promote the straight eights of its marketplace rivals.

[13] This is the author's conclusion based on inspection of the photos and drawings kindly provided by the sole surviving Buick twelve's keeper, Walter Marr's grandson Paul Durant Marr.

[14] Ironically Leo Goossen never saw the V12 he'd designed. By the time it arrived in Tennessee he had left for the southwest to cure a spot of tuberculosis – the same ailment that brought Walter Marr to Signal Mountain.

[15] Bore diameters of 60.3 and 68.3mm have also been mentioned for the Enger, but the author believes that the figure cited is the most likely.

[16] The author considers it likely – but cannot verify – that the cylinder head was designed as a single casting suitable for both banks of the engine, a valid and useful economy.

[17] Thermosyphon cooling takes advantage of the rising of heated water from the engine to the top of the radiator, from which cool water circulates back to the engine without the assistance of a water pump.

[18] G. Marshall Naul considered it likely that Weidely was in fact developing his V12 at Premier before that company had what he called its 'initial failure'.

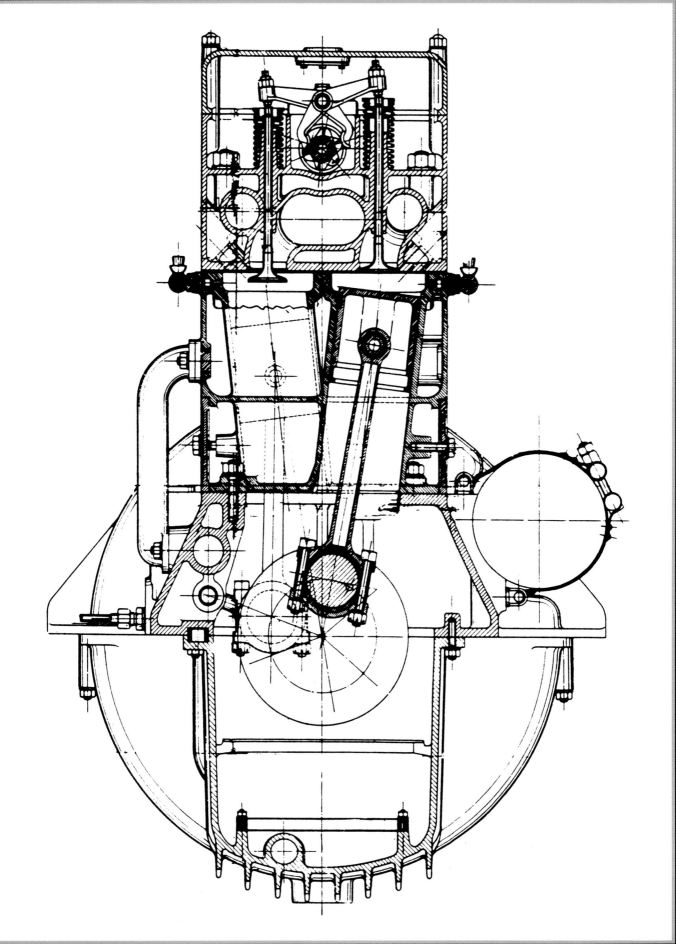

EUROPEAN TWELVES

We knew we weren't to expect a twelve-cylinder Sunbeam at the post-war auto shows. We've already heard Louis Coatalen's sour-grapes speech, grumbling that Packard stole the laurels that were rightly Sunbeam's. Also noticeable by its absence at the 1919 Paris Salon was one vee-twelve in particular. Europe's auto makers emerged from their wartime efforts with impressive new models that showed the inspiration, in many instances, of their aero engine designs for the military. One such powerplant, that of Hispano-Suiza, had gained particular success. It was a water-cooled V8, designed by Geneva-born Marc Birkigt, whose origins accounted for the 'Swiss' part of the name of this Barcelona-based producer of cars, trucks and aero engines.

The clean-lined overhead-cam 'Hisso' V8 was so successful and so much in demand that 21 companies – 14 of them in France – were asked to produce it during the war. In all 56,000 were supplied to Allied aircraft makers. To produce more than its 180 horsepower Marc Birkigt also designed a V12, but the war ended before it could be brought to the front. He could well have produced a smaller version and thus launched a V12 Hispano-Suiza for the post-war luxury-car market. Instead, he penned an in-line six closely derived from one bank of his V12, creating the superb H6. A twelve-cylinder Hispano-Suiza may have been among the missing at 1919's Paris Salon, but a dozen years later Birkigt would more than make amends for his truancy.

Also active during the war was France's proud Lorraine-Dietrich, which traced its origins to the 17th Century and built its first car in 1896. It too was building magnificent aero engines. They were designed by Marius Barbarou, a former Benz man who had been recruited from Delaunay-Belleville specifically for his knowledge of multi-cylinder power units. His wartime designs included several V12s and a 24-cylinder in W configuration.[1] At the Salon in 1919 Lorraine-Dietrich displayed his 6½-litre vee-twelve passenger car, bearing the company's distinctive Lorraine-cross badge, but this remained a prototype and a six was introduced instead.

Another explorer of vee-type engines during the war was Italy's Lancia. For its founder, burly racing driver Vincenzo Lancia, vee-type engines were an obsession. During the war he took care to patent several ideas for engines of very narrow vees, effectively in-line engines made shorter by staggering their cylinders to left and right. Lancia built two types of V12 aero engines, one with its banks at 50° and the other with a 53° vee. Both had vertical combustion chambers and lateral valves resembling those used by Miller and especially Duesenberg.

Lancia was the first to think of liberating the connecting rods of the facing cylinders of a vee-type engine from a single shared crankpin. When rods share

Opposite: *Brought to pre-production status and shown at salons in 1919 was a Lancia vee-twelve of 22½° vee. This had individual crankpins for each connecting rod and a single cylinder head carrying long vertical valves operated by an overhead camshaft through rocker arms. Lancia's channelling of exhaust heat into a central passage in the head was sure to have been a negative feature of the design, which did not reach production.*

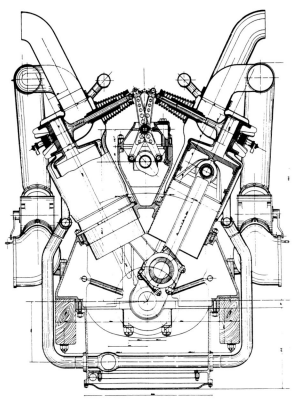

Vincenzo Lancia used a 52° vee angle for his aviation vee-twelve designs of 1917. Engines of this type were built with capacities of both 24 and 32 litres. A comparison is interesting with the contemporary Miller engine shown on page 29.

In 1918 Turin-based Lancia produced this prototype twelve with a vee angle of 30°. Twin camshafts operated side-mounted valves, while each connecting rod was given its own crankpin in search of the smoothest possible running.

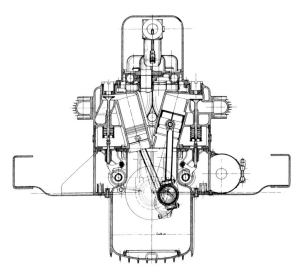

the same crankpin, by whatever means, obtaining evenly spaced firing in an engine depends on its bank angle. This makes 90° ideal for a V8, 60° optimum for a V12 and 45° correct for a V16. If you gave each connecting rod its own crankpin, reasoned Lancia, you could position it on the crankshaft where it ideally had to be to get even or near-even firing with almost any bank angle. This opened a door to new engine configurations through which Lancia strolled. He didn't use this technique on his aero engines, which had slightly uneven firing intervals due to their narrower-than-60° bank angles, but applied it instead to new engines for his post-war cars.

Vincenzo Lancia and his team in Turin warmed up with a design for a 30° V12 with L-head chambers and side valves on the outside of the engine, where its vertical valves were driven by twin camshafts flanking the crankcase. With the cylinders angled and the valves vertical this gave a good combustion chamber by L-head standards. His ultimate solution, however, was an even narrower V12, aimed to achieve the optimum in compactness and visual simplicity in a twelve-cylinder engine. In this it was a tour de force, resembling a swarthy silver-topped monolith with six spark plugs along each side – the antithesis of the bitty-looking American twelves.

Lancia's final design, a 22½° twelve with individual rod journals on a four-bearing crankshaft, was a layer cake of an engine. Its bottom two layers were in aluminium, a deep sump and a shallow trapezoidal-section crankcase. The next layer was its iron cylinder block, its combustion chambers contained in the block. Atop that was its flat-faced iron cylinder head with long-stemmed overhead valves placed vertically. Carried in its centre was a shaft-driven single overhead camshaft opening the valves through adjustable rocker arms. The topmost layer was an aluminium rocker cover. Similar covers at the sides of the block concealed its attachment studs and nuts to the crankcase. A magneto and its distributor were deployed laterally at the front.

Of the two versions of the engine tested, one of 7,238cc (80 x 120mm) and a shorter-stroke version of 6,032cc (80 x 100mm), the smaller one went through as a prototype for production.[2] Producing 100bhp at 2,800rpm, it was fed by a single Zenith carburettor plugged into the centre of its left flank. It supplied mixture to inlet manifolding cast into the periphery of the head, while the exhaust ports vented into a passage down the centre of the head to a single outlet at the rear. This was likely to have been the engine's Achilles heel, building up tremendous heat within the head. Inelegant though many of their twelves had been, the Americans always took care to hasten exhaust heat away. Although a handsome chassis strutted Lancia's stuff at 1919's Paris and London shows, and limited production was hinted at, this did not come to pass.

What Lancia could do, Turin's big battalions in the form of Fiat could do as well. That was the mindset of Giovanni Agnelli, his technical director Guido Fornaca and engineering head Carlo Cavalli as they contemplated the post-war auto market at home and abroad. During that war Fiat had produced some impressive V12 aero engines, from the 57-litre overhead-cam A-14 to the more compact experimental A-15-R of 20.3 litres with enclosed valve gear.

For ground-borne use Agnelli's engineers had weighed the merits of a vee-twelve as early as 1915, inspired by the eruption of engines in America. Not surprisingly their Type 43 proposal was Packardesque with its single central camshaft, integral L-head chambers and iron cylinder blocks at a 60° angle on an aluminium crankcase. They provided more generous water jacketing than Packard, solid instead of roller tappets and lower positioning – for a sleeker line – of the manifold that carried mixture to the blocks from its central carburettor.

Anticipating peacetime prosperity, Fornaca and Cavalli started work after the war on a superb new twelve for Agnelli. They gifted him a classical 60° V12, engine type number 120, rich in meticulous engineering detail. It outdid the Lancia with a bigger bore, 85mm, which with a similar 100mm stroke gave 6,809cc. This, the most-built version of the 120, developed 120bhp at 2,800rpm and 268lb-ft of torque at 1,500rpm. Under study as well was a longer-stroke variant of 7,490cc (85 x 110mm).

With a central chain-driven camshaft operating vertical overhead valves through pushrods and rockers, the Fiat's architecture was not unlike that of the valve-in-head American V12s. Twin coil springs closed each valve, and each roller-tipped tappet had an individual coil spring to keep it in contact with its cam lobe. The water pump was mounted in the central vee, whence it pumped coolant to both banks, and the long sump contained doubled oil pressure pumps. Ignition distributors were placed laterally at the front, where one of Fiat's own carburettors supplied the mixture to the centres of the two heads through a casting that also served as the warm-water takeoff.

After World War I Fiat got serious about a big V12 passenger car, developing its Type 120 engine in 1920–21 for its Type 520 'Superfiat' luxury car. A lateral section showed its centrally mounted water pump, its drilled connecting-rod shanks and its vertical overhead valves operated by pushrods.

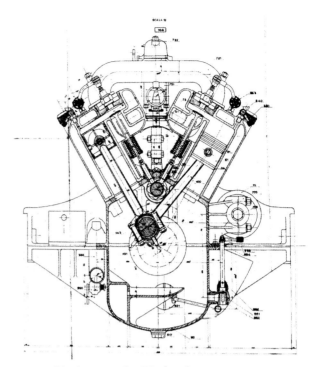

Inspired by the example of Packard, Fiat's creative engineers explored a vee-twelve passenger-car engine concept in 1915. In many respects it resembled the Packard, although its side valves were parallel to the cylinders instead of angled slightly away from them to improve gas flow as in the American engine. The Type 43 Fiat was not produced.

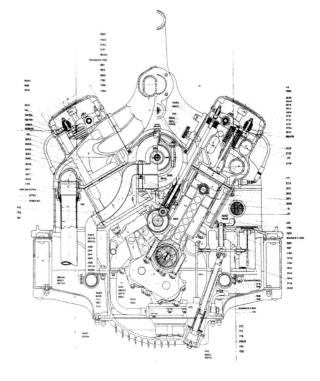

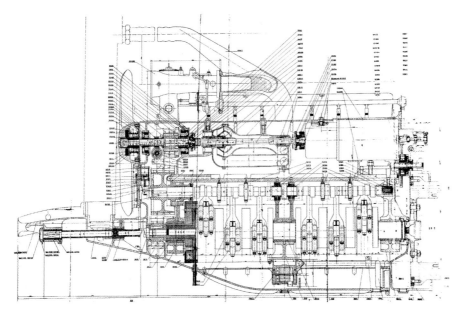

Deep iron cylinder heads contained the 120's combustion chambers and internal cored passages for both inlet and exhaust manifolds – the latter again a departure from American practice that was certain to retain heat before the exhaust escaped down a central pipe. Pistons were iron in short six-cylinder iron blocks that were bolted into the crankcase from below. The lower half of each bore, spigoted into the crankcase, was a separate cylinder screwed into the block and prohibited from unscrewing by a set screw. The blocks were opposite each other by virtue of fork-and-blade connecting rods, following the precedent set by the A-14 aero engine. Unusually, the I-section shanks of the rods were drilled for lightness. Divided at the crank centreline, the crankcase and its finned sump were aluminium.

This twelve was installed in the 152-inch wheelbase chassis of a magnificent big Fiat, the Type 520, whose chassis alone weighed 3,750lb and was priced in Britain at £1,800. Fully meriting its name – Superfiat – it was justifiably a sensation at the auto shows of 1921 and '22. Both touring-car and town-car bodies were seen on its robust chassis with a proud angular radiator. As market conditions for such luxury cars worsened, however, Fiat balked at committing its Superfiat to full production. Then, as later, Fiat wasn't always confident that its marque belonged at the top of the market. The 520 would, wrote Nick Baldwin, "have given the Silver Ghosts, Twin Sixes and other great cars a run for their money if more than a handful had been built." One source suggests three, another "no more than five".

The 1921 Paris Salon also saw a French twelve-cylinder entry, the work of the proud and eccentric Gabriel Voisin.

Having participated in the birth of aviation in France, Voisin decided to dedicate his exceptional – by his own lights – inventive talents to the world of the automobile. This he did with unfailingly intriguing and controversial results. His staple model was the M1, which he renamed the C1 in 1919 in honour of his late brother Charles. Voisin had adopted the patented Knight system of sleeve valves in which two concentric ported sleeves, forming the cylinder bore, slid up and down to open and close the inlet and exhaust ports.

Next on Gabriel Voisin's agenda was a twelve-cylinder luxury car, which was his C2 in chronological order. Emphasising the aesthetic in all his works, Gabriel Voisin rivalled Lancia in his fashioning of an engine of surpassingly elegant appearance for his new model. He chose the narrow vee angle of 30° to create an engine of such symmetry that it's impossible to say whether its cylinder banks were aligned or staggered.[3] All its main castings were aluminium, with the valve sleeves sliding directly in the light metal. Apertures along the sides of the blocks gave access for attaching the sleeve linkages to shafts that ran alongside, driven by a train of gears at the front that also turned the water pump, on the right, and twin Delco ignition distributors on the left. Its fan was belt-driven.

Though belied by the C2 twelve's smooth exterior appearance, its cylinders were in blocks of three with integral inlet manifolding fed by a rear-mounted Zenith HK carburettor – a reversal of the Lancia method. Three roller bearings carried its crankshaft, which "was in two parts, bolted and keyed together," wrote Cecil Clutton. "The inside of the water jackets was enamelled under pressure and stoved to prevent porosity. In fact,

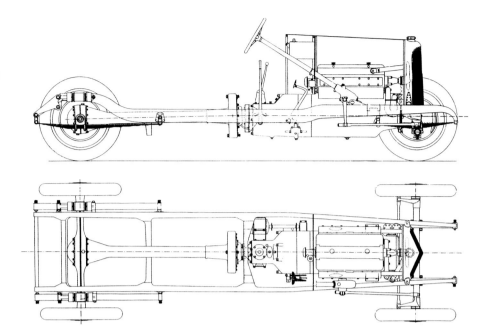

Looking for a form of propulsion that would approach the steam engine, France's Gabriel Voisin built two prototypes of his V12 C2 in 1920. As was customary with Voisin the 7.2-litre engine was beautifully clean-lined, even its spark plugs being concealed. Voisin decided against producing his C2, however.

everything about the engine seems to have been as difficult as possible." Its capacity was substantial – 7,238cc (80 x 120mm) – and its appearance indeed elegant, its rows of spark plugs on top concealed by hinged covers.

Gabriel Voisin installed his V12 behind an arched and veed radiator in his C2 chassis, stretching 150.6in from wheel to wheel, the latter being discs carrying 935 x 135mm tyres, the largest then available for automobile use. Two C2 chassis were built, one with semi-independent front suspension and open tourer bodywork. That no power figure was quoted for their engines suggests that they were never made fully customer-ready, although one was tested on the road from Paris to Cannes and back in April 1920.[4] It was premature to try to produce the twelve, Voisin said later: "It was too complex and therefore prohibitively expensive to produce in as small a factory as ours." *Le Patron* made use of one of the prototypes for personal purposes while he mulled the future of vee-twelve engines. He would not give up on the idea, which he saw as coming as close as possible to a steam engine's smooth propulsion.

Here were four attempts – Lorraine-Dietrich, Lancia, Fiat and Voisin – to launch a luxury V12 for Europe, all striking the buffers. The French and Italians had at least tried, but the English and Germans showed no signs of activity. German companies had been slow to embrace vee engines, even in wartime. "The Mercedes engines were all of the single in-line type," said engineer Sam Heron about their military efforts, "since the Germans appear to have considered that a vee engine would not work." (This despite numerous captured Allied vee engines, not to mention pre-war French and British engines.) There

were exceptions, notably Ferdinand Porsche's trend-setting Austro-Daimler V12 aero engine, but otherwise the more upwardly mobile German auto companies followed the star of the straight eight in the 1920s.

As for England, later in the 1920s Daimler would introduce a V12, but that's a topic for Chapter 6. Otherwise the British perspective could be summed up by a 1927 remark by Colonel Napier: "It may be said on the whole that the four-cylinder engine will continue to be thought good enough for most people and that no one can really need anything better than a six. The straight-eight and diagonal (or vee) twelve remain available for the wealthy faddists of exquisite sensibility." Nor were the sceptred isle's richest necessarily panting to splash out on lavish cars, as Rolls-Royce engineer Maurice Olley explained to Americans in 1921:

Many well-to-do city men living in London suburbs do not own cars to this day because the week-end is devoted to exercise of one sort or another, cycling, walking, tennis or cricket, and a car might break down those regular habits. His social status is not governed by the car he drives, or by his income, but rather by the particular accent with which he speaks the English language. Bear in mind that anyone may ride in the most peculiar or tiniest cars without loss of dignity.

In spite of his failure to move it forward on the commercial front, one man in England still had faith in the vee-twelve – a Frenchman of course, Sunbeam's Louis Coatalen. Having sold his rapid Toodles V to America, the impetuous and speed-mad engineer lost no

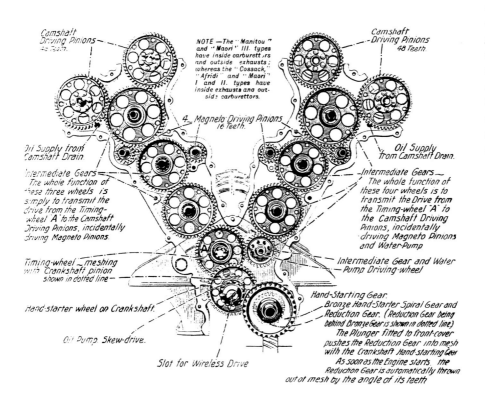

During World War I Britain's Sunbeam produced numerous vee-type aviation engines, including the vee-twelve Manitou of 15.4 litres. Its twin overhead camshafts and accessories were driven by a train of gears of no small elaboration.

Below: A single overhead camshaft on each bank of Sunbeam's Arab V8 of World War I operated a single inlet valve directly and twin exhaust valves through rocker arms. Although hopes were high for the 11.8-litre Arab, vibration problems severely limited its usefulness.

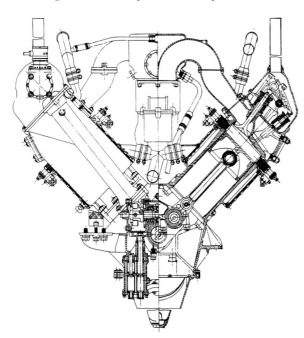

time in creating a successor to make post-war history. The result, wrote William Boddy, "was a most exciting car, destined to become one of the fastest ever to use the Track". The Track, of course, was Brooklands, by the spring of 1920 recovering from the ravages of heavy use during the war by the Royal Flying Corps and Vickers Aviation. The first race meetings were in April and as early as June Coatalen's new speed machine was ready to stretch her legs at Brooklands for the first time.

Never shy of twisting the facts to serve his purposes, Louis Coatalen confused generations of historians by writing that the new car's vee-twelve "was based, so far as its design was concerned, on the very latest development of the Sunbeam Manitou aviation engine". The four-overhead-cam 15.4-litre Manitou V12 was one of the engines that Sunbeam was eager to promote for post-war aviation, so its association with a very fast car was hoped to be as helpful as Toodles V was in launching the successful Mohawk. However, the new car's engine was actually a derivation of the V8 Arab, an engine that was mutually catastrophic for both HM Government and Sunbeam and thus hardly worthy as the inspiration of a new racing car.

It's easy to see why the War Office was attracted to Sunbeam's Arab when it was presented in prototype form in January of 1917. A 90° vee with shaft-driven single overhead cams, it had much of the neat look of the

Hispano-Suiza V8 and indeed shared the nominal dimensions (120 x 130mm, 11,762cc) of that engine. Each cam opened three valves per cylinder – a single inlet directly through finger followers and paired exhausts through short rocker arms. Cylinders of the two banks directly opposed each other, for Coatalen chose the master-rod and link method of joining the connecting rods to the crankshaft. This proved the Arab's Achilles heel, for the consequence was "alarming vibration problems" that made the vee-eight all but unusable.[5] "There is little doubt that the Arab was one of the worst engines of the First World War," wrote Alec Brew. Though 6,160 were ordered in the first glow of optimism, only 1,311 Arabs were delivered.

Louis Coatalen salvaged something of the Arab for the engine of the car that became known as the '350hp Sunbeam'. Its cylinder bore was the same 120mm and its stroke was slightly lengthened. Because it had the same master-and-link-rod big-end design as the Arab, its strokes differed from side to side. "The mean stroke is 138.5mm," wrote Coatalen, "and the total cylinder capacity 18,322cc."[6] With the included angle between the cylinder banks narrowed to 60°, the vibration problems experienced by the 90° Arab seem not to have been a hindrance. With its three-valve head and dual ignition the top end was exactly that of the Arab, although a significant difference was the use of a train of spur gears instead of shafts, at the front of the engine, to drive its overhead camshafts.

Cylinders and heads were cast *en bloc* of aluminium, in three-cylinder units, and bolted to a compact aluminium crankcase. Steel liners were pressed into the cylinders and valve seats were screwed into position. Takeoffs from the front spur-gear train drove a single water pump and a pair of BTH magnetos that sparked KLG plugs through a total of 120 feet of high-tension leads. Prodigality of hose clips was evident at the top of the engine, where 48 of them dealt with the water take-offs, numbering a total of eight from the four cylinder blocks. Seven main bearings carried the nickel-chrome-steel crankshaft, whose oil drillings were fed by one pump ganged with two scavenge pumps for the dry-sump system. As with Toodles V, the oil tank was in the tail.

Each 'vee-six' half of the engine was given its own induction system. Each had a central Claudel-Hobson HC7 Mark II carburettor with twin throats, both with 42mm venturis. The mixture rose from them into a water-heated T-shaped manifold that delivered it to the manifolds for each three-cylinder block. Rising up from the centre of the vee were 4-inch-diameter inlet pipes that curved down and then up to feed the carburettors.

The Sunbeam Arab's cylinder head configuration was carried over with little change to the vee-twelve engine of 18.3 litres that Louis Coatalen completed in 1920 to power a replacement for his Toodles V. In this he was successful, for the new engine produced 356bhp at 2,300rpm.

Imposing exhaust pipes trailed straight back along each side. According to a test on 29 September 1920 this engine produced 356bhp at 2,300rpm and could rev to 2,500. Its awesome peak torque, 873lb-ft generated at 1,750rpm, was ideal for quick getaways.

Impressive though the Arab-and-a-half engine was, Louis Coatalen's greatest feat was engineering a drive train to cope with this vee-twelve in a car weighing 3,140lb. The drive went from an exposed flywheel to a multi-plate dry clutch and thence to a four-speed transmission with a gated right-hand shift lever. The

Sunbeam's W. R. Perkins here made adjustments to the 350-horsepower Sunbeam, as the new racing car was known. We can be sure that the engine hadn't recently been run.

Built chiefly for record-breaking, the 350-horsepower Sunbeam did without front-wheel brakes. Like its predecessor Toodles V, its rear frame rails were lead-filled to improve weight distribution and traction. For 1920 this was heavy metal by any standards.

propeller shaft was open, with semi-elliptic rear springs taking all the axle's torque loadings, and after initial tests a differential was done without. Final-drive ratio was 1.5:1, which with the 880 x 120 tyres would have given a maximum speed of 200mph at 2,300rpm.

Foot brakes were on the rear wheels and an 18in

Seen at Brooklands, where he set a new official world land speed record at a two-way average of 133.75mph, Kenelm Lee Guinness was the first to flaunt the tremendous potential of the 350-horsepower Sunbeam. It was timed at Brooklands over a half-mile at 140.52mph.

finned-drum hand brake was at the output of the gearbox. The engine was subframe-mounted in a conventional channel-steel frame giving a wheelbase of 127in. As in Toodles V, the rear channels of the frame were lead-filled to improve balance and traction. Bodywork was single-seated, with upper surfaces left bare aluminium and lower areas plus the radiator cowl painted in Sunbeam's grey-green.

This supercar from Wolverhampton made a spectacular Brooklands debut in the worst way, crashing through a corrugated steel fence after a tyre failed during a practice run, fortunately with little damage to car or driver, Harry Hawker.[7] It then wore artillery wheels on knock-off hubs, soon replaced by wire wheels. The latter were in place on 10 October 1920 at Gaillon, along the main road from Paris to Rouen, where racers tackled a straight with a 9 per cent gradient and were clocked over a kilometre from a flying start. With a record time of 20.6 seconds René Thomas and the Sunbeam were a second faster than Thomas had been the year before in a 4.9-litre Indianapolis Ballot, also a record. An attempt to break records at Brooklands in December was thwarted by bad weather.

"It was never easy for Coatalen to find drivers sufficiently brave and experienced to handle the Sunbeam," wrote William Boddy. This was scarcely surprising, for it bid fair to be the world's fastest car. It was "all engine and bonnet and beautiful to handle, if it liked

you," recalled S.C.H. Davis. "That car handled best when not a trace of tyre tread pattern remained, at which point it could do just about ten laps before the tyre burst." Some drivers could have found this unsettling.

The first Englishman to master the Sunbeam was Kenelm Lee Guinness of KLG spark-plug fame, who was also competing in Grand Prix races for Sunbeam. Lapping Brooklands with it at 122.47mph in May of 1922, Guinness showed the 350hp's potential for record-breaking. This was verified on 17 and 18 May 1922, when KLG set new world speed records at Brooklands, running both ways over measured distances in what the track's historian William Boddy called "some really sensational motoring". The booty was as follows:

Standing kilometre	83.67mph	134.63km/h
Standing mile	96.63mph	155.48km/h
Flying kilometre	33.75mph	215.20km/h
Flying mile	129.17mph	207.83km/h
Flying 5 miles	116.75mph	187.85km/h
Flying 10 miles	113.13mph	182.03km/h

The flying kilometre figure was well short of the speeds that Packard's 905 had shown at Daytona in 1919, but by virtue of being a two-way average it was declared the new official world land speed record by the international authority, the AIACR[8]. The icing on KLG's cake included a new Brooklands lap record at 123.39mph and a one-way run over a half-mile timed at 140.51mph.

The 350hp Sunbeam's exploits – its final runs at Brooklands – were watched with special interest by a London insurance underwriter, not because he'd insured the effort but because he coveted the big car and its speed potential. "I'd give my heart and soul to get my hands on that car," admitted Malcolm Campbell to his mechanic Leo Villa. Campbell borrowed it from Sunbeam to set a two-way speed of 134.07mph on 17 June 1922 on Britain's Saltburn Sands, but because timing was by hand the slight improvement on Guinness's speed wasn't internationally recognised.

The speedy Scot had the same disappointment after being timed on Denmark's Fanoe Island at 137.72mph on 23 June 1923; again the timing equipment wasn't AIACR-approved. Third-time unlucky he was back at Saltburn on 21 June 1924, when his 145.26mph average went unrecognised because a timing tape failed to break. Neophyte Malcolm Campbell was discovering some of the hazards of the record-breaking business.

By 1923 Campbell owned the Sunbeam outright and by 1924, with the advice of aeroplane builders Boulton & Paul, he'd fitted it with a new longer-tailed body which reduced its tendency to veer to the right under power.

By 1923 the big Sunbeam had become the property of speed-mad insurance underwriter Malcolm Campbell, here leaning on its cowl. In search of a land speed record Campbell had abortive outings at Saltburn Sands in Britain and Fanoe Island in Denmark in 1923.

A return to Fanoe Island that year was marred by a spectator fatality caused by an errant tyre from the skidding Sunbeam. In the meantime the bar had been raised for Campbell by René Thomas at the wheel of a Delage – which we'll meet later in this chapter – and then by Ernest Eldridge in a powerful Fiat, the latter leaving the record at 146.01mph in July 1924. On 25 September of that year Campbell went to a new venue, Pendine Sands on the shore of Carmarthen Bay in South Wales,

Aerodynamic experts recommended a reshaped body with a longer tail for the Sunbeam, which Campbell used to good advantage to set a new world land speed record at 146.16mph at Pendine Sands in South Wales. Malcolm Campbell was now well and truly launched on his record-breaking career.

where the RAC timed him officially at 146.16mph – a new official world record by the slimmest of margins. The ambitious sportsman was in the record books at last.

Craving a bigger margin over his rivals, Campbell decided to return to Pendine in the summer of 1925. "We hotted the old Sunbeam up a bit," said Leo Villa; it was now running sometimes with exhaust pipes and sometimes with stub exhausts. "On 21 July," the mechanic continued, "with even less fuss than on the last occasion, he pushed the speed up to 150.6mph." His speeds, in fact, were 150.869mph for the kilometre and 150.766 for the mile. Campbell had finally outsped the one-way run of the Packard 905 and become officially the first man to be timed at better than 150mph. While Campbell would break more records in cars of his own, powered by W12 Napier and V12 Rolls-Royce aircraft engines, the 350hp Sunbeam was his entrée to this arcane world. He told his son that it had the finest acceleration of any car he'd ever driven.[9]

Within less than a year Campbell's new record would fall to another V12-powered Sunbeam – a car, astonishingly, with an engine of less than one-quarter the size. It was another product of the ever-questing imagination of Louis Coatalen. "About the middle of 1925," wrote racing driver Henry Segrave, "Mr. Coatalen expressed an interest in seeing what was the maximum speed which could be obtained with a racing car outside the limits of capacity that had been imposed in the events of the last few years. Presently the conception began to take definite shape, and a car was put in hand at the Sunbeam Works." The result would be the world's most elegant and efficient high-speed vehicle until the arrival of the ill-fated 1928 Stutz Black Hawk of America's Frank Lockhart.

With Grand Prix rules changing for 1926 to engines of 1½ instead of 2 litres, componentry was available from Sunbeam's successful Fiat-inspired 2-litre racing sixes to build a new vee-twelve. Its bore and stroke were identical to the GP engines, 67 x 94mm, giving a capacity of 3,977cc for the twelve. It was not Coatalen's manner to do this in the easiest way, however. While the Grand Prix engine had two fabricated steel monoblocs, each of three cylinders, the Frenchman specified three two-cylinder blocks for each bank of his new V12. Sunbeam's Captain J.S. Irving took charge of the new car's build, aided by chief mechanic and test driver Bill Perkins.

Each cylinder block's integral heads contained two valves per cylinder at the wide included angle of 96°, opened through finger-type followers. Bank angle was 60° on an aluminium crankcase.[10] The right-hand bank was shifted forward to permit the rod big ends to share

journals on the twelve's seven-bearing crankshaft, supplemented by an eighth bearing to take thrust loadings from the clutch. Rollers were used for both the main and rod bearings, for which an oil pressure of 14psi was sufficient. With the crankshaft solid, all the roller bearings ran in split outer races.

Each bank's twin overhead camshafts were turned by a train of gears up the back of the engine, from which a shaft protruded rearward into the cockpit to drive two Bosch magnetos. The nose of the crankshaft drove a huge Roots-type blower, mounted longitudinally, from which manifolds branched up into the centre of the vee. With a 5.9:1 compression ratio and 7.9psi of boost, drawing through a Solex carburettor, an output of 292bhp at 5,000rpm was measured. This was transmitted through a multi-plate clutch, three-speed transmission and torque tube to the live rear axle with 3.5:1 gearing. Installed in a chassis akin to that of the Grand Prix Sunbeams, with a wheelbase lengthened by four inches to 106 inches, this purposeful-looking racer weighed only 2,015lb dry. Its driver was offset to the right so that he could be seated low alongside the drive shaft; thus a passenger could be carried.

Wheelspin was acute when the four-litre Sunbeam was first tested at Brooklands at the end of 1925, but even with one cylinder not co-operating it was clocked at 145mph over a half-mile stretch. At the beginning of March 1926 the car was taken to Southport in Lancashire, where a seven-mile beach of indifferent quality was available about one-third closer to Sunbeam at Wolverhampton than the longer sands at Pendine in Wales. There a vertical cowl for the radiator replaced the

Another product of the restless mind of Louis Coatalen of Sunbeam, this 4.0-litre vee-twelve first ran in 1925. As shown here, the twelve first used a single large Roots-type supercharger driven from the nose of the crankshaft and delivering to the two banks down the centre of the 60° vee.

sloping mask that had first been tried at Brooklands, and body-side excrescences were given fairings.

The first tests at Southport showed carburation problems plus a tendency for the big blower to crack its housing when its rotating lobes expanded at speed. Capt Irving had already initiated work on a twin-blower setup and wanted to wait for this, but driver Segrave was eager to get on with it, so the équipe returned to Southport on 16 March with a supply of blowers. This was prudent, for the record attempt ended with six broken casings. To conserve the last one the Sunbeam was towed, not driven, to the start of the record track with its cooling water pre-warmed.

In fact that last casing broke during Segrave's final run through the measured distance, which slowed his speed over the measured mile. Over the kilometre, however, he was timed at an average of 152.336mph, a new world land-speed record by a slim margin. Allowing for wheelspin on the sand, an increase of the blower's clearances that certainly reduced its boost and Segrave's use of part-throttle on the first of his runs, this was well short of the feisty Sunbeam's real potential.[11]

Back at Wolverhampton the 230mm blower was replaced by two 140mm Roots-type units running at engine speed, each with its own Solex carburettor. Offering a boost of 7.2psi, these ran reliably and gave an output of 299bhp at 5,000rpm with peak torque of 340lb-ft at 3,500rpm. Joining the original car in 1927 was a sister, and they were aptly named 'Tiger' and 'Tigress'.[12] In May of 1928 Kaye Don used Tiger to break international Class C records at Brooklands over distances from one kilometre (136.39mph) to 100 kilometres (120.06mph). Don set a new standing mile average of 90.11mph that he upped with the same car to 100.77mph in 1929, when he went back to Brooklands to raise all his previous speeds by substantial margins and to add a new 200-mile class record of 115.05mph.

Although not designed for racing, both cars took part in Formule Libre events in Europe and contests at Brooklands, where they showed exceptional speed for such drivers as Don, Dudley Froy, John Cobb and Cyril Paul. An example was Kaye Don's new Brooklands lap record of 131.76mph in 1928, which he raised to 134.24mph in 1929 and a stunning 137.58mph in 1930. The three-speed boxes were a handicap in road racing and four-speed transmissions were made, though both were to prove fragile behind these potent V12s. By 1930 they were developing 340bhp at 5,500rpm on a racing fuel that mixed 60 per cent petrol with 40 per cent benzole.

Here were two more Sunbeams coveted by Malcolm Campbell. By 1931 the Scot held the land speed record at 246mph in his own Blue Bird, but this was hardly suitable

After a successful attack on the land speed record in the hands of Henry Segrave the Sunbeam twelve was rebuilt with twin Roots-type superchargers boosting in parallel, seen at the Sunbeam factory.

Badged for the occasion as a Talbot, the 4.0-litre Sunbeam was raced successfully by Albert Divo at France's Gaillon hill climb.

Two of the 4.0-litre vee-twelve Sunbeams were built, dubbed 'Tiger' and 'Tigress'. Here they were being readied for a 500-mile race at Brooklands, which required the fitting of specially designed silencers.

for Brooklands, where he still enjoyed competing. Having acquired Tiger and Tigress in 1930, he had them completely rechassised by Thomson & Taylor at Brooklands to designs by Reid Railton, who gave them an underslung frame at the rear and an I-beam front axle like those he would design for Britain's ERA racers. Front brakes were now hydraulic by Lockheed. Transmission trouble was overcome by installing four-speed Wilson planetary gearboxes which contributed to a weight increase of more than 200lb. With his rebuilt Sunbeam Campbell defeated John Cobb in another great V12, the 10.7-litre Delage, in the Brighton Speed Trials in September 1932. His time for the standing half-mile was 23.6 seconds against Cobb's 24.0.

After acquiring both Sunbeams in 1930, Malcolm Campbell had completely new chassis designed and built for them to Reid Railton's designs. Here Campbell raced one of them on the road circuit at Brooklands, using twin rear tyres to harness its power of more than 340bhp.

The rebuilt four-litre Sunbeams carried on racing through the 1930s, one being sold to another speed-obsessed Briton, John Cobb, in 1935. Though always awesome competitors, they suffered from both reliability problems and the heavy handicaps given them at Brooklands. Nevertheless these two vee-twelve Sunbeams closed out the decade among the fastest cars the Surrey speed bowl had ever seen. After the war, in the hands of new owners, they were converted to plain-bearing bottom ends to deal with the too-rapid crankshaft wear the roller bearings caused. Their fuel mix became a more radical 80/10/10 blend of methanol/benzole/petrol.

In the 1980s one of the Sunbeams was track-tested by Willie Green, who found its engine "sensational. The power starts to come in at 2,500rpm, and when it does it's something else again. By 3,000rpm it's really starting to go, and towards 5,000rpm the output is something prodigious. This must be the most gutsy, most torquey and simply powerful pre-war engine I've ever sat behind, and I'm not forgetting the Alfa Romeo P3. There is just instant, solid, *vast* power on tap." Acceleration times taken in 1969 showed a scintillating zero to 60mph in 6.4 seconds and to 100mph in 14.5 seconds. The standing quarter-mile was covered in only 13.4 seconds.

Intertwined with the sagas of Sunbeams both big and small were the exploits of another vee-twelve-powered car built by another Frenchman, Louis Delage. A maker of cars under his own name at Courbevoie since 1905, Delage had soon shown a knack for fast-car design. One of his 1913 Grand Prix cars won the 1914 Indianapolis 500-mile race in the hands of René Thomas, generating the massive publicity for his marque that Louis Delage loved – especially if he didn't have to pay for it, for Delage was known as a tough manager and frugal purchaser. The moustachioed, boss-eyed Delage enjoyed windfall profits as a maker of munitions during World War I.

Although Arthur-Louis Michelat was the designer of Delage's post-war product range, he departed during the war. In 1919, Delage recruited his cousin, Charles Planchon, as design chief. Like Delage himself, Planchon had studied at the École des Arts et Métiers, graduating in 1895. Subsequently he worked at Peugeot, Charron, Gnôme-Rhône and Panhard. A former Salmson and SCAP engine designer, Albert Lory, was engaged as his assistant. Louis Delage asked his new team to build a very fast car that could be taken around France to amaze the locals with the competence and excellence of Delage products. Here was a mission closely akin to Jesse Vincent's for his big Packards, the 299 and the 905 – especially the latter.

In fact Planchon and Lory built three special sprint cars. Two were in-line sixes, one of 5,136cc and the other

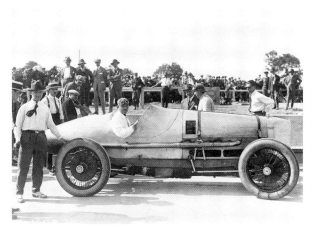

A very busy piece of machinery indeed was the Delage DH V12 built for Louis Delage by his cousin Charles Planchon. Individual cylinders and heads carried pushrod-operated vertical overhead valves. Carburation was in the central vee.

Albert Divo was assigned the wheel of the DH Delage, which was built principally to promote the company's products by demonstrating high speed at appropriate local venues. It had four-wheel brakes and a wheel base of only 110.8in.

5,954cc, while the third was powered by a vee-twelve of 10,688cc (90 x 140mm). Making a twin-six – by the 1920s a well-established concept – was a logical enough way to provide the cylinder displacement that a very fast car would need at a time when supercharging was still in its infancy.[13] On an aluminium crankcase, carrying its crankshaft in four roller bearings, individual cast-iron cylinders with welded-on water jackets were attached by four studs. Cast-iron cylinder heads – also individual – were detachable and carried two vertical valves apiece, inlets toward the inside of the vee and exhausts toward the outside.

Exposed pushrods and rocker arms opened the valves from a single central camshaft whose individual cam lobes were splined to the shaft.[14] Planchon provided for valve-clearance adjustment in the pushrods, but perversely at their virtually inaccessible lower ends. Camshaft, single water pump and twin magnetos were driven from the crankshaft nose. With the banks at a 60° vee, the right-hand row was set forward of the left to allow side-by-side rods on the crankshaft, which was of built-up design to accommodate the roller mains. Plain big-end bearings were lubricated by oil scooped up from troughs in the sump. These were kept filled by one of the three oil pumps. Another supplied the mains while the third scavenged oil to a reservoir under the seats.

Each cylinder bank was fed by its own manifold, topped by two bronze Zenith 48VI downdraft carburettors.[15] On each side small pipes from two exhaust headers provided heat to the manifolds at the bases of the carburettors. Revving to 3,200rpm, the Delage Type DH produced 280 horsepower on its original compression ratio of 5.5:1. A central lever in the two-passenger cockpit stirred its four-speed transmission,

behind a 12in multi-disc clutch. The big engine took up most of the DH's conventional leaf-sprung chassis with its 110.8in wheelbase and unladen weight of 3,360lb. The big machine enjoyed a bold square radiator and a sketchy body with a tapering tail.

Completed in 1923, the DH Delage was built, said W.F. Bradley, "as an advertising stunt. Practically every Sunday it was sent to some district where sales needed a boost, in order to climb a hill at a record pace or to enthuse the locals by a sprint down a deserted road. Any attempt at record-breaking," judged Bradley, "appears to have been an afterthought."

Its debut outing was at Gaillon on 7 October 1923, the first time a standing start was used. René Thomas covered the uphill kilometre in 31.0 seconds, setting the climb's new record. In 1925 the DH would climb in 29.6sec, again a record. Its time was reduced by one second in 1926 by Albert Divo in the four-litre Sunbeam twelve disguised as a 'Talbot' for the occasion. In a speed trial at Geneva the DH Delage was clocked at 129.3mph for the kilometre, proving that it was no slowcoach.

On 6 July 1924 the French Motorcycle Club organised a high-speed trial on more than four miles of the straight N20 highway some 20 miles south of Paris, near Arpajon and the site of the Montlhéry circuit, which was then under construction. It arranged for timing to be official so that records could be established over both the kilometre and mile. With all France converging on the Arpajon road for a Sunday festival of speed, the DH Delage and René Thomas would have been conspicuous by their absence.

When the racing cars took to the narrow tree-lined highway after lunch, the DH showed her capabilities. In

René Thomas took the wheel of the Delage DH in July 1924 for a speed trial at Arpajon near Paris. There Thomas and the DH set a new official land speed record of 143.312mph.

spite of losing a tyre tread on his return run, Thomas was clocked at an average of 143.312mph for the mile, an increase of more than 13mph on the previous official record. The Delage held the crown only briefly, for six days later it was seized by a 21.7-litre six-cylinder Fiat at 145.90mph, also at Arpajon. The speeds were so close that Delage and Fiat could be excused for simultaneously displaying their cars in Paris and hailing them as the world's fastest.

Throughout 1927, after which Delage withdrew from racing, the DH continued to thrill crowds in France in the hands of Thomas, Albert Divo and Robert Benoist. It was acquired by Thomson & Taylor's Ken Thomson in time to

Like so many fast cars of the era the Delage DH ended its contemporary racing career at Brooklands in the early 1930s. Seen on the bumpy banking in 1932, the DH won 13 of her 52 races up to 1933 in the hands of John Cobb.

be driven by John Cobb in the 1929 Brooklands season. With maintenance and tuning by Robin Jackson, in Cobb's hands the DH won thirteen of her fifty-two races up to 1933 and took seventeen second places. Cobb also broke records in international Class A, for cars over eight litres, setting the coveted one-hour record at 112.18mph on 11 September 1929. Post-1933 Oliver Bertram raced it, setting the DH's fastest-ever Brooklands lap at 136.45mph. Loaned to the elfin Kay Petre, it recorded the fastest-ever ladies' lap speed of 134.75mph.

If the DH was a vee-twelve Delage that achieved its aims more through brute force than finesse, Charles Planchon may be forgiven for he was at work in parallel on another twelve for Delage that is considered one of the enduring masterpieces of the Grand-Prix-engine art. The marching orders given him by Louis Delage were certainly sharpish, for the Delage chief had been mortified when his two four-cylinder entries in the 1922 French Grand Prix were found to be so unsatisfactory that he had to withdraw them before the race. That was the first season to be run under new rules that reduced the displacement of GP cars from three to two litres and slashed their minimum weights from 800 to 650 kilograms.

That a four-cylinder engine was no longer adequate for Grand Prix racing was shown by the straight-eights that raced in 1921 (Ballot and Duesenberg) and 1922 (Bugatti and Rolland-Pilain). Always looking for an advantage – he introduced desmodromic or positively closed valves in 1914 – Louis Delage experimented with an eight-cylinder two-stroke engine. Finding this too great a challenge, he decided on an equally ambitious step: the allocation of a dozen cylinders to an engine of only two litres. This carried the clear implication of a search for higher revs per minute, surpassing the peak speeds of around 5,000rpm that were then current for GP engines, if the advantages of his twelve's smaller cylinders were to be exploited.

Assisted by Albert Lory, Charles Planchon designed the new engine during three months over the 1922–23 winter. In March construction began with the aim of an entry in the French Grand Prix at Tours on 21 July 1923. This was achieved by the slimmest of margins. On 28 June the new model, Type 2LCV, was submitted for approval to the Bureau of Mines, which classified it as a 16CV for tax purposes. Competitions chief and driver René Thomas arrived at Tours too late for practice, but enjoyed a front-row starting spot by virtue of the early receipt of his entry by the French Automobile Club. He lasted only eight of the 35 laps, falling back after an early third place with an engine that was overheating so much, Thomas said, that it "was making *pommes frit*". The 2LCV finally retired with connecting-rod failure. No entry was made for the year's other Grand Prix at Monza.

Infuriated not only by this public display of incompetence but also by his discovery that Planchon was planning to sell drawings of his new engine to rivals, Louis Delage fired his cousin. After weighing the credentials of Swiss engineer Ernest Henry and rejecting them because the chap was a foreigner, Delage entrusted to Albert Lory the further development of his new V12. Although it hadn't yet delivered the goods, the new twelve certainly looked the goods, with its aluminium castings lovingly damascened. "The engine bristled with a seeming infinity of tiny nuts, bolts, studs and screws," wrote Griff Borgeson, "that gave it at one and the same time an appearance of hairiness, delicacy and mechanical elegance unique in history." It was as sophisticated as the more-than-five-times-bigger Delage DH V12 was, in its way, crude.

Although its dimensions of 51.4 x 80mm (1,992cc) gave a stroke more than half again its bore diameter, the Delage V12 had a piston area of 38.4sq in, almost as large as that of the 3-litre Duesenberg eight that won the 1921 French GP. Just over two inches in diameter, its full-skirted aluminium pistons looked no bigger than a hefty salt cellar. With crown cut-outs for valve clearance, they slid in six-cylinder blocks of fine cast iron that included integral cylinder heads. With their cylinders widely spaced to allow ample water passages between them, the blocks were cast with open-sided jackets that were closed by access plates. A 60° vee divided the cylinder banks, of

which the one on the left was offset forward to allow the use of side-by-side connecting rods.

Carried at the split line of the two-piece aluminium crankcase in seven main bearings, the 2LCV's crankshaft had circular webs. All its bearings, main and big-end, were Hoffman rollers in split races and spaced by duralumin cages, running on case-hardened crankshaft journals. Roller bearings also carried the four hollow steel camshafts, with their outer races held in two-piece aluminium cam carriers attached by studs to the cylinder heads. Finger followers were interposed between the cam lobes and valve stems, which were at an included angle of 100°. Triple coil springs closed each valve, and between them was an 18mm spark plug set back from the hemispherical chamber and linked to it by a small passage between the valve seats.

Oil demands of the twelve's complex top end, and the train of gears – with their ball bearings – at the front that drove it, justified a pressure pump dedicated to its supply. Another pressure pump fed the crankshaft, where overflow from the mains oiled the big ends, while a third pump scavenged oil from the sump and delivered it to a reservoir under the rear of the chassis and pierced by cooling tubes. The front-end gear train also drove a single water pump with dual impellers, delivering water to the outside of each cylinder block. At the front as well were the twin magnetos, each firing its six-cylinder bank.

Though the 2LCV seemed well-cooled, we can be sure that its overheating at Tours was aggravated by Charles

In its original unsupercharged form Delage's 2LCV vee-twelve of 1923 had central exhausts and four updraft carburettors feeding inlet manifolds at the sides of the engine. Designed by Charles Planchon with the assistance of Albert Lory, the 2LCV was built to the 2-litre Grand Prix regulations.

Flanked by a connecting rod and one of the ball-bearinged cam-drive gears, the aluminium crankcase of the 2LCV Delage was ready to accept the cast-iron six-cylinder blocks with their integral heads. Roller bearings were used throughout its bottom end.

The 2.0-litre Delage vee-twelve was raced in unsupercharged form in 1923 and 1924, bringing its power to 115bhp at 6,000rpm. The 2LCV achieved second and third place in the 1924 French Grand Prix.

Planchon's decision to take its exhaust gases from the centre of the vee via a simple log manifold which must have become very hot indeed – recalling Lancia's problems with a centre-vee exhaust. Unlike any previous twin-cam vee-twelve, the Delage's induction systems were outboard. Planchon gave both sides two updraft carburettors, each feeding three cylinders. As it appeared

As raced in 1925 the 2LCV Delage had dual Roots-type superchargers at the front, only one of which is in position here. Cradles above the superchargers were for its ignition magnetos. Power output was now 195bhp at 7,000rpm.

at Tours in 1923 the twelve produced 95bhp at 6,000rpm, with maximum torque in the range of 5,500 to 5,700rpm, in a chassis that was geared to reach 115mph at 6,000 revs. With its multiple-disc clutch and integral four-speed transmission the 1923 car showed impressive acceleration during its brief outing.

For 1924 Albert Lory tackled all aspects of this unique engine. For reliability he blended the I-section shanks of its connecting rods much more smoothly and robustly to their big ends, at the same time lightening the areas gripped by their bolts. For performance he began experiments with supercharging, Fiat having been the first in Grand Prix racing to show the benefits of boosting in 1923. In spite of his engine's small size Lory equipped it with two Roots-type blowers at the front in a special cradle. A pipe running back along each side pressurised a single carburettor which fed a six-branch inlet manifold. Exhaust pipes now rose up out of the central vee, where they were exposed to cooling air, and were gathered in a manifold that fed a single left-hand exhaust pipe. The engine's oil reservoir was relocated to the car's scuttle.

Lory and Delage decided not to use the blowers in the 1924 French Grand Prix at Lyons, *Le Patron* being distrustful of their reliability. Instead, at the eleventh hour before the race on 3 August, Lory fitted each side of the twelve with a special twin-throat Zenith updraft carburettor that had a single central float chamber serving both venturis. From the throttles three-branch manifolds – with a small balance pipe between them – rose to the inlet ports. On a compression ratio of 7.0:1 the 2LCV's output was now up to 115bhp at 6,000rpm.[16] Lory installed it in a new lower chassis on a wheelbase of 102in and reckoned to have slimmed his racer down to the minimum weight allowable.

Delage presented a trio of twelves for the '24 French Grand Prix. Given a preview at the factory, *The Autocar* concluded that "It is no exaggeration to state that these three cars are the finest examples of high-class engineering ever produced by a firm whose reputation is world-wide in racing." Nor did they let down the side. Among rivals that for the most part were supercharged, they placed second and third (Robert Benoist and Albert Divo) with Thomas in seventh, theirs being the only team to complete the race intact. Benoist was bested by a scant 66 seconds after seven hours of racing. Delage brought four cars to San Sebastian's Grand Prix on 25 September and saw two place third and fourth (André Morel and Divo) in a wet race. Benoist had taken the lead before crashing, while engine trouble eliminated Thomas.

With 1925 the final year for the 2-litre formula, it was now or never for the 2LCV. Delage and Lory made it 'now' after an abortive start in June's Belgian Grand Prix that saw several of their four entries wearing twin superchargers. Succumbing to the twelve's augmented power, their connecting rods cried out for more attention from Albert Lory. In Delage's home event on the new road circuit at Montlhéry all four cars were supercharged, their twin Roots blowers drawing from individual updraft Zenith carburettors with horizontal inlets. Introduced at Spa was an individual exhaust manifold for each cylinder bank, with piping that rose to two exhausts emerging from the left side of the bonnet, whose flanks were now comprehensively louvered for cooling. All four had Lory's latest connecting-rod design.

Its 195bhp at a heady 7,000rpm made the 2LCV easily the most powerful two-litre racer although, as T.A.S.O. Matheson wrote, "its tremendous performance was rendered less effective by virtue of bad brakes and indifferent roadholding which were inadequate for the increased speed." Although the Alfa Romeos were better-balanced cars, the crash of one and the withdrawal of the others left the way clear for Robert Benoist to win the 26 July 1925 French Grand Prix over almost nine hours for 621 miles. He was relieved by Divo, who set fastest lap. Another Delage was second in the hands of Louis Wagner and Paul Torchy. This was a signal victory, the first by a French car in the French Grand Prix since 1913.

Delage bowed to Alfa by not entering 1925's Italian GP but brought four cars to San Sebastian for 441 miles of racing on 19 September. While one crashed, killing the unfortunate Paul Torchy, the others placed one-two-three. Crashing with mortal consequences was also the fate in the 1926 Targa Florio of two-time winner Giulio Masetti, who had acquired one of the Delages. In his honour all three factory cars were withdrawn from this Formule Libre event, held over tortuous Sicilian roads which suited them not a whit. Run to free-formula rules in 1926, the Spanish Grand Prix saw the remaining three Delages on the grid. Benoist and Wagner took one of them to third place behind two works Bugattis.

Delage sold five 2LCVs in all to private parties – two to Italy, one to Sweden and two to Juan Malcolm in Argentina. In Malcolm's hands one of the latter won the 500-mile race at Rafaela in 1927; Caesare Millone also raced an Argentine car. Like most racing cars the Delages gradually faded away. One, which was raced at such venues as Rome and Alessandria by Valpreda and Aimini, later surfaced in Rome in 1932 as the Ardizzone Speciale, with "half of its twelve cylinders taken out of action" so it could compete in the 1,100cc *Voiturette* class. At Brooklands Dudley Froy, who had driven the four-litre Sunbeam V12, competed in a 2LCV chassis with a two-stroke four-cylinder engine in 1932 and '34 – not a race-winning combination.

Although seen here at the Gaillon hill climb in 1926, in the hands of Robert Benoist, this was the configuration of the supercharged Delage V12 that the same driver used to win the French Grand Prix of 1925. It was the first win by a French car in the national Grand Prix since 1913.

For the new 1½-litre Grand Prix formula of 1926 Delage put in hand an in-line eight. Reducing its already finicky 2-litre twelve to the smaller size the new rules required seemed a step too far, even for the ambitious Louis Delage. It was not out of the question, however, for Turin's Itala and that company's engineering consultant, Giulio Cesare Cappa.

Founded in 1904, Itala had explored such technical novelties as rotary valves and built Hispano-Suiza V8s toward the end of the war – an adventure that brought it under government control in 1924. It also precipitated the appointment of former Aquila-Italiana and Fiat man Cappa, whom admirers spoke of as "a poet of machinery, as much artist as engineer". This was evident in an aero engine he unveiled in 1926, the 18.3-litre Sauda Cappa 18. It was an elegantly compact 60° twelve consisting of two back-to-back vee-sixes whose power was drawn off at the centre by a 1.4:1 reduction gear.

For Itala, by 1926 Cappa had produced a mind-boggling new racing-car concept. Its engine, he said, was close kin to a 700-horsepower unit he intended to build for aviation use along lines different from his Sauda Cappa. While for the latter a V12 was ideal, it was a surprising choice for Itala's racer, which was to be an order of magnitude smaller in both 1.1- and 1.5-litre sizes as the Types 11 and 15 respectively. Their dimensions were 46 x 55mm (1,097cc) and 53 x 55mm (1,456cc). One engine was completed and installed in an equally radical chassis with front-wheel drive and all-independent suspension.

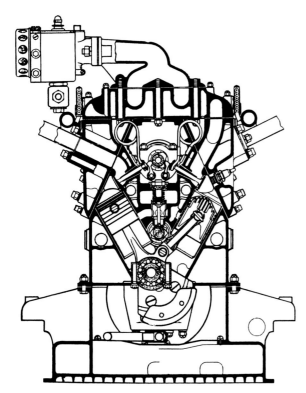

Few racing engines of any era matched the fantasy of the 1.1-litre Itala built by ex-Fiat engineer Giulio Cesare Cappa. Features visible here were master and link connecting rods, hairpin-type valve springs and a peculiar arrangement of porting to the cylinders controlled by a second camshaft just above the crankshaft.

Only the Itala's 60° vee angle was at all conventional. Cylinder banks faced each other directly, for which Cappa schemed two solutions. One was the use of a master rod on the right and link rod on the left, while the other was fork-and-blade. In both designs the connecting rods had tubular shanks. Split-race roller bearings were used for both the rod journals and six of the seven main bearings of the one-piece crankshaft, the nose bearing being ball-type.[17] Made of Holtzer P4H steel, the crankshaft had bolted-on bronze counterweights. Divided on the crank centreline, the block/crankcase was an aluminium casting into which steel cylinder liners two millimetres thick were pressed after the block was heated in oil. Unusually for a racing unit the crankcase was wet-sump.

From the cylinder peripheries upward, the sides of the Itala's block sloped inward at 25° to the vertical to form the flat surfaces to which the silumin-alloy cylinder heads were attached. These held the 12mm spark plugs, four exhaust ports per side and inlet porting – eight passages, some bifurcating to serve the twelve cylinders – from a top cover that also served as an inlet manifold from a central side-draft carburettor. Domed to match the

sloping heads, the internally ribbed Borgo pistons gave a 6.0:1 compression ratio.

Carried in the upper end of the block were paired valves for each cylinder, their stems at right angles to the bore centreline. Their position and the engine's geometry allowed a single cam lobe to operate the valves on both sides of the engine, through short finger followers, so there were a dozen lobes in all. The 24mm valves, very short (63mm) and light (20 grams) thanks to the innovative use of hairpin-type valve springs, slid in inserted iron guides and seated on bronze.

The Itala's novelties didn't end there. Down at the base of its vee was another camshaft, this one controlling vertical valves that admitted air to ports in the base of the cylinders from a central manifold fed by a nose-mounted vane-type blower.[18] Cappa's concept was that the air thus injected would cool the cylinders, speed the exhaust gas's exit and then mix with an extra-rich atmospherically inducted air/fuel charge to give the right proportions for combustion. Cappa envisioned this as a means of extracting optimum performance from the indifferent petrol fuels then available.

The helical three-gear train driving both camshafts was at the engine's clutch end, where it also turned two laterally placed Bosch magnetos through skew gears. The idler gear in the train was of Celeron composite to reduce noise. A water pump at the rear of the block – as the engine was installed in this front-drive chassis – was driven by the nose of the upper camshaft. Internal manifolding directed cool water to such hot spots as the exhaust-valve seats. In Cappa's pure monoposto Itala chassis the stylishly rectilinear engine drove a four-speed front transaxle, pulling a light (1,150lb) chassis on a wheelbase of 98in. Razor-edged bodywork was remarkably sleek, crisp and clean.

On the test bench the exotic Itala twelve posed some puzzles to its builders. Although its torque curve was virtually flat, when loaded by the dynamometer it seemed reluctant to maintain a given speed. Cappa concluded that he needed more sophisticated test equipment to evaluate it fully. Smoothness was an obvious virtue and it easily revved to 7,000 and beyond.

After only brief dynamometer running the twelve was installed in Itala's racer. It was tested at Monza by the experienced Meo Costantini, who reached 105mph and declared it promising. The cost of its further

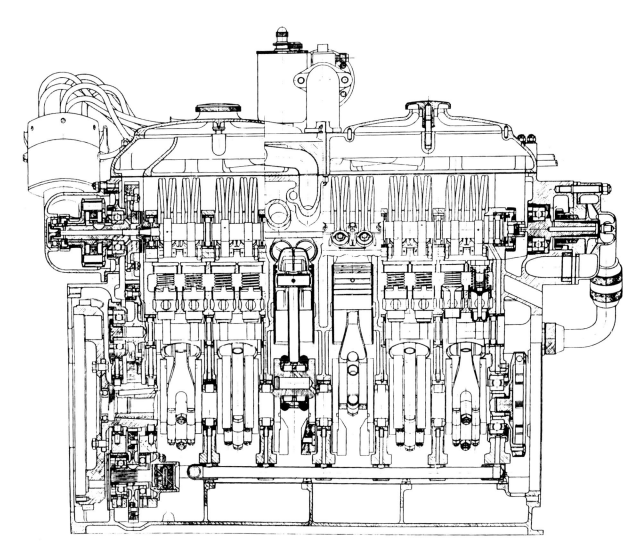

Below: *The 60°-vee Itala vee-twelve had an unusual combination of natural induction with a nose-mounted, vane-type supercharger which delivered pressure air via a central manifold to ports situated low in each cylinder bore.*

Below: *With front-wheel drive and all-independent suspension, the Itala powered by Cappa's twelve was as radical as its engine. Regrettably after only brief running at Monza Itala had to conclude that it couldn't afford to develop Cappa's spectacular brainwave.*

development was more than Itala could bear, however, and the Type 11/15 was shelved. It served only to prove the tart assessment of Alfa Romeo's Vittorio Jano, who said of Cappa that "My common sense is a hundred times better than all this theory." In 1935 loss-making Itala was folded into Turin neighbour Fiat's empire.

Until he moved across town to Itala in late 1924, Giulio Cesare Cappa had been one of the artificers of Fiat's successful racing cars and engines. He was one of the team that introduced new concepts such as roller bearings and two-valve hemispherical heads to Grand Prix engines in the early 1920s under Guido Fornaca and Carlo Cavalli, the latter a trained solicitor who had found his *metier* in car engineering. Bright in 1922–23, Fiat's star faded in the later years of the 2-litre formula when Alfa Romeo and Delage exploited its new techniques to even greater advantage.

When at the beginning of 1925 Fiat curtailed its racing programme, this was understood by the company's engineers as a signal that they were to carry on with new developments but quietly, behind the scenes. With their eyes on the new 1½-litre formula for 1926, they did this to remarkable effect. Their spur, extraordinarily, was the Indianapolis 500-mile race. In a semi-private effort works driver Pietro Bordino took a supercharged 2-litre straight-eight Fiat to the Indiana race in 1925 and finished tenth. Both the race's fascination and its rewards – Bordino collected $1,400 and the winner $27,800 –

A longitudinal section showed one bank of six cylinders of Fiat's Type 406 twelve-cylinder, built to power its Type 806 Grand Prix car. Properly this was a U12, with its twin crankshafts geared together.

worked their magic on the Italians. With Indy also adopting the new 1½-litre formula, a new car would suit both Europe and America.

Tranquillo Zerbi, Scipione Treves, Giuseppe Sola and a designer named Vagilenti were among the Fornaca/Cavalli team who tackled the challenge of a suitable engine. Their first effort, a two-stroke with twin crankshafts and pistons opposing each other in six cylinders, was powerful but tall, excruciatingly noisy and hard to master thermally. Soon after Bordino's return from America they turned their efforts instead to a twin-crankshaft engine of another kind: two three-quarter-litre sixes set side by side and geared together to make a U12 of 1,484cc (50 x 63mm). For secrecy it was built under a series-production type number, 504, but the engine was Type 406 and the car the 806.

In no wise an adaptation of existing engines, the 406 was a new design from scratch that fully integrated its two six-cylinder banks. It used Fiat's successful steel monobloc cylinders with welded-on water jackets, fabricated in pairs. This suited the engine's architecture, which carried each crankshaft in four 40mm plain main bearings. The rod journals were 40mm too and the big-end bearings remarkably long at 41mm. To allow the connecting-rod big ends to be one-piece for strength, that part of the crankshaft was built up, using the Hirth method of radial serrations held together by long finely threaded bolts. The I-section rods were 130mm long.

Operated through finger followers, the 30mm valves were inclined at the wide 100° angle popularised by Fiat. Circular retainers nearly as big as the cylinder bore held the tops of six small coil springs clustered around each valve stem – a novelty for Fiat engines.[19] KLG 348 spark

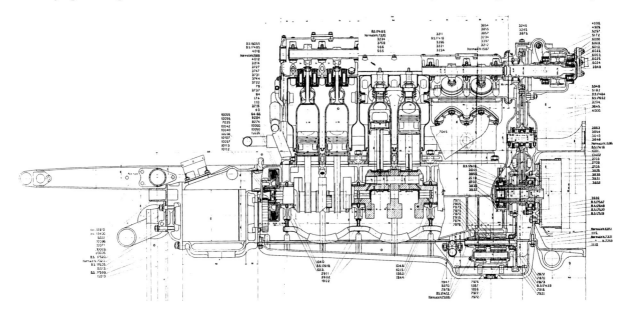

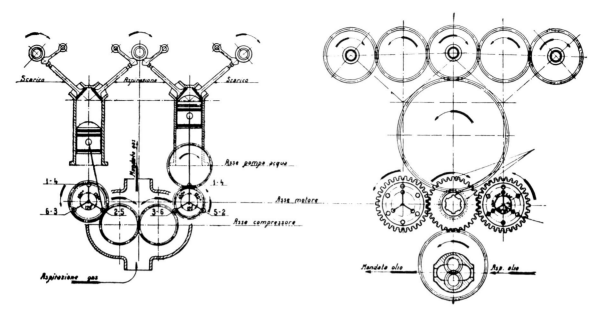

Above: *These sketches show the layout of the U12 Fiat Type 406, with triple camshafts, a single Roots-type supercharger and integrated gearing to the three cams and to its final-drive clutch.*

Below: *Fiat brooked no compromise in its design of the Type 806 Grand Prix car to compete under the 1½-litre formula of 1927, when the elaborate racer was completed. An offset drive line allowed Pietro Bordino to sit low in the chassis.*

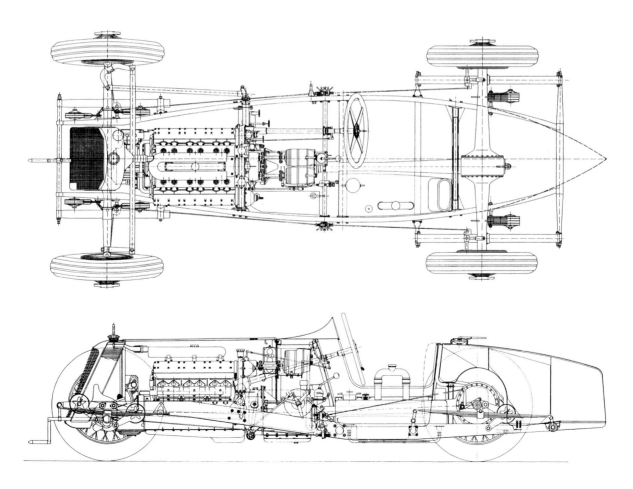

plugs of 18mm were set centrally and recessed from the top of the chamber, their sockets finned for cooling within the water jacket. Another Fiat concept was retained for the pistons: their rings, not their skirts, guided them in the cylinders. Wide lands held two pairs of rings above the gudgeon pin and one pair at the bottom of the full skirt.

The 406's full integration was shown by its valve gear, which used only one central camshaft to open the inlet valves of both banks, arranged so that a single cam lobe dealt with both opposing valves. Five spur gears across the top of the rear of the engine, joining the three camshafts together, were turned by a huge single gear from a small spur on the output shaft. The latter was a short shaft on one roller bearing and one ball bearing – to take clutch thrust – that was driven by gears at the back ends of both crankshafts. A gear downward from there drove the scavenge and pressure pumps of the 406's dry-sump system, which operated at pressures up to 130psi.

A single large aluminium crankcase carried the six pairs of cylinders and twin crankshafts, closed by a shallow sump casting. From the nose of the right-hand crankshaft a multi-disc coupling allowing slippage drove a gear pair to the single Roots-type supercharger, flat at the front of the engine. Drawing from a horizontal carburettor, it delivered 13psi boost to a pair of manifolds

Above: *In wet weather Pietro Bordino, in the foreground, prepared to start his second heat at Monza in the Fiat Type 806. Behind him was the Chiribiri 12/16 of Roberto Serboli, which finished third, and, most remotely, the Bugatti 37A of Nino Cirio which was second in the heat.*

Below: *Fiat's radical U12 Type 806 performed superbly in its short races at Monza on 4 September 1927. Bordino's performance suggested that the 806 was Europe's fastest 1½-litre racing car through 1927. This was, however, the last European race meeting under that Grand Prix formula.*

between the blocks. A single water pump was driven by a gear from the nose of the left-hand crankshaft. Twin Bosch magnetos were driven by the tail of the inlet camshaft through a gearbox that also contained an advance/retard mechanism.

A multi-disc clutch and four-speed transmission with attached brake-servo system drove through a torque tube to the 806's rear axle, which like the entire drive train was offset to the left to allow the driver on the right to be seated low in the chassis, next to the oil reservoir. Pietro Bordino hoped to be that driver in the 1927 Indy 500, but work on the 406/806 wasn't completed in time. In fact it wasn't completed in time for the crucial Italian Grand Prix at Monza on 4 September; reliability wasn't yet good enough for a 373-mile contest, according to Fiat chief Giovanni Agnelli.

On the same day as the Grand Prix, however, Fiat did enter its 806 in the Milan Grand Prix. Word was said to have come from Rome that it was high time to confront the French with Fiat's latest to enhance the prestige of Mussolini's Italy. An engine change the night before meant that Bordino had to compete with a twelve that wasn't fully run in. Nevertheless he was the star of two wet but short races.

Pietro Bordino raced against all comers – including supercharged 2-litres – to win both his 31-mile heat and the 31-mile final. His fastest lap of 96.50mph bettered the best lap of 94.31mph set by winner Robert Benoist during the Italian GP in his Delage, then by far the most successful European 1½-litre racer. Expectations that three Fiat twelves would compete in the Brooklands 200-mile race in October were, in the event, in vain.

Fiat's 406 U12 was undeniably potent. A July 1927 test showed peak output of 160bhp at 8,000rpm on alcohol-based Elcosine fuel, while maximum-boost trials registered outputs of 175bhp at 7,500 and 187bhp at a heady 8,500rpm. Its fuel consumption during trials at Monza was 8.3 miles per Imperial gallon. Although the engine's configuration threatened to make it massive, shrewd design held its weight to 381lb – not excessive for the time. Before the Monza races the new car was by no means fully proven. Only eleven days earlier Bordino's legs were scalded by hot oil from a broken rubber tube to the oil-pressure gauge.

Any thought of a further career for the 806 was ended by the expiration in Europe of the 1½-litre formula at the end of 1927, the death of Guido Fornaca in January 1928 and the implacable objection of Giovanni Agnelli to further competition by Fiat, which saw these and Fiat's other fine racing cars of the 1920s scrapped beyond recovery. The era nevertheless ended on a high note – the scream to more than 8,000 revs of the smallest twelve-cylinder engine yet to race.

Chapter 3 Footnotes

[1] The 'W' layout is usually taken to mean that an engine has three banks of cylinders disposed in a fan-like pattern. Lorraine's aero engine had three banks of eight cylinders.

[2] Michael Sedgwick wrote that "only parts of Lancia's abortive 6-litre of 1919 seem to have been made." The author relies on Wim Oude Weernik's in-depth research into early Lancias.

[3] A guess would be aligned, but the design of its connecting rods is unknown to this author.

[4] With a reputation as a Casanova that surpassed his engineering feats, Voisin certainly did not overnight alone in Cannes.

[5] Sunbeam historians may want to enquire after the reasons why the engine was not converted to fork-and-blade rods, which the five-bearing crankshaft would have accommodated.

[6] This was almost 20 per cent bigger than the Manitou that the engine purportedly resembled.

[7] Famous aviator Hawker was no stranger to big power. He had acquired two 225-bhp Sunbeam Mohawks and installed one in a Mercedes chassis for road use.

[8] The International Association of Recognised Automobile Clubs.

[9] Miraculously the 350hp Sunbeam has survived as a treasured exhibit of Britain's National Motor Museum.

[10] Numerous references, including Segrave's book *The Lure of Speed*, attribute a 75° bank angle, but the author prefers the 60° of Sunbeam expert Anthony Heal, which accords better with the engine's appearance.

[11] On 8 May 1990 the Sunbeam was timed at an average 157.44 mph over a kilometre at Elvington Airfield, North Yorkshire, driven by one of its restorers, John Baker-Courtenay.

[12] Sunbeam revived the 'Tiger' name for its Ford-powered sports car of 1964–67.

[13] Griff Borgeson speculated that the V12 may have been conceived for aviation purposes "in view of Lory's aero engine background [with Salmson], the aeronautical character of this powerplant, and the fact that a post-war boom in aero engine development was taking place at that exact moment." This possibility cannot be excluded. Only in the 1930s would Delage venture into aero engines, without success.

[14] A late drawing of the DH Delage shows rocker-arm covers, but it's difficult to see how these could have been accommodated.

[15] An alternative system used a single central updraft Zenith supplying all twelve cylinders.

[16] As restored by Sean Danaher in 2003 an unblown Delage produced comfortably in excess of 120bhp.

[17] The rearmost main bearing comprised in fact two roller bearings flanking the gear drive to the camshafts.

[18] Most reports mention a Roots-type blower, but visual inspection suggests a vane-type unit.

[19] Although some reports state that the springs were three in number, the author considers this unlikely. The number six is his speculation.

AERO SPEED

Henry Segrave's 1926 land speed record of 152.336mph in the astonishing Sunbeam four-litre V12 would be the last set by a car powered by an engine resembling that of a normal automobile – just as its creator Louis Coatalen had intended. Henceforward, until 1965 when Bob Summers broke the wheel-driven record with four Chrysler V8s, the most treasured of all land speed records would be set with cars powered by aeroplane engines. All, save one gas turbine, would be V12s or W12s.

Although Packard made much of its aviation intentions for the V12 engines it built before and during World War I, leading up to its 150-mph Type 905 single-seater, none actually took to the air. Sunbeam's Coatalen made better use of the V12 powering his Toodles V, transforming it into his successful Mohawk aero engine. His ill-fated airborne Arab V8 provided the basis of the V12 in his 350-hp Sunbeam, but the latter was not itself an aviation engine.

The first to use an actual aero engine to break the land speed record was resourceful Briton Ernest Eldridge, who acquired a surplus Fiat A-12bis six-cylinder of 21.7 litres giving more than 300 horsepower and a 1908 Fiat chain-drive chassis in which to install it, after its frame members had been suitably lengthened. It was Eldridge who snapped world-speed laurels from the Delage DH of René Thomas on the highway near Arpajon in July 1924 with a speed of 146.01mph.

Would-be record-breakers on the war's winning side had a remarkable range of vee-twelves from which to choose. American engines included the Duesenberg, Packard, Hall-Scott and Liberty. Britons could choose from one Napier, one Galloway-Atlantic, five Sunbeams and three Rolls-Royces, while Fiat had two and Renault and Panhard one apiece. All were 60° vees save the Renault, which was 47.5°, the Liberty 45° and the Napier Lion a W12 with its side banks of four cylinders at 60° to its central quartet.

Offering 450 naturally aspirated horsepower from 23,942cc, the oversquare (140 x 130mm) 24-litre Napier Lion was destined to enjoy an illustrious career as a record-breaker on land as well as in the air, where it powered the 1927 Schneider Trophy winner. Connecting rods in its central cylinder bank were the masters, joined to the outboard pistons by link rods.[1] Each bank had a pair of overhead camshafts operating four vertical valves per cylinder. Individual forged-steel cylinders were united by an aluminium cylinder head for each bank. Although its big-end bearings were plain, its crank ran in five roller main bearings.

Only one barrier blocked record-car use of the Lion: in the 1920s it was still a front-line engine for the RAF. "It was out of the question to contemplate buying a post-war aero engine," wrote Leo Villa; "apart from the cost, which would have been prohibitive, most of them were on the secret list and were not available to civilians." Thus Villa was all the more astonished when his patron, Malcolm

Opposite: *Although the White Triplex had no rear suspension, springing of a sort was provided at the front. Leaning on its cockpit was Ray Keech, who set a new land speed record with the Triplex at 207.55mph at Daytona in April 1928. James White stood just behind him.*

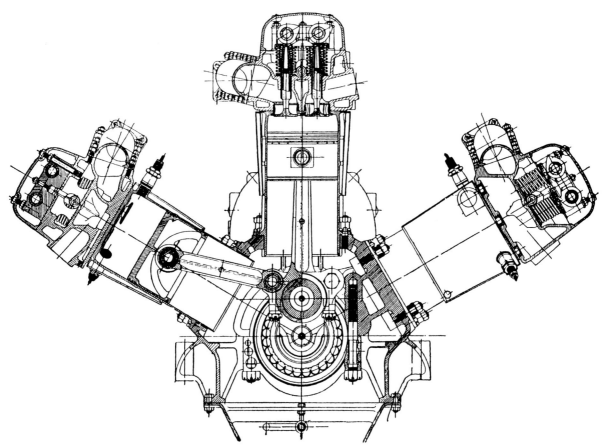

Napier's Lion stands in history as the most successful pure
W-type twelve-cylinder engine used both in aircraft and in
land-based record-breakers. A lateral section shows its twin
overhead cams for each of its three banks and its central
master rod paired with link rods for its outlying cylinders.

Its compactness and short overall length were assets of the
Napier Lion when attempts were made to install it in
record-breaking automobiles. This was the first such
installation, made in 1926 in a car with which Malcolm
Campbell set a new land speed record at 174.88mph in
February 1927.

Campbell, said out of the blue that "The Air Ministry have
agreed to let me have a Napier engine." Having broken
the 150-mph barrier in the 350-hp Sunbeam, the wily
Campbell now had his sights set on three miles a minute
and persuaded the Powers That Be that he was the man
to win that honour for Britain – and the Clan Campbell.

A straightforward car to carry the Lion was designed by
Amherst Villiers, succeeded by the author of its planetary
gearbox Joseph Maina, and built by Vickers and
Campbell's own crew. Under far-from-ideal conditions on
Pendine Sands, Campbell set a new record with his Blue
Bird in February 1927 at 174.88mph, topping another
aero engined rival. Deprived by Segrave of the honour of
being the first to 200mph, Campbell extensively rebuilt
his three-ton car and cadged a Schneider Trophy Lion
from the Admiralty with a 10.0:1 compression ratio that
produced 875bhp on exotic fuel. Taking it to Florida's
Daytona Beach, he set a new record at 206.95mph in
February 1928.[2]

Napier raised the unblown output of its Lion still
further to 951bhp at 3,600rpm, an astonishingly high
speed for such a big engine, to power the Irving Special,
a creation of Capt. J.S. 'Jack' Irving, late of Sunbeams.
Long and lean to reduce frontal area to a remarkably low
11.6sq ft when fully laden, Irving's car, nicknamed

Huge brakes and massive radius rods guiding the solid front axle were features of the Golden Arrow designed by Captain J. S. Irving to be driven by Henry Segrave. Its Napier Lion engine had been tuned to produce an unsupercharged 951bhp at the remarkably high speed of 3,600rpm.

Captain Irving shaped the body of his Golden Arrow around the three banks of its Napier Lion engine. Adding fairings between the wheels which also served as surface-type radiators, Irving's car for Segrave set a new record of 231.45mph at Daytona in March 1929.

'Golden Arrow', carried 7,694lb on a 168in wheelbase. Very low seating for Henry Segrave was achieved by twin drive shafts alongside his seat to the rear axle. Segrave and Irving made record-breaking look ludicrously easy at Daytona in March 1929 with a practice sally followed by a two-way run that averaged 231.45mph. A further attempt with the aim of surpassing four miles per minute was cancelled when the beach was closed after a fatal accident and the Golden Arrow never raced in anger again.

In the meantime Malcolm Campbell engaged the services of ace designer Reid Railton at Brooklands' Thomson & Taylor to update his Blue Bird to aim for 250mph. With faired wheels and a huge tail fin, the big car was fitted with a centrifugally supercharged Napier Lion that produced 1,480bhp at 3,600rpm. To ensure availability of a spare Campbell had obtained the use of two of these special engines which powered Gloster's contenders in the 1929 Schneider Trophy races. At Daytona Beach in February 1931 the speedy Scot was the first to surpass 240mph with an average of 246.09mph. A year later he returned with much the same car to put the record up to 253.97mph. For good measure Campbell set new speeds for five kilometres, five miles and ten kilometres.

In Australia a similar Napier twelve was borrowed from the British Air Ministry, via the Royal Australian Air Force, by expert mechanic and motor racer Norman 'Wizard' Smith. Born at Richmond near Sydney, Smith had previously obtained for the sum of £40 a 1922-vintage

Rolls-Royce Eagle giving 360bhp at 1,800rpm from 20,329cc (114.3 x 165.1mm) and installed it in a lengthened Cadillac chassis to create his 'Anzac,' an impressive two-seater machine with its bulky bonnet and stub exhausts. On Gerringong Beach in New South Wales he drove it to a new Australian speed record of 128.571mph in 1930. Then on New Zealand's Ninety Mile Beach,[3] on the west flank of a spit of land protruding north-west from the North Island, he drove the Anzac to a two-way speed of 148.637mph over a ten-mile stretch.

Updates to his Blue Bird by Reid Railton and a supercharged Napier Lion producing 1,480bhp allowed Malcolm Campbell to break the land speed record in 1931 and again in 1932. Here Campbell was demonstrating his awesome record-breaker to the crowd at Brooklands.

Norman 'Wizard' Smith's Anzac, with its Rolls-Royce Eagle engine, was a forerunner of a special car produced to be powered by a supercharged Napier Lion. Although patterned after the successful Golden Arrow, Smith's car proved unable to break even 200mph.

This would have been a new world record for the distance had his timing equipment met with approval.

Badly bitten by the record-breaking bug and relishing the monetary rewards it promised, Norman Smith commissioned a new car to carry his supercharged W12 Napier. It was built in Sydney by Don Harkness, himself a racer who had been the first to exceed 100mph officially in Australia in 1925 with an aero engined special. A partner in Harkness & Hillier, an engineering firm, he had been behind the building of the Anzac and even rode shotgun on Smith's 1930 runs. Harkness now took on a much

Designer Reid Railton was credited in the naming of a special high-speed track car built for John Cobb by Thomson & Taylor at Brooklands. It set many international records and left the fastest-ever Brooklands lap at 143.44mph.

bigger challenge. He and Smith unashamedly patterned much of their car after the successful Golden Arrow, including the hue of its paint. By combining the latter's low frontal area – they claimed even less – with 55 per cent more horsepower they had visions of at least 285mph.

Named the 'Fred H. Stewart Enterprise', after the Sydney businessman who put up a bond to secure the loan of the Napier Lion, the big machine with its Smith-Harkness hydraulic transmission was completed in 1931 and delivered at the end of that year to New Zealand. 'Wizard' Smith based his effort at Hukatere on the Ninety Mile Beach. That stretch of sand was capricious, however, denying its best to the Australian. On 26 January 1932 he successfully took the world's 10-mile record at 164.084mph, with a best one-way run just over 178mph. Conditions failed to improve, and when Smith essayed a kilometre run on 1 May 1932 a carburettor fire caused superficial damage. Lacking both the funding and motivation to take the Enterprise to an established record-breaking venue like Daytona Beach, Smith never ran his big racer again.

Back in Blighty 'ordinary' versions of the Napier Lion were available by the early 1930s and were even being converted for marine use by Thomson & Taylor. Thus when John Cobb – looking for something faster than his Delage DH and four-litre Sunbeam – decided to build a big fast car for Brooklands, the Napier was nominated. Tested by its makers, Cobb's W12 was the mild Mark XIA derivative delivering 564bhp at 2,700rpm. It was sparked by magneto and fed by a triple-throat Claudel Hobson carburettor. Installed in a conventional chassis underslung at the rear, the Napier drove through a single-disc clutch and three-speed gearbox to accelerate the Napier-Railton – for Reid Railton was its designer. On a

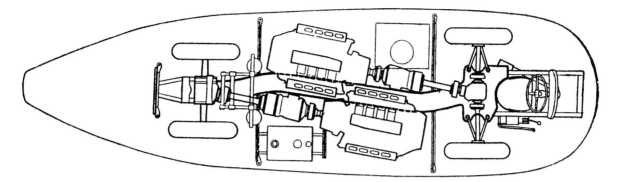

wheelbase of 130in Cobb's offset single-seater was not unduly weighty on its big Dunlops at 5,040lb, in view of its engine's 1,000lb weight. Mainly intended for fast-track use, it did without front brakes.

This was a big car among the big cars of Brooklands. On the bumpy Surrey bankings it set records that stand for all time: fastest lap at 143.44mph and fastest timed kilometre at 151.97mph in 1935 in the hands of John Cobb. Cobb also had his eye on the prestigious world's 24-hour record, but had been thwarted by poor conditions at Montlhéry. In July of 1935 he accepted the cost of shipping the Napier-Railton to Utah's Bonneville Salt Flats, where a 12½-mile circular course had been surveyed. With Tim Rose-Richards and Charlie Dodson and using National Benzole fuel, Cobb broke all the records from 50 kilometres to 24 hours, their speed for the latter being 134.85mph.

Rivals fought back, so in September of 1936 Cobb and the big car returned to Bonneville. "There is really something magnificent about the way in which the giant Napier-Railton tackles a job of work," said *The Autocar*. "Travelling across the Atlantic it arrives eventually at those bleak flats in Utah, and straight away, with the minimum of practice, it is started upon records, and it takes them." The car made two official runs, the first to set a new hour record at 167.69mph and the second to cover all the records to 24 hours, which was left at 150.16mph. This was its last hurrah as a record-breaker, for the attentions of Cobb and Railton now focused on the outright land speed record – still with Napier engines.

While his opponents turned to Rolls-Royce V12s, Cobb stayed loyal to the 'broad-arrow' W12 from Napier. For his new car he found two supercharged Lions which had been used in a racing speedboat in 1929. The same type of engine that Campbell had used in 1931 and '32, their sea-level output of 1,480bhp was reduced to 1,250bhp at the altitude of the Salt Flats. With its centrifugal blower each weighed 1,120lb. Reid Railton nestled these bulky engines at angles in his car's midsection, driving the front wheels with the left-hand

A plan view of the twin-engined Napier-Railton showed how ingeniously Reid Railton fitted its twin Lions diagonally into an S-shaped chassis, providing drive to all four wheels through separate power trains. A brave John Cobb sat right at the front.

W12 and the rear wheels with the right-hand engine – which was the more forward of the two. Both were cooled by water in a 75-gallon tank to which ice was added. The water also served to cool the contracting-band brakes on the car's two drive lines.

Rightly dubbed "amazing" by *The Autocar*, the bigger

Seen in its post-war configuration, John Cobb's second Napier-Railton housed two supercharged Napier Lions in an extraordinary streamlined shape by Reid Railton that also provided for four-wheel drive. It was one of auto history's most brilliant designs.

After successful record attacks before the war, John Cobb
returned to Bonneville in 1947 to set a new land speed
record of 394.196mph. This remained the fastest speed by a
wheel-driven car for almost seventeen years.

Napier-Railton was called "the most unorthodox record-
breaker ever built anywhere" by *The Motor*. "In order to
use four tyres," its designer said in relation to Dunlop's
proscriptions, "we had to keep the weight down to three
tons." It was in fact 3.15 tons on a wheelbase of 162in on
a chassis that was markedly crab-tracked at 66in in front,
42in in the rear to suit the car's teardrop-shaped form. No
conventional clutches were used, Cobb shifting with free-
wheeling devices instead, and the front and rear engines
and axles lacked any mechanical interconnection.

The ingenuity and daring of Railton and Cobb were
well rewarded. In the autumn of 1938 they took part in a
titanic battle of speed at Bonneville with George Eyston's
Thunderbolt, powered by two Rolls-Royce V12s. After
Eyston set the record at 345.2mph on 27 August, Cobb
began his trials. He made his first run without the car's
body to prove the four-wheel-drive system, and on his
second averaged 325mph. Finally on 15 September he
was timed at a record-setting 350.2mph. Extending his car
to the limit the next day, Eyston replied with 357.3mph.

Cobb, Railton and the Thomson & Taylor crew
decamped to their Brooklands base to regroup and
returned to Bonneville in August 1939. On the 22nd they
set a new record mile average of 368.85mph – the first to
six miles a minute. War was only days away. John Cobb
capped his second visit to Utah with world records over
five kilometres to ten miles, the first at 326.66mph and
the last at 270.35mph.

Confident that it had more speed to give, the team
returned in 1947 with much the same car, now the Railton

Mobil Special in recognition of welcome sponsorship.
This time Cobb was racing only himself and the tantalising
figure of 400mph. The old Lions roared again on the test
bed of Thornycroft at Caversham, revving now to
4,000rpm on more exotic brews than the aviation fuel
used before the war. Each was tuned to give more than
1,400 horsepower at Bonneville's high altitude.

In Utah one engine gave trouble, seizing a camshaft,
and spare parts had to be flown from England to effect
repairs. Salt conditions were poor on 16 September when
Cobb made his runs, but nevertheless he managed a
satisfying 403.135mph in one direction and an average of
394.196mph. This stood as the wheel-driven land speed
record until 17 July 1964 when Donald Campbell topped
it by a scant 8.8mph with his turbine-powered Blue Bird.

With its land-speed successes the Lion is the only
'broad-arrow' engine of W12 configuration to make a
significant mark in the history of the automobile. Few
have been built, and none has performed so well as the
Napier twelve. One last application deserves mention
because it involved a car that we met in the previous
Chapter, the Sunbeam 'Tigress'. After the war 'she'
sacrificed parts of her engine to keep Tiger running,
which 'he' did to excellent effect in VSCC (Vintage Sports
Car Club) races in 1965 and '66. Peter Morley and David
Llewellyn acquired the engineless Tigress and installed a
Napier Lion. This overparted even the doughty Sunbeam
chassis, which was replaced in 1972 by Bentley
underpinnings to transform the Napier-Sunbeam into
the Bentley-Napier. Rebodied in 1980, it was in the best
tradition of the VSCC 'Special'.

Marrying unusual engines and chassis enjoyed a long and
honourable tradition in Britain. The lure of Brooklands,
with its rewards for horsepower and disincentives for

All vee-type engines trace their origins to the narrow-angle twin produced in 1889 by Gottlieb Daimler and Wilhelm Maybach. While Daimler used it to power his own Stahlradwagen, the light and efficient wire-wheeled two-seater pictured, it was also manufactured in France by Panhard & Levassor. With cylinders opposite each other, it used fork-and-blade big-end bearings so that both connecting rods could share a common crankpin.

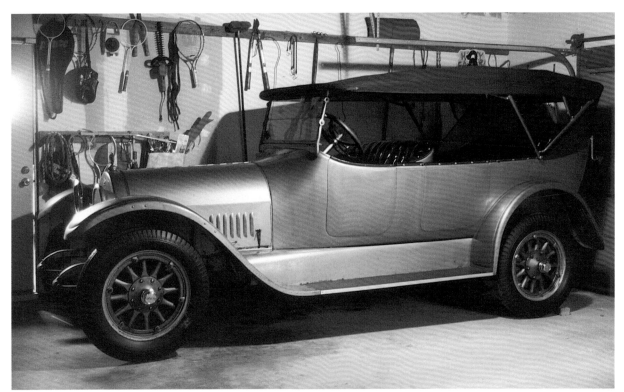

With the help of young draftsman Leo Goossen, Walter Marr prepared Buick to compete in America's booming market for twelve-cylinder cars with an overhead-valve engine of 8.2 litres, installed in its D55 chassis. Two prototypes were made of this robust V12, with exposed rocker arms, but with Buick's sixes selling well the twelve was not produced. Remarkably this Buick twelve prototype has survived in the hands of a descendant of Walter Marr. The other was acquired by Walter Chrysler. (Paul Marr)

In the 1930s America rediscovered the passion for twelves that had animated it before World War I. A leading producer was Lincoln, under the umbrella of the Ford Motor Company with the tasteful guidance of Edsel Ford. A 1932 Lincoln KB touring car is above. Packard revived its twelve-cylinder tradition with a fine engine that had its origins in racing. Below is a 1933 Model 1005, its headlamps 'veed' to match its radiator. (Robert J. Neal)

Twelves built strictly for speed were created on both sides of the Atlantic. Above is the 10.7-litre V12 designed by Charles Planchon for Louis Delage. Completed in 1923, its 280 horsepower took it to a new land speed record in 1924.

Though less powerful with 130bhp from its 4.9 litres, Packard's 299 of 1916, below, propelled a redoubtable racer. Competing in Europe, it fired the twelve-cylinder dreams of Enzo Ferrari. (Robert J. Neal)

Survivor of a pair of 4.0-litre Sunbeam V12 racing cars, *Tigress*, above, represents the determination of Louis Coatalen to set a new land speed record with a car that was not a freak of speed. In its day its output was 299bhp. John

Cobb's Napier-Railton, below, carried 23.9 litres in a W-configuration Napier Lion around which Reid Railton built a special car for record-breaking and racing at Brooklands. At the latter it left the lap record at 143.44mph.

The 6.0-litre V12 engine under the bonnet of the 1932 Type 670 Horch, above, was immaculately elegant. Its creators drew inspiration from the design of V8 engines recently introduced by divisions of General Motors. Displacing 7.3 litres, Rolls-Royce's Phantom III twelve, below, was introduced in 1935. Any prospects of a profit from its production were vitiated by its complex aviation-inspired design. (Stephe Boddice)

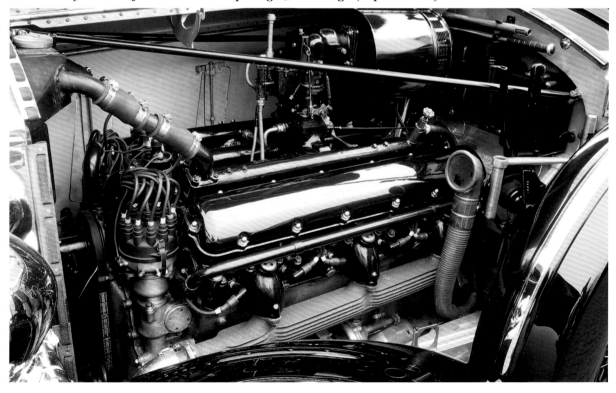

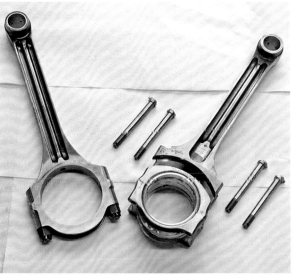

Above at left is the bottom end of the aluminium block of the Rolls-Royce Phantom III, showing its counterbalanced crankshaft and seven main bearings with caps fitting snugly into their webs. (Photograph courtesy of Fiennes Restoration Ltd) Above at right are the Phantom III's fork-and-blade connecting rods, showing how they allow the banks to be directly opposite each other. (Stephe Boddice)

A top view of the R-R Phantom III's block, below, reveals its many studs and the retainers for its tappet guides in the central vee. (Stephe Boddice) At right are the blade rod, on the left, and the forked rod, showing the way its big end was made as a separate component on the outer surface of which the blade rod had its bearing surface. (Photograph courtesy of Fiennes Restoration Ltd)

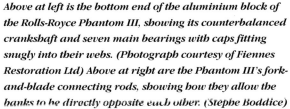

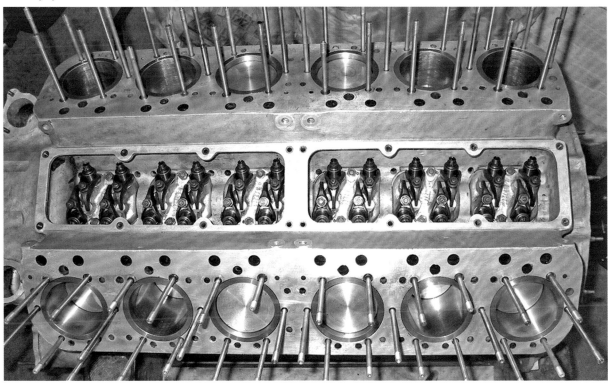

Two twelve-cylinder road cars of the 1930s gained a special reputation for sporting performance. In its lighter Rapide version, above, Lagonda's 4.5-litre V12 was capable of 112 mph. It was introduced just as war broke out in Europe.

Bodied as a sedanca coupé, below, the Hispano-Suiza J12 produced 190 or 220bhp to choice from its 9.4 litres. As a luxury car capable of astonishing performance it was without rival in its day.

handling and braking, was largely responsible. One aero engine that figured prominently was the United States Standard 12-Cylinder Aviation Engine, better known as the Liberty V12.

The Navy's chief construction officer, Admiral Taylor, christened as 'Liberty' the engine that one historian called "the most outstanding achievement in the history of mass production by the American automobile industry." It was the result of a decision taken in May 1917, a month after the United States entered the war, to design and build a new standard engine for US aircraft instead of copying one already being made abroad.

Primary parentage of the Liberty lay with two men and their organisations. One we've already met: Jesse Vincent and his team at Packard, who had been experimenting with aero engines. The other was Elbert L. Hall, chief engineer and production manager of San Francisco's Hall-Scott Motor Car Company, which was already in production with several aero engines and had just completed the prototype of its A8, a new big 60° V12. Both men had been eager to win orders for their engines, but at the suggestion of Edward Deeds of Delco they were brought together by the Aircraft Production Board to combine their skills and experience in the design of a new engine to be mass-produced by the American auto industry.

Their three-day around-the-clock marathon at the end of May to design such an engine in a suite at Washington's Willard Hotel is now the stuff of legend. While Vincent took charge of the lateral section, working with draftsmen who had been rapidly recruited and a set of Hall-Scott blueprints, Hall attended to the longitudinal section. Although they also envisioned four- and six-cylinder variants of the basic engine, with its individual cylinders, Hall and Vincent concentrated initially on V8 and V12 versions. The eight was first away, incredibly ready for its first test on 4 July 1917 thanks to the efforts of Packard's machine shops and skilled operators. By 25 August the first successful 50-hour test was passed by the Liberty V12. This became the mainstay of the new range.

Instead of the usual 60° vee angle, the Liberty was narrower at 45° to keep its frontal area at a minimum. With fork-and-blade rods on common crankpins this meant that firing intervals wouldn't be evenly spaced, which the team tolerated. It required the design of a special ignition system, unusually for an aircraft engine a coil and distributor system sourced from Delco. Jesse Vincent defended his use of coils in spite of "every kind of pressure," he said, from "certain people having magnetos to sell." His justification of the $112 Delco system included lighter weight and easier starting. The distributors were at the back ends of the single overhead cams on each bank, which opened two inclined valves

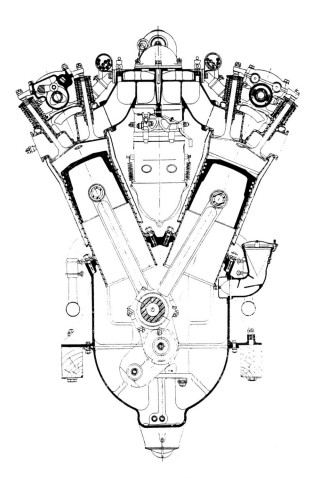

Features of both Packard and Hall-Scott aviation engines were combined by their designers in the famed Liberty V12 manufactured in America during the First World War. Two big valves topped each cylinder of the Liberty, whose banks were at a 45° angle to reduce head resistance to the minimum.

per cylinder through rocker arms with rollers contacting the cam lobes. Shafts and bevel gears at the rear of the Liberty drove its camshafts, while two updraft Zenith duplex carburettors huddled in its vee.

The Liberty V12 adopted Hall-Scott's cylinder dimensions of 5 x 7in for a displacement of 27,028cc. Made by Ford using a new process, its Mercedes-style steel cylinders sat on an aluminium crankcase with seven main bearings, the whole assemblage weighing 825lb. Its normal output was 421bhp at 1,700rpm, a speed that suited its direct-drive aircraft installations, and at 1,940rpm it produced 449bhp. Orders for 26,500 engines were placed by the government: 6,000 each from Packard and Lincoln, 5,000 apiece from Ford and Nordyke-Marmon, Cadillac and Buick 2,000 each and 500 from Trego Motors. Five thousand special jigs and fixtures were built to meet all their needs.

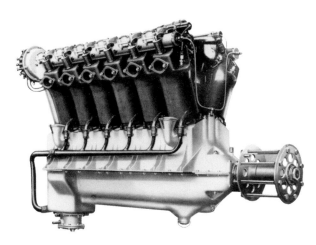

An external view of a direct-drive Liberty twelve showed its individual steel cylinders on an aluminium crankcase, and the shafts and double gears located at the rear of the engine driving a single overhead camshaft along each cylinder bank.

By Armistice Day in 1918 America's car makers had delivered 15,572 Liberty twelves. With run-on production the total came to 20,478. Packard's Liberties gained a reputation for unreliability, partly because it bore the main development burden, while those made by Henry Leland's Lincoln Motor Company were highly regarded. Some went abroad – 405 to France at $6,000 each and 980 to Britain at $7,300 apiece, which included spares.

Liberties were widely used as workhorse engines – especially in multi-engined aircraft – by the British as well as the Americans as late as 1933. They also saw service in World War II. Until the land-borne Meteor version of the Rolls-Royce Merlin was ready, Britain powered her Centaur medium-cruiser tanks with Leyland-built Liberties. Some saw service in, and after, the Normandy landings.

One Liberty had a quite extraordinary career in Britain. It was acquired soon after World War I by Count Louis Vorow Zborowski, who despite his exotic handle had English and American parentage. Passionate about cars and racing, the moustachioed Count had the wherewithal to buy and build them at his estate near Canterbury, Higham House. His aide in this was Clive Gallop, a knowledgeable engineer-driver. With Gallop's guidance Zborowski built a trio of Chitty-Bang-Bangs, huge cars on chain-drive Mercedes chassis using Maybach, Benz and Mercedes six-cylinder aero engines. Having acquired a Liberty, which far out-powered these, Zborowski decided to commission a purpose-built chassis to carry it.

Work on the new car began in 1923. For its drive line Gallop raided the Higham parts bins for a Mercedes scroll clutch and a 200-horsepower Benz four-speed

transmission, which drove the rear wheels through chains. On the left side, a chain to a cross-shaft at the front of the engine provided a point at which the Liberty could be cranked to start it. Clive Gallop knew well the merits of a deep-sided frame and front brakes, but Zborowski preferred slender truss-braced frame rails and rear-wheel brakes only. Bodied in typical early-1920s style with a bluff radiator, the white-painted Higham Special – as it was named – was remarkably light at 3,460lb. Its gearing gave 120mph at only 1,400rpm.

Count Zborowski had but one chance to race the Higham at Brooklands, in the 1924 Easter meeting, before his death at Monza later that year. When his estate was wound up the Higham Special was bought for £125 by a remarkable Welsh-born engineer who dwelled in a bungalow inside the track at Brooklands, John Godfrey Parry Thomas.

Although Thomas had made an outstanding reputation as a creative engineer with Leyland, including the design of a superb passenger car, the Leyland Eight, from 1923 he set up on his own to build racing cars of all kinds. No handicap to his new independent career, according to Reid Railton, was that Thomas "had the valuable knack of persuading others of the feasibility of any project in which he was interested, and furthermore of convincing them that he could carry it through."

In October of 1925 Thomas took the ex-Higham to Pendine Sands, where Campbell had broken the 150-mph mark in July. It was much as in Zborowski's time except for stub exhausts instead of manifolding and a sloping cowl for its radiator. Bad weather over the seven-mile speed course meant that nothing useful could be done. Thomas buckled down to a busy winter in the workshops adjoining his Brooklands home, The Hermitage.

In April 1926 the doors swung open to reveal a racer totally transformed. Although officially a Thomas Special it was affectionately nicknamed 'Babs.' Gone was Zborowski's conventional body and in its place was a highly aerodynamic form with a long, tapering tail. Its radiator was set lower and sloping backward behind an oval air inlet. In the manner recommended by aerodynamicist Paul Jaray, whose ideas were much in vogue at the time, Babs had a separate upper teardrop form on the right into which the cockpit was recessed.

Parry Thomas also attended to Babs's chassis. He fitted a Leyland Eight front axle, still innocent of brakes, and a multiple-disc clutch in place of the Mercedes scroll device. Containing new pistons and new camshafts supplied by Laystall to Thomas's designs, the Liberty was credited with 500bhp. A new induction system deployed two carburettors at front and two at the rear, all fitted with forward-facing air scoops. Although Babs was first rolled

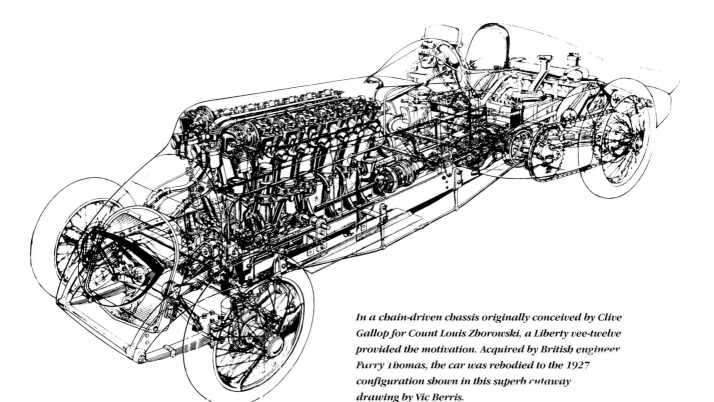

In a chain-driven chassis originally conceived by Clive Gallop for Count Louis Zborowski, a Liberty vee-twelve provided the motivation. Acquired by British engineer Parry Thomas, the car was rebodied to the 1927 configuration shown in this superb cutaway drawing by Vic Berris.

out in April with exhaust manifolding, she achieved her best performance with stub exhausts and running on a mixture of 60 per cent Shell aviation fuel and 40 per cent benzole. During his runs Thomas was kept busy by the hand pump on his left which pressurised the fuel tank.

With Shell sponsorship, Parry Thomas took Babs to Pendine Sands at the end of April 1926. Rolling out of the Beach Hotel's garage onto the sand he found it damp, so much so that the massive car – now weighing 3,920lb – would sink in without the large wooden platforms to which she was wheeled when at rest. Nevertheless Babs ran like a champ.

Greedily, Thomas in effect broke the record twice on successive days. On the 27th he averaged 169.30mph and on the 28th 171.02mph – nearly 19mph faster than Segrave's speed the month before in the 4-litre V12 Sunbeam. Never before had the record been broken by such a margin; not for the burly Welshman the style of inching speeds upward to save bites of the apple for later. His quickest runs were made with the carburettor air scoops covered over.

As mentioned earlier, Malcolm Campbell topped Thomas's speed with his Napier-engined Blue Bird in February 1927. Racers preferred the winter months at Pendine, when heavy seas smoothed and firmed the sand. Campbell's advantage was less than four miles per hour, however, so Thomas was confident that Babs could retake the record. Still suffering the aftermath of a bout of 'flu, he was back at Pendine in early March of 1927 with

a titivated Babs. Her cooling-air inlet was smaller, her stub exhausts faired closer to the bonnet and her driving chains covered by fairings.

On the 3rd of March Parry Thomas made several preliminary runs with the big Liberty audibly missing. On her first high-speed run Babs swerved violently after the

After successful attacks on the world land speed record in 1926 Parry Thomas returned to Pendine Sands in March 1927 with the Liberty-powered car he had nicknamed 'Babs'. It looked the most potent of record breakers in the hands of its Welsh constructor.

Babs was a sorry sight after she swerved out of control at the end of a first high-speed run by Thomas on March 3, 1947. Engineer Reid Railton concluded that breakage of the right rear wire wheel had been the catalyst for a crash that sadly killed Parry Thomas.

timed section, through which she'd peaked at some 180mph. The white car snaked and somersaulted before coming to a flaming stop in the sand. Engineer Reid Railton inspected its wreckage and concluded that the tragedy began when the right rear wire wheel collapsed. One of its spokes became entangled in the chain which then broke, the lack of drive to that wheel further exacerbating the swerve. Railton's friend and, indeed, mentor, was killed in the resulting crash at the age of only 41.[4]

Between Babs's first and last record runs she had

If brute force could be relied upon to set a new world land speed record, this was provided by Philadelphia businessman James M. White with three Liberty engines crammed into a special chassis which became known as the White Triplex. All three engines drove directly to a special rear axle with three sets of final-drive gears.

enjoyed a brief racing career at Brooklands. Both John Cobb and Thomas drove her in races during the summer of 1927. Although handicapped out of contention, she was a stirring sight at 160mph on the Railway Straight before her driver reached for the outside hand-brake to slow her. In 1927 the remains of Babs were interred in the sands at Pendine, an act that in effect brought down the curtain on the Welsh beach as a venue for the very highest speeds. Controversially but successfully, Babs was exhumed in 1969 and by 1984 was considered fully restored.

If Thomas's tragic end were to be seen as a hoodoo cast by his use of the Liberty V12 as a record-breaker, this could only be reinforced by the fate of another Liberty-powered machine, the White Triplex.[5] Justly maligned as the crudest contraption ever to make a serious attempt on the world land speed record, the Triplex was the creation of Philadelphia wire manufacturer and sportsman James M. White. Acquiring no fewer than three Liberties, he arrayed them arrow-fashion in a purpose-built chassis: one in the front and two side-by-side at the rear. Each drove without clutch or gearbox to a special rear axle sprouting three sets of ring and pinion gears.

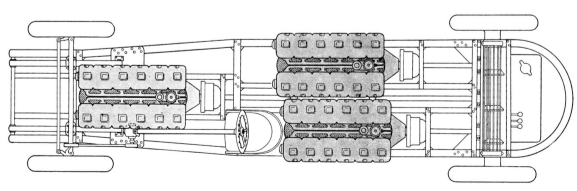

The Triplex driver – originally mooted as White himself – sat offset to the left in the niche between the front and rear engines. Unpretentious bodywork enclosed the front engine and left those in the rear of this 8,000lb vehicle exposed. No radiator was needed, for the engines were cooled by a supply of water in a tank under the chassis. While the front axle was conventionally sprung, that at the rear was attached to the frame. When a first attempt to provide an electric-motor reverse gear failed, White's crew fitted an extra axle at the rear that was driven from one engine by a worm gear with a 500:1 ratio and engaged with the ground by a hand lever. Fortunately this could be dispensed with during the record runs.

White's handsome emolument persuaded a fellow Philadelphian, Ray Keech, into the Triplex's cockpit. A gregarious and burly character, the red-haired Keech was beginning to make a name for himself in board-track racing. A first attempt to set a record on Daytona Beach at the end of February 1928 ended when Keech was scalded by a failed water hose on the front engine and had to be hospitalised. Only then was a protective barrier installed between engine and driver. Returning in April, the plucky Keech took the Triplex to a two-way average of 207.55mph. Although less than one mile per hour faster than Campbell's Napier-powered record, it was a new world's-fastest figure for 81,084cc of triple Liberty vee-twelves.

In May of '28 world-record-holder Ray Keech made his first appearance at Indianapolis, finishing fourth in a Miller. When in March 1929 James White decided to field his Triplex again to challenge Henry Segrave's new Napier-powered record of 231.45mph, Keech waved off, saying, "There's not enough money to get me back in that hot seat." White again considered taking the wheel himself, but then turned to up-and-coming racer Wilbur Shaw. At the time, however, Shaw was in hot water with the American Automobile Association, and the AAA was America's record-attempt timing authority. Lee Bible, 42-year-old owner of the Daytona garage where the Triplex was serviced, offered to drive her in Shaw's stead.

Powerful though the Triplex was, with at least 1,200bhp, chances of her breaking Segrave's record had to be slim. Nevertheless on 13 March 1929 the game Bible stepped aboard. Having practised the day before, he now satisfied the AAA timers with a run of 183mph that he could handle the Triplex. Then in the afternoon he made his first serious run. Northbound, Bible clocked 202mph through the mile. Thereafter he backed off too sharply, however, and 36 cylinders suddenly slowed the rear wheels, which skidded. The heavy car swerved left toward the dunes, killing a cameraman as it tumbled out of control.

Lee Bible, who had called this "the golden opportunity of a lifetime," expired after being thrown from the

Little that was recognisable remained after the 81.1-litre White Triplex crashed during a record attempt in March 1929. The crash killed a cameraman and the plucky driver of the Triplex, Daytona garage owner Lee Bible.

hurtling Triplex, which was a tangled wreck. Two and a half months later Ray Keech drove a steady race to win the 1929 Indianapolis 500-mile contest. Magazine reports on the race referred to him as 'the late Ray Keech', for only two weeks after the 500 he was killed on the Altoona, Pennsylvania board track when wreckage from another crash blocked his path.[6]

Less tragedy – so far as we know – is associated with another Liberty-powered vehicle charmingly described by one publication as "The Time Machine from Wagga Wagga". It began with a chassis, a chain-drive relic made by France's Malicet et Blin (MAB) circa 1908, which was unearthed in Australia's Wagga Wagga, New South Wales, in 1978. Stuart Saunders had the dream of building a Brooklands-style monster on its 126in wheelbase but needed a suitable engine. He found it in America, a 1918-vintage Liberty V12. Moving the four-speed gearbox rearward to accommodate it meant adding a primary chain that drove forward to the original drive sprockets and their shafts. This proved useful as an additional means of altering the MAB-Liberty's overall gear ratio, which saw it cruising at 75mph at only 1,400rpm. With external exhaust manifolding, a cylindrical fuel tank, monocle windscreen and tufted seats, Saunders's creation was the very essence of Edwardian road-eater.

Amongst the record-breaking efforts of Malcolm Campbell, Parry Thomas, Ray Keech *et al* at the end of the 1920s, another aero engined effort stood out for its resolution and effectiveness. Henry Segrave and Louis

Coatalen had shown phenomenal efficiency in raising the record to 152mph in the four-litre V12 Sunbeam in 1926. Now, however, Thomas had put the speed up to more than 170mph and Campbell was known to be building his Napier-powered car. "I went to see Mr. Coatalen again," Segrave related, "and asked him if he thought it would be possible to build a vehicle which would attain a speed of 200mph on land."

"I have shown what can be done by making a small engine super-efficient," the French engineer replied, referring to his four-litre car. "Let us now allow ourselves unlimited engine capacity and take, for example, a thousand-horsepower engine!" He had just such an engine, his Sikh III V12 of 64,126cc (180 x 210mm) under development to power airships. Producing 1,000bhp at 1,650rpm it had the required power, but its 5½-feet height and its weight of 2,760lb made it inconvenient to install. "Mr. Coatalen then conceived the brilliantly successful idea," said Segrave, "of splitting the power unit into two and fitting one half to the front of the car and the other to the back. A rough layout of the design was worked out by him and then handed to Captain Irving to complete and build."

The new concept wouldn't quite hit the 1,000-horsepower mark (although lettering on the car would claim that it had) but it was close enough at 870. From Sunbeam's extensive stores Capt Irving withdrew two Matabele V12s that had powered a racing speedboat, *Maple Leaf VII*, in 1920. In its specifications the Matabele was close

Sunbeam's Louis Coatalen re-entered the record-breaking scene in 1927 with the construction of a twin-engined car powered by two of his Matabele vee-twelves. Formerly aircraft engines, they had been used in a racing speedboat.

kin to the Liberty with its displacement of 22,445cc (122 x 160mm), weight of 1,100lb and output of 435bhp at 2,000rpm. In a de Havilland DH4 – the aeroplane most often Liberty-powered – it out-sped the Liberty at 122 to 117mph in spite of its wider vee angle of 60°.

A development of Sunbeam's Cossack range, the Matabele had two three-cylinder aluminium blocks per bank and gear-driven twin overhead camshafts opening four valves per cylinder. Bottom-end bearings were plain, including eight main bearings, and the connecting rods were of master and link type. To cope with its dual ignition, each engine had an impressive battery of four magnetos at its anti-drive end, above a single water pump feeding manifolding to both sets of cylinder blocks. Two Claudel-Hobson HC.7 carburettors nestled in the central vee.

"Seen in its chassis state," reported *The Autocar* about Sunbeam's new creation, "the machine is not so much reminiscent of a motor car as of the engine room of a battleship before turbines came in." No chances were taken with its frame, which had side members 14in in depth and massive cross members to cope with a wheelbase of 141 inches. Under the frame, said one report, was an undershield made of 6mm armour plate "to provide a firm and strong base on which the car can slide in the event of a wheel coming adrift."

Subframes carried the two Matabeles, one just behind the front wheels and the other over the rear wheels, with room for Segrave between them. Their business ends, taking direct drive from the engines, faced toward the car's centre. Both drove into an all-indirect three-speed gearbox from which power went to a cross shaft that drove the rear wheels through sprockets and chains. Armour-quality steel panels aimed to protect the driver from any chain failure.[7] Leaf-sprung axles were tubular, that at the rear curved deeply to pass under the aft engine.

Ingeniously, Capt Irving reduced stress on the gearbox by stepping up its input speed to it by a ratio of 2.5:1 and then reducing speed again by the same amount at its output. This allowed him to use a much lighter and more compact transmission than would otherwise have been required. In operation the rear Matabele was first started, using a supply of compressed air at some 1,700psi. Then the rear clutch was engaged and – with a hand lever – the front clutch was engaged to start the front engine. Once the latter was running a dog clutch locked the two engines together. Impressively, the entire drive train was thoroughly tested over eight hours at Wolverhampton with each rear wheel driving a Heenan & Froude dynamometer and a water supply cooling the engines.

Ultra-radically for 1926–27, the entire vehicle was encased in fully enclosed bodywork. Tests of a model in the Vickers wind tunnel forecast 700lb of front downforce and a modest rear lift of 200lb for its rounded nose and long tapering tail. A nose slot cooled the front engine's single radiator while side scoops admitted air to two flanking the rear engine. Although tunnel tests suggested enclosed wheels, the '1,000 hp Sunbeam' ran with its wire wheels and 6 x 35 Dunlop tyres exposed. Representing a new higher level of development by Dunlop on its special testing machine in the Midlands, the tyres were stated to be safe for 3½ minutes at a speed of 200mph for the 7,800lb car.

Henry Segrave and Sunbeam fell out on the issue of where the car should run. The British company thought a venue in Britain should be suitable, but Segrave "was equally certain that it was out of the question," observing that "it was my neck which had to be risked." The American-born Briton decided to take the car to Daytona Beach on his own recognisance and cost. Segrave was in fact the pioneer of the modern record-breaking era in Florida, personally initiating the many actions needed to have the AAA's timing equipment accepted for international record-breaking by the AIACR's successor in Paris, the FIA (*Fédération Internationale de l'Automobile*). The Atlantic-facing Daytona sand provided four hard and straight miles on both sides of the central measured mile.

"This was something more gigantic than any yet dreamed of," said Segrave of the awesome Sunbeam. "It is the only time I can honestly say when I have stood in front of a car and doubted human ability to control it." Hitherto abstaining, the tall, balding driver began cadging cigarettes and chain smoking a quarter-hour before the off in Florida. His first runs showed the rear engine to be starved of cooling air, so inlet scoops were added, and the steering ratio was speeded up. Through

In a robust chassis designed by Captain J. S. Irving, the big Sunbeam had separate radiators for its front and rear engines. Drive from both engines reached the car's rear wheels through a cross shaft and chains.

the gears Segrave accelerated to better than 70mph in first, 135 in second and a maximum of 212mph in top at the end of the measured mile. His two-way average over the mile of 203.79mph would stand for almost a year before being topped by Campbell's Napier-engined Blue Bird. The Sunbeam set a new five-kilometre mark as well at 202.67mph.

An extreme novelty for 1926–27 was the Sunbeam's fully enclosed bodywork. Not until the 1930s would full enclosure of the body be seen as productive by record-breakers. In March 1927 Henry Segrave became the first to be timed officially at an average speed of better than 200mph at Daytona, Florida.

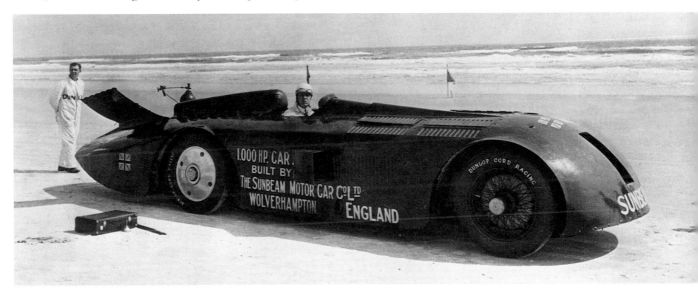

The next time Sunbeam went record-breaking, the practical talents of Capt Jack Irving were conspicuous by their absence. Both he and Segrave – now Sir Henry – had turned their attention to speed on water, which would kill the 33-year-old Segrave in June 1930. Such, however, was the passion for record breaking that Louis Coatalen could not resist another sally. Although the new effort was a costly one that Sunbeam could ill afford, Coatalen was not to be denied, for he "had true tenacity and definite character," wrote S.C.H. Davis, "getting his own way by truly Gallic methods, as befitted a Frenchman." His ambitions for the new car were high indeed: no less than 300mph.

Strangely Coatalen rejected the all-enveloping bodywork that had been so successful in 1927 and reverted instead to an exposed-wheel design. From his open-air drawing office on the Isle of Capri, the engineer produced instead a slim-cigar concept with the same twin propeller shafts that had worked so well for Capt Irving's Golden Arrow. Driving them was an all-indirect three-speed gearbox and a multiple-disc clutch that was locked when fully engaged. Execution of Coatalen's concepts,

With extreme profligacy Louis Coatalen built two special engines for a 1930 record contender dubbed the 'Silver Bullet'. Although he gave the engines only single ignition, Coatalen said that he had aviation ambitions for the aluminium-block units, each of which displaced 24.0 litres.

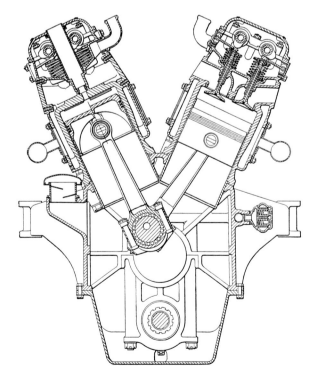

assigned to Hugh Rose, included the design and manufacture of no fewer than 300 special split-race twin-row roller bearings of unique design used throughout the vehicle.

For the new car Coatalen specified two completely new V12 engines which – shades of Toodles V and the Manitou – he hoped to evolve into a new family of aviation engines. The new unit's hallmark was high revolutions, abetted by a roller-bearing bottom end with split races and a one-piece crankshaft devoid of counterweights. Directly facing cylinders were accommodated by fork-and-blade connecting rods, each running on two rows of $\frac{1}{4}$-in rollers on 60mm journals.

"Oversquare dimensions of 140 x 130mm for 24,014cc were chosen," said Coatalen, "to minimise frontal area, as was the unusual vee angle of 50°." The twelve was constructed of two three-cylinder monobloc aluminium castings per bank. Cylinder liners were hard-nitrided steel with ultra-smooth bores, held in place by small flanges at the bases of the blocks. The cylinder blocks were bolted to an aluminium crankcase with four bearers along each side.

Coatalen's new V12 had four valves per cylinder opened through finger followers by close-spaced twin overhead camshafts akin to those of the Napier Lion. The cams were driven by a train of gears at the crankshaft's anti-drive end, while twin water pumps sat transversely at the rearmost or output end of the front engine, where they served the cooling needs of both twelves. Each engine had its own pair of dual oil pumps for its dry-sump system, using castor oil. Hollow exhaust valves were oil-cooled.

Oddly for an engine for which aeronautic ambitions were claimed, the purpose-built Sunbeam twelve had single ignition with its plug placed centrally in the combustion chamber. Each engine had two distributors separately serving its cylinder banks. Tested naturally aspirated, each 1,000lb twelve was said to produce 490bhp at 2,400rpm with a compression ratio of 5.6:1 and to be capable of development to a heady 2,000 supercharged horsepower on its fuel blend of half and half benzole and alcohol with a dash of ether "to give a wider range of explosive mixture" that was helpful for starting.

In the 'Silver Bullet', as the new car was dubbed with a cheeky reference to the Golden Arrow, the two twelves were placed in line ahead of the designated driver, Brooklands star Kaye Don.[8] Joining them was a special telescopic splined coupling that allowed relative movement of the two engines. Integrated into their dry sumps was a sub-shaft that turned at a stepped-up ratio of 0.43:1. Originally it was to drive a quartet of Roots-type blowers for each engine, but these proved troublesome

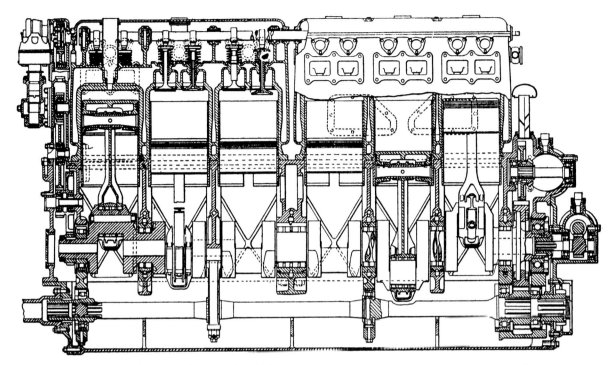

in trials and were replaced by a single centrifugal blower behind the rearmost V12, turning at up to 20,000rpm and drawing through two huge Amal carburettors. It fed ducting that led forward to the two engines, whose exhaust pipe-works were set flush with the Sunbeam's outer skin. Anticipating Railton's solution for John Cobb, the Silver Bullet's engines were cooled by water flowing through a tank containing 750lb of ice, which was enough to cool the engines for five minutes. Striking *empennage* was to provide both stability and air braking.

Conventional solid-axle suspension was guided by radius rods at both front and rear. Engines and gearbox

Coatalen and his designer Hugh Rose used roller bearings liberally throughout the two V12s of the Silver Bullet, including their fork-and-blade connecting rods. This was the forward engine beneath which a layshaft carried the drive rearward.

To say that the Sunbeam Silver Bullet of 1930 represented a radical conception would be to understate the case. Driver Kaye Don sat at the extreme rear of a vehicle whose 15.4 ft of wheelbase imposed massive bending loads on its chassis. The provision of supercharging for the engines became a knotty design challenge.

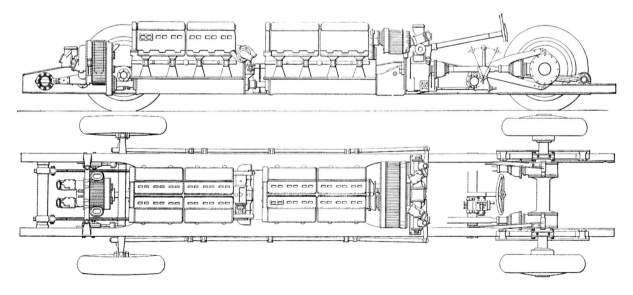

With tailplanes designed to aid both stability and braking, the Silver Bullet was a dramatic sight when it rolled out of Sunbeam's Wolverhampton factory. It was destined to be one of the last great follies of Louis Coatalen.

Later attempts to extract the potential of Sunbeam's Silver Bullet included a revision in which the exhaust pipes emerged directly from the bodywork instead of being deeply submerged within it. Efforts to make something of the awesome car by later proprietors were unsuccessful.

acted as cross-members for a massive frame that carried the Silver Bullet's 6,000lb on a wheelbase of 185 inches.[9] This huge wheelspan was found disadvantageous after the Sunbeam crew decanted their Bullet at Daytona Beach in March 1930 with the aim of reaching 250mph, the car's 300-mph design speed being held in reserve.

We can dismiss claims that each of the supercharged engines developed 2,000bhp, but even 1,000 apiece – not out of the question – should have powered a rapid motorcar. In Florida, however, she was a handful on a less-than-ideal beach surface and was afflicted by many technical gremlins during eighteen runs, the fastest of which was 'only' 186mph. Hopes of a return to Florida were dashed by Sunbeam's financial plight, which saw it in receivership in 1931.[10] Others, including famed tuner and driver Freddie Dixon, later tried to exploit the Silver Bullet's potential, but without success.

Having been first to top 250mph, Sir Malcolm Campbell – as he now was – set a new target of 300mph. This would test his powers of persuasion to the utmost, for the engine he had in mind to achieve this was made by Britain's most conservative car maker, Rolls-Royce. Fortunately for Campbell, Rolls-Royce had already been persuaded to do something outrageous, namely to build engines to power some of Britain's 1929 contenders for aviation's Schneider Trophy Race. Although Sir Henry Royce sketched a potential V16 for this assignment, lack of time meant that an existing engine, the H-Type or Buzzard, was taken as a basis instead.

Measuring 152.4 x 167.6mm, the Buzzard vee-twelve was a big bird at 36,696cc. Essentially an enlarged version of the Kestrel of the late 1920s, the Buzzard was made in

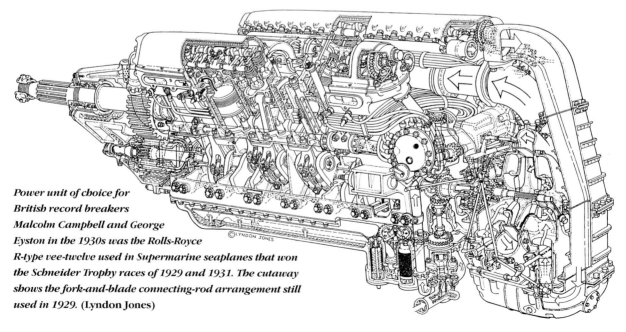

Power unit of choice for British record breakers Malcolm Campbell and George Eyston in the 1930s was the Rolls-Royce R-type vee-twelve used in Supermarine seaplanes that won the Schneider Trophy races of 1929 and 1931. The cutaway shows the fork-and-blade connecting-rod arrangement still used in 1929. (Lyndon Jones)

a run of only 100 in 1927, producing 925bhp from its 1,450lb. From this promising clay Royce fashioned the R-Type engine that powered Supermarine seaplanes to victory in the Schneider races of 1929 and 1931. By the latter year the supercharged R-Type was producing 2,350bhp at 3,200rpm with a manifold pressure of 33psi and weighed 1,630lb. Among the final changes to the engine was the replacement of fork-and-blade rods by an articulated-rod system. High-pressure boosting was accepted by its monobloc cylinders, cast of aluminium in two banks of six at a 60° angle. Four valves per cylinder were opened through long fingers by a single shaft-driven overhead cam on each bank.

As installed by Reid Railton at Thomson & Taylor in the stretched Blue Bird chassis, the R-Type Rolls-Royce could be uprated to 2,500bhp at 3,400rpm with manifold pressures of up to 36psi because its lifetime no longer had to be one hour at full power; scant minutes would suffice. From February 1933, when he set his first new record with the R-R-engined Blue Bird at 272.46mph at Daytona, the main challenge for Railton and Campbell was harnessing this magnificent engine's power.

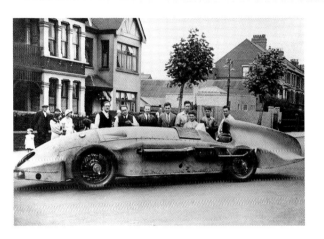

In February 1935, when a much-changed Blue Bird with full-width bodywork and twin rear wheels managed only 276.88mph in Florida, they realised that the car had become too fast for the venue. In September they repaired to Utah's salt flats, where without changes the tail-finned blue racer was clocked at 301.129mph. It was Sir Malcolm's ninth land speed record and his last, at the age of 50.

Another satisfied Rolls-Royce customer was Captain George Edward Thomas Eyston. Born in Oxfordshire in 1897, the tall, bespectacled Eyston was not only a hugely experienced racing driver but also an engineer well able to create his own record-breakers. One such was his

Right, top: *Huffing and puffing from the exhausts of its R-type vee-twelve, Malcolm Campbell's Blue Bird is shown during one of its last runs at Daytona in February 1935, when it was timed at 276.88mph. Later in the year the same car bettered 300mph at Bonneville.*

Right, centre: *Seen with silencers fitted for testing at Brooklands, the front-drive 'Speed of the Wind' was designed for George Eyston – the tall bespectacled figure behind the front wheel – by Ernest Eldridge, the shorter personality on Eyston's left. Its power was a 21.2-litre Rolls-Royce Kestrel V12.*

Right, bottom: *Finger-type cam followers figured in the valve gear of Rolls-Royce's Kestrel vee-twelve. Long through-bolts provided lateral bracing for its main-bearing caps.*

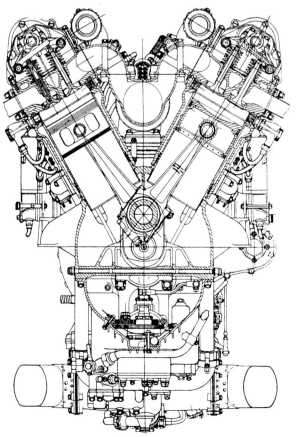

'Speed of the Wind', a front-driven car designed for Eyston by Ernest Eldridge. Built by L. T. Delaney and Sons, it was powered by an unblown Rolls-Royce Kestrel V12 of 21,236cc (127 x 139.7mm). Later versions of the Kestrel gave 625bhp at 2,900rpm for a weight of 900lb. At Bonneville Eyston drove Speed of the Wind to a new one-hour record in 1935 and raised it to 162.53mph in July 1936. In the latter session he and Bert Denly put the 24-hour record up to 149.10mph, only to see John Cobb and friends seize it in September with the Napier-Railton.

Eyston and Cobb were rivals for the outright speed record as well; both had their sights on Campbell's alluring 301mph target. For his contender, designed to reach 335mph, Eyston decided on not one but two R-Type Rolls-Royce V12 engines mounted amidships side by side.[11] His 'Thunderbolt', a juggernaut to challenge the record if ever there was one, had paired driving wheels at the rear and two sets of front wheels, the front pair much narrower-tracked than the other to suit the car's rounded nose. Parallel-wishbone suspensions were stiffly controlled by transverse leaf springs, with the rearmost front pair retarded by inboard clutch-type disc brakes driven by shafts from the hubs.

It took seven months to build Thunderbolt in the Bean factory at Tipton in Staffordshire, with its all-enclosed body made of corrosion-resistant aluminium by a firm of boat builders on the south coast. Eyston sat behind its front wheels and ahead of its engines, which drove though special dog-engagement clutches and a gear train to the three-speed gearbox and chassis-mounted differential. Lateral airbrake flaps and a big fin were features of the big car's tail. Weighing 13,900lb,

Although not visible here, George Eyston's Thunderbolt of 1937 had two pairs of front wheels and dual drive wheels at the rear. Powered by two Rolls-Royce R-type V12s, Eyston and Thunderbolt set land speed records at velocities of up to 357.50mph.

Thunderbolt needed every one of its potential 5,000 horsepower to accelerate up to speed in the measured mile, even at Bonneville.

After several runs were aborted by problems with its novel clutch, Eyston and Thunderbolt thundered to a new land speed record of 312.00mph in November 1937.[12] Accepting John Cobb's challenge, Eyston improved his car's streamlining, enclosing its cockpit and smoothing its nose. On 27 August 1938 he roared to a new record of 345.50mph at Bonneville, only to be topped by Cobb a week later. Undaunted, George Eyston stripped away his car's tail fin to reduce drag and removed its radiator, rounding the nose and substituting a water tank for cooling. The more slippery Thunderbolt responded on 16 September with runs averaging 357.50mph, handing victory to Eyston in his epic 1938 battle with John Cobb. The latter returned, as we know, in 1939 to set a new record that lasted through the war.

Only after the war did the world learn that Germany had been preparing a car to rival the achievements of Cobb and Eyston. In an historic alliance, it was designed by Ferdinand Porsche's Stuttgart engineering office to be built by Daimler-Benz and powered by one of its vee-twelve aero engines. Creation of the latter dated back to 1932, when Daimler-Benz began work on a liquid-cooled V12 for aircraft. The effort was overseen by the veteran Benz engine-design team of Arthur Berger under engineering chief Hans Nibel. Soon the experimental supercharged inverted-vee twelves of 35.7 litres were producing 800bhp.

In 1934 the Reich Aviation Ministry set up a new system of designations for aircraft engines. They allotted Daimler-Benz the initials DB and a number series from 600 to 699, so the new engine in carburetted form became the DB600 and its injected version the DB601. Not until 1937 would one of the DB600 engines be flown in public but in 1936 1,000-horsepower DB600s were being delivered to builders like Heinkel for experimental installations. And the DB601 promised a maximum of 1,300 horsepower.

Availability of such engines for record-breaking on land was as circumscribed in Germany as it was in Britain in 1936. Their price of some 9,000 marks apiece was academic, for the still-secret power units were built for and controlled by the Reich Aviation Ministry, just as Malcolm Campbell's Rolls-Royce engine had been British Crown property. It happened, however, that the man who wanted them, tall and likeable racing driver Hans Stuck, was a crony of old of the Third Reich's director of aircraft procurement, Ernst Udet, an aviation hero for his

With steel cylinder sleeves screwed into an aluminium block and fork-and-blade connecting rods, the Daimler-Benz DB601 vee-twelve was one of the major aero engines of World War Two. Built to be run inverted in the aircraft, its crankshaft would have been at the top.

exploits in World War I. Udet promised Stuck the engines he needed.

Now Stuck needed a car to carry the engines to attack Campbell's record, which was left at 301.13mph late in 1935 at Bonneville. Mercedes-Benz racing director Alfred Neubauer estimated the total cost of such a record attempt to be one million marks, roughly $300,000. "Now, Hans Stuck had no million," said Neubauer. "He didn't even have half. But what he did have was exceptional connections." He'd shown that with his successful appeal to Udet.

Another friend of Hans Stuck was Ferdinand Porsche. Stuck had raced Porsche's designs for Austro-Daimler, Daimler-Benz and Auto Union. He'd contributed some capital to the kitty that Porsche had drawn on to set up his own design office in Stuttgart in 1931. And he was a mainstay of the Auto Union racing team whose successful rear-engined cars were globally flaunting Porsche's abilities. Porsche was instantly excited when Stuck suggested that he design such a car, so much so that he offered to do it free of charge.

Porsche didn't have to make good on his offer, because the resourceful Stuck took his idea and his

promises from Porsche and Udet to Daimler-Benz chief Wilhelm Kissel. Though now an opponent on the track, Stuck was well regarded at the Daimler-Benz headquarters in the Stuttgart suburb of Untertürkheim. In fact he'd been invited to join the Mercedes-Benz team for the 1935 season. Now it was the Summer of 1936 and Stuck was asking the Swabians to build for him one of the most expensive automobiles ever conceived.

Wilhelm Kissel weighed many factors after meeting with Stuck. This was not a novel idea. Before his death in November 1934 Hans Nibel, one of the creators of the Blitzen Benz that once held the record, had suggested that it might be interesting to use their new aero engine in another land speed record contender. Yet Stuck was the first to come along with a concrete proposal and with the promise of a Porsche design as well.

As K.B. Hopfinger wrote, however, Kissel "did not particularly like Porsche, with whom he had some disagreement at the time when Porsche was chief engineer of his company." Chassis-design chief Max Wagner argued that Daimler-Benz should design the car itself, saying, "We'd be a laughing stock if we couldn't put a record car on wheels." Turning Stuck down could have unpleasant consequences, thought Kissel: "If we say no, then Stuck takes our two engines and goes to another firm to have the car built....."

From these considerations Wilhelm Kissel sifted the recommendation, ultimately accepted by his board, that they should undertake the construction of the car to the Porsche design. That way, Alfred Neubauer noted, "we killed two birds with one stone: for we kept the engines under our control – and if need be we could still disassociate ourselves a little from this fantastic undertaking." Daimler-Benz would build the car, and Stuck would raise the financing for the record attempt.

To exceed Campbell's speed, Porsche explained to Stuck, he'd need two of the DB601s. Well over 2,000bhp had to be available. Considering that the engines were to be used on the ground, said Daimler-Benz, they could promise much more power from a single unit. With this assurance, Porsche's team commenced design of a single-engined car that drove through a wet slipping clutch to a four-wheeled rear bogie, carried by swing axles. Front wheels were sprung by torsion bars and twin trailing arms. The Type 80, as it was designated in the Porsche office, was conceived as a slim machine of low frontal area with lateral stub wings to keep it on the ground.

Assuming that the power available was 2,200bhp at 3,500rpm, Porsche told his Daimler-Benz colleagues, the Type 80 would reach its design speed of 550 km/h, in 3.1 miles from rest. The car's design was complete and construction under way in late 1937 when George Eyston's

Allocated for test installation in the land speed record car designed for Daimler-Benz by Ferdinand Porsche was the third test sample of the DB603, measuring 44.5 litres and offering 2,800bhp in 1939. Its centrifugal supercharger was at the right and its drive to the wheels emerged at the left.

Designed as the Type 80 by Porsche's independent engineering office, the Daimler-Benz record car was to be driven by a quartet of rear wheels suspended by swing axles and torsion bars. Front suspension was by torsion bars and trailing arms.

twin-engined Thunderbolt roared to a new land speed record at 312.10mph This was followed by the staggering show of speed at Bonneville in September of 1938 in which Eyston first elevated his own record to 345.2mph. Then John Cobb lifted it to 350.1mph with his Railton Special. Eyston topped this with 357.3mph. This was rather faster than the Type 80's design target of 550km/h.

Ferdinand Porsche, ever adaptable, produced a new scenario for his car. He now aimed for a speed of 373mph, to be reached after 3.7 miles of acceleration, followed by a braking distance of 1.4 miles. For this, Porsche said, he

would need 3,000 horsepower. Could Daimler-Benz oblige? It could and would came the reply, with an engine in its early development stages, the DB603. The third experimental engine of this type, DB603 V3, was installed in the Type 80 chassis early in 1939 and became the only engine ever fitted to the car.

The new V12 was much larger than the DB601 at 162 x 180mm (44,522cc). It retained the same general design features, including the 60° vee with the cylinders hanging downward from the crankshaft to make a complete unit optimally suited to aircraft installation. It rested between the two big tubes of the Type 80 chassis in the same orientation.

Each bank of six cylinders was cast integrally with the head in Silumin-Gamma alloy, ported for two inlet valves and two exhausts per cylinder. A thin-walled dry liner of steel was inserted into each cylinder from the bottom and held by fine screw threads. The lower end of each liner was retained in the deep Silumin crankcase by a ring screwed onto the bottom, the six rings along each bank being the means of holding the cylinder blocks onto the crankcase. Forged aluminium pistons had concave crowns that gave a compression ratio of 7.5:1 for the left bank of cylinders, 7.3:1 for the right bank.

The DB603's forged and counterbalanced crankshaft was carried in seven main bearings of steel-backed lead-bronze, retained by cross-bolted bearing caps. Like the DB601, the DB603 had fork-and-blade connecting rods. The roller-bearing big ends used on earlier engines were replaced by more reliable plain bearings on the DB603. A system of gears capped by vertical shafts and bevels drove the single overhead camshaft along each cylinder bank. Through pivoted followers, two cam lobes opened and closed the facing pairs of inlet and exhaust valves in each cylinder.

Another gear train drove the in-line 12-plunger Bosch fuel injection pump placed in the central vee. Other drives, such as that to the Bosch magneto for the dual ignition, had to be changed to get the low profile Porsche wanted for his Type 80. The 2:1 reduction gear engineered into the nose of the DB603 for aeronautical use was omitted in the record car, in which the engine was mounted with its drive end pointing rearward. Ready for installation, fitted with a special 80lb flywheel, it scaled 1,778lb, some 500 more than the smaller DB601.

Hot-coolant off-takes were from the backs of the blocks, rising and running forward to a pair of vapour separators high at the front of the engine. Vapour released from the glycol-filled system was vented to an adjacent reserve tank that was part of the return flow, between the radiator and the coolant pump. The dry-sump system's oil reservoir warmed the bottom of the

driver's seat, just ahead of the engine. A starter was powered by a compressed-air supply.

What thrust could be expected from the huge DB603? At the same specific power as a special DB601 prepared for air-speed record-breaking in 1939 it would have produced just over the 3,000 horsepower (at 3,200rpm) that Porsche said he needed to reach 600km/h. When the Type 80 was nearing completion in 1939 the DB603 hadn't yet reached that stage of development. During the war a service version produced a takeoff 2,830bhp at 3,000rpm with a two-speed supercharger, but in 1939 its maximum output was 2,800bhp at 2,500 – insufficient to give confidence of surpassing John Cobb's final pre-war record of 367.7mph, set on 22 August 1939.

Then there'd been the nagging question of where to attempt the record. Its designers and builders had Bonneville in mind. In 1938, however, as news of this still-secret undertaking spread through ruling circles in Berlin and as international tensions intensified, the idea of an expedition to America became less and less realistic. With the famed *Autobahns* being built, viewed as a modern wonder, the search went out for a stretch under construction that might suit a very fast car.

A section was found north of Leipzig, through level, open country, that seemed promising. Belatedly, however, its builders realised that the road crossed the north-east corner of one of the two largest brown-coal deposits in Germany, one of the nation's most essential resources. The *Autobahn* had to be displaced. Curves were added at both ends of the section. Between them, over more than five miles, the central strip was paved

Although it was destined never to be driven in anger, the T80 record car was nearly completed at Daimler-Benz before the war. Both downforce-generating wings and anti-slip control of the driving wheels promised a stable ride for designated driver Hans Stuck.

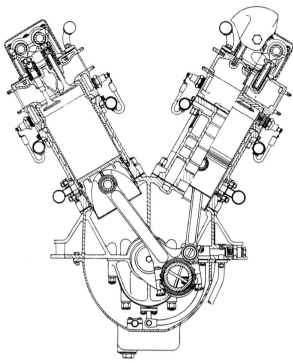

To take the fight to his English rivals at Bonneville, American racer Ab Jenkins acquired two Curtiss Conqueror vee-twelves. Displacing 25.4 litres, they were an evolutionary version of this Curtiss D-12, having twin overhead cams for each cylinder bank and master and link connecting rods.

Although designed to take two Curtiss Conqueror twelves, the Mormon Meteor III of 1938 made do with a single Conqueror for use in record breaking by Ab Jenkins. As late as 1950 this great car was still setting new world marks on the circular track at Bonneville.

over to make a smooth, straight concrete speedway some 100ft wide.

Although other records were set on this astonishing stretch between Bitterfeld and Dessau, including speeds of up to 248mph in a 3-litre V12-powered Mercedes-Benz, the Type 80 never turned a wheel there. Late in 1939 it was about a month away from readiness for a trial on the road. Hans Stuck had already been alerted to stand by for the first test drive. The authorities scheduled a Record Week at Dessau for 1940 at which the six-wheeled Mercedes-Benz would be the star attraction.

By the end of 1939 it was clear this wouldn't happen. When Stuck visited the factory he was told what so many in Germany thought was true at that time: "The war will be over in three months, and then you can begin again at once!" On 29 February 1940 DB603 V3 was returned to the aero engineers to resume its experimental role. In June 1940 the Type 80 chassis was parked, a mute phantom of speed on land, in Box E of the Daimler-Benz car park in Untertürkheim.

The Type 80 remained one of the mightiest of the might-have-beens of land-speed history. Could it have broken Cobb's record? After the British fur broker and his Railton upped the ante even further in 1947 to 394.20mph, well over the 600km/h mark for the first time, Daimler-Benz decided there was no point in reviving – indeed completing – its Type 80. Nor were the heart and soul of the factory and its management ever fully committed to this "fantastic undertaking".

A more-than-interested observer of the battles at Bonneville was David Absolom 'Ab' Jenkins, a Utah-born Salt Lake City building contractor and part-time record-breaker. Jenkins, who had done much to encourage the British drivers to exploit the salt flats, now found that Eyston and Cobb were toppling many of the records that he'd set in Pierce-Arrows and a Duesenberg.[13] "I realised that if I were going to keep in their company," he said, "I'd have to jettison my motors and search for more 'horses' in the hangars."

Jenkins set his heart on the Allison V12, but by now all the Allisons were earmarked for America's rearmament effort. Second-best turned out to be pretty good: "I found two Curtiss Conqueror motors to my liking in the possession of Clyde Pangborne, world famous air pilot living in Paterson, New Jersey. And so I made a deal with him." One would go into his existing Duesenberg chassis.

The clean-lined Conqueror was an evolution of Curtiss's D-12, a 60° V12 with master-and-link connecting rods. Each bank had four vertical valves in a detachable head, opened through mushroom tappets by twin overhead cams. Their gear drives were at the rear of the aluminium crankcase, which had aluminium six-cylinder blocks with wet steel liners bolted atop it. Twin Stromberg carburettors were used and ignition was by a single Splitdorf magneto with independent circuits and distributors for the dual ignition. Measuring 130.2 x 158.8mm, the 996lb Conqueror displaced 25,351cc and in a 1934 version was rated at 675bhp at 2,450rpm with a compression ratio of 7.25:1.

"I took these machines to Lycoming Motors at Williamsport, Pennsylvania," added Jenkins, "where they underwent quite an operation. A flywheel, clutch and bell housing were added to each one so as to 'automobilise' them. Then the machines were shipped to Auburn, Indiana where one was inserted into a Duesenberg chassis." This took, said Jenkins, "…from November of 1935 to the following June to complete – and we were working hard all the time." The existing two-seater body was given a stabilising tail fin and featured a low-placed headlamp and fairings ahead of and behind its wheels.

While Jenkins was completing his new car, christened 'Mormon Meteor' in a contest organised by the Salt Lake City newspaper, Eyston broke his old records up to 48 hours. In September 1936 Ab Jenkins replied, ultimately taking every record from 50 miles to 48 hours with his Curtiss-powered Duesey which, he admitted, was "for the first time a car capable of going at a faster speed than I could handle on the circular track." A year later he was relieved for three hours by Lou Meyer on his way to a new

24-hour record of 157.27mph. The teetotal Mormon rightly took pride in his ability to drive many hours without relief.[14]

For 1938 Jenkins and Augie Duesenberg, helped by young Marvin Jenkins and draftsman Rex Purtny, built a gorgeous new car – with quadruple headlamps this time – around their Curtiss engine, which they tweaked to 750 horsepower. This was Mormon Meteor III on a 142in wheelbase, carried by a deep channel-steel frame with semi-elliptic springing and de Dion rear suspension, the latter to overcome handling problems that Ab experienced with the V12 in the Duesenberg chassis when fuel loads were light.[15]

Constrained to wait for good conditions on the salt, not until July 1940 did Jenkins and Cliff Bergere extend the new car. They set new world marks for distances from 50 to 500 kilometres and from three to 24 hours. A final fling came in September 1950 when Jenkins, now 67 years old, set new marks on the Salt Flats including a speed for one hour of 190.68mph. It seemed that he was getting the hang of it.

Before they were displaced by turbines and jets, V12 and W12 aviation engines had wonderful innings in record-breaking on land. On this we should let Reid Railton – who had so much to do with taming these big twelves – have the last word: "We should consider ourselves very lucky in that the present-day racing aero engine is so admirably shaped for fitting into a motor car."

Chapter 4 Footnotes

[1] Owing to the use of this connecting-rod system the engine's actual displacement is slightly less than its cylinder dimensions would indicate.

[2] This qualified Campbell as the first holder of the Sir Charles Wakefield Trophy, which was presented to the AIACR to be awarded to the current holder of the world land speed record. Wakefield's Castrol also gifted a prize of £1,000 per annum, awarded on a pro rata basis to the holder according to the number of days he kept the record. The prize was no small incentive to the would-be record breakers of this era.

[3] Eoin S. Young reminds us that the length of the beach is 'only' 64 miles.

[4] The restorers of Babs, who were more familiar with its post-crash condition than most, were adamant that stories of Thomas being killed by the broken chain were just that. Evidence indicated that the chain flailed downward, not upward.

[5] Although the car's official name was 'The Spirit of Elkdom,' an apparent reference to the Elks Lodge, this was little used and on the car was painted 'Triplex by White.'

[6] Perhaps uniquely in the annals of motor racing, Keech – who was leading at the time of his crash – was posthumously declared the winner at Altoona.

[7] This was comforting to Segrave, but he was well aware that while he was waiting in Florida to make his record attempt the reports from Pendine stated – in error – that an errant chain killed Parry Thomas.

[8] Never short of a dramatic claim, Coatalen said that Don's silhouette was projected against a wall and the car's cross-section designed to fit as closely to it as possible.

[9] Is this the longest wheelbase ever used in an automobile – not including stretch limousines? The author believes it possible.

[10] The saga of the Sunbeam-Talbot-Darracq combine is a convoluted one, and the Sunbeam name did not disappear, but the 1931–32 period was one of crisis for the Franco-Britannic Group's UK arm.

[11] The engines already had record-breaking history. One powered the Supermarine S6B that gave Britain outright possession of the Schneider Trophy, while the other propelled another S6B to the exceptional speed of 407.5mph.

[12] Eyston credited Leo Goossen, draftsman of the Buick V12 and long-time Miller and Offenhauser design engineer, with the modifications that made his clutch function properly.

[13] Jenkins's record-breaking in Pierce-Arrow V12s is described in Chapter 8.

[14] When his first long-distance records were sent to Paris for approval by the authorities there, they were reluctant to rubber-stamp them because they didn't believe that one man could drive so fast for so long.

[15] Mormon Meteor III was designed to accommodate two engines, with its front hubs built to suit the provision of drive through the front wheels as well, but these options were never explored.

CLASSIC-ERA AMERICANS

Few auto shows were held under less auspicious circumstances than New York's in January 1930. Successive collapses of shares on that city's market the previous October had slashed billions from the value of America's leading industries. The immediate impact of the Wall Street Crash was harshest on that nation's wealthiest, those who held those shares. In 1929 one-third of all personal income had gone to the top five per cent of earners, men who'd boomed the American market for luxury cars to a heady 150,000 units, five per cent of the total. Although many still hoped for a fast recovery, others at New York's 1930 auto show were gloomy. Yet over at Cadillac's stand was the most elaborate and costly car in that proud company's history – a *sixteen-cylinder* luxury automobile.

With the Cadillac's launch the era of the 'multi-cylinder' automobile was reborn in the United States, that term being applied to any engine with more than eight cylinders. Cadillac had scored a coup by doubling up the straight-eight, then the engine of choice for the elegant motorcar. Only Marmon would rival it with another V16, first shown in Chicago that October.[1] Instead, America's multi-cylinder trophy would be fought for by makers of V12 engines, magnificent half-ton power units that would motivate some of the finest cars ever produced and give birth to the elegant autos that Americans have honoured since as 'classics'.

In retrospect it's easy to comprehend the hubris that inspired America's makers of luxury cars to splash out on the twelve-cylinder autos that only came to market after the Crash. Stock-market trading suggested that the US economy would continue to enjoy boom times; volumes on the Exchange more than doubled from 1921 to 1925 and doubled again from the latter year to 1928. In June of 1929 financial guru Bernard Baruch opined that the "economic condition of the world seems on the verge of a great forward movement" while in the autumn Yale's respected Prof Irving Fisher said, "Stock prices have reached what looks like a permanently high plateau." None begrudged the fortunes being made at a time when, said Richard Burns Carson, "wealth's prerogatives went unchallenged, and a man's money was his to spend as he pleased. If his plans included owning cars that aspired to be works of art, then this was no more than others would hope to do in his shoes."

Eager to offer this affluent market a car of iconic status, Lawrence P. Fisher launched work on Cadillac's multi-cylinder engines in 1926, only a year after he'd taken over as general manager of General Motors' most important division. His premier-engine programme for Cadillac would ultimately absorb an investment of $53 million. Franklin started work on 1927 on a vee-twelve to power what it dubbed – appropriately enough for the time – its 'banker's car'.

With rumours about Cadillac's project circulating among America's auto elite, Pierce-Arrow started designing its twelve in 1929. In the same year the Auburn

Opposite: *Displacing 6.0 litres, Cadillac's V12 of 1931 shared all its design details with its V16 sister, save for a cylinder bore one-eighth of an inch larger. The engines shared many common components as well as a vee angle of 45°, which was ideal for the sixteen but less so for the twelve.*

Cord Duesenberg Corporation initiated a V16 project that evolved into a V12 and Packard commissioned a front-driven prototype that fortuitously had V12 power. Only Lincoln found itself playing catch-up with its design of an excellent V12 in the months after Cadillac's announcement.

Lawrence Fisher, member of the clan that founded coachbuilder Fisher Body, had an excellent team at Cadillac. His chief engineer was Ernest Seaholm, who felt that he was awarded the job after an exodus from Cadillac of other talents early in the 1920s "due to my seniority, possibly, and knowing my way around in this area". Seaholm's assistant was W.R. Strickland. As engine designer they engaged Owen Milton Nacker, who had consulted on an overhead-valve V8 with Alanson P. Brush and on early V16 concepts with Howard Marmon. Nacker's visibility on the Seaholm radar screen intensified "when his performance marked him as a man of exceptional ability and one whom those working with him looked up to and accepted as a leader".

Fisher and his team took every precaution to keep their radical project under wraps. Though their aim was to derive both a V12 and a V16 from a common design, they mentioned only the V12 – *outré* enough in its own right – in their extra-Cadillac contacts. Even within the GM Corporation they labelled drawings as 'bus' or 'coach' to throw rivals off the scent. While the sixteen-cylinder version would be introduced first, Lawrence Fisher told his dealers, "The addition of the 12-cylinder line is a logical step and might well have preceded the introduction of the Cadillac V-16 which made its debut at the National Automobile Show in New York. The V-12 engine is of the same type and built to exactly the same standards as the V-16 – in fact, a duplicate of this engine in pattern and appearance but having 12 instead of 16 cylinders."

Nacker's concept for Cadillac was an intriguing blend of traditional and modern engine concepts. Although it had overhead valves with automatic hydraulic clearance adjustment – the first ever – it had cast-iron cylinder blocks atop an aluminium crankcase. Though the latter recalled the earlier V12 generation, in Nacker's design the blocks were very short and the crankcase exceptionally deep.

First thoughts were to adopt a narrow 28° vee, to allow a single cylinder head in the style of Lancia, but well-justified fears of problems with manifolding led to that idea's rejection. The angle finally adopted was 45°, shared by both the twelve and the sixteen. In terms of firing-impulse spacing this was right for the 16 but not strictly correct for the 12, which ran with satisfactory smoothness in spite of its 45°–75° firing intervals.

In cross-section, Cadillac's V12 differed from its V16 chiefly in its 0.125-inch larger bore, adopted to give the V12 a larger displacement than the company's V8. The twelve's dimensions were 79.4 x 101.6mm (6,033cc). The left-hand cylinder bank of an exceptionally handsome engine was shifted forward to allow the use of side-by-side rod big ends.

Both multi-cylinder Cadillacs shared the same forged molybdenum-steel connecting rods, which measured 235mm centre-to-centre and weighed 31.8oz – shorter and lighter than the Cadillac V8 rod. The poured big-end bearings measured 63.5mm while the twelve's four steel-backed main bearings were 66.7mm in diameter. A fraction under a yard long, the crankshaft carried a small harmonic damper at its nose. Attached to the rear main-bearing cap was the oil pump, driven by a long shaft from the back end of the camshaft in the centre vee. Oil level in the pressed-steel sump was signalled by a float which moved a left-side indicator from 'MT' through 'FILL' to 'FULL'. After 1932, oil to the valve gear was cleansed by a Cuno filter which self-scraped its disc-type elements every time the starter pedal was depressed.

The pushrod-and-rocker overhead valves were silenced by a pioneering hydraulic lash adjuster developed by

Silent running and easy servicing were the aims of an automatic valve-clearance adjuster developed for Cadillac's multi-cylinder engines by GM's Research Staff. This used a hydraulic dashpot acting against an eccentric which raised and lowered the rocker arm to effect lash-free valve adjustment.

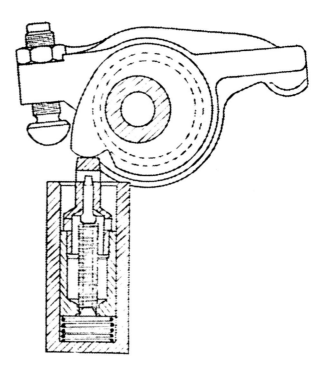

General Motors Research. It acted by rotating an eccentric sleeve between the rocker-arm bushing and the rocker shaft. The hydraulic dashpot which controlled the action of the eccentric was bolted to the head, between the tubular duraluminium pushrods. Roller cam followers were used, keyed to slots in their removable guides. Timing was mild, with inlets opening at top dead centre, a mere 5° of overlap and 8.7mm of lift. Twin valve springs closed inlet and exhaust valves of equal size: 33.3mm. Capping the valve gear were deep rocker covers cast of aluminium.

Four bearings high in the aluminium crankcase held the Cadillac's camshaft, driven by a Morse-type duplex chain 38mm wide. Tensioned by a spring-loaded ratchet-type automatic adjuster, the same chain drove the generator on the right-hand side of the block. An extension shaft from the rear of the generator turned the water pump, which had twin outlets – one directly to the right-hand cylinder block, the other to the left side by way of a duct cast into the top of the clutch housing. Just above this was a diaphragm-type vacuum pump, driven from the camshaft, to operate the windshield wipers.

A highlight of the Cadillac V-12 was its magnificent aluminium crankcase. By far the largest element of the engine, this extended half-way up the cylinder bores and reached down well past the crankshaft centreline. A shallow finned aluminium sump enclosed its lower aperture. Integral with the block was the larger part of the bell housing and the front-end chain case, which was covered by a steel stamping. Very deeply spigoted into the crankcase were the cylinders of the symmetrical cast-iron blocks, with relatively short water jackets at their tops. In a beautifully integrated piece of design, these blocks also carried the guides for the cam followers.

Flat-topped pistons were cast of nickel-iron, matching the material of the blocks to eliminate any chance of disparate expansion. With the valves placed parallel to the cylinder centreline in the cast-iron heads, the combustion chamber was a straight-sided bathtub bordered by small squish areas. A single Delco-Remy distributor incorporated twin breakers and circuits, treating each bank of cylinders like an in-line six. Its two coils were embedded in the radiator header tank, to clean up the compartment and keep them at a constant temperature. Concealed by a stylish enamelled cover, 18mm spark plugs were in the centre of the vee.

Each cylinder bank had its own induction and exhaust system, attached from the outside. An exhaust-heated inlet manifold was fed by an updraft air-valve carburettor of Cadillac's own design. Later these were replaced by more up-to-date 1½-inch Detroit Lubricator carburettors. With a compression ratio of 5.43:1 Cadillac's twelve produced 284lb-ft of torque at 1,200rpm and 135bhp at

Remaining in production throughout the 1937 model year, Cadillac's vee-twelve played a significant role in raising the profile of GM's luxury marque in the fine-car field. Both induction and exhaust systems were at the sides of the engine, not within the central vee.

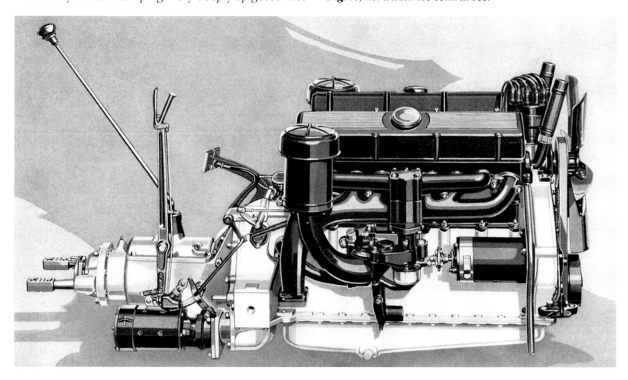

3,400rpm, although it was capable of revving to more than 4,000rpm safely.

Driving through a twin-disc clutch and three-speed transmission borrowed from V8 Cadillacs, the twelve was carried in conventional chassis with wheelbases of 140in and 143in, plus an alternative long chassis at 156in. Launched as a 1931 model, the Series 370-A, the V12 was given the shorter wheelbases of 134in and 140in in 1932 as the Series 370-B.

Opportunistically sharing most of its body panels with Cadillac's V8, the GM division's V12 was attractively priced at $3,895 in five-passenger saloon form, a heady $2,055 less than a similarly bodied V16. Production, a satisfying 5,725 in 1931, plummeted to 1,709 in 1932 and only 952 in 1933. "Fisher's prospects of closing the luxury gap were being shadowed by a gloomy economy and huge losses in luxury-car clientele," wrote Richard Burns Carson. "His team had redefined luxury motoring only to find that the luxury car itself was beginning to die." Nevertheless Lawrence Fisher had created a Cadillac so broadly based that it remained a major contender in the luxury-car market, surpassed in volume in the early 1930s by Packard alone.

"In 1934," wrote Carson, "Larry Fisher left Cadillac and was replaced by Nicholas Dreystadt, an executive of the dreary cost-accounting school." Fortunately by then the newly formed Art and Colour Section at GM was getting into its stride under the inspirational Harley Earl, for the Series 370-D V12 shared handsome new styling with its sisters. New features were divided windscreens (at a price premium of $500) and concealed spare tyres on chassis with front wheels independently sprung. Body-style offerings totalled a staggering 52, priced from $3,995 to $6,295, though less than half were actually produced. Elevating the twelve's compression ratio to 6.0:1 helped raise its output to 150bhp. Nevertheless V12 production fell to 683 in 1934 and then to 377 in '35.

Dreystadt's pruning of his Cadillac range resulted in 1936 twelves on wheelbases of 131 and 138in that were indistinguishable, except for badging, from their V8 sisters. From the standpoint of performance this was no bad thing, for they were some half a ton lighter than their predecessors and $1,000 cheaper as well. Carried over with the 138in wheelbase alone for 1937, this was the final year for both the vee-twelve and the 45° vee-sixteen that sired it. In 1938 Cadillac introduced a wide-angle side-valve V16, but without a twelve-cylinder sister. The total of 10,821 twelves built by the GM division from 1931 through 1937 would far surpass arch-rival Packard's production of comparable big engines.

No greater contrast could be imagined than that between Cadillac, in motor-city Detroit and backed by the might of General Motors, and proud independent Franklin in Syracuse in upstate New York. Franklin was the epitome of the idiosyncratic car maker, since 1902 a builder of air-cooled autos exclusively and an advocate of such arcane features as full-elliptic springing and, until 1928, chassis members primarily of wood. Still guided by its founder, Herbert H. Franklin, the proudly autonomous company hewed to the principles of the chief engineer, John Wilkinson, who espoused 'scientific light weight'. Franklins were expensive cars in the price range of $2,000–$4,000 at a time when the cheapest Chevrolet cost $510.

After Wilkinson and Franklin fell out in the mid-1920s, the founder named Edward S. Marks, only just in his thirties, as chief engineer. Marks realised that Franklins needed updating to keep pace with rivals in their price class who were embracing the popular new straight-eight doctrine. Thinking laterally, Marks tapped the talent at the Army's aviation centre, McCook Field at Dayton, Ohio. There he recruited F. Glen Shoemaker, who had been working on air-cooled aeroplane engines.[2] Shoemaker brought Franklin's staple sixes into the modern era by equipping them with aluminium cylinder heads, more apposite valve sizes, cross-flow cooling of the heads and cylinders and much more efficient squirrel-cage cooling blowers that ultimately required only four horsepower to drive them instead of the previous twenty. Shoemaker's changes helped Franklin output jump from 60 to 100 horsepower.

A straight-eight, however, was found to be a leap too far. The air-cooled Franklins required a cylinder centre-to-centre distance of 127mm for a bore of 88.9mm, the considerable excess being needed to provide adequate space for cooling fins. With seven main bearings Franklin's sixes could cope with the lengthy crankshaft this imposed, but when they tried it with eight cylinders and nine bearings the additional length was too great, with crankshaft whipping the audibly unpleasant result. The solution, Herbert Franklin decided, was to pair up two of his sixes to create a V12. In 1928 Glen Shoemaker was assigned the task of designing it. When he left after a year in Syracuse his work – including improvement of the sixes – was carried forward by engineers John Rogers, Carl T. Doman and John Burns under Edward Marks.

To his credit, Shoemaker configured his proposed twelve with a 60° vee to ensure equally spaced power impulses. In fact it was the only American twelve of the classic era to have this optimum vee angle. Versions of 5.6, 6.5 and 7.4 litres were mooted without departing from established Franklin cylinder proportions. Suggested too, was a central camshaft with pushrods operating overhead valves with finning and cooling on the new lines being introduced for the sixes. This meant vertical valves that were opened by individual rocker arms, each on its own pivot, so they could open valves that were placed in a transverse plane across the cylinder, allowing cross-flow porting, instead of the usual longitudinal plane.

Looking over Shoemaker's layouts, John Rogers is credited with having appreciated that pushrods emerging from a central camshaft would block the flow of cooling air if it were introduced into the central vee. He rejected the alternative; the cumbersome use of separate exterior fans blowing through the cylinders from the sides, with warm air exhausting into the vee.[3] To simplify its cooling arrangements the base engine was made more complex by giving it separate camshafts along each side of the crankcase, operating pushrods up the external flanks of the vee. This was a first in the history of the automotive V12. Previously National had used twin camshafts, but to operate side valves rather than pushrods. Separate silent chains at the nose of the crank turned the Franklin's forged-steel camshafts, the left one being adjusted automatically and that on the right tensioned by moving the generator, which it also drove.

Camshafts and crankshaft were carried in a deep crankcase, cast of aluminium by a veteran Franklin supplier in Syracuse, the Oberdorfer Foundries. Seven 66.7mm main bearings carried the fully counterbalanced crank, on whose 60.3mm throws the big ends of the I-section rods sat side by side, the left cylinder bank being shifted forward to permit this. Running in individual finned cast-nickel-iron cylinders, aluminium pistons were of Invar-Strut design to compensate for aluminium's greater expansion with heat than iron. Each carried two compression rings and two for oil control. Finally established for the V12 were dimensions of 82.6 x 101.6mm (6,525cc). Room for further expansion was there; simply using the larger 88.9mm bore of the Franklin sixes would have brought capacity to 7,568cc. With a longer stroke as well (120.7mm) its designers forecast a potential of 300bhp for a nine-litre version of their air-cooled twelve.

Finely finned, the Franklin's individual cylinder heads were cast of Y-alloy aluminium, each topped by a stamped-steel rocker cover held on by a spring bail. Under it were the short rocker arm for the exhaust valve, nearest the outside, and a longer rocker opening the inlet valve. Its experiments had convinced Franklin that it was best to cool the head from the inlet side, because cooling from the exhaust-valve side left the inlet passages so overheated that the fresh air/fuel charge was sharply reduced in density, decreasing power. Valve diameters differed sharply at 45.6mm for the inlets and 36.9mm for

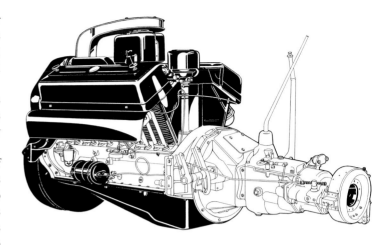

A glimpse under the shrouding of Franklin's V12 engine of 1932 showed housings for the pushrods that ran up from separate camshafts at both sides of the crankcase to operate overhead valves. This positioning of the camshafts and pushrods was adopted to provide better cooling of the cylinders with a blower providing air to the centre of the vee.

the exhausts, a configuration that Glen Shoemaker had recommended during his search for higher power. Valve springs were doubled up and differentially wound to discourage surge. Fashioned of Silchrome No 1 steel, the valves closed against inserted seats of Ni-Resist iron.

Six studs and nuts attached each head to its cylinder, which in turn was bolted to the crankcase. A log-type

A partially dismantled Franklin V12 showed its finned cast-iron cylinders at a 60° vee, topped by aluminium individual cylinder heads, each with its own rocker cover. Also shown was the small oil cooler at the rear of the vee.

exhaust manifold joined the heads along each side, leading to individual silencers and exhaust pipes. Exhaust gases were tapped to heat the inlet manifold, which was on a single plane with three branches to a side, each supplying two cylinders. Topping the manifold was a Stromberg carburettor with twin throats, each feeding its own side of the twelve. It received air from a cartridge containing copper turnings, as an air cleaner and flame arrestor, under mild pressure from a duct fed by the cooling blower. Franklin's advertising claimed a 'supercharging' benefit, but its effect was negligible and indeed the delivery duct was restrictive under some operating conditions. Ignition was by Delco, with a dual-breaker distributor. Cylinder banks were covered by shrouds – an early example of under-bonnet styling.

The nose of the crankshaft drove the Franklin twelve's 15in scirocco-type cooling blower at engine speed. Ducted up and back into the engine's vee, its output – 5,720cu ft per minute at 60mph – was tailored to cool the cylinders equally by meticulous experimentation which involved, at one stage, 144 heat-measuring thermocouples on the cylinders alone. Careful baffling, including a wedge-shaped diverter, achieved the engineers' aims. "This engine cooled perfectly," Carl Doman recalled. "It could be operated at full throttle, 3,500rpm, in a room 60°C continuously without troubles of any kind." Helping achieve this was a small oil cooler in the airflow toward the rear of the vee that reduced oil temperature from 170° to 115°C.

Of the three test engines built, two were installed in stretched Franklin Airman chassis for road testing. One of these mules was thrashed throughout the United States by Erwin 'Cannon Ball' Baker, then a Franklin employee, whose mission was to publicise the durability of the company's products with city-to-city speed feats. Delivering 150bhp at 3,100rpm, the twelve passed Baker's tests with flying colours. But Herbert Franklin, already in debt to the banks for investments intended to increase output of his mainstream models, had other priorities and vacillated over a production launch of the V12. Finally the decision was taken to show two cars in New York in January 1932. They were a stunning surprise, both to the public and to Franklin's dealers.

The show cars were of traditional 'scientific lightweight' Franklin design. Though the twelve weighed 500lb more than the six, cars of that ilk would still have scaled no more than 4,400lb and given lively performance.[4] But Franklin was destined to veer in a grander direction at the behest of the company's new chief, 63-year-old Edwin McEwen. Seven banks holding outstanding loans installed McEwen late in 1931 to see what he could make of Franklin, whose production had

collapsed from an all-time high of 14,432 in 1929 to 6,043 in 1930 and 2,851 in 1931. Nevertheless McEwen reasoned – like so many others – that good times could be just around the corner. Exploiting the V12, he would anticipate that demand by building the biggest, fanciest car that would ever carry the Franklin name.[5]

Although he'd pared Franklin's engineering staff to the bone, McEwen put their hard-pressed underpaid remnants to work on a crash project to create a big, luxurious car to carry their vee-twelve. From supplier Parrish they sourced a conventional frame with a 144in wheelbase, using semi-elliptic springs and proprietary axles from the Cord Corporation.[6] In the hope of becoming a supplier to the project LeBaron proposed some rakish body designs, which were bought by Franklin for peanuts when McEwen decided that the bodies would be built in-house. This was achieved in a cack-handed manner on the upper floors of Franklin's seven-storey manufactory, resulting in bodies that were off by as much as an inch side to side and burdened by 300lb of lead filler.

Plenty of problems cropped up when engineers Doman and Burns took the first prototype to California and back in two weeks at the end of March and beginning of April 1932, but by then 49 of the new cars were already being assembled. The new Series 17 model was hastily launched in May with advertisements that didn't do justice to its handsome lines. They claimed, however, that its engine required "100 less parts than comparable water-cooled engines" and gave "sensational performance which carries you to new luxury in travel".

With the big Franklins weighing 5,500 to 5,900lb their acceleration was not electrifying, but owners found the twelve "no slouch as a road car…could cruise comfortably at an honest 70mph. Its response to the throttle is lively and, in the middle to higher speed range, exhilarating. It is a real machine, and considering the pressure and handicaps when it was built, it is a remarkably good one." The selling position, however, was difficult. In 1932 the Series 17 was launched at prices ranging from $3,885 to $4,185, but in 1933 and '34 these were slashed by $1,000 in the hope of attracting customers for by far the biggest and most prestigious Franklin ever.

Meanwhile, the H. H. Franklin Manufacturing Company was collapsing. Production fell to 1,905 in 1932 and 1,011 in '33. The last year would be 1934 with 360 cars being made. Among these final Franklins were 217 Series 17 twelves. The negligible volume, reflected engineer Carl Doman, "…should not be charged to the design. Economic conditions simply eliminated the market. Otherwise, this car would have received great public acceptance. It was outstanding in appearance and performance, but just too costly for Depression days." Reportedly some of the big twelves were used in military vehicles, to which they would have been well suited. And the Franklin name lived on as a producer of aviation engines.

The challenge that faced Franklin – that of crafting a new model to preserve its upper-middle ranking in the marketplace – was the opposite of that with which Packard had to deal. Making the most of its side-valve in-line 'Single Eights' during the 1920s, the Detroit-based producer surveyed its segment from the lofty heights of dominant production, building just short of 50,000 cars in 1928 and registering 42,961, supplying one-third of all American luxury-car demand. Though 1929 registrations were even higher at 44,634, Packard chief Alvan Macauley was uneasy. His market was softening. Macauley's priority

Franklin's advertising agency flaunted the fact that the V12's cooling blower provided mild pressurisation of its carburettor at certain speeds. Although the Franklin's 6.5-litre twelve gave it performance that was 'no slouch as a road car', it wasn't so sensational as the ad men suggested.

*S*upercharging means super-performance
—Come Drive This New AIR-COOLED TWELVE

A supercharged airplane engine in a motor car! That's the formula for performance that only racing drivers and aviators have known. But why shouldn't motorists also demand the finest performance?

In the new Franklin Twelve a great, eager, super-charged stream of 150 horsepower waits to be loosed. This supercharged power is different from what you are used to. It's more like turbine power.

For three decades automobile engines have relied upon suction alone to draw gasoline into the cylinders. But now by Franklin supercharging, power-laden vapor is *forced* with terrific speed into the cylinders,

in *uniform, maximum quantity*. No starved cylinders, no gasping acceleration. No wasted or unvaporized fuel. Every thimbleful of gas is made to perform.

1940-performance! And when you look at the car we believe you'll recognize an equal achievement in style. Le Baron designed the Franklin Twelve, and every detail is the pattern for coming motor car beauty.

To know the most luxurious motor car transportation we invite you to examine and drive the new Supercharged Twelve—also to consider the new 100 horsepower Super-charged Airman. Franklin prices begin at $2,345 f.o.b. factory. Franklin Automobile Company, Syracuse, N.Y.

FRANKLIN
AIR · COOLED TWELVE

was to make a calculated move downmarket by creating a new kind of Packard that would be true to the quality of the house, yet appealing to a clientele that hadn't previously put Packard on its shopping list.

A competitive factor was also at work. "Buick had come out with their eights," said engineer Cornelius Van Ranst, "and they would beat the pants off a Packard – and of course they sold for a lot less".[7] As an independent consultant, Van Ranst was engaged by Packard early in 1930 to design a new model that "we were supposed to get down into the Buick price range".[8] That would mean between $1,200 and $2,000 when the cheapest Packard was $2,285. "They wanted something fast," the engineer added, "and they wanted a radical change in design." Van Ranst gave them that with front-wheel drive and a power unit that was true to Packard's traditions but entirely new: a vee-twelve.

Tommy Milton provided the link between Packard and Van Ranst. Though sighted in only one eye from birth, the gregarious Milton was a successful racing driver with two Indy 500 wins to his credit. His first victory in 1921 was in a Frontenac designed by Cornelius Van Ranst, who was one year Milton's senior. Later in the 1920s Milton segued smoothly into the role at Packard that Ralph DePalma had previously filled, that of senior advisor to Alvan Macauley and chief engineer Jesse Vincent, now 'Colonel Vincent' after his wartime exploits with the Liberty engine.

Settled into a prosperous middle age, this was no longer the racy Packard of the past, with its 299 and 905 speedsters. But it was still sparky enough to have bought a front-drive Miller in 1925 "for experimental purposes" and also to have commissioned a proving ground with America's fastest banked oval track – son of Sheepshead Bay. In 1928 racing driver Leon Duray lapped its 2½ miles at 148.2mph in his own front-drive Miller, then the fastest-ever speed for a closed circuit. Thus Milton's involvement was still in character for the ostensibly staid luxury-car maker.

"He was valuable to Packard," recalled Van Ranst's son of Tommy Milton, because "he could recognise good design and he certainly knew automobiles." Not an engineer, "he was more of a promoter and a get-the-job-done sort of fellow." When the Packard chiefs set out their aims for their new Buick-beater, Milton suggested Van Ranst for the job. Management saw the project as a joint effort by the two men, referring to it as the 'M&V car'.

At the age of only 37 Cornelius Willett Van Ranst was one of America's most experienced and able designers and developers of high-performance cars. In addition to his work on Louis Chevrolet's Frontenac racer, he had designed a Stutz racing engine and a 300-horsepower front-driven racer with two-stage supercharging. Van was able to drive them as well, as he proved with several stints in the 500-mile race. He'd completed his work on the first front-drive Cord, the L29 of 1929 – essentially Van's design – and a brief stint at Chrysler when the Packard opportunity arose. "We were given a corner of the engineering building," he said, "and left pretty well alone." His key lieutenants were the Storey brothers, Frank and Edward, the latter looking after the new car's engine.

Van Ranst's racing experience showed in several aspects of the new car's engine. One was in its nearly square dimensions of 85.7 x 88.9mm (6,157cc), laid out to permit higher revolutions than were then usual in road

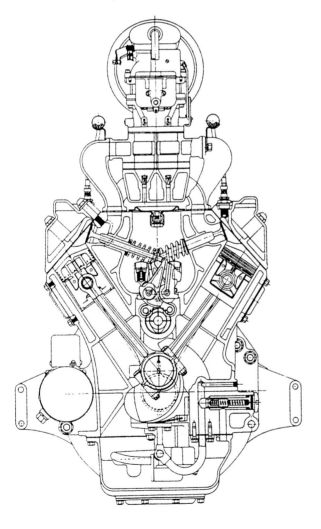

Designed by Cornelius Van Ranst under the auspices of racing driver Tommy Milton, Packard's 1930s V12 had race-bred features including its smooth-flowing manifolding and compact combustion chambers. Visible at the pivots of its rocker arms was the hydraulic valve-adjustment system licensed by Packard from General Motors.

cars. Another was in its inlet passages, which instead of being constricted into awkward meanderings flowed smoothly in an S-curve from the carburettor to the ports through an aluminium manifold that one writer likened to an octopus, another to a spider. Van kept the block as short as possible to reduce its weight and to suit a front-drive installation. To make room for its valve gear and ports he chose a vee angle of 67°.

Van Ranst also broke with convention by shaving the top of each bank of cylinders at an angle other than orthogonal. The surface to which each head was bolted was tilted up at an angle of 15° from the usual horizontal in relation to the cylinder centreline. Here was a solution not unlike that of the 1926 racing Itala designed by Giulio Cesare Cappa (Chapter 3). The Packard's head angle was less extreme; the comparable figure for the Itala was 35°.[9] Their aims were similar: to ensure good access for the entering gases, to concentrate the combustion chamber proper and to provide a squish area between the head and part of the piston crown to stimulate combustion and cool the end gases to discourage detonation or 'pinking'.

Packard's exceptional foundry skills were exploited by the new twelve's cylinder block, a complex iron casting which extended from a flat surface at the top, to which its manifolds were attached, down past the crankshaft centreline. Four 63.5mm main bearings carried a robust crankshaft with four counterweights. A tubular manifold delivered oil to them from below, through the main-bearing caps. Van Ranst specified a cast aluminium sump. I-section connecting rods were 238.1mm long and carried full-skirted aluminium pistons with three compression rings and one oil ring above their gudgeon pins. The right-hand cylinder bank was offset 32mm forward to permit side-by-side rods on their 63.5mm journals. The block's water jacketing was generous, especially around the critical inserted valve guides.

Nestling in the vee of Van Ranst's twelve was its single chain-driven camshaft and valve gear, operating valves placed above them at an angle of 20° from the horizontal. Closed by single-coil springs, the 42.1mm valves were opened by elegant I-section rocker arms with roller tips contacting the cam lobes. Van took particular pride in his successful adaptation of Cadillac's automatic valve-lash adjustment to his engine, a boon both to silence and to the knuckles of Packard mechanics. As in the overhead-valve Cadillac, the hydraulic adjuster shifted the position of an eccentric on which the rocker pivoted to provide consistent clearance. With its tiny precision parts the system was costly, over and above the royalty of one cent per valve that Packard paid to General Motors for its use.

As configured by Van Ranst for front-wheel drive, the M&V prototype had two six-cylinder ignition distributors driven from the camshaft nose, hence located next to the firewall. A pulley at the tail of the camshaft – at the front as installed – drove a fan and a generator above the vee. Spark plugs of 14mm were positioned vertically in the heads, opening onto the periphery of the combustion chamber. Lurking under the inlet manifold, a cast-iron exhaust manifold provided heat to the downdraft twin-throat carburettor and led spent gases away to the rear.

With its compact cylinder dimensions and light valve gear, Van Ranst's twelve was a high revver by the standards of 1930, when the first M&V test car was ready. It delivered its exceptional 150bhp at 3,600rpm and was capable of much higher revs. Among contemporary American passenger-car engines only the race-bred Duesenberg developed its peak power at the higher speed of 4,200rpm. On Packard's new track it propelled Milton and Van Ranst at speeds of up to 110mph. "It was the fastest passenger car in the US at the time we finished it," Van recalled.[10] But its novel four-speed front-drive transaxle suffered teething troubles that April 1931 improvements failed to solve. Meanwhile, of course, the economy was heading south. "Packard management felt that the time was not propitious to bring out an entirely new automobile," said Van Ranst in his typically understated way.

Patrician though it was and remained, Packard could not overlook Cadillac's cheeky attempt to seize the luxury-car high ground with its multi-cylinder motors. Though the front-drive M&V might not be ready for prime time, its engine certainly was. In the autumn of 1931 Packard paid Milton and Van Ranst $10,000 "for the use of their twelve-cylinder motor and any other parts of the M&V car for adaptation to our deluxe chassis." With its

registrations having declined to 28,318 in 1930 and on their way to only 16,256 in 1931, Packard sought refuge in "that exclusive and limited production field where the last word in motoring luxury is demanded and where prices are correspondingly higher." The M&V vee-twelve would be its key to that sanctuary.

A glossy display twelve was the centrepiece of Packard's exhibit at New York's Grand Central Palace in January 1932. Two 147in rear-drive chassis were equipped with it, one for the show and the other for testing by engineers Charlie Vincent and Clyde Paton. Car and engine were mismatched, however, Van Ranst remembered: "They weren't able to get it above 85mph." The bore had already been opened as much as the engine's compact architecture would allow, from 85.7 to 87.3mm, with which production of the engine was being tooled. That process was interrupted when Charlie Vincent, alarmed that the new twelve lacked hill-climbing torque, suggested that its stroke be lengthened as well.

Stretched to 101.6mm from 88.9mm, the stroke brought the final engine's capacity to 7,300cc.[11] In this form it developed 160bhp at 3,200rpm and a lusty 322lb-ft of torque at 1,400rpm on the same 6.0:1 compression ratio as the smaller prototype. Charlie Vincent concluded that "the engine performance problem was licked" when he kicked the throttle open at low speed and in his mirror, "saw black marks on the pavement that almost duplicated those made from a quick stop." With the

Packard initially used the 'Twin Six' appellation to remind customers of its earlier twelves. Introduced in 1932, the new 7.3-litre engine was installed in a rugged chassis with central X-bracing.

twelve able to rev to 4,200, top speeds on the banked track were consistently at 90mph and with low-drag body styles 100mph. Packard's new V12 was ready.

Other changes made in the production twelve from the M&V engine included the use of a single Auto-Lite dual-breaker distributor at what was now the front of the engine, skew-gear-driven from the front of the camshaft. Spark plugs were moved down from the tops of the heads to an upper surface where they were nearer the centre of the chamber and better cooled by its water passages. Crankcase ventilation was added and the main-bearing caps were better braced laterally and tied to their webs by two more studs and nuts. A special twin-throat Stromberg carburettor, the EE-3, was designed to include auxiliary venturis that improved mid-range response. Complete with clutch and transmission the power train weighed 1,320lb.

Initially dubbed the Twin Six, to evoke memories of earlier twelves, Packard's new motor was available in wheelbases of 142 and 147in weighing 4,980lb with open touring-car bodywork. In 1933 the model became simply the 'Packard Twelve' at prices from $3,790 to the $6,000–$7,000 range for custom bodies. With its three

Packard expert Robert J. Neal posed with family members at the rear of a 1936 Packard 12T with handsome coupé bodywork. Packard would continue to produce its twelve until August 1939. (Robert J. Neal)

speeds used to the full its acceleration to 60mph in 19 seconds was exceptional for such a massive machine, while it trickled easily away from 5mph in top gear. "You are propelled along as if by magnets," said a 1985 tester. "There is immense latent power there virtually from tickover and right through to top speed, and at no time does the engine take on a more urgent note."

Gaining more rounded styling for 1935, Packard's V12s received even longer strokes of 108.0mm to bring capacity to 7,756cc. With a compression ratio of 6.3:1 they now developed 175bhp at 3,200rpm. This was level-pegging with Pierce-Arrow's twelve and second only to Duesenberg and Cadillac's V16.[12] Heads were changed from iron to aluminium and steel-backed inserts replaced poured-babbitt big-end bearings. Packard continued to make them with tender loving care, motoring each for an hour electrically before six hours of running-in preceeding an hour and a quarter of dynamometer testing and, after installation, 250 miles at the proving grounds before delivery.

Nineteen-thirty-five also saw Packard's launch of its low-priced eight-cylinder 120, which helped its sales soar from 1934's 6,552 to a record 109,518 in 1937. The big twelves were still catalogued as 1939 models, of which 446 were made. Production of twelves was halted on 8 August 1939 with a total of 5,744 taking to the road. Though this was less than one-sixth the number of twelves that Packard produced in its pioneering Twin Six

era, it left behind some of the most elegant and imposing automobiles of the 1930s.[13] And in its future Packard would revisit the idea of another vee-twelve.

Although a pipsqueak compared to Packard, the Lincoln Motor Company was destined to be not only a leader in the production of twelve-cylinder cars in the 1930s – with output of more than 10,000 approaching that of Cadillac – but also the only one of America's luxury-car makers to continue with twelves after the war. It didn't harm Lincoln's potential, of course, that it had been a property of the Ford Motor Company since 1922. Prosperous Ford easily absorbed the losses that Lincoln made through most of the 1920s while it continued to produce V8-powered luxury cars to the exacting standards laid down by Lincoln's founder, Henry M. Leland.

We last met Leland in Chapter 4, when his Lincoln Motor Company was producing Liberty V12s for the war effort. The exacting engineer left a 1902 partnership with Henry Ford to found Cadillac, where his dedication to precision made it one of America's premier marques. Leaving GM-owned Cadillac in 1917, he and his son Wilfred began producing Lincoln autos on their own account in 1920, when the elder Leland was 73. For power they chose a V8 with a vee angle of 60°, chosen to reduce the vibration that other V8s were then generating with their 90° angles. Their rugged side-valve engine had individual cylinder blocks on an aluminium crankcase and fork-and-blade connecting rods, with the forked rods on the left side.

Heavy investment, reversals of America's economy and an unexpected tax bill combined to sink Lincoln financially in 1921. To the surprise of many Henry Ford stepped forward to acquire Lincoln from its receivers in 1922 for $8 million, saying, "We have built more cars than anyone else, and now we are going to build a better car than anyone else." Although Henry said that he wanted the Lelands to carry on as before, interference by his minions put their backs up. Brushing off attempts by the proud Lelands to buy back the company, Ford had them dismissed that summer of 1922. His son Edsel became Lincoln's new president. Its chief engineer remained Frank Johnson, who had been at Henry Leland's right hand since their first single-cylinder Cadillac of 1902.

Lincoln stood pat with its Series L V8 through the 1920s, with Edsel encouraging the use of custom bodies on its wheelbases of 130 and 136in. Wall Street Crash or no, it was evident to Edsel Ford by 1930 that tougher competition at the top of its market would oblige Lincoln to enter the multi-cylinder race. Edsel knew action was needed when one of his customers deserted Lincoln to buy a Duesenberg because he'd suffered the ignominy of being passed "as though he was standing still". With a V12

An important maker of Liberty vee-twelves during World War I, Lincoln – a Ford property since 1922 – introduced its own modern twelve-cylinder automobile in January 1932. All the engine's manifolding was within its central vee.

the obvious answer, Edsel authorised Frank Johnson and his colleagues Jack Wharam and Fred Wellborn to start work on one in the summer of 1930.

Conservatively, the engineers carried over many features of their eights. Close-grained iron blocks with detachable heads were still separate from an aluminium crankcase and rods were still fork-and-blade, similarly aligned. A widening of the bank angle from 60° to 65° provided more space in the central vee for the twelve's more elaborate inlet and exhaust manifolding. Recalling earlier American twelves was the practice of driving both the water pump and the generator, along the right side of the block, by the same automatically adjusted timing chain that turned the camshaft. Machined from a steel forging weighing 51lb, the final camshaft weighed 13½lb. It operated roller tappets opening 47.6mm valves.

Selected to differ in weight less than seven grams, aluminium pistons were full-skirted. Cylinder bore of 82.6mm was 6.4mm less than that of the eight, and with a stroke of 114.3mm gave a capacity of 7,341cc. Carried in seven 63.5mm main bearings, the Lincoln's crankshaft was whittled down to 57lb from a 117lb forging before bolting on the twelve counterweights that brought its final weight to 93lb, not including the vibration damper on its nose. It was little wonder that the new twelve scaled 1,070lb, carried in the 145in wheelbase Series KB frame on three rubber mountings.

Entirely within the central vee, the twelve's manifolds had to be removed in order to adjust its valve clearance. Placed relatively high, exhaust manifolding directed

THE WILLOUGHBY LIMOUSINE

The *LINCOLN*

THE LINCOLN, a versatile car, continually astonishes loyal owners who put it to supreme tests of one kind, and then, on another occasion, find that it can meet wholly new and different tests. Thus, a rancher in Wyoming, accustomed to mountain and desert driving, learns from his wife of the car's agility in city traffic. A business man, to whom the Lincoln is a triumph of engineering, suddenly realizes, as he emerges from the opera, how beautiful a car he drives. The Lincoln is all things to all people. . . . This is a luxurious car, a safe car, with a V-12 cylinder, 150-horsepower engine powerful enough to take steep hills in high and at an almost incredible pace. Lincoln engineers affirm it the finest they have yet designed, and experience on the road confirms that judgment. And it is a car which imparts to the owner, no less than to the maker, pride in its beauty and pleasure in its high achievements. Available in twenty-three standard and custom-built body types.

Lincoln found an appropriately patrician tone for its advertising of its new Model KB vee-twelve, producing 150bhp at 3,400rpm.

LeBARON CONVERTIBLE ROADSTER

The *LINCOLN*

A LINCOLN owner in California has driven his car well over 150,000 miles, chiefly over mountain and desert. A 1925 Lincoln has traveled 200,000 miles. . . . These are not solitary examples of the Lincoln's endurance. Staunchness, dependability evoke the loyalty of owners everywhere, even though they may never put their cars to supreme tests. . . . From the laying of the frame to the tailoring of upholstery, the Lincoln is soundly and beautifully constructed. And this, so true of Lincolns in the past, is even more characteristic of today's Lincoln. The new V-12 cylinder engine, developing 150 horsepower, Lincoln engineers deem unsurpassed by any they have thus far designed. Air-plane-type bearings, here first used in motor car engines, will withstand excessive temperatures as high as 750 degrees. Other achievements include an improved cooling system, aluminum cylinder heads, and a single-plate clutch, which at a touch fairly animates the car. Two wheelbases—standard and custom-built body types. From $3200, at Detroit.

PRESS OF
JUDD & DETWEILER, INC.
WASHINGTON, D. C.

With a LeBaron Convertible Roadster body the KB Lincoln of 1932–33 was more than enough automobile for the early years of the depression. Its successor, the KA, had a simpler engine, ultimately of 6.8 litres.

spent gases forward and then down along the left side of the crankcase. A 1½in Stromberg dual-throat downdraft carburettor was fed by a combined air cleaner and silencer. An ignition distributor was at the rear of the engine, driven by the tail of the camshaft. On the modest compression ratio of 5.25:1 Lincoln's massive twelve produced 150bhp at 3,400rpm and 292lb-ft of torque at 1,200rpm. It first ran on the dynamometer on 9 May 1931 and was dropped into a chassis only six days later. Commendably taking more time for development than some of its more impetuous rivals, Lincoln waited until January 1932 to unveil its twelve in New York.

At 5,600 to 5,900lb the KB was by far the heaviest Lincoln yet. Accepting the Depression's challenge, at $4,500 to $7,000 its pricing was generally comparable to that of the previous year's V8s, which in 1932 were offered at lower cost alongside the twelve. "Mechanically archaic" and "not terribly progressive" though its design was called, the 7.3-litre Lincoln KB was an engine with

which to reckon. In England *The Motor* timed its Lincoln saloon at 90.1mph at Brooklands, finding that "the engine (which will turn over at speeds up to 4,500rpm) remains absolutely silent and vibrationless. Indeed it is no exaggeration at all to say that the car cruises comfortably and with ample power in hand at 80mph. Few would believe it was capable of a performance exceeding by an enormous margin that of many so-called sports cars." Its acceleration to 60mph was clocked in 26 seconds *in top gear only*.

The seven-main-bearing KB twelve was offered throughout 1933, its sales declining sharply, and then discontinued. In all, 2,174 were made.[14] In 1933 it was joined by a sister twelve, the KA, which was destined to carry the big Lincolns through the rest of the decade. Again the work of Frank Johnson and his team, the KA twelve was a simplified and lightened successor to the KB. While keeping the latter's chain-driven generator and water pump and twin iron blocks on an aluminium crankcase, the KA adopted more conventional side-by-side connecting rods and offset cylinder blocks. Its main bearings were four instead of seven, allowing the engine to be shortened by 115mm, and both cylinder-block deck heights and connecting-rod lengths were reduced, narrowing the twelve by 25mm.

The new engine's vee angle was fractionally increased to 67°, the same as Packard's V12. In search of better torque, valve sizes were cut back to 42.9mm. While KA's stroke remained the same as the KB's at 114.3mm, bore was smaller at 76.2mm for 6,255cc. Thus configured the KA twelve, introduced in 1933 as a replacement for Lincoln's 60° V8, developed 125bhp at 3,400rpm. This was its only season at this size and power, for in 1934 Lincoln promoted it to the leading role in its product line. From '34 until the 1948 model year Lincolns would only be powered by vee-twelve engines.

To fulfil its new mission the KA was given a bore increase to 79.4mm that raised its displacement to 6,787cc. With new aluminium heads its compression ratio was raised to 6.38:1, helping boost output to the KB's level of 150bhp at 3,400rpm. To improve durability an oil/water heat exchanger was added and the rods were drilled to deliver pressure oil to the gudgeon pins. The new twelve's small valves, matched with smaller carburettor bores of 1¼in, gave it even higher torque than the bigger KB with 312lb-ft at 1,200rpm.

In this form the KA V12 was produced through 1939 for wheelbase lengths of 136 and 145in, mounted in the chassis at four points.[15] Improvements made in 1937 included hydraulic self-adjusting tappets and steel-backed copper-lead rod and main bearings. These internal changes were complemented by handsome new body styles that integrated headlamps into the wings, while still catering to such custom-body builders as Brunn, Willoughby and Judkins.

The car that Richard Burns Carson derided as "a rolling exhibit of discarded automotive ideas" served admirably in 1939 as the basis for an open Presidential car, Franklin Delano Roosevelt's Brunn-bodied 'Sunshine Special' on a 160in wheelbase. One KA was hopped up with twin Carter carburettors and a pair of horizontal Vertex magnetos to power the handsome roadster belonging to a Los Angeles restaurateur.

Sales of the big Lincoln twelves dropped into triple digits in 1937 and their last year, 1939, saw 133 produced. Not until July 1940 was the last one sold. "We did not stop producing luxury cars," Edsel Ford later remarked; "people stopped buying them." Edsel hadn't given up without a fight. In 1939 he had a team working on an all-

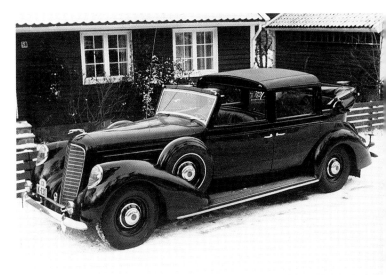

One of Lincoln's coachbuilders, Brunn, produced this semi-collapsible cabriolet on a 1937 Model KA chassis. It was a majestic town car suitable for any occasion.

new luxury Lincoln, the 05L, that he hoped to launch in 1940 to rival Cadillac's final side-valve V16. It was to be powered by an all-new V12 with a one-piece block. Although handsome clay models and body layouts of the 05L were produced, Edsel – to his great regret – was unable to marshal the engineering resources needed to create its engine. A different V12 Lincoln, the smaller Zephyr, would have to represent Ford's premier marque in the luxury-car market.[16]

Like Lincoln, Pierce-Arrow built its vee-twelve on classical lines with two iron cylinder blocks on an iron crankcase. Pierce, after all, was not a company to rush to embrace fads. Not until 1930, for example, did it give up the huge sixes it had been building since 1907 to succumb to the craze for new-fangled and vogueish straight-eights. Pierce-Arrow's styling hallmark was its wing-mounted headlamps, introduced as a patented feature in 1913. Until 1932 conventional headlamps would be an option, but most buyers preferred the distinctive lamps on the wings that set Pierces apart from lesser cars.

If egalitarian, puritanical America could be said to have made a motorcar for its nobs and nobesses, that would be the Pierce-Arrow. First a car maker in 1902, Pierce traced its origins to an 1865 maker of birdcages in Buffalo, New York, not far from Niagara Falls. Moving spirit George Pierce died in 1910 but his company persevered, renamed Pierce-Arrow in recognition of its successful Great Arrow models. Wounded by the 1921 recession that was nearly fatal to Lincoln, Pierce-Arrow carried on independently until 1928, when it fell into the welcoming arms of Studebaker. The latter's chief, Albert Erskine, became Pierce's leader as well in 1929.

Although the proud company's alliance with lowly Studebaker in far-away South Bend, Indiana was controversial, Pierce-Arrow nevertheless benefited significantly from a relationship that was far more collegial and productive than that between Lincoln and Ford. Studebaker provided the foundry that Pierce lacked and produced all-steel bodies for its base models. Its distribution network was a boon as well. Thanks to Studebaker's support, Pierce-Arrow was able to design and produce a vee-twelve to make it a runner – albeit a late starter – in the multi-cylinder race among luxury-car producers.

The twelve's designer was also a boon from Studebaker. In 1929 Karl M. Wise was transferred from South Bend to Buffalo to take over as Pierce-Arrow's chief engineer. A key assistant, also from Studebaker, was

Karl W. Wise was the architect of Pierce-Arrow's V12, which had the widest vee angle of any American twelve at 80°. Each row of cylinders had its own induction and exhaust manifolding, above mushroom tappets which, from 1933, included hydraulic valve adjustment.

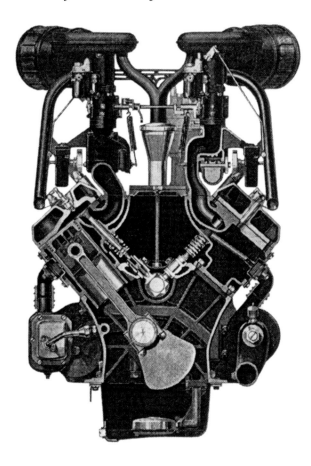

Maurice Thorne. Prudently, Wise counselled that at its small production volumes – its break-even was 3,000 cars a year – Pierce should err on the side of over-design for reliability. "Wise was convinced," said Thorne, "that we could not afford endless experimentation and development required for the sole purpose of penny-saving on elements of design." The big car makers needed and could pay for such squeezing of costs through trial and error. Wise realised that this would not suit the pocketbook of Pierce-Arrow, which needed to earn its place as part of Studebaker.

Moustachioed and grave, Karl Wise dedicated much of 1930 and '31 to the design and development of Pierce's twelve, which entered production on 9 November 1931 as a 1932 model. Primarily to provide reasonable valve-gear access in the engine's vee, he gave it the generous angle of 80° – widest of all the American twelves. A deep cast-iron crankcase went down well past the crankshaft centreline to a shallow sump and carried two six-cylinder blocks, also iron castings. Living up to his name, Wise designed the blocks so that one part could be used for both banks. With their cylinder bores spigoted down into the crankcase, the blocks were attached by studs along their bases whose tightly recessed nuts were anything but mechanic-friendly.

A single central camshaft, carried by four bearings, was driven by a 38.1mm silent chain and opened the side valves through mushroom-shaped tappets. Valve stems were angled away from the bore centreline by $5\frac{1}{2}°$ to make the combustion chamber more compact and improve gas flow. Closed by single coil springs damped by coils of steel strip, valves were 42.1mm for the inlets, 39.7mm for the exhausts. Ports in their blocks curved upward to horizontal surfaces to which each bank's individual inlet and exhaust manifolds were bolted. Feeding forward and to the right and down, the exhaust manifolds were outboard of the inlet manifolds, to which they provided hot spots under their carburettors. The latter were single-throat Strombergs, one for each bank, their throttles co-ordinated by a short shaft. A forked manifold from a single cleaner delivered air.

Skew gearing from the tail of the Pierce's camshaft drove its dual-coil twin-breaker ignition above, either Delco Remy or Owen Dyneto, and its oil pump – with a floating pickup – below. Piped into the lubrication system, a Harrison oil/water heat-exchange matrix was on the right-hand side of the crankcase. It was fed by a passage through the crankcase from the left side, where the water pump was driven from the tail end of the generator and fed the left-hand block directly. Coolant entered the blocks through manifolds, built into their steel access plates, that piped water directly to the hot

valve guides and seats. Twin vee belts from the crank nose drove the generator and a six-bladed cooling fan.

Also at the nose of the crankshaft was a vibration damper for the forged-steel crank with its twelve integral counterweights. It was held by seven 63.5mm main bearings and had 56.3mm crankpins carrying connecting rods side by side, thanks to a forward shift of the left-hand cylinder bank. Forged-steel connecting rods 252.4mm long were rifle-drilled to provide pressure lubrication to the gudgeon pins. Bohnalite aluminium pistons had Invar-Strut compensation for differential expansion and carried four rings: two compression, one scraper and one oil-control ring. The first twelves of 1932 had the moderate compression ratio of 5.05:1.

Erskine and Wise elected to launch their twelve-cylinder engine in two cylinder sizes. Both had a stroke of 101.6mm, relatively short by American classic-car standards. The smaller unit had a bore of 82.6mm and the larger 85.7mm for respective capacities of 6,525 and 7,037cc. With conservative valve timing both delivered exceptional torque at 1,250rpm: 355lb-ft for the smaller unit and 375lb-ft for the larger. Their power levels at 3,400rpm were 140 and 150 horsepower respectively. They were offered on wheelbases of 137, 142 and 147in powering Pierce-Arrows weighing 5,200 to 5,500lb and costing from $3,650 to $7,200.

One design feature had not been ripe enough to be risked on the launch version of Pierce's twelve. This was a novel automatic valve-lash adjuster, the first hydraulic unit

In 1936 the Pierce-Arrow twelve, America's largest at 7.6 litres, was given aluminium cylinder heads with a higher compression ratio that helped produce a proud 185bhp at 3,400rpm.

of its type to be an integral part of the cam follower. The conception of Carl Voorhies, these hydraulic tappets were introduced in 1933, when the smaller twelve was dropped from the range. The larger one was continued with its compression ratio raised to 6.0:1 and its power elevated to 160bhp. It now had a bigger brother, the Pierce-Arrow V12 in its final form, a 7,568cc titan – America's biggest twelve of this period – with the unchanged stroke of 101.6mm and the enlarged bore of 88.9mm.

Both the bore enlargement and other improvements in the 7.6-litre Pierce twelve were, in significant part, the work of the teetotal Mormon we met in Chapter 4, David 'Ab' Jenkins. Salt Lake City, Utah native Jenkins chose a Studebaker when he raced a train from there to Wendover in 1925, crossing part of the Great Salt Lake on the way. Jenkins was again Studebaker-mounted in 1931 when he set new official records for stock cars on some 65 hill climbs in 35 states. When their confrères in Buffalo decided that their new V12 needed a bit more in the way of salt and pepper, the Studebaker engineers know just whom to recommend.

"After completing the hill climbing campaign," wrote Jenkins, "I was asked by the Pierce-Arrow people to come to their factory in Buffalo, New York. They asked me if I would see whether I couldn't get some of the 'bugs' out of the engine and put more 'horses' in it. That I consented to try to do." Accompanying Ab Jenkins to Buffalo was senior Studebaker engineer Omar J. Diles. With Karl Wise's team they made a number of changes, including new circular-section inlet manifolds instead of the original square-section design, carrying Stromberg EX32 carburettors with automatic chokes. Camshaft timing was much more radical as follows:

Inlet opens	19° BTDC	Exhaust opens	56° BBDC
Inlet closes	69° ABDC	Exhaust closes	28° ATDC

The changes made Pierce's twelve distinctly racier. Though still substantial, its torque was less than its predecessors at 350lb-ft, which it could maintain from 1,000 to 2,000rpm, while its power was up to 175bhp, available from 3,400 to 3,800rpm, on a compression ratio of 6.0:1. Its toughness was verified by 150 hours on the test bench at 4,000rpm.[17]

This wasn't the limit for the Pierce-Arrow twelve. A swathe of changes in 1936 included aluminium cylinder heads with the higher compression ratio of 6.4:1 and individual air cleaners for the twin carburettors. Power was now 185bhp with a peak at 3,400rpm. This matched the power of Cadillac's V16 and was only surpassed by the Model J Duesenberg among American autos.

The changes gave a fillip to the fortunes of Pierce-Arrow, which had been owned by a syndicate of Buffalo businessmen since Studebaker's bankruptcy in 1933.[18] The fillip was of negligible value, however, lifting 1936 production of twelves to a scanty 270 units from 1935's even more scanty 205. Only 71 were made in 1937 and the final 22 in 1938, the year in which Pierce-Arrow too was declared bankrupt.[19]

No rescuer came forward for the Buffalo firm, which folded just short of the rearmament boom that might have given it a new lease of life. In all it built 2,168 twelves, among them some of America's most magnificent and imposing custom-bodied cars with coachwork by Rollston, Le Baron, Dietrich and Brunn.[20] Pierce's twelve itself lived on, with fire-engine-maker Seagrave acquiring the patterns and tooling to produce it. Seagrave used it for many years, eventually enlarging it to 8.7 litres by changes to both bore and stroke.

Another American vee-twelve of the 1930s survived in a similar manner and expanded to a similar size. When Lycoming stopped manufacturing engines for automobiles, it sold the tooling for Auburn's V12 to another producer of fire engines, American LaFrance. The Auburn twelve's lifetime was the shortest of all these

American engines of the classic era, but by no means the least spectacular, for anything the auto empire of Errett Lobban Cord did in those days made news. E.L. Cord was only 30 in 1924 when he plucked Indiana auto-maker Auburn from a virtual scrapheap and began its urgent and profitable restoration.

"One of my principles is to be different," said the plain-spoken Cord. "Not spectacular or contrary, but different." A salesman through and through, Cord grasped the meaning of perceived value in automobiles long before his contemporaries. Seizing on the craze for straight-eights, he had Lycoming-built eights in Auburns by 1925. From its first stuttering single-cylinder models of 1902 Auburn was transformed by Cord into a stylish alternative to the offerings of mainstream makers. Cord having added Lycoming to his growing empire, an eight from that Williamsport, Pennsylvania company powered the rakish front-drive Cord L-29 which came to market only weeks before the stock-market panic of October 1929.

With Duesenberg under his auspices as well, E.L. Cord entered the 1930s in ebullient form in spite of America's struggling economy. The new catch phrase was 'vee-sixteen' with Cadillac having introduced one and Marmon soon to do so. Cord put the Lycoming engineers to work on an all-new V16 to power his future models.[21] By the autumn of 1930 they had three prototypes under test. Their vee angle was 45°, as best suited a bent sixteen, and their capacity was 8,044cc (79.4 x 101.6mm). Developing some 175bhp, one was installed for trials in a strengthened L-29 front-drive chassis whose wheelbase was extended a full 20in from its usual 137½in. Dubbed the E-1, this prototype was given a luxurious seven-passenger saloon body and unique front-end styling resembling a more muscular L-29.

Following Cadillac's example, Cord seized on the idea of producing a V12 version of this new sixteen. The busy engineers at Williamsport built this in two versions. One, intended for rear-drive Auburn models, had the same dimensions as the V16 and thus a capacity of 6,033cc. The other had the larger bore of 82.6mm for 6,525cc and was earmarked for a front-drive model, possibly a smaller L-29. However, these twelves ran into trouble. They'd been created by lopping off the rearmost four cylinders in a manner that compromised their main-bearing layout and crankshaft oilways. Although some progress was made in overcoming balancing anomalies, the engines' lubrication and durability remained suspect.

By late 1931 Lycoming had regrouped by designing a new V12 from the ground up. It retained the sixteen's 45° vee angle, which kept the engine narrow enough to fit within the slim bonnets that were then fashionable. Again the engine was built in two sizes. The larger, Type BA for front-drive models, at 8,041cc (88.9 x 108mm) was virtually as big as the vee-sixteen that had started this programme. Its sister, the Type BB, had the smaller bore of 79.4mm and was seen as a potential Auburn engine. With both having the same cylinder-centre distance of 100mm, the larger-bore version had slimmer water passages between its cylinders.

Installed for tests in the E-1 chassis, the big V12 offered ample performance with its output of 200bhp at 3,400rpm.[22] Here was an engine to reckon with for a future Cord, and E.L. lost no time in alerting his dealers to its imminence:

After two and one-half years of development work a new Cord Front-Drive will be brought out during the year of 1932. It will be 200 Horse-Power. We predict this new Cord Front-Drive will be the sensation of the automobile world.

With his existing L-29 struggling, however – only 1,416 were sold in 1931 – and the economy anything but lively, Cord finally balked at introducing such a costly mastodon.[23] With 335 final sales the L-29 ran out in 1932 instead, The auto world would wait until 1936 for another Cord and this one a V8 rather than a V12.

Auburn, instead, would be the beneficiary of this development programme. When the 1932 Auburn range was introduced it included the Model 12-160 – a twelve-cylinder car on a 132in wheelbase in six handsome body styles offered at startlingly low prices which by June 1932 had been slashed to $975 from $1,145. "The Auburn Twelve was mind-boggling," wrote Griff Borgeson, "it was so inexpensive, yet it was a terrifically good car – perhaps too good to be credible, as it deserved to be. The cheapest of its peers cost 2.7 times more." Auburn declared its objective for the model as follows:

Our aim for these new Twelves is to enable owners to enjoy a performance combining speed, power, smoothness and economy, the like of which they have never experienced. And – to make it available at a price that will force a complete revision of standards for comparison of values.

Auburn said it had spent a million dollars developing the new engine – $400,000 on design and engineering and $600,000 on manufacturing tooling and facilities. Initiated in December 1931, production was planned to ramp up to 1,600 vee-twelves per month.

With its dimensions of 79.4 x 108mm the Type BB Lycoming V12 for Auburn displaced 6,410cc, making it similar in size to the Franklin twelve and smaller than all the

To suit new products being developed by the Auburn Cord Duesenberg Corporation, the company's Lycoming arm produced a 45° V12 in 1931. Designated the type BA, this displaced 8.0 litres and developed 200 horsepower.

other American twelves save Cadillac's. Lycoming mastered the casting of its iron block in a single piece, extending down past the crankshaft centreline. Sized to suit its eight-litre sister, the Type BA, the crankshaft was massive with four 76.2mm main bearings and 63.5mm rod journals. Rods sat side-by-side on the latter with the left

For testing, Lycoming's BA vee-twelve was installed in a unique experimental front-drive chassis, the Cord E-1. Cord came close to offering such a car in production but decided against it. From it evolved the series-built BB twelve.

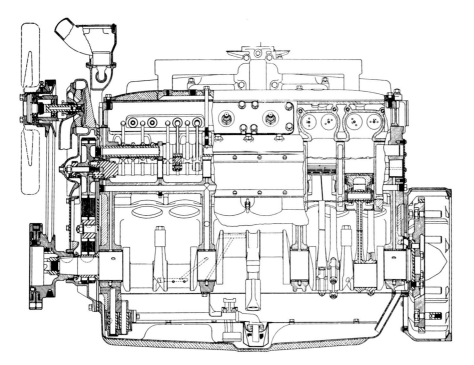

A longitudinal section of Auburn's Type BB V12 showed the four main bearings of its counterbalanced crankshaft and the front-end chain drive to its single camshaft. Also shown was the unusual shape of its combustion chambers, which debouched upon the main cylinder volume.

cylinder bank offset forward. Three counterweights were bolted to the crank, which was oiled from a gallery down the centre of the vee. Skew gearing at the front of the camshaft drove the oil pump, in the front of a cast aluminium sump, and the distributor at the engine's prow.

Auburn's Type BB enjoyed one of the most unusual combustion chambers of any twelve and indeed of any engine. At top dead centre the flat-topped piston was virtually flush with the top surface of the block. The chamber proper was a pocket in the cylinder head in which the valves formed most of its inboard surface and the spark plug was located outboard. The plugs screwed into water-cooled mini-heads, one to each pair of cylinders, without which it wouldn't have been possible to insert the valves into their guides. For the valves were placed horizontally, which obliged the chamber pockets to be inclined $22\frac{1}{2}°$ inboard from the cylinder centreline. The pockets themselves were significantly larger than the apertures through which gases flowed in and out of the cylinder, the 41.5mm inlets being placed nearer those apertures than the 39.2mm exhausts.

This unique chamber was credited by Lycoming engineers with a high resistance to knock on the poor

The Auburn twelve's combustion-chamber design had much in common with that of the Miller aviation V12, shown on page 29. Although Miller was from time to time a consultant to the Auburn-Cord Group, he is unlikely to have been the source of the design, which featured horizontal valves operated by roller-tipped rocker arms.

grades of petrol that was then in use, saying that on the test bench "you could advance the spark until the engine would slow down, and you wouldn't get any knock out of it." Its compression ratio was 5.75:1. The horizontal valves were opened by robust I-section rocker arms that offered a high ratio of multiplication from the cam lobe's profile. Instead of the solid shoes that gave trouble

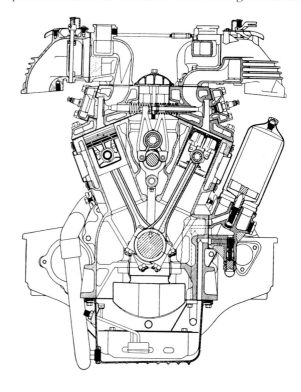

during the V12's development, the rockers had rollers following the cam. Each rocker had drillings to pressure-oil its rollers and a screw adjustment at its tip for clearance, readily accessed through apertures down the centre of the vee. A single coil spring closed each valve.

A duplex silent chain drove the camshaft from the crank nose, which also carried a vibration damper. The latter was grooved for a pulley to drive the coaxial fan and water pump through a single vee belt. Twin outlets from the pump supplied water to distribution manifolds inside the water jackets of each bank. Water surrounded the top two-thirds of each bore, within which was a full-skirted piston with pairs of compression and oil rings. Their gudgeon pins were pressure-oiled through drillings in the I-section connecting rods, 246.3mm long. To reduce the need for added material in the rod's shank, the drilling was slightly offset from the rod's centreline.

All the ports emerged from the horizontal top surfaces of the cylinder heads, the inlets being paired so they could be fed by siamesed passages in the inlet manifolds. Each bank had its own inlet and exhaust manifolds, the latter finned for heat dissipation on their outer surfaces. Exhaust heated the inlet manifolds, each of which carried a 1¼ inch Stromberg downdraft carburettor. The dualism carried through to the exhausts, which were individual systems all the way to the tailpipes. For an extra sensation of speed and power a floor-mounted control opened a silencer bypass.

Coming to market with 160 horsepower at 3,500rpm and torque of 286lb-ft at 1,500rpm, Auburn's V12 shared its body styles with the company's 100hp straight-eight, up to and including a spectacular boat-tailed Speedster. Although their engines alone weighed 1,096lb, the Model 12-160 Auburns were commendably light at 4,235 to 4,615lb. An added feature, new and exclusive to Auburn, was a Columbia two-speed rear axle that offered a choice between final-drive ratios of 4.55:1 and 3.04:1. To flaunt the twelve's performance Auburn took three cars to California's Muroc Dry Lake in July 1932. They demonstrated top speeds of 93mph for closed cars, 96 for the convertible and 101mph for the Speedster. Zero-to-60 acceleration took 15 seconds.[24]

As Griff Borgeson remarked, this was "a product that should sell itself. How good could a better mousetrap be?" Yet the high hopes and ambitions of Cord, Auburn and Lycoming were dashed by a stubborn marketplace. Instead of tens of thousands of twelves, only 2,550 were produced in three model years. In their final season, 1934, carryover bodies were used while the main Auburn line was converted to a new style. Auburn was still sitting on 400 unused engines in 1935, the marque's penultimate year. In the twelve E.L. Cord had given Auburn a car that

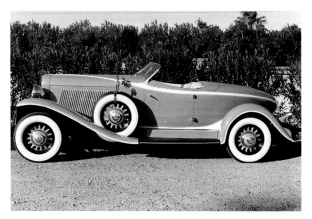

Few American cars offered more performance per dollar than the vee-twelve Auburn, especially when bodied as a Speedster. Nevertheless the twelve-cylinder model did not enjoy the sales success that it so profoundly deserved.

was "not contrary, but spectacular and different," to amend his phrase. With Cord increasingly remote from his auto empire in 1934 and afterward, it quietly expired after the last hurrah of the Cord 810 and 812.

The early years of the Great Depression were no kinder to another ambitious effort of America's classic-car era, the Marmon Sixteen. Nordyke & Marmon of Indianapolis, Indiana traced its origins to the middle of the 19th Century and began making cars in 1902. Chief engineer Howard Marmon's first cars had vee-type engines, including experimental V6s and V8s. His straight six was the first Indy 500-mile winner in 1911. In the 1920s he pioneered the extensive use of aluminium in Marmon's engines, and capped this in 1931 with the introduction of a magnificent vee-sixteen of 8,044cc in which all major static components excepting its wet steel cylinder liners were cast in aluminium.[25] Though elegant in both styling and engineering, the Indianapolis-built Sixteen was a car out of time. Marmon quietly closed its doors in 1933 after 390 had been made.

Howard Marmon, however, went out with a bang. Around the time that his eponymous company folded he rolled out a prototype that was rife with radical engineering ideas. With Marmon itself in trouble, the engineer financed the project with $160,000 from his own pocket. This meant that the rights to the HCM Special's design remained his when Marmon's assets were sold off. It was novel from stem to stern with sliding-pillar front suspension *a la* Lancia, inboard rear brakes with transverse-leaf independent rear suspension and a backbone-type frame *a la* Tatra. And powering the HCM, derived from Marmon's V16, was an all-aluminium V12.

Marmon's capable mechanicians made their V12 by

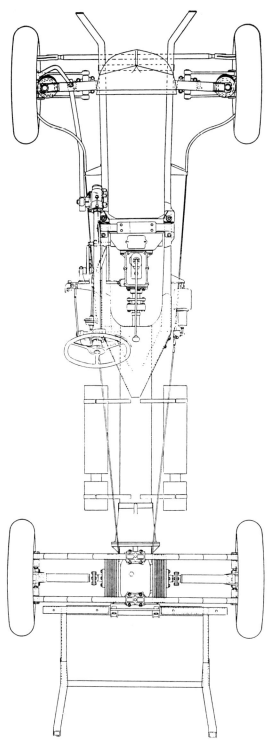

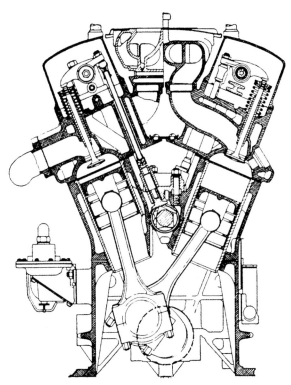

*With its cross-flow porting and wet iron cylinder liners the
Marmon engine was advanced for its time. As modified to a
vee-twelve configuration for Marmon's HCM Special it
retained its 45° vee angle and displaced 6.0 litres.*

cutting out cylinders six and seven from both banks and
welding the one-piece aluminium block casting back
together, treating the heads, manifolds, valve covers and
sump similarly. Though this was not unlike the way
Lycoming's engineers had treated their V16 to make an
unsatisfactory V12, the Marmon's truncation was more
successful. As in the Auburn instance both the parent
sixteen and the resulting twelve had a vee angle of 45°.
Thanks to the extensive use of aluminium both engines
were light for their size and configuration: 930lb for the
sixteen and 850lb for the twelve.

With the same cylinder dimensions as the sixteen
(79.4 x 101.6mm), the HCM's twelve displaced 6,033cc.
Cutting out four cylinders was made easier by the design
of the larger unit, which placed its cylinders directly
opposite each other and used fork-and-blade connecting
rods, with forked rods along the right bank. Valves were
overhead, opened through adjustable rockers and
aluminium pushrods by a single central camshaft. It was
driven by a chain which also turned the generator and,
behind it, the water pump on the right side of the block.
A new camshaft and crankshaft were of course made for
the V12, which used the V16's rugged 203.2mm I-section
rods and aluminium pistons.

*In 1933 Howard Marmon, formerly producer of the
eponymous automobiles, built a radically advanced
prototype with pillar-type independent front suspension
and transverse-leaf rear springing, carried by a tubular-
backbone frame. The engine of the HCM Special was a V12
derived from Marmon's all-aluminium V16.*

Porting to and from the HCM's combustion chambers with their 6.0:1 compression ratio – high for the time, akin to Packard – was strikingly forward-looking. Exhausts were piped to the outside of the head, while only the inlet manifolding was in the centre, fed by a single central Stromberg twin-throat downdraft carburettor. Water instead of exhaust gases warmed the inlet manifolding. The ignition distributor rose vertically at the front of the engine. Howard Marmon's twelve was high-revving for its era and its size, producing its peak of 151bhp at 3,700rpm. Maximum torque was 262lb-ft at 1,200rpm, maintaining 244lb-ft at 2,800rpm.

Handsomely styled by W. Dorwin Teague Jnr, with a two-door coupé body on its 134in wheelbase, the 4,600lb HCM Special was rolled out in 1933 by its 57-year-old creator. Capable of more than 90mph and impressive acceleration, it seemed a convincing demonstrator of the advanced ideas it embodied.[26] However, in the straitened circumstances of most of America's car makers in the 1930s it was not convincing enough to win a manufacturer for Marmon's design. Nor was another of Howard Marmon's advanced projects, his aerodynamic rear-engined Model D, ultimately realised. Marmon died a decade later, a disappointed but honoured pioneer.

Thus ended what some have termed the "second generation" of American V12s, a reference to the wave of twelves that ended the straight-eight's domination of the luxury-car world during the 1920s after the "first generation" faded away. One American vee-twelve would remain, however, and live on well into the 1940s. Lincoln's Zephyr and its descendants deserve appreciation in that context. They were no match for these proud and powerful engines, which were rivalled only by their classic contemporaries in Europe.

Chapter 5 Footnotes

[1] Peerless produced a lone V16 prototype but expired before it could be produced.

[2] Said a colleague, "Probably the most important asset possessed by Mr Shoemaker was his very delightful wife who guided him and encouraged him to do the unusual."

[3] This was the method adopted for its automotive V8 engines by Tatra of Czechoslovakia.

[4] Though none of these early prototypes survived, Franklin enthusiast and restorer Tom Hubbard has built a replica, his 'Super Merrimac' dual-cowl touring car, which hints at what might have been.

[5] McEwen and his banking consortium accounted for the nickname 'banker's car' given to the Franklin V12.

[6] LeBaron designer Hugo Pfau understood that the frames were left-overs from the collapse of Cleveland's Stearns, where McEwen had been an executive. The largest Stearns had a wheelbase of 145in, close enough to the big Franklin's 144.

[7] In fact Buick's sensational across-the-board conversion from sixes to eights took place in its 1931 models, introduced on 26 July 1930, but few such initiatives remained secret for long in Michigan's motor industry.

[8] Although work on the new car must have begun earlier, the project was officially approved by the Packard board on 25 June 1930.

[9] The possibility cannot be excluded that Van Ranst was aware of Cappa's solution, which had been described in the American technical press. "We all borrowed ideas from each other," he once said. "I borrowed from Miller, Miller borrowed from Duesenberg, Offenhauser and Bugatti borrowed from Miller, Milton borrowed from Peugeot and all our cars were better for it."

[10] The author saw one such car in the late 1940s when its keeper was Joe Rempson, who looked after the cars in Briggs Cunningham's collection. It still survives.

[11] These changes were made so late that the data published on 27 February 1932 by Automotive Industries still described the M&V engine with the smaller bore.

[12] Power was officially 180bhp with optional 7.0:1 cylinder heads. Packard expert Robert Turnquist says that its power ratings were conservative and that the respective outputs of the twelves were actually 192 and 202bhp.

[13] There could have been a British-built Packard V12. Napier ran a ruler over Packard in 1932 when it was considering a return to car production. It weighed the idea of making Packards under licence but finally decided to stick to its successful aero engine production.

[14] Production and sales figures for the KB Lincolns are conflicting and confusing, ranging from 2,048 to 2,210 for the number made over two years.

[15] Lincoln would have been challenged if asked to do much more. After he completed his work on the 1934 engine Frank Johnson was told by Henry Ford to fire everyone on the engineering staff except his closest lieutenants. Fifty men were laid off.

[16] The story of the Zephyr is told in Chapter 12.

[17] Their high-performance work on the Pierce V12 took Jenkins and Diles to Utah's Salt Flats for their first record-breaking effort in September 1932. This is recounted in Chapter 8.

[18] Studebaker of course was restructured and carried on for another twenty years.

[19] Oft repeated is the assertion that Karl Wise, who left to join Bendix, had a final V12 assembled from the receiver's stocks for his personal use. His daughter dismisses this as a canard.

[20] The production figures are estimates published by the Pierce-Arrow Society. Another estimate suggests that total V12 production was 1,878.

[21] Many accounts credit Auburn assistant chief engineer George Kublin with authorship of that company's vee-type engines, but former Lycoming engineers assert that Lycoming alone was involved in their design.

[22] After research and restoration efforts bordering on the superhuman, the V12 was reunited with its E-1 chassis by Paul Bryant and Stan Gilliland. Having run again for the first time on 7 August 2003, she is on view at the Auburn Cord Duesenberg Museum in Auburn, Indiana.

[23] Cord may also have been wary of offering a car which could rival his range-topping Duesenberg. Although placarded at an unblown 265bhp, the Duesenberg eight actually produced 208bhp in production form.

[24] Later in the year they also broke records there, as related in Chapter 8.

[25] We recall that Owen Nacker, credited with Cadillac's V16 and V12, had previously worked with Howard Marmon.

[26] Thanks in no small part to its conservation by industrial designer Brooks Stevens, the HCM Special has survived.

BRITISH AND FRENCH CLASSICS

It was fitting that one of Europe's oldest car companies, dedicated to the production of luxury carriages for the noble and/or wealthy, should be the first on that continent to produce twelve-cylinder road cars in significant volumes. Though Europe's major auto makers produced a spasm of V12 production prototypes at the beginning of the 1920s, none had gone forward to the market. Europe left it to the Americans to produce a plethora of roadgoing twelve-cylinder cars, meanwhile tearing up the tracks with some impressive racing twelves. The gap was bridged in October 1926 with the announcement of a production vee-twelve by the Daimler Motor Company of Coventry, England.

The UK-based Daimler Company was formed in 1896 to begin manufacturing cars in Britain according to the patents of the Daimler Motoren Gesellschaft. British Daimlers began to be produced in 1897. A twin-cylindered car from the Coventry firm was delivered in 1900 to HRH The Prince of Wales, soon to become King Edward VII. "What the Prince did, others did after him," wrote St. John C. Nixon. "'From that moment, the Daimler was the royal car."

After 1909 a characteristic of Daimler engines was their use of sleeve valves instead of the usual poppet. In a system licensed by American inventor Charles Knight, two sleeves surrounded each piston. Ingenious porting in the reciprocating sleeves carried out the opening and closing functions of the four-stroke cycle.

Six-cylinder engines were Daimler's stock-in-trade in 1925 when the company engaged a new chief engineer. Though only 42, Laurence H. Pomeroy had already enjoyed a notable career at Vauxhall, where he rose to general manager, and as a consultant and vehicle designer in America, where he advised Pierce-Arrow. Early in the 1920s Pomeroy showed his interest in the twelve by compiling the parameters of large sixes, eights and twelves, listing seven of the last including the Sunbeam Maori, Napier Lion and Liberty 12. In a 1919 technical paper the engineer argued that a key benefit of what he called the "super-multi-cylinder" engine was the lower 'recoil torque' that it imposed on the engine mountings, thus on the car's frame and body. Wrote Pomeroy:

Increasing the number of cylinders, keeping the torque the same, will reduce the torque recoil effect in proportion to the increase in the number of explosions per minute. The point at issue is as to how far it is really necessary to increase the number of cylinders to avoid the manifestation of torque recoil in such a degree as to exact the sensitiveness of the expert driver. The super-multi-cylinder engines now used on certain celebrated makes give a smoothness of pick-up which seems superlative and obtained at the expense of more desirable qualities such as absence of fuss at high speeds, high petrol-consumption, complication of design, etc. From the aspect of the user the super-

Opposite: *At its front end the Bentley-designed Lagonda twelve used a combination of helical gears and chains to drive a single overhead camshaft for each cylinder bank. A lower chain drove the generator and water pump along the left side of the engine, the pump's impeller being visible here.*

multi-cylinder engine is regarded as advantageous in respect of high gear work on the hills and on the level, characteristics in which such engines have certainly no advantage in respect of the number of cylinders per se...

Here was a knowledgeable interest in the attributes of the twelve-cylinder engine, and at the same time a frank appreciation of its merits and demerits. Pomeroy found himself accentuating the positive after he joined Daimler in 1925. According to one of the company's directors, "Shortly after the war the Daimler Company recognised the fact that the final product would lack an essential refinement of performance so long as so much power was divided among only six cylinders. Under certain conditions it was undeniable that the explosive force per cylinder became the dominant factor limiting the perfection of top-gear road performance." Daimler elected to bypass the eight and go straight to the twelve, this decision supported at a marketing level by Pomeroy's views on "the psychology of numerical appraisal, by which he meant that in choosing a car, the ignoramus assumed that an eight-cylinder model must be twice as good as a four and so on, pro rata."[1]

With both the vee-eight and straight-eight still problematic from the standpoint of vibration control, it was

One of the most extraordinary cross-sections of automotive V12 engines is that of the Double-Six Daimler of 1927. Its creator, Laurence Pomeroy, married two six-cylinder blocks of Daimler's sleeve-valve engines. Adjacent to the crankshaft were the two eccentric shafts that operated two sliding sleeve valves in each cylinder.

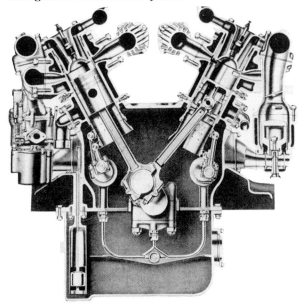

easy enough for Pomeroy and his chief at Daimler, Percy Martin, to decide to trump their rivals with a twelve – then the ultimate in the psychology of numerical appraisal. Even better, the chief engineer had come up with an ingenious way to give Daimler its first twelve; he married two of Daimler's sixes on a common aluminium crankcase. This meant that he could use the blocks – cast in threes – and all the sleeve valves and many of the reciprocating parts of an engine that was already in production.

Surprisingly, this was a new idea. Other car makers had built twelves using their contemporary technology, but none had simply combined two of its existing sixes to make a twelve. With beguiling candour the engine was dubbed the Double-Six, an honourable echo of Packard's famous – and by then defunct – Twin Six. The first such unit, the Double-Six 50, was announced in October 1926 for 1927 production.[2] Using the blocks of Daimler's 25/85 Six, its displacement was 7,137cc (81.5 x 114mm).

Major parts not shared with the sixes were the connecting rods. Pomeroy placed the blocks directly opposite each other at a 60° vee angle and used fork-and-blade I-section connecting rods, the forked rods being those of the right bank. Innocent of balancing masses, the nickel-chrome-steel crankshaft was carried in seven main bearings in a crankcase that was cut off at the crank centreline and enclosed by a deep cast-aluminium sump. Flanking the crank were two eccentric shafts that operated the twin sleeves in each cylinder through short duraluminium links. Turned by silent chain from the engine's flywheel end, the sleeve-driving eccentric shafts were carried by four bearings apiece.

At the crank nose a skew gear powered transverse shafts above and below it. The lower shaft drove two dual-entry water pumps, one for each bank. Unlike some makers of sleeve-valve cars, who took advantage of the clean and pure shapes of their water jackets to rely on thermosyphon cooling, Daimler encouraged the coolant's flow with pumps. Water was piped to each block through a manifold and extracted from the top of each head, which had deep water jackets surrounding the spark plugs and the tops of the sleeves. The upper transverse shaft turned a magneto at each side. From there, vertical shafts motivated two distributors, which could supply sparks from the magnetos or from a coil ignition set, to the driver's choice, in a belt-and-braces system. A Lanchester vibration damper at the crank nose, containing oil-bathed multiple discs, did double duty as a pulley to the fan.

Before starting, the driver could pump oil directly to the port-controlling sleeves to be sure that they were well oiled when the engine was awakened.[3] To the same end, oil was added to the fuel/air mixture during starting.

Firing up a Double-Six from cold was an arcane ritual that tended to limit sales of such cars to those with chauffeurs. Failure to follow the ritual – and omitting an oil change every 1,000 miles – led to seizing and damage that ended the careers of many of these smooth but delicate engines.

Oiling of the lower ends of the Daimler's steel sleeves was aided by patterns of perforations while a 'wash' of white metal on one sleeve avoided the friction of steel on steel. Some engines also had channels at the bases of the sleeves to draw off excess oil to overcome the tendency of sleeve-valve engines toward smoky exhausts. The full skirts of the flat-topped aluminium pistons were split so that an internal spring could ensure an absence of piston slap when starting from cold. Each piston carried five rings: three compression rings above oil drain holes, and below them two oil rings. Clamped in the rod's small end, the gudgeon pin was free to turn in the piston.

Log-type exhaust manifolds ran down the centre of the vee to the rear, underneath a cowling which was directly cooled by the fan's rearward draft. Warm air from this central vee was piped downward and then out to the inlets of the Daimler carburettors. These updraft units had internal air-metering dashpots that progressively uncovered fuel jets as required. The mixture rose to a pipe the length of the engine which, in the big Double-Six, also carried warm engine water away. Downward-facing ports near the ends of this pipe delivered the mixture to downward-sloping manifolds, each of which fed three cylinders. The circuitous system was justified as giving good distribution of a thoroughly warmed and thus vaporised mixture.

Emphasising smoothness in Daimler's big Double-Six meant that its output of 150bhp at the moderate speed of 2,480rpm was significantly below the figure of 170bhp that would have been twice the power of the 25/85 six. Driving through a four-speed transmission, it propelled chassis lengths of 155½ and 163in weighing 4,250lb in the shorter version. All four speeds were scarcely needed, for a speed range from 2 to 82mph could be coped with in top gear alone. Said *The Autocar*, "It is quite possible for a passenger, whilst the car is travelling dead slow on top gear, to get out of the car, walk round it and get in again."

Should one cylinder bank be out of commission, said the Daimler's designer, "the horsepower of the engine is reduced to some 40 per cent of what it is with two banks, and the car can get home correspondingly more slowly, but does get home." This would have been comforting to King George V, who had Daimler twelves retrofitted to two of his chassis and ordered a complete Double-Six as well. This added credibility to the forecast of *The Autocar* that "Fortunate beings in the immediate future will leisurely survey the moving surface of the earth through

Renowned as cars for Britain's royalty, the big Double-Six Daimlers produced 150bhp at 2,480rpm to power luxury carriages like this one with Daimler's distinctive fluted radiator.

the clear windows of their Daimler Double-Sixes as they pass onward in silent dignity."

Daimler itself asserted that with improved roads and better braking, the engines of big automobiles "are now used more frequently at their full power, and the great force of the explosion that occurs in cylinders of large size becomes increasingly liable to attract undesirable attention." The Double-Six was the answer, it said:

While the primary reason for the multiplication of cylinders in the development of automobile engine design has been the sub-division of the explosive force, many other advantages attend this form of construction. When the power is developed in several cylinders it is possible for them to be connected to the crankshaft in such a way that their impulses overlap so as to produce a very smooth torque on the transmission. In the case of a properly designed "double-six" the effect is that of a turbine, and so perfect are the new Daimler engines in this respect that their smoothness of operation far surpasses anything that has hitherto been available in any car.

The arrival of a smaller sister, the Double-Six 30, was announced in the summer of 1927. Using the cylinder blocks of the 16/55 six, its capacity was 3,743cc (65 x 94mm). Against its theoretical output of 110bhp it did relatively well, delivering 103bhp at 3,700rpm, sufficient for a top speed of 75mph. The smaller Daimler twelve

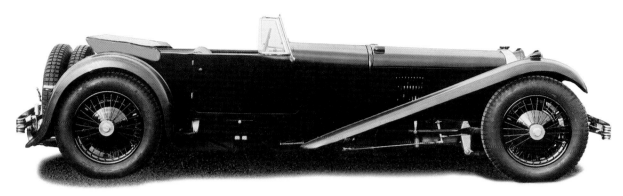

Two special chassis were designed by Reid Railton to take the large Double-Six 50 engines. The result was a spectacularly low and rakish Daimler with a surprising turn of speed.

completed a 50-hour test at 4,040rpm and was capable of revving to 4,600rpm for brief periods. Although its torque peak of 166lb-ft came at 2,500rpm, it delivered more than 160lb-ft from 1,500 to 3,000rpm. The engine weighed 785lb in a chassis that scaled 3,025lb without bodywork. The least costly Double-Six 30 was priced at £1,570, well down on the £2,450 of the comparable Double-Six 50. Their respective fuel economies were measured at 16.5 and 10.0mpg.

The year 1931 saw the launch by Daimler of a completely new range of sleeve-valve V12 engines, again making use of cylinder blocks from in-line sixes in the company's range. Two versions of the engine had common strokes and different bores to give displacements of 5.3 and 6.5 litres.

While the new smaller Daimler twelve was offered from 1928 into 1932, the larger unit was phased out at the end of 1929. Some of the big engines remained, however, and in 1930 Pomeroy interested Thomson & Taylor at Brooklands in building ultra-low 150in wheelbase chassis to take them. Their design was the work of Reid Railton, who set the engine well down and back to create a car of vivid sporting looks. At Daimler, Simpson modified the sleeve-valve phasing to give a more racy state of tune. One of these late Double-Six 50s was equipped with the hydraulic coupling 'fluid flywheel' and preselector transmission that Daimler introduced in 1930. The two cars that were built on this low chassis – one bodied by Corsica – are among the most spectacular ever made.

Astonishingly, in view of the state of the world economy in the early 1930s, Daimler not only persisted with its vee-twelves but also introduced an entirely new generation of these ambitious sleeve-valve engines in 1931. As before the twelves made use of the cylinder-block assemblies of Daimler's in-line sixes, in this case the new-in-1930 Model 25 of 81.5 x 114mm (3,568cc). This new generation of sixes had one-piece aluminium cylinder blocks in which the port-controlling sleeves rubbed directly against the aluminium. Extremely neat and clean in design, they had combustion chambers that were conical rather than the previous hemispherical. As before L. H. Pomeroy used two such blocks at 60° to create his V12.

Again there were two versions of the twelve, but this time based on a common architecture. At 104mm their strokes were shorter than that of the six and their bores were 81.5 and 73.5mm for respective displacements of 6,511 and 5,295cc. No clue as to their actual power output could be gleaned from their designations as the Double-Six 30/40 and 40/50 models, which were redesignated simply as the 40 and 50 models for 1933. They could be fitted to long, standard or short chassis with a price differential of £200 between the two engines. A standard 40/50 chassis cost £1,450, for example, against £1,250 for the smaller 30/40 Daimler.

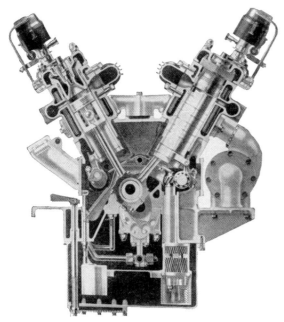

Taking advantage of advances in his sleeve-valve sixes, Laurence Pomeroy's new Daimler twelves for 1931 had conical rather than spherical combustion chambers. Carried over from the previous design were a vee angle of 60° and the use of fork-and-blade connecting rods.

Far neater in appearance than the earlier twelves, these new engines were founded on an aluminium crankcase that extended well down past the crankshaft centreline. Main bearings were again seven in number

and fork-and-blade connecting rods were still used, oiled by a pressure pump whose auxiliary gears circulated oil through a cooler built into the water radiator. Chains at the Daimler's flywheel end turned the two sleeve-controlling eccentric shafts and, on the left, the generator and the single water pump supplying both cylinder banks.

Each cylinder bank had its own coil-ignition distributor mounted at the rear, its drive shaft in line with its cylinders. Induction went from the previous twelve's complexity to stark simplicity, with an updraft carburettor at the front of each bank supplying a log manifold that ran back along the block. Mixture entering the log was further vaporised by a hot spot provided by the exhaust pipe, which ran forward along each bank and down the front of the engine.

That the new Daimler twelves could declare 'mission accomplished' was acknowledged in April 1931, when five of the new chassis – four with the larger engine and one with the smaller – were delivered to the Royal mews for the transport of the King and Queen. All of course had the new 'fluid flywheel' transmission. The order for these, placed in the autumn of 1930, was seen at the time "as an encouragement to the motor trade and with the object of helping reduce unemployment," according to Daimler, who averred that "this statement was received with general satisfaction throughout the industry."

When four years later King George V required two new state limousines – his 30th and 31st Daimlers! – the Coventry firm powered them with new poppet-valve V12

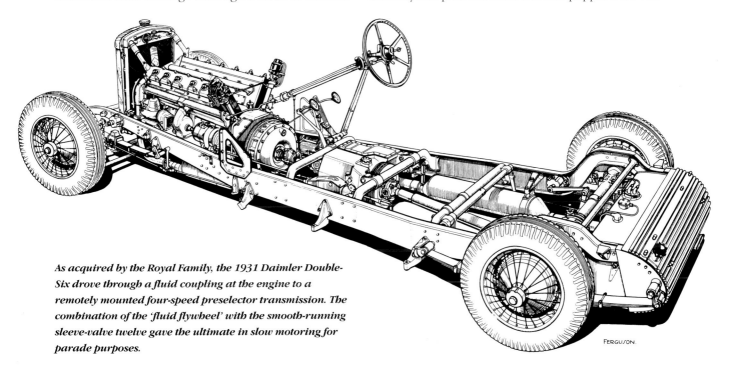

As acquired by the Royal Family, the 1931 Daimler Double-Six drove through a fluid coupling at the engine to a remotely mounted four-speed preselector transmission. The combination of the 'fluid flywheel' with the smooth-running sleeve-valve twelve gave the ultimate in slow motoring for parade purposes.

FERGUSON.

Last of Daimler's twelve-cylinder family in 1935 was a new engine based on the final sleeve-valve twelves but using overhead poppet valves operated through pushrods by dual camshafts flanking the crankshaft. Inlet and exhaust manifolding shared the engine's central vee, unencumbered by pushrods. These ultra-rare engines were built chiefly for Royal use.

engines – fifth and last of this Daimler twelve-cylinder dynasty.[4] This was a final project by L.H. Pomeroy, who had been Daimler's managing director since 1929 and would leave in 1936. Although records show that nine chassis were planned, only a few were assembled. In all, Daimler would build no more than 150-odd of all types of its Double-Sixes.[5]

Pomeroy based his farewell twelve on the larger Double-Six 40/50, using the same crankcase and 6,511cc displacement while replacing its sleeve-driving eccentric shafts with camshafts that operated pushrods travelling through the outer passages of its cast-iron blocks. With rockers operating overhead valves under Cadillac-like cast covers, this was akin to the valve-gear layout of Franklin's vee-twelve. The nose of each camshaft drove a vertical shaft to a distributor at the front of the engine.

While spark plugs were on the outer surfaces of the cast-iron heads, all the porting was in the inner vee. Exhausts ran forward as before while the inlet manifold was fed by a single dual-throat Stromberg downdraft carburettor with an automatic choke. To assist the Royal chauffeurs, the system of pre-lubricating the cylinders before starting was employed, although the sleeve valves that had benefited from it were gone. The twelve's output in the 140–150bhp range at 3,200rpm, on a compression ratio of 5.5:1, was more than adequate for the King's stately carriages.

These developments at Daimler had not gone unnoticed to the north at Derby, where the year 1929 saw the introduction of a new model, the Phantom II, powered by a six-cylinder engine of some 120bhp. Rolls-Royce took pride in its standing as 'The Best Car in the World' and its provision of powerful coachbuilt automobiles that suited the driver as well as the chauffeur. The world was moving on, however, with both Daimler and the cheeky Americans powering their luxury cars with impressive multi-cylinder engines. Laurence Pomeroy's "psychology of numerical appraisal" was a phenomenon that Rolls-Royce could not ignore, depression or no depression.

Knighted in 1930 for his outstanding aero engines, Sir Henry Royce remarked that same year of the luxury-auto scene that "we have to pay for our reputation as well as live up to it." His company would soon invest in a new automobile powered by a vee-twelve that mirrored its great work in the aviation field.

Several considerations led to the decision to build a twelve. As described in Chapter 4, the achievements of the company's twelves in record-breakers in the air and on the ground could not be overlooked. Engineer Maurice Olley also elicited from the Rolls-Royce men that "They feel exactly the reverse of Cadillac that they would rather have the job of [fuel/air] distribution for a 12 or 6 cylinder engine than for a 16 or 8." This ruled out the V8 that they also considered for the new model. A final damper on any temptation to challenge Cadillac with a V16 was imposed by Royce, who "suggested that if Rolls-Royce built a 16-cylinder car everyone would have thought he was mad." A twelve it would be, with the first outlines sketched as early as 1930.

Still under the supervision of the semi-invalid Royce, long-time associate Albert G. Elliot had been in charge of design of both cars and aero engines since 1929. Other key members of the team were Arthur J. Rowledge, a recent recruit from Napier, and Ernest Hives heading the experimental department. When serious work began on the new twelve in the summer of 1932, Henry Royce was still active, but it was apparent to him that this was one new model he would not see out. Sir Henry died in April 1933. "Suddenly Royce, who was not only designer but also a practical engineer, was not there any more," wrote Wilton Oldham. "For the first time decisions had to be made by Elliot, who, brilliant designer though he was, was not a practical man." This would have its consequences in the design of the new model.

Adding to the challenge facing the sixteen-strong Rolls-Royce engineering team was the decision to marry the new engine to a completely new chassis with independent front suspension and a remote-mounted four-speed transmission. Given the 'Spectre' code name, three experimental prototypes were built.[6] The first of these was running as a chassis in June 1934 and in fully bodied form that November. In the traditional manner these were driven hard on tough continental roads, starting in the spring of 1935.

Surprisingly soon, in early October of 1935, the new model was announced. No fewer than nine coachbuilt examples were on display at Olympia – many on dummy chassis. In mid-1936 production of the first Rolls V12 began. To the disappointment of engineer William A. Robotham – "I feel that it is most important to give a new model an attractive name" – after two high-level board meetings to discuss the subject it was prosaically dubbed 'Phantom III'.

Although observers noted that the new engine's dimensions of 82.3 x 114.3mm were the same as the contemporary Rolls-Royce 20/25 six, the perfectionist R-R engineers had no thought of the opportunistic – albeit economical – methods employed at Daimler by Pomeroy. The 7,341cc twelve was a new engine from scratch, equipped with aluminium cylinder heads and a block of aluminium as well, using the special Hiduminium RR50 alloy that High Duty Alloys and Rolls had jointly developed for aero engines.

The cylinder block extended downward well past the crankshaft centreline so the aluminium caps for its seven main bearings could be given lateral support by their webs. Wet cast-iron cylinder liners were clamped at their tops by the cylinder heads and sealed at the bottom by two O-rings in grooves in the block. Save for a wider gap between the middle pairs of cylinders on each bank, the centre-to-centre distance was a generous 120.7mm.

The PIII's crankshaft was fully balanced by eight bolted-on counterweights, the most massive of which were at the extreme front and rear. All the journals were bored hollow and then sealed at both ends by caps which were tensioned against each other by central nutted bolts.[7] A shallow cast sump, deeper at its rear, enclosed the bottom of the block. It was equipped with a baffle plate and a swing valve to prevent fore-and-aft surge.

As in their aviation engines, the Rolls-Royce designers used fork-and-blade rods for their automotive V12. Elegantly shaped, the I-section rods had raised ribs along their shanks to accommodate pressure drillings to their small ends. Achieving this in the forked rod required some clever passageways. This was doubly difficult because the rod's big end was formed in two pieces which mated at a curved surface. Akin to the arrangement of Rolls-Royce's Merlin, this allowed the

When Rolls-Royce decided to meet the challenge of its luxury-market competitors by building a V12 of its own, it spared no expense in creating an elaborate engine for the model that was introduced as the Phantom III. With 7.3 litres it was expected to give power which, in the Rolls-Royce tradition, would be 'adequate'. (**Sir Henry Royce Memorial Foundation**)

Rolls-Royce engineers under Albert Elliot carried over the fork-and-blade connecting-rod configuration from their V12 aviation engines. While the forked rod rode on a full-width big-end bearing, the blade rod had its own individual bearing surface inside the big end of the forked rod. (**Sir Henry Royce Memorial Foundation**)

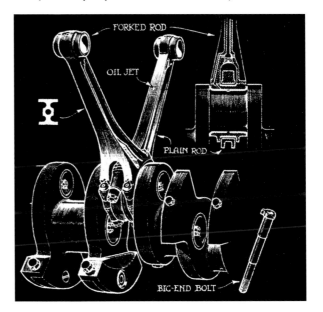

Fitted with wet cylinder liners, the aluminium cylinder block of the Phantom III Rolls-Royce had a closed top deck and carried its crankshaft in seven main bearings. The massive 'slipper flywheel' vibration damper was seen at the right. **(Sir Henry Royce Memorial Foundation)**

As viewed from the rear, on the test bench, the Rolls-Royce PIII vee-twelve was an impressive piece of kit. Built regardless of cost, it developed 165bhp at launch from 7.3 litres. **(Sir Henry Royce Memorial Foundation)**

portion carrying the blade rod's bearing to be made of nickel steel, hardened in a manner that the complete rod did not require. The forked rods, with their four-bolt big ends, were on the left bank. A separate manifold under the main-bearing caps supplied them with pressure oil. Flat-topped aluminium pistons had two compression rings, one oil ring and very long slotted skirts.

At the front of the crank, inside the timing chest was a large vibration damper – called a 'slipper flywheel' by Rolls – driven through a ring of coil springs. A helical gear at the crank nose turned a fibre idler on the left. This in turn drove gears turning both the central camshaft and the generator, behind which was the water pump. A skew gear at the nose of the camshaft turned a cross shaft which drove two vertical shafts to the engine's two twelve-cylinder distributors for its dual ignition system. As usual, Rolls-Royce produced its own ignition apparatus at Derby; before making cars, Royce had been a successful producer of electrical equipment.

In search of the ultimate in silence, the Rolls-Royce designers equipped their twelve with hydraulic cam followers. This followed the 1933 example of Pierce-Arrow and preceded their later use by Lincoln. It proved to be a decision in advance of its time, however, unless the chauffeur was well trained both to check for sludging of the oils then in use and to clean the relevant filters and traps, as any small particle could, and often did, disable the automatic valve-lash adjustment. Reacting to many field complaints, Rolls started testing solid lifters in 1937 and fitted them as standard from 1938, exciting no complaints on the grounds of excessive noise. The curved-face lifters, which worked against individual coil springs, slid in iron guides that were held in sets of quadruplets in an aluminium block by forked clamps.

Holes through the closed top deck of the PIII's block accommodated its pushrods, which opened vertical valves through rockers with valve-clearance adjustment on their pushrod ends in the engines with solid lifters. Dual-coil valve springs were tapered to smaller diameters at their tops. Combustion chambers were entirely in the heads in the form of a deep bathtub into which the compressed gases were swirled by wide squish areas in what Rolls-Royce called a 'turbulent' head. A 14mm spark plug was set into each side of the chamber in a manner directly analogous to the design of Rolls aero engines. In early twelves the timing of the plugs was given a 2° difference, though this was later changed to simultaneous sparking. Dash controls allowed either ignition system or both to be used.

In a manner recalling Fiat's prototype twelve of 1921, the PIII's three siamesed exhaust ports on each head curved out and downward. Also akin to the Fiat was the way these exhaust spouts were water-jacketed. Bolted to them was a finned log manifold that took the gases forward to keep them away from the footboards. On the inlet side of the head the ports were joined by a manifold partly in the head and partly covered by a plate. The mixture reached this manifold from yet another manifold with four outlets in all for each side.

From a water-warmed central mounting, each cylinder bank was fed by one throat of a two-barrel Stromberg downdraft carburettor. This replaced the battery of four downdraft Rolls-Royce instruments in a row that were used on the first cars. They were rejected because they gave less-good low-speed pickup, were hard to adjust to get a good idle and had to be removed completely to extract the inboard spark plugs. Nevertheless the four carburettors and their long cylindrical air cleaner were still on view when the first descriptions of the new chassis were written – a sign of the haste with which the new model was brought to the market.

When Maurice Olley visited Rolls-Royce in October 1934, just as the first twelve was being readied for the road, he found its engine "not silent but smoother than any twelve I have seen. I should say as good as the 16 Cadillac, but not better." Added Olley, "General appearance of engine is complicated but mechanical. Since this is scheduled for the large car, cost has not received any consideration." An example was the aluminium cylinder head, each of which had 74 drillings, 25 of which were for screwed-in steel core plugs of five different sizes.

This was typical of the approach taken throughout the engine and indeed the car. Wrote Ian Lloyd, "Little attempt had been made to produce an economic design. The Phantom III was the result of an all-out attempt to regain technical supremacy rather than an attempt to control costs." Rolls did have a cost-accounting system, but it kicked in after a new model's production began, not before. As a consequence for Rolls-Royce the PIII was "the most disastrous model financially which they had ever made."

The chassis alone was priced at £1,850 in 1936; bodied as a seven-passenger limousine a Phantom III cost £2,600. In spite of its unladen weight of 5,800lb the PIII offered acceleration that *The Autocar* called "thrilling" and "amazing". It accelerated from nought to 60mph in 16.8 seconds and to 70 in 24.4 seconds, timings that few non-sporting cars achieved. It was capable of 73mph in third gear and 89mph in fourth. Top speed rose to 100mph in 1938 when changes to the engine's timing and porting raised its output from 165 to 180bhp in the Series D models.

In 1937 a lighter 'Continental' version was prototyped

but not proceeded with; by the end of that year sales were no better than three cars per week and forward development of the PIII was terminated. When production stopped in 1938 only 727 had been made.[8] The last cars languishing at British agents were shipped to J.S. Inskip in New York to be sold to Americans, who were not yet at war.

Acquired for the use of no fewer than 131 titled owners, this first Rolls-Royce V12 had all the makings of magnificence. Certainly those owners received a car whose price inadequately compensated Rolls for the cost of making it. It didn't help that it was rushed to market by the company's chief, former head of sales Arthur Sidgreaves. "The Sales Department at Rolls-Royce were pushing the Design Department too hard," wrote Wilton Oldham; "consequently the model was put on the market before all the teething troubles were overcome." Its tappet idiosyncrasies were exacerbated by a marked tendency to overheat.

Oldham, himself a PIII owner, added that "Where the Phantom III is to be criticised in its design, is that no real thought was ever given to the time when an overhaul would have to be done and the question arose of having to dismantle and re-assemble it." Indeed, Rolls-Royce never got around to preparing a service manual for this, its most complex car by far. All in all, Wilton Oldham concluded, "The Phantom III is probably the most

Fine-pitched helical gears at the nose of the Rolls-Royce PIII crankshaft drove the single central camshaft and accessories. aero engine practice was followed in the positioning and firing of two spark plugs per cylinder, the driver having the option of using either or both systems to choice. **(Sir Henry Royce Memorial Foundation)**

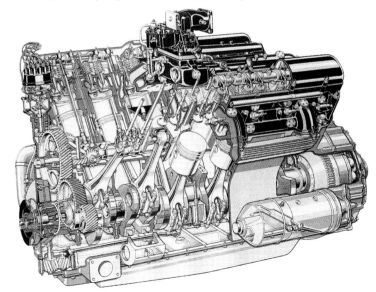

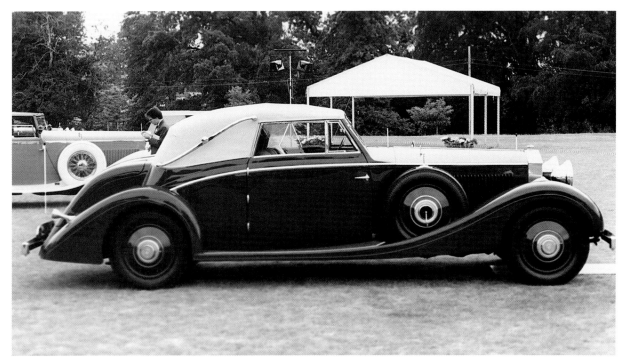

Eminently suited to powering the most elegant carriages in the Rolls-Royce range, especially after its output was raised to 180bhp for 1938, the Rolls-Royce PIII suffered from being launched prematurely to a demanding market. It thus gained a controversial reputation among Rolls-Royce automobiles.

controversial model which Rolls-Royce Ltd have ever made; it has been called 'Best of the Best' by some owners who possess and love the marque; it has also been described as the most diabolical car that has ever been made!" Sixty years would pass before Rolls again essayed a twelve.

Anyone viewing the PIII launch as hasty would be horrified by the timetable set for a comparable project by the new proprietor of Britain's Lagonda in June 1935. A City *Wunderkind* at the age of only 29, Alan P. Good made a bid for Lagonda, then in receivership, that trumped that of Rolls-Royce. A maker of quality cars with a sporting edge, Lagonda had been in business since 1898 at premises near Staines Bridge over the Thames River. Good and his managing director Richard Watney recruited as chief engineer none other than Walter Owen Bentley, who was thrilled to be designing cars again after his chiefly decorative role at Bentley Motors following its acquisition by Rolls-Royce in 1931.

The Irish-born Good paid a total of £71,500 for Lagonda and its stores and committed to raising a quarter of a million pounds sterling to fund its revival. He referred

to this when he gathered his 25-strong staff together and delivered their standing orders. "We are going to build the best car in the world," Good told them, "and have just two years to do it in. That is your part of the job – mine is to find the money." The latter was a relief to Bentley, who found the company's Staines plant "a dilapidated wreckage, and I was thankful that responsibility neither for rebuilding and expanding the works, nor the finances, were mine". But Bentley's job was to meet the two-year timetable, imposed by Good because he knew his capital wouldn't hold out much longer.

Walter Bentley and his team had to begin their work in "an ancient tumbledown shed" in which "spiders and water fell freely about us." They also had to contemplate making their engine on equipment for which the word 'antiquated' would be charitable. Lagonda's big six was produced for them by Meadows; nothing on this scale had been made there previously. In 1936 the Staines machine shop was effectively sold by Alan Good to F. Wyndham Hewitt, who carried out independent contract work as well as machining for Lagonda. Hewitt was later to say that he was "amazed at their temerity in even attempting to make a top-quality car on the equipment available."

In spite of these handicaps W.O. Bentley's reputation was such that he was able to recruit an outstanding team to build his new Lagonda. An engineer who worked for both Henry Royce and Walter Bentley found them both "very much concerned with the final details of their designs, the 99 per cent perspiration component of

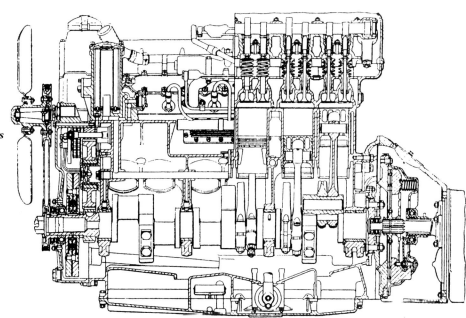

Britain's Lagonda, anointed by its new proprietor Alan Good as a fresh challenger at the top of the marketplace, powered its entry with a new 4.5-litre V12 designed by a team under Walter O. Bentley. The drawing shows a longitudinal section of the engine in which such details as the oil filler and gearbox attachment are not representative.

genius, and both obviously had the remaining one per cent too. Both had the quality of great determination. Sir Henry seemed the more extreme and intolerant, W.O. the more human and tolerant and I think the more balanced. He had the gift of inspiring affection as well as respect in those who worked for him." Several came from his old Bentley team, including Charles Sewell, Eric Easter and Frank Ayto, while engineers from Rolls-Royce were Leslie Stark and Stewart Tresilian. William G.J. 'Willie' Watson also worked as a designer under Bentley.

Middlesex-born Tresilian, a talented engineer and Bugatti enthusiast, significantly influenced the design of Lagonda's engine. The tall, bespectacled designer agreed with Bentley that with Rolls-Royce plumping for a vee-twelve, Lagonda had no option but to do likewise if it wanted to challenge 'The Best Car in the World'. It also suited Bentley's goal for the new model, which was "mechanical refinement and silence combined with turbine-like power, particularly in the higher speed range." A twelve, he said, reflecting the view of L.H. Pomeroy, "would provide us with the advantage of the highest possible number of impulses per mile, an important factor in a town carriage at low speed." Displacement was modest at 4,480cc with unfashionably short-stroked dimensions of 75 x 84.5mm.

Stewart Tresilian pressed for aluminium for the block and heads, following Derby practice, but this was rejected as a development risk too far for the understaffed team. As well, vibration-damping iron was more certain to produce the ineffable refinement that

Bentley desired. By July 1936 the drawings of the heads and block were ready, soon to be cast by Midland Motor Cylinder. In the style of his eponymous company, Bentley cast the sides of the block open and closed them with aluminium access plates. He set the bank angle at 60° and offset the right bank 27.9mm forward to facilitate side-by-side connecting rods – a simplifying departure from the PIII's design.

The bottom of the Lagonda cylinder block was cut off on the centreline of the crankshaft, which was carried in four 63.5mm main bearings. Each of their massive caps was retained by four studs and nuts. The cylinders separated by main bearings were on a 117.5mm centreline spacing while those between bearings could be spaced more closely at 92.1mm. Made of Nitralloy to facilitate hardening of its bearing surfaces, the forged crankshaft had bolted-on counterweights at its centre and between the end pairs of cylinders. To ease the burden of the counterweight the crank throws were made hollow and given aluminium plugs into which the various oil passages were drilled. Closing the bottom end was a deep aluminium casting with a detachable bottom cover that carried baffles and one-way valves to keep oil at the pickup under braking and acceleration.

Like Rolls's twelve, Lagonda's had a large-diameter vibration damper at the nose of the crank, hidden inside the timing case. Behind it was a helical gear that drove a large central gear which turned two more gears near the tops of the cylinder banks. Sprockets driven by these gears powered short double-roller chains to the single

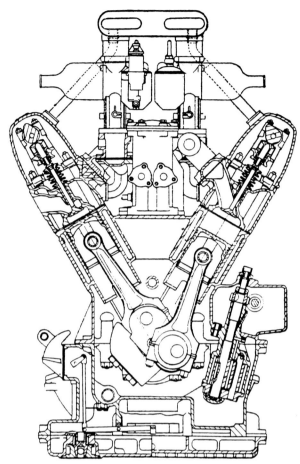

An early drawing of the Lagonda V12 showed its aluminium connecting rods and single oil pump, replaced before production began with a dual pump that lubricated the engine's accessories at lower pressure than the main and rod bearings. Carburation was by twin SU downdraft units.

Detail drawings show the mushroom-type cam follower used in the Lagonda vee-twelve and depict, as well, the manner in which exhaust gases heated a copper hot spot underneath each carburettor.

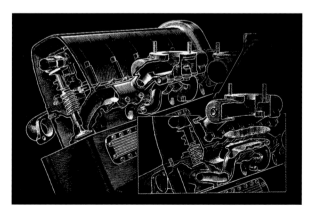

camshaft above each head.[9] Sheet-steel carriers for the Weller-type spring-blade chain tensioner also served to hold the upper sprockets in place when the heads were removed – an engineering first for an overhead-cam engine. A short chain from the left-hand idler turned a shaft that drove the water pump, at the front, and the generator toward the rear.

At the middle of this accessory shaft a skew gear drove the oil pumps in their own niche in the sump. Pumps were in the plural because one supplied only the main and rod bearings at a pressure of 70psi, while the other lubricated all other engine functions at the lower pressure of 15psi. A modern touch was the main pressure delivery through drillings in the block instead of the added-on piping others were still using. By May of 1939, when the twelve's firing order was changed, all engines enjoyed 70psi delivery from both pumps and wider big-end bearings and journals. Only later was a restriction discovered downstream of the pressure-relief valves that was blocking oil flow; Lagonda modified customer engines to relieve this constraint.[10]

Availability of a generous flow of oil was important because Bentley and Tresilian had elected to use connecting rods forged of aluminium whose big ends rubbed directly on their hardened 57.2mm journals without the intervention of bearing shells. Chosen for its lightness, aluminium was also used by Standard, Jaguar and Aston Martin for connecting rods.[11] The usual alloy included copper, magnesium and manganese. With aluminium expanding more with heat than steel, this meant that the running clearance would open from those of a cold engine, passing more oil. The pump had to be able to cope. As well, clearance with a cold engine had to be tight, but not too tight – a delicate balancing act. Small-end lubrication was by splash, against gudgeon pins that floated in the Specialloid pistons and were retained by circlips. Four rings were above the pin on the flat-topped, full-skirted aluminium piston.

Bathtub-shaped combustion chambers slightly overlapped the cylinder bores longitudinally to make more room for the valves, which were placed in line. The chamber opened out around the 40.1mm inlet valve to improve its ability to breathe; the exhaust valve measured 33.7mm. Twin coil springs closed the valves, which were opened by mushroom-topped tappets that had radiused tops and so were prevented from rotating. They slid in phosphor-bronze guides in a bolted-on aluminium carrier that held the cast camshaft in seven bearings. Valve clearance was adjusted by a screw and lock nuts at the bottom of each tappet. Skew gears at the tails of the camshafts drove Delco Remy distributors for the ignition, which was dedicated to each bank.

Smooth-flowing exhaust manifolding, with a central outlet, showed the benefit of racing experience. Each bank supplied its own piping and silencer. Two passages in each head diverted some exhaust gases to warm a copper-sheet hot spot below the carburettor that served that head. On each bank a special SU downdraft instrument fed a log-type manifold with two passages to another log, partially recessed in the head that supplied the inlet ports. The first engine ran on a single downdraft Stromberg carburettor like that used by Rolls-Royce. Bentley hoped to use this in production, but Rolls paid Lagonda the compliment of applying commercial pressure to deny it to the Staines company.

The difference between gross and net horsepower can perhaps be invoked to gain an appreciation of the Lagonda's power ratings. While publicly the engine was said to develop 180bhp at 5,500rpm, actual power curves showed a peak of 157bhp at 5,000 with the standard compression ratio of 7.0:1. "The V12 would run happily up to 6,000rpm," Bentley recalled, "and was still quiet at this speed." Net torque was 209lb-ft at 2,000rpm.

Road testers found that Bentley-bred horses were real percherons. In March, 1938, a month after production began, *The Autocar* tried a saloon on the shortest chassis of 124in; the others were 132 and 138in. Weighing 4,435lb unladen, their Lagonda V12 sprinted to 60mph in 12.9sec, with second gear taking it to 63mph. Top speed was timed at 103.45mph. At Brooklands that October Earl Howe sensationally covered 101.5 miles in an hour in spite of a 2½-minute stop to change a tyre, albeit helped by the built-in jacking system.

"The twelve cylinders made it very smooth running as well as quiet," said renowned car connoisseur Briggs Cunningham of his open Lagonda, "and the chassis was excellent with good roadholding." "The V12 in its brisker form," wrote Dennis May of the short-chassis car, "was

An imposing sight under the bonnet with its cast-aluminium camshaft covers, the Lagonda twelve developed 180bhp gross and 157bhp net. It suited drivers who were prepared to rev it to get the best performance.

the fastest closed or convertible car on the British market in the immediate pre-war period." This was underlined by the performance of its Rapide version with skimpier but still luxurious drophead bodywork as introduced at the October 1939 Earls Court show. May credited it with a top speed of 112mph.

Assessing a Rapide, Brian Palmer found that "a steady turbine-like build-up of speed is the order, punctuated only by gearchanges" and that "70–80mph was an easy cruising gait on main roads." Trying a Lagonda twelve in

Lagonda's new twelve was put through its paces at Brooklands by racing driver Earl Howe. Here the new twelve was in the foreground next to one of Lagonda's sixes which it comfortably outperformed. Within an hour Howe covered 101.5 miles with the new model.

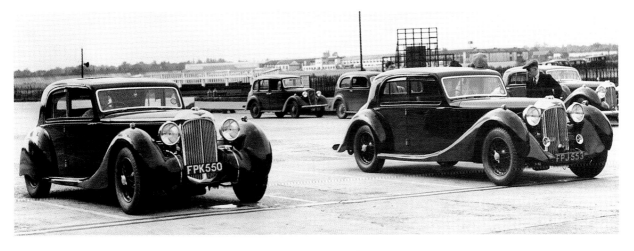

Drivers who were willing to use the Lagonda vee-twelve to the full found its performance outstanding, especially in lighter short-wheelbase models such as this handsome drophead styled by Frank Feeley.

1991, Mike McCarthy said driving it was like "cream, pure cream, double, not whipped, just gently poured." In his view "the Lagonda V12 Rapide could be regarded as the pinnacle, the ultimate, of pre-war British motoring achievement, both technically and visually" – paying a deserved compliment to the body designs of Frank Feeley.

The ultimate in rakish pre-war Lagonda V12s was represented by two open sports cars that the company prepared to compete at Le Mans in 1939. Although Walter Bentley, amply experienced at Le Mans, had misgivings about the effort, he and his crew brought great experience to the preparation of their pair of twelves.

Walter Bentley was more modest in assessing his V12 as "a good luxury semi-sporting car with quite considerable power. But it was by no means perfect," he added, "even after a year of production. The main trouble was that it was produced in a hurry and under management pressure. Also the power of the V12 was not good low down, where it is most wanted, on British roads anyway." Historian Anthony Blight thought the Lagonda's design "was a strange mixture of decision and hesitation, ambition and humility, advance and retreat, as if every feature identified with high performance had been deliberately neutralised by its opposite." Ironically, these very dichotomies were responsible for the engine's remarkable versatility.

Lack of low-rev power was a not a problem for the two open two-seaters that Lagonda built to compete at Le Mans in 1939. Weighing only 3,025lb they had lighter engines, with sumps cast of magnesium and lowered to hold more oil, topped by a quartet of SU carburettors.[12] A higher compression ratio of 8.8:1 and other tuning tweaks brought net power to 206bhp (220bhp gross) at 5,500rpm and torque to 225lb-ft at 4,000rpm.[13] Special American valve springs allowed them to rev safely to 6,500.

Though preparation was hasty, it was also thorough. The combined experience of W.O. Bentley and Lagonda contributed to a smooth run to third and fourth places at

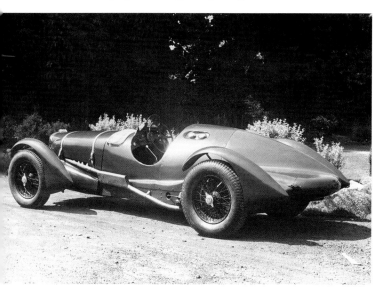

The two Lagondas more than repaid the effort made by their creators with finishes in third and fourth places at Le Mans in 1939, in spite of their hasty preparation. This was the fourth-placed car of Selsdon and Waleran. Had Lagonda competed again in 1940, shorter-wheelbase cars would have been built.

Le Mans in spite of the breakage of all but a handful of the special valve springs. The racing car's pace was highlighted by a lap of Brooklands at 127.70mph in August – just before war's outbreak.

Here, then, was a magnificent motorcar still in its swaddling clothes that had come amazingly close to meeting the demanding objective set by Alan Good. In its brief production life the more sporting models dominated with 113 made on the short wheelbase. One of these was a magnificent streamlined coupé with a Le Mans engine, bodied in aluminium by Lancefield, the prototype of a £2,000 high-speed grand-touring car. Sixty twelves were built on the medium-length chassis and a dozen on the long wheelbase, bringing the pre-war total to 185 cars. Production ceased on 26 September 1939, though cars were available for sale into 1940.

Lagonda's first post-war catalogue listed the V12. Two were made initially, one a handsome coupé by H.J. Mulliner. "The sales people were very keen that we should market it again," recalled W.O. Bentley, who volunteered however that he accepted "the entire blame" for its failure to revive: "I was very keen to drop the V12. I didn't think there would be a market for that kind of car. But how wrong I was! By lightening the frame and improving the steering, by modifying the camshafts to produce more power low down, and a few other modifications, we could have had a car to stand without disgrace alongside other high-performance cars in the higher price range, anyway for quite a few years after the war." Bentley, who died in 1971 at the age of 83, lived long enough to see Lagonda take another stab at the vee-twelve – with far less satisfactory results.

Britain's vee-twelve-developing engineers had not been altogether unaware of parallel activities in other parts of Europe. In 1934, for example, a team of engineers from Derby paid a call at 36 Boulevard Gambetta in Issy-les-Moulineaux on the south-west periphery of Paris. There Gabriel Voisin took pride in showing them the remarkable vee-twelves he'd been producing for sale since 1930. By then the coming Rolls-Royce V12 was well along in development, but that wouldn't deter the egotistical Frenchman from imagining that he had influenced the great car maker's decision to build a twelve.

No greater difference could be imagined between the over-engineered Derby engine and the spare, cubist vee-twelve first displayed by Voisin at the Grand Palais in Paris in October 1929. To be sure the cubism was not so extreme as in his abandoned prototype of 1921 – this time the individual cylinder banks could be discerned – but the latest V12 from Voisin displayed his usual attention to aesthetics as well as technology. Like the big

A handsome Lagonda V12 coupé bodied by Mulliner in 1949 hinted at what might have been, had Lagonda continued with its twelve after the war. Walter Bentley, who rejected the effort of Lagonda's sales people to carry on with such a model, later admitted that he had erred.

vee-twelve he built for record-breaking in 1929[14], its cylinder banks were at 60° instead of 30° and set in direct opposition to each other. As in all his other engines – and akin to the contemporary Daimlers – Voisin remained faithful to the Knight system of twin sleeve-valves.

The Voisin twelve on show in 1929 was his Model C19, with the modest displacement of 3,860cc (64 x 100mm). Perversely, it must be said, this was far smaller than his largest current six-cylinder, the C16 and its successor the C22, which displaced 5,829cc. Rated at 100bhp at 3,900rpm, only three C19s were made, for Gabriel Voisin decided to increase the bore diameter to 72mm and the displacement to 4,886cc to cope more robustly with both the coachwork and the competition. Voisin was virulently antipathetic to the American cars that were invading France and Europe; this car was mustered as his weapon for "thrashing" the despised Americans.

Gabriel Voisin stepped back a number to C18 as the designation for his new twelve in standard touring form on a 141in wheelbase, which made its bow as the 3,860lb Diane at the Paris Salon of 1930. He also offered it in a lower underslung chassis that afforded the creation of spectacular coachwork. This came in a similar wheelbase, the C20 Simoun, and in a shorter 126.7in version – the C21 Mistral – that was usefully lighter at 3,340lb.

Of the C18 89 were made, and of the C20 and C21 30 and 40 respectively. Including the C19, this brought to 162 the number of twelves that Voisin built from 1929 to 1937, when the last C20 left Issy-les-Moulineaux. Considering the economic conditions and the price –

Introduced in 1930 to power his C18, C20 and C21 models, Gabriel Voisin's twelve had a 60° vee. Here stripped of its cylinder blocks, the 105-horsepower twelve flaunted its Knight-patent sleeve valves and, at the front of the crankshaft, a huge dynamotor.

Gabriel Voisin relied on a single central eccentric shaft to operate all the sleeve valves of his C18 vee-twelve. Their linkages were specially designed to fail safe in the event of a seized sleeve, so as to cause the minimum of damage to the engine.

almost triple that of a Type 35A Bugatti and the same as an eight-litre Hispano-Suiza – this was a more than respectable performance

Voisin founded his twelve on a shallow crankcase cut off at the bottom on the crank centreline and at the top below the mounts for a central eccentric shaft. Voisin contrived to operate all 24 sleeves from this one shaft and, as well, to design a link to the sleeves that would fail safely if a sleeve seized instead of shattering the surrounding metalwork. A triple chain from the nose of the crankshaft drove the eccentric shaft, from the centre of which a bevel gear turned a vertical Delco Remy distributor. Coupled to the crank's nose was a massive combined generator and starter that was fed 24 volts from a system that otherwise functioned on 12 volts. This eliminated the raucous clash of Bendix drive against flywheel, which Voisin rightly detested as "the noise that disgraces the automobile". Both the water pump – like Daimler eschewing thermosyphon cooling – and the fan were belt-driven.

Like Voisin's sixes, his twelve had only three main bearings. A deep cast-aluminium sump closing the underside of the crankcase was finned for cooling on its bottom surface. Mirroring its multitudes of attachment studs were those holding down the iron blocks that comprised each bank of six cylinders. Unlike the C19, which had its inlet ports on the exterior and the exhausts in its vee, the larger C18 had outside exhausts. Vertically finned manifolds were provided for groups of three cylinders, each having its own downpipe. Two Cozette DH-21 carburettors fed the inlet ports from the central

True to his architectonic principles, Gabriel Voisin produced an extremely handsome power unit for his C18, C20 and C21 models, which were produced from 1929 to 1937. This display engine showed a belt drive to its high-mounted water pump and lacked carburettors.

vee. The twelve's neat appearance was completed by cast covers for its cylinder heads that concealed the spark plugs and their wiring.

With its compression ratio of 5.5:1 the C18 twelve produced 105bhp at 3,500rpm and was capable of revving to 3,800. A more powerful engine for the low-chassis cars had 6.5:1 compression and could produce 125bhp at 3,800rpm. While the C18 had a multiple-disc clutch, the C20 and C21 had single-disc clutches driving through a massive four-speed transmission in unit with the engine.

Under Voisin, André Lefèbvre and Marius Bernard were allies in the creation of these cars, some of which are among the most striking ever conceived. While the former left to design Citroëns, the latter worked with Gabriel Voisin through the 1930s in the engineer's drive to create what he called "a steam car activated by an internal combustion engine" – a good definition of the sensation that a twelve-cylinder could evoke. In 1937 this led him to initiate the design of a model confusingly called the V12L, powered by an in-line twelve. Conceived to shift more of the engine's weight rearward in the chassis to improve balance and handling, the V12L used two Voisin sixes coupled together to provide 5,988cc (76 x 110mm). Only four such cars were produced in 1937 and '38.

If Voisin had a French rival in the production of motorcars of the most outré aspect, that rival was certainly Bucciali. Builders of extraordinary automobiles, front-driven from 1926, the Bucciali brothers used one of Voisin's vee-twelves to power what Griff Borgeson called "the last and probably the most gorgeous of all the front-

Under the low bonnet of a C20 Simoun of 1930, Voisin's V12 showed its twin downdraft carburettors and, between them, the distributor whose wiring was concealed by a cover along each cylinder bank. Its exhaust manifolds were finned for heat dissipation.

wheel-drive Buccialis, the TAV12." With its body by Saoutchik it was one of the super-stunners of the 1932 Paris Salon. Of Corsican ancestry, the Buccialis flattered the Voisin engine by claiming 180 horsepower for it. Their search for a suitable engine continued; reportedly they were unhappy with the sleeve-valve Voisin's tendency to puff blue smoke.

Even more short-lived than the fanciful Buccialis was the contemporaneous Lorraine twelve. For the second time Marius Barbarou sought to translate the aeronautical achievements of Lorraine-Dietrich into a twelve for the road. Lorraine-Dietrichs won the third and fourth 24-hour races at Le Mans in 1925 and 1926 – interrupting a string of Bentley successes – and took all three podium places in the latter year. After 1928, when the cars were known simply as Lorraines, Barbarou began work on a new V12 that he hoped would enter production, unlike his aborted effort of 1919.

When word of his new car leaked out in 1931 it was expected to be something special, a new Lorraine that would both serve the luxury-car market and challenge again at Le Mans – an earlier version of the Lagonda twelve. Each bank of six cylinders was topped by an overhead camshaft and sparked by aviation-inspired dual ignition. A duplex carburettor fed its 4,984cc (72 x 102mm). Again, however, Lorraine balked at commissioning production. This time the company's twelve didn't even appear at the Salon. Though its last car was made in 1934, Lorraine carried on as an aero engine producer.

As in World War I, so too in the 1930s Lorraine's main French rival in the aviation-engine field was Hispano-Suiza. Great engines emerged from the latter's factory at Bois-Colombes, in the Seine's sweeping bight on the north-west outskirts of Paris. There Marc Birkigt continued as technical director and owner of 51 per cent of the company's shares, thanks to wealth accrued from royalties on the manufacture of his designs. His principal technical lieutenants were drawing-office chief Ferdinand Fouré, head of product development Edmond Bellinger and chief test engineer Louis Massuger, whose skills had supported Hispano since its racing days. François Victor Bazin was the sculptor of the marque's elegant flying-stork mascot, adapted from the badge of French flying ace Georges Guynemer, whose Spad was Hispano-powered.

During the 1920s Hispano's six-cylinder H6 of 6,597cc (100 x 140mm) brooked few rivals as a powerful luxury tourer with sporting attributes. As the passion for straight-eights grew, however, and as the noise emissions of the overhead-cam six became less acceptable, workaholic Birkigt decided that Hispano-Suiza needed a

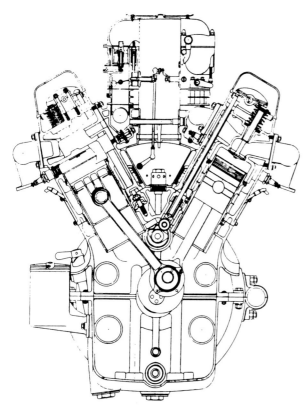

With 'square' cylinder dimensions of 100 x 100mm Marc Birkigt gave his Hispano-Suiza's V12 the proud capacity of 9.4 litres. Designed as the Type 68 and marketed as the J12, the magnificent new Hispano engine was introduced at the Paris Salon in 1931.

multi-cylinder engine. This was no committee edict, the designer's grandson recalling that "Marc Birkigt decided what should be made and how." The sales staff's job was to market what Marc wrought, all of which were sold as chassis for the attention of custom body makers.

Designed as the Type 68, Birkigt's twelve was marketed as the J12 on four wheelbases: 134.6in, intermediate choices of 146.0 or 149.6in and a long chassis of 157.5in. In unit with the engine and a single-disc clutch, its transmission offered three speeds. The lower two were all but redundant in the face of the massive torque of the J12's vee-twelve of 9,425cc. With contemptuous disregard of the taxation by cylinder-bore

In many respects resembling aviation techniques rather than automotive design ideas, the Hispano-Suiza J12 had steel cylinders screwed into its aluminium combustion chambers. Main bearings were nominally seven in number although the rearmost main was split to straddle the gear drive to the single central camshaft.

size used in important Hispano markets, Birkigt kept his H6's bore diameter for his new twelve and married it with a similar stroke to create a 'square' engine. Unlike Lagonda, he didn't exploit this to aim for high revolutions. No J12 engine was rated for its maximum power at more than 3,000rpm.

Contemplating calm, quiet luxury-car propulsion by a slow-revving engine, Marc Birkigt had no reason to continue using the aircraft-inspired overhead cams of his H6. On the other hand he wanted to retain the efficiency of overhead valves, so he operated them by pushrods and rocker arms from a single central camshaft gear-driven from the rear of the crankshaft. Seven bearings supported the camshaft. Sliding in guides clamped in place, the tappets contacted the cam lobes with roller faces. Aluminium pushrods operated rockers to vertical valves that were closed by twin coil springs. Valve timing gave no overlap and very early exhaust-valve opening as follows:

Inlet Opens   7° ATDC   Exhaust opens   60° BBDC
Inlet closes 45° ABDC   Exhaust closes 5° ATDC

Short and elegant with no appreciable multiplication factor, the rockers lacked any provision for clearance adjustment. This was provided by making the valve stem hollow and screwing into it, for adjustment, a threaded member. The collar at its top was locked in place by radial serrations that matched those on the surface of the coil-spring retainer.[15]

All the Hispano's major castings were of aluminium by Montupet, with the cylinder blocks pressure-enamelled to seal any porosity. Bolted to an aluminium crankcase, the blocks were relatively short, holding water around the upper halves of the bores. Housing six cylinders, each block was of integral-head monobloc construction, with nitrided steel cylinders screwed into the combustion chambers as were those of the H6. Sealed at their

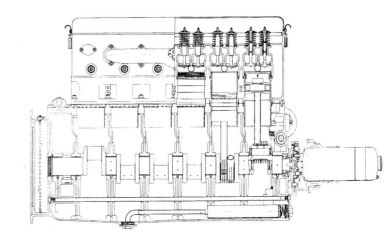

peripheries where they mated with the top of the crankcase, these wet liners were spigoted deeply into the latter. The right-hand cylinders were shifted 26mm forward of those on the left to permit side-by-side rods on the 55mm crank journals.

Machined from a 970lb forged-steel billet, the crankshaft weighed 70lb. With exemplary stiffness by virtue of its large 70mm main bearings and the substantial journal overlap given by its short stroke of 100mm, the crank needed only a small vibration damper behind the dynamotor at its nose. Nominally the counterweight-free crank was carried in seven main bearings, but in fact there were eight with two bearings at the rear flanking the cam-drive gearing.

Closing the twelve's bottom end was a deep aluminium sump into which the main-bearing caps were integrally cast, thus marrying with the crankcase at the crankshaft's centreline. They were snugged together by studs reaching down from the block to the bottom of the sump. At the front a vane-type oil pump supplied a central tubular gallery below the main bearings.

Throughout the Hispano-Suiza twelve its design and execution bordered on the exquisite. Its aluminium castings were ultra-thin and its steel components pared to an ineffable minimum. Nowhere was this more obvious than in the design of its connecting rods. Machined from the solid, the 250mm rods had tubular shanks, formed by drilling down from the top with the resulting aperture in the small end left open. Drillings admitted oil into the rod's shank to lubricate the small-end bushing.

The rods' big ends were unique. Meshing teeth formed on both the rod and the big-end cap were drilled so the cap could be secured by two tapered pins, inserted through the teeth along the engine's longitudinal axis. Though demanding impeccable machining skills, this was an ultra-light configuration completed by ribbing for strength around the big end. The latter's journal was 55mm in diameter.

Full-skirted aluminium pistons carried four rings above the steel gudgeon pins, which were held in place by aluminium plugs. Initially flat-topped to give a compression ratio of 5.0:1, pistons were also supplied with a raised crown to give a 6.0:1 ratio. The combustion chamber was fully open, bowed outward next to the valves to improve gas flow, and fired by dual ignition with horizontal plugs on both sides of the chamber.

At the rear of the engine, animated by the camshaft drive, two vertical SEV distributors sparked the plugs. Each was a 12-cylinder distributor serving both banks; not for Hispano the concept of limping home on one bank alone. Wiring to all the plugs went under a cover down the central vee, from which the wires to the outer plugs passed through apertures in the head to give an

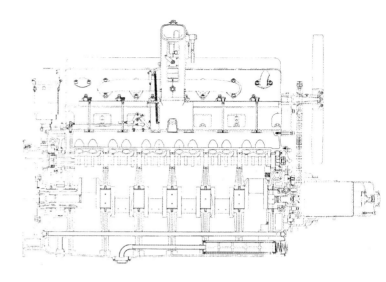

Like Voisin, Birkigt elected to provide both generation and starting by means of a single dynamotor at the nose of the crankshaft. Carburation and inlet manifolding were within the central vee, each bank of cylinders having its own Hispano/Solex carburettor.

Partially dismantled, a Hispano-Suiza J12 engine showed off its fine aluminium castings by Montupet, its integral-head cylinder blocks pressure-enamelled to eliminate porosity. Multiple studs were in place on the right-hand cylinder bank, uncovered, to accept installation of the carriers for the rocker-arm shafts.

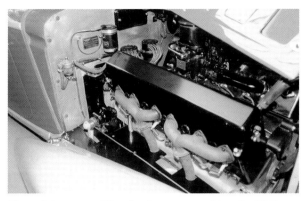

The quintessence of the classic era was achieved with the under-bonnet appearance of the Hispano-Suiza J12, sober yet ineffably powerful. It quickly drew recognition as one of the finest cars of its era or indeed of any era.

Credited as being no less luxurious than its contemporary the Rolls-Royce Phantom III but offering a more aggressively sporting performance, the Hispano-Suiza J12 established a position for the French company at the apogee of the market. For those who required even more performance an 11.3-litre longer-stroke version of the engine was available.

exceptionally neat appearance. In later engines distributors were replaced by Scintilla Vertex magnetos.

Skew gearing from the nose of the camshaft drove a cross shaft that turned the water pumps, one at each side of the crankcase. These delivered to passages in the crankcase feeding the water upward to the cylinder blocks. Water was drawn off from the front of each cylinder head. Six ports in each of the latter took exhaust gases away to two triple-branch manifolds and double downpipes. Within the vee, compact four-outlet inlet manifolds served the part-siamesed porting in each head. Each bank had its own carburettor, a single-throat Hispano/Solex Type 40IEF instrument, joined to its mate by linkages and an air-inlet casting. Cast-in passages from the exhaust ports provided inlet-manifold hot spots.

All these exterior features, topped by smooth enamelled rocker covers so precisely made that they required only front and rear clamps to retain them, were on display in chassis form at the 1931 Paris Salon. Small wonder that *Omnia* verged on incoherence when informing its readers that "Marc Birkigt's twelve-cylinder dominates the Salon and will widely disseminate the reputation of its incomparable superiority." Hispano-Suiza was on safe ground in promising its customers "*vitesse, sécurité, confort, silence, élégance*". J.R. Buckley called the Type 68 "almost certainly the most magnificent motor-car ever to be built in series production." William Boddy compared it to the Rolls-Royce Phantom III, saying that the Hispano, "while extremely flexible and quiet, delivered its performance with a trace of arrogance, so that whereas the English car was luxury personified, the car from France was of more sporting aspect."

The performance was certainly there. On the lower compression ratio the rated power was 190bhp and on the higher 220, which many felt was conservative. Torque was outstanding, on the order of 465lb-ft at 1,700rpm, while acceleration was enhanced by relatively low weight for this class of car at some 4,400lb in short-chassis form. *The Autocar* called its test car's performance "astonishing" and "amazing", recording acceleration from rest to 60mph in 12sec, to 70 in 15 and to 80mph in 19sec. With Brooklands lapped at a timed 95mph, top speed was comfortably in excess of 100mph. Although acknowledging that a car costing £3,500 would only be of practical interest to a wealthy minority, the weekly called the Type 68 "unquestionably one of the world's finest cars in both design and performance on the road."

Marked by a broader radiator – not for Hispano the cooling problems of its rivals – the J12 was bodied by all the greats of the era from Chapron to Franay, Million-Guiet to Letourneur et Marchand, Vanvooren to Binder,

Saoutchik to Kellner and the flamboyant Fernandez et Darrin. One owner was so taken with the engine's appearance that he specified glass inserts in the bonnet of his J12. The best bodies on this superb chassis were described as achieving "restrained dignity overlaying the veiled impression of enormous power." Among the world's great cars only the J-Type Duesenberg and the Bugatti Royale – the latter at twice the price – could be ranked as rivals. Such was the confidence of the French company in its product that it thought it unnecessary to have its name visible on any part of its exterior.

An even more potent Hispano V12 was created at the request of Raoul Dutry, director of the French railways; he had inspired the creation of the Royale-powered Bugatti railcar. He saw in the mighty Type 68 the makings of another railcar engine. To fulfil this mission Marc Birkigt lengthened his engine's stroke to enlarge its displacement to 11,310cc (100 x 120mm). Under France's tax rules this was a 66CV engine, the country's largest save for the 72CV Bugatti Type 41. It developed 250bhp at a still-lazy 3,000rpm and 557lb-ft of torque at 1,700rpm. Here was an engine with which to conjure, rivalled in its era solely by the supercharged SJ Duesenberg.

Only a few J12s were powered by this Type 68-bis engine. Among them were the Hispanos of wealthy American racing driver Whitney Straight and Italy's Count Carlo Felice Trossi. Driving one such, Cecil Clutton credited it with a "mighty, effortless surge of power which completely grips the imagination." A 68-bis may also have powered the stunning streamlined Xenia built on a Hispano chassis for André Dubonnet.

Britain's Peter Hampton installed a 68-bis in his Saoutchik cabriolet on the 146in chassis. Shrugging off its weight of 4,750lb, the acceleration of this magnificent carriage was timed by *The Autocar* at 11.5sec to 60mph from rest 25 years after it was built. This was in spite of taking 4sec to 30mph out of respect for its clutch. The Hispano reached 100mph in 35.7sec and returned a fuel consumption of 9mpg, somewhat thirstier than the usual 11mpg. "Except when the engine is started from cold there are no individual noises under the bonnet," wrote Ronald Barker, "and the unit is quiet as a club library."

From September 1931 to November 1938 the Bois Colombes factory produced 114 vee-twelves. Ten were factory test cars, 47 on the short chassis, 44 on the medium-length chassis and only 13 on the longest, showing a distinct slant toward the more sporting configurations. Reversing the sequence followed by Daimler, in 1934 Birkigt cannily introduced his K6, an in-line six derived from one bank of his vee-twelve. With dimensions of 100 x 110mm, its capacity was 5,184cc. Unlike the twelve it had a detachable head – Hispano's first – and simpler provisions for its wet cylinder liners. However, with French Rail's Raoul Dutry becoming armaments minister, car production was stopped at Bois Colombes after 1938 to concentrate on aero engines. One of the last of the 204 K6 Hispano-Suizas was acquired by Dutry.

Its cylinder capacity made the J12 Hispano Europe's largest twelve-cylinder auto engine in the years before World War II. In 68-bis form it was even bigger than the largest sprint Delage, the DH of 1923, and a stunning 50 per cent more voluminous than America's largest twelve of the classic era, the Pierce-Arrow. But Germany has not yet been heard from. Car builders there were said to take some pride in a Maybach curiously called the 'Zeppelin'. Could anything smack more of grandiosity?

Chapter 6 Footnotes

[1] Pomeroy was quoted by engineer Maurice Platt, then a journalist at *The Motor*. The psychology he promulgated has changed little over the years.

[2] Initially simply the Double-Six, it was given the '50' suffix in 1928 when a smaller sister was introduced.

[3] In later Double-Six 50 engines this feature was deleted.

[4] Brian Smith wrote that the change from sleeves to poppet valves was made "with the concurrence of His Majesty".

[5] Regrettably Daimler's production records were bombed out in 1941. Daimler authority Brian Smith has estimated, from coachwork records and other sources, that Daimler built "something approaching 150–200 Double-Sixes".

[6] While two of these were scrapped, one was rehabilitated and sold.

[7] Used since the 1920s in Rolls-Royce aero engines, this feature was shared with the Napier Lion and Maybach's roadgoing V12s. Although it usefully lightened the crankshaft, it also provided traps for sludge that could menace efficient lubrication.

[8] Quoted by Malcolm Bobbitt, the figure is credited to the chassis-record research of Nick Whitaker and Steve Stuckey.

[9] An early drawing of the engine suggests that it was initially built with longer chains running all the way from the half-speed gear to the camshafts.

[10] This discovery was made during wartime development of the V12 as a potential engine for a Vosper-built attack hydroplane. It was only used in the prototype, the production boats being Ford-V8-powered.

[11] After the War, Bentley would say that he'd concluded that aluminium rods did not have a weight advantage over steel.

[12] Four SUs had given good results during the standard engine's development but had been rejected by Bentley as too hard to synchronise.

[13] Equipped with as many as six downdraft SUs, Lagonda twelves are said to have been developed subsequently to as much as 275bhp.

[14] This car and engine are described in Chapter 9.

[15] This was a neat and unique technological transfer of the adjustment method used for the direct-acting tappets of overhead-cam Hispano engines.

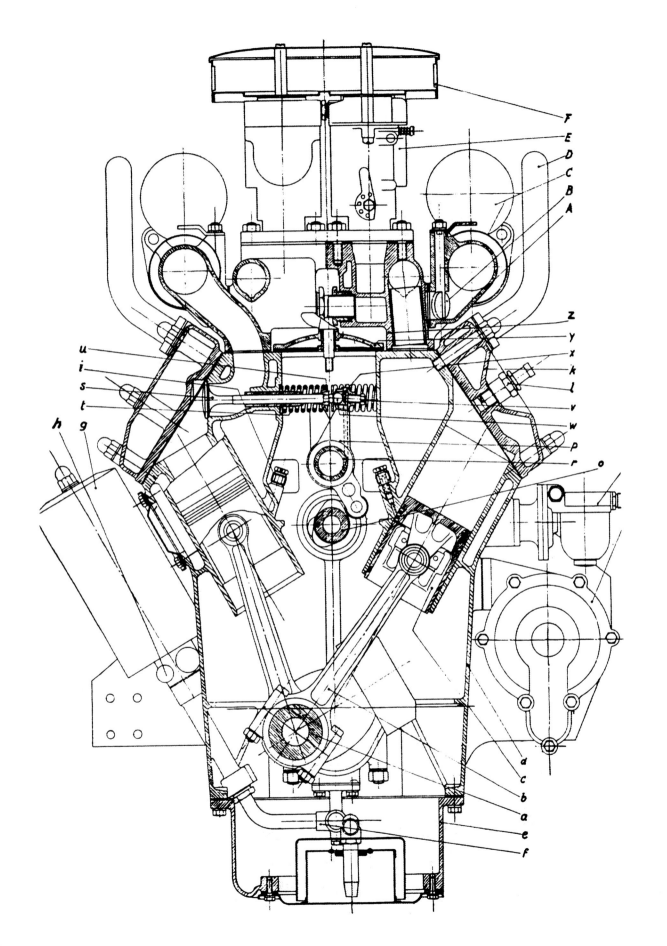

F
E
D
C
B
A

z
y
x
k
l
v
w
P
r
o

u
i
s
t
g

h
g

d
c
b
a
e
f

TEUTONIC TWELVES

"The Tatra company can always be depended upon to have one of the most interesting exhibits in any automobile exhibition at which they are showing. The present instance was no exception," praised *The Automobile Engineer* of the Czech company's stand at the Paris Salon in November 1930. They'd come to expect the exceptional from Hans Ledwinka, an Austrian who'd been with Tatra since 1897 apart from two sojourns with other firms, one to explore steam-powered vehicles in 1902–05 and the other to create a new range for Steyr in 1916–21.

Renowned for its railway carriages as the Nesselsdorf Wagon Factory, Ledwinka's employer adopted the Tatra name for its products in 1919 in honour of the highest peaks – reaching 8,700 feet – in the mountain range that snaked just to the east of the works. In 1927 the name of the company became 'Tatra' as well. Since 1923, when Hans Ledwinka introduced his radical T11, the name had stood for advanced design that was creative and at one and the same time practical. The T11 had its flat-twin air-cooled engine at the front, with its gearbox bolted to a central tube that was joined to the final-drive gear casing and swing-axle rear suspension. This backbone-type frame became the hallmark of whole generations of Tatra cars and trucks.

The T11 and its successors helped move Tatra into a prominent position among the dozen or so companies making motor vehicles in Czechoslovakia between the wars. With its products among those most recognised and purchased in other lands, Tatra decided it would do no harm to aspire to a prestige vehicle that would buff its reputation to a high gloss and appeal as well to the Czech

great and near great. This initiative was supported by Tatra's owner, Baron Hans von Ringhoffer, who moved in the circles that might appreciate such a car. At Paris in 1930 he and Ledwinka posed proudly next to a display chassis that showed that their backbone-chassis concept was by no means limited to small cars.

The Tatras T70 and T80, launched simultaneously, were anything but small. They shared a wheelbase of 149.6in and, with the exception of some front-suspension differences, were identical apart from their engines. The T70 was powered by an in-line overhead-cam six of 3.4 litres which, said Tatra, could be swapped in only two hours with the alternative V12 that made it a T80. In both instances the crankcase was strong enough to cope with the entire bending and torsional loadings that were imposed on the chassis, of which it was an integral element.

Cast of high-silicon aluminium, the crankcase that fulfilled this demanding requirement had to be – and was – of unusual design. It was shaped as a completely enclosed barrel into which the crankshaft was inserted from the rear through a central tunnel and into the foremost of eight main bearings. At the bottom of the tunnel were the lower halves of the main bearings, to which the upper halves were bolted down as the main-

*Opposite: **Although admittedly inspired by American V8s, engineers Fritz Fiedler and Werner Strobel at Horch innovated independently in their design of a 6.0-litre V12 for that company, launched in 1931. Horizontal valves were a feature, as were cylinder heads angled well away from the horizontal with respect to each cylinder bore.***

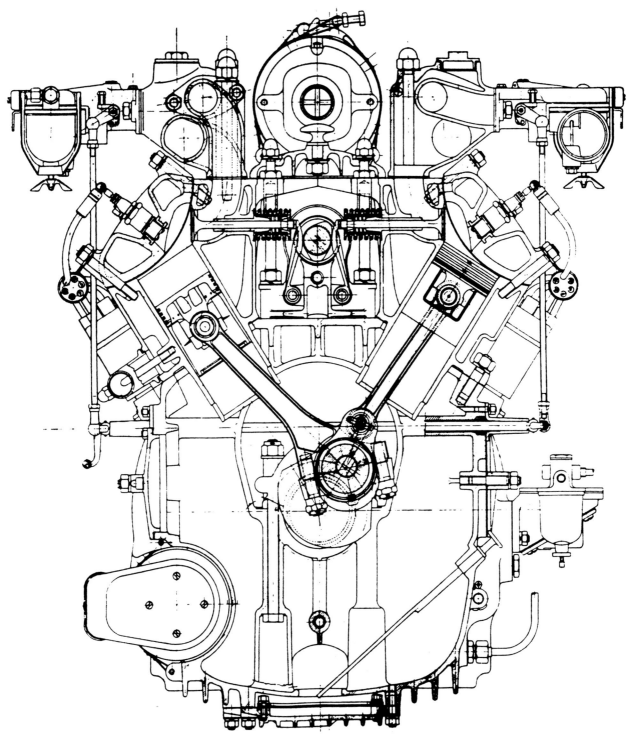

Hans Ledwinka's flair for creativity was amply on display in the cross section of his T80 V12 of 1930. Inclined at a vee angle of 65°, its cylinders were directly opposite each other thanks to the use of master and link connecting rods. A single central camshaft operated horizontally placed valves through finger followers.

bearing caps – inverting the usual arrangement. Along each side of the crankcase three large circular access ports were held in place by clamps – a hallmark of Ledwinka design.

Deeply spigoted into the upper surfaces of the crankcase were two cast-iron six-cylinder blocks at a 65°

included angle. Generously water-jacketed, the blocks contained inlet and exhaust porting that rose vertically to top surfaces that were planed off flat. Resembling such engines as the Auburn and later Packard vee-twelves, Tatra's T80 had valves placed horizontally to create a modified side-valve layout which allowed more compact combustion chambers. By virtue of its wider angle, Ledwinka's twelve was able to operate its valves directly through pivoted finger followers, working against double coil springs.

From the rear of the crankshaft, a silent chain between the rearmost main bearings drove the camshaft. Also driven from the rear were the individual six-cylinder ignition distributors for each block. The camshaft's nose drove another chain which rotated the cast six-blade fan, the single water pump and, through a shaft to the rear, the generator. The water pump's output was split to supply cool water to the base of each cylinder block, at its centre, while warm water was drawn off from the front of the heads.

Each block was topped by a high-silicon aluminium cylinder head, into which a spark plug was inserted above the centre of each chamber. Instead of the usual flat joint between head and block, Hans Ledwinka mated the two on surfaces that were sections of a cylinder. The block was the concave element, generated on a radius of 120mm, and the mating head surface was convex, nestling into the block. Cavities in the heads, above the cylinder bores, formed the main combustion chambers at a compression ratio of 5.3:1 to suit Central European fuel quality.

The T80's cylinder blocks were set directly opposite each other, thanks to Ledwinka's use of I-section master and link connecting rods. The link rods served the left-hand cylinder bank. Use of this system meant that although the engine's nominal dimensions were 75 x 113mm, its actual capacity would differ from the 5,991cc that that would delineate.[1] Flat-topped Nelson-Bohnalite aluminium pistons carried four rings above their gudgeon pins.

Each cylinder bank had its own manifolding, with inlet and exhaust logs placed next to each other in a low-profile array. Downpipes at the front led the exhaust gases away, keeping them clear of the footboards. A side-draft Zenith carburettor fed each inlet manifold. Their close synchronisation was assured by a rotating shaft that passed through the cylinder block. Tuning was more for smooth torque than potency, with 100bhp being produced at 2,500rpm and a maximum of 115bhp at 3,000rpm. The Tatra twelve could rev smoothly to 3,600rpm if required.

Although the T80's chassis weight was modest enough at 2,650lb, the imposing bodies mounted on it by

Characteristic of Hans Ledwinka's designs were the three access ports whose covers were held in place by clamps. Thanks to his use of side-draft carburettors, Ledwinka achieved a low profile for his 6.0-litre T80 V12.

Tatra itself and such coachbuilders as Josef Sodomka meant that the finished vehicles scaled nearer 5,500lb. Thus acceleration was leisurely through its four speeds to a maximum around 85mph. This was more than adequate for the luxurious Tatra's users, among whom were Czech president Tomáš Masaryk and foreign minister Edvard Beneš.

Fitted with disc or wire wheels to choice, the T80 Tatras were handsome beasts with ample space for side-mounted spares. Sodomka fitted some with two-door bodies with a distinctly sporting aspect. Priced at the equivalent in Germany of $6,800, however, and up

Designed as it was to be an integral part of the T80's tubular frame, the aluminium crankcase of its twelve-cylinder engine had to be especially robust. Production of T80 Tatras amounted to only 22 units from 1930 to 1935.

Another Czech entry in the supercar sweepstakes of the 1930s was the Walter Royal designed by Vitezslav Kumpera, introduced in 1931. Gearing at the front of its 5.9-litre twelve drove its six-bladed aluminium fan directly as well as accessories in the central vee.

against tough competition in a difficult economy, sales were not brisk abroad. In all, Tatra made 22 complete T80s from 1930 to 1935. Parts for three more cars were produced but retained as spares. Its less costly six-cylinder sister fared little better, with 65 produced of the T70 and its T70a successor. The last of these – the terminal water-cooled Tatra – was delivered in 1947 to Edvard Beneš, now the nation's president.

Having peaked in the realm of quasi-conventional cars with its T80, Tatra turned to the spectacular streamlined air-cooled models advocated by the company's new product-development chief, Erich Übelacker. In the meantime another Czech car builder had stepped into the ultra-luxury market with a vee-twelve-powered model that had even more lofty aspirations. "The twelve-cylinder Walter was beyond doubt the most elaborate and luxurious automobile that was ever produced in Czechoslovakia," wrote Hans-Heinrich von Fersen. "It was individually built by a staff of qualified aviation-engine engineers and workmen of the finest materials without regard to cost."

Although Prague's Walter had been making engines for aircraft since 1922, it was founded in 1896 and had been producing motorcycles since 1902 and cars since 1908. When in 1922 its founder Josef Walter sought other pastures, engineer Vitezslav Kumpera took over at Walter. With car production only slightly in excess of a thousand a year at the end of the 1920s, Kumpera moved

upmarket with the launch of a new range of overhead-valve Walter sixes that even included a supercharged version whose top speed of nearly 120mph made it useful in competitions.

In 1931 Vitezslav Kumpera unveiled his masterwork, the Walter Royal.[2] At least in principle and perhaps in fact it aligned two of his iron six-cylinder blocks on an aluminium crankcase at a 60° vee angle.[3] The detachable iron heads held vertical overhead valves operated by pushrods from a single central camshaft turned by helical gears. The central vee contained the generator, which with the water pump and six-bladed fan were driven from the upper gears of the front-mounted timing case. Scintilla supplied the magneto ignition – also in the central vee – and the 12-volt electrical system.

Carried in seven main bearings, the Royal's crankshaft was fully balanced both statically and dynamically and carried a large vibration damper at its nose. Cut off at the crankshaft centreline, the bottom of the crankcase was enclosed by a cast-aluminium sump with finning for oil cooling. Induction and exhaust were both on the outside of each head, with the exhaust manifold placed higher and leading the gases forward. Beneath it, on each bank, was the inlet manifold, fed by one horizontal Solex carburettor. Its fuel was supplied by an electric pump.

Adorned with its winged-W emblem, the Walter Royal was first shown abroad at Paris late in 1931. There its engine "made an exceptionally smooth-surfaced and clean impression." Its dimensions were 76 x 108mm – sharing its stroke length with the sixes – for 5,879cc. Its compression ratio at launch was a modest 5.0:1. In this form the Royal produced 120 horsepower. Installed in a conventional X-braced chassis, it drove through a four-speed transmission that made use of Maybach's vacuum-

By placing his inlet and exhaust manifolding on the outside of each bank, in the manner of Cadillac's V12, Kumpera made room in his Walter's central vee for the water pump, magneto and distributor. Beneath each bank's cover were rocker arms and pushrods from a single central camshaft.

assist patents. Coachwork by Sodomka and other leading Czech firms adorned its 141.7in wheelbase, fronted by a bold radiator wider at its top than its bottom.

With Walter's automotive jewel for the wealthy egregiously unsuited to the 1931–32 marketplace, its sales were outpaced by snails. Nevertheless Kumpera – who in the meantime started making Fiats under licence – updated his Royal. By 1934 its bore was enlarged to 82mm and its capacity to 6,844cc, changes that helped increase its compression ratio to 5.75:1. Now fed by twin downdraft Stromberg carburettors, the bigger twelve produced 140bhp at 3,200rpm.

Production of the Royal didn't greatly burden the company's aero engine builders, for experts agree that total production did not exceed a dozen units. More engines were made, however, for Walter used them to power its fast intercity coaches. For this mission a final bore enlargement (85 x 108mm) brought displacement to 7,354cc. After 1937 Walter gave up all car production to concentrate on its aero engines. The name is still alive in the Czech Republic as an aviation-engine maker, but no example of its vainglorious Royal is known to survive.

To the south in the old Austro-Hungarian Empire a car of exceptional standing had been produced since the century's first years. The Emperor Franz Joseph rode in a Gräf & Stift, as did the Archduke Franz Ferdinand at the time of his assassination, catalyst for the First World War. Renowned as 'the Austrian Rolls-Royce', Gräf & Stift cars – produced in Vienna – proudly carried as their mascot a

Respected as the most prestigious maker of automobiles in the Austro-Hungarian Empire, Gräf & Stift was near the end of its life as an auto producer in 1938 when it introduced its 4.0-litre C12. With a side-valve engine developing 110bhp, this C12 was the only such car produced by Gräf & Stift before the war.

silver lion that was every bit as prestigious as the British flying lady.

Through the 1930s Gräf & Stift delivered to order its straight-eight SP8 with an overhead-cam six-litre engine of 125 horsepower. A smaller sister eight had side valves, the solution adopted in 1938 when Gräf & Stift decided to add a vee-twelve to its range. By luxury-car standards this model, the C12, was relatively small at 4,036cc but it produced as much power – 110bhp at 3,500rpm – as the company's 4½-litre eight.

The prototype twelve was installed in a handsome side-mounted saloon with a split windscreen, still with free-standing headlamps. This remained the one and only C12, for Austria was now part of Greater Germany, where the von Schell Plan to rationalise the region's vehicle production limited Gräf & Stift to the output of trucks and coaches.

Germany herself had seen ambitious efforts to enhance prestige through the introduction of multi-cylinder engines. Saxony's Horch stole a march on its home-country rivals when, near the end of 1926, it introduced Germany's first straight-eight production model. This was

Developing 120bhp, the Horch V12 was an impressive sight under the bonnet of Type 600 and Type 670 models which were styled with considerable flair. Its recessed sparkplugs gave it a superficial similarity to Tatra's T80 V12, although the Horch was considerably more successful commercially.

engineered by Paul Daimler, who had joined the Horch-Werke AG in 1923. Daimler moved laterally from Berlin engine-maker Argus, which like Horch was majority-owned and controlled by Moritz Strauss. The company's founder, August Horch, who launched his first car in 1901, had left Horch in 1909 after disagreements over his stewardship of the company's products.

Like others whose cars competed with American imports of high quality and low prices, Horch struggled during the 1920s. Late in the decade, however, it turned in some acceptable financial results, though not enough to erase the debts it had accumulated. As well, its unique positioning as a maker of straight-eights had rapidly been eroded; by 1929 ten more German companies were offering them. Strauss and his board decided that it was time to leap ahead of the direct competition – read Mercedes-Benz – once more with a multi-cylinder engine. The assignment went to Fritz Fiedler, who joined Horch from Stoewer in 1929 to take over the technical chair from Paul Daimler, who was kicked upstairs to the supervisory board.

Fiedler in turn relied on Werner Strobel, who had headed engine design at Horch since 1928. "At the time we were all possessed by the burning ambition to be

better than the competition in Untertürkheim," said Strobel, referring to the company that had gained new momentum with the 1926 amalgamation of Daimler with Benz. "With the twelve-cylinder," he added, "we entered completely uncharted territory." He and his colleagues were shrewd enough to find some guidance across the Atlantic. "With a sideways glance toward America," Strobel said, "where General Motors was building a successful V8, we developed a twelve-cylinder that had several similarities to the American motor."

In fact GM proffered two vee-eights for the edification of Fiedler and Strobel. Oldsmobile introduced its Viking V8 in March 1929 and Oakland its similar eight in January 1930. Both were available in good time for the engineers' assignment, which saw work getting under way in 1930. The main gift to Horch from the American engines was the use of a single central camshaft operating horizontally placed valves through pivoted rocker arms that contacted the cam lobes through roller tips. Notably, as well, the American eights were the first in volume production to have a one-piece iron cylinder-block-cum-crankcase. This too was a feature of the Horch design.

The very deep and complex block casting of Strobel's twelve extended from its flat top, from which the inlet and exhaust ports emerged, to well below the crankshaft's centreline. Carried in seven main bearings, its crank had twelve bolted-on counterbalancing masses and a vibration damper at its nose. I-section connecting rods 230mm long, drilled to carry oil to the gudgeon pins in aluminium pistons, sat side-by-side on the 60mm rod journals. The left-hand row of cylinders was offset forward to permit this. A shallow cast aluminium sump closed its bottom end (see page 150).

A triple-row roller chain drove the camshaft with its roller-rocker valve gear. Each rocker had an adjustment screw at its valve end and opened its horizontal valve against its single coil spring.[4] Unlike the American V8s but foreshadowing the later Packard V12 design, Horch's V12 had cylinder-head joints that were angled away from an orthogonal relationship to the cylinder bores. They were sloped upward at a 27° angle to the flat piston crown, more than the Packard's 15° and less than the Itala V12's 35°. The space created in the block by this slope constituted the combustion chamber, formed by a head face that was flat-surfaced save for small indentations giving valve clearance. Compression ratio was 5.2:1.

Inlet and exhaust manifolds ran the length of the block, just inboard of the heads. Outermost were the log-type exhaust manifolds, which vented forward and down to the left. Inboard of these were the inlet manifolds, warmed as needed by exhaust gases controlled by a butterfly valve. Induction initially was through a twin-throat downdraft Solex 32JFFP carburettor, and from 1933 provided by a D-3 twin-throat Stromberg, with each throat supplying one bank. Driven from the camshaft at the rear of the block was a vertical Bosch distributor which sparked a plug in the centre of each chamber.

An accessory drive at the front of the Horch turned its fan and, along the right side of the block, its generator. In line with the latter and driven by it was a single water pump that delivered to both sides of the cylinder block. Warm water was drawn off the top of each cylinder head at points both forward and rearward. Above the water pump was a mechanical fuel pump, worked by a pushrod from the camshaft.

As in the sleeve-valve Daimler twelves, a driver-operated plunger delivered engine oil through nozzles, near the camshaft, to the lower one-third of each cylinder bore. This was to be operated before starting the engine, especially in cold weather, to be sure that the bores were well oiled. Intriguing though this was, it hinted at engine-development difficulties at Zwickau.

In lovely round numbers the dimensions of Horch's vee-twelve were 80 x 100mm (6,032cc). Its output was 120bhp at 3,200rpm, delivered through a single-disc clutch and a four-speed ZF transmission. As Type 670 on a wheelbase of 135.8in, the twelve was launched spectacularly as a yellow sports cabriolet by Gläser at the 1931 Paris Salon. Its top was tan and its upholstery green Morocco leather. Visitors were stunned by the contrast of this flamboyant display of excess with Europe's straitened economy. Explained Hans-Heinrich von

Fersen, "It was intended for those customers for whom the normal Horch was still insufficiently exclusive and pretentious." Prices ranged from 23,500 to 26,000 marks – around $6,000.

Even more lavish was the Horch twelve shown at Geneva in 1932 on the longer wheelbase of 145.7in released that year, as the Type 600. Again bodied by Gläser, it flaunted magnificent four-door cabriolet coachwork in metallic silver. Other Horch bodies were designed by Hermann Ahrens, who gave them strikingly sporting lines. Ahrens would soon be snapped up by Daimler-Benz to design the custom bodies it built at Sindelfingen. A completed Type 600 could scale 5,500lb, which meant less-than-sparkling performance and a top speed little more than 85mph. Nor did its ultra-conventional solid-axle chassis command much respect, gaining as it did a reputation for 'swimming' on straights.

The attack on Untertürkheim seemed to be going well; in 1932 the tally for German-market sales of cars over 4.2 litres was 472 to Horch versus 282 for Mercedes-Benz. Nevertheless production of Horch twelves was halted at the end of 1933, when 78 in all had been made. Twenty were the long-wheelbase model and 58 the shorter Type 670. Horch buyers demanding the pretentious continued to buy models that looked much the same as the twelve but with less elaborate engines under the bonnet – from the end of 1931 including a V8 of 3½ litres that closely resembled its American inspiration. Slow sales of the twelve meant that the final example only left the Zwickau factory in February 1935.

Excision of the 600/670 from the Horch range was one consequence of the rationalisation that followed the

A cabriolet on Horch's Type 670 chassis of 1931 showed the styling talent of Hermann Ahrens. Although its performance was adequate, the big Horch failed to win praise for the deportment of its antiquated running gear.

company's merger with Audi, DKW and Wanderer in June 1932 to form the Auto Union combine. Its failing finances meant that from 1930 onward Horch was effectively under the control of the state of Saxony, which engineered the Auto Union alliance to prop up its local motor industry. A Horch man, William Werner, took over his company's technical directorship in 1932 when Fritz Fiedler moved to BMW. Werner, a production expert, was to become a leading light of Auto Union. He'd found little to admire in the knife-and-fork fabrication of the Horch vee-twelve.

No campaign to scale the heights of the German auto market at the beginning of the 1930s could ignore its looming Matterhorn, the Maybach Zeppelin. Here indeed was a machine of extremes, save for the Hispano-Suiza Europe's biggest vee-twelve of this era in its ultimate eight-litre form, typically carrying three tons of elaborate coachwork on a 147.0in wheelbase. The price for its chassis alone rose to $10,100 in New York and depending on its bodywork a complete Zeppelin could cost as much as $13,000. In price it was only rivalled in Germany by the supercharged 'Grosser Mercedes' eights from Untertürkheim with their limousine or cabriolet bodies. Globally, only Duesenbergs and Rolls-Royces were pricier.

The 'Zeppelin' model deserved its peculiar name, for it was Graf Ferdinand Adolf August Heinrich von Zeppelin who had backed the effort of Wilhelm Maybach and his son Karl to set up a company to make aviation engines in 1912. Since the century's dawning von Zeppelin, a German army officer, had been experimenting with lighter-than-air craft. He'd powered some with Daimler engines, but when the genius behind Daimler's designs, Maybach the elder, left that company in 1907 and offered his services to von Zeppelin the latter knew when he was on to a good thing. Wilhelm and Karl were each 20 per cent shareholders in the Maybach Motorenbau GmbH at Friedrichshafen, set up close to von Zeppelin's operations on Lake Constance in southern Germany.

With von Zeppelin building more than 100 airships for use in World War I, each needing four, five or even six engines, the new business was off to a lively start. Maybach engines also powered Rumpler aircraft. After the war, however, with a defeated Germany disarmed, this trade vanished. Karl Maybach, who had been well trained in all aspects of technology at the feet of his father, thought to make engines for motorcars. Finding only moderate success, such as a sale of 150 engines to Holland's Spyker, he decided to bite the bullet and build complete automobiles. The first Maybach car, an in-line six of 5.7 litres, was revealed at 1921's Berlin Show.

By the late 1920s both Zeppelin and Maybach were back in the dirigible business with impressive success. Hugo Eckener, who led the airship maker after its founder's death in 1917, commanded the *Graf Zeppelin* in the first passenger-carrying voyage across the Atlantic at the end of 1928. Propelling it were five Maybach vee-twelves, each with a cruising power of 450bhp. In 1929 the *Graf Zeppelin* made a precedent-shattering round-the-world voyage that seemed to portend an age of the airship. Karl Maybach concluded that the time was right to raise his game as a car producer by launching what the Germans call a *Repräsentationswagen*, best translated as a vehicle that will make the biggest possible impact at the embassy, the opera or the country club. Like the *Graf Zeppelin*, it would be vee-twelve-powered.

If Walter's launch of its Royal was an act of sheer vainglory, it was surpassed in hubris by Maybach's new venture. Neither car production nor airship engines had netted a *pfennig* for Maybach Motorenbau during the 1920s. Because the company's products tended to test the limits of the available technology they frequently required costly fixes in the field that mopped up what little profitability remained. Nor did Karl Maybach feel constrained to seek simple solutions. Some of his car designs boasted dazzling complexity, especially in their transmissions, an area in which he was driven to innovate. Consequently there was no lack of tension between Maybach and Hugo Eckener of Zeppelin, which with its banks was obliged to shoulder the burden of the Maybach company's rising debts.

Though a commercial man, Julius Bernhardt, was installed at Friedrichshafen, he seemed incapable of curbing Karl Maybach's technical excesses. In 1928 work was well under way on the car that would be introduced late in 1929 simply as the '12'. Its engine was conceived not only as a car unit but also as a potential prime mover for industrial purposes, marine use and for coaches; although Maybach was well aware that in these spheres the efficiently manufactured American engines were tough competitors. "The production of the new car can only be contemplated," Maybach accordingly informed Zeppelin in December 1928, "if the tests we are about to conduct on the foreseen five to six experimental engines as well as vehicles offer us absolute confidence that lengthy development work and its consequent high development costs can be ruled out."

In the layout of his new car Karl Maybach made a valiant effort to achieve what was, by his lights, a measure of simplicity. Among his aides were gearbox specialists Glücker and Maier and chassis man Stump, who provided a conventional design with solid axles front and rear that would be kept for all the twelves. The somewhat bizarre features of earlier Maybachs were to be eschewed in favour of a more conventional configuration that would not alarm purchasers who were as conservative as they were wealthy. The 12's main technical distinction would be – as usual – in its transmission, which had an automatic overdrive, at first, and later a special vacuum-actuated ZF gearbox that offered up to eight forward speeds.

That's not to say that the 12's engine lacked engineering interest. Its crankcase was cast of aluminium alloy, with its cylinders formed by dry iron liners pressed into the block and retained by the cylinder heads. The liners extended down well past the limits of the block surfaces and the generous water jacketing that fully surrounded each cylinder. Cut off at the crankshaft centreline, the block was double-walled for stiffness along its flanks. A wide cast-aluminium sump closing the bottom end had a bulge on its left side for the low-placed oil pump, driven by a shaft from a skew gear on the single central camshaft. A sophisticated lubrication system included a filter and oil cooler. The left hand row of cylinders was offset forward to allow side-by-side connecting rods to be used.

Complexity crept into the top ends of the cylinder liners, for instead of being circular these were bowed out to form pockets toward the front and rear of the block to give added clearance for the heads of the valves, which stood vertically in line down the cylinder heads. This was necessary because the valves seated directly against the flat faces of the iron cylinder heads and opened down into the cylinder bore. Giving a 5.6:1 compression ratio, the combustion chamber consisted of the top of the cylinder as defined by the piston's flat crown. Nelson Bohnalite pistons with automatic wall-clearance compensation carried three compression rings, one oil ring and a steel gudgeon pin held in place by circlips. Forged-steel connecting rods 225mm long featured I-section shanks.

Like the Hispano-Suiza V12, Maybach's 1929 twelve nominally had seven main bearings although the rearmost bearing was split to flank the gear drive to a single central camshaft. Karl Maybach was generous in the cylinder spacing of his twelve, which had ample water capacity around each bore.

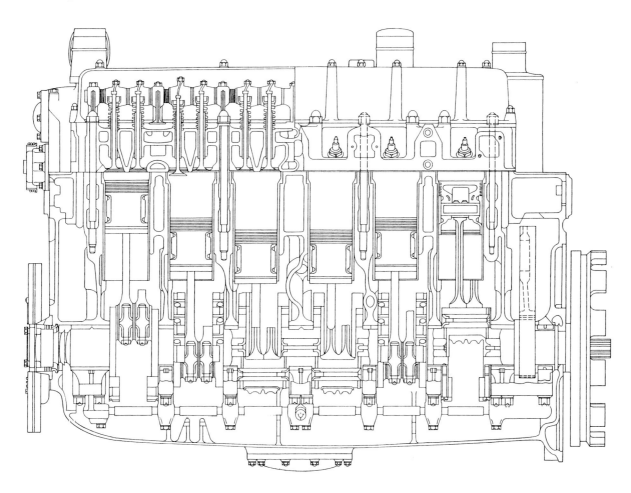

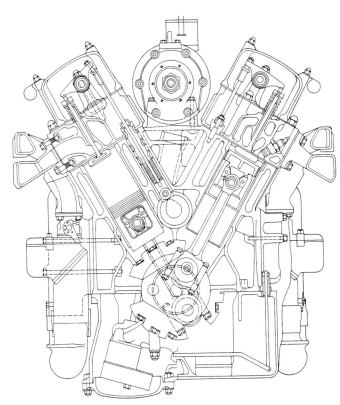

Bolted-on crankshaft counterweights were a feature of the Maybach, which displaced 7.0 litres. Both induction and exhaust manifolding were on the outer flanks of the Maybach twelve, with its single central camshaft operating its valves through pushrods and rocker arms.

At its late-1929 introduction the Maybach 12 measured 86 x 100mm for a capacity of 6,971cc. This was virtually the same displacement as the Maybach six that the twelve replaced, albeit with much less extreme proportions than the long-stroke six's 94 x 168mm. Determining the stroke was the crankshaft of chrome-nickel steel supported by seven 73mm main bearings plus a rear outrigger bearing, next to the flywheel, of 66.5mm. All the main bearings were retained by massive caps, with the front, centre and rear mains significantly wider than the rest and given four bolts instead of two. Crankpins, relatively small at 55mm, were between circular cheeks and opposite pairs of triple-bolted counterbalances with which both static and dynamic balance were achieved. All the bearing journals were bored hollow for lightness and sealed off by caps tensioned against each other by central bolts and nuts. A large-diameter vibration damper was at the crank's nose.

The rear outrigger bearing – which also took clutch thrust – was needed because a pair of helical gears there drove the camshaft, which seven bearings supported. The driven gear was cut from Novotex, a resin-impregnated fibrous material which encouraged silent running. At the nose of the camshaft was another Novotex gear – indeed the same part – which drove a gear above it that turned the six-blade fan and another gear above turning a shaft down the central vee. At the input end of the shaft was one of the two Bosch distributors for the coil ignition, the other being behind the generator which the shaft also rotated.[5] En route to the generator the shaft turned a central water pump, uniquely of axial-flow design, which delivered cool water to the heads and central vee.

Long and well-cooled guides carried the valves in the shallow iron cylinder heads. Closed by single-coil springs, they were opened by rocker arms that gave a slight mechanical advantage and had screw adjustments for clearance at their pushrod ends. At its bottom each pushrod rested in a short tappet with a roller contacting the cam lobe. In an inserted carrier that guided the tappet, a single coil spring held it against the lobe. The rocker gear was encased by cast aluminium covers that carried the distinctive Maybach double-M emblem.

A sign that Karl Maybach was at least trying to curtail costs was his use of a cylinder head that was common to both banks of the 60° vee twelve. All its ports were on the outside, three exhaust ports neatly siamesed from pairs of cylinders plus four inlet ports. The compact exhaust manifolds, which led the gases rearward to twin pipes and silencers, were below the aluminium inlet manifolds. Feeding each of the latter was an updraft twin-throat Solex carburettor, Type MMUVS35. Induction warmth was controlled by mixing the flow of air to the carburettors, which could be delivered either from the radiator or from air warmed by passing through the hollow flanks of the crankcase. Petrol flowed by gravity to the carburettors from an Autovac, a small tank which used the engine's vacuum to draw fuel from the main tank. To top up manifold vacuum as required, a wobble plate on the nose of the camshaft drove a small piston-type vacuum pump.

Scaling 1,125lb, this imposing engine was rubber-mounted at three points in its chassis, which at launch had a wheelbase of 144.1in. Output of the 1929-model Maybach 12 was 150bhp at 2,800rpm, equalling the power production of the slightly larger sleeve-valve Daimler. The latter was Europe's first vee-twelve in production. Voisin and Maybach virtually dead-heated for the honour of being second. The German firm had high hopes for its new model, saying that "in the near future the sales of the new 12-cylinder motor will be aggressively pursued." In 1930 it envisioned supplying 70 in cars and 100 more as power units for coaches.

Karl Maybach didn't quite achieve his goal of an engine that would be so well designed that its development costs would be minimal. Tests on Alpine passes in the hot summer of 1929 revealed the need for changes. In March of 1930 Maybach was assuring Hugo Eckener and his colleagues at Zeppelin that he'd deal with its teething troubles "with all available means" and "as soon as possible". He took a sample car with him on a trip to America, hoping to sell licences for some of its features.

During 1930, dreams of selling 100 engines per month to Büssing for its coaches were dashed. Maybach's DSO-8 version was developed for this purpose, and for other utility uses, but it overran its forecast costs and could only meet Büssing's price expectations if it were sold at a loss. With Maybach Motorenbau already deeply in the red, this was judged to be a drain too far. In April 1931 Maybach disposed of its stock of more than 300 DSO-8s at distressed prices that "scarcely cover more than material and production costs."

For the 1930 selling season Karl Maybach newly designated his twelve as the DS7, standing for Double Six (*Doppel Sechs*) of seven litres. The longer wheelbase of 147.0in was also introduced. Challengingly, in view of the strained relations between Motorenbau and its parent, the new model also proudly carried the 'ZEPPELIN' name on an arched bar between its headlamps, in front of its radiator.[6] Thus was born one of the motor industry's

most compelling binomials (a two-part name), for 'Maybach Zeppelin' would forever stand for a plutocratic extreme in the production of massive motorcars for the obscenely wealthy. Purchasers, said a contemporary report, were "owners of factories, company presidents, high-ranking government officials, owners of large farms and other important personages, seldom under 50 years of age and mostly around 60."

There were not enough such personages to support the new car programme, Maybach ruefully reported in April 1931, saying that "not only in Germany but also throughout the world the buyer segment that can afford expensive products at the peak of the market is steadily contracting." With sales of the Maybach twelve only trickling along, its production was generating "not insignificant losses" and "constantly growing stores of unsaleable engines, cars and transmissions."

If product improvement could make a difference, Maybach was trying. At 1930's Paris Salon one of the most eye-catching exhibits was a Saoutchik-bodied cabriolet, black with silver striping, on the Maybach stand. This heralded the availability of the DS8 Zeppelin, its

In 1930 Maybach introduced its DS8 Zeppelin, with a larger bore that brought capacity to 8.0 litres and output to 200bhp. On conventional solid-axle chassis the Zeppelins were imposingly bodied by such coachbuilders as Spohn, which fashioned this striking sports cabriolet in 1937.

designation marking its increase to eight litres – 7,977cc to be exact. While its stroke remained 100mm, its bore was enlarged to 92mm with new sleeves in the aluminium block. With a 6.3:1 compression ratio the twelve's power rating rose disproportionately to 200bhp at the higher speed of 3,200rpm.[7] Its gearbox later became more elaborate, with vacuum controls operated by levers at the hub of the steering wheel that produced clutchless changes of the intermediate ratios. Eerily, the system automatically raised engine speed when downshifting. Irrespective of its body style, the DS8 could comfortably exceed 100mph.

Piloting a Zeppelin imposed certain demands. First of all, in Germany its driver had to have the special commercial-vehicle licence required for operators of vehicles of more than 2½ tons. Then he had to master the starting procedure, which the manual set out as follows:

◇ Switch on the contact-body ignition.
◇ Activate the fuel injection pump four or five times, then wait for two or three minutes.
◇ Turn the manual throttle lever slightly so that the carburettor is opened by about a quarter.
◇ Adjust the manual ignition adjuster to 'ignition advance', i.e. push the button.
◇ Move the gearshift lever into centre – i.e. idle position.
◇ Pull the starter flap and release slowly again after the first firing (starter flap should be in use above all at low ambient temperatures).
◇ Allow the engine to warm up slowly until operating temperature is reached.

Once under way the Zeppelin's demeanour was beguiling, one passenger reported: "It's hard to believe that the car is actually moving, because there is no noise, no feeling of vibration, no tendency to stall or buck as you ooze along at one or two mph. The tachometer needle indicates that the engine is turning at less than 250rpm. With a touch of the accelerator, you can often keep moving along in traffic jams without a stop." Highway running was relaxed as well: "The sixth speed is direct drive, and the eighth is an overdrive. In final drive the Maybach can cruise at 55mph with the engine turning over at only 1,300rpm."

Maybach chassis were bodied with appropriate pomp by Erdman & Rossi and especially by Spohn at Ravensburg, a convenient 12 miles north of Friedrichshafen. In 1932 the two collaborated on a radical show-stopper, a four-door saloon with full envelope bodywork that easily seated three abreast at both front

and rear. Spohn struggled vainly to marry Maybach's more traditional front end to the huge car's aerodynamic lines in this early – and indeed worthy – attempt at streamlining. Nor did Maybach succeed in developing a distinctive radiator design that would have added character to its offerings. Only their sheer bulk set them apart from lesser cars on the road.

Struggling for market acceptance, Maybach made other cars as well, including from 1935 a new smaller six with – amazingly! – independent suspension at all four wheels. As early as March 1933 Karl Maybach put its development in train, having concluded that "the times of the big luxury car seem – at least for years ahead – to have passed." Nevertheless the solid-axle Zeppelin continued to be catalogued right up to the war, by which time Maybach had made some 1,800 cars *in total*. Of these 183 are thought to be twelves.[8] Maybach Motorenbau continued to struggle throughout the 1930s in a state of virtual bankruptcy. Rearmament came to its rescue. During World War II it built some 140,000 engines, putting 40 million horsepower to work for the *Wehrmacht*.

Even in its heyday, critics questioned the premise of the big Maybach. "A really productive mindset" seemed somehow to be missing, commented one journalist, who felt that massive though it was, the Zeppelin lacked a convincing mission. Although most of the cars would be chauffeur-driven, great effort seemed to have been made to ease the driver's task – something that the car's owner would not in fact worry about very much. While the Zeppelin was a powerful car it was resolutely unsporting, both in its mode of motoring and in its appearance, thanks to Spohn's less-than-sparkling efforts. Pretentious though it indubitably was, the Zeppelin utterly lacked charisma.

At the heart of the big Maybach's failure to command greater respect in the world's motor markets, said company historians Wilhelm Treue and Stefan Zima, was that the "disagreements between the technical and sales departments then led to the consequence that the engineers under Maybach's direction took too much time and cared insufficiently about costs and prices, customers and the performance of the competition." Making the cars had become more of an obligation, as a form of advertising for the company's heavy engines, than a mission in its own right.

Although its heavy-engine business revived after the war, in the 1950s Maybach Motorenbau relapsed to money-losing. Industrialist Friedrich Flick became the company's majority shareholder in 1952 and in 1960, the year Karl Maybach died at the age of 80, transferred that interest to Daimler-Benz. By 1966 Maybach was wholly in the hands of Stuttgart's Daimler, which in 1969 merged it with veteran engine-maker MAN. Some three decades later DaimlerChrysler, looking for a range-topping model that could rival BMW's acquisition of the Rolls-Royce brand, discovered that it owned a marque that had once been at the very apogee of the German hierarchy.

Long before these post-war events Daimler-Benz had run a ruler over its rival at the very southern border of its home state of Baden-Württemberg. Overlapping as they did both in motor vehicles and heavy engines, it was inevitable that they should keep a close eye on each other. In 1937, for example, Daimler management-board chairman Wilhelm Kissel unburdened himself on the subject to his colleagues:

I've often thought about the reaching of an agreement with Maybach, on our side to give up the big propulsion engines to Maybach and thus to gain a free hand in automobile production; or Maybach could continue to build its designs and entrust us with their sales; or Maybach could order the bodywork for its cars from us. There are thus a number of possibilities for the reaching of an agreement with Maybach, and in this respect we could perhaps speak to Maybach on a non-binding basis.

Kissel's remarks were prompted by a suggestion from Jakob Werlin, whose membership of the Daimler-Benz board was not unrelated to his intimacy with Adolf Hitler, whom he informally advised on automotive matters. In February 1937 board meetings Werlin expressed doubts about Mercedes's ability to carry on competing in the market for *Repräsentationswagen*. It only had a dozen sets of parts remaining for its 7.7-litre straight-eight 'Grosser' model, he said. The 540K was regarded as a sports model, not a prestige car, while the dull side-valve five-litre Nürburg "didn't come into consideration for such requirements".

Although Maybach had lacked the management skills to profit from its production of luxury cars, the launching of its Zeppelin into a small but perfectly formed pond made a considerable splash. Germany's wealthiest individuals were not easily deceived. They were well aware of the value that Maybach built into its cars, the very value that drove its costs even higher than its astronomical prices. As a consequence, Jakob Werlin told the Daimler board, "unfortunately all the prominent people are going over to Maybach. We absolutely have to do something in the big-car class." While the majestic Type W07 Grosser Mercedes had started strong with 42

sales in 1931, its first full year, its rate had subsequently fallen to one a month or less. Even cheeky Horch was seen as muscling its way into Mercedes territory.

Munich-based Werlin had a recommendation for the board: obtain a licence from Maybach and produce its DS8 as a Mercedes-Benz. Without such a car, he asked, with the supply of Grosser Mercedes running out, what would we be able to offer as a really large *Repräsentationswagen?* The answer came from a man relatively new to Daimler-Benz, its board member for engineering Hans Gustav Röhr. He pointed out that the ageing W07 would be replaced by the "completely changed and fundamentally improved" W150. Still using the supercharged 7.7-litre straight-eight, the W150 was introduced in 1938 with a tubular chassis and de Dion rear suspension. On the heels of the 117 W07s made, the W150 saw 88 delivered into 1943.

In the February 1937 board meetings the balding, toothbrush-moustached Röhr reminded his colleagues that he had new engines in his pipeline. One was a V8 and another a V12, closely related to give an economical sharing of components that Daimler-Benz had not enjoyed since the two companies were merged in 1926. The twelve, he said, could power a future range-topping car. "The six-litre 12-cylinder vee-engine," said Röhr, "will be fully comparable to the Maybach vehicle as a *Repräsentationswagen*, but certainly substantially cheaper." The engine was drawn, he added, and the casting patterns and crankshaft were being made. He foresaw the possibility of taking orders for the new twelve in December 1937 and delivering cars in May 1938.

Hans Gustav Röhr had parachuted into Daimler-Benz at a very high level indeed. He'd most recently headed engineering at Adler, which produced advanced front-drive cars under his aegis. He was looked upon favourably by Emil Georg von Stauss, the Deutsche Bank executive who was chairman of Daimler's supervisory board, the body that represented the company's owners. Death had toppled Benz man Hans Nibel from the Daimler-Benz technical chair in November 1934, with the post going to veteran Max Sailer. Considering that this wasn't a good enough appointment, von Stauss applied pressure to the management to engage Röhr.

There were misgivings. Röhr was an 'outsider', for a start. He lacked impressive academic credentials. At only 40 he was young for a Daimler board member. He'd created advanced designs, including his own straight-eight Röhr automobile, but that company had folded. He was expensive, not only for his own salary and patent rights but also for the engineering team he insisted on bringing with him from Adler. Paramount among them was Joseph Dauben, a skilled engineer who had long been helping Röhr realise his radical concepts. Agreement was finally reached, with the Röhr team arriving in Untertürkheim on 17 September 1935. Some compartmentalisation of their work was accepted, with house engineers Wagner and Nallinger retaining authority for certain sectors in co-operation with Röhr and Dauben.

It was soon obvious that Hans Gustav Röhr felt no obligation to respect the shibboleths of Daimler-Benz tradition. With Dauben he embarked on a new range of front-drive small Mercedes. He even dared to suggest that for many models live rear axles could be cheaper and better than the sacred swing axles. Indeed, Röhr proved it by inviting his colleagues to compare a 500K with an Auburn Speedster at the Nürburgring. The American car surprised with its superior handling.

In February 1936, five months after his appointment, Hans Gustav Röhr presented his plans for larger Mercedes power units to his board. He would make a four-litre V8 and a six-litre V12, which would allow many parts to be shared between the two engines. The twelve would supplant the supercharged 5.4-litre straight-eight of the 540K, whose unsatisfactory chassis would also be replaced by a new model to be sold in both 'cheap' and 'deluxe' versions. The V12, he said, would be made in both naturally aspirated and supercharged versions and could have either a live axle or de Dion rear suspension. Röhr's boss, Wilhelm Kissel, found this "a programme about which there was nothing to criticise".

Röhr assigned the engine-design task to Wilhelm Syring, a trusted member of his peripatetic team. Syring in turn remained true to the task Röhr had set, giving both versions of the engine the same dimensions of 82 x 95mm so that the maximum number of parts could be shared. This gave the M147 V8 a capacity of 4,014cc and the M148 twelve 6,020cc. As completed in 1938, the V8 produced 105bhp at 3,500rpm and powered a tubular chassis with de Dion rear suspension. Sixteen prototypes of the W147[9] took to the road, but in January 1939 the programme was terminated. Germany had other tasks for Daimler-Benz. Hans Gustav Röhr would not be involved because this creative engineer, felled by a virus, died prematurely on 10 August 1937.

By 1938 the first prototypes of Röhr's twelve were on the road. Innovative in many ways, his M148 foreshadowed features of many post-war production engines. Most striking of its attributes were its vee-inclined overhead valves in hemispherical combustion chambers. Hans Gustav Röhr favoured overhead valves for engines in which cost was not a dominant factor, and in this he was in harmony with his boss, Wilhelm Kissel.[10] He pointed out, however, that the added power that overhead valves brought over side valves was "not substantial, as long as the valves were lined up in a row. Only when valves oppose each other is there a substantial advantage. However, such a design is not cheap and generally requires two [overhead] camshafts. We're looking for a simpler and more usable solution."

Röhr and Syring found that solution in the pushrod operation of vee-inclined overhead valves from a single central camshaft in a layout that strikingly foreshadowed Chrysler's famed Firepower 'Hemi' V8 of 1951.[11] Opening vee-inclined valves by pushrods and rockers was by no means new; the Belgian Pipe of 1905 had this feature. It did it with two camshafts, however. Achieving this with only a single camshaft (and without using the pushrod as a 'pull rod' as well) was a relatively new idea. In 1924 Swiss engineer George Roesch patented such an arrangement for the British arm of Talbot that had the disadvantage of requiring one pushrod to pass between the cylinders; it seems not to have been implemented.

A quite different Talbot, the French company, took an important step forward with its new T150, first shown at the Paris Salon in October 1935 – the month after the Röhr team decamped to Untertürkheim. In Walter Becchia's design of its six-cylinder engine, a single low-placed camshaft used pushrods and rocker arms to operate valves inclined equally at an included 72° angle in a configuration that required very long rockers for the exhaust valves. German engineers paid close attention to the Talbot engine on display in Paris. Two went back to Munich, inspired to create the great BMW 328 six.[12] It's likely that some members of the Röhr team saw the T150 as well.

Whether or not the Talbot was their inspiration, the Stuttgart engineers came up with a distinctly better design. By raising the camshaft just enough, and by accepting a narrower 45° angle between the valves, they succeeded in giving equal proportions to the inlet and exhaust rocker arms. Both were compact, to reduce inertia, and gave a multiplication ratio from the cam lobe of 1:1.29. Adjustment screws were at the pushrod ends of the rockers, which had to be angled in plan view to allow them to reach their respective valves. Coil springs along the two rocker shafts held them in place against the shaft

Provocation from Horch and Maybach led to a decision by Daimler-Benz to develop a twelve-cylinder engine of its own. Under Hans Gustav Röhr, the twelve was designed by Wilhelm Syring. He gave his M148 engine an 80° vee angle, in common with its sister V8, and inclined overhead valves operated by rocker arms and pushrods from a high-placed central camshaft.

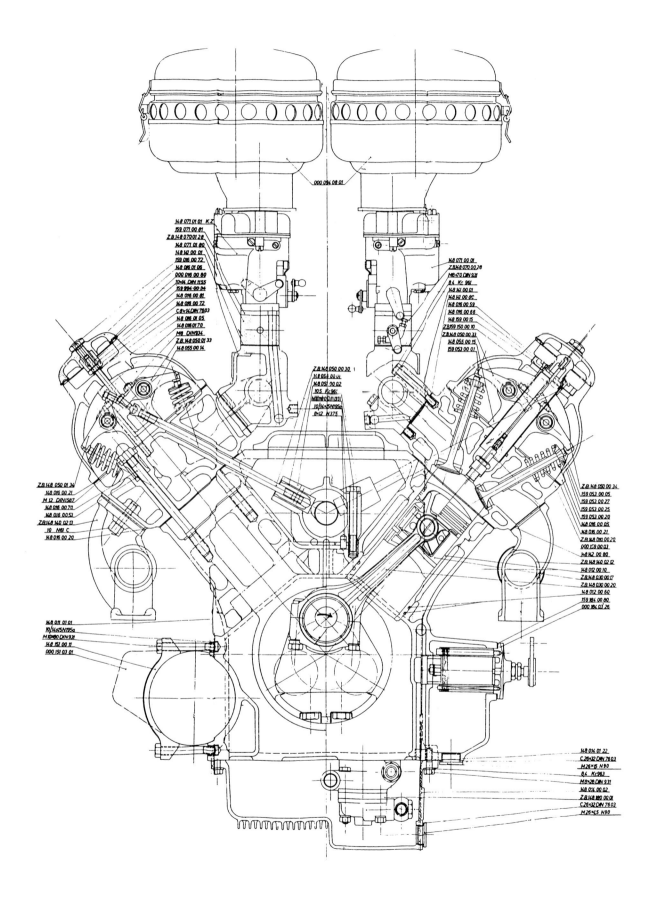

stands. A simple flat-faced tappet 23mm in diameter transmitted cam thrust to the pushrod, which was aluminium with inserted steel end-pieces.

Spark plugs were placed smack in the centre of the hemispherical combustion chambers, which slightly overlapped the bores adjacent to the valve heads to grant the gases free passage. Inlet-valve heads measured 40mm and the exhaust 38mm. Although Wilhelm Syring originally suggested two coil springs to close each valve, only a single spring was needed. Cylinder heads were aluminium; while Syring at first proposed seating the inlet valve directly on the light alloy, seat inserts for both valves were found in the final M148 vee-twelve. Again recalling the later Chrysler Hemi, a tube from the head to the top of the cast-aluminium rocker cover provided access to each spark plug, whose wiring had its own concealment cover.

A longitudinal section of Syring's M148 vee-twelve showed (indicated by arrows) the large-diameter main bearings that were one of the engine's controversial features. Although they aided compactness and crankshaft stiffness, the two big bearings threatened to generate excessive heat.

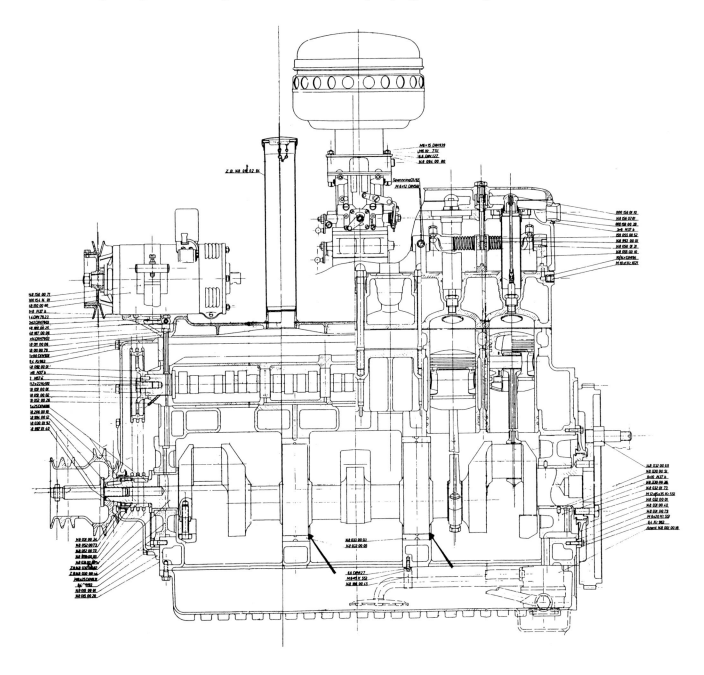

The M148 cylinder head was a true crossflow design, with six outboard exhaust ports flowing into manifolds with central offtakes. Each head had its own water-warmed log-type inboard inlet manifold, fed by a twin-throat Solex 32IFF carburettor. Ample space between the cylinder banks for the twin downdraft carburettors and their Knecht air cleaners was provided by the engine's wide 80° bank angle, shared not only with the M147 V8 but also with Pierce-Arrow's twelve. Under a central cover was the single camshaft, carried in six bearings and driven by a triple-roller chain from the crank nose. From the camshaft's tail a drive went upward to the ignition distributor. Vee-belt pulleys at the crank nose powered the generator, in the front of the vee, the fan and the single water pump, which was offset to the left of the front of the block.

Notable for its absence from the M148 was a crankshaft vibration damper, either internal or external. This implied a crankshaft that was so stiff that no suppression of any significant torsional orders within its operating range was required. Its unusual design contributed to that result. Its general layout was conventional enough, with 60mm big-end journals that carried two connecting rods side by side, the left bank being offset forward. Its front main bearing of four was 55mm – taking clutch thrust – and its rearmost bearing 65mm, next to the flange to which the flywheel was bolted. Balancing masses were cap-screwed to the crank's foremost and rearmost cheeks and another mass was forged integrally at its centre.

Usually at the other two main-bearing locations one would find a pair of crank cheeks flanking a bearing. Those cheeks, at locations on the crankshaft where no counterweighting was required, had no other function than degrading the crank's stiffness. Syring's design replaced both cheeks and bearing with a single large bearing journal a massive 160mm in diameter. The crankshaft with these two huge journals, together with their full-circle white-metal bearings, was inserted into the rear of the barrel-type crankcase and slid into position. Both the front and rear main bearings were carried by iron diaphragms bolted into the aluminium crankcase, the rear one a very substantial casting. Passages for cooling water passed around and under all four main bearings.

Here was a highly novel bottom end. Plain bearings as large as the middle pair were rare indeed. Such large bearings were used in heavy V12 engines by both Tatra and Maybach, but with balls or rollers, not plain bearings.[13] At risk in the design was the relatively high sliding speed generated at the bearing surface; the 160mm journal's surface speed was more than $2\frac{1}{2}$

times that of a conventional 60mm main bearing. The higher its surface speed the more heat a bearing generates, which Röhr and Syring aimed to dissipate by making the journals wide and surrounding them with cooling water.

Fully enclosing the crankshaft, and sealed at its bottom surface by a finned aluminium sump, the crankcase was a sophisticated aluminium casting. Thanks to its unique main-bearing design, it was able to carry its cylinders close together and at almost equal centre distances. The end and centre pairs were spaced at 108mm and the pairs between them at 113mm. Each cylinder was an iron wet liner, clamped at its top by the cylinder head against the block through a collar 35mm deep. The bottom end of the liner was sealed by two O-rings in grooves in the liner. The design's logic and simplicity were such that only 14 studs were enough to retain each cylinder head.

The gently domed crown of a full-skirted aluminium piston gave a 6.3:1 compression ratio. Its gudgeon pin was lubricated by a drilling up the I-section shank of the forged connecting rod, 190mm long. The rod's big-end journal was split at a 45° angle to permit pistons and rods to be drawn up and out of the bore for servicing. The tail of the camshaft drove a shaft downward to the oil pump, placed at the sump's extreme rear and drawing from its centre. An oil filter was on the left side of the block, into which the starter motor was recessed at the right rear.

While some members of the Röhr team carried on at Daimler-Benz, among them Joseph Dauben, their leader was gone after August, 1937. Others, including Fritz Nallinger, filled the technological gap. Development continued on the M148 and the new chassis designed to carry it. Tests found the engine revving normally to 3,800rpm and developing its maximum 155bhp at 3,400rpm. Peak torque of the six-litre twelve was 285lb-ft at 2,000rpm.

Daimler-Benz records indicate that a 170-horsepower M148 was also developed; this may have been the fuel-injected version that was being experimented with in the early months of 1941. Problems were indeed encountered in assuring the lubrication of the two big main bearings, but these seemed superable.

Two chassis, both with de Dion rear suspension, were designed for the twelve. One, for the *Repräsentationswagen* and named the 600V, was the W148 with wheelbases of 148.8 or 152.8in. This suited Sindelfingen's most capacious coachwork. The chassis to replace the sporty 540K was the W157, to be called the 600K. Its wheelbases were more modestly dimensioned at 129.1 or 134.4in. Ideal for the latter would have been a

During the war a new version of the Mercedes-Benz V-12, the M173, increased displacement to 6.5 litres and used iron instead of aluminium for both block and heads.

After its installation in a handful of automobile prototypes, the M148 was used during the war to power searchlight generators. Fuelled by natural gas, it delivered the reduced output of 105bhp.

Another change in the M173 V12 during the war was the narrowing of its vee angle to 60°. Although this was done specifically to produce an improved engine for searchlight batteries, the narrower angle was certainly also foreseen by the Daimler-Benz engineers as a better proposition for future passenger-car use. Remarkably, however, the engine was not revived for that purpose after the war.

supercharged version of the engine, rated at 240bhp at 3,600rpm and offering 416lb-ft of torque at 2,200rpm. Other engine/chassis combinations were tried as well, such as a 540K engine in the W157 chassis and a 12-cylinder engine powering a W150 Grosser.

At Sindelfingen former Horch man Hermann Ahrens fashioned special bodies for prototypes on both chassis. Front wings were deeply rounded, running boards were *de rigueur* and headlamps were faired into position between the wings and grille. Among the long-chassis bodies were a Pullman limousine and a seven-passenger touring car, while a handsome two-door cabriolet was mounted on the 600K chassis. Although some were nominally allocated to Nazi bigwigs, none was ever seen in public in their company. To the end of 1941 eight 600Vs were built and no more than seven 600Ks.[14] Thereafter the cars were withdrawn from service and not seen again.[15]

The onset of war opened new opportunities for the M148 twelve. Two producers of anti-aircraft searchlights had long been using the five-litre Nürburg eight to power their mobile batteries, but this engine wasn't up to the latest demands. Cue the Daimler-Benz twelve, converted to run on natural gas and throttled back to 105bhp at a steady 2,200rpm. To save on scarce aluminium, cast-iron

cylinder heads were phased into its production. With its dual magneto ignition the wartime M148 weighed 948lb.

War's demands even led to a further development of this Mercedes-Benz twelve. The M173 carried over the M148's cylinder heads and married them with a new cast-iron block whose bore was enlarged to 85mm, which with the 95mm stroke brought capacity to 6,469cc. At the same time the M173 was made more compact by narrowing its vee angle to 60°. The new block kept similar internal components but relocated the water pump to the centre of the engine's front end. Both rocker covers and sump were now steel pressings. With the higher compression ratio of 7.0:1 and running on gas fed to a single carburettor, the M173 produced 110 to 125bhp at 2,200 to 2,600rpm and weighed a much heftier aluminium-saving 1,135lb.

Syring's twelve turned out to be a useful wartime money-spinner for Daimler-Benz, which produced 3,420 such engines in both versions. With its tooling still available after 1945, it would seem to have been the answer to the desire of chairman Wilhelm Haspel, expressed at the end of 1947, for a new model that would again enhance the reputation of the marque. This, said Haspel, could be either a sports car or a *Repräsentationswagen* with a displacement of four to five litres.

As if by magic, a proposal for such a car arrived on Haspel's desk early in 1948 from Rudolf Uhlenhaut, the brilliant development engineer who had headed the company's pre-war racing effort. One engine for such a car, said Uhlenhaut, could be a 6.6-litre V12 with a 60° bank angle – close enough to the wartime M173. If a supercharged engine were to be preferred, he said, the twelve could be a higher-revving 4.5 litres with a Roots-type blower. The engineer suggested dimensions of 78 x 78mm for 4,473cc and a wider angle between inclined overhead valves, 60° instead of 45°. Hydraulic valve-lash adjustment should be provided, Uhlenhaut said.

In the end, Daimler-Benz decided against reviving the M173 to power a post-war model. Reasons given included the relatively high friction of its big main bearings, the limit on high revs imposed by its valve gear and, reportedly, the constraints of its combustion chamber on valve and port diameters. The latter, it would seem, could easily have been remedied by setting the spark plug to one side to grant more space to the valves.

Most compelling, to be sure, must have been the parlous economic condition of post-war Germany, to which a big petrol-swilling vee-twelve would have been utterly unsuited. Mercedes-Benz would introduce a 3-litre six instead – with the same cylinder bore as the M173.[16] Twelves would return in Germany; BMW and Mercedes would race to introduce them. But that would be decades in the future.

Chapter 7 Footnotes

[1] One source gives 5,976cc, another 5,950cc.

[2] Walter had a penchant for noble British names. Other models of the 1930s were called the Lord and Regent.

[3] The Walter's cylinder banks appear to be directly opposed but the author is in the dark about its connecting-rod arrangements.

[4] Some reports attribute a hydraulic means of automatic valve-clearance adjustment to the Horch V12, describing a 'helper piston' under engine-oil pressure that took up the clearance. A system akin to that used by Packard would have been suitable, and may indeed have been adopted during the engine's lifetime. However, our drawing of the engine shows no such system or any other.

[5] In later engines a single distributor, mounted at the front, supplied sparks to all twelve cylinders.

[6] We can reasonably surmise that this honour was granted to its daughter, at the request of Julius Bernhardt, by Zeppelin in the hope that it would improve sales so that Maybach's financial demands on its parent would be lessened.

[7] Maybach's New York importer, A.J. Miranda, Jnr., claimed 230bhp.

[8] Some sources, including Maybach expert Michael Graf Wolff Metternich, say that production was "about 300" twelves. Regrettably no factory archives seem to have survived.

[9] The Daimler-Benz internal model-designation system distinguished between M prefixes for engines (*Motor*) and W prefixes for cars (*Wagen*).

[10] He and Dauben used side valves for their smaller front-drive prototypes, both to reduce cost and to keep their engines narrow.

[11] One of Hans Gustav Röhr's close associates, Otto Winkelmann, joined Chrysler after the war. Although Chrysler has laid down clear domestic bloodlines for its Hemi, the possibility cannot be excluded that Winkelmann – although chiefly a chassis expert – was able to provide his new employer with information on these Mercedes-Benz engines.

[12] Fritz Fiedler and Rudolf Schleicher ended up with a different configuration, using extra cross-head pushrods to open the exhaust valves.

[13] In defending his concept Röhr told the Daimler directors that a similar bearing design was used in a truck engine by Hanomag. The author hasn't been able to verify this assertion.

[14] Jan Melin's research into these rare cars has been relied upon.

[15] General von Schell's programme for curtailing the ranges of Germany's car makers to gain greater efficiency seems not to have played a part in the extinction of these models. Luxury Mercedes-Benzes were excused from its strictures.

[16] Its DNA, in fact, came straight from the twelves of Röhr and Syring. The latter had designed an in-line six, the M159, that used essentially one cylinder head from the twelve. It was produced in volume during the war to power light trucks, and the machinery to bore its cylinder blocks was still available. Thus, for practical reasons, Syring's M159 was adopted as the basis for the M186 six which ultimately powered the Mercedes-Benz 300, 300S and 300SL.

Chapter 8

RACERS IN AMERICA

Errett Lobban Cord and his colleagues built a firecracker of a car in their 1932 Auburn vee-twelve. With its 160 horsepower from 6,410cc of Lycoming twelve the Model 12 160 Auburn offered serious speed at prices so low they verged on the incredible. Since the late 1920s California tuner and racer Eddie Miller – no relation to Harry – had been demonstrating the durability and speed of Auburns with long-distance record runs. Here, surely, was a new model that deserved the Eddie Miller treatment.

It was Miller who piloted a trio of Auburns to high speeds on California's Muroc Dry Lake, a convenient 60 miles north of Los Angeles. Budding hot-rodders had been testing the top speeds of their creations on its dried-mud surface for several years before Miller arrived with his Auburns in July 1932. His fastest speed was the 100.77mph he recorded in the Speedster with its hood erect. Clocked under the auspices of the American Automobile Association (AAA), this marked the first time that any American production car had been timed officially at better than 100mph.

Miller added to his tally that July with a one-hour run in the Speedster at an average 92.2mph and 500 miles at a speed of 88.95mph on a five-mile circular course. These, plus a standing-start-mile speed of 67.03mph, established 26 new American stock-car records. To boot, new records for closed cars were set by an Auburn Custom Brougham at speeds that included 82.7mph for 500 miles.

Eddie Miller mulled over the Auburn's quick times, reflecting on the fact that the first-ever average of more than 100mph had just been recorded in the Indianapolis

500-mile race that May. Could a Speedster do better than that? If so it would be quite a publicity coup for Auburn. Miller gained E.L. Cord's backing for another sortie to Muroc in December of 1932. Stripped of its bumpers, wings, lamps and windscreen, the Speedster presented a slimmer profile to the wind. Now its one-mile speed was 117.89mph, taking full advantage of the high 3.04:1 ratio in the Auburn's novel two-speed rear axle.

On 29 December Miller set out on a surveyed circle at Muroc. His early milestones set American records, but by the time he hit the 200-mile mark, at a speed of 112.93mph, he was setting new records for the International Class B for cars with engines of up to eight litres. His 500-mile speed was even higher at 113.38mph – easily besting the Indy average. Miller broke records all the way to 2,000 kilometres (105.93mph) and 12 hours (105.83mph) in the doughty Auburn. In all they set nine new International records that December, toppling speeds set at Brooklands by Parry Thomas in his Leyland-Thomas and at Montlhéry by a Graham-Paige.[1] The V12 Speedster averaged 6.75 miles per US gallon during the run.

More than any other American car, the rakish two-seater Auburn V12 Speedster had the goods to appeal to the young men who were pacing that nation's budding enthusiasm for road racing European-style. In August

Opposite: *A master and link rod of Charles Voelker's 1937 5.4-litre V12 were set out on one of its exhaust manifolds for inspection in Indy's Gasoline Alley. Induction was through three Zenith downdraft carburettors.* **(Indianapolis Motor Speedway)**

THE V12 ENGINE

171

1932 one of that movement's leading lights, Samuel Carnes Collier, bought a black Model 12-160 which he promptly nicknamed 'Beelzebub' after the Devil's right-hand man. He had no illusions about his new mount's capabilities:

The Auburn was very fast, but no great joy to drive on twisting roads. It was very nose-heavy from the huge V-12, understeering like crazy, ate tires at a prodigious rate, had a distinct lack of rear-end traction and gulped fuel at an alarming rate. On damp roads it was always a toss-up as to which end of the Auburn would wash out first, the front or rear.

Sam Collier had every chance to experience these and other idiosyncrasies of his new acquisition when he and his brother Miles entered it in the Coupe Internationale des Alpes in July and August 1933. Beelzebub was the sole American entry in this gruelling five-day hegira through the French, Swiss and Italian Alps. Both car and crew overcame starting problems, overheating, ignition maladjustment, locking rear brakes and a cracked sump to finish the arduous Alpine Rally fifth in class. The sump problem was solved by Miles Collier climbing out on the running board and topping up with two quarts of oil every hour while the Auburn was on the move.

Although the Colliers bought more suitable foreign machinery for the road races of the newly formed Automobile Racing Club of America (ARCA), Sam wheeled out Beelzebub for an 88-mile race on the streets of Memphis, Tennessee on 13 May 1936. Against token opposition, to be sure, Collier's Auburn was the winner of the Cotton Carnival Race. In July the big Auburn competed in the climb up New Hampshire's Mount Washington, in which Sam Collier was fifth of nine entries. His time was thought excellent, wrote ARCA historian Joel Finn, "considering he had never seen the mountain before, much less ever having driven up it." Although slower than he'd been the year before, Sam Collier placed second to a 2.3-litre Alfa Romeo in his 1937 climb with Beelzebub.

Advantageous both in Alpine rallying and in hill climbing was the Auburn's good steering lock. This was exploited in 1932 in mountains near Los Angeles, where a vee-twelve raced to eight hillclimbing records at altitudes as high as 6,050ft. Also in 1932, sixty cars started the society-rich rally from Paris to Nice. Best placed at the finish was Prince Nicolas of Romania in his Auburn V12 Speedster. The prince, who was highly partial to E.L. Cord's products, raced a Duesenberg at Le Mans in 1933.

Hillclimbing in America reminds us of that Salt Lake City, Utah native, David Absolom 'Ab' Jenkins, who with Omar Diles sparked up the performance of Pierce-Arrow's new V12 for its launch in 1932. Jenkins was thought to be the first man to ride a motor vehicle on the nearby Bonneville Salt Flats, a motorcycle in 1910. Although rock salt and potash were already being extracted from its surface, Jenkins felt that an area 10 by 15 miles could be made available for motor racing and record-breaking. Another promoter of the salt's merits was William Rishel, the state of Utah's first motorist. In 1914 he lured Teddy Tetzlaff and the 200-horsepower 'Blitzen' Benz to the salt to set an unofficial land speed record of 142.85 miles per hour.

Ignoring the demonstrated suitability of the Salt Flats, record breakers went to more accessible Daytona Beach instead. Jenkins and Rishel felt they'd have to do something spectacular to convince them that the salt's merits were worth a journey to western Utah and the hamlet of Wendover, on the state's border with Nevada. This was much on the mind of Ab Jenkins when he saw the kind of power the Pierce-Arrow twelve could produce. Why not take a well-prepared Pierce to Utah and set some speed records? The Buffalo, New York company, then suffering a sales decline, decided to back Jenkins's bold initiative.

At Buffalo Omar Diles supervised the car's preparation, running its engine at 4,000rpm on the dynamometer for 151 hours – an ample margin. The V12 had the larger bore that was due to be introduced soon on 1933 models, with a displacement of 7,568cc, plus the livelier valve timing that Diles and Jenkins had conjured. Carburation was adapted to Bonneville's 4,000-foot altitude. Diles prepared a special 3.00:1 rear-axle ratio that gave 126mph at 4,000rpm. Shorn of its wings, the roadster-bodied Pierce-Arrow carried a single central headlamp for night-time running, linked to turn with its front wheels, and a tonneau cover over its passenger seat.

Meanwhile in Utah the state's road commission surveyed a ten-mile circle on the salt and provided twenty oil flares to delineate its periphery at night. Bill Rishel took care of the timing, which although to AAA standards was not sanctioned by that body owing to lack of time. A compound was set up with tents for the Pierce-Arrow men and the Salt Lake City Chamber of Commerce, plus barrels high on stilts for gravity refuelling.

After warm-up laps by Omar Diles, Ab Jenkins took the Pierce's wheel on the morning of 18 September 1932. His goal was a 24-hour run; Pierce-Arrow officials had ridiculed his target of 2,400 miles or a day's driving. In fact he covered 2,710 miles to average 112.91mph for the 24 hours. At 115mph its engine was turning a comfortable

3,600rpm. Although Jenkins made a dozen stops for fuel, not once did he alight from the cockpit – establishing an 'iron man' reputation that the teetotal Mormon would more than uphold in years to come.

The AAA not only failed to sanction Jenkins's records but also fined him $500 for his temerity in attempting them without their blessing. To put things right he and Pierce-Arrow returned to the salt in 1933. Although the car was much the same, still with a single two-throat carburettor, its compression ratio was upped to 7.5:1 and its porting and combustion chambers refined. Together with a more radical camshaft these changes raised its output to 207bhp. Back on Bonneville's shimmering white expanses in August 1933, the Pierce-Arrow team was met by a full complement of AAA officials and their timing equipment.

Starting on 6 August, Jenkins set a cracking pace. From the 200-mile mark onward he was breaking not only International Class B records – wiping out Eddie Miller's Auburn marks – but also outright world speed records irrespective of category. Early records fell at 124mph speeds and the average at 12 hours was 120.58mph. From 2,000 miles onward and at 24 hours Jenkins undercut the times that a Voisin had set at Montlhéry. He pressed on

undaunted through a heavy rainstorm and high winds. Leaving the 24-hour record at 117.82mph, Jenkins carried on for another hour and half – solo as usual – to collect the 3,000-mile prize at 117.98mph.

The V12 Pierce-Arrow set no fewer than 38 American records. It was also the holder of 14 new outright world and class records – the holder, that is, after the sceptical Paris authorities finally satisfied themselves that one man alone could have achieved what relays of drivers had normally accomplished in setting previous day-long records. "No matter how enduring he might be," wrote fellow record-breaker George Eyston, "no man, they declared, was capable of holding the wheel for twenty-four consecutive hours and more than 110 miles an hour." They'd have been even more dubious, added Eyston, "had they known that Jenkins was fifty years of age."

Although looking relatively tame when converted to a road car, the 'Ab Jenkins Special' still manifested the 'sportiness' that allowed this specially prepared Pierce-Arrow to set numerous International speed records at Bonneville in 1934. Ab Jenkins, by its cockpit, could be proud of what he and Pierce-Arrow achieved. (Gordon E. White)

These new trophies adorned the boardroom of a Pierce-Arrow that had been rescued from the hold of a floundering Studebaker by a group of Buffalo businessmen. Their enthusiasm and that of Pierce boss Alfred Chanters for record-breaking Jenkins style was such that another more ambitious iteration of the flying twelve was authorised. "During the winter of 1933–34," wrote Jenkins, "I was busily engaged in designing a new car in the laboratories of Pierce-Arrow in Buffalo, New York. I was determined to turn out a car which would boost my then existing endurance marks so high that the Britishers would simply have to come out on the salt if they were to regain them."

Here, for the first time, was a purpose-built record-breaker from Buffalo. Its two creators shared the credit, for it was dubbed both the 'Ab Jenkins Special' and the 'Pierce 12 Special', the latter with its distinctive arrow motif. This looked built for speed. Its all-new aluminium body had a cowled radiator and below it a single 'Cyclops' headlamp. Ab still sat offset to the left with a headrest on a long, pointed tail, in which two fuel fillers were set. From the sides of the engine bay, which were left open, long external exhaust manifolds trailed to the rear. Wheels were wire with knock-off hubs.

The rugged Pierce-Arrow twelve was taken to the gym for a thorough workout. Complementing its free-flowing exhaust manifolds was a new inlet manifold carrying six downdraft carburettors. New cylinder heads gave higher compression, contributing to its output of 235 horsepower.[2] With its new gearing the 1934 Pierce 12 Special was capable of 150mph, as it proved when it returned to the ten-mile circle at Bonneville on 16 and 17 August.

As good as his word, Ab Jenkins elevated his own previous records substantially and also lifted some speeds to 1,000 kilometres that Europeans had seized in the meantime. For three hours his average was 132.59mph, for six 130.80, for twelve 129.74 and for 24 hours 127.22mph. This time in his solo run Jenkins comfortably collected the 3,000-mile record within the 24 hours, averaging 127.53mph.

Ab was right; the British could no longer ignore the salt. In 1935 John Cobb arrived with his Napier-engined Railton Special to commence a battle with Jenkins, who switched to supercharged Duesenberg power and later to his Curtiss Conqueror twelves, as related in Chapter 4. The Pierce era was over – Jenkins converted the Special into a road car – but the last Buffalo-built record-breaker had more than done its job.[3]

Subsequently, of course, Utah's unique saline arena saw many more record-breaking attempts and successes. In 1935 a 12½-mile circular course was established, and at its best the salt offered straight courses of 11 and later 13 miles. The annual Bonneville National Speed Trials attract a bizarre and thrilling range of four-wheel and two-wheel record setters, but few have used twelve-cylinder engines, preferring to rely instead on proven American V8s.[4]

Nor, intriguingly, were America's great mavens of speed in the 1920s and 1930s advocates of the vee-twelve for motive power. The Duesenberg brothers had made their name with straight-eights, for both road and race track, and remained loyal to that configuration when commissioned by E.L. Cord to create their ultimate production car. The protean Harry Miller, never short of an idea and with designers Leo Goossen and Everett Stevenson at his elbow to realise his every whim, never powered a racing car with a twelve. Like the Duesenbergs, Miller's reputation had been built on his elegant supercharged straight-eights and the four-cylinder version thereof which evolved into the immortal Offenhauser.

Harry Miller had, as we know, once essayed a vee-twelve as a potential aviation engine, and not without elegance and ingenuity. His successor, Fred Offenhauser, returned to the theme in September 1941 with a proposal for an aero engine drawn by Leo Goossen. This was to be a classic 60° vee twelve with its left-hand cylinder bank offset forward. Six-cylinder blocks were to be cast of aluminium with integral heads, holding two valves at a 70° included angle and pressed-in iron cylinder lines. Goossen allocated four main bearings to its crankshaft, which had the gear drive to its camshafts at its anti-drive end. Shrewdly he took the drive to its rear-mounted centrifugal supercharger from the crank's nose so that the shaft to the blower, running back through the engine's centre, would absorb torsional vibrations.

Offenhauser's proposal to the Army Air Corps was for a supremely elegant power unit that would have fitted nicely into an automobile with its 6,149cc (88.9 x 82.6mm). It would weigh only 500lb, Goossen forecast, complete with its reduction gear, and develop the same number of horsepower at 4,500rpm. This would have matched the best aircraft-engine specific-power achievements of that era. It had dual ignition, of

Clear potential for automotive as well as aviation use was evidenced by Leo Goossen's design of September 1941 for Fred Offenhauser of a 60° V12 displacing 6.1 litres. Goossen liberally finned its external parts to gain maximum cooling from its proposed aircraft application.
(Leo Goossen Archive / Gordon E. White)

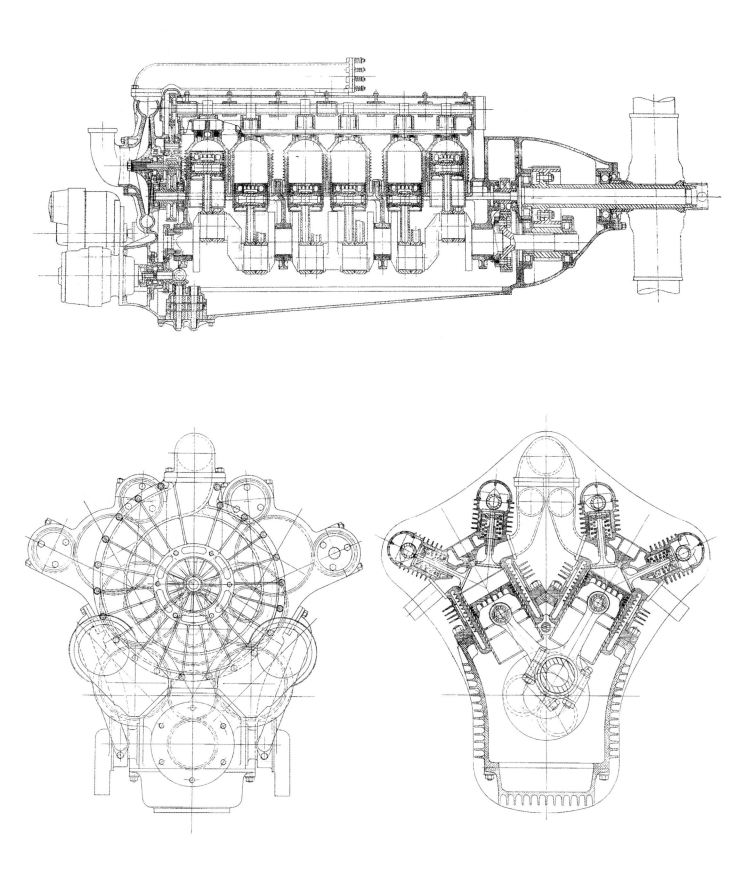

Above: *A proud Charles Voelker stood behind the Kimmel Special powered by 5.4-litre his vee-twelve at Indianapolis in 1937. The failure of Henry Banks to qualify the car at the Speedway that year was attributed to problems with the engine's carburation.* (Indianapolis Motor Speedway)

Below: *With the Voelker twelve's displacement reduced to 4.4 litres to meet new regulations in 1938, Henry Banks successfully qualified the Kimmel Special, albeit at the back of the field. Banks retired past half distance in this, the only occasion on which a Voelker-powered car qualified for the 500-mile race.* (Indianapolis Motor Speedway)

course, and the classic Miller-Offenhauser tubular connecting rods.

Earlier in the 1930s Harry Miller himself had committed to New York industrialists to produce a new family of engines based on a 60° vee with a cylinder diameter of 4¼ inches or 108mm. One was to be a vee-eight and another a vee-twelve with the same stroke, giving a capacity of 11,856cc. Drawn by Everett Stevenson, the twelve had twin overhead cams on each aluminium bank of two-valve cylinders with integral heads and wet steel liners screwed into its combustion chambers. Main bearings in an aluminium crankcase were seven in number, with master and link connecting rods allowing the cylinders to oppose each other. Centrifugal supercharging was provided.

The New York project's aim was to create an ultra-light twelve that would produce 1,000 horsepower at 6,000rpm with aviation applications in view. At least one was made and tested in a Manhattan loft before Harry Miller upped stakes to seek greener pastures. He found these in 1936 in a wealthy Canadian who needed an engine for his Gold Cup racing hydroplane. The vee-twelve fitted the bill perfectly. After many travails the Miller twelve, still wearing its aviation dual ignition, did produce more than 1,000 horsepower and powered Miss Canada III to victory in the 1939 President's Cup race in Washington, D.C. Observed Miller historian Mark Dees, "This was the last design of Harry Miller to actually win a race."

In 1939 Tommy Hinnerschitz tried to qualify the twelve-cylinder Kimmel Special but failed to make the field. By now the car's relatively primitive chassis had to be a significant hindrance. **(Indianapolis Motor Speedway)**

Vital contributions to the twelve's development were made by Charles Voelker, described by Dees as "a well-known Detroit engine expert." Over the winter of 1936–37 he dealt with manifold overheating by introducing water cooling and with valve float by providing triple instead of single valve springs. A knotty problem was the twelve's habit of failing its connecting-rod assemblies. Studying their geometry, Voelker concluded that the link bearing on the master rod's big end was wrongly positioned. The resulting disparities in stroke length meant that if ignition were timed correctly for one bank it was wrong for the other. Charles Voelker designed and made new rod assemblies that transformed the big Miller's throttle response and reliability.

The Detroit engineer's skills were also on display in 1937 at the Indianapolis Motor Speedway. That was the last year in which the rules allowed great latitude in engine configuration within a six-litre limit. New for 1937 were the imposition of petrol as fuel and permission to use superchargers, which had been prohibited since 1931. Rolling into Gasoline Alley was an elderly two-man Miller chassis with something unusual under its bonnet: an

Above: *In 1946 a much more purposeful proposition was a completely new chassis by Singer housing Charles Voelker's 4.4-litre vee-twelve. This looked the business but Charles Van Acker was unable to qualify and did not make the starting field.* (Indianapolis Motor Speedway)

Below: *In 1946 one of the Le Mans Lagondas, seen here at a race in Jersey, was significantly slimmed and lightened to be entered as an unlikely contender at Indianapolis by Robert Arbuthnot. Damaged in a pre-race incident, it was unable to qualify.*

unblown vee-twelve designed and built by Charles Voelker for sponsor Louis Kimmel.

Voelker's twelve was broadly on Miller lines with two valves per cylinder and twin overhead camshafts for each bank, driven by a gear train at the front. A novelty by Miller standards was the use of detachable heads on an aluminium crankcase. Cylinder banks opposed each other, with Voelker – an expert on this technology – using master and link rods. Both rods had tubular shanks, with the link rod having needle bearings at both ends. A Bosch magneto was driven transversely at the engine's front, while a central log manifold carried three downdraft Zenith carburettors (see page 170).

This handsome engine measured 77.8 x 95.3mm for 5,430cc at its 1937 Indianapolis debut. Nominated by Kimmel to drive the Miller-Voelker was Henry Banks in his second outing at the Speedway. The combination was not yet ripe enough to make the programme, carburation troubles being blamed for its failure to qualify. On 11 July the car was entered for the George Vanderbilt Cup at Roosevelt Raceway on New York's Long Island, with Banks again the pilot. He qualified 19th in the 30 car starting field, which included works teams from Mercedes-Benz, Auto Union and Alfa Romeo. On the 24th of 90 laps Banks and the 'Jumire' – as it was named for the occasion – retired when a rear-axle shaft came adrift.

In 1938 Indianapolis adopted the new Grand Prix Formula that limited blown engines to 3 litres and unblown units to 4½ litres. To meet this requirement Charles Voelker reduced his engine's bore to 69.9mm and, thereby, its displacement to 4,380cc – giving away, strangely, 2.7 per cent of the available capacity.[5] The Kimmel Special's chassis weighed in at 2,077lb, up some 100lb from the year before.

Henry Banks again got the nod from Kimmel. Qualifying his blue machine at 116.279mph in a year in which the fastest qualifier ran 125.769mph, Banks started from the inside of the last of 11 rows of three cars per row. At the half-way point of the 500 miles Banks was still motoring, albeit having made six pit stops, but after completing lap 109 of 200 he was sidelined by – of all things – a 'burned' connecting-rod bearing.

If Voelker's twelve could be said to have had its day of glory at the famed Speedway, that was it. In 1939 Tommy Hinnerschitz tried to put it into the field but failed in his first attempt at the Speedway. His third time at Indy was not the charm for Louie Webb in 1940 with the Voelker-powered Kimmel, which failed to qualify. The same fate met Ira Hall in 1941 for more specific reasons; he wrecked the car in practice.

Charles Voelker's 4½-litre twelve was back in some style in 1946 in a new chassis, a Singer-built single-seater that was a much more modern racing car. Louis Kimmel was no longer involved, for the unique V12 was entered by Charles Van Acker and to be driven by him. Van Acker averaged 115.666mph for his four qualifying laps, which even allowing for the Speedway's wartime deterioration wasn't up to Banks's speed in 1938. He was second reserve but none of the qualified 33 obliged him by dropping out.

Voelker's engine made at least two more Speedway appearances. In 1948 it was entered by Lawrence Jewell with an eponymous chassis and driven by Charles Rogers in his only attempt to qualify at Indy. He wasn't successful. Nor was Hal Robson in 1953, when he took over from Bill Doster in the Voelker entered by Stanley Olszewski. Thereafter this racing twelve vanished from Gasoline Alley.[6]

After the war the Voelker wasn't the only twelve hoping for glory in the world's richest race. In 1946 an unlikely contender was Robert Arbuthnot's Le Mans Lagonda, stripped of its wings and lighting. Damaged in a towing incident near the Speedway, it was repaired but never made a serious attempt to qualify.

A much greater threat in 1947 was Tommy Lee's W154 Mercedes-Benz, a 1939 supercharged 3-litre racing car that was the very cream of the glorious pre-war years of Grand Prix racing. During the 1930s the Europeans invested both their pride and their patrimony in some of the greatest racing cars ever created. Not surprisingly, vee-twelves were among them.

Chapter 8 Footnotes

[1] This was one of the few recognised record-setting efforts at Muroc, from which the hot-rodders were shooed by the Army Air Corps in 1938 to make way for what became Edwards Air Force Base, the hub for testing of advanced aircraft. Limited timing of cars there was still tolerated until 1942.

[2] We can safely surmise that Jenkins used prototypes of the new aluminium cylinder heads that were fitted to the Pierce-Arrow twelve's 1936 models.

[3] The Ab Jenkins Special is not known to exist, but with the help of Ab's son Marvin an Arkansas enthusiast has built a replica. It returned to Bonneville for a demonstration run in 2003.

[4] After World War II the Allison V12 was the sole exception. Its exploits on land are described in Chapter 10.

[5] This anomaly may be related to the aberrant effect on cylinder capacity of the use of master and link rods.

[6] Though respected Miller historian Mark Dees wrote that Voelker's twelve was still entered "as late as the 1970s", the author has not found evidence of this. To be sure, many Speedway habitués entered cars without a ghost of a chance of qualifying simply to enjoy the Gasoline Alley camaraderie.

Chapter 9

GRAND PRIX GLORIES

"Nineteen thirty-nine was surely the period of the V12," wrote Anthony Blight, "with no fewer than four sports racing types in this configuration, and a further three in the Grand Prix category." As we've seen, the 1930s were exceptional years for vee-twelves in road cars, on both sides of the Atlantic. Blight's point was that they'd also become important – indeed even dominant – in road-racing cars as well.

We've already met one of the sports-racing types: the V12 Lagonda that performed so well at Le Mans in 1939 and was denied further glory by the onset of war. Another car that first competed in 1939, Alfa Romeo's magnificent 4½-litre 412, did at least enjoy a post-war career. The third end-of-decade sports-racer was the roadgoing version of Delahaye's Type 145, a versatile competition car in the French tradition. Last of the four was a rare machine indeed, a one-off vee-twelve Delage. Both French cars had 4½-litre engines.

Twelves in Grand prix racing were represented by the stripped version of Delahaye's 145 and its *monoplace* iteration, the 155. The other two competing in both 1938 and 1939 were the supercharged 3-litre V12s of Mercedes-Benz and Auto Union, both of which rank among the finest racing cars ever created. It was, indeed, a great year for twelves.

In motor-sporting terms the decade started early with a dramatic record run by a car created by the indomitable Gabriel Voisin. The pioneer Parisian aviator and successful car builder had frequent recourse to record-breaking as a means of publicising his cars and his company. Since its high-banked concrete 1.58-mile oval

was opened at the end of 1924, Montlhéry Autodrome fifteen miles south-east of Paris had been a lodestone for the speed-crazed. Unlike Britain's Brooklands, nestled in leafy Surrey, Montlhéry allowed round-the-clock running with no exhaust-strangling silencers. A special Voisin first broke records there, including the world six-hour mark, in 1925.

Gabriel Voisin saw record-breaking as one weapon for his attacks on the hated Americans and their insurgency in Europe, a dramatic means of asserting the superiority of French technology. After a 1927 session with an eight-cylinder car, Voisin renewed his interest in 1929 when his company was at such a low ebb that he was obliged to cede his last shares to a Belgian group that promised fresh financing. Though his 1929 record car was built on a shoestring, it in no way lacked the elan for which its designer and his aide, André Lefèbvre, were now famed.

Its engine made use of two cylinder blocks from his C12 production model, which with its dimensions of 86 x 130mm added up to 9,062cc.[1] As usual the blocks contained the double sleeve valves that were used in all Voisins, driven by links from a central eccentric shaft, and inside them magnesium pistons. The cylinder blocks were mounted opposite each other on a crankcase fabricated from sheet steel, an expedient that avoided the need to make costly casting patterns. As in the six that donated its

Opposite: *Two Roots-type superchargers in parallel provided the boost for the M154 Mercedes-Benz 3.0-litre vee-twelve of 1938. Although one 1938 engine produced 474bhp, most were at the 440bhp level.*

In 1929, strictly for record-breaking, Gabriel Voisin built a 9.1-litre V12 by marrying two cylinder blocks from his C12 production car on a fabricated steel crankcase. The sleeve-valve engine had central carburation and individual exhaust stacks for each cylinder.

With eyes painted on its bonnet giving it a demonic aspect, Gabriel Voisin's underslung record-breaker set new speed marks over long distances in September 1929.

blocks, main bearings were three in number. They were lubricated by pressure and scavenge pumps in the engine's dry-sump system with a remote reservoir.

A high-mounted front water pump was belt-driven from the V12's crank nose, which carried a massive dynamotor. Vertically mounted at the rear of the twelve, the big Voisin's Delco ignition distributor and two coils fired a plug in the centre of each cylinder head. Individual rectangular exhaust pipes jutted through the bonnet, while in the central vee two Cozette carburettors flanked a fabricated manifold feeding the dozen inlet ports. On a *pro rata* basis from the 105bhp C12 the record twelve should have produced at least 200bhp at 3,000rpm, and indeed more in view of its special petrol-benzole fuel mixture.

Innocent of any gearbox, the big twelve was offset slightly to the left of its underslung right-hand-steered chassis to offer a bit more room to the driver. The latter was most often César Marchand during extensive tests in which a variety of open-wheeled body styles were tried. The final shape was purposeful with down-sloping nose and tail and an aero-screen for its intrepid pilot. Its sloping oval 'mouth' inspired the painting of two bold eyes atop its bonnet.

The third week of September 1929 at Montlhéry saw Marchand at the ready to commence a gruelling endurance run in the company of Messrs Morel, de Présalé and Kiriloff. Their aim being to set new records at 5,000 miles and far beyond, they could allow the twelve to loaf at 1,800rpm which gave an average of 91.17mph at that distance. Their speed at 10,000 miles was a still-

respectable 85.25mph and at 20,000 miles their average had only fallen to 82.73mph. The 48-hour record went at 91.10mph. After nine days the big Voisin was still going strong until it left the track in the hands of Serge Kiriloff, through either fatigue or a wheel failure.

With the run having been sponsored by oil firm Yacco, a scurrilous accusation that the Voisin had barely been able to run when it crashed had to be countered. Its creator announced that its teardown would take place in public at the Issy-les-Moulineaux works; all were invited. They saw components that were still in good order – a double triumph for Gabriel Voisin.

Frustrated at not having won for France some of the longest-distance records, still held by a hated American Studebaker, Voisin returned to Montlhéry in September 1930 with one of the most bizarre-looking record-breakers of all time. It was a standard C18 Diane 4.9-litre vee-twelve-cylinder chassis, minus wings but complete with bonnet and closed coupé body, behind which was an open rear deck and two huge cylindrical tanks, one for fuel and one for oil. His driving team persevered this time to 17 days, at which the record speed was 74.48mph. New records were set from 30,000 miles (74.44mph) to 50,000km (74.53mph). Gabriel Voisin now could – and did – claim for *La Belle France* all the speed records from 500 kilometres to the ultimate time and distance limits that had been explored by man.

While Voisin's record-breaking tractor – for that's what it looked like – was pounding around Montlhéry's banked oval, engineers in far-away Milan were mulling the challenge of the AIACR's latest attempt to impose order on a chaotic Grand Prix scene. Unlike America, Europe had given up the costly 1½-litre supercharged formula after the 1927 season. Anarchic conditions thereafter allowed race organisers to frame events as they saw fit. The only car-related rule promulgated by the AIACR for 1929 and 1930 was a minimum weight of 900kg, with a suggestion of a limit on the allowable consumption of fuel and oil. Even these were thrown aside for 1931, when open-wheeled racing was Formule Libre except for a requirement that to be a Grand Prix a race should last for a gruelling ten hours.

Seizing the day, Milan's Alfa Romeo reacquired three of its successful 1924 P2 racing cars and began entering them on behalf of drivers such as Achille Varzi. The old two-litre eight-cylinder racers were updated in their suspension and body shape to resemble the current 6C 1750 Gran Sport model and their supercharging systems modified to bring their power to 175bhp at 5,500rpm. By 1930 Tazio Nuvolari was driving the resuscitated P2 Alfas for Enzo Ferrari's newly formed

Scuderia Ferrari, which was to carry the Alfa Romeo banner in racing through 1937.

With its engineering led by former Fiat man Vittorio Jano, creator of the 1924 P2, Alfa was also challenged to muster a rival to cars that were being built for sheer speed on fast tracks such as the 4.9-litre Type 54 Bugatti and the V4 Maserati, which married two eights to make a four-litre sixteen. When someone jestingly said to Jano that "You should make a better car by putting two together", he responded by building a twin-engined car. He placed two six-cylinder engines side by side, driving separately to each rear wheel. The sixes were the successful Roots-supercharged 6C 1750 units of 56 x 88mm, which combined as a twelve to displace 3,504cc and produce a total of 230bhp at 5,200rpm. Although they started out as wet-sump engines, they were modified to dry sumps during development.

In fact only the left-hand engine resembled a standard 6C 1750, because the right-hand six was mirror-imaged so that all the inlet piping would be between the engines and the exhausts on the outside. Each six was cooled by its half of the radiator. Completing the mirror-imaging was the positioning of the two rings and pinions in the live rear axle, which required counter-rotating engines. Shrewdly, this had the added advantage of improving traction by cancelling out the torque that usually lifts the right rear wheel. With each engine driving its own wheel, a connection between them having been tried but

Viewed from the rear, the twin engines of Alfa Romeo's Type A showed an essentially standard 6C 1750 six on the left and a mirror-image unit on the right, so arranged as to allow exhausts to be outboard and induction systems to be between the two engines.

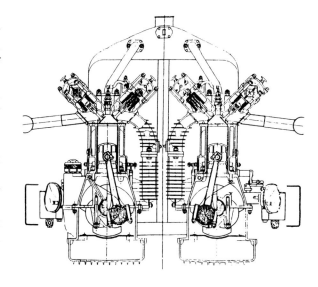

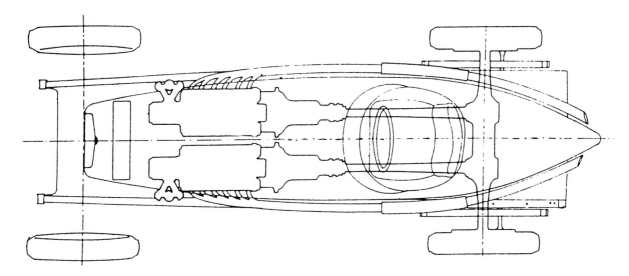

The driver sat centrally above the two counter-rotating drive shafts of Alfa Romeo's Type A of 1931. Although not a true V12, the Type A was an opportunistic effort that marked time until Alfa Romeo could produce an authentic twelve-cylinder engine.

abandoned, a differential effect was provided by giving the output shaft of each three-speed gearbox an overrunning clutch. A transverse shaft allowed a left-hand lever to shift both boxes.

Dubbed the Type A, this novel device made history in Alfa's annals by being its first *monoposto*, with a centrally seated driver.[2] In fact its pilot was very deeply enclosed in his cockpit by the standards of the day in order to improve the A's streamlining for fast circuits. The first race that met that definition was the Italian GP on 24 May 1931 over the full Monza road and track circuit. Two As suffered a tragic debut, with Luigi Arcangeli's killing him in practice and Tazio Nuvolari's breaking after two of the ten hours. Giuseppe Campari placed his fourth on 2 August in a race for which it was eminently unsuited, the Coppa Ciano,[3] and then won the 188-mile Coppa Acerbo on the fast Pescara circuit on the 16th with Nuvolari having to settle for third after one of his sixes blew its head gasket.

The Coppa Acerbo result showed that Jano had not blotted his copybook with his Type A's design, opportunistic though it undoubtedly was. At the Monza Grand Prix in September the two twelve-cylinder Alfas (out of four made) were seen to out-corner the Type 54 Bugattis, although the French car had a speed advantage over the Alfa's 150mph. The race itself was anticlimactic, with Nuvolari and Campari third and fourth in their heat and the latter non-starting in the final, while Tazio retired after challenging for the lead.

Jano's Type A had been built as a stopgap until his classic Type B – designed in parallel – was ready. His hugely successful 1932 Type B reverted to a proven straight-eight engine with a drive line inspired by his experiments with the Type A. Early in 1933, however, shortage of funds obliged Alfa Romeo to suspend its participation in racing. Later that year Alfa was restructured and taken under the wing of IRI, the government-owned industrial holding company, which was formed that same year to prop up selected enterprises in Benito Mussolini's Italy. In 1933 Alfa would make only 408 cars, but it was growing in importance as a supplier of trucks and aircraft engines to a rearming Italy and in that light deserved and received national support.

When Alfa Romeo officially returned to the Grand Prix wars in 1934 it soon discovered that its revised Type B was no match for the new cars that Mercedes-Benz and Auto Union tailored to that year's new Grand Prix formula, which limited car weight to a maximum of 750 kilograms or 1,654lb without tyres and liquids and required a body width of 33.5in. "This was intolerable to national pride," said one observer of Alfa's eclipse, "not only for sporting enthusiasts, but also for the national fascist hierarchy." In 1934 Alfa's management commissioned Vittorio Jano to commence work on a new Grand Prix car to uphold Italy's honour.

In the circumstances Jano's assignment was no sinecure. Instead of desperately needed money and men, wrote colleague Gioachino Colombo, his bosses motivated Jano with "more or less authoritative messages, directives and appeals." In the factory, he said, there was "great confusion about roles, too many people all wanting their own way in the matter of planning. It's a matter for amazement that he managed to build a vehicle at all under those conditions."

In 1939 Lagonda prepared two of its V12s for entry at Le Mans. Experienced there as he was, designer W. O. Bentley had his doubts about the enterprise, but it was rewarded when the teams of Dobson/ Brackenbury and Selsdon/ Waleran finished third and fourth respectively behind a Bugatti and Delage. While the works competition cars had four downdraft SU carburettors, this Lagonda racer has been equipped with six.

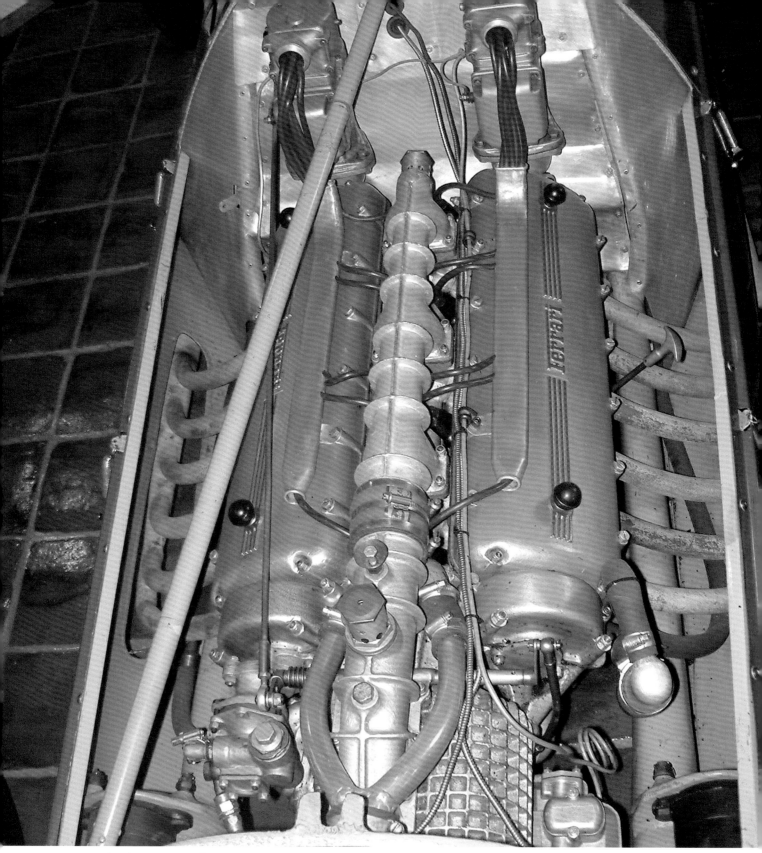

Based on his Ferrari 1.5-litre V12, Gioachino Colombo evolved a full Formula 1 version with a single Roots-type supercharger at the front of the block. Twin magnetos stood tall at the rear. Such single-seater Ferraris first raced in 1948's Italian Grand Prix and scored Ferrari's first Formula 1 victory in 1949 in the Swiss GP in the hands of Alberto Ascari. With changes of engine this green car was raced in Formulas 1 and 2 by Briton Peter Whitehead.

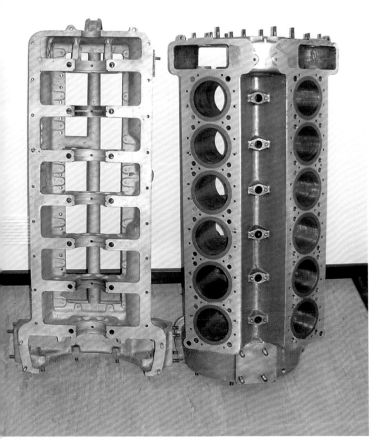

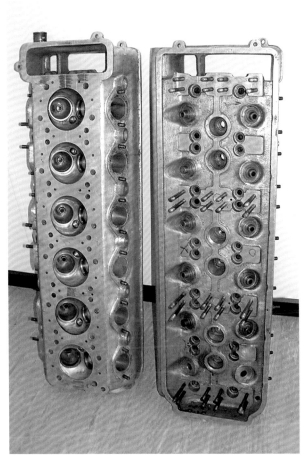

In 1949-51 the Maserati brothers, at their OSCA in Bologna, built an ambitious 4.5-litre twelve for Formula 1. Their Type G was to be shared with France's Gordini, which however was unable to fund its leg of the project. Above left are its aluminium cylinder block and magnesium main-bearing carrier, while above right are its cylinder heads. Below is the forked connecting rod, showing its V-shaped join between the separate big end and the rod proper.

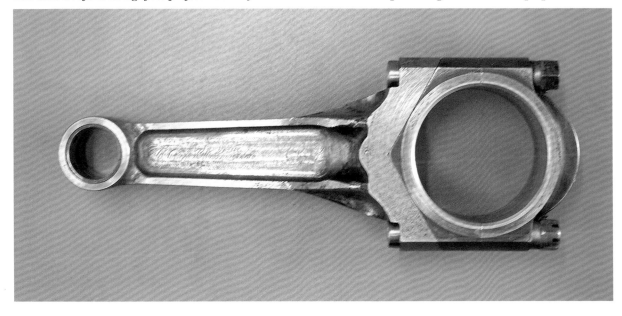

OSCA completed two Grand Prix cars powered by its 4.5-litre V12 engine, both of which were converted into sports cars. Above is one of these, resigned to life in a French museum. In the mid-1960s Ferrari fielded four-camshaft twelves for both Formula 1 and sports-car competition. The handsome unit below, a wet-sump engine for a sports-car application, had downdraft ports between its camshafts, fed by slide throttles and Lucas fuel injection.

In 1957's Sebring 12-hour race Ferrari fielded a team of sports-racers powered by a new generation of four-cam twelves of 3.8 and 4.0 litres, developing up to 390bhp. Potent though they were, they were overmatched that year by Maserati's 450S, though Piero Taruffi drove one to a win in the Mille Miglia. This was destined to be the last Mille Miglia, for a sister car crashed late in the race, killing its occupants and nine spectators.

It amused Enzo Ferrari to contemplate that after the war only one other auto company was using V12 engines, America's Lincoln. Here in a Continental, the side-valve Model H Lincoln was a far cry from Enzo's exotic engines.

Nevertheless with its aluminium heads and 75° vee angle the Lincoln was a unique creation, by no means the clone of Ford's V8 that it's often accused of being. From 1937 into 1948 it powered some 220,000 Lincolns.

190

Early in the 1960s GM's Cadillac Division developed a twelve in 7.4- and 8.2-litre sizes that was radical by GM's standards with its chain-driven single overhead camshafts on each cylinder bank. The 'V-Future' V12, right, failed to make it to production. Luxury-car buyers in the 21st Century have their pick of twelves, including the BMW-derived 6.7-litre unit in the Rolls-Royce Phantom, below, capable of 453bhp and 531lb-ft of torque.

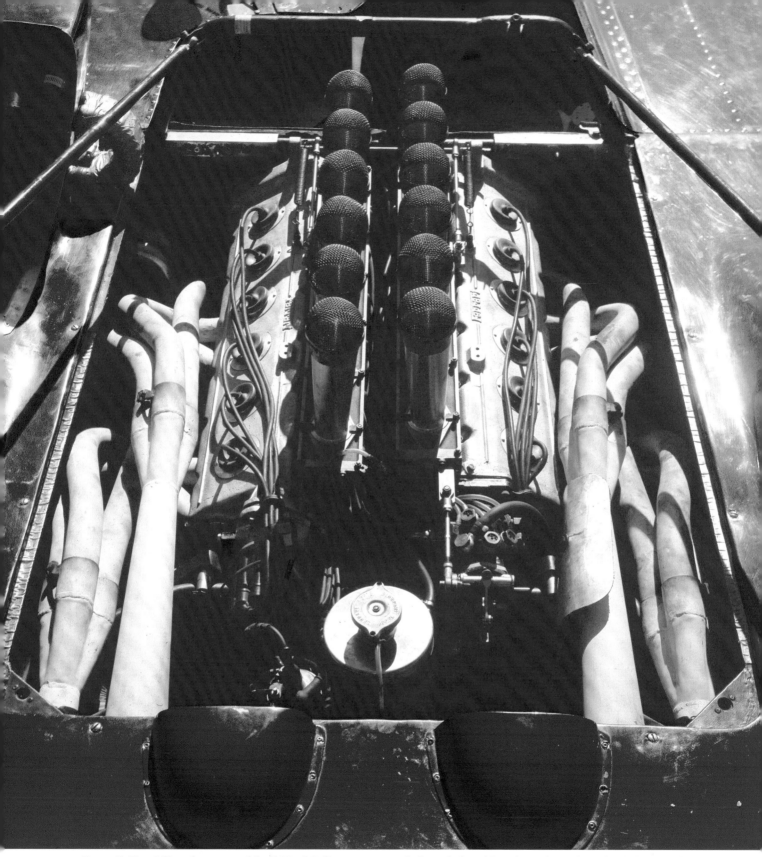

Ferrari's Type 261 twelve powered the 612P of 1969, Maranello's most ambitious contender for top honours in the rich Can-Am series. Producing well in excess of 600 horsepower, the engine began the season with 6.2 litres and ended it with 6.9. Although it achieved two third places and one second in the hands of entrant Chris Amon, unreliability kept it from posing a more consistent challenge to the dominant McLaren-Chevrolets.

THE V12 ENGINE

Jano's new car had all-independent suspension with trailing arms and coil springs in front and swing axles with a transverse leaf in the rear, carried by a frame of box-section tubes. Its transmission was rear-mounted while its clutch remained at the engine. Jano also planned a new twelve-cylinder engine for the chassis, but with that unready the new model was launched as the 8C, with an updated Type B engine, in September 1935. On 10 May 1936, at the Tripoli Grand Prix, it made its bow as originally planned with its V12 engine as the 12C.

Jano entrusted a newcomer to Alfa with the task of detailing the new twelve's design under his direction. This was 43-year-old Bruno Trevisan, a reserve major in Italy's Air Force. An engine expert at Fiat, Trevisan moved to Milan in October 1934, just in time to start work on the new twelve. Their engine was a work of commendable purity. Its vee angle was 60° with its right bank offset forward to allow side-by-side connecting rods. Two valves per cylinder were angled symmetrically at the wide spread that Jano favoured of 104° and equal in diameter at 35mm. With cylinder-centre distances of 95mm, the twelve's dimensions were 70 x 88mm for a capacity of 4,064cc.[4]

All the engine's main castings were in light alloy, with the crankcase cast of magnesium alloy. Pioneered for

The extremely wide valve angle of 104° was chosen by Bruno Trevisan in his design of a 4.1-litre racing V12 for Alfa Romeo, under the supervision of Vittorio Jano. Its cylinder blocks were aluminium and its crankcase castings of even lighter magnesium.

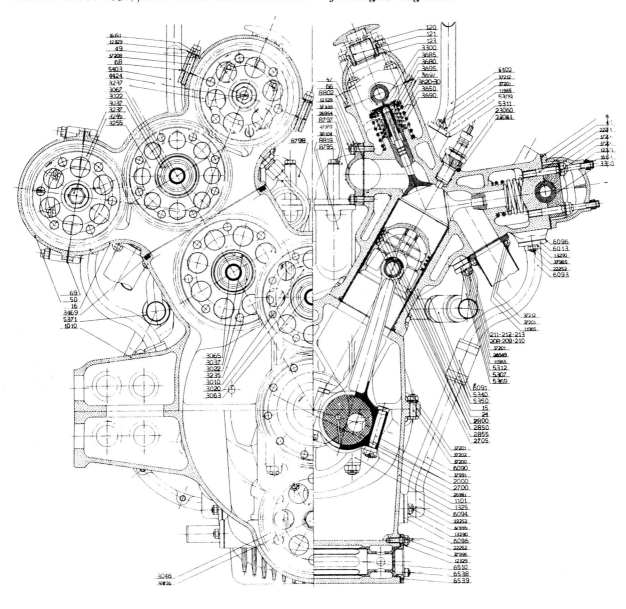

Gearing at the front of Alfa Romeo's 1936 vee-twelve turned a single Roots-type supercharger, beneath which two horizontal Weber carburettors provided mixture.

Bruno Trevisan's design for Alfa Romeo's 1936 vee-twelve placed its camshaft-drive gear train at the rear of the engine, adjacent to the clutch. The transmission of the 12C-36, in which it was installed, was a transaxle at the rear of the chassis.

racing cars by the Maserati brothers, magnesium had been used successfully in the 3.8-litre eight that powered the chassis in its original form as the 8C. Extending down to the crank centreline, where a deep magnesium sump added stiffness, the crankcase was literally that, with two aluminium cylinder blocks bolted to it. Each had integral heads and bores protected by thin dry steel liners, held in place by a small flange at the base of the block.

If there was a fault in Trevisan's layout it was its lack of full cooling around the valve guides in the symmetrical heads, although this was not untypical of Jano's designs. Each connecting-rod journal was hollow-bored to reduce its mass and opposed by double counterbalances. The forged-steel crankshaft was carried by seven 65mm main bearings, which were oiled from a gallery running the length of the engine's central vee.

Slim-shanked I-section connecting rods for the twelve measured 190mm between their 22mm small ends and 60mm big-end bearings. High-domed aluminium pistons, giving a 7.1:1 ratio, carried four rings and were well braced internally. Above them the valves were closed by triple coil springs, one large external spring and two shorter ones inside it. A thin mushroom tappet was screwed around the end of the valve stem and held laterally by the top of the valve guide, an exceptionally compact and light valve gear. Four plain bearings supported each of the four overhead camshafts.

Trevisan divided the accessory loads between the front and rear of his twelve. At the output end, a gear train

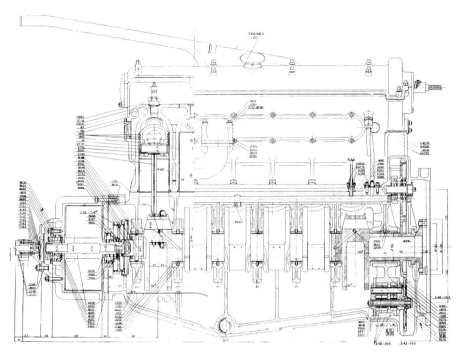

A complex coupling at the nose of the crankshaft, left, provided a cushioned drive to the large-radius rotors of the Alfa Romeo's single Roots-type supercharger. An extremely wide rear main bearing provided support for the cam-drive gear train of the 12C-36, the drive gear of which was machined integrally with the crankshaft.

ran upward to the camshafts and downward to the two-section oil pump, integral with the massive rear main-bearing cap, for the dry-sump system. Driven directly from the nose of the crank was one 200mm lobe of a Roots supercharger that blew upward and back into the centre of inlet manifolds which were partly integrated with the blocks. Under it was the inlet ducting for two horizontal twin-throat Weber carburettors. Other gears turned the single magneto and the water pump on the right, from which two manifolds ran back along the blocks to inlets below the exhaust ports.

By Alfa Romeo's racing-car standards this was an epic engine, its most potent yet. Boosted at 11psi, it produced 370bhp at 5,800rpm. "They were confident," wrote Laurence Pomeroy Jnr, "that with the extra power available from this they would be able to take full advantage of their new independently sprung chassis and reassert in 1936 the supremacy which had been theirs only two seasons before." The Scuderia Ferrari had high hopes for the new 12C-36. Six in all were made, plus four spare engines.

The first race outing at Tripoli in May 1936 was not without promise. On this very fast circuit the Alfas were only two seconds slower than the Mercedes on a lap of 3¾ minutes. At the finish, however, the three twelves were sixth, seventh and eighth and, indeed, behind an 8C Alfa in fifth, trailing the German cars. On a more challenging track at Barcelona's Montjuich Park on 7 June, Tazio Nuvolari drove the sole 12C-36 to a tremendous victory over both German teams in spite of two pit stops

over 188 miles; the new car was proving hard on its tyres. Nuvolari would win three more times that year in the new twelve, at Milan, Modena and – most importantly – the 300-mile race on the new Roosevelt Raceway on New York's Long Island for the George Vanderbilt Cup. Though no Germans were present, this gave both Tazio and Alfa major bragging rights over the winter.

Nevertheless this hadn't been a good Mercedes-Benz season. Vittorio Jano knew he had to extract more power from his twelve for 1937, terminal year of the 750-kilogram formula. He and Trevisan enlarged both bore and stroke to 72 x 92mm to bring the twelve to 4,495cc, with the compression ratio rising to 7.25:1. Boost pressure went up to 12psi with higher supercharger efficiency thanks to the use of two 105mm Roots blowers running at one and a half times engine speed. High-speed durability benefited from caged roller bearings at the connecting-rod big ends, on journals which were no longer bored for lightness.

Weighing 474lb, the revised engine produced 430bhp at 5,800rpm. This was as naught, however, against the 575bhp of Mercedes-Benz and Auto Union's 520-plus. In the major races the best that Alfa Romeo could muster was Nuvolari's fourth in the German Grand Prix. In minor events, against occasional Auto Union entries, wins were achieved at Turin, Naples and Milan. Laurence Pomeroy wrote that "during 1937 so far from narrowing the gap, Alfa Romeo fell farther behind."

The Milan firm nursed high expectations for a new low-chassis model that made its debut at Pescara in August. Marrying the existing power train and suspension

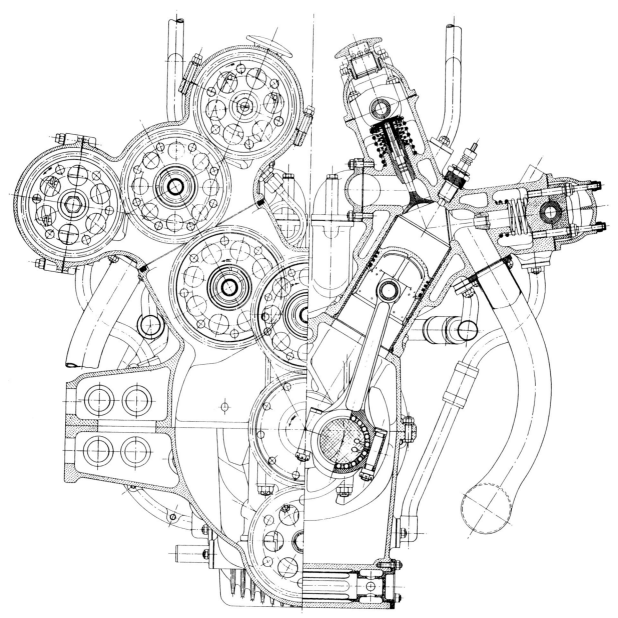

With increased bore and stroke to bring capacity to 4.5 litres for the 1937 racing season, Alfa Romeo's twelve now had roller-bearing big ends. It carried over Jano's favoured compact valve gear with a flat circular tappet screwed into the stem of the valve for clearance adjustment.

to a narrow chassis – virtually a backbone – and a much lower profile, a quartet was put on wheels. The new model was far off the pace, and of the two entries only one started for Nuvolari, who struggled to run ninth before handing his car to Nino Farina, who retired.

This catastrophic launch on home territory, said Alfa engineer Luigi Fusi, "cost Jano his parting with Alfa Romeo." "The management was very hard, very severe," recalled another engineer. "However good you were, whatever brilliant work you had done in the past, if you did not deliver you could be dismissed." Earlier in 1937 Vincenzo Lancia had died and, partly to fill the vacuum left by the founder, Jano returned to Turin and Lancia.

Nineteen thirty-seven had been a transitional year in racing for Alfa, which acquired 80 per cent of Scuderia Ferrari in March and by the end of the year was ready to open its own racing department, Alfa Corse, in new buildings in Milan. For 1938 Grand Prix cars could be 4½ litres unblown and 3 litres supercharged. With odds strongly favouring the latter, Alfa shrank its twelve to 2,997cc (66 x 73mm) and without greatly changing its blowers or boost pressure extracted 350bhp at 6,500rpm.

This, in the lower chassis, was Alfa's Type 312 for 1938, for which the 35-year-old Gioachino Colombo, a close ally of Jano, had some design responsibility. Three of the new cars were built, cadging components from their predecessors.

The 312's performance in its few 1938 appearances led many to suggest that this Alfa could be a contender if its maker were inclined to back it with conviction. Problems in setting up the new Alfa Corse didn't help, nor did Alfa's dalliance with eight- and 16-cylinder engines for the new formula and its heightened interest in the 1½-litre *Voiturette* category, for which it had the eight-cylinder Type 158 designed by Colombo and built in Ferrari's Modena workshops.

All three 312s were at Tripoli in Libya, one of Italy's African protectorates, for the first big Grand Prix of '38 in mid-May. Two started, with the thrusting Nino Farina showing the 312's potential but crashing out – as he often did. The other twelve crashed as well, killing its unfortunate driver, Eugenio Siena. Of two cars in July's German GP one crashed and the other retired. Duos competed at home in August in the Coppa Ciano and Coppa Acerbo. In both they had to give best to a Mercedes, but nevertheless took second and third places. In the Swiss Grand Prix on 21 August Nino Farina was fifth behind three Mercedes and an Auto Union, albeit two laps behind the winner after 50 laps. Jean-Pierre Wimille was seventh in a sister car.

Wimille and Piero Taruffi had 312s for the Italian GP at Monza, where both retired. No more entries of the twelve were made until the Belgian Grand Prix on 26 June 1939, where one was entrusted to Frenchman Raymond Sommer. He was fourth, twice lapped, behind the Germans in the wet race in which Britain's Richard Seaman was killed. This – just missing the podium – would be the 312's best performance in a major Grand Prix.

To power the Type 312 Alfa Romeo of the 1938 season the twelve's capacity was reduced to 3.0 litres. Fitted into a new lower chassis, the 350-horsepower twelve showed considerable promise in its few 1938 racing appearances.

Nor did the single-seater Alfa V12 star in a series for which it should have been tailor-made: the Formule Libre races in Argentina at the beginning of 1948. Achille Varzi, who had raced there in 1947, arranged for Alfa Romeo to build a 'special' for his next campaign. The Milanese married a pre-war chassis which had been used for a 3-litre V16 with a 1937-style 4½-litre supercharged twelve to create as formidable-looking a racing car as has ever been contrived. Its looks flattered to deceive, however, for the best that Varzi could manage with it was a second at Mar del Plata.[5]

At Buenos Aires in 1948 Achille Varzi raced a magnificent Alfa Romeo 'special' which married a 4.5-litre version of the V12 with a redundant pre-war chassis. Awesome though it looked, it was not a match for the latest post-war designs.

An unsupercharged version of the Grand Prix vee-twelve was used by Alfa Romeo to power two sports-racing cars, dubbed the 412. They first raced and won in May 1939.

Fed by three twin-throat downdraft Weber carburettors, the unsupercharged Alfa Romeo V12 delivered 220bhp from its 4.5 litres. This engine powered the car in which Felice Bonetto placed sixth in the 1951 Mille Miglia.

In a 'waste not, want not' frame of mind, Alfa Corse itself made use of redundant 4½-litre V12s before the war. In 1939 it used its GP-car componentry to build a sports-racing car on the lines of the famous 8C 2900B Mille Miglia model but powered by an unblown version of the big vee-twelve to compete in events where superchargers were banned. With its blower deleted, the twelve had new inlet manifolding carrying three downdraft double-throat carburettors. Its compression ratio raised to 8.15:1, the engine's output was 220bhp at 5,500rpm.

Swiss sports-car champion Willy Daetwyler rebodied his 412 for the 1953 season in a lighter style better suited to post-war sprint racing. He also obtained supercharging equipment from Alfa Romeo to raise its power still further.

Dubbed the 412 and bodied by Touring, a pair of these formidable sports-racers was ready to race over the streets of Antwerp, Belgium on 31 May 1939.[6] They finished one–two against opposition largely from France, where this category was very popular. They were due to meet the French again at Liége on 20 August, and were fastest in practice, but the imminence of war forced the race's cancellation.

After the war the 412s were recovered from safe storage. "Everything was covered in thick grease," an Alfa man remembered. "It was just a question of cleaning it all carefully and with nothing more than normal preparation we could immediately race again." One car was sold to Felice Bonetto, who won with it in Portugal in 1950 and had it magnificently rebodied by Vignale for the 1951 Mille Miglia, in which he was sixth. Its sister was acquired by Willy Daetwyler, who raced it extensively and successfully in and around his Swiss homeland. For the 1953 season he had his 412 rebodied in a lighter style, and from Alfa's stores he obtained a supercharging kit which would have given it power akin to the Varzi single-seater. Ultimately this potent machine was acquired by the Schlumpf Collection in Mulhouse.

Remote from Alfa's racing travails in these last years of the 1930s, Bruno Trevisan moved to Alfa's production-car side, where he designed an engine that's among the great might-have-beens of Alfa Romeo history. He prepared two new car ranges in 1938: the V8 S11 series of 2.3 litres and the V12 S10 model of 3.6 litres. Both were to be all-independently suspended. The smaller car would have been a monocoque design tooled for large volume, while the separate frame of the larger would have suited custom coachwork.

Trevisan's vee-twelve for the S10 was a 60° design with

From his racing-engine work Bruno Trevisan transferred to production-car engineering at Alfa Romeo, for whom he designed the 3.6-litre S10 V12 in 1939. Angled at 30° in cylinders inclined at a 60° vee, its valves were vertical in wedge-type combustion chambers.

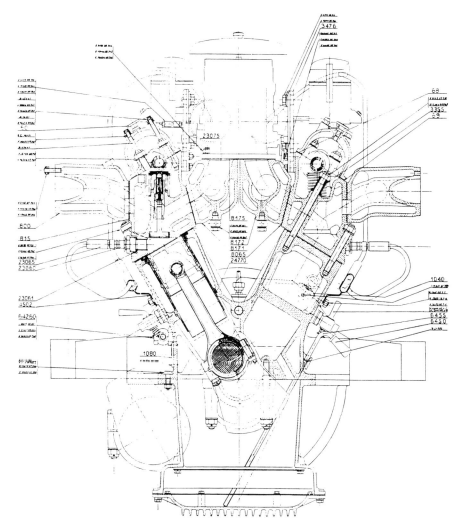

aluminium heads and block, the latter cut off at the crankshaft centreline. Its finned wet sump was also an aluminium casting. Two 30mm valves per cylinder were in line in the heads, inclined at 30° to the cylinder axis to form a wedge-type combustion chamber and to align the valve stems vertically in the engine. Jano's compact and light valve gear was carried over for the single overhead cam above each head, driven by chains from the crankshaft nose. The front accessory drive also turned the water pump, fan and – through a belt – the generator. At the rear of the camshafts vertical distributors were driven; various versions had either one or two.

The S10's cylinders were formed as wet liners of steel, which were pinched by the heads at flanges at their tops and seated against the block at their bottoms. With a bore

Compact and designed for economical production, Trevisan's 3.6-litre S10 V12 was a canny conception that could have been of great value to Alfa Romeo. A sporting version, with twin overhead cams for each bank, was also schemed before the war.

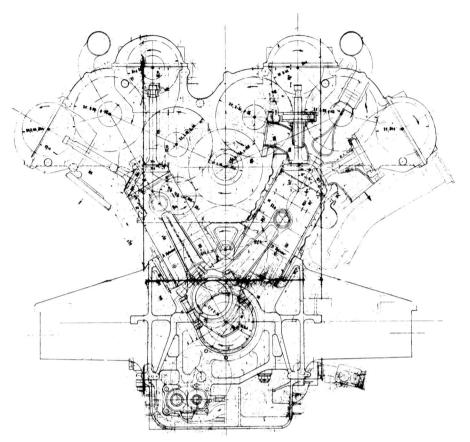

of 68mm – shared with the V8 – and a stroke of 82mm the S10's capacity was 3,574cc. Its right cylinder bank was offset forward to suit the side-by-side rods on its seven-bearing crankshaft. Porting was cross-flow with outboard exhausts, in water-shrouded manifolds recalling those of the Phantom III, and water-warmed inlet manifolding in the central vee. Fed by one double-throat downdraft carburettor it produced 140bhp at 4,700rpm on a compression ratio of 7.0:1.

The S10 would have given Alfa a worthy upscale model, with half as much power again as the 6C 2500 introduced in 1939. Two experimental cars were built, but wartime exigencies meant that the model wasn't proceeded with. Its sporting sister, the S10 SS, failed to reach the prototype stage but its engine, with twin overhead cams and 165bhp at 4,700rpm, was built in two test samples. Thoughtfully designed to be both powerful and producible, the S10 was the right car for Alfa Romeo but at the wrong time.

By far Alfa's most successful Grand Prix season with its twelve was 1936. Ironically, part of the responsibility for this lay with the failure of Mercedes-Benz to make good use of a twelve of its own. Its master plan for the 1936 season was to build an 'SSK' version of its existing eight-cylinder W25 GP car. Making it lower and shorter, especially at the rear, would lighten it so that it could also be powered by a new and more powerful engine without exceeding the Formula's 750kg maximum weight.

Conceived for this mission by the Daimler-Benz engine-design group under Albert Heess was a 60° V12 using exactly the same construction techniques as existing eights, namely fabricated-steel cylinders with four valves apiece on an aluminium crankcase. The first of these 'D-series' engines was designated DAB because it had the same bore and stroke as the eight-cylinder M25AB, 82 x 88mm to give 5,577cc.[7] It made use of the existing forged-steel cylinders as the B-series eight, with its four 35.5mm valves at a 60° included angle. The same angle was used for the two banks of cylinders, each composed of two triple-cylinder blocks.

Normal M25 top-end components, including finger-type followers and double-coil valve springs, were used inside the aluminium castings that tied each pair of blocks together along the rows of valves, carrying each camshaft in four bearings. The gear-drive train to the four camshafts ran up the back of the engine, where it also turned the tachometer, magneto and oil pumps. A straight-sided aluminium crankcase accommodated the steel blocks, extending downward 90mm below the centreline of the crankshaft. Caps for the seven main bearings were tied in by cross-bolts as well as two vertical studs apiece.

Main-bearing size was 63mm except for a smaller front main, while rod journals were 55mm. They carried fork-and-blade connecting rods like those in contemporary Daimler-Benz aircraft engines. The blade rods were on the left bank, with dual rows of 8mm big-end bearing rollers. Embracing them at the journals were the forked ends of the rods from the right bank, each side of the fork enclosing a single row of 8mm rollers. Both types of rods measured 171mm from centre to centre and had four bolts holding the big end together at their deeply serrated joint faces.

Oil pumps were placed low at the right rear of the shallow finned sump. A bevel gear at the front of the crankshaft drove the Grätzin fuel pump with its Daimler-Benz pressure regulator, on the right, and the water pump on the left. Its coolant output was split through a 'Y' manifold to the two cylinder banks. Further forward a hollow extension of the crank nose drove twin Roots-type superchargers at a 2:1 step-up in speed through a circular cage containing multiple sets of coil springs. Facing the drive and deceleration forces, the springs gave flexibility to the drive train.

At the ends of this case were two bevel gears, each driving a Roots-type supercharger mounted at right angles to the crankshaft. As viewed from the front the blowers were splayed to the right and left, the right one in line with its cylinder bank and the left one tilted a little more, at 32°, to gain the space needed for its mounting. The use of two facing drive bevels meant that the compressors turned in opposite directions; this was intentional so they could draw air from their outside faces and pump it into a common central manifold. With lobes 180mm long, the blowers delivered pressure air to two Daimler-Benz twin-throat carburettors and thence to the inlet valves through the central manifold.

When in the late summer of 1935 the first DAB engine was finished it was judged disappointing, not in its power – which easily exceeded 500bhp – but in its weight. It scaled 620lb, over 200lb more than the various M25 eights. Having the same rear engine bearers as the eights cast integral with its crankcase, the first DAB was installed without undue difficulty in a W25 chassis for testing. During trials on a new section of *Autobahn* at Echterdingen, just south of Stuttgart, the engine was badly damaged when it was over-revved. Repairs were easy enough; parts for ten engines had been commissioned.

It wasn't the Grand Prix Formula's weight limit that excluded the DAB from Grand Prix consideration,

As viewed from the front, the Daimler-Benz DAB V12 had its twin Roots-type superchargers approximately in line with its cylinder banks. Supercharging was by the method still used by Mercedes-Benz in 1935 and 1936: compressing fresh air and delivering it to the carburettors.

Fork-and-blade connecting rods allowed the two banks of the DAB V12 to be opposite each other. Following the practice of the straight-eight Mercedes-Benz racing engines, the gear drive to the camshafts was at the clutch end of the engine.

testified Rudolf Uhlenhaut, who headed the engineering side of Mercedes-Benz's *Rennabteilung* or racing department. Rather in the car as it wasn't well enough balanced to be a successful road-racer: "Although the new car was within the 750kg limit, it had too much weight at the front end. It was quite good for setting records on a straight road but quite unsuitable for the Nürburgring, for example." For setting records on a straight road, the DAB V12 was ultimately to be unsurpassed.

With 1936 a forgettable racing year for Untertürkheim, its managers decided to buff the Mercedes-Benz reputation – in the year celebrating the 50th anniversary of the first Daimler and Benz cars – with an attempt on Class B records, for engines of up to eight litres. In September the racing department assembled a DAB engine with a compression ratio of 9.1:1. By mid-October engine-test chief Georg Scheerer despatched it from his test bench with a peak reading of 616bhp at 5,800rpm. Maximum boost was 18.2psi after the blowers, 14.9psi at the most remote inlet valves. Its torque was formidable, registering 585lb-ft and better over the speed range from 3,000 to 5,000rpm. These readings were obtained on fuel of 86 per cent methanol, 4.4 per cent nitro-benzole, 8.8 per cent acetone and 0.8 per cent ether that was used for record-breaking.

The chosen chassis was one of the now-redundant Model 1936 Grand Prix cars for which the engine had been built, keeping all its main suspension and drive features. Its body was fully enveloping, at the time a radical experiment. In mid-1936 few cars of any kind had been built with their wheels fully enclosed within an unbroken aerodynamic shell. None had been completed and driven at high speed with this type of body.[8] Not until late 1937 did the concealed-wheel juggernauts of Eyston and Cobb begin their epic joust of speed at Bonneville.

The German sporting authority closed the *Autobahn* section just south of Frankfurt, toward Darmstadt, along the eastern boundary of Frankfurt Airport, for record attempts in late October 1936. The western or southbound lane was used for Rudy Caracciola's runs in both directions, allowing about two miles to accelerate before reaching the timed section. Recorded were new World Class B records of 226.4mph for the kilometre and 228.0mph for the mile. On a German highway Caracciola had gone virtually as fast as the land speed record holder of 1929 had travelled at Daytona Beach. One more two-way drive netted the Class B record for five kilometres at 211.6mph. In November Rudy returned to cover five miles at an average of 209.3mph, ten kilometres at 206.2 and ten miles at 207.2mph. The last was an outright world record as well as a Class B mark.

In 1937 the German authorities staged an official

One DAB vee-twelve was installed in the 1936 single-seater chassis for which it was originally intended. Arched induction passages took pressure air to its carburettors. Although effective in a straight line, the resulting car was too nose-heavy to be a useful road racer.

Record Week or *Rekordwoche* on one lane of the Frankfurt-Darmstadt *Autobahn* from 25 until 31 October 1937. A specially prepared 15.5-mile stretch of the concrete roadway and about 30 feet wide was closed to traffic, which was shunted onto the other carriageway. The timed section would allow record attempts over distances of up to 10 miles. Daimler-Benz readied new cars for this occasion that were intended to allow Rudy Caracciola to retain his old records and set some new ones.

On 14 October the dynamometer tests were complete on DAB engine number three, prepared for these attempts. It was fed by blowers that drew fuel/air mixture from two Solex carburettors plus a special boost-controlled supplementary carburettor. Its output was now a stunning 736bhp at 5,800rpm on a boost pressure of 18.2psi and a 9.17:1 compression ratio. Torque was 725lb-ft and more from 3,000 to 4,000rpm. These were figures to conjure with, the highest ever recorded on the dynamometers of the Daimler-Benz *Rennabteilung*. An attempt to take a power reading at 6,000rpm resulted only in the awed notation: "brake shaking".

The DAB twelve was installed in the much-improved 1937 W125 Grand Prix chassis and fitted with a body based on the '36 design but narrowed and lowered. It proved a disaster at the *Rekordwoche*, 'aviating' alarmingly at the front. As well, wrote John Dugdale, "the big Merc was a pig to start. A mechanic had to stand in the engine compartment and prime or maybe choke the carburettors while the car was push-started."

Hectic activity at Christmastime in 1937 was owed to another record attempt planned for late January 1938, just before the February opening of the auto show in

Berlin. The Nazis had declared that records would be set only during the official October week, but Hitler-intimate Jakob Werlin – a Daimler board member – pulled some strings at the Reich Chancellery to arrange a special face-saving session for Daimler-Benz. Major changes in the car included the use of an ice-cooling system, eliminating the drag of a radiator, and a superb new shape with an extended tail that brought the car's overall length to 248in and its weight to 2,608lb dry.

It was overcoat weather but there was no snow on the ground at Frankfurt on the cloudy morning of 28 January 1938, which the weather section at the nearby airport said would be suitable for the running of this very fast car. It had been rushed to completion the night before and trucked to the *Autobahn* in time to meet Alfred Neubauer and Rudy Caracciola at 5:00am. Rudy decided to wait until the frost had cleared from the roadway. By nine that morning they were having a celebration breakfast at the Park Hotel in Frankfurt. Caracciola made one reconnaissance run just after eight, then a serious attack. "The car hugged the road beautifully – I was aware of that even on the starting run. It drove altogether differently from the car they had the year before."

The brutal boom of its side-spewing exhaust stacks rattled onlookers as the silver car hurtled by. Its two-way average was 268.712mph for the kilometre, 268.496mph for the mile. It was a sensational speed, a great achievement. No faster speeds have ever been officially timed on a public highway.

The DAB twelve also had one chance to do a bit of racing. Daimler-Benz counted on this as its major weapon for Formule Libre races that were staged on 30 May 1937 at Berlin's rebuilt AVUS track, with its new 43° banked north turn. Trials at the end of April, however, suggested that tyres – already under strain at the speeds being reached – were overloaded by the extra weight of the twelve. One streamlined DAB-engined car was entered for Manfred von Brauchitsch, while Geoffredo Zehender drove a 1936 Grand Prix car with the DAB engine – the Grand Prix car that Mercedes-Benz might have fielded in 1936.

Zehender's car was a non-starter after suffering engine trouble in practice. In his 83-mile heat, however, von Brauchitsch was the winner at the average speed of 160.27mph. This was not only a first victory for the DAB twelve but also the fastest motor race ever held. The average of the 96-mile final – from which von Brauchitsch retired early with clutch trouble – topped this by more than two miles per hour. In his heat, however, von Brauchitsch turned one lap at a stupefying 174.83mph. This was to remain the fastest lap, either race or practice, recorded during the entire meeting.

Their work on the DAB twelve could be considered a warm-up lap for the Mercedes engineers' design of a new engine for the 1938-39 Grand Prix formula. Like Alfa Romeo, Mercedes-Benz and Auto Union chose the supercharged 3-litre option, and both the German companies selected 60° vee-twelves as well.[9]

The Stuttgart twelve's mechanical design resembled that of the DAB V12, with dimensions of 67 x 70mm (2,962cc). A major difference was the forward offsetting of the left-hand cylinder bank by 18mm to allow for side-by-side connecting rods. Main-bearing journals measured 60mm except for the 52mm journal at the

In January 1938 Rudy Caracciola used the latest DAB-powered Mercedes-Benz streamliner to set a new record for its class at 268.7mph over the flying kilometre on the Autobahn between Frankfurt and Darmstadt. No-one has ever travelled faster officially on a public highway.

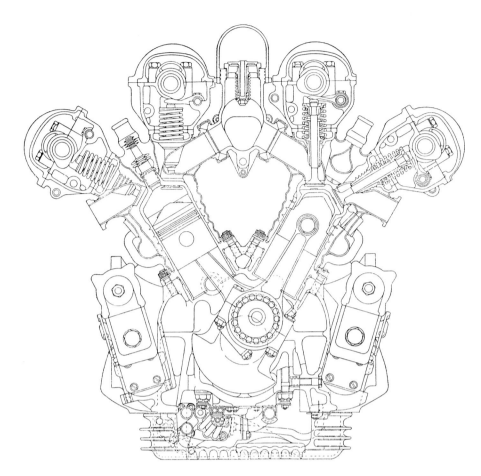

front, and ran on 10mm rollers. At the big ends, rollers 8mm in diameter and 12mm long ran on 54mm journals. Connecting-rod length was 155mm, forged of nickel-chrome steel with I-section shanks. Cylinder-centre distance within each steel three-cylinder block was 93mm.

The M154, as the new unit was known to the engineers, was also DAB-like in the placing of its cam-gear and oil-pump drive at the crankshaft's output end. Other drives were provided at the rear for fuel-injection pumps, a six-cylinder pump along each flank, but the injection wasn't ready so these were used for extra oil-scavenge pumps instead. Four bearings supported each camshaft within the full-length aluminium cam housings, also enclosing the finger-type followers and double-coil valve springs. Symmetrically disposed at a 60° included angle were four valves per cylinder, each with a 30mm head diameter.

From the time the new engine first drew breath in January 1938 until the racing season was well under way in May, the V12 was troubled by a limitation on revs caused by valve bounce in the new high-speed regimes it reached. This meant early valve contact with the pistons,

whose crowns had been pushed exceptionally close to the chamber walls in this large-bore, short-stroke (by previous standards) cylinder to get a compression ratio of 7.8:1 in the first engine. To gain reliability the piston-crown height had to be dropped, reducing the compression ratio of the 1938 M154 to the range of 5.9–6.2:1. At some sacrifice in maximum power, this made the engine serviceable for the 1938 season.

Induction in 1938 was through two Roots-type compressors operating in parallel. Their steel rotors in magnesium casings measured 106mm in diameter and 150mm in length. Protruding forward from the front of the engine, they were driven by a train of spur gears from the nose of the crank at a step-up of 1.5:1. Their pressurised air-fuel mixture was supplied to a single central manifold from which individual branches led downward to oval inlet ports. The blowers were fed by a single Daimler-Benz carburettor with a boost-controlled supplementary fuel delivery.

Hermann Lang's engine for Reims showed the highest reading obtained in 1938: 474bhp at 8,000rpm. Lang was fastest qualifier and race leader until his car proved hard to restart after his pit stop – a chronic 1938 problem. The

This display V12 was fitted with the new two-stage supercharging system developed for the 1939 racing season by Mercedes-Benz. Nearest the camera is the large primary Roots-type blower, which delivered to a smaller neighbouring unit, from which boost was passed to the engine.

In his cutaway drawing clearly based on the preceding photo, Vic Berris showed the four valves per cylinder of the Mercedes-Benz M154, the spur-gear drive to its twin Roots-type superchargers and the heavy counterbalancing given its roller-bearing crankshaft.

engines sent to Donington Park in October produced between 433 and 444bhp at 8,000rpm.

Problems notwithstanding, Mercedes won three of the major 1938 Grands Prix to Auto Union's two. Rudolf Uhlenhaut set new objectives for the 1939 version of the V12: "From the driving point of view a speed of 8,500–8,800 would be of great advantage, even if the power remained constant from 8,000–8,500 or fell off slightly." Standing in the way, he acknowledged, were shortcomings of the valve gear and the connecting rods.

Extensive revisions to the base engine improved its ruggedness, serviceability and oil-tightness, leading to a new designation: M163. Both this and the M154 accepted the same supercharger assemblies, valves and valve gear and accessories. Bore and stroke were unchanged. During 1939 four of these new engines – also known as K-Series – were completed for use by the team.

Breakup of the main-bearing journals, which had been a problem in 1938, was still troubling the twelve, as was valve bounce. To ensure reliability the racing red line was lowered to 7,200rpm, so instead of rising in 1939, as Uhlenhaut had hoped, the speed limit had to be lowered. Not until this new red line was enforced in the last two races of 1939 was the V12 judged to have attained "complete operating reliability".

Another change for 1939 was the adoption of two-stage supercharging. This helped the late-1939 engines produce seven per cent more power on ten per cent less manifold pressure than the 1938 engines of the same compression ratio. The rotors of both blower stages were given the same diameter, 125mm, their lengths differing at 220 and 125mm. Both were driven at 1.25 times crankshaft speed. The more efficient two-stage system reduced the amount of power that was needed to drive the blowers, helping net engine output rise at every engine speed. The peak power figures of 470 to 480bhp that had been recorded before at 8,000rpm were now achieved at 7,500. Torque was 365lb-ft at 5,500rpm. Power was increased by 25 and 30bhp handfuls all the

Seen at the 1939 French Grand Prix, the M154 V12 still required tender loving care if it were to deliver its full performance throughout a Grand Prix. The 1939 two-stage engines were rated at 480bhp at 7,500rpm, although late in the season a 7,200rpm rev limit was imposed.

Manfred von Brauchitsch was at the wheel of this Mercedes-Benz W154 in the last Grand Prix of 1939, held at Belgrade on September 3rd, two days after German troops invaded Poland. In an 87-mile race von Brauchitsch placed second to an Auto Union.

way up the curve while specific fuel consumption remained almost unchanged.

The Mercedes racing engineers weren't yet home free. A spate of engine failures in mid-season had them scratching their heads until they diagnosed and solved a fault in the carburettor and its controls. After rectification, the 1939 W154 Mercedes-Benz swept the board in the Swiss Grand Prix on 20 August, placing one–two–three in both a preliminary heat and the final. This was the last of the season's four major races, three of which the W154 won. The Mercedes-Benz V12 was

finally race-ready – just in time for Grand Prix racing's pre-emption by war.

The final pre-war Grand Prix, at Belgrade in Yugoslavia, was won by Tazio Nuvolari, who had deserted Alfa Romeo to assist Auto Union after its star, Bernd Rosemeyer, was killed trying to top Rudy Caracciola's speed at Frankfurt in January of 1938. With Ferdinand Porsche's engineering team now helping Mercedes-Benz, the Auto Union men, led by Robert Eberan von Eberhorst, designed their own new vee-twelve. In-house experience was available in the person of Werner Strobel, the Horch veteran who had designed that company's roadgoing twelve. The Horch workshops at Zwickau were commandeered as well to make components for the new D-Type Auto Union engine and car.

A single deep aluminium casting formed the new engine's cylinder block. Forged-steel wet cylinder liners were deeply spigoted into the block and sealed at their tops by the cylinder heads. Within cylinder centres of 86mm, bore and stroke were 65 x 75mm (2,986cc). Connecting-rod length of 168mm was the same as that of the company's previous V16, as was the main-bearing diameter of 70mm.

Plain mains were used at first, but during 1938 a significant horsepower gain was achieved by installing roller mains, each with 24 rollers measuring 7 x 10mm. The big ends used 22 rollers each of 7.5 x 11mm, running on the 66mm rod journals of a Hirth built-up crankshaft. While Auto Union's 1934–37 V16 crankshafts were only

Looking remarkably like a three-bank engine, the 1938 Auto Union D-Type V12 was in fact a 60° vee with triple camshafts. The central camshaft opened the inlet valves of both cylinder banks. Like its predecessor, Auto Union's Porsche-designed V16, the 3.0-litre 1938 engine was mounted at the rear of the chassis.

Components of the Auto Union D-Type's crankshaft showed the serrated joints with which its various segments were joined together. This method of construction, held together by the Hirth differential-thread system, allowed roller bearings to be used together with one-piece connecting-rod big-ends.

In 1938 a single vertical Roots-type blower, drawing from twin carburettors, provided the boost for the Type D Auto Union which developed 450bhp at 7,000rpm.

partially counterweighted, in its final edition the V12 crank was completely counterweighted to cope with its much higher engine speeds.

A single central overhead camshaft opened the inlet valves of both banks through finger-type followers. It was driven by a vertical shaft and bevel gears at the rear of the engine. The bevel gear at the inlet camshaft then drove bevels to short cross shafts which extended out to camshafts along the tops of the exhaust valves, again working through finger followers. Double coil springs closed the valves. Thus the D-Type was a triple-cam engine with inlet/exhaust valves 34/31mm in diameter. Made of cobalt-nickel-alloy steel with solid stems 8mm in diameter, the valves were equally inclined at an included angle of 90° and rested on inserted bronze seats.

Three compression rings were above the gudgeon pin and a single oil ring was at the bottom of the forged Mahle piston's full skirt. Two Bosch six-cylinder magnetos, driven by the bevel gears at the rear of the engine, sparked plugs that were placed centrally at the top of the combustion chambers. A single Roots-type supercharger had a finned Elektron (magnesium alloy) case. Displacing almost 1.4 litres per revolution, it was driven at 2.4 times crank speed – up to 17,000rpm – to produce a boost of 17psi. With this single vertically mounted

blower the D-Type engine developed 460bhp at 7,000rpm, enough to power Nuvolari to wins at Monza and Donington at the end of 1938.

For 1939 the Zwickau racers developed two-stage supercharging, using it for the first time in racing at the French Grand Prix in July. The smaller second-stage blower was a shorter-lobe version of the one used in 1938, displacing 1.2 litres per revolution. It was driven from the same idler gear as before, but swung around 90° so that the charge passed through it from right to left and was then ducted forward into the engine. To the right of it the larger, first-stage blower was placed, a shorter edition of the supercharger used on the earlier V16s, sweeping 2.25 litres per revolution. Both were driven at 1.63 times engine speed, delivering a 24psi supercharge to the engine. Thus equipped the V12 produced 485bhp at 7,000rpm and could attain 500bhp at 7,500, although this wasn't always used in racing. Peak torque was 405lb-ft at 4,000rpm, a remarkably low speed for a racing engine.

The D-Type started out with Solex carburation, but for 1939 Auto Union worked with SUM to make a four-throat float-free instrument. Each jet block drew from a chamber which was kept full by one fuel pump and was constantly tapped off, at a precise level, by a second pump. All four throats were controlled by a single vertical barrel-type throttle valve, arranged so that it progressively uncovered a second main jet as it opened.

For Robert von Eberhorst the two-stage blower was only a stopgap measure until he could perfect a vane-type supercharger which, with its internal compression, is a more efficient instrument. Based on the Centric design,

The D-Type Auto Union of 1938–39 was a well-balanced car that frequently took the fight to Mercedes-Benz, especially when driven by Tazio Nuvolari, seen here during the Swiss Grand Prix of 1938.

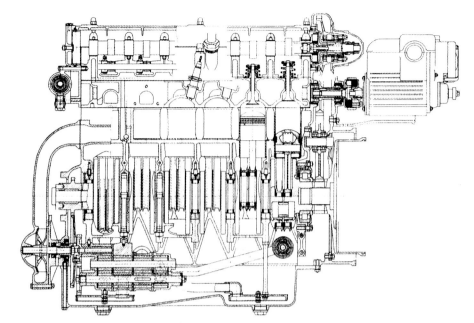

a pair were being developed in 1939 for use on the planned 1½-litre V12 E-Type Auto Union engine. Designed as the Type 537, this was to have 1,483cc (53 x 56mm) to give them an entry in the increasingly popular *Voiturette* category, which was being trailed as a likely Grand Prix formula for 1941. It was hoped to have a car ready to compete during 1940.

For its mini-twelve Auto Union would have given up the Hirth assembled crankshaft in favour of a forged crank with split roller bearings for both mains and big ends, sharing a diameter of 55mm. Cylinders were spaced at 76mm distances. The 130mm connecting rod would have a needle bearing at its small end. Flow-bench tests showed advantages for four valves per cylinder, which were to be validated by trials on a single-cylinder test unit.

Another test-bench result in the Chemnitz laboratories proved the valve gear's reliability to 11,400rpm, while other investigations pursued the idea of hydraulic valve-lash adjustment to achieve a zero-lash valve gear, "which seems particularly important for high revolutions". Twin overhead camshafts were foreseen for each bank, driven from the clutch end of the crankshaft by a train of gears that also drove the magneto for one plug per cylinder. Oil and water pumps would be low at the front of the twelve, gear-driven from the crank nose.

SUM had delivered a sample of its special triple-throat carburettor, while tests of fuel injection were progressing in 1940 on a 3-litre D-Type V12. A special Schenk dynamometer to cope with the smaller engine's higher speeds was on order and expected by the end of 1939. An ultra-high compression ratio of 10.0:1 and output approaching 300bhp at 8,500rpm were foreseen for Auto Union's Type 537, a potential rival to the W165 V8 of Mercedes-Benz and Alfa Romeo's Type 158.

Block and heads were to be of high-silicon aluminium. Free-standing wet steel cylinders would have been squeezed down by the heads in a manner that might have become problematic when the engine was developed to very high boost pressures. The E-Type's twelve was well along in construction, with single-cylinder tests under way and casting patterns made, in 1940 and indeed into 1941. Only in the second half of that year was it clear that Germany's motor industry had to devote all its attention to the war effort.[10]

Toward the end of the 1930s other engineers in Greater Germany were asked to turn their thoughts to Grand-Prix-car designs. Hermann Goering, always keen to carve out a distinctive role for himself in the Third Reich, had a special interest in the armament factories at Steyr in Austria. A maker of fine cars, Steyr also had the ability to design racing cars. With Goering's encouragement its engineers began penning Formula car proposals, including vee-twelves. Before they could progress very far, however, Steyr's factories were needed for other tasks.

Another stillborn engine project of the late 1930s aimed to create an unblown 4½-litre V12 for the 1938–39 Grand Prix races for France's Talbot, enjoying a lusty revival since 1933 under the leadership of Paris-based Italian Antony Lago. Lago, said René Dreyfus, "was an

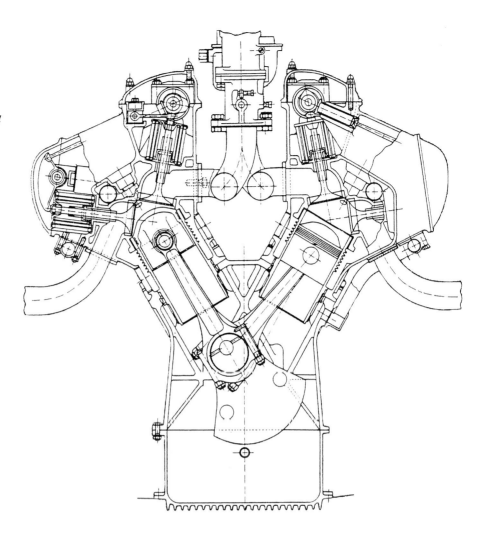

In 1937 Walter Becchia designed a 4.5-litre unsupercharged V12 for potential use by France's Antony Lago. Becchia proposed a single overhead camshaft for each bank, operating inlet valves directly and exhausts through pushrods and rockers. Tony Lago made other engine plans for his Talbots, however.

interesting man, gregarious, loquacious, full of fun" and "a motor sports enthusiast *par excellence* and when it came to racing he was very serious indeed."

At his "efficient, compact" factory at Suresnes Lago had a talented chief engineer in Walter Becchia, who provided a link with the great days of Sunbeam in the 1920s. Louis Coatalen had recruited Becchia, with Vincenzo Bertarione, from Fiat in 1922 to design his Grand Prix contender for 1923. In Italy both men created successful racing Fiats under Guido Fornaca and Giulio Cesare Cappa, whom we remember from the radical V12 Itala of the late 1920s.

Walter Becchia, who of course was intimately familiar with Coatalen's four-litre V12 Sunbeam of 1926, proposed to Antony Lago that he design a 4½-litre unsupercharged twelve to suit the new 1938 Grand Prix formula. He laid down the design of an unusual engine measuring 74 x 87mm (4,490cc).[11] Becchia's Talbot twelve would have been light, with an aluminium block extending down past the crank centreline and unified

aluminium cylinder-head-*cum*-block castings into which the wet steel cylinder liners were screwed. The liners extended well down into the crankcase, which carried the crankshaft in seven main bearings. Induction was central, to be fed by downdraft carburettors into log manifolds, and exhausts outboard.

The Becchia design was straightforward enough in its 60° bank angle and the forward offset of its right-hand cylinder bank, but novel in the manner of its use of only one overhead camshaft per bank. With its two valves per cylinder symmetrically inclined at a wide 92° included angle, something special was needed. Becchia provided it by placing his lone camshaft above the inlet valve, interposing a finger follower, and operating the exhaust valve through a tappet, pushrod and rocker arm. His use of triple coil valve springs was a trademark of the 1920s–1930s Italian design school. It was a valve gear that would have suited an engine running up to 6,000rpm or so – sufficient for a 4½-litre twelve – but would have been hard-pressed beyond that.

In the summer of 1937, however, Tony Lago changed tack. He asked Becchia to turn his talents to an improved in-line six for the 4½-litre category. Also, with his sights set on a potential grant from the French government for a new racing-car design, Lago set work in train on the design of a supercharged 3-litre V16. For this Becchia reversed his valve gear, putting the camshafts above the exhaust valves and opening the inlets through pushrods and rockers. This project, though never completed, was a success in one important respect: it won for Talbot the government's grant of 600,000 francs, then close to $17,000.

Needless to say, others among France's car makers thought they might be entitled to their government's largesse. Though Louis Delage's eponymous firm was no longer the powerhouse it had been in the days of its magnificent four-cam two-litre vee-twelve – in fact it was bankrupt by 1935 – in 1936 it was reviving as a member of a group that included the stronger Delahaye. As always, motor sports were not far from Delage's mind. "My greatest wish would be to take part in Grand Prix races," he said in January 1937, "for the rules for 1938–40 seem reasonable and in any case more acceptable than those that are current. Regrettably, I don't have the wherewithal. Thus I'm preparing a vehicle for sports-car races."

Given permission to put a single new prototype on wheels for 1937, veteran Delage engineer Albert Lory plumped for a 4½-litre vee-twelve. To fit his suit to Louis Delage's cloth, however, he was obliged to use as his

A rare glimpse under its bonnet showed the vee-twelve that Albert Lory fashioned from two Delahaye cylinder heads for Louis Delage in 1937. Lory's opportunistic Delage engine produced 190bhp.

starting point the cylinder head of Delahaye's successful 3½-litre six, dubbed 135S in its sporting version. The head was in its normal position on the twelve's right-hand bank, with both inlet and exhaust manifolding on its right side, and reversed – with a special casting – on the left bank so that the pipe-work would also be outboard on that side of the engine. This left the central vee clear for a single camshaft operating the pushrod and rocker valve gear of both heads. Here, driven by practicality, was a return to the layout of such twelves as the Maybach and Cadillac. To make his engine as compact as possible Lory placed the two cylinder heads virtually back-to-back for a narrow vee angle, on the order of 25°.

Albert Lory had to cope with a mismatch between the bore size of the Delahaye, 84mm, and the 73.5mm bore that he chose for the twelve, which with a stroke of 88mm gave 4,481cc. With the Delahaye having four main bearings, Lory chose a similar layout for his Delage V12. Connecting rods were side-by-side, their big-end width constrained by the cylinder-centre distances that the heads mandated. With an eye toward eventual production, Lory specified plain bearings for the bottom end. Along each side of the engine he arrayed three downdraft carburettors for a total of six. Lory's imposing power unit was credited with 190bhp at 4,500rpm.

Driving through a twin-disc clutch and Cotal gearbox, the Delage twelve was installed in a Delahaye Type 148 touring-car chassis shortened to a wheelbase of 116.1in. This was sent to Jean-Henri Labourdette, who fitted it with a magnificent finned coupé body incorporating the latest aerodynamic ideas of Jean Andreau and a *Vutotal* windscreen that eliminated the front pillars. The right-hand-drive coupé's weight came to 3,470lb.

"Breathtaking beast" (Anthony Blight) though the new Delage certainly was, it was outclassed in the company it found at Montlhéry, venue in July 1937 for the French Grand Prix, run that year for sports-racers to exclude the annoying silver cars. Setting the scene, Louis Delage said it was only entered to show what a grand-touring car could do over a 500-kilometre Grand Prix distance. It was denied a chance even to do that. In trying to lap quickly enough to qualify the coupé, experienced works tester Frettet overdrove its brakes and dented its snout. Prudently, it was withdrawn.

Its nose repaired and two-tone paint applied, the striking Delage starred on Labourdette's stand at the 1937 Paris Salon. When in May of 1938 it appeared at Brooklands to compete in the Junior Car Club's International Trophy, it was seen to be wearing a simple offset two-seater open sports body, minus its cycle wings. Driven by experienced albeit ageing veteran Joseph Paul, during the race the Delage caught fire as it passed the

Albert Lory's unique V12 powered a shortened Delahaye type 148 touring-car chassis badged as a Delage and magnificently bodied by Labourdette. It was later rebodied as an open sports-racer, in which form it made only a handful of competition appearances.

pits. In trying to pull to the side Paul tangled with another car and both overran the protective banking to plunge into a spectator area. Ten were injured and two killed, Miss Peggy Williams and talented Austin racing engineer Murray Jamieson.

Joseph Paul was the Delage's entrant for the Twelve Hours of Paris in September 1938 at Montlhéry, where Roger Loyer and Jean Tremoulet were its drivers. It proved neither fast nor durable, first breaking a valve and then finally a piston after only 109 miles of racing. After an entry of the unique Delage V12 in the Brussels Grand Prix of 16 June 1946 was recorded, for Lucien Langlois, no later verified racing appearance of the Delage has come to light.

Nor did Albert Lory's vee-twelve have a production successor. "The car always gave trouble," said historian Serge Pozzoli, "because of the con-rods whose big ends were side-by-side on the same crankpin and too narrow." Roller big ends would have cured this, but only by taking the engine away from its simple specification. As well, said Pozzoli, "roadholding was bad" with the road-car-derived chassis.[12] Thus ended the brief and indeed sorry saga of this last lone vee-twelve Delage.

Far more ambitious – and ultimately successful – was the twelve-cylinder engine project of Delage's rescuer, Delahaye. The latter was one of France's motoring pioneers, having first exhibited in Paris in 1895. In 1898 an Alsatian, Charles Weiffenbach, joined the firm at the age of only 28. In the 1930s, concluding that the best way to cope with the depression was to move upmarket, Weiffenbach and his main shareholders instructed their Jean François to aim higher.

In François they had a creative new chief engineer who had joined the company in 1933 at the age of 29. August and conservative Delahaye, they decided, would even compete in racing. Accordingly, wrote Anthony Blight, "the ancient firm of Delahaye discarded its corsets and

stays, hitched up its skirts and, with much caution and some trepidation, set out to court the favours of the young man and woman about town."

Eager and able to encourage this dramatic transition was a wealthy American couple living in Paris and Monte Carlo: Laury Schell and his wife Lucy O'Reilly Schell. With firm orders for suitable cars, they and their friends launched Delahaye into the sports-racing-car market. Their next step was even bolder. If Delahaye would build a suitable car for the coming Grand Prix formula, the Schells told Charles Weiffenbach in the spring of 1936, they would pay for the effort and set up their own team, Ecurie Bleue, to race them. Appraised of this ambition, Jean François's head was swimming as he headed for the Place Périere and its nearby Duplantin restaurant. He returned from his lunch with a tablecloth embellished by sketches that suggested the configuration of a new vee-twelve Delahaye engine.

Although Jean François was bidden to build an engine that could be used for road cars as well as racing, and had to fit in the existing Delahaye chassis, he brooked few compromises in his 60° twelve's design. One peculiar compromise, however, was that although he deployed three camshafts, none of them was overhead. One was in the centre of the vee and the other two were at the sides, all operating their valves through pushrods and short rocker arms. Their positioning allowed the inlet pushrods to be shorter, at 240mm, than the 290mm exhausts. Rocker arms were highly polished and angled in plan view to keep the pushrods from interfering any more than necessary with the ports. The rockers gave a

With backing from wealthy Americans living in Paris, engineer Jean François designed this 4.5-litre V12 for Delahaye in 1937. A front-mounted cluster of accessories included two Bosch magnetos, the water pump and twin mechanical fuel pumps.

high multiplication ratio and had no clearance adjusting screws, this being the function of inserts of differing lengths at the tops of the pushrods. Each row of rockers had its own individual cast-magnesium cover.

While the centre camshaft dealt with all the inlet valves, each of the flanking cams coped with the exhaust valves on its side of the block. All were driven by a gear train at the nose of the crankshaft, inside a magnesium cover. Jean François gave his new twelve hemispherical combustion chambers in its aluminium heads with 42mm valves set at a 62° included angle and sparked by

At the 1938 Cork Grand Prix a rare glimpse of the Delahaye V12's valve gear was obtained by John Dugdale. Visible were the engine's twin spark plugs for each cylinder and short and stiff rocker arms, operating inclined overhead valves from a single central camshaft, for the inlets, and outboard camshafts for the exhaust valves.

twin plugs. The gear train at the crank nose drove twin Bosch magnetos, placed laterally, and a large central water pump with takeoffs to both banks. Above them were two mechanical fuel pumps, feeding triple dual-throat downdraft Zenith-Stromberg carburettors. Each of these delivered to a four-branch manifold that coped with its quartet of cylinders.

With its left cylinder bank offset forward, the Delahaye's block extended down past the crank centreline. Seven 65mm plain bearings supported the one-piece crankshaft, which however used 8mm roller bearings for its split rod big ends, running directly on 54mm hardened races on their journals.[13] A duplex oil pump provided pressure and scavenging for a dry-sump lubrication system. Wet steel cylinder liners were clamped in place by the head, against flanges, and sealed at their bottoms with a pair of O-rings in grooves in the block. With dimensions of 75 x 84.7mm, François's twelve had a capacity of 4,490cc.[14]

One of the new twelve's most advanced features was its one-piece cylinder block of ultra-light magnesium, a feature it had in common with Alfa Romeo's V12. Magnesium offered the ultimate in lightness, volume for volume, weighing 35 per cent less than aluminium. Making the blocks, however, was a major challenge. When the first blocks were cast at the beginning of 1937 their porosity was all too obvious, either immediately or after machining. Then when the engine was assembled and running, magnesium's higher rate of expansion with heat – 21 per cent greater than that of aluminium and indeed 160 per cent more than steel – brought more problems with the engine's melange of materials.

By April 1937 the new twelve was running on test, weighing 591lb. Ultimately it was developed to produce 245bhp at 5,500rpm on Ternaire fuel, a tripartite blend of petrol, methanol and benzole with a dash of castor oil. It drove through a multi-disc clutch and conventional four-speed gearbox. The Type 145 Delahaye – as the new model was named – rolled onto the track at Montlhéry for the first time on 25 June. It was in a right-hand-drive two-seater which, said one journal, "cannot be said to be a good-looker" with its blunt front and awkward lines.

Although little more mature than the V12 Delage that had been withdrawn from the French Grand Prix on 4 July, the Delahaye at least qualified well, on the front row, but in the race was out early with oiling maladies. Two cars were prepared for another sports-car Grand Prix at Reims two weeks later, where troubles with their Goodrich-Colombes tyres stopped both.

Stripped of its sketchy aerodynamic cycle-type wings, the Type 145 was back at Montlhéry in August. Its mission was to lap the track for 200 kilometres, 124 miles, at a specific increment faster than the winning average in the 1934 Grand Prix on the same circuit. If it could achieve this by 31 August 1937, and not be bettered, Delahaye would pocket a prize of one million francs, some $37,000, offered by a state fund[15] to encourage the development of French cars for the 1938 GP formula – to which the car would have to conform. This time on Dunlop tyres, the mission was entrusted to René Dreyfus. On the 27th of August, in one of the toughest drives of his life, Dreyfus topped the target figure by a scant 4.9 seconds after an hour and 22 minutes. A counterattack by Bugatti failed, and in one of the most dramatic happenings of the year in France, Dreyfus and Delahaye won the Million.

In 1938 Type 145s were campaigned in Grand Prix races by Ecurie Bleue for René Dreyfus and Gianfranco Comotti. In the first such race, at Pau in France on 10 April, they made history. Dreyfus's Delahaye became the only non-German racing car to win any Grand Prix in 1938 or 1939. Over 172 miles of a tight street circuit, the race pitted the French cars against a singleton Mercedes-Benz W154 started by Rudy Caracciola and taken over, after refuelling, by Hermann Lang.

In practice Dreyfus and Caracciola lapped at similar speeds, while a second car for Lang was withdrawn after practice problems. Not needing to add fuel, Dreyfus rolled through with a victory margin of almost two minutes in the same car, remarkably, that he'd driven to fourth place in the Mille Miglia only a week earlier. In the sister 145 Comotti was third at Pau.

This was destined to be the high point of 1938 for the V12 Delahayes, which competed in most of the Grand Prix races with Dreyfus and Comotti, the latter replaced toward the end of the season by Raphaël Béthenod de Las Casas, who raced as 'Raph'. René Dreyfus did win at Cork on 23 April, against modest opposition, but in the rest of the season the best he could manage was fifth in the German Grand Prix and the Coppa Ciano. Comotti was fourth in the Coppa Acerbo.

In 1939 the best result of far fewer entries by the disillusioned Schells was fourth and fifth at the 'Ring for Dreyfus and Raph. After the war a 145 made only one Grand Prix appearance, finishing sixth at St. Cloud in June 1946.

Most disappointing for Laury and Lucy Schell was the complete failure of the special single-seater Delahaye, the Type 155, built fully to exploit the vee-twelve. It looked the goods, with its central seating, rear-mounted gearbox and de Dion rear suspension, but a failure by Jean François to master the latter's geometry meant that Dreyfus would try it but usually prefer the 145. He raced it only once, at Donington late in 1938, where he retired with an oil-pipe failure. After the war Paul Friderich, son of Ettore Bugatti aide Ernst Friderich, took on the 155 but

Two of the V12 Type 145 Delahayes cornered at Thillois on the Reims Grand Prix circuit in 1939. The car in the foreground was in the same configuration in which René Dreyfus had won the French million-franc prize with a drive at Montlhéry in August 1937. At Reims they were also-rans behind the German cars.

even after modifying its troublesome suspension was denied success in 1946. Nor did Jean Achard in 1947 or André Simon in 1948 achieve anything with this unique Delahaye.

On the brink of war Delahaye realised its dream of launching a production model, its Type 165, powered by François's V12. For this mission the engine was extensively revised by the chief engineer and his drawing-office chief Georges Monciny. A conventional crankshaft

An attempt at a more attractive Type 145 Delahaye, still in two-seater form, was fielded in 1939. Capable of being raced as a sports car as well, the Delahaye had provisions for headlamps in its frontal cowling.

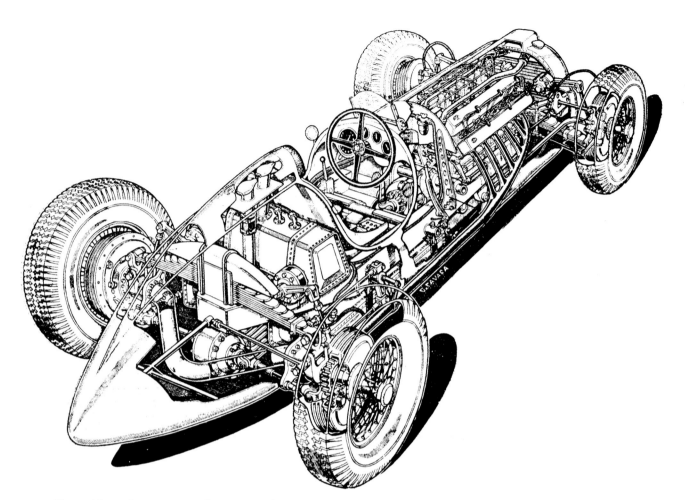

Above: *A huge disappointment for Laury and Lucy Schell, sponsors of the Delahaye racing effort, was the failure of the central-seated Type 155 to reach raceworthiness. Still powered by the 4.5-litre unsupercharged V12, it seemed to have all the right features but they failed to function well in combination.*

Below: *René Dreyfus competed at England's Donington in 1938 with the Type 155 central-seater Delahaye, but retired with an oil-pipe failure. Efforts to revive the car and compete with it after the war were doomed to failure.*

Below: *Commendably, Delahaye's Charles Weiffenbach achieved his goal of launching the V12 as a production-car engine in the company's Type 165. Although the road-car engines generally had single carburettors, this one had triple carburation atop an engine whose crankcase was of aluminium instead of magnesium. Single ignition was judged sufficient for road-car use of this impressive V12.*

was fitted entirely with plain bearings in a crankcase of aluminium instead of magnesium.[16] 'Quietened' front-end accessory drives turned a distributor instead of magnetos to spark only one plug per cylinder. The sump was wet instead of dry, while the compression ratio was reduced to 7.2:1. Although triple carburettors were tried, a single two-throat Solex was fitted to the production 165, of which a dozen sets of parts were laid down. The revised engine was credited with 165bhp at 5,500rpm.[17]

Charles Weiffenbach gave the 165 the launch it deserved. At the Paris Salon late in 1938 it rested on a rotating turntable, unusual in those days. On the 126.4in wheelbase of the first chassis Figoni et Falaschi fashioned a red two/three-seater roadster with the most voluptuous lines imaginable, fully enveloping its wheels. Its bonnet side was cut away to reveal the magnificent engine. The twelve-cylinder chassis alone was priced at $3,700 and a completed car of this type at nearly $8,000.

A similar Delahaye was one of the stars of the French Pavilion at New York's 1939 World's Fair. Its engine was incomplete because François and Monciny had not finished their work on the hydraulic valve lifters which they felt the car needed to be marketable in America. They did complete such an engine, but it was never married with the car.

Only four Type 165s were bodied before Hitler stopped play. Still in business after the war, but not able to afford the racing of its twelves, Delahaye offered its redundant Type 145 racing chassis to the coachbuilders – albeit fitted with the remaining road versions of the V12 engines and Cotal gearboxes. Four in all were put to work for the company in this way. One was an *ultra-surbaissé* or ultra-low roadster by Franay and two were coupés by Henri Chapron. A fourth Type 145 is thought still to exist in racing-engine trim.

As Anthony Blight said, it had indeed been quite a decade for sporting vee-twelves. Two of them, those of Alfa Romeo and Delahaye, segued smoothly from racing cars to sports cars. Another, Lagonda's, began as a luxury sporting car and became a racer. Neither Mercedes-Benz nor Auto Union made road versions of their Grand Prix twelves – but they might have.

Soon after the war Daimler-Benz weighed the idea of basing a sports car on the chassis of its supercharged 3-litre W154. As either racer or road car it would have been quite a machine. But with Daimler still rebuilding its war-torn factories, this was judged a step too far. Mercedes-Benz would have to wait a little longer for its twelve-cylinder road cars.

Chapter 9 Footnotes

[1] Voisin expert Pascal Courteault – to whom the author is indebted for information on these cars – suggests that the engine was unlikely to have had the larger blocks of the 1930-model C16, which with its 94 x 140mm dimensions would have given it 11,659cc. The author's information, otherwise complete on records of this era, is silent concerning the Voisin's displacement.

[2] This defied the AIACR's ruling that Grand Prix cars should have two-man cockpits. France's hegemony in Italy had ended in 1848.

[3] Oddly the Scuderia Ferrari entered the Coppa Ciano instead of the race on Berlin's flat-out Avus on the same day, which would have suited the Type As admirably. Starting money must have been better at Montenero.

[4] When originally drawn its bore was 68mm, which would have produced 3,835cc. The bore increase was made before the twelve was raced. The Italians would continue to struggle to keep up with the development pace set by their partners in the Pact of Steel.

[5] The big Alfa was sold to Clemar Bucci, who raced it in Argentina from 1949 to 1953. Rebodied as a sports car, it was entered in the 1956 Buenos Aires 1,000 Kilometres for Bucci/Suarez, but didn't start. It was later converted back to a single-seater.

[6] Although Alfa Romeo says four were made, specialist historian Simon Moore has been able to identify only two.

[7] The DAB remained at the same size throughout its career. There was neither opportunity nor need to develop the DA, the smaller Class C version that had originally been proposed. It would have used an under-bored A-series cylinder giving dimensions of 77.5 x 88mm for 4,980cc.

[8] The only exception is Henry Segrave's '1,000-horsepower' Sunbeam.

While this had an envelope body, it set its records with wheels exposed rather than enclosed.

[9] To cover its flanks Mercedes commissioned studies of 4½-litre unsupercharged units from the Porsche office, with which it then had a consulting contract, but these were never given serious consideration.

[10] This engine has acquired a legendary reputation, many enthusiasts suggesting that it was actually completed. This was definitively not the case. A car that has sometimes masqueraded as the E-Type Auto Union is described in Chapter 10.

[11] An authoritative reference source on the racing Talbots gives dimensions of 74 x 85mm, but these don't approach 4½ litres. The figures given are the author's best assessment.

[12] The chassis was at least good enough to be used for record-breaking on the banked track at Montlhéry in 1949, powered by an MAP diesel engine. Many contemporary references to this record-breaker call its chassis a 'Delahaye', which of course it originally was.

[13] A French Delahaye reference states that the crankshaft was built up and that roller bearings were used for both mains and rods. The description given, that by Anthony Blight, is the author's preference, although both types of crankshaft may have been used.

[14] Anthony Blight noted that the bore diameter was "the classic French artillery bore".

[15] Contributing to the fund was a hike in the cost of driving-licence renewals from 50 to 60 francs, half the increase going into the pot.

[16] This is the author's assumption. The ultra-lightness of magnesium wasn't needed in a road car.

[17] Some sources cite 175bhp at the higher compression ratio of 7.5:1.

Chapter 10

POST-WAR POTENCY

If speed maniacs didn't sweep up aero engines after World War II with quite the same enthusiasm that they showed after the earlier conflict, there was reason enough. Engines were altogether bigger and more powerful, less easy to drop into a redundant Edwardian chassis for a spot of go-faster gratification. Let it be said, however, that this didn't stop some of the world's more adventurous engineers.

Among English enthusiasts who stepped up to this challenge was Ted Lloyd Jones. A tough character who relished cocking a snoot at the establishment, Lloyd Jones acquired a Rolls-Royce Kestrel V12 of 21,236cc (127 x 139.7mm) that was capable of as much as 625bhp at 2,900rpm and weighed 884lb.[1] Unsupercharged, the overhead-cam Kestrel carried two duplex carburettors in its central vee. Lloyd Jones coupled it to a Vauxhall 30/98 transmission, which drove the transfer box from a Daimler Dingo scout car to power all four wheels of his Flying Triangle Special.

Courageously, Lloyd Jones mounted the Kestrel above his car's rear wheels, placing a radiator ahead of the engine which collected air from big scoops just behind the intrepid driver. The Dingo's rugged frame conjoined the whole, which included coil-spring independent suspension at all four disc wheels. Although one of the more ungainly-looking cars ever made, from 1950 the Flying Triangle gave a fine account of itself in both hillclimbs and sprints in spite of problems with its transfer box. It competed at Prescott and Shelsley Walsh hillclimbs and was the outright winner over the standing kilometre of the Brighton Speed Trials in 1952.

As late as 1957 the Triangle was still Flying in the hands of a new owner, F. Michael Wilcock, owner of Worthing's Swandean Garage. He renamed it the Swandean Flying Saucer to distinguish it from his own Swandean Spitfire

Opposite: *Franco Rol's OSCA Type G was an entrant at Turin in April 1952 but failed to complete its first lap. This and a sister car were both later converted to sports-car configurations.*

Below: *Marrying a 21.2-litre Rolls-Royce Kestrel vee-twelve with a Daimler Dingo scout car's four-wheel drive was Ted Lloyd Jones's formula for his spectacular Flying Triangle Special sprint and hillclimb car. Lloyd Jones, here competing at Prescott, enjoyed many successes with his ambitious special.*

Onlookers at Shelsley Walsh hill climb observed with interest the Kestrel engine of Ted Lloyd Jones's Flying Triangle Special, a cross-section of which may be seen on page 99. Just forward of the engine Lloyd Jones mounted cooling radiators which were adequate for the short, sharp sprints in which the car specialised.

Special, which was powered by a supercharged Mark XXV Rolls-Royce Merlin engine normally found on one wing of a de Havilland Mosquito. Offering 27,022cc (137.2 x 152.4mm) in twelve 60° banked cylinders, this weighed 1,450lb and was rated at 1,620bhp at 3,000rpm for takeoff. Its toughness was such that Wilcock took it to

4,000rpm several times with no negative consequences.

Wilcock and his experienced mechanic/builder Bill Hyder mounted this massive unit at the front of their 'special', which they thought at first to base on the chassis of a Daimler Double Six that had once graced the Royal Mews of George VI. Instead they rescued only the steering gear from that chassis and mounted it on two Daimler Dingo frames welded together to provide the longitude needed to house the massive engine and a 60-Imperial-gallon fuel tank cadged from a Spitfire. The result was a magisterial wheelbase of 162in connecting the coil-sprung suspensions and four-wheel drive of the doubled-up Dingo.

A clutch from a Leyland truck and a gearbox from a heavy-duty Crossley were the Swandean Spitfire Special's drive train, placing a heavy strain on its reinforced Dingo transfer box, which was perilously close to the driver. The latter was Michael Wilcock, who competed with the 5,400lb juggernaut eight times, including its clutch-slipping debut at Brighton in 1953. He found it capable of more than 150mph in the third of its four gears and never extended it in top. "It was built for fun and was never meant to be taken seriously," wrote historian Michael Ware, "but it gave Swandean Garage very good publicity."

Another big-power enthusiast, Briton Paul Jameson, warmed up in 1974 with a car powered by the unblown tank version of the Merlin, the Meteor, and then in 1975 went the whole hog with a six-wheeled creation powered by a supercharged Merlin for which 1,760bhp was claimed. With its four rear wheels driving, it was timed at 10.4sec from rest to 100mph in 1976.

A Meteor was the engine selection of Briton Graham Moss, who used his vintage Bentley restoration skills to

Specialist Bentley restoration company R.C. Moss naturally used chassis components from that marque when creating its Thunderbolt, powered by a Rolls-Royce Meteor V12. Patterned after the great Brooklands racers, the Thunderbolt set British records at distances up to 200 kilometres at Millbrook on 2 August 2003.

Graham Moss of R.C. Moss built and drove the Thunderbolt, which was propelled by a Meteor V12, the tank-powering version of the aviation Merlin. In its record-breaking exploits at Millbrook the Thunderbolt's fastest timings were 143.44mph over a distance of 5 kilometres from a flying start, and 143.22mph over 5 miles.

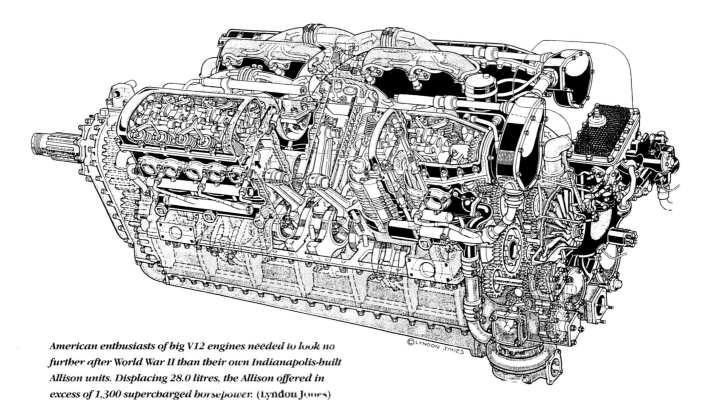

American enthusiasts of big V12 engines needed to look no further after World War II than their own Indianapolis-built Allison units. Displacing 28.0 litres, the Allison offered in excess of 1,300 supercharged horsepower. (Lyndon Jones)

craft a chassis that used many Bentley parts and a car that seemed a clone of the 1930s Brooklands racers. In 2003 the Thunderbolt, as Moss named it, broke British records at speeds up to 143mph on the banked track at Millbrook Proving Grounds.

For speed-hungry Americans the aero engine of choice was, of course, their Allison V12. Slightly larger than the Merlin at 28,032cc (139.7 x 152.4mm), it weighed around 1,400lb with supercharged power of up to 1,325bhp at 3,000rpm. In 1954 its dimensions didn't deter Nebraskan Ed Cramer, who built a tubular-steel chassis to carry an Allison on his own independent suspension at front and rear. Inspired by GM's LeSabre dream car, Cramer styled a fin-tailed roadster body that hid the cooling radiator under its rear deck. A GMC truck clutch and four-speed gearbox channelled the power of Cramer's 5,200lb roadgoing roadster.

In 1961 Midwesterner Jim Lytle, a talented designer and fabricator, acquired his first Allison V12, still in its crate, for $100. It would be the first of many. He drag-raced it successfully in a 1934 two-door Ford, then in 1965 built 'Quad Al' – a four-wheel-drive dragster, with dual tyres front and rear, powered by *four* Allisons. With its 112 litres and more than 8,000 horsepower it won a place in the *Guinness Book of World Records* as the most powerful piston-engined car. At the other extreme, Jim Lytle powered a tri-

wheeled motorcycle and – wait for it – a BMW 600 mini-car with Allisons. Into the 1990s Lytle was still at it, stuffing an Allison V12 into a Volkswagen Microbus.

Other dragsters and would-be record breakers embraced the Allison. Californian Ed Lytle installed one inside a two-door 1934 Ford sedan with a chopped roof and made room for himself, as driver, in the back seat. He relied on a quadruple-disc slipping clutch and direct

In the early 1960s American Jim Lytle built an Allison-powered dragster he dubbed Big Al II. He used a quadruple-disc clutch and a Pontiac rear axle to take its 2,500 lb-ft of torque. (Jim Lytle)

Another Jim Lytle creation of the 1960s was Quad Al, driving twin wheels at all four corners from four Allison V12s. With its counter-rotating engines Quad Al gained a listing in the Guinness Book of Records *as the most powerful piston-engined automobile.* **(Jim Lytle)**

drive to motivate his 'Grinder Griper III'. Another Allison found a home in Norm Taylor's dragster-type chassis in 1955, driving through a five-speed White truck transmission mounted in reverse to step up the speed of the slow-revving aircraft engine. We don't know what success either hot-rodder enjoyed.

Allison twelves also powered the early racing cars built in Akron, Ohio by Art Arfons and his sidekick Ed Snyder. For feed-supply businessman Arfons, called "remarkably inventive and resourceful", the purchase of war-surplus Allison engines was a low-bucks way of building exciting cars. Fascinated by drag racing, the rugged Arfons installed one of his Allisons behind the driver's seat of a skimpy machine with a huge wheelbase and dual rear tyres. When at one drag strip the track announcer boomed, "Get that green monster out here!" Art Arfons had found a name for his creations.

In 1954 an Arfons Green Monster won the World Series of Drag Racing and in 1956, at the same event, clocked a winning 152.542mph at the end of the quarter-mile. Its event-winning time in 1959 was 156.25mph in a shorter Monster whose Allison was elevated for more weight transfer to the rear – and so it would fit in the converted coach in which Art transported his cars.

Still loyal to the Allison, in 1960 Arfons raised his game with a streamlined all-wheel-drive car that one onlooker said looked like "an anteater with shoulders". Its two-stage-blown vee-twelve was credited with 3,800 horsepower. In several seasons at Bonneville his best effort with this latest Green Monster was a one-way ride at 313mph. In 1965 Art Arfons would go almost twice as fast on the Great Salt Lake – with a huge jet engine alongside him.

An Allison V12 inspired the speed-record dreams of a Salt Lake City, Utah garage owner, Athol Graham. With the enthusiastic support of wife Zeldine, Graham invested more than a decade of his spare time in a mid-engined streamliner powered by an Allison that had formerly rested in an unlimited-class hydroplane. Supercharged to a reputed 3,000 horsepower, it was Graham's ticket to tackle the wheel-driven land speed record of 394mph held by the Napier-Railton of John Cobb.

Bonneville officials took a dim view of some of the design features of Athol Graham's 'City of Salt Lake' when he first presented it in 1958 and made a few 100mph runs. In 1959, however, he was clocked at an impressive 344mph. This drew the attention of Firestone, which assisted with both tyres and forged-aluminium wheels. Graham booked 1st to 4th August, 1960 for officially timed runs at Bonneville. On his initial run on the first day he'd exceeded 300mph within three miles when his Firestone-red car veered off line and turned turtle.[2] A badly injured Graham died in hospital three hours later. His widow persevered with the rebuilt car and other drivers, but without success.

High-speed incidents with cars enjoying vee-twelve power are not rarities, as we've seen. We recall, for example, the Baroness Avanzo having to plunge her Packard 299 into the North Sea to extinguish a fire during a battle of speed at Fanoe. After her subsequent swap of her Packard to Antonio Ascari, she said, it "went from owner to owner, and no-one managed to get any good results from it except Enzo Ferrari, who said that it had given him the inspiration for his future twelve-cylinder cars."

This would be an exaggeration, albeit a delightful one. The recommendation that Ferrari build a twelve came from the engineer whom he chose as his collaborator, Gioachino Colombo. The two knew each other well from their pre-war associations, with Colombo designing racing Alfas, including the low-chassis 312 and the 158 *Voiturette*, and Ferrari organising their racing entries until his Scuderia was bought out by Alfa Romeo during 1937. With his long-time technical ally Luigi Bazzi, Ferrari himself had built such cars as the 1935 Alfa-powered *Bimotore*, with engines both front and rear, the first car ever to carry the prancing horse above its grille.

Although only 100 miles south-east of Milan, Modena seemed much more remote to Gioachino Colombo in the war-ravaged Italy of late July 1945. Ferries took cars across the River Po during that hot summer before the bridges were rebuilt. "However, it was unthinkable for me not to make the trip," Colombo reflected on his arduous journey from Milan. "A call from Enzo Ferrari absolutely could not be ignored." The invitation was all the more important to Colombo, who at the age of 42 had just been laid off by the company for which he'd worked since 1924, Alfa Romeo.[3]

The engineer was well aware that he was speaking to a man who possessed a substantial manufactory where they met at Maranello, ten miles south of Modena. Ferrari's copies of fine German grinders were in such demand that he was asked to move his workshops to escape the Allied bombings. From 1943 he built up a factory of 40,000 square feet with 140 to 160 workers. Although it was damaged in air raids during November 1944 and February 1945, Enzo Ferrari still had a plant capable of making aircraft components, precision machinery – and automobiles. Moreover, having bought out his former partners in the Scuderia, it was all his.

In 1945 Enzo established Auto Costruzioni Ferrari – a clear sign of his intentions. "I had had ambitious plans for launching out into the manufacture of high quality cars," Ferrari said later. "I remembered that I had joined Alfa Romeo when they were endeavouring to produce a car a day, and I too had hopes of achieving this same target." Quite without small talk, Ferrari made his aims clear to the swarthy, balding engineer. "Colombo," he said, "I want to go back to making racing cars instead of these machine tools! Tell me: how would you make a fifteen-hundred?"

Gioachino didn't have to ask what he meant. Before the war the popular 1½-litre category had already been tipped as a likely future Formula 1, with superchargers allowed. Any newcomer to the sport would want a 1,500cc engine in his armoury. The size could also be attractive for a sports car in a straitened post-war world in which big engines would – at least at first – be extravagant rarities.

Having already considered his reply, Colombo was quick off the mark.

"Look," he said, "Maserati has a first-class four-cylinder; the English have the six-cylinder ERA and Alfa Romeo has the eight-cylinder. You, in my view, should be building a twelve-cylinder!"

Ferrari's smile confirmed to Colombo that he'd divined the entrepreneur rightly.

"My dear Colombo," he replied, "you've read my thoughts! For years I've been dreaming of building a twelve-cylinder. Let's get to work right away!"

With their limited resources, Ferrari and Colombo knew they couldn't challenge the might of Alfa Romeo, which was bound to revive the Type 158 that they knew so well, with an equal number of cylinders.[4] By going from eight to twelve they opened up an avenue of broader piston area and higher revolutions that might offer a chance for success. In Britain BRM would take this idea a step further with a 1½-litre V16, which would prove four cylinders too far.

"I had always hankered after a 12-cylinder," Ferrari confided in his memoirs, "recalling early photographs I had seen of a Packard that had raced at Indianapolis in 1914 and a Delage that came in second at Lyons in 1924.[5] I had always liked the song of twelve cylinders; what is more, I must confess that the fact that there was then only one firm in the world making such engines acted on me as a challenge and a spur."

"He talked to me about his passion for the twelve-cylinders a thousand times," said Ferrari engineer Mauro Forghieri about his boss. "It is a beautiful, balanced engine. He told me that he was already thinking of the twelve-cylinder as far back as 1925." Ferrari did not want to go to the extreme of exotica that the roller-bearing Delage represented, however: "All we wanted to do was build a conventional engine, but one that would be outstanding."

Enzo Ferrari admitted that many thought him mad: "I came in for a great deal of criticism; it was forecast that I was bringing about my own downfall, the experiment being too daring and presumptuous." "It was an *idée fixe* with him," recalled racing-driver Franco Cortese, "and one for which he was heavily criticised. Several forecast, 'He's a nut case. It will eat his money and finish him.' In particular the Maserati brothers were highly critical. But if he'd made a four, or a six or even an eight, Ferrari wouldn't have enjoyed the great success he's had."

It was one thing to think of making a twelve, another to design it. After their July 1945 meeting, in which they settled Colombo's fee, the two men lunched at the *trattoria* opposite the factory before the engineer began his tortuous trip back to Milan. His brain was abuzz: "I was delighted, both because of the trust that Enzo Ferrari was placing in me and because I was finally getting the chance to design something really new, into which I could put all my best ideas. In effect, I began the planning of the first Ferrari twelve-cylinder on the journey back to Milan from Modena."

Early in August during the *Ferragosto* holiday, Colombo and his family went to Castellanza, north-west of Milan, to lunch with his sister. After lunch he left the table to sit "under a tree with a pen and a big sheet of rough paper in my hand. And it was there, all in one go, that I drew the design for the cylinder head." Back in Milan he borrowed a drafting board from his cousin and set it up in the bedroom of his flat. There he designed not only the engine but also the whole of the first sports Ferrari, the 125S. With colleagues and emissaries from Maranello, Colombo recalled "long hours spent in my bedroom, debating every detail around the big drawing board where the new twelve-cylinder was taking shape."

From August until November of 1945 – when Colombo was rehired by Alfa Romeo – the engineer's drawings were hand-carried to Maranello, where "Ferrari had created a small but very efficient group of designers who transformed my layouts into working drawings in their format." Luciano Fochi, a recent graduate, was among the engineers who completed this task by the spring of 1946.

As early as April of 1946 the first raw engine castings arrived from the Calzoni foundry, which had the merit of being in Bologna, in the opposite direction from Milan, where Alfa Romeo would be wondering what its former racing chief was up to. An Alfa technician, Giuseppe Busso, joined Ferrari in June 1946 to oversee the new car's gestation. From September 1946 to March 1947 he had the help of an ambitious young engineer, Aurelio Lampredi.

Ferrari's V12 first ran on 26 September 1946. At first it was no power prodigy, with its single Weber carburettor. "It gave 60 to 65 horsepower," said Lampredi, "and revved up to 5,600 – not even 6,000. The problem was the ignition, which was outdated. Nobody had done anything new since 1937–38." Work on the engine continued after road trials of the new model began on 12 March 1947. Finally it was encouraged to produce 72bhp at 5,400rpm, the figure quoted in the first sales brochure for the 125 Sport. With triple carburation for the 125 *Competizione* its output was 118bhp at 6,800rpm on a compression ratio raised from 7.5:1 to 9.5:1, which required special fuel.

In its 125C version the twelve was capable of revving to 7,000rpm – very fast for that time. "You had to pay very close attention to the revs with this engine," said Franco Cortese, the first man to race it. "It was a somewhat different engine, one that went up to speed very quickly. If you were used to normal fours and sixes, this twelve was like an electric motor. It revved so easily that you always had to be on your guard. You had to drive with your head…and with your eye on the tachometer." With an eye to its torque characteristics, Colombo had given the 125 a five-speed gearbox – very unusual for those days.

The twelve's rev-readiness was a factor of its short stroke and oversquare dimensions of 55 x 52.5mm

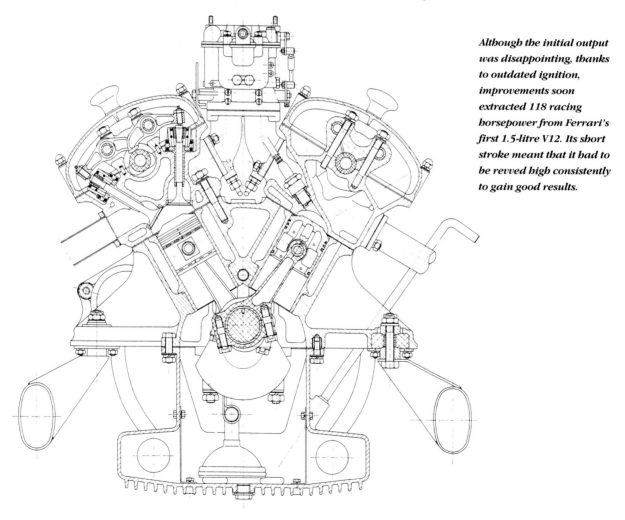

Although the initial output was disappointing, thanks to outdated ignition, improvements soon extracted 118 racing horsepower from Ferrari's first 1.5-litre V12. Its short stroke meant that it had to be revved high consistently to gain good results.

(1,497cc). This was a daring choice by Colombo when set against the Alfa Romeo tradition, acknowledged at Ferrari in many respects, which favoured long-stroke engines. With smaller bore diameters, the under-square engine was easier to make shorter and lighter in a long configuration like a V12 or straight-eight. Against this background the oversquare proportions selected for the first Ferrari engine look all the more surprising.

Gioachino Colombo's choice of a short stroke – the shortest yet for a V12 engine – was one of the novelties he was eager to employ, drawing on "certain experiences in the world of motorcycling which interested me." The latter also accounted for his use of hairpin-type valve springs. Though ultra-rare in car engines, among them Cappa's design for Itala, such springs were used in racing motorcycles and in several Alfa Romeo engines of the 1930s. In one design they served to close the exhaust valves of a two-stroke Alfa diesel engine; one of Colombo's collaborators in the Ferrari job was Giovanni Nasi, who had headed Alfa's diesel-engine department.

To open the valves Colombo used a single central camshaft for each head, working through rocker arms. Later these rocker arms were given roller tips at the cam lobes to combat wear. Hairpin springs continued to be used for all Ferrari engines of all categories, racing and production, for a decade. Beginning in 1959, a transition was made to coil springs for Ferrari engines. By then advances in manufacturing methods and materials had improved the performance of coil springs, as had a better understanding of the dynamics of valve trains and cam-lobe design.

Colombo's use of a single overhead cam for each bank, operating vee-inclined overhead valves through rocker arms, was new to twelve-cylinder engines. It was common in aviation twelves, even before the days of the Liberty, but had not yet been used in a V12 built for cars. He chose a symmetrical valve layout with an included angle of 72°. With the camshafts blocking access to the centre of the chamber, he faced a challenge in positioning the spark plugs, which he inserted from the carburettor side. The cams were driven from the crank nose by a single triple-roller chain, which also drove the water pump and generator on road cars.[6]

The engine's vee was a conventional 60° with its right-hand cylinder bank offset forward, like that of the pre-war Alfa Romeo V12 with which Colombo was familiar. He chose very long wet iron cylinder liners inserted in an aluminium crankcase cut off at the centreline of the crankshaft with its seven main bearings. The 112mm connecting rod's big end was split at an angle to allow it to be drawn up through the cylinder bore for servicing.

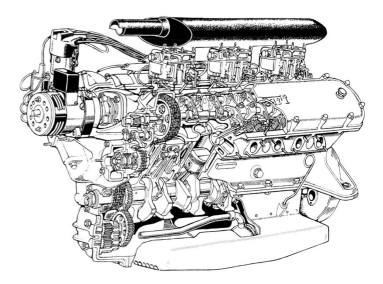

New to the world of twelve-cylinder automobile engines was Gioachino Colombo's concept of inclined overhead valves operated by rocker arms from a single central overhead camshaft. In spite of his use of hairpin-type valve springs, this created a congested top end that required him to tuck the spark plugs away on the inlet side of the cylinder head. Triple twin-throat Weber carburettors were used on competition versions of Ferrari's new twelve.

The engineer secured his engine's future by giving it the generous cylinder-centre spacing of 90mm.

Though high crankshaft speeds were essential to the 125's success, achieving them posed knotty problems. Colombo's idea had been to use a conventional babbitt bearing that was free to rotate against its outer surface as well as against its journal, his theory being that the respective sliding speeds would thus be halved. Lampredi recalled this floating bearing as "a disaster". The only workable solution was to use needle bearings 3mm in diameter, with every other needle a minuscule fraction smaller to act as a separator. With needles the crankshaft journals had to be especially hardened, which gave immense problems in achieving a crankshaft that was still straight after the hardening process.

The solution came from England. Former Alfa Romeo mechanic Giulio Ramponi, who had lived there for some years, knew that Vandervell Products was making a new type of steel-backed bearing insert, based on Glacier designs that had been proven in aeroplane engines. "For me the visit of Mr. Vandervell was a revelation in every respect," said Aurelio Lampredi, who judged that the British bearings "saved" the engine. Enzo Ferrari too acknowledged that "we were enabled later to develop this engine fully and perfectly only by the use of special materials not then available," such as the Vandervell

A typical early road-car version of the Ferrari V12 had a single Weber carburettor feeding a dozen cylinders through a water-warmed inlet manifold. This was a 2.0-litre Type 166 version of the 60° Ferrari vee-twelve.

bearing with its lead-indium-plated copper-lead surface on a steel backing.[7] Nevertheless needle bearings remained in use in Ferrari's supercharged Grand Prix engines at least as late as 1951.

Only two months after this new Ferrari car first ran, it was raced. "We raced every Sunday to prove the car," said Franco Cortese. "Against the Maseratis, more than others. But we had an advantage. The Ferrari was a more modern machine, indeed exceptional for those days." "They took part in ten races," added Colombo: "they won six of them, were second in one and had to withdraw from three." This was an outstanding performance for a radical new design.

Next Giuseppe Busso was tasked with the V12's enlargement to two litres. "We approached it in stages," he said, "first with the 159, whose engine was fired up at the end of July, and later with the 166, which gave its first sneezes at the end of November." That final step was taken under the supervision of Gioachino Colombo, who joined Ferrari on a part-time basis from September 1947 and full-time from the beginning of 1948.

From the original proportions of 55 x 52.5mm the bore and stroke were initially enlarged to 59 x 58mm to bring capacity to 1,903cc. With each cylinder displacing 159cc, this provided the engine's '159' designation. Over the winter all Ferrari's engines were rebuilt to new bigger bores of 60mm, bringing displacement up to 1,968cc. Soon enough the stroke was also lengthened to 58.8mm to create the 166's final displacement of 1,995cc. With a compression ratio of 8.0:1 and triple 32mm Weber twin-throat carburettors this, the 166SC, produced 130bhp at 7,000rpm. It was deservedly successful, both in sports form and powering the dominant Formula 2 Ferrari

As an unsupercharged unit Gioachino Colombo's design for Ferrari came into its own at the 2.0-litre Type 166 capacity. From the first such engine, which ran in November 1947, units were developed which took Ferrari to a dominant position in the 2.0-litre Formula 2 category throughout 1951.

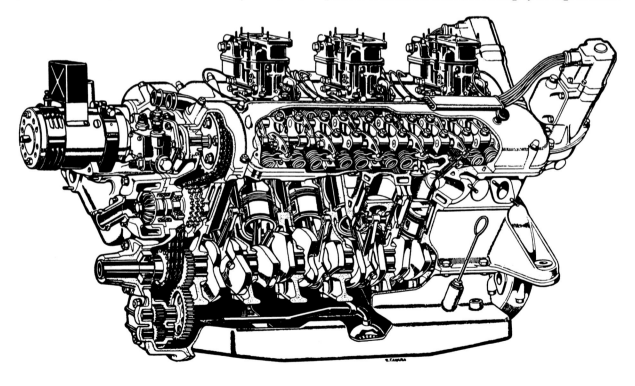

Although Enzo Ferrari had high hopes for a supercharged version of his 1.5-litre V12 that would compete in Grand Prix races, it did not produce the desired success against the dominant Alfa Romeo Type 158. A single front-mounted Roots-type blower delivered its boost to the twelve cylinders through a central manifold.

For the 1949 Grand Prix season Gioachino Colombo produced a completely new 1.5-litre supercharged V12, his GP49. This had twin-cam cylinder heads to which the individual cylinders were clamped by bolts, fed by two-stage Roots supercharging. Design flaws led to the abandonment of this costly and ambitious exercise.

through 1951, when it produced 160bhp at 7,200rpm on alcohol fuel and a compression ratio of 11.0:1.

Giuseppe Busso also gave some thought to a Formula 1 version of the engine, and when Gioachino Colombo returned to Maranello he found evidence of his efforts on both a single-seater car and its engine. By November of 1947 Colombo had laid out a design for the car that became known as the 125 F1. Among the 1947 intake of engineers assisting him were three men who had been working together during the war at aircraft-engine maker Officine Reggiane-Caproni. They were Aurelio Lampredi, Franco Rocchi and Walter Salvarani, all of whom would be vital to Ferrari's future. The prematurely balding Lampredi had returned after a mid-1947 spell with Isotta Fraschini to find a better-organised Ferrari that was more to his liking. Born in Livorno on 16 June 1917, the Swiss-educated Lampredi was destined to perform great deeds at Maranello.

Driven from the front accessory case of the Ferrari V12 for Formula 1 was a single Roots-type blower, fed by a Weber carburettor. Its output was delivered down the centre of the vee to six cylinders on each side. Reports at the time spoke of a scheme to add two more superchargers, the idea being that these would comprise the first stage of a two-stage blower system, but the single-cam V12 never raced with more than one blower.[8] Initially it developed 225bhp at 7,000rpm, which in 1949 was raised nearer to 250bhp. With its clutch the engine weighed 430lb.

Ferrari's ultimate effort to crack the puzzle of the supercharged 1½-litre Formula 1 was a completely new design by Gioachino Colombo – its ambitious GP49. This kept only the 55 x 52.5mm dimensions of the single-overhead-cam engine and the rudiments of its crankcase, adding twin-camshaft cylinder heads in which the valves were opened through short finger followers by gear-driven cams. Two-stage supercharging was provided by twin blowers driven from the timing-gear case at the front. To avoid gasket problems, the individual steel cylinders were bolted to the detachable heads.

Although the GP49's 305bhp at 7,500rpm took Alberto Ascari to a victory in the 1949 Italian Grand Prix, Colombo's elaborate twelve was beset by maladies that included severe overheating and by early 1950 it was abandoned. "This supercharged 12-cylinder engine didn't work – a fact which we repeatedly confirmed," said Aurelio Lampredi, adding that "the supercharged car couldn't be driven…out of the garage." This was only a slight exaggeration. Lampredi, with supercharging experience from his aero engine days, begged Ferrari to let him have a go at a new blown engine of his own design, but Enzo turned him down. "They are one of the regrets of his life," said Griff Borgeson of Ferrari's denials to Lampredi.

While Ferrari as a marque was a brash Formula 1 newcomer, a veteran of the Grand Prix wars was contemplating a return to top-line racing in 1951. Daimler-Benz's initial plan was to build an updated version of its 1939 V8 Voiturette, the W165, which in turn was patterned after the V12 W154. However, after witnessing the titanic battle between Alfa Romeos and Ferraris in the German Grand Prix on 29 July 1951 its executives changed their minds. At a meeting on the following day "all those gentlemen present," summarised Alfred Neubauer, "shared the view that there was no longer a question of building our earlier Type W165 racing car, since this design promises at best equality, not, however, superiority." The management decision to produce more W165s was superseded by the need to design an entirely new Mercedes-Benz racer.

In 1951 Daimler-Benz was designing its M195, a supercharged 1.5-litre vee-twelve engine for a Grand Prix racer. This drawing delineated the features of its cylinder block, which was to be fabricated of sheet steel as a six-cylinder unit.

Under Fritz Nallinger's direction a small group in the central design office had already started outlining a supercharged 1½-litre V12 racing car as the W195. The choice of 12 cylinders followed a recommendation made by the *Rennabteilung* late in 1939 that a cylinder of 125cc be developed as a test unit so that it could be the basis of either a 1,500cc V12 or, if the formula of the time continued, a 3,000cc W24. In 1951 they envisioned a front-engined car with provisions for four-wheel drive.

With its deep aluminium crankcase and fabricated steel cylinders the 60° vee M195, as the engine was known, had much in common with the company's 1938–39 M154/163 V12. Unlike that unit its cylinder blocks were complete sets of six instead of pairs of three-cylinder blocks, with cylinder-centre spacing of 80mm. The German engineers settled on the same 55 x 52.5mm dimensions as Ferrari, specifying the roller-bearing bottom end with which they were comfortable and which, as Ferrari's experience indicated, was in fact the only bearing technology that would permit very

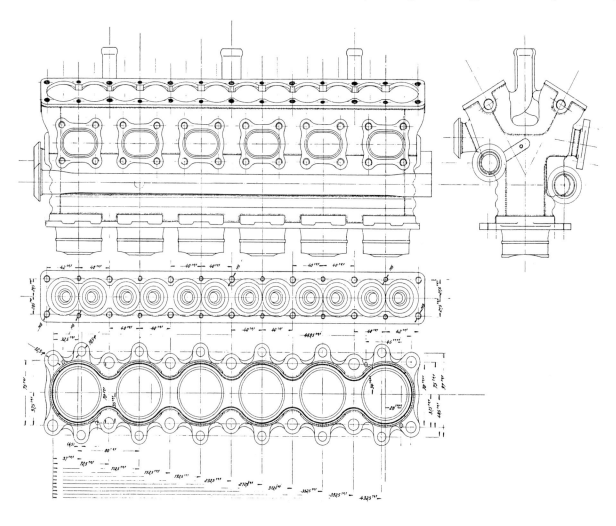

high engine speeds until Vandervell's product became available.

Nallinger's team carried over to the M195 the four valves per cylinder that had worked well before the war to dissipate the heat generated in a highly boosted engine. Their included angle was 60°. As well, in the longitudinal plane the pairs of valves were angled away from each other at 3° each, a total of 6°. This gave more room for valve springs, enhanced gas flow and improved the shape of the combustion chamber with its central spark plug.[9] Completed in September and October of 1951, the M195 design did not provide for direct-cylinder fuel injection and would have incorporated high-pressure supercharging, either two-stage Roots-type or vane-type by Centric or Zoller.

Here was potentially an electrifying engine capable of some 450bhp at crankshaft speeds approaching 10,000rpm. Neither it nor the W195 could be running until the summer of 1952, however, and would not contest a full season until 1953, so a continuation of the formula beyond 1953 was essential if the cost and effort of building it were to be justifiable. When in October 1951 the FIA's Sporting Commission announced new rules for 1954 that slashed supercharged engines to only 750cc, the M195's fate was sealed. It remained a paper study.

The spirit, if not the reality, of Auto Union's pre-war plans for a 1½-litre vee-twelve racer was evoked by a hugely ambitious undertaking in East Germany in the early 1950s. The creation of the ATB Type 650 was one of the many schemes implemented by the occupying Russians to extract technology from the annals of the Third Reich. The Soviets were expert at putting German engineers to

Details of the cylinder block for the Mercedes-Benz M195 of 1951 showed the way in which its pairs of valves were respectively vee-angled and the method by which its forged-steel cylinders would have sheet-steel water jacketing welded around them. It would have been a sound basis for a new twelve easily capable of a race-winning 450bhp.

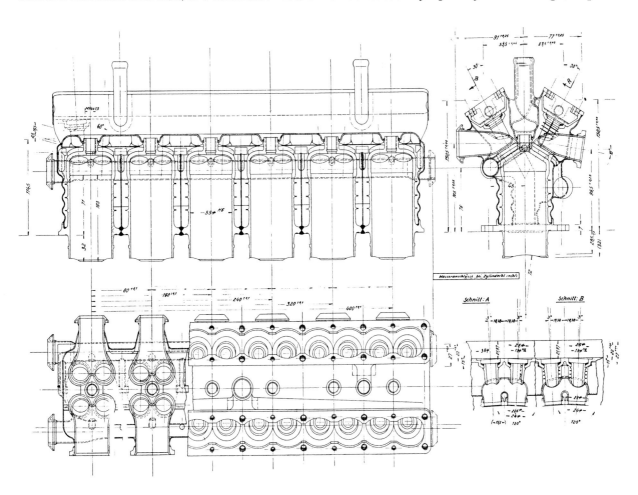

Former Auto Union racing engineers, working at that company's sometime experimental department in Chemnitz, were commissioned by the Soviets to design modern racing cars that embodied Auto Union ideas and experience. Their only effort to reach completion was a 2.0-litre V12 dubbed the Type 650. Completed in 1952, the two Type 650s followed Auto Union practice with their mid-mounted engines and tubular frames.

Four downdraft single-throat carburettors served the induction needs of the Type 650, designed by the Automobile Technical Bureau (ATB) at Chemnitz. Twin overhead cams operated two valves per cylinder in the East German V12, a version of which was also being developed for supercharged 1.5-litre competition.

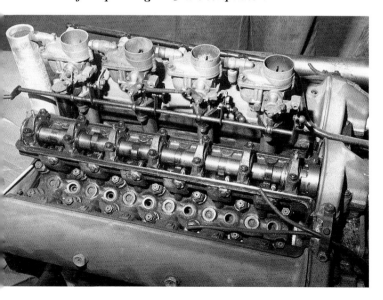

work on projects that seemed to have value for the participants but in reality were tailored to transfer useful technology to the USSR.

Before the Russians in their Eastern Zone lay the principal factories and test facilities of the Auto Union combine. Many of its great racing cars went eastward to be pored over by technical institutes before falling into disrepair. At Chemnitz, in the former Auto Union experimental department, an Automobile Technical Bureau (ATB) was set up in June, 1946 to assess the state of Auto Union's art. In mid-1948 it was brought into the orbit of the Soviet Awtowelo, which was also responsible for the former BMW factories in Eisenach. There BMW-like cars were made under the EMW marque and a skilled collective, the Automobile Workshop Eisenach, built sports-racing cars under the AWE name.

The ATB was preternaturally active, carrying out some 80 design projects. After it produced its report on the Auto Unions, Awtowelo commissioned the ATB to design and build modern racing cars, embodying Auto Union principles, to compete either as two-litre cars in Formula 2 or as 1½-litre supercharged machines in Formula 1 – much the same course that Ferrari followed with his first cars.

The racers designed as the ATB's Type 650 were the work of a team that included engineers Gottfried Heinke, Arthur Kordewahn, Hermann Lange and, for the engine, Werner Wolf and Walter Träger. Their single-seaters were rear-engined, of course, with twin-tube frames, side-mounted fuel tanks, five-speed transaxles and torsion-bar springing for the de Dion rear suspension and front trailing arms.

Although the 650's engine broadly resembled that intended for the E-Type Auto Union it differed in important respects. Vee angle was 65° instead of 60° and cylinder-centre distance was 84mm instead of 76mm to accommodate the two-litre version. Bearing diameters were smaller, 50mm instead of 55mm, and the connecting rod 2mm shorter at 128mm. A strong similarity was the placing of the gear train to the four overhead camshafts at the rear of the block.

Wet-steel cylinder liners were inserted in a high-silicon aluminium cylinder block that went well down past the crank centreline. Both plain-bearing and Hirth-type roller bottom ends were built for the twelve, whose frontal package of single water pump and oil pumps closely resembled that of the Type E Auto Union's layout. Cast of bronze, to obviate the need for valve-seat inserts and to evacuate heat rapidly, the cylinder heads had bolted-on carriers for their twin camshafts above valves at a wide vee angle. In two-litre form the Type 650's dimensions were 62 x 55mm (1,993cc).[10]

That the East-German twelve was laid out chiefly for

supercharged operation as a 1½-litre was obvious from the cramped conditions in which its manifolding had to operate. In unblown form it was fed by four single-throat downdraft carburettors, each with a manifold to three cylinders of one head. Although calculations indicated an output of 152bhp at 8,000rpm for the two-litre version, doubtless on methanol-based fuel, this may be thought optimistic in relation to the similar power achieved by Ferrari's two-litre 12-cylinder Formula 2 engine.

The ATB made two single-seater Type 650 cars and a total of three engines. One of these was readied for supercharging, although no test results are available. The first tests of the Formula 2 version took place in the spring of 1952, when one was reported to have reached 109mph during 37 miles of trials on a stretch of *Autobahn*. In a bizarre episode in the summer of 1952 the two cars were shipped to Moscow were they were to race, but without the attentions of the mechanics familiar with their fuel and tuning. While there they briefly acquired the nickname *Sokol* or Eagle.

With failure in Moscow preordained, the cars returned to Germany and the hands of the Eisenach AWE collective. They tested them but never committed them to a race. Preparations were made, but never completed, to install the supercharged engine in an AWE sports-racer of new design. While one of the single-seaters remained in the hands of the Dresden Technical University, the other came to the west to be rebodied as an exhibit at Britain's Donington Park.

The eclipse of supercharged Grand Prix engines was accelerated by Ferrari, which introduced a 4½-litre unblown V12 in 1950 to compete against the prevailing 1½-litre boosted engines. A racer whom Enzo Ferrari esteemed, Parisian Raymond Sommer, had driven both the unsupercharged 4½-litre Talbots and the early GP Ferraris and, before the war, the Type 158 Alfas as well. He told Enzo that the much better fuel economy of an unblown engine, with adequate power, would be a strong combination. Similar arguments advanced by Ferrari engineer Aurelio Lampredi were accepted by Ferrari, who was at a dead end with his only-marginally serviceable GP49.

Before Enzo could unleash Lampredi on a big new engine project he had to find a way to finance its construction. He turned to his tyre supplier and sponsor Pirelli, requesting and receiving a grant of some $20,000 for this purpose, £8,000. The amount seemed so trivial to Piero Pirelli that he double-checked to make sure that that was all Ferrari really needed. Also justifying the investment was the engine's planned suitability to sports-racing and production Ferraris.

Hairpin-type valve springs continued to be a feature of the larger V12 designed for Enzo Ferrari by Aurelio Lampredi in 1950. By extending cylinder-centre distance to 108mm from the former 90mm Lampredi made room for much larger cylinder bores in an engine that was initially built to reach 4.5 litres for Grand Prix racing.

Although he kept the general concept of Colombo's design, with its single overhead cams on each bank and rocker arms, Aurelio Lampredi created an engine of his own. He added roller tips to his rocker arms to give them better durability and allow the cam lobes to be narrow. Symmetrically disposed at a 60° included angle, the valves did not oppose each other directly but were slightly offset longitudinally to allow their actuating rocker arms to be straighter than would otherwise have been the case. Spark plugs angled in from the sides of the head to cavities in the chamber; the developed 1951 version had two plugs per cylinder. A single triple-roller chain drove both camshafts.

Lampredi extended the cylinder-centre distance from 90mm to 108mm to provide room for bigger bores, which he fashioned as wet steel cylinders that screwed into the heads. The latter were deep, extending almost two inches below the combustion chambers to form the upper water jacket. The bottom ends of the cylinders were sealed to the crankcase by two O-rings in grooves in their outer surfaces. A Lampredi trademark in the crankcase was his doubling up of its flanks to give added stiffness to an aluminium-alloy casting that was cut off at the crankshaft centreline and enclosed by a deeply finned sump. Racing versions had dry sumps, with a triple-gear scavenge pump, while road applications had wide wet sumps.

Assembly of a large Lampredi-type Ferrari vee-twelve showed the great depth of its cylinder heads, into which individual steel cylinders were screwed from below. This allowed more compact construction for its crankcase, with all the main components being cast in aluminium.

Depicted with a modified front-end accessory drive, as developed when such an engine was raced by the Vandervell team in England, Lampredi's 4.5-litre Type 375F1 V12 displayed its gear-driven oil pumps at the front of its sump and the slight longitudinal offset of its valve pairs to allow the rocker arms to be as straight and stiff as possible. **(Vic Berris)**

"I believe that the best approach is to make small engines and then make them grow," said Aurelio Lampredi, who proved it by baptising his new V12 as the 275F1 at 3,322cc (72 x 68mm) for the Belgian Grand Prix in 1950. This was in fact an experimental outing, using a version of the 275S sports-car engine tuned for alcohol fuel, but its success in powering Alberto Ascari to fifth place in Belgium was encouragement for his unblown-engine project. During that year Lampredi's twelve was enlarged to 4,102cc (80 x 68mm). With 230bhp at 6,000rpm the 4.1-litre version powered the 1951 Type 340 America, Ferrari's first sports-racing car to use the long-block engine.

Fed by three double-throat 42DCF Weber carburettors, the new twelve was bench-tested by Luigi Bazzi in 4.1-litre form in the summer of 1950. "Bazzi thought the test bench was out of order," Lampredi related, "as the power recorded seemed too high. The test bench was stripped and reassembled twice, until he was convinced that the power reading was correct." On the special fuel needed by its 12.0:1 compression ratio the 4.1-litre V12 was giving 335bhp at 7,000rpm – more power than any Ferrari yet built.

With the longer stroke of 74.5mm the twelve was opened out to the full allowable capacity of 4,494cc for the last championship race of the year at Monza. As the

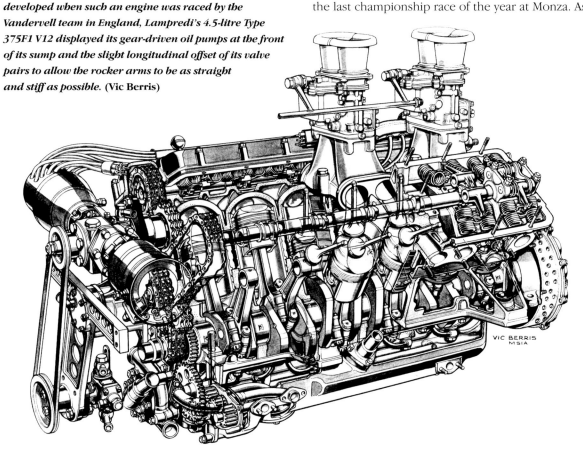

375F1 it was now rated at 350bhp at 7,000rpm. In speed it was breathtakingly close to the Alfas and placed second behind one of them after a hammer-and-tongs battle of attrition and car-swapping.

With dual ignition and larger 46DCF/3 Webers in 1951 its power peak was raised to 7,500rpm and its output to 380bhp to complete what Lampredi regarded as his 'real' Formula 1 engine. Its punch was enough to allow the Ferrari to beat the Alfas at last in Britain and Germany, although not quite sufficient to seize the World Championship. In 1952 one car of a new design evolved from this type qualified to race at Indianapolis, its output stepped up to 400bhp with three four-barrel 40IF4C Webers, but it retired with a rear-hub breakage.

Ferrari wasn't alone in exploring the potential of an unsupercharged vee-twelve as a post-war 4½-litre Grand Prix engine. Although with Lago-Talbot and Delahaye the French were leaders in the use of engines of this size before the war, neither firm was in a position to attempt a twelve in the difficult post-war economy. A new face, however, among France's racers was willing to make the effort. This was Amédée Gordini, born as Amedeo near Bologna in 1899. Since 1922 Gordini had lived and worked in France. By the 1940s he was building and racing small sports and single-seater cars with the backing of French auto maker Simca and, remarkably, Vietnam's Imperial dynasty.

Although his contract with Simca barred him from racing cars with more than four cylinders, Gordini was hankering to field a more ambitious engine in Formula 1. In this he was encouraged by Guglielmo Carraroli, active as a racing driver through much of the 1930s and now an entrepreneur. By arranging to design and build the car outside France, he assured Gordini, Simca needn't be troubled. And he had just the men to do it: the Maserati brothers, who at the end of 1947 had established their own company, OSCA, in Bologna to make racing cars after their ten-year contract with Maserati expired.[11] As a youngster Gordini had been apprenticed to Alfieri and Bindo Maserati at Isotta Fraschini before leaving Italy.

With Carraroli's help, by early 1949 Gordini had contracted with OSCA to create his car's new engine. At the Italian company the prime movers were Ernesto, 51, Ettore, 55 and Bindo, 66. They agreed on the project's budget and parameters with Amédée Gordini, 50. The latter would design and make the chassis in his own workshop. Its chief was Antoine (Antonio) Pichetto, whose pedigree extended back to work on the 12-cylinder Itala racing car of 1927. Gordini and Pichetto both influenced the design of the engine, which the Maseratis named 'Type G' in honour of their customer.

Their twelve's square dimensions of 78 x 78mm (4,473cc) harked back to successful 1½-litre racing engines made by both parties. Vee angle was 60° with cylinder centres spaced at 100mm. Wet steel liners were used in an aluminium-alloy block with detachable aluminium heads which were mirror images of each other. Each cylinder was surrounded by its own set of four studs, adding up to 24 per bank. The block was cut

With its wet steel cylinder liners inserted, the aluminium block of the Type G OSCA vee-twelve showed its closed-deck design with minimal water passages between the block and heads. Cylinders were directly opposite each other.

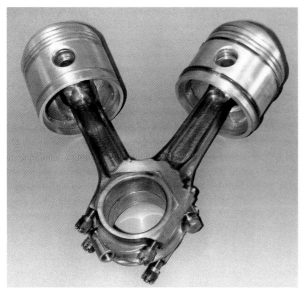

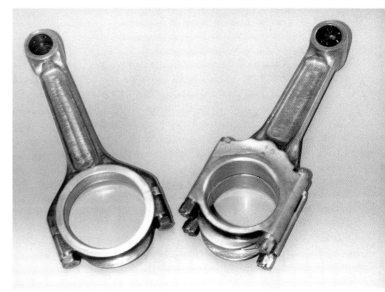

Developed for the use of both Gordini and OSCA, the Bologna-built Type G V12 used fork-and-blade connecting rods. They were topped by full-skirted pistons that had oil rings below their gudgeon pins.

The Type G OSCA carried the big end of its blade rod on a separate bearing surface built into the big end of its forked rod. This created a forked rod that weighed substantially more than its blade counterpart.

off at the centreline of the steel crankshaft, which was carried by seven 61.4mm main bearings. Two-bolt main-bearing caps were cast integrally with the magnesium sump, which was closed at its bottom end by a simple magnesium plate. A central oil-delivery gallery was integral with the sump as well.

Full-skirted pistons carried two compression rings and one oil ring above the gudgeon pin and one oil ring below. Any need for cylinder offset was avoided by the use of fork-and-blade connecting rods – a unique initiative among post-war automotive vee-twelves. The forked rods were in the OSCA's right bank, blade rods in the left. Bearings for both were white metal applied directly to the rod surface. Journal size for the forked rod was 50.7mm in diameter and 42mm wide, while the blade rod ran on a journal 60mm in diameter and 17mm wide at the big end of the forked rod. Both rods had I-section shanks and were 151mm long.

A feature of the forked rod was that its four-bolt big end was made in three pieces instead of the usual two, echoing the design of Rolls-Royce's Phantom III V12. The removable big-end cap was as normal, but its opposing surface, normally part of the rod, was detachable. It mated closely with the main part of the rod at surfaces machined at a 120° vee angle. This allowed the two pieces constituting the big end to be made of nitride-hardenable steel, as was needed because they also supplied the bearing journal for the blade rod. The rest of the rod was made of a steel better suited to durability. The cost of this

construction in performance terms was that while the blade rod weighed 530 grams, the forked rod was almost twice as heavy at 962 grams. Understandably, each rod journal had its own pair of counterweights.

A train of spur gears up the front of the Type G OSCA drove the oil pumps, a single water pump with dual outlets, a gearbox with a spiral-bevel drive to two transverse six-cylinder Marelli magnetos and a fuel pump on its way to turning two overhead camshafts in each bank. Set low, the cams opened inclined overhead valves through short roller-tipped rocker arms whose two arms were significantly offset. Splayed equally at an included angle of 80°, the valves measured 43mm for the inlets and 36.5mm for the exhausts. The former were fed by three double-throat Weber carburettors on short two-cylinder manifolds down the centre of the vee. Magnesium covers for the valve gear were held on by the individual screwed-in pipes that gave access to the spark plugs.

The Maseratis reported to Amédée Gordini that his engine first ran in February of 1950 but was initially "erratic" between 3,000 and 4,500rpm. After attention to its Webers it held solidly at 4,200rpm and produced an early 215bhp. Pichetto was at work on its chassis, with a five-speed transaxle, inboard rear brakes and independent suspension at all four corners, and by July had completed his layouts. Apprised of the project by a hopeful Gordini, Simca definitely turned it down. Although some funding was provided by His Imperial Majesty Bao Dai of Vietnam it was not enough to allow

Gordini to continue and he withdrew from the project. He salvaged something from his investment by basing the design of his four-cylinder Type 16's twin-cam cylinder head on that of the single Type G that he received.

Dedicated as they were primarily to small-displacement racers, the Maserati brothers had to regroup after Amédée Gordini's defection. Continuing work through the 1950–51 winter on the twelve, now their sole property, they claimed 295bhp at 5,600rpm on alcohol fuel with a compression ratio of 11.5:1. Shrewdly they offered the unit as a replacement for the supercharged 1½-litre engines of the 4CLT/48 Maseratis, which by now were distinctly fatigued. They found a customer in Birabongse Bhanudej Bhanubandh, Prince of Siam, who raced as 'B. Bira'.

With incredible speed – only ten days, they claimed – the Maseratis installed their twelve in Bira's Maserati in the spring of 1951, also giving it an OSCA-styled oval nose with vertical grille bars. He won a 12-lap race in its first appearance at Goodwood on Easter Monday, setting a new lap record, in spite of his concerns that the car wasn't running as he'd like. At San Remo on 22 April he retired with radiator damage after an early shunt, and a week later placed fourth in the inaugural Bordeaux Grand Prix.

May saw Bira third in his heat at Silverstone but nowhere in the rained-out final. In a heat at Goodwood later in the year he again raised the lap record but the engine failed in the final, as it was to do at the start of the only championship Grand Prix he entered at Barcelona in October. A June 1952 outing in Ulster's Tourist Trophy, in which it crashed on the first lap, was the final European appearance of Bira's OSCA-Maserati. In 1955 Bira took it to Australia, where he used it at Orange when his Maserati 250F failed, only to have the unprepared OSCA break as well. Through the 1950s it continued racing down under in the hands of Australian owners.

Finding customers in Luigi Piotti and Franco Rol, the Maseratis designed and built two pukka OSCA GP racers. Only Rol's was completed in time to race under the Formula 1 for which it was built. With coil springs in front and a torsion-bar de Dion axle at the rear, it was a purposeful-looking machine in the brothers' style. Gentleman driver Rol qualified it a quarter-minute off the pace for the Italian Grand Prix at Monza in September 1951 and trailed behind the field to finish ninth and last, 13 laps behind the winner and unclassified. Overhauled, with an airbox above its carburettors and a concave grille, Rol's Type G appeared at Turin in April 1952 but expired on its first lap.

This was the downbeat conclusion of the Gordini/OSCA effort to offer opposition to the big battalions of Formula 1. Both Grand Prix chassis were later rebodied as sports cars, with compression ratios lowered

In the Type G OSCA vee-twelve, twin overhead cams operated inclined valves through short roller-tipped rocker arms. While this contributed to a low profile for the engine, it was not the most rigid or light valve gear available. Valves were inclined at an included angle of 80°.

As installed in OSCA's own chassis, the Type G vee-twelve was an impressive unit. Its first outings in 1951 were inconsequential, although it did win one short British event in a Maserati 4CLT/48 chassis.

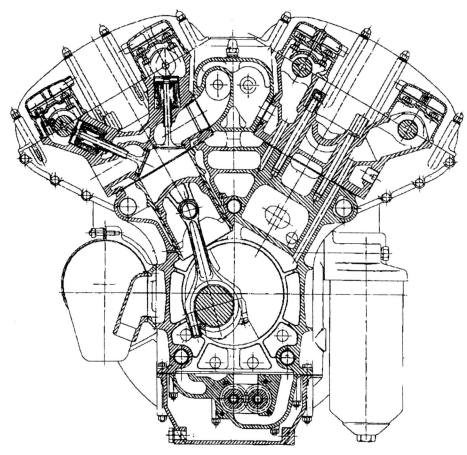

In 1953 Lagonda again attempted a V12. The company was now in the hands of businessman David Brown, who had taken on Aston Martin as well. The 60° twelve was intended to help Lagonda challenge Ferrari both on the road and on race tracks.

to 8.0:1 and developing 220–240bhp at 5,500rpm on petrol.[12] However, neither was destined to find a buyer who had the wherewithal to complete the development and race preparation of these elaborate cars. Nor had little OSCA itself been able to develop the engine to the 350bhp at 6,500rpm that had been its original target. Of the planned eight engines, only four were made.

Work on another 4½-litre V12 began in 1951 in Britain under the best possible auspices. Successively in 1947 and '48 the assets of both Aston Martin and Lagonda had been acquired by industrialist and enthusiast David Brown. While still under Walter Bentley's technical direction Lagonda had elected not to continue with its vee-twelve after the war, making instead a new 2.6-litre in-line six designed by Bentley and Willie Watson which ultimately powered both Lagonda and Aston Martin cars.

David Brown was not unlike his Lagonda predecessor Alan Good in having upmarket ambitions for his illustrious marque. In 1951, accordingly, he asked his team to create a big V12 engine that could power a future Lagonda, both on the road and in racing. Ferrari had already laid a marker down with its Lampredi twelve, and Brown hoped for a British equivalent. As his design chief

he engaged Robert Eberan von Eberhorst, whose credentials included the 1938–39 Auto Union 3-litre V12. The very picture of the German boffin with his tall stature, prominent beak, moustache and spectacles, von Eberhorst brought rigorous Teutonic analysis to a small company that was more used to making and mending.

To design the engine under von Eberhorst, Willie Watson was engaged. Watson, wrote his colleague John Wyer, "was a senior design engineer and a very good one but he did have this tendency to get bored with what he was doing, or supposed to be doing, and start working on something else. If you tried to keep his nose to the grindstone he just dried up completely." Nevertheless Watson had worked on Lagonda's pre-war V12 and had current knowledge of Aston Martin Lagonda's people and facilities. A reading of the runes thus suggested a successful outcome for the engine designated DP100.

With the American market high on the agenda, the DP100's dimensions were expressed as 3¼ x 2¾in. This made 82.6 x 69.9mm for 4,486cc, just six cubic centimetres more than Lagonda's pre-war twelve. Watson arrayed his two banks of six cylinders at 60°, with seven main bearings spacing them evenly instead of the uneven separation imposed by the four main bearings of both the pre-war engine and Watson's Aston Martin six. Although the design was said to provide for a bore increase to five litres, its cylinders were closely spaced longitudinally. The left-hand cylinder bank was offset forward, the opposite of the pre-war Lagonda.

Individual wet-steel cylinders were inserted into an aluminium block, clamped at their tops in much the same manner as the Colombo-designed Ferrari. Extending down well past the bottom of the crankshaft, the block was closed at the bottom by a shallow dry sump that carried its scavenge and pressure pumps at the rear. As in the Aston Martin six and a similar engine he'd designed for Invicta, Watson carried each main bearing in a split aluminium disc, known as a 'cheese' after its shape. The counterbalanced crankshaft, complete with its assembled cheeses, was inserted into the heated block from the rear of the engine, the cheeses being gripped by their matching bores when the block cooled.

A sign of roadgoing intentions for the twelve was the twin-belt drive to its front-mounted water pump, which could also carry a fan. All the other accessory drives were at the rear, where sets of primary helical gears provided the drive to the double-roller chains that turned twin overhead camshafts for each bank. Skew gears from the helical-gear shafts drove two magnetos in the DP100's racing version, each firing twelve cylinders in the engine's dual ignition. Chambers above the camshaft housings were used to keep the ignition wires tidy. Carburation was by triple four-throat 40IF4C Webers.

Von Eberhorst dedicated time and attention to the V12's all-important cylinder-head shape and porting. Watson followed what was to be a new post-war trend in two-valve hemispherical chambers in departing from symmetrical valve inclination to favour the space available to the inlet valve. The latter's inclination was only 28°, against 36° for the exhaust valves. Valve gear was inverted piston-type tappets, sliding directly in the aluminium head, concentric with the coil valve springs and their retainers. Piston tops were crowned to give an 8.5:1 compression ratio and studs for the big ends of the connecting rods were machined integral with the bodies of the rods, following normal Aston Martin practice.

The first DP100 coughed into life at the end of 1953, just as von Eberhorst completed his contract and returned to Germany. He was not replaced, so racing manager John Wyer "reluctantly became the godfather" of the vee-twelve, which "for the next eighteen months…was to absorb a tremendous amount of our time and effort." It was installed in a chassis that resembled an enlarged version of the successful DB3S sports-racing Aston

Seen at Le Mans in 1955, the Lagonda V12 showed off its four overhead cams and the airbox built to provide pressure air to its three quadruple-throat Weber carburettors. Dual ignition by magnetos was a feature.

Martin and first tested in April 1954, when it caught fire with David Brown at its wheel.

Developing 280bhp at 6,000rpm, the twelve was entered in a 50-mile sports-car race at Silverstone on May 15th for Reg Parnell, who outperformed the works DB3Ss to place fifth behind a 4.9-litre Ferrari and three 3½-litre Jaguar-powered cars. By Le Mans in June output had been raised to 300bhp but the Lagonda – not the easiest car to handle – crashed out after only 25 laps.

Even after its long gestation the DP100 was far below its hoped-for output of 350–375bhp at 7,500rpm. The reason for this was a stunning miscalculation in the design of its bottom end. Independent analysis suggested that its cramped main bearings – especially the highly stressed centre bearing – were too narrow. Even worse, the bearing cheeses weren't tightly supported. The concept worked with aluminium cheeses in an iron block, as in the Aston engine, with aluminium expanding much more than iron as temperature rises. With both block and cheeses made of aluminium, however, the whole expanded instead of tightening with heat.

To give a semblance of proper hot-engine running clearances the main bearings were set up extremely tightly when cold, so much so that the starter motor sometimes couldn't cope. As a result, said a mechanic, "John Wyer gave the very firm instruction that before any V12 was started, the cooling system had to be filled with hot water and the car left alone for ten minutes."

Even with this drastic measure the engine couldn't maintain oil pressure. At Le Mans in 1955, running in a new space-frame chassis, oil pressure started out at 90psi

In ninth position after seven hours at Le Mans in 1955, the vee-twelve Lagonda was retired by fuel-leakage problems. The unfortunate choice of aluminium for its bearing supports as well as its crankcase settled the engine's future before it even ran for the first time.

and gradually faded to 60psi, which was only maintained because the drivers backed off the throttle several times each lap – hardly the way to go racing. Oil drained away not only through the bearings themselves but also through the widening interstices between cheeses and block. Fuel leakage forced retirement at Le Mans after seven hours, when the Lagonda was lying ninth. The condition of its bearings suggested that it wouldn't have completed 24 hours.

Le Mans in '55 was the last hurrah for the V12, which was never even installed in the several big Lagonda four-door prototypes that had been built to receive it. Finally appointed technical director in 1955, after Le Mans John Wyer "scrapped the 12-cylinder Lagonda. We had wasted quite enough time and money on that particular white elephant." "It was a fiasco, really," said the mechanic quoted above. Aston designer Ted Cutting called it "a disaster for AML of the first magnitude, both technically and financially." The best skills and intentions had failed to produce a world-beater in the DP100.[13]

In the meantime Ferrari had not been idle in the exploitation of its own big V12 engine. Although the 4.1-litre 340 Mexico didn't win the 1952 race for which it was

designed, in 1953 Ferrari's 4.1-litre vee-twelves developed 300bhp at 6,600rpm and won the Giro di Sicilia and the Mille Miglia. For Le Mans in 1953 Ferrari introduced its 375MM. Although the sports-car versions of the big V12 shared their architecture with their Grand Prix sisters, they differed in cylinder dimensions (84 x 68mm) for 4,522cc. For 1954 their stroke was lengthened to 74.5mm to create the 344-horsepower 375 Plus of 4,954cc, winner both at Le Mans and the Mexican Road Race.

The awesome power of the long-block twelve was also exploited for Ferrari road cars, such as the 1953 375 America of the same cylinder dimensions as the 375MM and producing 300bhp at 6,500rpm. Introduced at the 1953 Paris Salon, the first 250 Europas used the same basic engine with dimensions of 68 x 68mm 2,963cc and 220bhp at 7,000rpm. In 1956 the 68mm stroke was married with a bore of 88mm to create the Type 126 engine, powering the 410 Superamerica of 4,962cc and 340bhp at 6,500rpm. Its successors, with the same capacity, were the aptly named 'Superfast Ferraris'. Versions of the Superamerica also raced as the 410 Sport.

In 1954–55 Ferrari began a flirtation with in-line six-cylinder engines which ended with the departure of Aurelio Lampredi during the latter year. Alfa Romeo and Lancia veteran Vittorio Jano became an advisor to Ferrari, where young engineer Andrea Fraschetti was a key member of the team. Their first vee-twelve effort, the 290MM of 1956, was based on the rugged Lampredi-designed crankcase and heads to enclose 3,491cc (73 x 69.5mm) and produce 320bhp at 7,300rpm, enough to

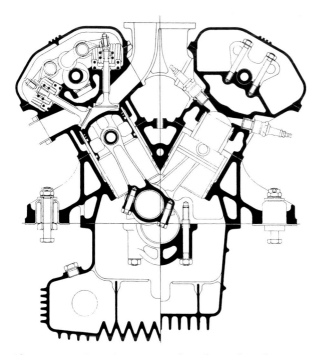

win the Mille Miglia, the Swedish Grand Prix and, in 1957, the 1000 Kilometres of Buenos Aires.

Jano's distinctive valve gear, with its tappet screwed directly into the valve stem, was adopted by Fraschetti and Franco Rocchi for a new range of twin-overhead-cam racing engines based on the 290MM block. From half-speed gears at the crank nose they drove the cams with individual double-roller chains for each bank. The new units came in three sizes: the 335S of 4,023cc (77 x 72mm) and 390bhp, the 315S of 3,783cc (76 x 69.5mm) and 360bhp – both at 7,800rpm – and the 312S of 2,953cc (73 x 58.8mm) and 320bhp at a heady 8,200rpm. The 315S took Piero Taruffi to victory in the 1957 and final Mille Miglia in the last year in which the displacement of world-championship sports-racing cars was unlimited. In 1958 the four-cam engine's ultimate version powered Ferrari's entry in the 500 Miles of Monza. In the single-seated 412 MI it was the most powerful Ferrari car engine yet with 415bhp at 8,500rpm.

Above: Ferrari's racing engines of 1956 were based on Lampredi's block construction with modifications by Andrea Fraschetti and new consultant Vittorio Jano. This was the engine of the 290MM of 1956 which, with dual ignition as shown, brought racing successes.

Below: Based on the block of the 290MM, Andrea Fraschetti and Franco Rocchi developed a new range of four-cam Ferrari racing engines for the 1957 sports-car season. They drove their camshafts through a combination of gears and roller chains and adopted the compact screwed-on tappet that Jano had favoured in his Alfa Romeo years.

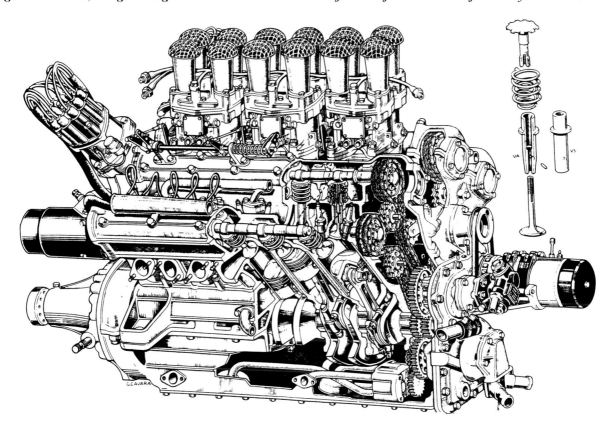

With its spark plugs in the process of being changed, this was the Ferrari 315S vee-twelve of 3.8 litres at Sebring in 1957. It was credited with 360bhp at 7,800rpm.

One of the first of Ferrari's great 250MM V12s of 3.0 litres was shown at the Paris Salon in October 1952. In its 3.0-litre form the original Colombo-designed engine would achieve great things, both on the track and in Ferrari's road cars.

In the 1950s Ferrari didn't fail to exploit the potential of his original Colombo V12. Its 212 version was introduced in 1951 with 2,563cc (68 x 58.8mm) and 1952 brought the 225 of 2,715cc (70 x 58.8mm). It reached full flower in 1953 as the 250MM of 2,953cc (73 x 58.8mm), producing 240bhp at 7,200rpm from a 9.5:1 compression ratio. This was the first of Ferrari's fabulous clan of 250-series engines used in racing under the 3-litre limit, even though it gave away 1½ per cent of the allowable capacity.

The Colombo-based engine powered Ferrari's 235bhp 250GT road-car models, starting in 1958.

Nineteen fifty-eight found the international authorities playing into Ferrari's hands with the imposition of a 3-litre limit on the engines of sports-racing prototypes. Here Colombo's V12 came into its own. In his press conference on 22 November 1957 Enzo Ferrari presented his 250 *Testa Rossa*, based on a prototype he'd raced earlier that year. Still of 2,953cc, it was fed by six Weber twin-throat

With six dual Webers giving an individual throat for each cylinder, the Ferrari 250 Testa Rossa made its bow in 1957. Producing 300bhp at 7,200rpm, it was destined to power many successful sports-racing Ferraris through 1963. (James A. Allington)

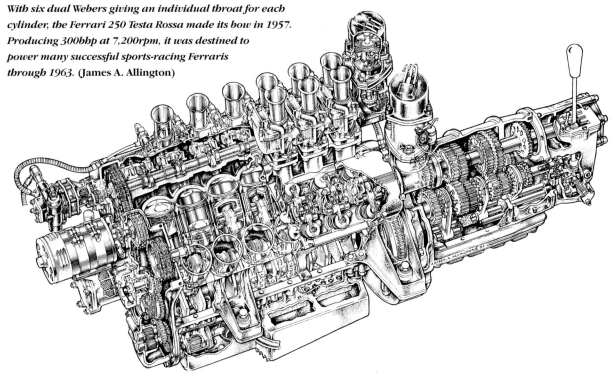

38DCN carburettors and was rated at 300bhp at 7,200rpm. With the exception of a championship just nipped by Aston Martin in 1959 and occasional intervention from Maserati, the 250TR and its successors ruled world sports-car racing through 1962. Then in 1963 much the same engine powered the mid-engined 250P, winner at Sebring, the Nürburgring and Le Mans.

With the rise in importance of Gran Turismo racing, Ferrari fashioned, first, the short-wheelbase 250GT berlinetta or coupé in 1959, then from experiments in 1961 the 250GTO berlinetta for 1962. The latter's engine was close kin to the 250TR V12, differing in its front-end accessory arrangements with a dynamo driven by belt instead of directly from the timing chain. Quoted at 290bhp at 7,400rpm, the GTO's twelve powered this handsome aluminium-bodied coupé to many successes.

Some GTOs raced as prototypes with four-litre vee-twelves. Their engines were based on the Type 209, introduced in Brussels in 1960. This was a Colombo-based replacement for the costly big-block Lampredi twelves that had hitherto powered the most luxurious road Ferraris. The Type 209's cylinder-block deck heights were raised to accommodate a longer 71mm stroke. When this was combined with a 77mm bore, the largest that the block could tolerate, a capacity of 3,967cc resulted. Powering the 400 Superamerica, on a 250GT chassis, the Type 209 developed 340bhp at 7,000rpm.

Although keeping to the principles of Gioachino Colombo's original design, a new Ferrari production-car engine introduced in 1964 had lengthened cylinder-bore centres that gave it the potential for increased cubic capacity. Its first users were the 330GT and 330GTC Ferraris.

In 1964 a completely overhauled Colombo-style four-litre engine of the same bore and stroke was introduced, with its cylinder-bore centres increased from 90 to 94mm to enable it to act as a foundation for future Ferrari twelves. Initially these powered the 330GT and 330GTC Ferraris, developing 290bhp at 7,000 from three 40mm twin-throat Webers. A version of it propelled the 1965 mid-engined 330P2 sports-racer with 410bhp at 8,200rpm.[14]

Surprisingly Ferrari's great Italian rival Maserati, founded in Bologna in 1926 and based in Modena since 1937, had never numbered a vee-twelve among its four-, six-, eight- and sixteen-cylindered cars. It remedied this omission in 1957 with a spectacular 60° V12 to suit the 2½-litre Formula 1.

Automobili Alfieri Maserati had long been owned by the Orsi family, led by Adolfo with his son Omer. From the 1955 season onward, Giulio Alfieri was their man in charge of all engineering for both road and racing cars.[15] Born in 1924, Alfieri received his engineering degree

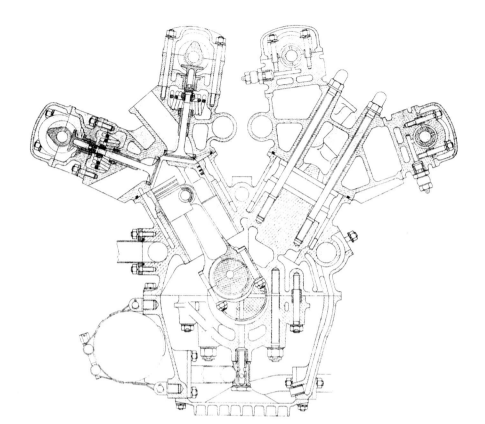

*Looking ahead to a change
in the Grand Prix Formula
1 for 1958 that would
require petrol instead of
alcohol-based fuels,
Maserati's Giulio Alfieri
recommended the building
of a new 2.5-litre V12. This
was a spectacular unit with
hairpin-type valve springs,
downdraft inlet ports and
massive four-stud main-
bearing caps. Pistons were
steeply crowned to obtain a
high compression ratio.*

from the Milan Polytechnic in 1948. He arrived at Modena and Maserati on 1 August 1953 when the company was readying a major thrust in the new two-and-a-half-litre Formula 1 with its 250F model for 1954.

The handsome six-cylinder 250F was successful as a car for Maserati's customers but only occasionally a contender for outright success. The factory team could only gain competitive power by adding oxygen-bearing nitro-methane to its methanol fuel. Thus when in mid-1956 rumours circulated that from 1958 Grand Prix cars would run on petrol only, albeit aviation-grade, Omer Orsi feared that his cars would suffer even more at the hands of the Lancia-derived eight-cylinder Ferraris. In September of 1956 he met with Alfieri to discuss countermeasures.

Within days Giulio Alfieri presented Orsi with a plan to build a twelve-cylinder engine. With smaller cylinder bores, he reasoned, the detonation problems suffered by high-compression engines running on petrol would be easier to master. Higher revolutions would be achieved, aiding the extraction of more power. Engineer and entrepreneur agreed to put the work in hand at once so they could test-run the twelve in 1957 in preparation for '58.

Alfieri's initial thought was to build a flat-opposed twelve in a completely new chassis, but as 1956 turned into 1957 Maserati, busy with its new 450S sports-racer as well as its revised 250F, realised that a new car would be too ambitious. Instead, Alfieri transformed his flat-12 into a V12 with 60° between its cylinder banks to create an engine that could be installed in the existing 250F chassis. He offset the right cylinder bank forward and gave his 250F T2 twelve dimensions of 68.7 x 57mm (2,491cc). Markedly oversquare, the shortness of its stroke among vee-twelves was only undercut by the Ferrari 125C's 52.5mm and the Itala's 55mm.

With weight the implacable enemy of a V12, its main castings were of aluminium and many minor parts and covers cast of magnesium alloy. The block extended down from the tops of the cylinder banks to the centreline of the crankshaft, whose seven Vandervell main bearings were retained by massive caps held by four studs apiece. Inserted cylinders were made of nitrided iron, only their upper one-quarter being exposed to the cooling water where they were pinched between head and block. Coolant was delivered by twin water pumps to the bases of the water jackets and extracted through a cast-in manifold adjacent to the inlet valves.

Fourteen studs retained each Maserati cylinder head. Machined from a steel forging, the crankshaft had supplementary balance weights welded to the faces of its cheeks. Although its main journals measured 60mm the rod big-ends were relatively small at 43mm. Only 117mm long centre to centre, the forged-steel connecting rods had I-section shanks and studs machined integrally with the rod. Grouped at the front of the sump, the twin oil scavenge pumps – with two pickups in the dry sump – and pressure oil pump were driven by gears from the crank nose.

Full-skirted Borgo pistons carried two compression rings and one oil ring. Tall crowns protruded deep into the hemispherical combustion chambers to provide compression ratios ranging from 11.3:1 to as high as 12.4:1. The two valves per cylinder were inclined at 38° for the inlets and 40° for the exhausts, giving the high included angle of 78°. Inlet valve-head diameters were 37.5mm while exhausts were 33.5mm. With space in the engine's central vee at a premium, the inlet tracts came down from the top of each head in the midst of the vee formed by the twin camshafts.

In every aspect Giulio Alfieri laid out his V12 to achieve high speed. "Ten and a half thousand rpm was a lot for 1957," he said. This was especially evident in its valve gear. For the first time a Maserati used hairpin-type valve springs instead of coils. Placed longitudinally within the valve chambers, the hairpins allowed the valve stems to be particularly short and thus light. Between cam lobe and valve were short, light mushroom-type tappets, sliding in inserts in the bolted-on camshaft carriers. The four cams were driven by a train of gears from the nose of the crankshaft.

The 250F T2 was the first unsupercharged Grand Prix engine in history designed to develop power at and above 10,000rpm. With dual ignition to 10mm plugs as well, this set Magneti Marelli a challenge. Its final choice rejected magnetos in favour of a system that gave each spark plug its own small ignition coil. Twenty-four coils were grouped under the car's scuttle and covered by a wire-mesh grille that shielded them electrically without interfering with their cooling. Two distributors were mounted at the front of the engine, each connected to three groups of four low-tension wires to its bank of coils. A small aircraft-type battery behind the driver provided the needed voltage and a Marelli 190-watt generator was on the right side of the crankcase.

Concerns that the unit might be too heavy were assuaged when it weighed in at some 10lb less than the six-cylinder 250F engine. Its carburation was by special Weber units designated 35IDM, with the 'M' standing for Maserati. The *dodici* – as it was known – was developed during 1957 to produce 310bhp at 10,000rpm on a methanol/nitro fuel mix. "We destroyed many in early tests," Alfieri recalled, "running late at night and keeping all Modena awake!" Attention to the base of the con-rod shank stopped the destruction.

Standing on its head, this Maserati V12 had been sectioned as part of an exploration into its castings and structure. Its two-part aluminium crankcase was split on the crankshaft centreline, dry-sump lubrication being a natural requirement for racing.

The new engine was installed in a standard 250F chassis for the race at Syracuse in April 1957, where it practised but didn't compete. This car was entered in the Reims Grand Prix in July, where it burned a piston. A similar 250F T2 practised at Monaco and Rouen but was not raced.

The bottom end of Maserati's vee-twelve was extremely robust with its quadruple-studded main-bearing caps and forged-steel crankshaft with supplementary balancing masses.

The definitive Maserati 250F T2 was based on one of the low-profile 'offset' chassis that had been built for the 1956 Italian Grand Prix. Here was an awesomely impressive car, with its long nose, deep-set cockpit and NACA ducts set into its bonnet to deliver air under pressure to its six carburettors. A refinement was a set of step-down gears behind the clutch with ratio choices of 1.39, 1.35 or 1.26:1 to adapt the engine's high speed to the existing transaxle.

After practising but not racing at Reims and Pescara, this magnificent Maserati was entered in the 1957 Italian GP for Frenchman Jean Behra, who had strongly encouraged its development. He qualified it in the second row for the race only 0.3sec slower than Fangio in the fastest Maserati. The *dodici*, its shrill exhausts screaming in anger, led several early laps of the hard-fought Grand Prix but had to succumb to overheating that led to engine damage.

The 2½-litre Maserati V12 did not race again. In 1958 Maserati adapted it to the petrol-fuel era for which it had been created, seeing output of 275bhp at 10,500rpm, but

A staunch advocate of Maserati's V12, Frenchman Jean Behra raced this one in 1957's Italian Grand Prix. Installed in a special low-profile chassis, it was an extremely fast motorcar that led some early laps of the race but retired with engine damage after overheating.

after 1957's expenditures and some business disappointments the company was too poor to race it. As well, Giulio Alfieri had second thoughts. "The twelve has too much friction loss, too heavy fuel consumption and a longer time of acceleration than engines of similar capacity but fewer cylinders," he concluded from this experiment. "In 1956–57 I did not know this, but I learned."

Alfieri also produced a sports-car version of his twelve by enlarging both bore and stroke to displace 3,491cc (73.8 x 68mm). The 350S in which it was installed was entered in several 1957 events but suffered from underdevelopment and had no finishes. The big engine was dropped into a single-seat chassis for the Race of the Two Worlds at Monza but also failed to make its mark. With the new 3-litre sports-car limit of 1958 one engine was resized to that capacity and tested by Stirling Moss at Spa and the Nürburgring but never raced.

Responding to the needs of such customers as American Briggs Cunningham and Count Volpi's Scuderia Serenissima, Maserati built several mid-engined racers in 1961, its Type 63. Initially they were powered by four-cylinder engines, whose vibration was unkind to their multi-tubular space frames. With this in mind, Giulio Alfieri unpacked his V12s, engines whose smoothness would better suit the Type 63. He extended their cam-drive gear train upward at the front to relocate

POST-WAR POTENCY

their distributors between the two rows of carburettors. This, plus a little encroachment on driver legroom, fitted them well into the mid-engined racers. Using a 10.0:1 compression ratio the twelve was rated at 320bhp at 8,200rpm in its 3-litre form.

The Cunningham team took two such Type 63s to Le Mans in June 1961 while Serenissima fielded one. On the apparent assumption that one was bound to be right, each of the three V12s had different cylinder dimensions: 68.3 x 68mm, 70.4 x 64mm and 75.2 x 56mm. Although all suffered from overheating, one Maserati, a Cunningham entry driven by Dick Thompson and Augie Pabst, survived to finish fourth. It was the car with the most oversquare dimensions and the same stroke as the 1957 V12.

Thereafter Cunningham's two cars went to America, where Walt Hansgen won two major events in 1961, one at Bridgehampton in August and another at Elkhart Lake in September. Although converted into Type 64s for the 1962 season, the cars enjoyed little subsequent success.

This wasn't Briggs Cunningham's first brush with vee-twelves. He owned a superb 1933 Packard V12 touring car, the first Ferrari imported into America, a cycle-winged Type 166, and in 1954 a Type 375 Ferrari that he rebodied and entered at Le Mans. Having raced his Cunningham sports cars with Chrysler V8 power since 1951, Briggs and his colleagues were looking for a lighter engine around which to build a lighter car. Good ones were hard to find, especially in America,

and Cunningham wanted his car to be all-American.

A customer for Cunningham's first production car, a C-3 coupé, was Wisconsin industrialist Carl Kiekhaefer. Also a great fan of motor sports, the cigar-chomping Kiekhaefer produced Mercury two-stroke outboard motors. In the early 1950s he was also producing an inverted vee-four to power target drone aeroplanes, a compact two-stroke delivering 90bhp. His Aeromarine, Kiekhaefer told Cunningham, would build an inverted vee-twelve to power the new C-6R racer that was on the stocks in 1954.

Although based on the drone engine, the two-stroke vee-twelve would be hopped-up by Aeromarine chief engineer Charlie Strang to deliver a minimum of 400 horsepower. The engine would also be used for marine purposes, said the hard-driving Kiekhaefer. Exciting though this sounded – not to mention the noise that such an engine would make – the idea quietly fizzled out. Carl Kiekhaefer went the Chrysler route instead, fielding a stock-car-racing team in 1955, while Briggs powered his 1955 C-6R with a 3-litre Offenhauser four.

From his Cunninghams Briggs would progress to Jaguars and then, after falling out of like with Ferrari, to Maseratis. He and his skilled team made the best possible fist of the V12 powered Type 63. This sports-racer was but the second wind for Maserati's ambitious vee-twelve. It would enjoy a third wind as well. But before that both Maserati and Honda would astonish the world with some of the smallest vee-twelves ever made. One of them would even win a race.

Chapter 10 Footnotes

[1] His Kestrel was one of two that had been installed at the estuary of the River Avon to power blowers that would engulf any wartime invaders in flaming petrol.

[2] According to Harold Pace it shed a wheel.

[3] One source suggests that Colombo's absence from Alfa Romeo, which was to prove temporary, was enforced until the completion of an investigation into his wartime career as a member of the Fascist Party.

[4] After the war the works Alfa Romeo team competed on 21 July 1946 in the GP des Nations at Geneva, regarded as the first revival of true Grand Prix racing. They entered four cars and were 1–2–3 in the final.

[5] Ferrari could have seen pictures of the Packard 299 being tested at the Speedway in 1916 or being raced there in 1919, but not in 1914. His recollection of the Delage was correct.

[6] Several $1\frac{1}{2}$-litre engines were built with gear drive to their camshafts. They are identifiable by the absence of the chain tensioner on the right side of the timing case.

[7] The backing was a steel strip 0.060in thick, carrying a bonded coating of copper alloyed with 20–26 per cent lead and 1–2 per cent tin to a thickness of 0.010in. As a protection against both wear and corrosion this was then plated to a depth of 0.001 to 0.002in by a soft but durable alloy of lead and indium that helped the bearing cope with severe conditions.

[8] Surviving hardware suggests that some single-cam engines were equipped for two blowers, but these may have powered racing motorboats.

[9] Porsche experimented with such a splaying of pairs of valves in a 1971 eight-cylinder engine and introduced the technique (with half the angle) in its turbocharged V6 for TAG in 1983. At that time it was considered an important innovation.

[10] This is the author's calculation, based on the cylinder spacing and published displacement.

[11] OSCA standing for *Officine Specializzate Costruzioni Automobili* or Workshop Specialising in Automobile Construction.

[12] The owner of one was Turin's Paolo Cordero di Montezemolo. His nephew, Luca Cordero di Montezemolo, rose to head Ferrari, Maserati and ultimately the Fiat Group in the 21st Century.

[13] Last shout for the 1954 and '55 Lagondas was masquerading as 'Warren-Ingrams' in the 1956 Rank Organisation film *Checkpoint*, starring Anthony Steel, Stanley Baker, James Robertson Justice and Odile Versois.

[14] The author has refrained from detailing the many interesting features of these and other Ferrari V12 engines and their evolution in recognition of the fact that they are well recorded elsewhere. He hopes for his readers' indulgence.

[15] It was a nice twist of history that his surname was the same as the given name of the Maserati who had taken the lead in founding the company.

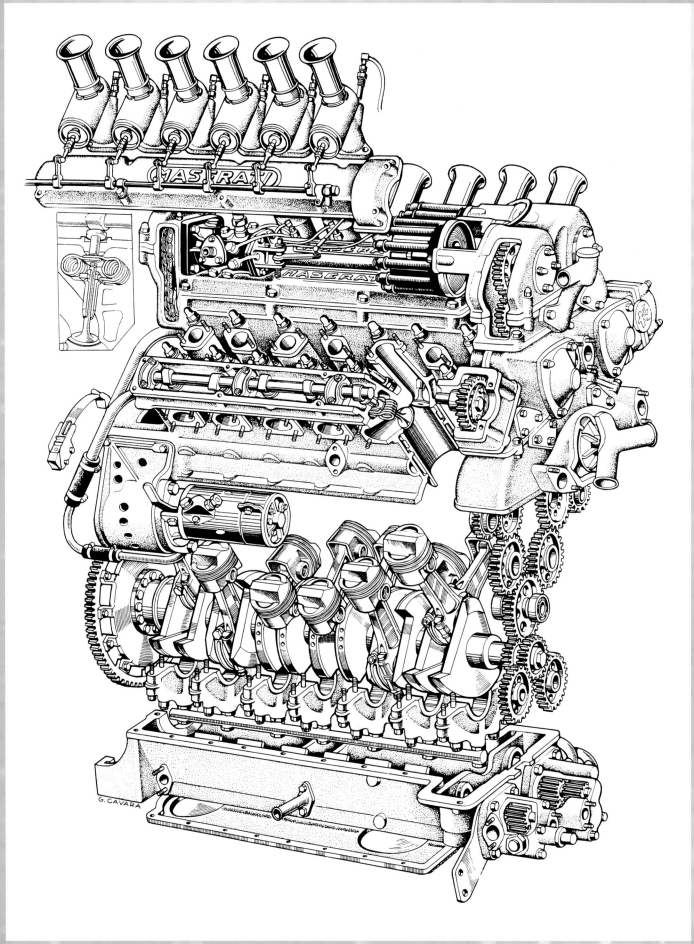

G. CAVARA

Chapter 11

COMPETITION
AMBITIONS

It scarcely seemed likely that engines with as many as twelve cylinders would be built for the new Formula 1 of 1½ litres that took effect in 1961. As we've seen, power units as small as that with a dozen cylinders were ultra rare. Nevertheless at least three were designed, two made and one raced during the formula's life through 1965.[1]

The one that didn't progress from the drawing board was a 1962 engineering study as a graduation thesis project by a young engineer studying in Zürich. He laid out a twelve-cylinder air-cooled Grand Prix engine in such detail, including crankshaft torsional calculations that suggested that a drive takeoff from the centre of the crank might be advisable, that his professor accused him of getting help from his uncle's company. Since his uncle

was 'Ferry' Porsche this was understandable, but as the student was Ferdinand Piëch – soon to carve out an outstanding engineering career in his own right – his precocity was comprehensible as well.

Piëch's conclusion was insightful, for both V12s built for the 1½-litre GP formula did extract power from the centre of the crankshaft. The one that did not race was Maserati's Type 8, designed by the irrepressibly creative Giulio Alfieri. With a team of three draftsmen led by Ennio Ascari, he started the project in October 1961 and completed the drawings by the year's end. His company's financial constraints were such that the engine was only assembled in April 1963 and later given four hours of testing, culminating in a brief trial in a Formula Junior chassis.

With a 60° bank angle, Alfieri's Type 8 was designed to be placed transversely in the chassis and angled forward, so much so that the forward cylinder bank – offset to the left – was almost horizontal. Given symmetrical 80° inclination of the two valves per cylinder, with their

Opposite: *An exploded view of the 3.0-litre Type 9 Maserati V12 of 1966 showed its downdraft inlet ports, hairpin-type valve springs and extra gearing added above its inlet camshafts to drive the ignition distributors in such a way that the unit could fit neatly in the mid-engined Cooper chassis.*

Left: *A view of the top of Maserati's Type 8 V12 of 1.5 litres showed the carburettor bodies that served as the slide throttles for its Lucas fuel injection. A special distributor was driven from the end of one of its camshafts.*

With its sump removed, the two scavenging oil pickups of Maserati's Type 8 vee-twelve were visible. The drive from the crankshaft was taken by two gears, embracing a special clutch designed by Giulio Alfieri.

Removal of one of the cylinder heads of the Type 8 Maserati V12 showed its wet cylinder liners and one of the drive gears to its twin overhead camshafts. An impressive and elegant design, the Type 8 never had a chance to strut its stuff.

overhead cams and finger-type followers, the Type 8 was like its Maserati predecessor in having downdraft inlet ports between the two camshafts. Each was topped by a Dell'Orto carburettor body serving as a slide throttle for Lucas port-type fuel injection.

Closed by hairpin springs, the valves were opened by cams driven by gear trains upward from two gears near the centre of the crankshaft, the two gears also taking the drive to a transverse drum containing an 11-disc wet clutch. Each crankshaft gear initiated the camshaft drive to one of the cylinder banks. The crankshaft of chrome-molybdenum-vanadium alloy steel was carried in seven main bearings, the outer ones being rollers and the rest 44mm plain bearings. Forged-steel rods 118mm long had 33mm big ends and carried high-domed full-skirted pistons giving an 11.5:1 compression ratio.

The Type 8's dimensions were 55.2 x 52mm (1,493cc). Its wet steel cylinder liners were carried in an aluminium casting that comprised the cylinder block, gearbox housing and half the enclosure for the final-drive gears. A large light-alloy sump enclosed the machinery and supported an ultra-compact transverse six-speed gearbox, all the components being lubricated by the same oil. Manifolding from a single water pump, driven from the left side of the gearbox, took coolant to both the blocks and heads. Although a Marelli system firing one plug per cylinder was used for the prototype, transistorised Lucas ignition would have been used in racing.

Weighing 315lb, Alfieri's complete package would have fitted neatly in the back of a small Grand Prix car. No in-house chassis was designed for the Type 8 when work on it was suspended. At that time it was producing 170bhp at 12,000rpm against a hoped-for peak of 14,000 and at least 225bhp. The cost of such a quixotic experiment to a struggling Maserati was certainly high, as Omer Orsi's son Adolfo remarked: "Engineer Alfieri was a mixed blessing. He was very creative, but often too much so with fantastic ideas. These could have been very expensive for Maserati at a critical time."

Maserati revealed details of its Type 8 in 1964 when rumours were flying that in far-away Japan an engine of similar design was being readied for Grand Prix racing. The rumours were true, as became clear in August of '64 when a white car, the Honda RA271, came to the Nürburgring to compete in the German Grand Prix. It had little luck that first short season but in 1965, with American Richie Ginther at its wheel and in a new RA272E chassis, the vee-twelve Honda won the season's final race – and the last of the formula for which it was built – in Mexico City.[2]

Although the broad similarities to Maserati's engine were notable, the Honda had many features unique to the

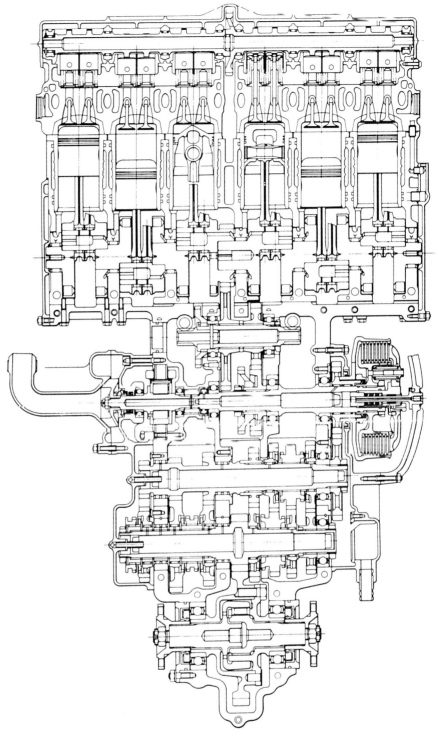

In parallel with Maserati, Honda developed a remarkable transverse V12 for the 1.5-litre Grand Prix Formula 1 of 1961–65. From the centre of its crankshaft a drive rotated successive transverse shafts to the gearbox and finally to the differential. Unusually, its pistons are shown in both profile and side view.

Japanese company's technology, honed with successes in motorcycle racing that included the 1961 Isle of Man TT, where its cycles swept the top five positions in both 125cc and 250cc classes on their way to World Championships. Ready to reach out into the world of automobiles with its S600 and S800 sports cars, founder Soichiro Honda found it natural enough to signal the seriousness of its intentions with a Grand Prix car. The design of his entry was led by Yoshio Nakamura while Tadashi Kume was especially concerned with its engine.

Work on a Formula 1 Honda engine began early in 1962 with the building of a vee-twin research unit, the K005. With just over 36bhp at 12,000rpm the K005 showed that some 220bhp should be produced by a twelve. Soon, in parallel, a vee-twelve was running, the RA270E. By mid-1963 the Honda engineers were ready to begin work on the RA271E, the first engine they would race. Like Alfieri at Maserati, they had the inspiration of placing it transversely behind the driver. Its drive was taken from a spur gear at the centre of the crankshaft at

The developed version of Honda's RA271E used the company's own low-pressure fuel-injection system. Slide throttles controlled the air inlets, seen at Monaco in 1965.

a reduction of 1.85:1 to a short transverse shaft. From this two skew gears drove shafts going downward to the gear-type oil scavenging pumps mounted in the sump.

From the transverse shaft another gear pair drove yet another east–west shaft, this one quite long. It was driven at a further reduction of 1.21:1, so this shaft turned at 44.7 per cent of engine speed. On the right end of this shaft was the multiple-disc clutch that drove the gearbox – two more transverse shafts – at another speed reduction of 1.14:1 through a pair of gears that could easily be changed to adjust the overall ratio.

On the long shaft's left end was the engine's single water pump. Its twin outlets delivered directly to coolant passages cast into the block and heads. Near the centre of the long shaft was a spur gear from which a drive progressed up the V12's centre to all four camshafts. A very large idler gear at the centre of each cylinder head drove its two cam gears; the gearing from the long shaft to these idlers established the necessary half-speed ratio for the cams. From the top of the gear at the centre of the rearmost exhaust camshaft another gear drove the fuel-injection distributor that was used for the developed version of the engine. It first raced in 1964 with six twin-throat downdraft Keihin carburettors.

Remarkably, the RA271E's cylinder size of 125cc was larger than any that Honda had used in its racing cycles. Its dimensions were more oversquare than those of the similar Maserati at 58.1 x 47.0mm (1,495cc). The bore was large enough to accommodate a single central 10mm NGK spark plug, two 24mm inlet valves – 1mm less than

in the RA270E – and two 22mm exhaust valves. Valve inclinations from the vertical were 30° for the inlets and 35° for the exhausts. The Honda's was, and has remained, the smallest auto-racing engine cylinder to make use of a four-valve head.

The valves were closed by conventional paired coil springs, shrouded in long-skirted cup-type tappets which slid in bolted-in carriers in the head. A single aluminium alloy casting constituted the head for each six-cylinder bank. In a unique Honda process the head was cast around chamber 'roofs' made of an aluminium-bronze alloy which bonded to the head material. These formed the complete surface of the pent-roof combustion chamber and provided durable valve seating and spark-plug threading.

Matching the chamber shape, the pistons had distinct roof peaks which were flattened at the top to provide a compression ratio of 10.5:1. Pistons were full-skirted, save for crescent cut-outs for crank counterweight clearance. Deeply ribbed under its crown, each piston carried two thin compression rings and one oil ring. A plain bushing joined the piston to the I-section connecting rod, which was steel and 119mm long.

One single complex aluminium casting, adroitly ribbed for stiffness, constituted both the RA271E's cylinder block and its gearbox and final-drive housing. After the insertion of all the gears and reciprocating parts its bottom was closed by another large aluminium casting

Light weight was not a feature of the complex RA271E, with its integral transmission and final drive. The complete unit weighed 475lb.

which provided a common sump for the entire unit. The weight of the complete assembly was 474lb, half again as heavy as Maserati's Type 8.

Each cylinder was an individual ferrous wet liner, ribbed around its circumference and sealed at its bottom end by O-rings in grooves in the block. The liner's square top was clamped directly by the head and the 16 studs along each cylinder bank. The crankcase casting extended down well past the centreline of the crank, which was carried in seven main bearings. All the bearings were rollers because, as engine-designer Yoshio Nakamura said, Honda "found that ball and needle type bearings are always superior in performance to plain-type bearings in high-speed operations – especially when the power required for bearing lubrication is taken into account."

Desiring to keep all bottom-end bearings as small as possible to reduce both friction and mass, Honda varied their diameter. The central main bearing next to the drive gear had a 40mm journal. The next two moving outward were 36mm, the next two 33mm and the outermost mains only 30mm. Uniquely, the connecting-rod journals were dealt with similarly. While the outer four rod journals were 27mm in diameter, the inner pair was 32mm in order to add strength to the crankshaft adjacent to its output gear.

The challenge of high-speed ignition was met by combining a six-coil breaker-type system with a high-tension magneto which came into effect at speeds above 7,000rpm. Nevertheless the Honda offered very little performance below 8,000rpm and was a poor starter both from cold and from the fall of the flag. The engine was fully reliable at 13,000rpm and was red-lined at 14,000. One of its drivers (American Ronnie Bucknum) once saw an engine survive being revved to 16,000rpm. That the Honda was peaky was indicated by the 11,000rpm at which it generated its maximum torque of 116lb-ft. Output ultimately reached 222bhp at 12,000rpm, which just out-powered the flat-12 Ferrari's 220bhp to make the Honda the 1½-litre Formula 1's most potent power unit.

Twelve-cylinder creativity wasn't denied to sports-car racing in the 1960s. As he and his engineers gained familiarity with his new generation of mid-engined prototypes, Enzo Ferrari added displacement and power to produce cars that could only be beaten by even more displacement and power from V8-engined cars by Ford and, occasionally, Chaparral. Nineteen sixty-four saw, first, the 330P of 3,967cc (77 x 71mm) giving 370bhp at 7,300rpm and, second, the 365P of 4,390cc (81 x 71mm) producing 380bhp at 7,300rpm, both with single-cam heads and six twin-throat Weber carburettors.

Under the rear deck of Ferrari's magnificent 330P4 of 1967 was a 4.0-litre V12 developing 450bhp. Curved ram pipes descended to ports which were of downdraft configuration, between the camshafts of each cylinder head.

In 1965 Ferrari introduced its first twin-overhead-cam power units for its mid-engined sports-racers, using Jano-type valve gear like that of its 1957 cars but placing the inlet ports between the pairs of cams as Maserati had done. The 330P2 had the same capacity as its single-cam predecessor but delivered 40 horses more at 8,200rpm. Its smaller sister was the 275P2 of 3,286cc (77 x 58.8mm) producing 350bhp at 8,500rpm. Both were Weber-carburetted.

This line of development progressively culminated in the 1966 330P3 of 3,967cc (77 x 71cc) of 420bhp and the 1967 330P4 of the same capacity and peak-power speed of 8,200rpm but developing 450bhp. Both had Lucas fuel injection which helped tolerate compression ratios raised to 10.5:1 from the 9.8:1 of the carburetted engines.

Meanwhile another Italian entrepreneur, more used to competing in the smaller sports-car classes, had his eye on the possibility of outright victory. This was Turin-based Carlo Abarth, who had close links to Fiat as a 'house tuner' of its production cars and builder of quick Zagato-bodied derivatives. Hearing that Fiat money was likely to go to Ferrari to help it build bigger-engined racers, Austrian-born Abarth's pride was pricked.[3] He feared that Fiat would dismiss his home-town potential, saying, "Oh, Abarth can't build such a car." He resolved to prove them wrong.

The remarkable Type 240 engine designed by Luciano Fochi for Abarth in 1966 was created by marrying two vee-sixes, each with its own sump.

The engineer behind Abarth's creations was Luciano Fochi, the same designer who as a callow graduate had detailed Gioachino Colombo's layouts for the first Ferrari V12. Later he followed Colombo to Bugatti and from there moved to Abarth in the early 1960s. He brought with him some concepts he had developed at Bugatti (see Chapter 12), setting out designs for 60° V12 engines of 4.2 and 5.2 litres in 1963. By 1965 Abarth, Fochi, Mario Colucci and his other engineers were preparing the design of a big-engined sports car they called the T-140. Its chassis-to-be was patterned after that of the Lola T70, a sample of which was acquired by driver Umberto Maglioli for Abarth on 29 May 1966.

Fochi's engine for the T-140, designated the 240, harked back to some earlier V12s in having triple-bore cylinder-head pairs along each bank and went even farther in marrying two aluminium cylinder blocks to complete the engine.[4] Ingeniously and economically he arranged for one block casting to serve for both ends of the engine.[5] Extending down well past the crankshaft centreline, the blocks carried wet-steel cylinder liners and had the left bank offset forward. They were stoutly knitted together by heavy bolts on both sides of the

crankcase. Each block had its own cast and finned sump, wet or dry to customer choice. For Abarth's T-140 both would certainly have been dry.

Relying as it did on sheer displacement to make its point, 5,983cc (92 x 75mm), Fochi's V12 was configured with single overhead cams and in-line valves along each bank. In case it should be needed the engineer also prepared a twin-cam layout. The camshafts were driven from the centre of the engine, where Fochi devised unique arrangements for marrying the two crankshafts and the camshaft pairs. While a large single water pump was driven by the nose of the crankshaft, the central accessory drive turned the twin Marelli distributors for quadruple-coil dual ignition, with spark plugs on the inner and outer head surfaces.

In several respects Luciano Fochi's design set the engine very low in its chassis. One was that it adopted the wide bank angle of 120°. Like 60°, this was fine for the acceptance of evenly spaced impulses from the cylinders of a vee-six or vee-twelve. Although Ferrari had previously built and raced a 120° V6, this was the first use of the wide-angle concept in a V12.

Also allowing low positioning was Fochi's choice of a gear and shaft from the central drive, running above the crankshaft, to take the engine's output to its triple-disc Borg & Beck clutch. As with the much smaller Maserati and Honda engines, this central takeoff avoided the

torsional problems that could be provoked by a long twelve-cylinder crankshaft.

In 1966 the T-140 was taking shape in the Abarth workshops, where it was known as the 'big secret'. Visitors found other programmes grinding to a halt with all hands working on the 240 engine, five-speed transaxle and Mario Colucci's design for a glass-fibre coupé body. Fitted with four triple-bodied Weber 40IDA3C1 carburettors the twelve was found to produce 610bhp at 6,700rpm on a compression ratio of 12.0:1 for a car that would weigh 2,450lb. Here indeed was a vehicle with which to reckon for overall sports-racing honours.

Carlo Abarth waited until his T-140 was virtually

Below: A single very large water pump driven from the nose of the Type 240's crankshaft provided coolant to both banks of the aluminium-block Abarth engine. Tests showed its output to be 610bhp at 6,700rpm, potentially important power for a sports-racing contender.

Drawing on experience from a Lola T70 that Abarth had acquired, Mario Colucci designed a handsome coupé body for a car that would be by far the largest to emerge from Abarth's workshops. This was the full-scale model of the planned T-140 sports-racing car.

A high level of professionalism was shown in Moteur Moderne's design for a new racing engine in 1966. Unusually, each connecting rod was given its own individual journal on the crankshaft. The engine, with a 60° vee, was designed to be built either as a V6 or a V12.

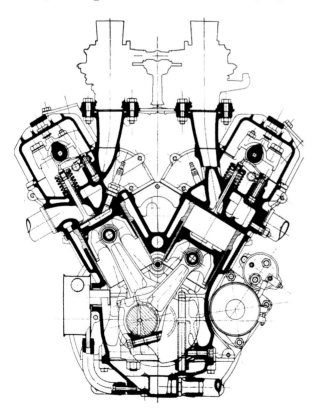

complete before he invited the Fiat brass to his small but well-equipped manufactory at Corso Marche 38 on the west side of Turin. With justifiable pride he presented the results of his team's efforts, a car that had cost them five times as much as the most expensive automobile they'd ever made. He was dismayed by their reaction. "You don't need to do that, Carlo," he was told. "Ferrari will build the big-engined cars." The brush-off was final. There'd be no funding from Fiat to make the T-140 a running reality.

In 1967 Abarth revealed the 240 engine, easily the most remarkable of the many to leave his workshops. He couldn't very well admit that he'd been trumped by Ferrari in the game to get Fiat's cash to go racing. Conveniently, the FIA had just announced that from 1968 all prototypes would be limited to three litres and production sports-racers constrained to five litres. This became the published rationale for Abarth's failure to carry his ambitious project through to front-line combat. Although credible enough, it wasn't the real reason.

Parallels are striking between Abarth's 240 and another engine developed at the same time by a Paris-based engine research company, Moteur Moderne. Led by Jacques Pichard, this French counterpart of Britain's Ricardo had enjoyed success in tuning racing engines for Renault and Peugeot. Picturing themselves as a Cosworth rival, Moteur Moderne's engineers started work in their spare time on a new racing engine. It could be built either as a 1,600cc V6 for Formula 2 racing from 1967 or – with two engines combined as one – as a 3,000cc V12 for the new Formula 1 that took effect in the 1966 season.

Among the similarities between the two concepts were single overhead camshafts operating vertical valves, deep aluminium blocks with wet cylinder liners, and a central geared takeoff of the drive to the clutch. Among differences were the French engine's vee angle of 60°

instead of 120° and its use of three instead of two valves per cylinder: two 27mm inlets and one 33mm exhaust. They faced into a shallow combustion chamber in the crown of a slipper-type piston that gave a 12.5:1 compression ratio. Short finger-type followers on spherical pivots were interposed between cam lobes and valves.

Substantially oversquare at 80 x 49.7mm for 2,998cc, the Moteur Moderne twelve had 130mm titanium connecting rods forged by Ugine. Their big ends were split diagonally at their 48mm big ends, the caps mating at serrated joints. Although not essential with a 60° vee, Jacques Pichard's engineers gave each rod its own journal on the forged-steel crankshaft. Deeply spigoted caps for the 55mm main bearings were side-bolted from the crankcase flanks. The gear drive to the camshafts was at the output end of the block, where the two blocks were mated to create a V12.

Fed initially by four triple-throat carburettors but designed to accept electronic fuel injection that Moteur Moderne was also developing, its twelve was a commendable effort for a small firm – another similarity to Abarth. There's no evidence, however, that it ever raced in anger either as a 3-litre or as a 1.6-litre V6 with a 53mm stroke. Although the French government was offering financial backing to its racing-car makers, none of this windfall would benefit Moteur Moderne.

The new 3-litre Formula 1 was widely viewed as a gift to Ferrari. "Everyone was expecting Ferrari to be the one company properly prepared for the new formula," recalled their 1964 world champion and team leader John Surtees, "but they weren't." For the early-1966 races Surtees was keen to use a 2.4-litre V6-powered car that had raced successfully in the Antipodes, but with a commercial policy heavily biased toward V12-powered road cars Maranello's Grand Prix campaign had to use that engine type. Competing as it was across a broad range of disciplines, however, and facing Ford's challenge at Le Mans, Ferrari wasn't able to marshal its forces to produce the new three-valve engine it wanted in time for the start of the 1966 season.

With dimensions of 77 x 53.5mm (2,990cc) the first Ferrari engine for the new Formula 1 was a short-stroke version of the contemporary 330P3 sports-racing twelve with two valves per cylinder. "Its power was announced at 310bhp," Surtees recalled, "but I saw the test sheets and the reality was about 280bhp." This was inadequate in a car which was excessively heavy. By June engineer Franco Rocchi had persuaded more than 300bhp from it and Surtees won at Spa in the 312F1-66, triumphing in his last drive for Ferrari.

In time for the 1966 Italian GP at Monza and a popular win for Ludovico Scarfiotti a new V12 with three valves

In its vee-twelve configuration the Moteur Moderne engine was mocked up, resembling the Abarth in its marriage of two vee-six units. Lacking a customer for its initiative, Moteur Moderne did not pursue this effort.

A front view of Ferrari's 3.0-litre V12 F1 engine of 1967 showed the scoops ingesting air for its inlet pipes and its centrally mounted exhaust. A single water pump delivered coolant to passageways down the centre of its 60° vee.

Its principal weapon for the 1967 Grand Prix season was Ferrari's V12 F1-67, having single exhaust valves and twin inlet valves fed by downdraft ports between the camshafts. It was rated at 375bhp at 10,000rpm.

per cylinder – two inlets and one exhaust – was finally mustered. Its inlet ports moved from the central vee to positions between its camshafts in Maserati fashion, while its exhaust pipes remained outboard. Ferrari was well aware of the advantage offered by four valves per cylinder, a technology just coming back into use, but deliberately chose three valves because the engine's

Ferrari's Type 261 vee-twelve was produced in 1968 for Can-Am racing, initially at the capacity of 6.2 litres. In 5.0-litre form it was later adapted as the Type 261C to power Ferrari's 512S of 1970.

bottom end was still the old sports-car design, not well suited to high crankshaft speeds and loads.

Through most of 1967 Ferrari raced an improved version of its 36-valve engine in its 312F1-67, in which the exhaust pipes were moved to its central vee. This allowed both smoother pipe flows and higher flanks for the monocoque frame, since the engine was not designed to be used as part of the chassis.[6] Quoted power was now 375bhp at 10,000rpm. At the end of the 1967 season a new four-valve V12 arrived. This kept the central exhausts and moved the inlet pipes and slide throttles outboard. In 1968 Ferrari claimed 410bhp at 10,600rpm for this Lucas-injected engine. In 1969 it moved the inlets to the centre of the vee and the exhausts outboard – as they'd begun in 1966 – for an engine producing 436bhp at 11,000rpm.

Nineteen sixty-nine was Ferrari's last with vee-type Grand Prix engines before adopting the 312B flat-twelve. Twenty years would pass before Ferrari returned to V12 engines for its Formula 1 machines. The 3-litre GP engines were also used in the beautiful open 312P spiders that contested the 1969 endurance-racing season. With an 11.0:1 compression ratio they produced 420bhp at 9,800rpm. The 312P was quick but had to yield that season to the Porsche 908.

The lines of the 312P had much in common with a stunning new Ferrari that appeared at the end of the 1968 Can-Am series, the 612P, powered by a completely new engine of 6,222cc (92 x 78mm). This was the Type 261, a classic modern Ferrari 60° vee-twelve with four overhead camshafts and four valves per cylinder. Working to the broad concept laid down by Mauro Forghieri, the engine was the detailed work of Franco Rocchi. Giancarlo Bussi oversaw its development.

In the manner well-established by Ferrari, the right bank of the 261 was offset forward and each bank had its own double-roller chain to its camshafts, driven from one of the two half-speed gears turned by a gear on the nose of the crankshaft. The nose of each half-speed gear also drove a magnesium-housed water pump, one for each bank. External pipes carried water well to the rear of each side of the block. Each cylinder had a single central 10mm plug sparked by a Marelli distributor on the rear of the left-hand inlet camshaft; its right-hand sister drove the Lucas injection's distributor.

Vee-inclined at an included angle of 24°, the Ferrari 261's valves were opened by bucket tappets and closed by single coil springs. Slide-type throttles in the central vee were atop short stub manifolds within which the mixture began to be spread to feed the bifurcated inlet ports. Exhaust ports, on the outside, were circular. Aluminium heads clamped wet iron cylinder liners against low-placed abutments in the block, also of aluminium alloyed with nine per cent silicon for toughness. Handsomely waffled on its exterior, the block extended down to the very bottom of the engine and was closed by a shallow cast-magnesium pan. This allowed the two-bolt main-bearing caps to be cross-bolted through the sides of the block for the ultimate in rigidity.

Seven main bearings carried the Type 261's forged-steel crankshaft, which was most heavily counterweighted at its ends and centre. Connecting rods had tapered I-section shanks. Carrying two compression rings and one oil ring, the pistons had shallow crown depressions for valve-head clearance. Pistons were slipper-type, with only slim vertical surfaces in the plane of the connecting rod to contact the cylinder walls. They were novel in that the hardest-worked piston face for side thrust, the one on the right side of the engine, was more robustly braced than the face on the left side, behind which the bottom of the piston curved up for lightness.

Along the exterior of the left-hand side of the block was a battery of oil scavenging pumps in magnesium housings, supplying the reservoir of the Ferrari's dry-sump oiling system. The pressure pump and filter were there as well, also driven by a cogged-rubber belt from a reduced-speed gear below the crank nose. Although protected by an aluminium shield, this would prove to be a vulnerable feature of the engine. Mastering its oil cooling would also prove to be a challenge.

The left-hand cylinder bank of a Ferrari Type 261C vee-twelve showed the roller-chain drive to its twin overhead camshafts, its circular exhaust ports and its camshaft bearings placed between its cylinders.

Initially credited with 620bhp at 7,000rpm on a 10.5:1 compression ratio, the 261 twelve was installed in the 612P spyder for New Zealander Chris Amon to drive at Las Vegas in 1968. Its engine sound "a heavy mechanical rasp overlaying a frantic animal moan", the Ferrari practised only briefly and was knocked out in a first-turn melee. Although arriving late for the 1969 Can-Am series the

From the rear three-quarters a Type 261C Ferrari vee-twelve displayed the outer housing of its multiple-disc clutch and the closed top deck of its cylinder block with its inserted wet iron cylinder liners.

An extremely deep aluminium crankcase gave rugged lateral support to the seven main bearings of Ferrari's Type 261C V12 of 1970. Flanking its bottom end was a gang of scavenging oil pumps feeding an oil filter.

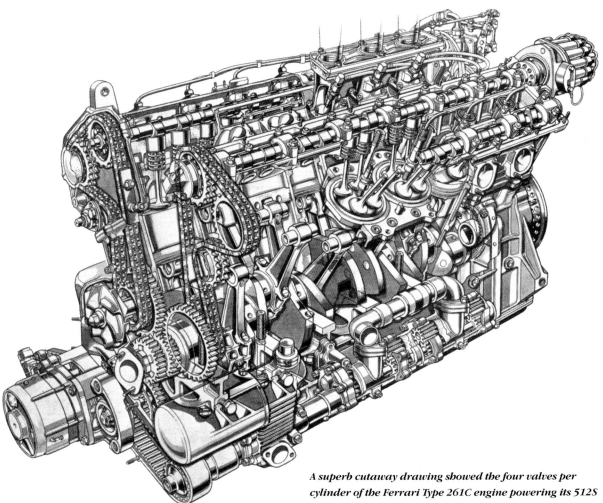

A superb cutaway drawing showed the four valves per cylinder of the Ferrari Type 261C engine powering its 512S sports-racing car. Clearly shown is the classical Ferrari method of driving twin overhead camshafts by roller chains which were turned by twin low-speed gears driven by the crankshaft nose. Visible at the front was a cogged-rubber belt driving oil pumps that would prove to be a weak point of the design. (Vic Berris)

612P was said to be more powerful, with 660bhp at 7,700rpm. A California dynamometer, however, suggested no more than 618bhp at 7,500rpm and torque of 476lb-ft.

Raced on a shoestring as a private venture by Chris Amon, the 612P had the speed to keep the dominant Chevrolet-powered McLarens honest with two third places and one second place in 1969, but its underdeveloped engine lacked reliability. This was not improved by the late-season use of a special long-stroke crankshaft increasing displacement to 6.9 litres. A similar big engine was used in some fitful Can-Am entries of another Ferrari spyder in 1971 for Mario Andretti.

In American hands Amon's big red roadster continued in the 1970 and '71 Can-Am races as a 512P. As such it was using a further iteration of the engine, the Type 261C, that Ferrari developed from the same basis to power its 512S of 1970. Produced in a series of 25 to be able to compete against Group 6 prototypes in the endurance races as a Group 4 sports car. With the latter

category having a capacity limit of five litres it was an easy matter to reduce the bore 5mm to 87mm and the stroke 8mm to 70mm to create a twelve of 4,994cc.

Externally the engine looked much the same, save for simplification of the water delivery to the flanks of its block. Each bank of the engine had its own water radiator as well as pump. Its compression ratio was higher at 11.0:1 and its initial output given as 550bhp at 8,000rpm, with torque of 372lb-ft at 5,500rpm. Developed versions would have 580bhp at 8,500rpm on a higher compression of 11.8:1.

Thanks to the signing of a pact between Fiat and Ferrari in mid-1969 the funds were available to manufacture a score plus one of the 261C and the

From its Can-Am engine Ferrari evolved its Type 261C V12 of 5.0 litres, the maximum allowed for a Group 4 sports-racer produced in a 25-off series. In 1970 and '71 it powered the 512S and 512M, delivering 550bhp initially and 580 in developed form. At right in the process of assembly and below in completed form, this big twelve powered Maranello's entries in epic battles with Porsche, as in Steve McQueen's movie Le Mans.

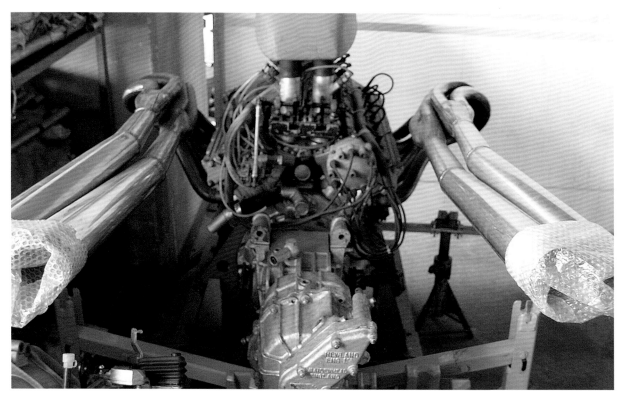

When Can-Am fever swept Japan, Toyota and Nissan fought hammer and tongs. Nissan's entry was this 60° twelve, initially of 5.0 litres but enlarged by Shinichiro Sakurai to 6.0 litres for 1969's Japan Grand Prix. Installed in the R381 chassis, it took Nissan's entries to a one-two finish in the season's most important race. Toyota prepared a turbo-charged rival, but concerns about an escalation of power and speed relegated both cars to museum exhibits. (Jack Yamaguchi)

Twelves have powered the world's most exotic cars. Above is the central-seated Yamaha GP SuperCar OX99-11, introduced in 1993 for '94 production, which failed to eventuate. It was powered by the 60-valve Yamaha V12 used in Formula 1 by Brabham in 1991 and Jordan in '92. Below is Ford's Indigo concept car of 1996, powered by an experimental 6.0-litre V12 of 435bhp derived from two of Ford's 3.0-litre Duratec vee-sixes. It would have a British future.

Developed by Jim Clark, head of the Core and Advanced Powertrain Engineering team in Ford's Advanced Vehicle Technology Group, the V12 in the 1996 Indigo proved to be just the new engine that Aston Martin needed to take a step forward. Introduced in 1999 with 414bhp for the DB7 Vantage, it was tuned to 460bhp for the Vanquish of 2001, above. For the DB9, below, torque was emphasised by efficient inlet manifolding and power was 450bhp.

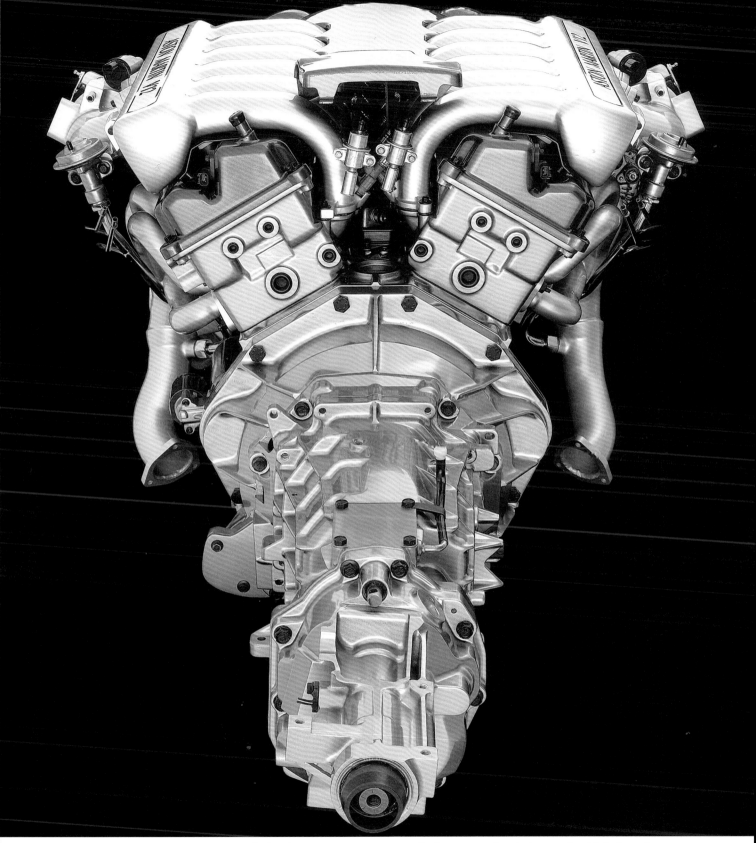

Complete with transmission as installed in the DB7 Vantage of 1999, Aston Martin's 60° V12 showed its inlet ram pipes from outboard plenum chambers, each with its own throttle valve. Aston's engineers were proud of their ability to meet both power and emissions goals with their twelve without such 'gimmicks' as variable valve timing and changes in inlet-passage volume. Their engine's stirring performance belied its humble Ford vee-six origins.

With 3.5-litre Grand Prix Formula 1 engines eligible from 1987 and turbos banned from 1989, BMW's Paul Rosche led a team to design suitable engines. They settled on a 60° V12 with fibre-reinforced magnesium cylinder block. Gear trains to the camshafts were tucked into the spaces remaining when the right-hand cylinder bank was offset forward. Above left is the four-valve version of the BMW twelve built in 1990-91.

On the same cylinder block the BMW team built an experimental five-valve Formula 1 engine, above. To gain optimum positioning for the central inlet valve they added a third camshaft on each bank. In the event this proved insufficiently advantageous to justify the added weight and complication, both engines producing around 720bhp. Never raced, the twelves prepared the way for BMW's return to Formula 1 in 2000.

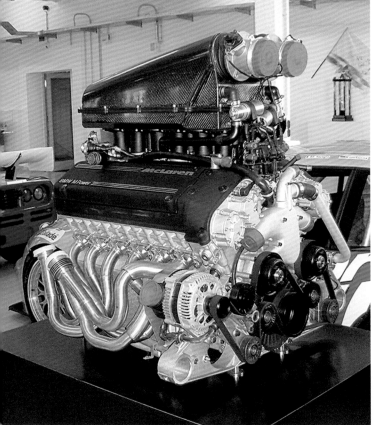

Although McLaren's F1 was conceived as the ultimate road-going sports car, its genetics were such that it turned out to be a success as a racer also. At left is the 6.0-litre S70/3 engine prepared by BMW for racing, with twin restrictors on its airbox.

From the 5.0-litre M70 V12 powering its 750i and 850i,
BMW derived this S70 twelve to motivate its 850Csi coupé.
Produced from 1992 to 1997, the S70 was enlarged to 5.6
litres by increasing both bore and stroke. Its oil cooler
visible at the front, the S70 had low-back-pressure silencers
and catalysts to help its output reach 380bhp at 6,300rpm.

Under the glistening glass-fibre skin of Group 44's XJR-5 at Le Mans in 1984, above, was a race-tuned Jaguar V12 developing some 600bhp. Although built to race in America under IMSA's GTP rules, this was the car that brought Jaguar back to Le Mans after an hiatus of 20 years. It and a sister were as high as fifth in the race but succumbed to tyre and gearbox troubles. (LAT) With its XJR-9LM the works Jaguar team run by Tom Walkinshaw Racing won Le Mans in 1988 against strong Porsche and Sauber-Mercedes opposition and triumphed again in 1990, left, with its XJR-12 driven by Price Cobb, John Nielsen and Martin Brundle. The Walkinshaw-built Jaguar was designed by Tony Southgate and powered by the company's V12, race-tuned to more than 700 horsepower and transmission-defying torque with the help of Cosworth. (Paul Skilleter)

aggressive-looking coupé that carried it, the 512S. Its production began in October and in January 1970 the FIA certified that all 25 512Ss had been built, even if eight of them still had to be assembled.

In March 1970 the 512S scored its first victory in the 12 Hours of Sebring. Porsche's new 917 was tough competition, however. During 1970 work began on a 512M for 'Modificata' with a revised cylinder head that raised output to 620bhp at 8,750rpm accompanied by peak torque of 401lb-ft at 5,500rpm. The engine was safe to 9,500rpm, as Mark Donohue found when qualifying at Daytona. Victory came at Kyalami in November of 1970 and in a round of Europe's version of the Can-Am, the Interserie, at Imola in 1971, but otherwise this ambitious vee-twelve Ferrari had to give best to the Porsche 917. The rules under which it could be raced expired after 1971.

Like Ferrari, Modena's Maserati took part in the first years of the new 3-litre Grand Prix Formula 1, starting in 1966, and also began its campaign with veteran material. In April of the previous year Britain's Cooper Cars had been acquired by a car-sales company, the Chipstead Group, which sold Maserati cars in the United Kingdom. When Cooper looked ahead to the new Formula 1 it was natural enough to check with Maserati to see what it could offer.

"Heaped in a corner of the Maserati workshops were a number of the old 1957 Formula One 2.5-litre V12 engines with twin overhead camshafts," recalled British driver Roy Salvadori, who had just been named Cooper's racing manager. "These formed the basis for Giulio Alfieri's development work." Chipstead contracted with Maserati for three engines for its team cars and engines for Cooper's customer cars as well.

Alfieri lived up to his reputation for creativity with wave after wave of developments and updates for his Grand Prix engines for Cooper. Having already built his twelves in sizes of 2½, 3 and 3½ litres, the engineer had no problem settling on the dimensions of his 1966 Type 9 engine. (In his remarks above Salvadori overlooked the sports-racing engines of 1961–62.) He chose the 70.4 x 64mm measurements of one of the engines he raced at Le Mans in 1961 – the median between two extremes of proportions – for 2,989cc. With its clutch his twelve weighed 420lb.

By relocating the distributors to suit the Type 63/64 sports-racers Alfieri had already taken the first step toward adapting his twelve to a mid-placed installation in the T81 Cooper, whose monocoque chassis was designed by Derrick White. The first tests were made in 1965 by Salvadori himself with carburettors, but for 1966 the Type 9 was fed by Lucas fuel injection, initially with two six-cylinder metering units in the central vee and

driven by gears from the tails of the inlet camshafts.[7] Though Dell'Orto carburettor bodies were used as throttles at first, these were soon replaced by bespoke rotary throttles for each cylinder. While the twin water pumps of the earlier engine were carried over initially, some were cooled by a larger single pump driven from the crank nose.

"Initially the engines were not producing much over 300bhp," wrote Roy Salvadori, "but by the middle of 1966 Maserati were claiming 360bhp at 9,200rpm" for the injected engines, with a 10.0:1 compression ratio. However, a check on the test bench of engine maker Coventry Climax showed 30bhp less than this. In their favour, added Salvadori, "these engines proved reasonably reliable during two seasons' racing."[8] For the fast Italian GP at Monza in September 1966 the Type 9 received a top-end overhaul that tidied up its central vee to allow the throttle bodies to be sloped inward, out of the airstream.

Already competent, the Cooper-Maserati package received a boost in mid-1966 when John Surtees arrived, eager to even the score with Ferrari. Surtees won in

His experience in building sports-racing versions of his 1957 V12 prepared Giulio Alfieri well for the creation of a 3.0-litre version of the engine to power Grand Prix Coopers in 1966. This was the first version of his 1966 Type 9 V12, which used Dell'Orto carburettor bodies as throttles for its Lucas fuel injection.

Mexico and placed second in the drivers' championship with team-mate Jochen Rindt third and Cooper third in the constructors' championship. With the Lotus-Ford getting into its stride in 1967 Cooper-Maserati was still third among constructors in points and satisfyingly ahead of Ferrari, whose advantage had been only one point in 1966. Best-placed Cooper driver was new man Pedro Rodriguez, who won 1967's first race in South Africa.

Cooper's spare car for Monaco gave first sight of Giulio Alfieri's *chef-d'oeuvre* for 1967, his Type 10 V12. Based on the underpinnings of the Type 9, it used the most extreme stroke/bore ratio of the 1961 Le Mans engines, 75.2 x 56mm (2,983cc). Topping it were new cylinder heads with two close-spaced camshafts, running in roller bearings that operated vertical valves – two inlets and one exhaust per cylinder – through cup-type tappets. Coil valve springs replaced the previous hairpins. As in Moteur Moderne's V12 the face of the head was flat, with the piston crown's recesses providing the combustion chamber's volume for a compression ratio of 11.8:1.[9] The new layout made for a much slimmer base engine.

Bifurcated inlet ram pipes for the Maserati Type 10 were topped by slide throttles for the first time. Each cylinder had dual ignition, 10mm spark plugs flanking the exhaust valve, with front-mounted distributors driven by cogged-rubber belts. Also contributing to a lighter engine, a similar belt at the rear drove the fuel-injection

Late in the 1966 season the Type 9 Maserati had rotary-type throttles whose bodies were inclined inward to provide less air resistance at the rear of the chassis. The Cooper-Maseratis usually raced without rear bodywork.

Alfieri's Type 10 vee-twelve for the 1967 Grand Prix season used two close-spaced camshafts to open three valves per cylinder, two inlets and one exhaust. In its ultimate form of development, the Type 10 had triple ignition.

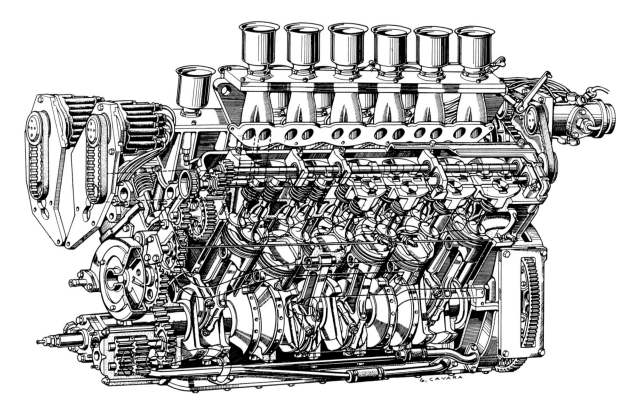

Above: *Over its Type 9 predecessor the Maserati Type 10 offered advantages in compactness and light weight. Cogged-rubber belts were used to drive both its distributors and the Lucas fuel-injection pump, which fed inlets in the central vee with slide throttles.*

Left: *Contemplating one of their BRM engines in Bourne in Lincolnshire in 1969 were the company's chief engineer Tony Rudd, left, and design engineer Frank Aubrey Woods. Initially wary of four-valve V12s, they designed a two-valve unit, their P101, instead.*

distributor. Nominal power for 1967 was given as 380bhp at 9,800rpm.

An ultimate refinement for the '67 season's last two races was an engine with an additional spark plug in the centre vee, between the two inlet valves. Demanding even more distributors, coils and wires, this triple ignition – unique in Formula 1 – nullified some of the weight reduction achieved with the Type 10, although Alfieri sought to compensate by making some crankcases of magnesium.[10] The engine raced twice, blowing up in America and finishing sixth in Mexico.

Although the Italians – with Alfa Romeo in the 1930s, Ferrari in the 1940s and Maserati in the 1950s – were seen as leaders in Grand Prix twelves, an explosion of such engines in the 3-litre Formula 1 was sparked in Britain. At the nexus of these developments was a research company based in Rye, Sussex since 1947: Weslake and Company, Ltd. A successful tuner of racing motorcycles, Harry Weslake had become renowned for his artistry in shaping combustion chambers and ports to improve performance while reducing fuel consumption. One of his satisfied clients was Tony Vandervell, who asked him to massage the ports of the Ferrari 4½-litre V12 he was racing in the 1950s as the 'Thinwall Special'.

In 1961–62 Weslake helped Britain's BRM improve the performance of its 1½-litre Formula 1 V8, which won the 1962 World Championship for Graham Hill. Friendly relations with industrial group Rubery Owen, owner of BRM, led to its 1962 investment in one-fifth of Weslake's shares and the deputing to Rye of two men from BRM, its former chief engineer Peter Berthon and design engineer Frank Aubrey Woods. Henceforth Weslake was considered a research arm of BRM and thus responsible for forward-looking projects. Fuel-supplier Shell and its research labs were important allies of both organisations.

Debate was intense and protracted between BRM and Weslake about the right type of engine for the coming 3-litre formula. While Berthon and Weslake were keen to build a V12 with four-valve heads, BRM was not, as its technical chief Tony Rudd said: "Somehow I and my team began to associate four-valve V12s with trouble." Such an engine, it was finally decided in April 1965, would be built by Weslake at Rye while BRM in Bourne, Lincolnshire would make an H16. Both engines were to be supported

Although initially conceived for sports-car racing, the BRM P101 vee-twelve of 3.0 litres was raced in Grand Prix cars by McLaren, Cooper and BRM itself into the 1968 season.

by single-cylinder test units, partly funded by Shell, to be built and tested at Rye.

Later in 1965, however, the three-year contract between Weslake and Rubery Owen expired. The alliance was dissolved and with it, for the moment, so was the four-valve V12, even though its single-cylinder test engine was developing the equivalent of 158bhp per litre, which for a 3-litre engine would be an awesome 474 horsepower. While BRM went ahead with its exotic H16, it also started work on a 3-litre V12 intended for customer use in sports-racing cars, its P101.

With 2,999cc (74.6 x 57.2mm), BRM's new twelve was based on a 2-litre V8 that had been successful in Tasman racing, said BRM designer Geoff Johnson: "We used chain drive to the cams, two valves per cylinder and the whole thing was simple, cheap and built very simply." Like the V8 from which it was derived, the V12 had its inlet ports between its overhead camshafts. Weighing 328lb less clutch, it delivered 389bhp at 10,000rpm.[11] Its price was a modest £2,000, well under half the cost of a Ford-Cosworth V8.

Bruce McLaren raced the BRM P101 several times in his own chassis in 1967 before defecting to Ford power in 1968. Cooper replaced its Maserati V12 with the P101 and BRM used it early in 1968 in 2½-litre form in the Tasman races in a chassis designed by Len Terry; this became the basis of BRM's Grand Prix car for 1968, a season which went reasonably well with BRM fifth in makers' points, up from 1967's sixth. With the V12 established as the team's main engine, in mid-1968

Rubery Owen's Sir Alfred Owen approved making four-valve heads for it.

The 48-valve P142 twelve, Geoff Johnson's design, had the narrow included angle of 13° between its rows of valves. Close-spaced camshafts were still chain-driven, though a geared design was prepared, and were carried in magnesium trays separate from the aluminium heads. Exhaust piping was in the centre vee with the inlet ram tubes along the sides of the heads.

The first P142 was tested for power on 13 February 1969. Though its medium-speed torque was down on the 24-valve it gave much more power at the top: 444bhp at 10,750 and a peak of 464bhp. This proved frustratingly hard to extract in the chassis, however, poor oil scavenging being a suspected culprit.

In the meantime the Weslake connection was having other consequences. Former BRM man Aubrey Woods had come to know American racer Dan Gurney when the latter drove for BRM in 1960. Their relationship revived, Weslake and his team carried out successful work for Gurney's All American Racers (AAR) on special cylinder heads for the Ford V8, the Gurney-Weslake heads that won Le Mans in 1968 and '69 in GT40 Fords.

Acquainted with the power that the Shell-financed single-cylinder test engine was producing, Gurney agreed that it would make the basis of a fine V12 for his All American Racers Formula 1 campaign. In August 1965 Woods started work on the final design and in October AAR contracted with Weslake for six engines. Its complete expenditure with Weslake would amount to £72,000.

Aubrey Woods patterned the engine's bottom end and gear drive to its camshafts after the practices he knew well from BRM. The aluminium alloy crankcase was the same as that of the 2-litre V8, with seven instead of five main bearings, its ribbed sides extending down well past the crank centreline and embracing close-fitting two-bolt bearing caps. Also identical to the BRM was the cylinder design, with thin-wall centrifugally-cast-iron wet liners held in place by a top flange nipped between the cylinder head and the closed top face of the block. A Cooper ring provided the fire seal around each combustion chamber.

Like all the engines in these families the right-hand cylinder bank was offset forward. The fully machined titanium H-section connecting rods were the same length (124mm) and design as those used by the 2-litre BRM V8 and in fact were supplied by BRM.[12] The forged aluminium piston's mechanical design below the crown was also the same, with narrow slipper skirts and only two rings: a Dykes-type compression ring and an Apex oil ring.

The four valves per cylinder were at a 30° included angle and operated by valve gear of BRM derivation: dual

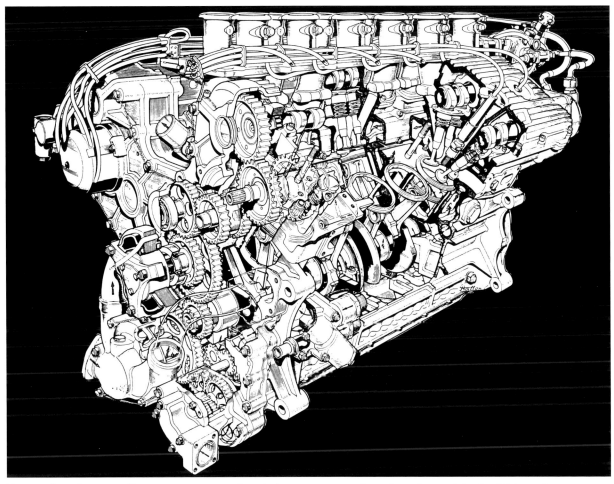

Terry coil springs, small cup-type tappets placed above the springs, a bolted-in ferrous carrier for each tappet, and camshaft support by seven crowded-roller bearings, each in a steel carrier that also formed the outer race, held down by two cap screws.

Of the classical 60° vee layout, the Gurney-Weslake Type 58 twelve was oversquare with dimensions of 72.8 x 60mm (2,997cc). Laystall made the steel crankshaft with its nitrided bearing surfaces of 60.3mm main diameter and 41.3mm rod journals. A departure from BRM methods was Woods's design of the aluminium cylinder-head casting to suit both banks of the vee to make manufacturing and servicing easier. Valve sizes were 30.5 and 25.0mm for inlets and exhausts respectively. Short stub manifolds down the centre of the vee joined each cylinder's separate inlet ports together to a single throat that was fed fuel by a Lucas injector nozzle located beneath the slide throttles.

During August 1966 the first engine was assembled, a job requiring 1,200 man-hours; by the 18th the 390lb V12 was ready for testing. After a week it was yielding 364bhp at 9,500rpm – vastly short of expectations. To Dan

Research conducted at Weslake for BRM was drawn upon for the design of a 3.0-litre V12 built for Dan Gurney's All American Racers Grand Prix team. Aubrey Woods was the designer of what became known as the Gurney-Weslake Type 58 engine.

Gurney's utter dismay, the arrow-straight inlet tracts of the Shell test engine had not been incorporated in his V12. Instead the inlet path was kinked where the vertical inlet pipe met the slope of the port. Astonishingly, no effort had been made to reproduce the efficient straight porting that had helped achieve such promising test results. Although higher figures were quoted from the untrustworthy Weslake dynamometer, Dan later admitted that "I never raced it with 400 horsepower or more."

Nevertheless the stars and stripes were waved proudly by the Gurney-Weslake twelve in its Len Terry-designed chassis. Dan and his team-mate, fellow Californian Richie Ginther, dominated the two heats of the Race of Champions at Brands Hatch on 12 March 1967 and Gurney won the final. Then in June at the Belgian Grand Prix Dan's

When it first appeared at Monza for the Italian Grand Prix in 1966 the Gurney-Weslake V12 was notable both for the base engine's compact dimensions and its magnificent array of exhaust pipes. The engine was destined to disappoint in both its power and its reliability.

Taking over construction of his engines from Weslake, Dan Gurney prepared a Mark 1A version of his V12 to be raced in a new titanium-skinned chassis for 1969. Lack of funding forced him to suspend an effort that, in fact, had never been adequately budgeted.

lone Eagle set a new lap record for Spa at 148.85mph and outlasted Lotus and BRM challenges to win the first GP victory for an American driver and car since Jimmy Murphy and his Duesenberg at Le Mans in 1921. Never well financed, however, Gurney had to give up his Grand Prix quest at the end of an erratic 1968 season. A search for buyers for the engine project turned up no takers.

After the collapse of the AAR project – which saw him join a separate company set up by Gurney in 1969 to build engines – Aubrey Woods returned to BRM in January 1969. For 1970 he reversed the BRM twelve's porting, putting the inlets in the central vee and the exhausts outboard. Internal revisions were aimed at the cooling problems that plagued the unit in 1969. Cross-bolting strengthened the block, allowing it to take some – but not all – the stresses at the rear of Tony Southgate's new chassis. The modest claim of 425bhp was made for its output, which took Pedro Rodriguez to victory in 1970's Belgian Grand Prix.

For 1971 refinement of the BRM, including work on its porting to give it useful torque from 6,500 instead of 8,500rpm, paid off handsomely. BRM was second among makes in points behind Tyrrell-Ford with two strong victories, Jo Siffert's in Austria and Peter Gethin's at Monza. The 48-valve engine was little changed in a new chassis for 1972, which saw Jean-Pierre Beltoise win at a wet Monaco – the last-ever victory for BRM. It was only

For the 1970 season Tony Rudd and Aubrey Woods revised BRM's four-valve V12, putting its inlets in the central vee and its exhausts outboard. Credited with 425bhp, it scored a victory for BRM in the 1970 Grand Prix of Belgium.

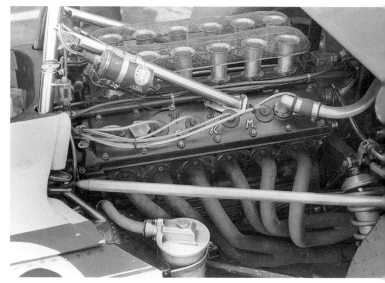

Heavily finned for both stiffness and cooling, BRM's vee-twelve was redesigned for 1971 to provide a fuller torque curve. The result was a good season for BRM, which placed second among manufacturers in Grand Prix points.

seventh in constructors' points, a standing it repeated in 1973. With much the same engine BRM limped on, its last season in championship racing being 1977 and the last appearance of a BRM-branded Grand Prix car in minor races in 1982.

Yet another offshoot of the Weslake-BRM-Gurney relationship traced its origins to a meeting during the 1970 British Grand Prix. Well established in Formula 1, the Ford-Cosworth V8 met as well the sports-car racing engine-size limit of 3 litres for prototypes, but it wasn't welcomed in endurance racing because the vibration of its single-plane crankshaft tended to shake the cars apart. At Silverstone Harry Weslake chatted with Ford's motor sports chief, Stuart Turner, and his house sports-racer designer, Len Bailey, about the engine requirements of long-distance racing. The Ferrari example suggested that a smooth vee-twelve could be the answer. As well, such an engine could cope with future Formula 1 competition if the Cosworth looked like faltering.

The outcome was a complex tripartite agreement. Weslake would develop a 3-litre vee-twelve and pay for its development in hopes of finding customers for the engine. Ford would subsidise Weslake's effort by paying for the first engines in advance, and then would sell them to J. W. Automotive, which was an unenthusiastic user of Cosworth V8s in its Gulf-sponsored Mirage cars. Essential

In 1971 Harry Weslake had another go at designing a racing V12, this time with subsidy from the Ford Motor Company. His new design, the WRP-190, differed in all respects from the Gurney-Weslake engine, with which it shared only a 60° vee and four valves per cylinder.

to the project's success, of course, was that the experienced John Wyer and John Horsman of JW should find the engine up to the demands that they would impose. Wyer, we recall, had already been massively let down by one V12 at Lagonda.

The year-long project to design and make the new 60° vee engine at Weslake was overseen by Michael Daniel, Harry's son-in-law, who had come into the picture near the end of the Gurney-Weslake adventure. He gave close attention to the twelve's robust crankcase, sized to suit 24-hour racing. Its cylinder dimensions were more oversquare than those of the AAR engine at 75 x 56.5 (2,995cc), in a block designed to take bores up to 80mm so that enlargement up to 4 litres could be achieved if necessary for other applications.[13] An important partner for Weslake in the project was British components supplier GKN, which supplied the engine's crankshaft as well as all its major castings.

Instead of the Gurney twelve's wet liners the WRP-190 – as it was designated – had dry cylinder liners pressed into its aluminium block. A front-mounted gear train drove the twin overhead cams on each bank, opening four valves per cylinder through cup-type tappets. Oil pressure and scavenge pumps were exterior to the crankcase, following Cosworth practice, while injection

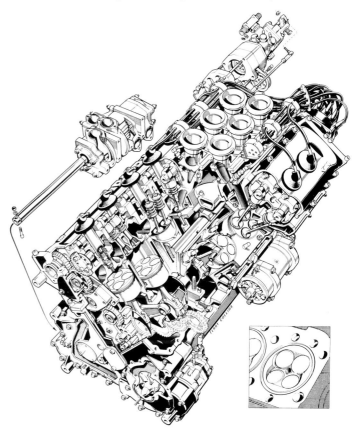

and ignition were driven from the rear of the camshafts. The package scaled 385lb less clutch. With a 22° included valve angle and high-turbulence Weslake chambers allowing a compression ratio of 12.0:1, the engine showed 455bhp at 10,500rpm on the oft-questioned Weslake dynamometer not long after it first ran on 20 December 1971. With a compression ratio of 11.5:1, peak torque was reported as 240lb-ft at 8,500rpm.

Now it was up to JW's men to render a verdict on what Weslake had wrought. John Horsman related that "nine test sessions were conducted – a total of 1,627 miles – using three V12 engines between August 1972 and April '73. Four of the tests were at Goodwood, two at Silverstone and one each at Daytona, Vallelunga and Le Mans. Harry Weslake came to all four Goodwood tests, but no-one from the Weslake factory attended our tests thereafter." In its trials in a Mirage M6 the WRP-190 competed against the Cosworth DFV V8 in a similar chassis, a combination that was 70lb lighter.

One engine, 001, gave performance similar to that of the Cosworth in tests at Goodwood and Silverstone, but the other two performed poorly, were hard to start and/or failed. When Gulf Oil tested one of the units on its own dynamometer it found a less impressive 410bhp. The net result discouraged the Gulf-Wyer team from racing the Weslake unit. "I believe we gave the engine a fair chance," said JW's John Horsman.

Combined with the team's lack of enthusiasm, the Energy Crisis later in 1973 gave Ford the excuse it needed to stop funding the programme after expending £39,000. This was well short of the £150,000 Weslake claimed to have spent building six engines, so when JW refused delivery of two engines it found itself being sued by Weslake. An out-of-court settlement was reached.

Harry Weslake pushed hard to gain Formula 1 interest for his twelve. He found a willing risk-taker in Bernie Ecclestone, whose first full season as owner of the Brabham Grand Prix team was 1972. Looking for an edge for his floundering team, he asked his designers Ralph Bellamy and Gordon Murray to build a car around the WRP-190 to see if it could live up to its audacious power claims. They fitted it into the one-off BT39, a Formula 2 monocoque with Formula 1 suspension, tankage and BT34-style 'lobster claw' nose.

When tested at Silverstone in the autumn of 1972, the Brabham-Weslake failed to impress. "It wasn't a fair test of the engine," Murray admitted later, "because the car was so awful, a lash-up. Graham said it was just diabolical." Negative press fallout from the supposedly secret test was another nail in the WRP-190's coffin. Neither did any joy result from a test of the Weslake twelve by Jean-Pierre

A partner in Weslake's WR-190 project of 1971 was Britain's GKN, which displayed its logo on the cylinder-block casting. Although the engine was tested in both sports cars and Grand Prix cars it failed to find a satisfied customer.

Beltoise in a BRM P160 chassis at the Paul Ricard circuit in 1973.

Weslake offered his project to Ford, but the latter declined to meet his £40,000 price. It was sold instead – doubtless at a keener figure – to Aston Martin Lagonda, which was looking for an engine to replace its veteran four-cam V8. Envisioning a detuning of the WRP-190 to transform it into a road-car engine, AML acquired all the parts, patterns, drawings and rights to the design. In 1979, under former Cosworth engineer Alastair Lyle, it began work on the engine as its Project DP1080.

A first disappointment was AML's discovery that the promised enlargement to 4.0 litres wasn't feasible after all. The limit looked like being only 3.4 litres. Also, said Michael Bowler, "it readily became apparent that the claimed figures were not true steady-state outputs and that torque was inadequate. The V12's ports were far too large and it was going to need a lot of other redesigning to get it into a useable production unit." The best that AML saw was 380bhp at 9,500rpm in an engine that was a long way from being a production proposition.

In the second half of 1980, AML cancelled Project DP1080. It would take a while longer to get V12 power for an Aston Martin. Its resourceful chairman, Victor Gauntlett, found a new home for the materiel at Jaguar rebuilders Lynx Engineering. Lynx had thoughts of using the ex-Weslake to power a Le Mans racer but was unable to raise the necessary sponsorship. It installed the only complete twelve in one of its D-Type Jaguar replicas, which, its former managing director said, "went rather well!"

From Lynx the project was sold on in 1989 to JHS Engines Ltd., a joint venture of former Cosworth engineer

Graham Dale-Jones, engine builder Terry Hoyle and wealthy American enthusiast Bob Sutherland. They acquired one engine, four-fifths of another and all the drawings and test data. Their interest resembled Weslake's original motivation, with the partners looking for an engine that would run smoothly enough to be a threat at Le Mans. Sutherland was interested in a road-car version as well.

"We bought it because we thought it could be a quick route to a vee-twelve," recalled Dale-Jones, "but once we got it we found it was a disaster area." The data showed an unhealthy torque curve, even with Weslake's tests having been run at unrealistically low coolant temperatures, and suggested that the mechanical Lucas injection had never been properly calibrated.

Their major step was expansion of its displacement to 3,494cc, to suit the capacity limit for the new post-1991 Group C regulations, by enlarging its bore from 75 to 81mm. To achieve this increase, which was beyond the tolerance for which the engine had been designed, Graham Dale-Jones omitted the dry liners and asked the pistons to run directly on Nikasil-coated bores in an aluminium block. He eliminated the separate front timing case, to reduce overall length, and mounted the cam-drive gears directly to the front of the block. Pumps were swept away from the front and repositioned along the sides. Water and oil-pressure pumps were on the left and the four scavenge pumps on the right, together with a centrifugal de-aerator for the oil. Among many other modifications, amounting to a completely new engine, were bigger titanium valves.

Looking for a backer for their engine, the JHS partners found engineer-entrepreneur John Mangoletsi, who was willing to build and field a car. Mangoletsi in turn found a sponsor in British industrial company Rubery Owen, which allowed its BRM brand name to be used. Announced at the beginning of 1991, the alliance saw its first engine run on 23 August of that year. Five BRM Type 290 twelves in all were made, with respectable power of 625bhp at 11,500rpm being registered.

Under-funded and under-developed, however, the carbon-chassis BRM P351 struggled and failed in its 1992 outings at Silverstone and Le Mans. At the end of the season the formula for which it was built expired. The 290's last hurrah was in an Arrows chassis competing in Britain's BOSS series for superannuated Formula 1 cars in 1998 and '99. Gearbox problems blunted its attack.

What Harry Weslake hoped to do was achieved – and in some style – by France's Matra. It possessed the talent, the determination and – most importantly – the pocketbook to make the most of a vee-twelve in both Grand Prix and endurance racing. French aerospace company S. A.

Engins Matra found itself in the automobile business in 1964 when it bought René Bonnet's small sports-car company. Acquiring with it a taste for automotive competition, Matra used its excellent government contacts to obtain a loan of $1.2 million toward the construction of a French Formula 1 engine, to be drawn down over three years. Additional support of $400,000 per year starting in 1967 came from a newly formed French fuel and oil distributor trading as Elf.

Hitherto a maker of cars but not engines, Matra appointed former Simca engineer Georges Martin as its head of engine design. In 1967 Martin in turn quietly negotiated a contract to design much of the engine with BRM, whose V8 engines Matra had used in some of its sports-racing cars. "They would contribute to the head design with ports and valve sizes," BRM's Tony Rudd said of Matra, "but we had to design camshafts, drives, tappets etc, together with the rest of the engine." Rudd and Geoff Johnson drew on their experience with their own V12 in the layout of the Matra engine, which was to have gear instead of chain drive to its camshafts.

All was going well until Sir Alfred Owen, boss of BRM owner Rubery Owen, bragged at a British motor-industry dinner that BRM was designing a Formula 1

France's Matra spared no expense in the photographic presentation of its MS9 3.0-litre V12 of 1968, which was viewed as an engine which would carry the colours of France in international racing. Its inlet ports were between the camshafts of each cylinder head.

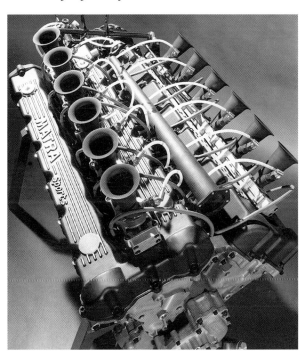

engine for Matra. "Matra were livid and in dead trouble," Rudd recalled, over the revelation of this British involvement in a French-flag-bearing project. BRM's contract was cancelled and the government's funding for Matra was jeopardised. Nevertheless Matra's own project went ahead with the support of the aforementioned Moteur Moderne. When completed there were still resemblances to the BRM, said Rudd: "Not surprisingly it looked like a four-valve version of our engine, inlets between the camshafts. [One of our mechanics] eventually found some of the parts were interchangeable."

Launched in 1967, Matra's first V12 had four-valve chambers with the valves inclined at an included angle of 55° 59' – 28° 22' for the inlets and 27° 37' for the exhausts, with respective diameters of 29 and 27mm. Cylinder dimensions were well oversquare at 79.7 x 50mm (2,993cc). Giving 390bhp at 10,500rpm, the MS9 engine first ran in its Matra MS11 chassis on the perimeter roads of Villacoublay Airport on Leap-Year Day of 1968.

Its first race was at Monaco. Although it retired, the Matra's shrill exhaust note brought an exciting new

Raced in 1967 and '68, Matra's MS9 brought an excitingly shrill new sound to Grand Prix racing but failed to deliver the victories that France had been counting on.

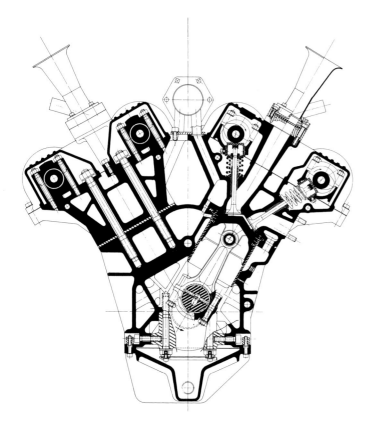

sound to Formula 1. In July at Zandvoort, helped by Dunlop's rain tyres, Jean-Pierre Beltoise's MS11 placed second to Jackie Stewart's winning Matra-Ford. "*Le jour de gloire est arrivé*," trumpeted *L'Equipe*.

The glory was premature so far as the MS9 V12 was concerned. Too thirsty and behind the latest technology, at the end of the '68 season it was withdrawn while Matra regrouped. New heads were designed on the lines of the findings of a single-cylinder test engine built by Moteur Moderne with a narrower valve angle and a flatter piston top.

Under the finned magnesium cam covers of the 1970 MS12 V12 were inlet valves inclined at 16° and exhaust valves at 17½° for a total included angle of 33½°. Valves were enlarged to 31mm for the inlets and 27mm for the exhausts.[14] Not used was another concept tested by Moteur Moderne: individual inlet tracts, throttles and injection nozzles for both inlet valves of each four-valve chamber.

To keep them small and light, the Matra's inverted-cup tappets didn't extend down around its dual-coil valve springs. The latter were individually checked before assembly by cycling them at a speed equivalent to 14,000rpm for six hours in a special rig. A train of narrow case-hardened spur gears at the front of the block drove the camshafts.

Located below the crankshaft in the earlier MS9, the oil scavenge and pressure pumps were taken out of the sump and mounted ahead of the front end of the engine, below the water pump, to help lower the installed profile of the MS12. Study of the Cosworth V8 led to a tighter encasement of the crank for reduced windage losses, above a curved baffle that aimed to keep outgoing oil away from the crank webs.

Matra's 1970 plan was to use the engine as part of the chassis, Cosworth-style. The sump casting was designed to take most of the lower-level stresses, while those at the top were fed into the new cam/tappet layer bolted atop each cylinder head. The latter, like the block, were cast of AS9KG aluminium alloy. Combustion chambers were very shallow in the surfaces of the heads, which were retained by 14 studs. The compression ratio was 11.0:1 in cylinder dimensions that were unchanged.

Because the MS9's steel crankshaft was one of the most expensive parts of the engine to make, machined as it was from the solid, and with several in the manufacturing pipeline, it was carried over generally unchanged to the MS12. Also continued was the forward offset of the right-hand cylinder bank. Retained were the 52mm main bearings and their caps, which were held in the deep-sided block by two vertical studs and two side-bracing cap screws. Other shared parts were the 116mm

*Right: Based on the bottom
end of the MS9, Matra built
a new vee-twelve, its MS12,
for 1970 with narrower
valve angles and inlet
passages in the central vee.
This was to be the
foundation of a highly
successful power unit.*

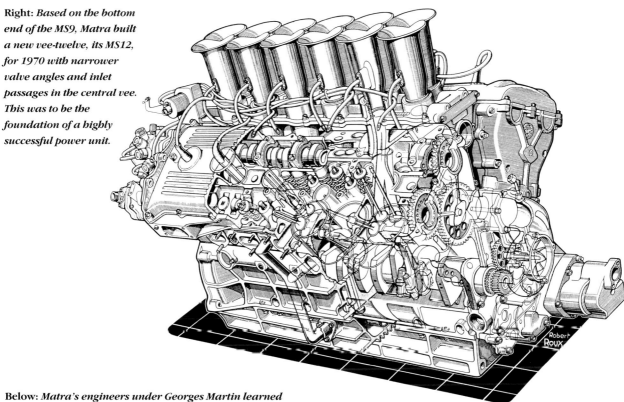

*Below: Matra's engineers under Georges Martin learned
from Cosworth's successful designs in the layout of their
MS12 for 1970. The narrow valve angles and baffled sump,
the better to control pressures and reduce windage losses,
were tested Cosworth techniques.*

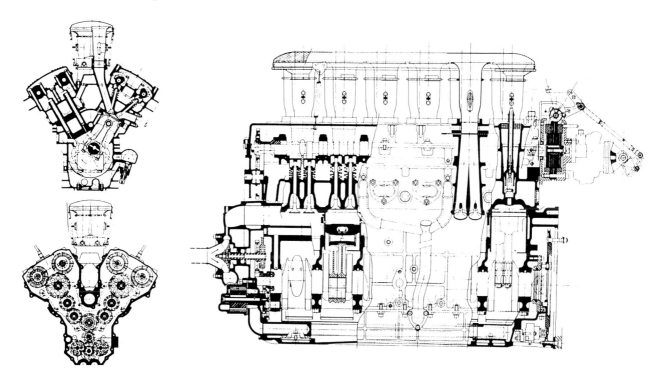

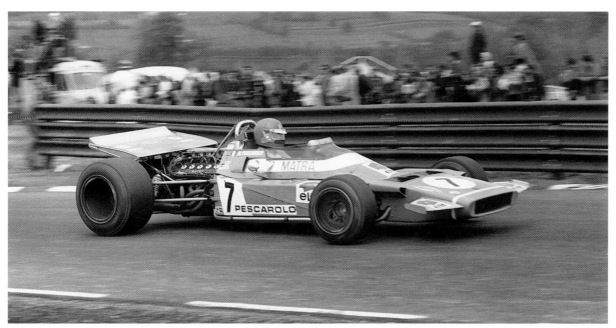

Driven here at Watkins Glen by Henri Pescarolo, the Matra MS120 Grand Prix car enjoyed some good performances with its revised V12 from 1970 to 1972. Chris Amon scored a victory in the non-championship 1971 Argentine Grand Prix with the reworked twelve.

Henri Pescarolo was at the wheel again at Le Mans in 1973, driving the Matra Simca 670B with which he and Gerard Larrousse won the twenty-four hour race at an average speed of 125.67mph.

titanium connecting rods with 44mm big ends running, like the mains, on Vandervell bearings.

Late in 1969 Matra was ready to put the MS12 to the test on its dynamometer at Saclay, five kilometres from the handsome Matra plant at Velizy, an aerospace centre south of Paris. The new cylinder heads brought a substantial improvement to 450bhp at 11,000rpm with the potential to rev even higher.

In Matra's MS120 GP car for 1970, its all-French pairing of Henri Pescarolo and Jean-Pierre Beltoise managed a

In 1981 Matra provided an overview of the performance development of its 3.0-litre V12 engines, showing an average rating with a dotted line and maximum and minimum power outputs. From 1976 the engine raced again in Formula 1 throughout 1978 and in 1981–2.

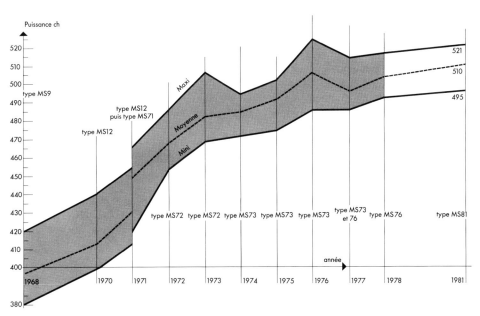

few finishes on the bottom step of the podium. New Zealander Chris Amon joined Matra for 1971. That year and in 1972, when Matra ran a single car for him, Amon showed tremendous pace with several record laps and a win in the non-championship 1971 Argentine Grand Prix.

The MS12 found a new home in the open MS660 sports-prototype that Matra built around it. It required few changes for its new mission, one being the use of steel instead of titanium for its connecting rods. The twelve demonstrated its speed in 1971 and then in 1972, in developed MS72 form, achieved Matra's goal of a Le Mans victory. The team of Pescarolo with Graham Hill won and François Cevert was second paired with Howden Ganley. This basic engine was still used in 1973 and 1974, when Matra won both the constructors' championship – defeating Ferrari in 1973 – and Le Mans. The 24-hour race was won both years by Henri Pescarolo driving with Gerard Larrousse.

After a break from Formula 1 the Matra twelve returned to the Grand Prix wars in 1976 as the MS73, further developed by Georges Martin with Jean-François Robin. It made a cameo appearance toward the end of 1975 in a Shadow chassis but for '76 Matra's customer for the engine was Guy Ligier's Formula 1 team, backed by the Gitanes cigarette brand that had also supported Matra's Le Mans campaigns. Ebullient Frenchman Ligier was no stranger to V12 power, having raced a private Cooper-Maserati in 1966 and part of '67.

For three seasons through 1978, evolving into the Type MS76, Matra's twelve powered Ligiers. Some podium positions for Jacques Laffite in 1976 led to a win

in Sweden in 1977. Although the Ligier-Matra was reliable, only two third places came Laffite's way in 1978.

In 1981 the veteran twelve was lured out of retirement, again by Guy Ligier in a new sponsorship deal that branded it a 'Talbot'. Now the MS81, it was rated at 510bhp at 12,500rpm with the occasional engine reaching 12,800rpm and 520bhp. Victories came in Austria and Canada for Laffite in 1981, plus three seconds,

With the help of Jean-François Robin, Georges Martin continued to develop the Matra V12, seen on the company's dynamometer at Saclay, south of Paris, in January 1981. Concluding a remarkable career, the Matra engine was retired after the 1982 season.

For the 1979 season Alfa Romeo's Autodelta arm converted its flat-twelve into a 60° vee to allow Brabham designer Gordon Murray to exploit the ground effects that were then revolutionising Grand Prix racing. With exhaust pipes curving up and away, space was freed under the car for rising venturis that accelerated air away, creating under-body suction.

The BT48 that Brabham's Gordon Murray designed around Alfa's new twelve was one of his most dramatic creations, with warm air from its side radiators exiting through huge louvres. The Brabham-Alfa failed to realise the promise of its appearance, however, and with Alfa Romeo building a Formula 1 car of its own the Anglo-Italian partnership was severed after a single season.

one third and two fourths. This helped place Ligier-Talbot fourth among manufacturers, but only eighth was the tally for 1982. Thereafter the durable Matra V12 was definitively retired.

The inexorable rise of turbocharged 1½-litre engines, dominant by 1983, was responsible for ending the unblown Matra's career. The turbos also ended the life span of a racing vee-twelve that Alfa Romeo had built, first for Brabham and then on its own account. From 1976 through 1978 Autodelta, a racing arm of Alfa led by former Ferrari chief engineer Carlo Chiti, had supplied flat-twelve engines to the Brabham team. Blocking the rear of the chassis as they did, such engines weren't ideal for the underbody ground-effects venturis that were coming into use, so for 1979 Chiti converted his flat-twelve into a 60° vee-twelve.

To the disappointment of Brabham designer Gordon Murray, at 375lb the new narrower Alfa engine was no lighter than its flat forebear. The Type 1260's capacity of 2,991cc (78.5 x 51.5mm) was fed by four valves per cylinder – 30mm inlets and 25mm exhausts – opened by four gear-driven overhead cams. With a 12.0:1 compression ratio it produced 525bhp at 12,300rpm.

In Murray's spectacular new Martini-sponsored BT48 chassis the Alfa twelve was unsuccessful, the team standing only eighth in 1979 manufacturers' points. Even worse from the standpoint of Brabham and its owner Bernie Ecclestone, Alfa Romeo introduced a Grand Prix car of its own, the Type 177, in 1979. At the end of the year Brabham and Alfa parted company.

Though a new model was introduced, the Type 179, Alfa Romeo's effort struggled. The team was 11th and last in points in 1980 and eighth in 1981, when the team wasted Mario Andretti's skills. In 1982, the last in which it relied on the twelve before switching to turbocharged V8s, Alfa Romeo was tenth in makes' points with its Type 1260 developed to 548bhp.

Alfa's engines were provided to the little Osella team for 1983, but they failed to propel its robin's-egg-blue car to any points whatsoever. When the Osella-Alfa succeeded in qualifying, its best finish was tenth in Austria. Thus ended Alfa Romeo's effort with its twelve and, indeed, the use of twelves in Formula 1 until turbocharged engines were outlawed in the 1989 season.

The 3-litre Grand Prix formula would not be without its Japanese entrant. With Honda having chosen a V12 for the 1½-litre Formula 1, speculation was rife that it wouldn't enter the new 3-litre era in 1966 with less than 32 cylinders. In fact it did give consideration to a sixteen, but when Honda's white and red contender was rolled out for the Italian Grand Prix at Monza on 4 September 1966 it was seen to have 'only' twelve cylinders. State-of-the-art though this was for Grand Prix cars at the time, the Honda RA273E twelve was shot full of typically distinctive Japanese design solutions.

The new engine's principal designer was Shoichiro Irimaji, working under Honda's experienced and dynamic chief racing engineer Yoshio Nakamura. Looking over their shoulders was the boss, Soichiro Honda, who continued to take a close personal interest in his company's racing engines. They considered the 120° vee angle that Abarth had used, but with this the narrow tub of a Formula 1 car would have little space. The alternative was to use the engine as a stressed member, but this was not attempted. The final choice was a 90° vee with the left-hand cylinder bank offset forward. Here, remarkably, was a reversion to the vee angle of the first-ever vee-twelve engine, the Craig-Dörwald of 1904.

To leave room for chassis longerons the exhaust ports were in the central vee, while the inlet ports were downdraft, between the twin overhead camshafts. The configuration was not unlike the contemporary Matra MS9, although the Honda had even wider angles for its four valves at 35° for inlets and 40° for exhausts for a total of 75°. Surprisingly these were larger valve angles than had been used in the 1½-litre RA271 V12 at a time when racing-engine designers were moving toward narrower included angles to make combustion chambers more

compact. Inlet valves were 29.5mm and exhausts 26mm in diameter, akin to those of the Gurney-Weslake twelve but smaller than the valves used by Matra. Valve-seat inserts were individual instead of the complete chamber roofs used in the 1½-litre twelve.

As in the RA271E roller bearings – a pet solution of Soichiro Honda – were used throughout the RA273E to support its camshafts, shafts and gears. Facing connecting rods were side-by-side on common journals, which meant that power pulses were irregular. The rods had one-piece big ends thanks to a built-up crankshaft, carried in eight roller main bearings. In retrospect the built-up crankshaft, less rigid than a solid crank, was a weak point of the V12's design. Save for the endmost mains, which were smaller, the RA271E's subtle variation of bearing sizes was not indulged in.

The extra eighth bearing was needed at the centre of the crankshaft, which carried an integral gear to drive the cogs to the camshafts and also to power a shaft to the multiple-disc clutch. As in the Abarth V12, this engine-output shaft ran above the crankshaft to allow the latter to be as close to the ground as its dry sump would permit. The long shaft also served as a damper of resonances between clutch and crankshaft. Oil was scavenged by six pickups, each of which had its own suction pump. The latter were in packs of three at both ends of the crankcase, gear-driven from the crankshaft. The front end of the output shaft drove the single water pump.

Japan's Honda chose a 90° vee angle for its RA273E V12, built to compete under the new Grand Prix regulations that from 1966 required 3.0-litre unsupercharged engines. The engine made liberal use of roller bearings, carrying the camshafts and, thanks to a built-up crankshaft, the connecting-rod big-ends as well.

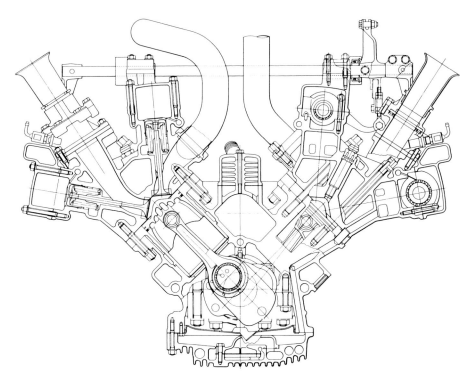

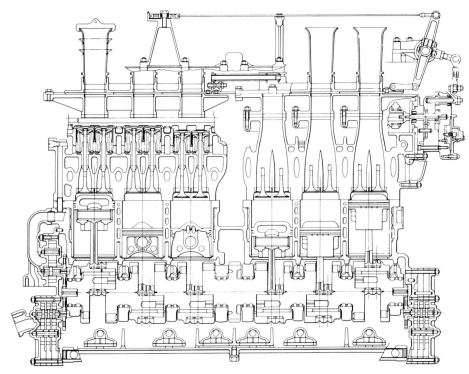

A longitudinal section of the 1966 RA273E Honda showed the construction of its built-up crankshaft, numerous scavenge pickups for its dry-sump system and its domed pistons in both profile and end view. Oil pumps were driven by both ends of its crankshaft.

Extending down well past the crank centreline, the crankcase was an aluminium casting. Inserted into it were the ferrous cylinders, which instead of being individual as in the RA271E were cast as units of three with a cylinder-centre distance of 92mm. They were knitted in place by a multiplicity of studs: 13 reached down from each head and 16 penetrated them from the block.

Cylinder heads were massive, with huge water chambers, although cooling water encirclement of the exhaust-valve guides was not achieved. Cup-type tappets slid directly in the aluminium head and were concentric with twin coil valve springs. Honda's own constant-flow fuel injection delivered petrol to each port below the throttle slides. With one 12mm NGK plug per cylinder, ignition was by Honda's 'energy transfer' system, combining coils and magnetos as in the RA271E.

The Honda twelve's dimensions were 78 x 52.2mm (2,993cc). No lightweight at 485lb, it made up for this with its initial output of 400bhp at 11,000rpm. After its first public airing on Honda's own test track on 23 July

No lack of fantasy animated the Honda RA273E V12 of 1966. Its central gear train rotated the camshafts and drove, as well, a multiple-disc clutch at the input to its transaxle. Its wide valve included angle of 75° went against the trend of the time. (Yoshihiro Inomoto)

1966 it was tested at the Suzuka circuit before being airlifted to Monza to make its racing debut. Onlookers there were awed by its size. "One is tempted to wonder why little men should make such a big car," remarked Edward Eves.

In spite of enjoying one of the smallest drivers in Richie Ginther, the Honda had the longest wheelbase, at 98.8in, and weighed 1,590lb dry at Monza. Comparable weights were 1,320lb for the Cooper-Maserati, 1,330 for the Ferrari V12 and 1,270 for the Weslake-powered Eagle against the FIA's mandated minimum weight of 1,102.5lb. This was a hefty handicap for the Japanese car.

That the horses were there was evident in the Honda's performance in the last races of 1966, with Ginther briefly leading in Mexico before finishing fourth. Promising though this was, Honda – far from the powerhouse company it later became – was dismayed by the cost and prepared to quit Formula 1 unless it could find an ally in a team that was prepared to race its cars. At Mexico City Nakamura-san found the man he wanted: John Surtees. "We had already set up Team Surtees to run the Lola sports cars," John recalled, "so, after giving the matter considerable thought, and once again being ruled by my heart rather than my head, I considered what Honda had achieved in motorcycle racing and decided to take on the project." In Slough Surtees set up Honda Racing, with Firestone tyre support, as the base for the team.

Weight was the enemy at the start of 1967, said Surtees: "It felt like a tank and was built as solidly as the Forth Bridge." Lighter magnesium cylinder heads were tried but proved unreliable. Surtees was unimpressed by the low-pressure fuel-injection system, finding it "very vulnerable and sensitive to changes in ambient temperature and general climatic conditions," but it was a personal pet of Mr. Honda and thus sacrosanct. Nor was an all-out attack at all circuits possible because engines were in short supply and often had to be nursed to a finish. "It could put up a respectable show," Surtees found of Honda's racer, "by running it with very low gears and letting the engine rev for short periods to 10,500rpm."

Carrying on with the RA273, Surtees's best performance with that chassis was third in the first race of 1967 in South Africa. With a lighter chassis from Japan slow to materialise, John gained Honda's permission to build a new car to take the RA273E in Britain at Lola, which was "just round the corner" from Honda Racing in Slough, convenient to Heathrow Airport. Called the RA300, the hybrid 'Hondola' took advantage of Lola's Indianapolis-car technology to produce a more compact car weighing 1,340lb dry, more competitive with its V12 rivals.

First seen at Monza in September 1966, Honda's RA273E vee-twelve impressed with its sheer size and showed no little pace in its first races.

In Japan Nobuhiko Kawamoto and Tadashi Kume tweaked their twelve's top end, increasing valve sizes to 31mm for the inlets and 30mm for the exhausts. The extremely large size of the latter was counterbalanced by reducing exhaust-valve lift from 8.5 to 7.0mm. Less-extreme valve timing urged a fuller power curve from the peaky twelve, now reaching 420bhp at 11,500rpm. The combination seized a dramatic debut victory for the RA300 at Monza on 18 September. It was destined to be Honda's only win during this 3-litre Formula 1.

For 1968 Kume and Kawamoto came up with a heavily revised V12, the RA301E. They based it on the roller-

A big car from a small country, the 1966 Honda Grand Prix car had the longest wheelbase and the highest weight of all entrants. In 1967 Honda entered into a racing partnership with the team of Englishman John Surtees.

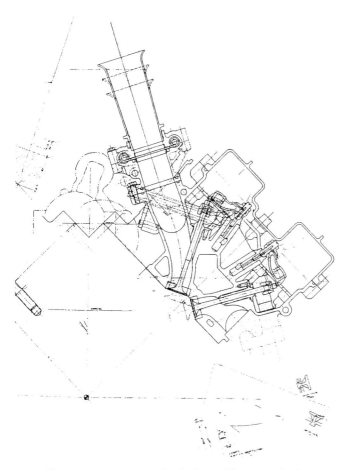

Above: *An engineering sketch showed the new cylinder-head design adopted for the Honda V12, now the RA301E, for 1968. This closed its valves with torsion-bar springs, a technique successfully used by Honda in Formula 2, and had the narrower valve included angle of 58° for a much-improved combustion chamber.*

A Nissan team under Shinichiro Sakurai built a V12 for Group 7 racing in Japan which was enlarged to 6.0 litres from its initial 5.0 litres for the 1969 Japan Grand Prix. It was credited with 600bhp from its Lucas fuel injection.

bearing bottom end of the 1966–67 engine, keeping the same cylinder dimensions. Completely new cylinder heads had the narrower valve inclinations of 28° for the inlets and 30° for the exhausts, adding up to 58°. This improved the combustion chamber, which allowed an 11.5:1 compression ratio.

Honda's pet constant-flow injection system fed inlet ram pipes that were now in the central vee, with the exhausts outboard. The valves, resized at 33.6 and 29.3mm, were opened by finger-type followers and

Below: *Installed in the Nissan R382, the company's big vee-twelve proved to be the class of the field in the 1969 Japan Grand Prix. Obviously inspired by British chassis designs, the V12 Nissan seized victory with a one–two finish.* **(Yoshihiro Inomoto)**

closed by the torsion-bar springs that Honda had used successfully in Formula 2 in 1966. Lifting the valves by forked arms, these allowed higher valve lift and the most radical valve timing yet used in a Grand Prix Honda while, at the same time, suppressing the high-speed valve bounce experienced with coil springs.

From its new unit Honda extracted 440bhp at 11,500rpm and a more useful torque curve from an engine that was significantly lighter at just under 400lb. Contributing to the latter was a simplified version of the output shaft to the clutch. It no longer turned the water pump, which was now driven by the crankshaft nose.

The new twelve was given a new chassis with the handier wheelbase of 94.8in. Built as before at Slough, it used titanium suspension components fabricated by Honda and magnesium instead of aluminium in its monocoque. With weight now down to only 1,170lb, the new package looked highly promising. Among twelve 1968 races, however, Surtees failed to finish a dispiriting eight times.

Further improvement of the revised twelve was halted in Japan, where Soichiro Honda urged the development of an air-cooled V8 that proved a costly dead end.[15] The best Surtees could eke from his season was pole position at Monza, second in the French Grand Prix and third in America. After his retirement in the last race in Mexico a sorrowful Nakamura-san turned to him and said, "John-san, it's the end." As Surtees later said, it was the end of one era for Honda, yet the beginning of a new era as well, leading to the end of air-cooled adventures and the launch of the Civic, the car that made Honda.

Honda wasn't the only Japanese car maker to go racing with vee-twelves in the 1960s. The major domestic battle, both on the tracks and the showrooms, was between Toyota and Nissan. North America's Can-Am competition with Group 7 sports-racers was mirrored in Japan, with Toyotas and Nissans the chief rivals.[16] In 1968 Toyota had a purpose-built racing V8 of 3 litres while Nissan fielded its R381, a Lola-like coupé designed under Shinichiro Sakurai. With 5.5-litre Chevrolet V8 power it won that year's premiere race, the Japan Grand Prix.

Both companies raised the ante for 1969. Toyota built a new 32-valve V8 of 5 litres producing 530bhp. Not to be outdone, Sakurai and his team created a 60° racing vee-twelve. Initially in the R381 chassis it too was sized at 5 litres, but in preparation for the '69 Grand Prix it was enlarged to 5,954cc. Producing 600bhp with its Lucas fuel injection, this lusty lump was fitted in a new roadster dubbed the R382. With the 1969 Grand Prix open to international competitors for the first time, the R382 was up against tough competition, but it walked the event with a one–two finish, led by Motoharu Kurosawa.

Even more ambitious Group 7 cars were planned for the 1970 Grand Prix – including a twin-turbo Toyota – but this fevered speed escalation was too much for the conservative Japanese authorities, who cancelled the 1970 race. Though it would take a while, both Honda and Nissan would be back, building new vee-twelves for Formula 1 and endurance racing. Twelves were not out of the racing picture – not by a long shot.

Chapter 11 Footnotes

[1] This tally does not include Ferrari's flat-12, the Type 512 F1.

[2] This was also notable as the first Formula 1 race success for Goodyear tyres.

[3] Although Fiat and Ferrari would become business partners with the Dino V6 engines in 1967, not until 1st August 1969 would the larger firm take its first shareholding in Ferrari.

[4] The author considers it likely that this construction method was adopted because larger components, such as longer blocks, camshafts and crankshafts, were too big to be machined on Abarth's equipment.

[5] This is the author's conclusion based on inspection of the engine's exterior.

[6] This was ironic in view of the fact that Ferrari was the first, in 1964, to make a Formula 1 engine serve as the rear portion of a mid-engined car's frame.

[7] One mid-engined racing car of 1966 did use the Maserati V12, in 2½-litre form, with carburettors. This was a Brabham prepared for Frank Gardner to drive in the Australia-New Zealand Tasman series. The Brabham-Maserati had such inconsistent throttle response – not unlike Maserati's own 1957 experience – that it practised but was never raced.

[8] It must have helped that Heini Mader, a Swiss engine builder, was engaged by Cooper to oversee the maintenance and supply of the engines. He was at the beginning of gaining an excellent reputation in this field.

[9] Such bowl-in-piston chambers were much in the wind at the time, having been used in production by Rover from 1963, by Ford in its English 1.3-litre four and soon thereafter by Cosworth in its SCA Formula 2 engine. They were known as 'Heron' chambers after Sam Heron, who experimented with them at the Ethyl Corporation in 1947–49.

[10] BMW used triple ignition in its four-valve Formula 2 engine of 1969.

[11] BRM's customer for the engine, Bruce McLaren, said that the power was 365bhp and the weight 385lb.

[12] Initially Weslake sought to source the rods from a common outside supplier but was told that the latter considered it 'immoral' to supply what was clearly a BRM-design connecting rod.

[13] Many reports say that the engine had the same cylinder dimensions as the AAR twelve. This is not the case. Indeed, with Gurney retaining the design rights to his engine, Weslake was prudent to choose different dimensions.

[14] A later development of the 1970 engine had valves 33.0 and 27.2mm in diameter.

[15] It also proved deadly to Frenchman Jo Schlesser, who crashed it on his third lap in the French Grand Prix and died in the ensuing conflagration. It never raced again.

[16] Although Nissan then sold its cars under the Datsun brand, its sports-racing cars and engines were branded 'Nissan'.

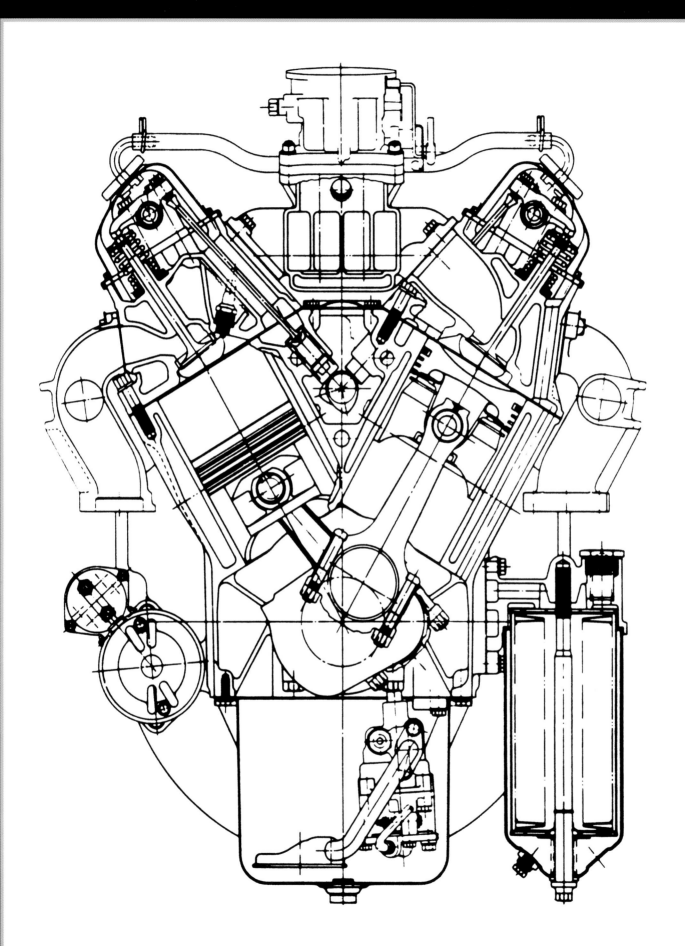

ENGINES FOR THE ELITE

"I must confess that the fact that there was then only one firm in the world making such engines acted on me as a challenge and a spur." Enzo Ferrari gave that as one of the reasons for his historic decision to plump for a vee-twelve for his first post-war automobile. That firm, the only one producing twelves after the war, couldn't have been less like Ferrari. Nor did its engine resemble Ferrari's in any way. But the remarkable role of Lincoln in maintaining continuity of vee-twelve production before and after Hitler's war deserves our attention and, indeed, our praise.

This is not to say that the twelve to which we refer was a model of its kind. The vee-twelve that began its life in the Lincoln Zephyr of 1936 had more than its share of critics in its day. "Youngsters often quipped that a lingering puff of smoke at a stoplight meant a Zephyr had just left," wrote one historian. Yet the Zephyr's V12 was built with the best of intentions by capable men to power a radical new Lincoln that had even more radical antecedents.

The Zephyr's origins were traceable to elegant and advanced streamlined rear-engined prototypes built by Detroit's Briggs Manufacturing Company to designs by Dutch émigré John Tjaarda. Briggs was a body supplier to Ford-owned Lincoln, then being guided by the astute and sensitive Edsel Ford – son of the crusty Henry. A mock-up of a car reflecting Tjaarda's ideas was the hit of the big expositions of 1933 and '34. To the delight of Briggs, Edsel saw in it a potential addition to his Lincoln range, which since 1932 had been dedicated solely to large and costly vee-twelves.

Assessing the prototype's potential, Ford's cost analysts judged that such a car held promise for the medium-price range, from $700 to $1,500, where Ford had no entries. A decision was made to have Briggs build the car as an addition to the Lincoln line, but with a front-mounted engine, Ford-style solid axles and transverse leaf springs front and rear. As in Tjaarda's prototypes it would have a monocoque integral body/frame construction. This was created at a time when such structures were rare in the industry, especially in a relatively large car.

John Tjaarda had equipped his prototypes with aluminium-block V8 engines of only 2.7 litres, taking advantage of their light weight and low drag to gain good performance with only 80 horsepower. For the less-optimised production car something with more muscle was needed; a large eight was the first choice. Edsel, however, demurred. The new car would have a vee-twelve engine, he decided, to give it a strong affinity with the costly and elegant bigger Lincolns. "Remember," his company would advertise, "that the Lincoln-Zephyr has been designed by Lincoln, is built by Lincoln."

While John Tjaarda oversaw the body's engineering at Briggs, the assignment to create the new car's engine went to the veteran Frank Johnson, whose association with Lincoln and Henry Leland dated from the turn of the century. It came at an awkward time, for Henry Ford had

Opposite: *For truck use in 1960 the GMC Truck and Coach Division of General Motors introduced a new family of 60° vee engines with this cross-section. They were built in both V6 and V12 versions to power GMC's trucks.*

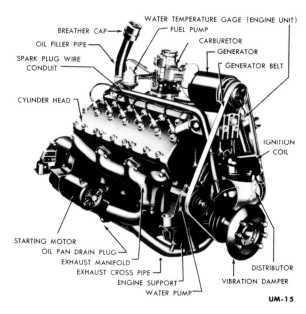

BREATHER CAP
OIL FILLER PIPE
SPARK PLUG WIRE CONDUIT
CYLINDER HEAD
WATER TEMPERATURE GAGE (ENGINE UNIT)
FUEL PUMP
CARBURETOR
GENERATOR
GENERATOR BELT
IGNITION COIL
STARTING MOTOR
OIL PAN DRAIN PLUG
EXHAUST MANIFOLD
EXHAUST CROSS PIPE
ENGINE SUPPORT
WATER PUMP
DISTRIBUTOR
VIBRATION DAMPER
UM-15

The weakness of Frank Johnson's design of the Lincoln Zephyr V12 was that it followed Ford V8 practice in taking its exhaust porting through the block, where it transmitted heat to the coolant. Nevertheless the side-valve vee-twelve powered Lincoln automobiles for more than a decade.

ordered Johnson to show the door to most of his engineering cadre in 1934. Also, Johnson was under pressure to create an engine that could be built at low cost to meet the mid-range price objective for the new car, coded as the Model H. If he could use existing Ford components and concepts in the engine, so much the better.

Although often denigrated as a bog-simple extrapolation of the Ford V8, the Zephyr V12 in fact incorporated a number of distinctive features. Eschewing the 67° vee angle of his other Lincoln twelves or the 90° angle of the Ford eight, Johnson selected a 75° vee. This gave a compact build while allowing adequate space for its central induction manifolding. With a conventional crankshaft this gave uneven firing intervals, but the Zephyr was respected for its smoothness. "Listening to the lively little 75° engine come to life with its firing couplets of 75°–45° was exhilarating," wrote Richard Stout; "the magic of twelve cylinders was heady fare in the middle-priced field."

The left-hand cylinder bank was offset forward to accommodate side-by-side connecting rods. An unusual feature adopted by Frank Johnson for his new twelve was *désaxé* or laterally offset cylinders. Instead of being aimed directly at the centre of the crankshaft, the centreline of each cylinder was offset 6.4mm to the right as viewed from the front of the engine. Well-known early

in the industry but less common in modern engines, the *désaxé* cylinder reduced piston side thrust against the cylinder wall during the downward power stroke.

Unusually as well in the 1930s, the Zephyr had full-skirted pistons of steel alloy, carrying two compression rings and one oil ring. In the year of its launch only Ford, Chevrolet, Pontiac and Willys still used iron or steel pistons in America. In spite of their rejection of aluminium, however, the Lincoln and Ford pistons were among the US industry's lightest.

The Model H's stroke was the same as that of the Ford V8, 95.3mm. Combined with a bore of 69.9mm this gave a capacity of 4,380cc. By American standards this was modest for a mid-range car; LaSalles and Buicks were 20 per cent bigger. However Lincoln's 'little' V12 was substantially larger than the engines that John Tjaarda had considered sufficient for his prototypes and displaced 21 per cent more than the Ford V8. With the new car's low drag and light weight the engine's size was thought adequate with good fuel economy the potential beneficiary. It also opened clear water between the Zephyr and the big Lincoln KA's 6,787cc.

Like the KA the Model H had four main bearings. These measured 61.0mm in diameter, the same as the Ford V8's. Rod-bearing journals were bigger, however, at 54.0mm versus the Ford's 50.8mm, and connecting rods were longer at 188.0mm against 177.8mm and meatier as well.[1] The rod big ends were cut on the diagonal to permit their withdrawal through the bore. Fully and massively counterbalanced, the crankshaft had lightened rod journals that were drilled out and then closed by Welch plugs. It carried a small vibration damper at its nose.

Cast in a single piece, using the foundry techniques developed for the Ford vee-eight, the Zephyr's iron block was cut off at the crankshaft centreline. Also following Ford practice the wet sump was pressed steel. The oil pump was driven by a skew gear from the tail of the single central camshaft, which was gear-driven from the crank nose. Powered by the nose of the cam was the characteristic Ford unified ignition coil, breaker and distributor. Fitting into apertures in the front of the block, at both sides, were twin water pumps, driven by a belt that also turned the dynamo. The cooling fan was attached to the damper on the nose of the crankshaft, while cooling-water capacity was generous at 6 US gallons.

An aluminium cylinder head capped each side of the block. Its recesses concentrated the L-head combustion-chamber volume over the valves so the pistons could induce turbulence with a squish effect above their crowns. As in the Ford V8 and many other side-valve engines the valve stems were not parallel to the cylinder axis but were angled slightly away at their stem ends to

ENGINES FOR THE ELITE

give more favourable flow conditions in and out of the chamber. In the Lincoln the inclination was more marked for the inlet valve, by 4°, than for the exhausts.

At 38.9mm the valves were the same size as in Ford's V8 and were interchangeable between inlets and exhausts.[2] This represented a relative increase in valve area because the twelve's per-cylinder volume was 19 per cent less than the eight's. Additional help for the Lincoln came from inlet-valve lift of 8.7mm against the Ford's 7.4mm, which was common to the Zephyr's exhaust lift. Initially solid, the tappets were replaced in 1938 by hydraulic lifters.

As in Ford's V8 the exhaust ports meandered down and outward, through the block, to four outlets on each side in the V12. Here was a departure from other L-head vee-twelves, which took care to extract the hot exhaust gases as quickly as possible through manifolds close to the valves. The Model H layout simplified the central vee, allowing an aluminium inlet manifold to do double duty as its cover. With some inlet as well as exhaust tracts siamesed, the manifold fed four inlet ports on each side of the twelve. It was topped by a single two-throat Stromberg carburettor.

Throughout his twelve Frank Johnson took care to keep weights and dimensions to a minimum, not only because this was Ford policy but also because it would best suit the engine for use in a new modern Lincoln in which lightness was a virtue. At 3,350lb on a 122-inch wheelbase the new model was competitive with others in its class and lighter than many. With its initial output of 110bhp at 3,600rpm from a compression ratio of 6.7:1 the twelve gave the Zephyr good performance. Torque was 186lb-ft at 1,800rpm.

In November of 1935 Ford sales manager William C. Cowling unveiled the Lincoln Zephyr, hailing it as "a sensational, completely new motor car". The Zephyr was priced right, at $1,275, to compete with the Packard 120 and the LaSalle, and advertised with emphasis on its vee-twelve: "Have *you* ever driven a twelve-cylinder car? Now *you* can drive and *own* one!" In 1936 17,715 found buyers. The Zephyr's pre-war peak came in 1937, with 25,243 examples sold. This was a breakthrough for Lincoln, which sold only 3,915 and 6,502 of its KAs in 1935 and 1936 respectively.

In the pre-war years Lincoln exported 3,404 right-hand-drive Zephyrs. Many came to the United Kingdom, where they were seen as good value at £500. Tests there showed them capable of 87mph and acceleration from rest to 50mph in 10.8sec and to 60 in 16sec – very respectable timings.

With the Ford Motor Company a major presence in Britain, it wasn't long before this lively new engine came to the attention of that nation's automotive entrepreneurs. One such was Nottingham's George

Above: *Exceptionally light and aerodynamic for a luxury car of its era, the Lincoln Zephyr filled a hitherto-vacant niche in the Ford Motor Company product range. This 1941 model had the low-positioned grille that evolved from efforts to provide better cooling for its twelve-cylinder engine.*

Left: *With its aluminium cylinder heads the Zephyr twelve could be polished to a high gloss, as in this Lincoln Continental. Like its Ford V8 counterpart, the inlet manifold also served as the cover for its central vee.*

Britain's Atalantas were handsome sporting cars with all-independent suspension and, in six made before the war, Lincoln Zephyr vee-twelves. Their coachwork was by Abbott.

Brough, justly famed for his fast motorcycles. When in the 1930s he began to produce cars as well he used Hudson engines and components for his Brough Superiors. In 1937 he sought to raise his game with a new model, the XII, powering it with the complete Lincoln

The first Allard to be powered by a Lincoln V12 in 1937 was 'Tailwagger I', built to the order of Ken Hutchison. He is seen competing with it in a speed trial at Lewes on England's south coast.

vee-twelve drive train. Although three chassis were laid down only one was bodied, an elaborate and – at £1,250 – costly Charlesworth four-door saloon.[3] Completed in 1938, it still needed development when war intervened. Brough didn't resume car production after the war.

A more sporting application of Zephyr power was in Atalanta cars, named after a fleet-footed Greek goddess. Although Atalanta Motors in the London suburb of Staines made only a score or so of cars in 1937–39, they broke new ground for Britain with their all-independent coil-spring suspension, the design of Albert Gough.

When the girlfriend of an Atalanta customer crashed his car in Germany, the owner suggested that while they were repairing it the works might install a Zephyr twelve in place of the small proprietary fours they'd been using. When it found that a complete V12 engine and transmission could be bought for only £112, Atalanta embraced the idea enthusiastically.

Not including this opportunistically-engined prototype, Atalanta built half a dozen Zephyr-engined cars before war stopped play. Bodied by Abbott, the V12 Atalantas were good-looking cars and fast. In the hands of *The Autocar* a two-door saloon was timed at 91.84mph at Brooklands and sprinted from rest to 60mph in 13.7sec. A car with more sporting bodywork reached 101mph for *Motor Sport*.

Atalanta was just getting into its stride as a car producer, enjoying some success in competitions, when the demands of war preparation switched its production to aircraft subcontracting. Although Atalanta was briefly revived after the war, its Lincoln-engined days were over.[4]

Another satisfied Zephyr customer was a garage in London's Putney, Adlards Motors. As a Ford dealer, Adlards had close links with the Dagenham company. Its moving spirit was Sydney Allard, an enthusiastic competitor in sprints and trials.[5] In 1936 Allard completed his first 'Allard Special', the success of which sparked demands for replicas. Before the war Sydney Allard and his small team completed a dozen such cars, all with Ford power save three which had Lincoln V12 motivation.

The first such car, registered as ELX 50 in December 1937, was equipped with the twelve instead of the smaller Ford V8 at the request of customer Ken Hutchison. With its skimpy body and cycle wings it was intended for competitions, in which it performed well. After the war this car was owned and raced by motorcyclist Len Parker, who later converted it into a mid-engined special.

Hutchinson took a second bite at the cherry with another Lincoln-Allard in 1938, FGF 290. He'd originally planned on Ford power for this even more sketchy machine but switched to the twelve because he missed its insouciant thrust.

In 1939 Sydney Allard's budding motor makers raised their game in response to an order from Commander Derek Silcock for a roadgoing sports car powered by the Lincoln V12. Bodied by Whittingham and Mitchell, this was a superbly stylish open roadster that hinted at post-war Allards to come. Under its bonnet the firewall was damascened and every eligible engine component chromed. Registered as FLX 650 in March 1939, it was the last of the vee-twelve Allard Specials and the most attractive to boot.

Silcock actively raced and rallied FLX 650 in the few months before the war. It competed in the La Turbie hill climb and covered more than 100 miles within the hour at Brooklands. Allard produced a more aggressive camshaft for the vee-twelve, and also fitted Silcock's car with a special manifold carrying three Stromberg carburettors. For wartime motoring, rods and pistons were removed from one bank of the engine and its inlet ports blocked off. Performance was still decent and fuel consumption much improved. Although she deserved to survive as the iconic pre-war Allard, FLX 650 was regrettably written off by a crash during the 1950 Alpine Rally.

In Britain's Midlands another company, Jensen Motors, was fitting American Ford and Nash engines in its bespoke motorcars. From 1936 Alan and Richard Jensen were badging their products with their fraternal surname. Attracted by the smooth running promised by the Zephyr engine, at a time when twelves were in the ascendant at both Lagonda and Rolls-Royce, Jensen fitted three Model H engines into its H-Type model range in 1938–39.[6] One of these was acquired by actor Clark Gable. Jensen were said to be disappointed with the engines, however, on the grounds of poor reliability.

The British experience suggests that Frank Johnson's twelve thrived in sporting applications but enjoyed less success in more banal touring roles. This mirrors its travails as power for the Zephyr. One problem area was cooling. With twelve exhaust ports blending through the coolant into eight outlets, overheating was easily provoked. This in fact contributed a styling breakthrough for Lincoln. Experiments led to a lower, wider radiator and grille openings that were lowered to suit. Introduced in the 1938 Zephyrs, this was the industry's first use of so-called 'catwalk cooling' that soon led the general transformation of American and European cars to wider and lower grilles.

Oil burning was another crime laid at the Lincoln's door. Although engineering writer Roger Huntington blamed this on "bore warpage, excessive bore wear, ring

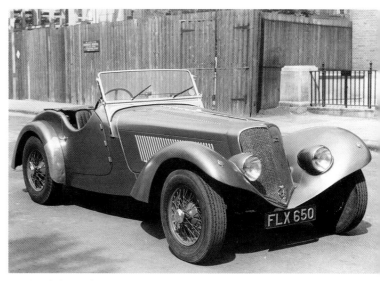

A splendid Lincoln-powered Allard that deserved to survive was FLX 650, which took the road just before the war. For competition purposes she was later fitted with skimpier wings but ultimately crashed beyond repair in 1950.

wear", it's seen now as related to failure of the available piston rings to seat well in the Lincoln's cylinder bores, which were America's smallest with the exception of Ford's 2.2-litre V8-60.

Where there are ring problems there is blow-by into the crankcase, and here the Lincoln had serious problems with the snug dimensioning that Johnson had given his engine and its block. Sludging of the oil easily developed and clogged the crankshaft's internal passages. The only solution in the field, said Lincoln, was to replace the crankshaft. Such problems were minimised when the twelve was revved freely and often and its oil changed frequently, but these practices weren't on the agenda of Americans. Lincoln owners took advantage of the Zephyr's torque and flexibility by lugging it in top gear – just what it most disliked.

Then when oiling problems arose, the Model H's original oil pump couldn't cope. With twelve instead of eight cylinders, and after 1938 hydraulic lifters as well, any slackening of clearances found oil escaping through too many interstices and pressure falling. After the war a new pump was fitted that had a gallon per minute more capacity. Owners have found it beneficial to fit an oil filter, improve oiling of the timing gears and drain lubricant better from the central valley.

However, this wasn't quite the end of the Zephyr's problems. A positive step in 1940 was a bore increase to 73.0mm, bringing capacity to 4,787cc, power to 120bhp and torque to 225lb-ft with a 7.2:1 compression ratio. For the short-lived 1942 model year the bore was bigger still at 74.6mm for a displacement of 4,996cc. With iron cylinder heads – aluminium in short supply in wartime – and a 7.0:1 compression ratio its power was 130bhp at 3,600rpm and its torque 235lb-ft at 1,800.

This was the liveliest version of the Model H. "I'm immediately amazed at the agility and acceleration of the V12 engine," wrote the driver of a 1942 Lincoln 56 years later. "This car would do very well in amateur stoplight racing, and must have surprised a few people in its day."

The last enlargement, however, was a boring-bar too far. The engine had been stretched, said one expert, "to within a millimetre of its life". Cylinder walls were now so thin that not all the castings could be bored without breaking through; scrappage rates were high. Similarly, reboring an engine to revive a worn block was a risky business. Not all could survive the process. In 1946, accordingly, Lincoln reverted to the 1940–41 specification of 4,787cc for the post-war era, in which the small vee-twelve was its sole power unit for a range of cars derived from the Zephyr.

In 1945 Ford set up a free-standing Lincoln Division for the first time. When in early 1946 plans were being made for future Lincolns, a V12 was very much on the cards. However, when on 13 June 1946 the Ford Products Committee reached its final conclusion, the twelve was out and a vee-eight of 160bhp was in. With eights powering all the Division's 1949 models, the final Lincoln vee-twelve was assembled on 24 March 1948. It was the last of a remarkable line. Flawed though the Model H may have been, in all it powered some 220,000 Lincolns,

Settling down to the displacement of 4.8 litres, Lincoln's V12 continued after World War II to power Lincoln cars through the 1948 model year, which included this handsome Continental coupé.

among them the justly revered Continentals.[7] It could hardly be assessed a flop.

Of course Lincoln wasn't the only American auto maker with a proud vee-twelve tradition. Packard said goodbye to its last twelve in 1939 and entered the post-war world with powerful straight-eights for its prestigious cars. From 1952 Packard had an ebullient new president, James J. Nance, who was well aware of the strong appeal of new product in the auto industry. With the arrival of GM's exciting new V8 engines in 1949, Nance and his colleagues realised that Packard had no alternative but to go and do likewise.

In 1951 Packard's Operating Committee first discussed the company's need for a vee-eight. With Jesse Vincent still leading the company's engineering, work was put in hand and by early 1953 the first prototypes were ready. In May of 1953 Jim Nance had a brainwave. What would it cost us, he asked Vincent, to build a V12 version of our V8 as well? Here would be an echo of Packard's greatest years, a dramatic product story that could attract new buyers to a marque that was in desperate danger of disappearing up its own exhaust pipe.

Hitherto Vincent had been planning an eight of 95.3 x 88.9mm for 5,068cc. Considering that adding four cylinders to this would be excessive, on 27 May 1953 he suggested a shorter stroke for both engines. Their dimensions would thus be 95.3 x 82.6mm, which would give 4,706cc for the eight and 7,059cc for the twelve. A nice differentiation would be achieved, with the V12 almost as big as the similar Packards of the 1930s. Pistons, rods and valves would be shared by both versions, with the twelve's block machined by shifting it along the transfer line for the boring of four more holes whenever demand for the eight was slack. Evenly spaced firing with the 90° twelve would be achieved by giving each connecting rod its own crank journal, offsetting the big ends of facing pairs by 30°.

The cost of the tooling needed to add the twelve to Packard's range was initially estimated at an affordable $750,000. By June of 1953, however, after other implications had been assessed, including knock-on effects on vehicle cost and timing, the idea of a twelve was dropped.[8] It was an opportunity missed. "No one else was building such an engine," said Packard product-planner Richard Stout, "and it was very much in the traditional Packard role. It could have been spectacular. Packard could have used some grand-standing in those days. The company and its customers were almost in a world of their own, buying, selling the same stuff time after time. The rest of the world held it in respect, but not too much interest."

By 1957, with Packard in terminal decline, James Nance was at the Ford Motor Company. There, when suggestions for Lincoln's future were raised, the idea of a V12 surfaced again. Here too was a chance to break away from the ordinary and celebrate a storied legacy. With the tooling for Packard's V8 being mothballed, the idea arose of acquiring and adapting it to build V12s for Lincolns. This didn't pass the stage of informal discussion, however.

In Europe, meanwhile, another maker of cars for the upper crust was struggling to regain its footing after the war. Among his future projects, Ettore Bugatti announced from Paris, would be "a Grand Sport de luxe with an engine of four litres capacity." This failed to take account of the chaotic state of his factory in Alsace, which at the time of his death on 21 August 1947 was still occupied by the French marines. Under Pierre Marco's direction order was gradually restored, a handful of Type 101s, based on the pre-war Type 57, being produced into the 1950s.

Another initiative on Marco's watch was the creation of a 2½-litre Grand Prix car, the Type 251. None other than Gioachino Colombo was the designer of this exotic racer with its front and rear de Dion axles and transverse eight-cylinder engine. Assisting him was one of his former colleagues from Ferrari, Luciano Fochi. A 1½-litre sports car was also proposed and prototyped, the Type 252, but was given up when its potential profit margins were seen to be too small. Instead, Bugatti returned to the concept that Ettore himself had proclaimed after the war.

Pierre Marco had retired and Noël Domboy was in charge of the Molsheim works in 1962 when the Type 451 project was launched to build 'a Grand Sport de luxe'. Its principal designer was Colombo protégé Luciano Fochi. He planned for the new Bugatti a 60° vee-twelve engine of 4,464cc (80 x 74mm) with the potential for 300 horsepower. Its suspension was to be all-independent by coil-spring struts, with its clutch and transaxle grouped at the rear in the manner of the Lancia Aurelia.

First components for the space-framed Type 451 were being made when, in July 1963, the works and its assets were taken over by Hispano-Suiza – not for its cars but for the defence contracts it was fulfilling in order to survive. Car production at Molsheim ended, but the dream of a Bugatti V12 – one of the few engine types Ettore had never built – would not easily die.

One car maker that most certainly had built vee-twelves and had a hankering to do so again in the post-war years was Cadillac. In 1960 a sister company in the General Motors family, GMC Truck and Coach, had introduced a new range of petrol engines based on a 60° V6 with a bore

of 90.9mm. Included was what GMC called a 'Twin Six', a vee-twelve of 9,026cc (90.9 x 115.8mm), which used two of the vee-six cylinder heads along each side of its one-piece cylinder block, each facing pair served by its own manifold and downdraft carburettor. The V12 produced 275bhp at a governed 2,400rpm and peak torque of 630lb-ft. While not a car engine, this GMC effort was a pioneering power unit for its time, in both its versions (see page 284).

In parallel with the GMC effort, GM's Cadillac Motor Division started developing a V12 of its own in 1959. Harold Warner was the division's general manager, Fred Arnold its chief engineer and James Roche – a future head of GM – its sales manager. Paul Keydel was assigned responsibility for the new engine's creation, which was supported right up to the top of the Corporation, said one engineer: "Ed Cole, and people like him, who knew about cars, thought Cadillac should have something more than a V8." [9] The project was launched as the 'V-Future' programme.

The Keydel design was unconstrained by an any existing GM engine. It was a 60° V12, initially of 7.4 litres, with a single chain driven overhead camshaft along each bank, the left bank being offset forward. Each cylinder head's spark plugs were fired by a distributor driven from its camshaft's nose. Its heads were aluminium as was its cylinder block, which was pressure-die-cast by GM's two-stage AcuRad process. This allowed the use of high-silicon aluminium alloys which in turn permitted the pistons to

A front view of Paul Keydel's V-Future engine for Cadillac showed the mountings of its twin distributors, which were driven from the front ends of its overhead camshafts. Keydel chose a 60° vee for this Cadillac twelve of the early 1960s.

Numerous manifold designs were tested on the six V-Future twelves that were produced as prototypes for Cadillac. This one enjoyed a free-flowing exhaust manifold, but its sump was a provisional fabrication.

From its 7.4 litres the V-Future Cadillac vee-twelve gave just short of 300 horsepower when equipped with twin carburettors. This test engine had two four-throat carburettors, their secondary ports opening progressively.

run directly in the bores without intervening liners. Valve gear was by finger followers whose pivots were mounted on small hydraulic cylinders that automatically held the valve lash at zero.[10] This maintained the tradition of hydraulic clearance adjustment that Cadillac had established with its 1931 twelve.

Cadillac's prototype V-Future twelves – six in all – were built and tested by GM's Engineering Staff in the Technical Center at Warren, Michigan. Run for the first time in May 1963, the impression the V-Future gave its developers was deeply disappointing. Against its current target, the slightly smaller 7.0-litre Cadillac V8, the twelve gave similar peak power – 295bhp at 4,400rpm – but, as a report stated, "very low torque values at intermediate engine speeds". This was not at all what Cadillac wanted. Its owners were accustomed to a rewarding sensation of limitless thrust at moderate engine speeds from what Cadillac called a "dome-shaped" torque curve.

Suspecting manifolding to be the source of the problem, the engineers fitted individual inlet and exhaust pipes to a fuel-injected engine to take manifolding out of the equation. With more torque throughout its range and 354bhp at 4,600rpm on a curve that was still climbing, a test gave confidence that "the basic V-Future engine design [was] acceptable". Indeed, a trial of a fine-tuned version of the racing-style individual ram pipes and an improved free-flow exhaust system showed 394bhp and maximum torque of 506lb-ft at 3,600rpm. When exhaust back pressure akin to that of a Cadillac silencer was imposed, peak power fell to 340bhp at 4,400rpm – less but still respectable. Development work thereafter concentrated on valve timing, tests of five different cam contours, and on manifold design.

The original inlet manifold had a single central four-throat carburettor feeding logs along each cylinder bank. With this, found the Cadillac men, "cylinder to cylinder distribution of fuel is extremely poor, varying from as lean as 16:1 to as rich as 9:1." Though they knew that this alone didn't account for the performance shortfall from their V8, they tried "all manner of skimmers, dams, risers and baffles" in the manifold to improve distribution, without success. A plastic-topped manifold was made to allow direct observation of the flow. Warmth helped vaporise the fuel-air mixture, but as they planned an aluminium manifold they couldn't use direct exhaust heat and had to rely on water heating.

Hand-fabricated induction systems were designed and tried, including twin four-throat, twin two-throat and triple two-throat carburettors, in search of the ideal layout. Tests of alternative designs, assessed in 204 dynamometer runs, continued to April 1964. Best, the engineers concluded, were a split exhaust manifold and a two-twin-throat-carburettor manifold giving 240° intervals between induction events. With this the V-Future gave 294bhp at 4,400rpm and 418lb-ft of torque at 2,400rpm. Though not 'dome-shaped', its torque curve looked a lot better. To be on the safe side, however, an 8.2-litre version of the V-Future was also put in hand.

Meanwhile in 1963–64 at GM's Engineering Staff development was under way on dramatic new front-drive trains for GM's big cars. These featured transverse or east–west positioning of V8 engines. Cadillac protested at this, pointing out that it would be barred from using the new front-drive transaxle because its vee-twelve wouldn't package transversely. The GM engineers then dreamed up ingenious monkey motion that met Cadillac's

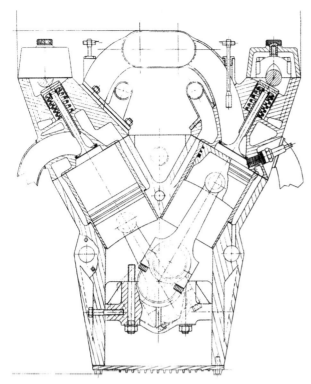

An Italian engineer working in Canada, Francesco Romanelli built this ambitious 60° vee-twelve for a sports car he hoped to produce in 1970. Romanelli adapted Fiat's cam followers to open the vertical valves of his twelve, using a design that had been developed by Aurelio Lampredi after his move to Fiat in 1955.

requirement with transaxles that aligned the engines north–south instead.

As the V-Future programme matured, GM's divisions were planning the new 'personal cars' that its engines would propel. Oldsmobile signed up for front-wheel drive for its new V8-powered Toronado, while Cadillac planned to install its V12 in its front-driven Eldorado. By 1964, however, its managers had lost faith in the potential of the twelve, which still seemed to be struggling to give the kind of power and torque that Cadillac required. Nor did it seem adaptable to the new controls on exhaust emissions that were beginning to be imposed. The Division had no choice but to revert to its eight for the Eldorado. The change in transaxle design for which Cadillac had lobbied successfully had gone for naught. V-Future was consigned to the past.[11]

Not long after these adventures at the world's biggest car company another overhead-cam aluminium-block V12 took shape under vastly less pretentious circumstances. At Montreal, Canada's auto show in January 1970 an Italian émigré, Francesco Romanelli, unveiled a stunning glass-fibre-bodied coupé which he hoped to produce and sell for $9,000. At the time it was powered by a Buick V8, but the ambitious Romanelli had designed and built a bespoke V12 which he planned to put under its sloping bonnet.

A 60° twelve with its left bank offset forward, Romanelli's engine had a very deep cylinder block into which wet steel cylinder liners were inserted and clamped between head and block. Rugged caps for its seven main bearings were side-bolted for added rigidity. Enclosing the bottom of the block was a finned plate, all that was needed for the twelve's dry sump.

Gears from the crankshaft drove a half-speed shaft, which in turn powered the Romanelli's single overhead cam on each bank through a double-roller chain. Vertical with respect to the cylinder bore, the valves were in line. They were opened by cup-type tappets that the designer appropriated from contemporary Fiat overhead-cam engines. In a design originated by Aurelio Lampredi, these had their clearance-adjustment discs set into the top of the tappet, in contact with the cam lobe, where they could easily be checked and changed.

For induction Francesco Romanelli provided a central plenum chamber from which ram pipes fed the individual cylinders. In each was an injection nozzle fed by a Bendix-patent electronic injection system developed by Conelec of Elmira, New York. A capacitive-discharge ignition system was also electronically controlled. With a compression ratio of 10.0:1, the Romanelli twelve developed 460bhp at 7,000rpm from its 5,742cc (92 x 72mm). Maximum torque was 380lb-ft at 5,000rpm.

The Montreal engineer bedded his twelve in a multi-tube chassis stiffened by a floor reinforced by rigid foam. Its drive was through a rear-mounted five-speed transaxle. All in all his package was an attractive one, well

Francesco Romanelli produced a coupé for his planned sports car that was exceptionally handsome by the standards of 1970. Regrettably he was unable to bring this ambitious project to fruition.

Engineers working for Alejandro de Tomaso used the then-fashionable cogged-rubber belts to drive the four overhead camshafts of his Type 105 V12 of 1970. They fed overhead inlet ports from side-draft Weber carburettors, which were significantly less expensive than downdraft Webers.

up to the standard of its badge with the she-wolf of Rome and the suckling Romulus and Remus, but the distance from a prototype to production in the motor industry is long and hard. Romanelli turned his talents to innovations in motorcycle engines and suspensions and parked his promising GT project.

Almost as ephemeral as the Romanelli were the vee-twelve engines which emerged from the fecund Modena workshops of Argentine racer-entrepreneur Alejandro de Tomaso. In 1970, newly flush with Ford funding for his Pantera production car, de Tomaso and his engineers produced a plethora of twelve-cylinder prototypes. Two had the same capacity, 4,782cc, and some commonality through their bottom ends, which had crankcases split on the crankshaft centreline, with the bottom half cast integral with all seven main-bearing caps. Right-hand banks were offset forward, in the Ferrari fashion. Aluminium blocks carried wet steel cylinder liners with collars at the top that were pinched in place by the heads.

Both versions of the 4.8-litre de Tomaso had twin overhead camshafts on each bank and four-valve combustion chambers. Intended for road cars, the Type 105 had valve angles of 23° for its inlets and 28° for its exhausts. The head casting was designed so that it served for both banks of the engine. Downdraft inlet ports, between the camshafts, were fed by half a dozen twin-throat side-draft Weber carburettors. At the nose of the crankshaft two cogged-rubber belts from a pair of half-speed gears drove each bank's twin camshafts. Like Romanelli, de Tomaso used Fiat-style cup-type tappets for his Type 105 V12. Weighing 440lb, the twelve was credited with 390bhp. Suited though it might have been to de Tomaso's XJ Jaguar look-alike, his Deauville, the 105 was never offered for sale.

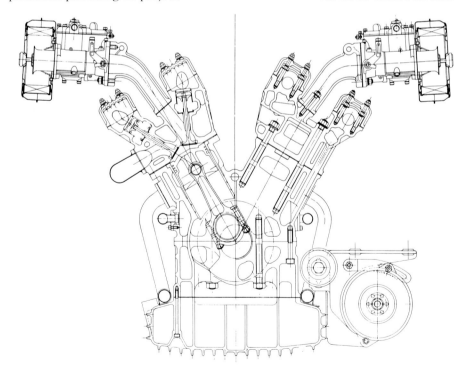

Fiat-type tappets, with large-diameter adjusting shims between the cam lobe and the tappet body, were used in the 4.8-litre de Tomaso Type 105 vee-twelve. The caps for its main bearings were an integral part of the casting that served as the lower half of its crankcase.

The Type 105 V12 would have been eminently suitable for use in de Tomaso's Deauville, his four-door counterpart to Jaguar's XJ saloon. However, no such automobile was ever brought to market.

Built on the same basis as the Type 105, de Tomaso's Type 102 was a dry-sump unit intended for Can-Am competition. Although this was an impressive engine with significant power potential, its 4.8 litres meant that it wasn't big enough to keep pace with the power race in the unlimited Can-Am series. It was never used in anger.

The sister 4.8-litre twelve, Type 102, was intended for Can-Am racing. Its sump was dry instead of wet and its camshaft drive a pair of enclosed chains instead of belts. With its camshafts closer together for a narrower valve angle, the Type 102 had one-piece cam covers and injection-fed inlet ports in its central vee. Impressive though it was, with 540bhp from 420lb, de Tomaso's 102 failed to keep pace with the horsepower escalation in the Can-Am series and never raced.

The same held true for another twelve, a 3-litre, that de Tomaso was building for Formula 1, for which he produced Cosworth-powered cars for the Frank Williams team in 1970. This engine had narrow-angle four-valve heads and cams driven by cogged-rubber belts, chosen for their lightness. There's no evidence that this engine was ever completed.[12]

No one in Italy – least of all de Tomaso – could avoid being influenced by the engines that Ferrari was producing for its road cars. The original line, the legendary series of Colombo-based single-overhead-cam engines that had made the company's reputation, was finally winding down in the late 1960s. The last new engine of this configuration was the Type 245, a 4,390cc (81 x 71mm) V12 introduced in 1967 to power the elegant four-seater 365GT 2+2.

Its increased bore a beneficiary of cylinder-centre distances increased from 90 to 94mm, the Type 245 was used as well in the 365 California, GTC and GTS. A direct

Bodied by Pininfarina, the Ferrari 365GT 2+2 of 1967 was one of the last of the company's cars to use an engine of the original Colombo-type single-cam design. It was motivated by 320 horsepower from the 4.4 litres of its Type 245 vee-twelve.

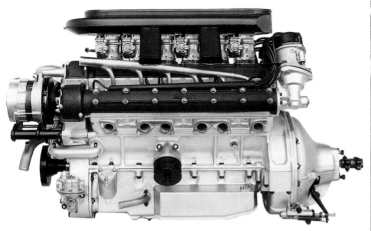

The first road-going Ferrari to be powered by a four-cam V12 engine was the 275GTB/4 of 1966. The 280bhp of its 3.3-litre Type 226 twelve were delivered through an engine-mounted clutch that drove a remote transaxle.

Seen during assembly at Ferrari in 1967, a Type 226 engine displayed the mounting of its oil pumps to its main-bearing caps and revealed the faces of its cup-type tappets with Fiat-style clearance-adjusting inserts.

descendant of the engine used in the 1964 racing 365P, the 245 was loafing by comparison with its three carburettors instead of six, 8.8:1 instead of 9.0:1 compression ratio and 320 instead of 380 horsepower, reached at 6,600rpm.

In the meantime Ferrari responded to heightened competition – not least from an upstart named Lamborghini – with its development of twin-overhead-cam engines for its twelve-cylinder road cars. The first of

With its transaxle configuration and four-cam 3.3-litre engine the 275GTB/4 Ferrari was handsomely bodied by Pininfarina to take the marque to a new level of technical and aesthetic sophistication.

these was the Type 226 for the 275GTB/4 introduced at the Paris Salon in October 1966. This four-cam engine of 3,286cc (77 x 58.8mm) replaced a two-cam engine of the same capacity. Its camshafts were chain-driven and its valve gear Fiat-style cup-type tappets. Fed by six Weber 40DCN twin-throat carburettors, it delivered 280bhp, a bonus of 20bhp, at the higher revs of 7,700 against 7,400 for its predecessor.[13] Both had a 9.3:1 compression ratio.

The 275GTB/4 was a relatively short-lived model, its export to the important US market curtailed by that country's new exhaust-emissions rules. To meet those increasingly demanding regulations, Ferrari and Pininfarina were already working on a new super-sports model they would launch at the 1968 Paris Salon.

Ferrari's first iteration of the new model's engine was its Type 243, using the same bottom end and dimensions as the 365 vee-twelve, 81 x 71mm for 4,390cc, but with two close-spaced camshafts on each bank operating two inlet and one exhaust valve per cylinder. In the Type 243 the valves were vertical, their seats flush with the face of the head and opening on a combustion chamber set entirely in the crown of the piston, our friend the Heron-type chamber. Two spark plugs for each cylinder were provided, inserted from the outside of each head and flanking the exhaust valve, and carburation was by sextuple twin-throat Webers.

Working in parallel on their Type 251 with classical twin-cam cylinder heads, Ferrari's engineers were able to achieve emissions results that were good enough to render the prosaic three-valve redundant. For the 365GTB/4, better known as the Daytona, they inclined the two valves per cylinder at an included angle of 60°, with diameters of 42 and 37.4mm for the inlets and exhausts respectively. Ingeniously the cams for both banks were driven by a single double-roller chain that drove a half-

speed sprocket in each head. From the sprocket a helical gear turned both camshafts. Carburettors were six 40DCN Webers. European compression ratio was 9.3:1 and output was a stirring 352bhp at 7,500rpm with peak torque at 5,500rpm of 315lb-ft.

With mid-engined sports cars all the rage at the time of the Daytona's launch, some were critical of Ferrari's decision to introduce a front-engined supercar, but its stunning looks and outstanding performance – 175mph and 5.8sec from 0 to 60 – soon silenced the querulous. Production of 1,284 coupés and 122 Spyders spoke for itself, as did the building of 15 special cars strictly for competition use. In 1972 these filled places five through nine in the 24 Hours of Le Mans. They won the GT category then and in 1973 and '74 as well.

While the 365GT4 BB with its flat-opposed twelve would be the Daytona's direct replacement in 1973, 1971 saw the launch of a new front-engined vee-twelve sports Ferrari in the 365GTC4. Its engine's basic specification was akin to that of the Daytona, with the same cylinder dimensions and 94mm cylinder-centre distance, the

Left: During a visit to Ferrari's Maranello factory in 1967 Raymond Firestone, directly behind the engine, listens to Enzo Ferrari, in sunglasses, who describes his Type 243 V12 of 4.4 litres with its three valves per cylinder. Production-ready though it looked, this design was replaced by a conventional two-valve engine with hemispherical combustion chambers for the Ferrari Daytona.

Below: In 1970 this Type 251 vee-twelve was being assembled at Maranello for installation in the 365GTB/4, the Daytona. Visible was the helical gearing to its twin camshafts, driven by a double-roller chain.

Introduced in 1971, the Ferrari 365GTC/4 was powered by an F101 vee-twelve, a refinement of the Daytona's 4.4-litre engine. Throughout 1972 five hundred such Pininfarina-bodied cars were produced.

The aluminium cylinder block of the F101 vee-twelve of 1971, showing its closed top deck and inserted wet steel cylinder liners. Small collars held by three of the studs kept the liners in place during assembly of the engine.

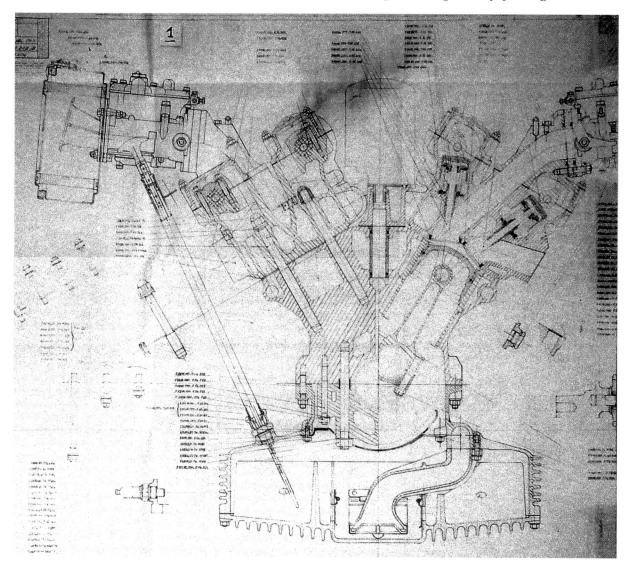

same rugged four-stud main-bearing caps and crankshaft machined from a solid billet, with 63.0mm main bearings and 43.6mm rod journals. Its connecting rods were 137mm long. It carried the first of a new type-number series as the F101, following a system more compatible with that of the new majority owner of Ferrari's production-car operations, Fiat.

The F101 V12 was topped by completely new cylinder heads. Its valve inclinations were narrower at a symmetrical included angle of 46°. Inlet-valve size remained the same at 42mm and exhausts were slightly bigger than those of the 251 at 36.8mm. Though space was reduced between the camshafts, that very valley was now used for the inlet ports, which sloped outward and at a smooth 43° angle to the inlet-valve stems. The repositioning of the ports, said Ferrari, was made in order to achieve a lower bonnet line in co-operation with Pininfarina. As well, it allowed the use of much cheaper side-draft Weber carburettors. The layout did, however, inevitably resemble the manifolding that new rival Lamborghini had previously adopted for its front-engined cars for similar reasons.

Tamer than its Daytona forebear, the F101 carried carburettors of 38 instead of 40mm and was compressed at an 8.8:1 ratio. Weighing 556lb less clutch, it produced 310bhp at 7,700rpm and 311lb-ft of torque at 4,600rpm. Through 1972 it powered the 500 365GTC/4s that left the Maranello factory. Next its stroke was lengthened to 78mm to increase its capacity to 4,823cc to help it cope with a GM-sourced automatic transmission in the four-seater 400 Automatic, introduced in 1976. In this form, still with Webers and an 8.8:1 compression ratio, it produced 340bhp at 6,500rpm.

An important change in this engine came in 1979, when for the first time it was equipped with Bosch K-Jetronic fuel injection and digital ignition control. Each cylinder bank of what was now the Type F110A was allocated its own measuring unit and fuel distributor. Emissions-constrained power was down further to 310bhp, still at 6,500rpm to suit the automatic transmission's speed limits. Ferraris thus-equipped became the 400i.

The final gasp of this generation of Ferrari vee-twelve was heard in a new version of the 400 introduced in 1985, the 412. It gained a one-millimetre bore increase for a capacity of 4,943cc (82 x 78mm). Its compression ratio

Opposite: The wet-sumped 4.4-litre Ferrari V12 introduced in the 365GTC/4 in 1971 was designated the F101 to make it more compatible with the systems used by Fiat, which had become the majority owner of Ferrari's production-car operations. Its wet sump was well baffled with trap doors to the left and right of its central oil pickup to keep the lubricant as close as possible at all times.

During assembly of an F101 Ferrari V12 in 1970, a paper protector kept debris from falling into the inlet ports between the camshafts of each cylinder head. Space in the centre of the vee could now be used for oil filters.

was boosted to 9.6:1 and its power to 340bhp at the customary 6,500rpm. Torque was a respectable 333lb-ft at the lower revs of 4,200. Motivated accordingly, the 412 continued in production into 1989. Its successor, the 456GT, would arrive in 1992 with a completely new V12 that broke all links with the old Colombo/Lampredi era. The sole saga in the long history of vee-twelve engines that bears comparison with that of Enzo Ferrari is that of his compatriot Ferruccio Lamborghini. If Ferrari was daring to begin his enterprise with a twelve – and he was – the feisty, independent Lamborghini took even greater risks in exactly the same manner. Ferrari made his choice with the benefit of a lifetime's experience with sporting and racing machinery of the highest quality. Twelve-cylinder cars that dated to before World War I were on his

Enlarged to 4.8 litres, the F101 Ferrari vee-twelve found a new home in the 400-series four-passenger models. Its power curve was tailored to peak at 6,500rpm to make it compatible with the GM-sourced automatic transmission used in the 400 Automatic.

agenda. Ferrari took a risk, but hedged it with knowledge gained over decades and the proven skills of Gioachino Colombo and Luigi Bazzi.

Lamborghini, in contrast, was an upstart industrialist, a maker of tractors, oil burners and air conditioning, who seemed to plunge headlong into the world of luxury sports cars without the slightest preparation – and with a vee-twelve engine. Many forecast financial suicide for Ferruccio. Ferrari and Maserati built all the sports cars that Italy needed, it was said; he'll go the same way as Spain's Pegaso and Italy's ATS and ASA, building a few cars and then failing.

Born in Emilia, like Ferrari, the stocky, forthright Lamborghini had the advantages of a degree in industrial arts from a Bologna institute and practical experience in the creation of his successful businesses. He spotted demands and sought to fill them. He did likewise in the world of cars.

"Before 1960," he said, "I had already worn out three Ferraris." Lamborghini was not easy on his cars, said a colleague: "A little rough and heavy-handed. Not a quick driver, and very sort of mediocre." "I had a very heavy gas foot," the industrialist admitted. "When I accelerated too hard I always fried the clutch." He asked his own technicians to have a look at his Ferrari's clutch, and found it to be a proprietary Borg & Beck not unlike the ones in his tractors. Perhaps the world of exotic cars wasn't as remote from his own activities as he'd previously supposed.

In 1962, at the age of 46, Ferruccio Lamborghini ordered a small area in his tractor factory to be cleared for the making of a prototype engine and car. "I have bought some of the most famous *gran turismo* cars," he explained, "and in each of these I have found some faults. Too hot. Or uncomfortable. Or not fast enough. Or not perfectly finished. Now I want to make a GT car without faults. Not a technical bombshell. Very normal. Very conventional. But a perfect car."

His assessment was not invalid. Although famous for their great engines, Ferrari and Maserati paid less attention to the niceties of the rest of the car. Details were dubious and serious development all but ignored. Customers were the first to endurance-test new models.

For his vital engine Lamborghini found a man who was much in need of just such an assignment. Tuscan Giotto Bizzarrini, equipped with an engineering degree from Pisa University, first worked at Alfa Romeo as an engineer and test driver and then joined Ferrari in a similar capacity in 1957. His was the development work that led to the famous short-wheelbase 250GT Berlinetta and the GTO. But in November 1961 Bizzarrini found himself among the eight men who, frustrated by the constant interference in their work of Ferrari's wife Laura, felt honour-bound to leave the company when one of them was fired. After a short spell with ATS, Giotto left to set up his own consultancy at Livorno, Societa Autostar, to gain freelance engineering assignments.

For his new car's underpinnings Lamborghini had engaged Modena coachbuilders Neri & Bonacini, and when he mentioned his need of an engine they suggested Bizzarrini. While the 36-year-old engineer was not known as an engine specialist, he'd been immersed in all Ferrari's affairs at a time of great creativity with the launch of new mid-engined cars by Carlo Chiti. He would also have had access to drawings of Ferrari's engines.

At the end of 1962 Autostar received the commission to design a V12 engine that would surpass Ferrari's. The fee was 4½ million lire – around £2,000 – for Bizzarrini's design and supervision of the engine's assembly. The contract was results-driven, imposing penalties if the output of 350bhp were not achieved and bonuses if it were surpassed. Half the fee was payable when the work began and the balance at its conclusion. Lamborghini would arrange to have the prototype's components made, sourcing its aluminium castings from Carlo Chiti at ATS and machining its crankshaft in his own tractor plant.

With Ferrari as the target, making the new engine a vee-twelve was the obvious option. It also allowed Bizzarrini to take full advantage of his knowledge of Ferrari engines in shaping the new power unit.[14] His first decisive step was to choose a capacity of almost 3½ litres, which would allow his contracted output to be reached if he could extract just over 100bhp per litre. This represented sports-racing output at the time; Ferrari's 3-litre 250P of 1963 produced 300 horsepower.

For the cylinder bore Bizzarrini chose 77mm, the same dimension that Chiti had used in a number of experimental Ferrari engines in 1961 and '62 and also the bore of Ferrari's 400 Superamerica of 1960. For the stroke he chose 62mm to give 3,465cc. Giotto secured his engine's future with a generous cylinder-centre spacing of 95mm.

The forward offset of the twelve's right-hand cylinder bank was another Ferrari-like feature. An advantage over Ferrari's road-car engines was Bizzarrini's choice of twin overhead camshafts, which offered the potential for higher engine speeds with reliability. Valve gear was of classical inverted-cup design, large enough to shroud the twin coil springs, with traditional adjustment by sized caps over the valve stems. At the front of the engine its camshafts were driven by a separate triple-roller chain for each bank, each powered by its own half-speed gear turned by the crank nose. The drive layout, the same one Carlo Chiti had used for his 1961 Formula 1 Ferrari V6, would later be adopted by Ferrari for its F101 V12.

Giotto Bizzarrini chose the included vee angle of 70° for his engine's valves. A compromise between the 60° angles lately used by Ferrari and the 78° of Maserati's V12, it allowed the use of generous valves: 42mm inlets and 38.2mm exhausts. The wide valve angles combined with the engine's 60° vee angle to congest the central vee, so Bizzarrini adopted Giulio Alfieri's Maserati solution of downdraft inlet ports between the camshafts of each head. The angle of inlet port to valve stem was a relatively large 55°, 5° more than Alfieri had managed. Distributors driven from the rear of the inlet camshafts fired a single plug per cylinder in the prototype engine.

In spite of his twin-camshaft configuration Giotto Bizzarrini achieved simplicity in his design of the Lamborghini's aluminium cylinder heads, which had integral tappet carriers and only four bearings for the camshafts, which were enclosed by finned covers. Fourteen studs clamped each head to the closed top deck of an aluminium cylinder block, in which cast-iron wet liners were inserted. Their fit into the block over their bottom two or so inches was tight enough not to require O-ring sealing. The block extended down well past the crankshaft centreline, a significant departure from Ferrari practice which gave a more robust join to the bell housing and transmission.

In no aspect of the Lamborghini vee-twelve was its Ferrari ancestry clearer than in its bottom-end bearing sizes, 63mm for the mains and 43.6mm for the rod journals. Maranello's bearings were identical. Each of the seven main bearings was held in place by a rugged four-stud aluminium cap. The I-section connecting rod, forged of SAE 4340 steel, was relatively short at 119mm.

Domed forged-aluminium pistons were full-skirted and carried three rings. Weighing 53¼lb, the counterbalanced crankshaft was machined from a 204lb billet of SAE 9840 steel. Bizzarrini gave his prototype a dry-sump lubrication system with both pressure and scavenge pumps driven from the crank nose. An idler sprocket for the right-hand cam-drive chain also drove the single water pump.

With its twin overhead cams, dry sump and 38mm downdraft Weber racing carburettors Giotto Bizzarrini's first prototype was a speed demon, as it demonstrated from its first dynamometer runs on 15 May 1963. It soon

When Ferruccio Lamborghini, in foreground, first unveiled his 3.5-litre V12 engine it was in the racy configuration as originally produced by Giotto Bizzarrini. Joining him at the launch were Giovanni Canestrini, cigar-smoking editor and journalist, and driver-engineer Piero Taruffi, in Argyle jumper.

Tasked with taming Bizzarrini's engine and making it suitable for a Lamborghini road car were, from left, Gian Paolo Dallara, Paolo Stanzani and Bob Wallace. Wise beyond their years, they were a young team dedicated to creating the best possible car for Lamborghini.

surpassed its contracted target by producing 358bhp at a scintillating 9,800rpm.[15] Peak torque of 240lb-ft was at the equally elevated speed of 6,000rpm. The Tuscan engineer had met his objective, but with an engine suitable for a racing car, not a road car. Indeed, he asserted that with 40mm carburettors it should be capable of 400bhp at a tooth-shattering 11,000rpm.

Lamborghini had to admit that Bizzarrini had done what he promised, but he wasn't thrilled to be given a race horse instead of a percheron. In fact he cavilled over the contract so obdurately that Bizzarrini had to go to court to collect the balance owed him. For his part, the racing-mad Bizzarrini was genuinely disappointed to find that the tractor builder was wary of building a competition car, that Lamborghini wasn't convinced that racing success was essential to achieving his goals. The two strong-willed men clashed with a result that was easily forecast: Bizzarrini left the project and, initially at least, was erased from the official Lamborghini history.[16]

While the first engine was installed in a Ferrari so Lamborghini could experience his new creation, the job of taming this tiger of a twelve was assigned to a Milan graduate in aeronautical engineering, Gian Paolo Dallara. He had worked at Ferrari under Chiti and at Maserati under Alfieri before coming to Lamborghini in 1963 at the recommendation of Giotto Bizzarrini.

Though only 26 at the time, the bespectacled engineer from Italy's Parma region was named the new company's chief engineer. "At that time," said the modest Dallara, "I was so young that I simply didn't know I needed much more experience to handle a job like that." He recruited two designers from Abarth, Oliviero Pedrazzi and Giorgio Bellini, and was joined by a Bolognese engineer a year younger, Paolo Stanzani, and a test driver/developer from New Zealand, Bob Wallace, also 25.

Enzo Ferrari was well aware of his drain of talent and designs in Lamborghini's direction. "I had several of

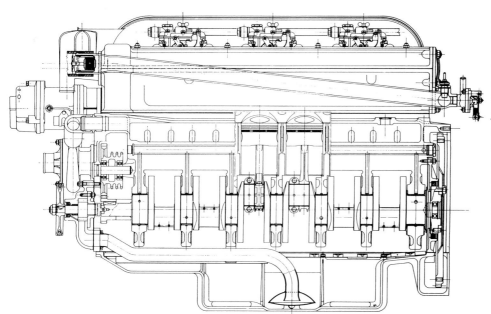

A longitudinal section of the Lamborghini V12 showed its wider front and rear main bearings and the upward-sloping duct that took warm water away from the engine, a thermostat at its left. Keyed to the nose of the crankshaft was a drive gear to the two half-speed gears which, in turn, drove the camshafts through roller chains.

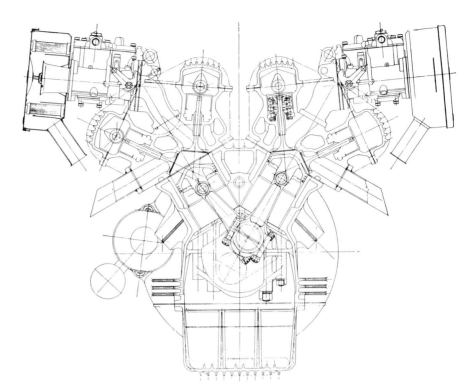

A classical 60° vee-twelve, the engine of Lamborghini's 350 GT had very large cup-type tappets enclosing two coil springs and clearance adjustment by a small cap between tappet and valve stem. Full encirclement of the exhaust-valve guides by water passages for optimum cooling was not achieved.

Ferrari's good technicians working for me," Ferruccio said of his early days. "From then on he didn't even greet me any more. With the others, like Maserati or Alfa Romeo, we never had problems. We always got along quite well, but not with Ferrari." The exoticism of Lamborghini's project had been a lure for Dallara, who hoped to see the new company move toward the racing he had come to enjoy at Maserati. In the meantime, however, his assignment was more prosaic: to make a sophisticated touring pussycat of Bizzarrini's wild beast.

First to go was the complex, heavy, costly and noisy dry-sump oiling system. The distributors were moved to the noses of the exhaust camshafts where they could be serviced more easily. Port sizes were reassessed, valve timing tamed and less-costly side-draft Weber carburettors fitted, resting above the exhaust-cam housings. Low-speed durability of the tappets was a problem; after testing of four different alloys case-hardened SAE 8640 steel gave good results on Dallara's test rig. Oil consumption also had to be controlled by reducing the losses down the valve stems from the overhead cams.

As completed for the Lamborghini 350GT the twelve gave an official 270bhp at 6,500rpm on a compression ratio of 9.5:1 but was known to deliver as much as 297bhp. The official figure pipped by ten horsepower the rating of Ferrari's 3.3-litre 275GTB of 1964. Torque was akin to that shown previously, 240lb-ft, at the more useful

speed of 4,000rpm. The 'full-race' V12 was still catalogued as the 350GTV, but none is known to have been delivered. Less clutch the engine weighed 513lb.

At the end of 1964 the first of the Touring-bodied Lamborghinis – a baker's dozen – were delivered. Their manufacture in the immaculate new plant that

Seen during assembly at Sant' Agata in 1967 was a Lamborghini crankcase showing its depth, fully enclosing the crankshaft, its side ribs for stiffening and its massive main-bearing caps.

New Zealander Bob Wallace, here preparing a 350GT for a test run, deserved much of the credit for the highly sophisticated running of this first production Lamborghini, which impressed experts in all parts of the world.

Lamborghini built at Sant' Agata Bolognese, between Modena and Bologna, was as meticulous as *Le Patron* had decreed. Machining the vee-twelve's block required 23 hours, the crankshaft 30 hours and each cylinder head an awesome 144 hours. The 20-hour test given each engine began with ten hours of being motored electrically. Four hours of low-speed running ensued, followed by

An air-conditioning compressor dominated the frontal view of the 3.9-litre Lamborghini twelve being prepared for installation in a 400GT. Its output was 320bhp at 6,500rpm.

increasing loads and speeds until full-power tests could safely be made.

Road testers found all this effort well worth the trouble. "The car was extremely quick and very, very quiet," said company tester Bob Wallace later, "and, for its day, was a very, very good-handling car." Experienced tester and racer Paul Frère agreed, saying of Lamborghini that "his 12-cylinder engine is one of the finest car units ever made. Rather surprisingly, the engine is almost inaudible at idling speed in spite of its 12 separate chokes and four camshafts, and remains so up to its recommended limit of 7,000rpm. The car as a whole is probably the quietest I have driven above 130mph."

Sampling a 350GT in Italy, Edward Eves recalled "the various moods of the motor, a hum at most speeds, low-pitched in town, high-pitched at the 120mph cruising speed, rising to a subdued, turbine-like whistle at maximum speed" – which he timed at 158.2mph on the *Autostrada del Sole*.

Also impressed was *Car and Driver*. "We were immediately astonished by the car's utter lack of temperament," it declared, and "it's so *smooth*, and so *quiet!* The car's engine and gearing are so good that you actually need only four of the five speeds, and any four will do. This no-sweat, American-car flexibility simply doesn't seem compatible with the car's genuine thoroughbred GT performance. It runs the quarter like one of our Super Cars, and cruises for days at 140. As Toad said in *Wind In the Willows*, 'A most unusual motor car!'" Its 0–60mph acceleration was in 6.4sec, standing quarter-mile in 15.2sec and top speed 156mph.

Geneva in 1966 saw the launch of a new version, modified to give two-plus-two seating, still on a 100.4in wheelbase. A bore increase to 82mm brought its capacity to 3,929cc, justifying a new designation of 400GT. With the higher compression ratio of 10.2:1 this produced 320bhp at 6,500rpm and 276lb-ft at 4,500rpm.

Opposite, top: *In 1966 Lamborghini created a sensation by mounting its V12 transversely in its mid-engined Miura sports car. This mirrored the transverse placement of twelves in Grand Prix cars practised in the early 1960s in prototype form by Maserati and in competition by Honda.*

Opposite, bottom: *In an extremely impressive and ingenious package, Gian Paolo Dallara led the engineering effort necessary to position the Miura's V12 transversely and to integrate with it a transaxle and final drive. With its engine behind the driver the Miura could have downdraft Weber carburettors to give it the direct gas flow that designer Giotto Bizzarrini had envisioned from the outset.*

Paolo Stanzani directed the engineering work necessary to mount Lamborghini's twelve longitudinally at the rear of its LP400 sports car, better known as the Countach. Although a 5.0-litre version was initially planned, the Countach was launched with a 4.0-litre engine.

Autocar found that this new model "seems to have the greatest range of smooth torque of any we have driven. From as low as 1,000rpm it will zoom sweetly to 7,000rpm, pulling hard all the way with no perceptible steps in the torque delivery. The engine is so smooth and so nearly silent it is hard to believe that 12 pistons and 24 valves are shuttling up and down just ahead of one's feet. Indeed, if the driver were told this was a 1975 electric car, or even a 1985 gas turbine car, he would find no reason to doubt the fact."

These were stunning expressions of praise for the work of Dallara and his team on the basis given them by Bizzarrini. Beyond question one of the greatest vee-twelves of all time had been created. Still as a 4.0-litre, the engine was uprated later in the 1960s to 350bhp to power the Islero S and to fit transversely in the mid-engined

Stanzani's ingenious conception for the Countach carried the engine's drive forward to an all-indirect gearbox, from which a pair of offset gears turned a shaft to the rear-mounted differential. This clever layout would lend itself to a four-wheel-drive version in the future.

Miura. The Miura S offered 370bhp and in 1971 the Miura SV was released, giving 385bhp at 7,850rpm and 286lb-ft of torque at 5,000rpm. For a semi-official 'racing' version of the Miura Bob Wallace extracted 430 horsepower.

In 1968 Gian Paolo Dallara left Lamborghini in search of the competition assignments that he craved. Thereafter Paolo Stanzani took charge at Lamborghini. His creation was the Countach, for which he readied a 4,971cc (85 x 73mm) version of the durable vee-twelve, mounted longitudinally and, like the Miura, integrating elements of the transmission with the engine. Although shown in 1971 this proved premature, and the Bertone-bodied LP400 Countach was launched in earnest in 1974 with 375bhp at 8,000rpm from an extensively revised 4.0-litre twelve, now with 42mm Webers.

In the wake of the Miura, the Countach "brought to the automotive world an original look that has characterised Lamborghini as a trendsetter of supercar style ever since," as *Autoweek* commented. "The engine combines the howl of a Ferrari V12 with the guttural rumble of a small-block Chevy," the magazine added.

With this stunning super-sports car Lamborghini

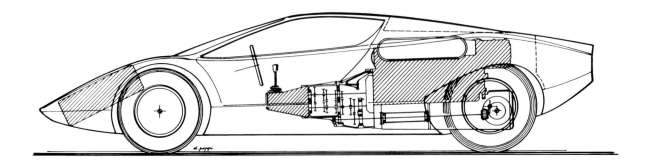

firmly cemented its place among the world's producers of exotic cars. "It took me a few years to accept that a man who set out to tap the Ferrari market could actually do so," wrote Michael Bowler in 1977, "but Lamborghini is now a well and truly established manufacturer of fine Italian cars."

Although its Countach was a sensational visiting card, the company was not so "well established" as many thought. Its cars were in demand, but Lamborghini laboured under such debts that it could scarcely afford to produce them. When the receivers seized control in 1978 they appointed as technical director none other than the 57-year-old Giulio Alfieri, author of many great Maserati products including its racing vee-twelves. Joining him at Sant' Agata was Ferrari and Maserati engineering veteran Vittorio Bellentani. Only after another financial collapse in 1980 and the takeover of Lamborghini by the Swiss Mimran brothers, Patrick and Jean-Claude, could forward progress be made.

The new team overhauled the Countach's vee-twelve, enlarging both bore and stroke (85.5 x 69mm) to give it 4,754cc. This justified calling it the LP500S at its 1982 introduction. With a 9.2:1 compression ratio and bigger 45DCOE Webers it generated 375bhp at 7,000rpm and, at 4,500rpm, 302lb-ft of torque. The modest speed of peak torque reflected Alfieri's effort to make the engine more civilised, but he realised that he "shouldn't go too far down that road" with one of the world's most electrifying sports cars. He was rightly proud of having reduced the Countach's specific fuel consumption by 20 per cent with its larger engine.

Lamborghini's twelves were eased into life over a two-day regime that began with six hours of electrically 'motoring' a non-running engine. Then it was fired up and for periods of 1½ to 2 hours run under load at speeds between 2,000 and 6,000rpm. Finally full-power runs verified that the unit was up to standard – or not. With an engine that "pulls superbly, with no hesitations or flat spots," *Autocar* measured 5.6sec to 60mph for the LP500S and a top speed of 164mph.

Next notch in the Countach's pistol grip was its four-valve version, introduced in 1985. Its bore was unchanged but its stroke was lengthened (85.5 x 75mm) to give the Quattrovalvole 5,167cc. This iteration was made "to meet the competition challenge without turbochargers", said Giulio Alfieri, who felt that the turbocharged engine "is only really good at the top end, and it sacrifices bottom end. You never use it properly for most of the time." The Quattrovalvole was seriously more potent with 455bhp at 7,000rpm and 369lb-ft of torque at 5,200rpm. A super-tuned version, built experimentally in 1987, produced 490bhp at 7,500rpm. This Evoluzione model was capable of 205mph.

With vee-twelve power, newcomer Lamborghini had successfully shouldered its way onto the world's supercar stage. By now, however, it needed a new engine. Alfieri and Bellentani would be just the men to provide it.

Chapter 12 Footnotes

[1] Most accounts of the Lincoln V12 state that it borrowed components from the Ford V8 and, when pressed for specifics, say that the connecting rods were common to the two engines. They definitely were not.

[2] This is a likely instance of the use in the Lincoln of Ford components.

[3] Another Lincoln-powered chassis is rumoured to have been completed as a cabriolet after the war.

[4] Although some of the V12 Atalantas later had Ford engines fitted, and one was given a Rolls-Royce tank engine (!), at least one Zephyr-powered car is thought to survive.

[5] The similarity of names was both coincidental and confusing.

[6] The coincidence of Jensen's H-Type and the Zephyr's Model H is just that.

[7] Their various problems led to the V12s being replaced by modern V8s in many Lincolns, especially the Continentals. Most notable of these swaps, from our standpoint, was the installation of an air-cooled Franklin V12 by a Wisconsin Continental convertible owner in 1954. With its 6.5 litres and more than 150bhp it was a bulging bonnetful that gave robust performance.

[8] Packard-history sources state that one pre-war V12 was installed by the factory in a special long-wheelbase 1951 Patrician at the request of the British-born wife of a Cleveland, Ohio "iron and coal mogul". Completed in 1953, the conversion was judged unsatisfactory and the twelve was soon replaced by an eight.

[9] At the request of Bill Mitchell and Chuck Jordan of Styling Staff, the author, then at GM, drew up a list of V12-powered cars of the past to help bolster the case for Cadillac's use of such an engine.

[10] In 1966 GM's Pontiac Motor Division introduced a single-overhead cam six, for its Tempest, with similar valve gear.

[11] Disappointing though the engine was to Cadillac's engineers, the Division's twelve continued to lurk in the background as a menace to its rivals. As late as 1988 GM officials were denying that it would be produced in response to BMW's newly launched V12.

[12] The author saw components for it being prepared at de Tomaso in 1970.

[13] Also quoted for this engine is 300bhp at 8,000rpm. Some reports credit it with dry-sump lubrication but the author's observations suggest otherwise.

[14] An oft-repeated story is that Bizzarrini scaled up the Lamborghini V12 from a 1½-litre Grand Prix engine he had designed on his own. Another and more outlandish assertion is that the engine was actually designed by Honda. The author judges both these stories to be smokescreens disseminated at the time to deflect attention from the engine's clear derivation from Ferrari's designs. With Enzo Ferrari in a position to make life very difficult for Bizzarrini and Lamborghini, both sought to avoid this to the extent possible by suggesting other origins for the engine's design.

[15] Other observers at Lamborghini credited it with 370bhp at 9,200rpm.

[16] In 1966–68 Bizzarrini would build half a dozen open sports-racers, his mid-engined P538, three of which carried Lamborghini Miura power trains.

CAT, ROUNDEL AND STAR

While a new Italian producer of spectacular sports cars was evolving an ultra-refined example of the genre, a British car maker known for its smooth, suave saloons was creating a new vee twelve to tear up the world's sports-car tracks. This was none other than Jaguar, whose reputation since the war had been founded on its magnificent XK twin-cam six-cylinder engine. Under chief engineer William Heynes this was designed by Claude W.L. Baily and developed by W.T.F. 'Wally' Hassan to meet the express request of Jaguar chief Sir William Lyons, who wanted an engine that was glamorous as well as powerful, "something like the old racing Peugeots and Sunbeams".

Surprisingly soon after their six was introduced in the sensational XK120 in 1949, Jaguar's engineers were thinking about doubling the number of cylinders. As early as 1951 one of its designers, Tom Jones, sketched a potential Jaguar vee-twelve. The job was next tackled in 1954 by Claude Baily, who based his ideas on a doubling-up of the XK six. Since the latter was made in versions of 2½ to 3½ litres, the twelves he laid out could have had from 5 to 7 litres. Such an engine could have challenged Ferrari's 375Plus, the 1954 Le Mans winner, but at the end of 1956 Sir William decreed a withdrawal from factory involvement in racing and the project was shelved.

Baily pulled out his drawings again in the early 1960s when his boss, Bill Heynes, thought it might be safe to think about Le Mans again. As well in 1961 Jaguar had introduced a big new production car, works-coded as the XJ5 and dubbed the Mark X, the motivation of whose two tonnes would benefit from additional power. A project to design and build a twelve was put in hand under works

code XJ6,[1] with the idea that the engine could also be useful for motor racing. By August of 1964 the first three of eight such V12s made were installed in Mark X saloons and propelling them at unaccustomed velocities.

Although at a glance the XJ6 looked like two six-cylinder heads on a common block, this was deceptive. Accounting for the resemblance was the twelve's use of the six's inverted-cup valve gear and cam-cover configuration, though the new engine had a symmetrical valve inclination at a 60° included angle instead of the six's 70°. In accord with this its combustion chamber was shallower, promising more efficient combustion. The twelve's capacity was 4,994cc with dimensions of 87 x 70mm, much more oversquare than the 83 x 76.5mm of the Jaguar 2.4 saloon with cylinders of similar size. Importantly its displacement suited it to the FIA's 5-litre sports-prototype racing category.

Instead of the iron of the six's block the twelve's was cast of LM8 aluminium alloy with slip-fitted dry cylinder liners of iron, flanged at the top for retention by the heads. The left bank of the 60° vee engine was offset forward by 19.1mm. Pistons were gently domed with flats for valve clearance, full-skirted and carrying three rings. Forged En 16 steel connecting rods had I-section shanks and big ends riding on generous 55.5mm journals. Main bearings were substantial as well at

Opposite: *Inspired by a casual conversation between two BMW executives, the Munich company produced its M33 prototype vee-twelve in 1974. It was powerful – so much so, in fact, that it was in advance of BMW's ability to provide a car for it.*

As prepared for installation in the Jaguar Mark X with its six side-draft SU carburettors, Jaguar's experimental 'XJ6' vee-twelve was a formidable piece of equipment. Its sump was cast aluminium and at each side its exhaust manifolds consisted of a pair of three-cylinder collectors.

A cross-section of the 'XJ6' Jaguar V12 showed its original inlet ports, on the left bank, and the straighter ports as revised for the racing engine on the right. Visible as well are its dry cylinder liners inserted in the aluminium block and held in place by flanges at their tops.

76.2mm. Seven in number, they were attached by robust four-bolt caps to a block cut off at the crankshaft centreline. Eight counterweights were forged integrally with the steel crankshaft.

A finned cast-aluminium pan enclosed the bottom of the wet-sump road version of the XJ6. At the nose of its crankshaft a roller chain downward drove the oil pump and another roller chain went upward to sprockets which drove, in turn, an upper chain to the twin cams of each head. The lower chain's idler sprocket turned a jackshaft in the central vee, from which a pair of near-vertical six-cylinder distributors was driven by skew gears. Space was available there because the inlet ports were downdraft, between the cams on each head. This was chosen as the only layout that would allow the engine to fit into its planned applications. For the Mark X installation the six ports in each head were fed by individual twin-cylinder manifolds from horizontal SU carburettors, six in all.

Jaguar never released power figures for the road version of its V12, but it must have produced in the ballpark of 300 horsepower at some 6,000rpm. All was not well, however. The two-stage chain drive was both unreliable and noisier than desired. The twin distributors resisted precise synchronisation. These annoyances would be dealt with later, but in the meantime the Jaguar engineers concentrated on the XJ6's competition version with the objective of a Le Mans entry in 1965.

Their strength was augmented in 1964 with the return of Wally Hassan through the Jaguar Group's acquisition of Coventry Climax, for whom he was creating successful Formula 1 engines. Hassan in turn recruited Harry Mundy, former BRM engineer and designer of the Lotus-Ford twin-cam head. As Hassan said, "This completed a really formidable team of engineers at Browns Lane."

To overcome the cam-drive failings they gave the racing version an even more raucous drive by replacing the upper chains with sets of spur gears. The twin distributors were used initially, and then replaced by a single Lucas Opus 12-cylinder ignition distributor adjacent to a Lucas injection pump, both in the central vee. Under the block was a new dry sump, scavenged by two gear-driven oil pumps with a vane-type pump providing the pressure.

The special crankshaft was of En 40 steel, suitable for nitriding of its bearing surfaces for added hardness. Main-bearing caps in the racing engine were of forged steel. As in the road-car version, the single water pump at the front of XJ6's block was vee-belt-driven. Special mounts attached to the block allowed it to serve as the structure at the rear of a mid-engined car.

Nimonic 80 steel valves in the racing V12 measured 47.6mm for the inlets, 34.9mm for the exhausts. Angled at first at 60° to the inlet-valve stems, the better to suit the outboard carburettors, the inlet ports weren't ideal for power production. In this trim the twelve delivered 446bhp at 7,250rpm. Power was better with a 48° angle and finally the head casting was changed – raising the cams by a quarter-inch – to reduce the angle between stem and port to 41°. With matching ram pipes, controlled by butterfly throttles, and a 10.4:1 compression ratio, this gave the engine's best output of 502bhp at 7,600rpm with 386lb-ft of torque at 6,300rpm.

Used to seeing 130bhp per litre from his Grand Prix engines, Wally Hassan was unimpressed by 100bhp per litre. He and Mundy concluded that, at least in this application, the downdraft inlet port was inferior to side porting. "Not only was there a lack of top-end power," he wrote, "there was also a distinct lack of low-speed and mid-range torque. An engine lacking both top-end power and mid-range torque was not my idea of a potentially successful racing unit. In a way it reminded me of the elegant engine my old boss, W.O. Bentley, designed for Lagonda; his V12 looked good and sounded splendid, but it suffered the same characteristics as this Jaguar, namely a lack of low-down power."

In parallel with work on the engine a chassis to house it was created. Its aluminium monocoque was the work of talented South African Derrick White. In mid-1965 White left to join Cooper, there to design a chassis to carry the 2½-litre Maserati V12. The special projects team for the XJ13, as it was named, was led by famed

aerodynamicist Malcolm Sayer, reporting to Bill Heynes. With White's departure a rising Jaguar apprentice, Mike Kimberley, took charge of the XJ13 project. The twelve drove through a twin-plate clutch and ZF five-speed transmission to power a superbly streamlined open sports-racer on a 96in wheelbase.

In its racing version the XJ6 twelve first ran on the dynamometer on 11 August 1964. Le Mans 1965 slipped by; late in 1965 engine and car were married. No timetable was pressing for the car's completion, so not until mid-summer of 1966 was it considered ready to run. Its fate was sealed in July when Sir William Lyons announced that Jaguar was to merge with BMC (British Motor Corporation), whose corporate policy was anti-racing. Although operating autonomously at the time, and not obliged to follow BMC's policy, Lyons fell into line. Not destined to be a works racer, the XJ13 was parked in a corner of the experimental shop.

Finally Bill Heynes decided that the car should at least be driven, so he and Jaguar tester Norman Dewis conspired to take it to Britain's motor-industry test grounds, MIRA, for trials on its 2.9-mile banked track in March 1967. Dewis took the wheel for tests in which lap speeds of up to 139mph were reached. Mike Kimberley supervised the tests, which continued in July on the road course and banking.

Kimberley was sitting next to driver David Hobbs when he clocked the fastest official lap of MIRA at 161.6mph, which put the XJ13 in *The Guinness Book of*

There was room in the central vee of the dry-sumped racing version of the 'XJ6' for the distributor serving its Lucas fuel injection. With its hemispherical two-valve chambers the engine's best output was 502bhp at 7,600rpm.

Installed in Jaguar's XJ13, its four-cam vee-twelve lapped Britain's MIRA high-speed backed track at better than 160mph, driven by racing driver David Hobbs. Its usual tester was the experienced Norman Dewis.

In 1966 Jaguar began serious work on a production V12 engine under the direction of Wally Hassan, centre, and chief designer Harry Mundy, right. Trevor Crisp, left, was responsible for achieving the new engine's emissions performance – no small task at the time.

Records. The maximum lateral g that it generated on the skid pad was 1.09. Also driven at Silverstone by Richard Attwood, the sleek mid-engined Jaguar was respectably quick but its configuration crucially ruled out the use of the new wider tyres that were revolutionising racing in the 1960s. This time it was parked definitively.[2]

Although racing would not (yet) be a venue for a Jaguar V12, the itch to have a new twelve-cylinder engine for Jaguar's road cars was being scratched in the meantime. Work accelerated at the beginning of 1966 when Wally Hassan finally left Coventry Climax to become a full-time Jaguar man.[3] "Jaguar policy at the time," he wrote, "envisaged two types of engine being evolved from one basic design – hopefully a high-powered sports-car version with hemispherical combustion chambers and twin-cam cylinder heads, and a second version intended to be much cheaper to manufacture, saving money, weight and complication by having single-cam cylinder

heads." The twin-cam version was especially dear to the hearts of senior engineers Bill Heynes and Claude Baily, said Hassan: "Somehow, a twin-cam head seemed to be an integral part of Jaguar's image, and they thought the vee-twelve should retain this if at all possible."

To cope with this panorama of requirements Wally Hassan and Harry Mundy built and ran a plethora of cylinder-head designs on three fuel-injected single-cylinder engines. Hassan joked that a spy in their engine shops might have concluded that Jaguar was preparing to launch a range of motorcycles! Testing included several types of hemispherical heads and four different versions of flat heads with vertical valves and chambers in the piston crown – the Heron-type head that was much in vogue in late 1966 when serious work on the final engine, coded XJ25 began. A hint that the Heron-chamber concept was promising was given by a vee-eight that Hassan's team at Coventry Climax had developed, the 2½-litre CFA that never saw production. Its performance was so convincing that classic wedge-type chambers were never considered during the twelve's genesis.

The test heads proved that air-flow characteristics with the vertical inlet valve improved the smaller the angle was between the valve stem and the port centreline. The best performance was achieved with a 35° angle, but to achieve a compact head design the final engine design had ports at 45° to its valve stems, sloping toward the centre of the engine's vee.

Thus the flat head with a bowl-in-piston chamber became the choice for the production Jaguar V12 – to the astonishment of a leading British engine designer. "I can remember arguing like hell with Harry Mundy about this," said Cosworth's Keith Duckworth, who had used the concept for his first engine, the single-cam SCA, then abandoned it to become one of the successful modern revivers of four-valve cylinder heads. "I was staggered when he used a Heron head on the Jaguar V12."

A major consideration during the XJ25's design was meeting the new emissions rules in America; these were a moving target during the engine's gestation. This imperative also gave good grounds for the use of a bowl-in-piston chamber. With vertical in-line valves a challenge is getting adequate valve sizes, which the designers helped with their over-square dimensions and addressed further by increasing the bore to 90mm which gave 5,344cc with the 70mm stroke.

Valve sizes were 41.3mm for inlets and 34.6mm for exhausts. They were closed by twin coil springs – the same as in the 2.8-litre Jaguar six – and opened by carryover chilled cast-iron cup-type tappets from the six, with clearance-adjusting 'biscuits' between stem and tappet. The valve gear was bounce-free to 7,400rpm.

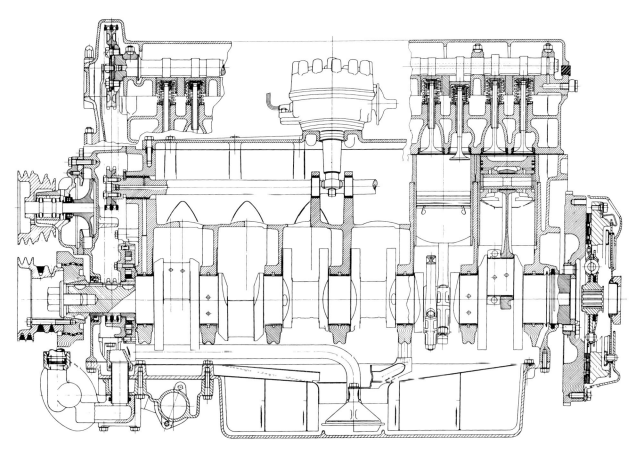

The rearmost cylinder, at right, of Jaguar's XJ25 V12 showed its bowl-in-piston Heron-type combustion chamber. Seating in the flat cylinder head, vertical valves were opened through cup-type tappets with clearance adjustment by caps between the valve and the tappet body.

Camshafts and tappets turned and slid directly in a bolted-on aluminium tappet block, which simplified the head castings. The designers kept a system they knew well, a duplex timing chain, to drive the cams at a time when cogged-rubber belts were coming into fashion. A single Morse chain did the job, though it had to be just over 5½ft long. Flanking it were damper pads and, on the slack right-hand side, a long Nylon-faced tensioner in which an infinite ratchet prevented loosening of the chain when any reverse rotation occurred, as could happen when the timing was being checked. This configuration was the end result of a lengthy development effort to eliminate all chain resonances.

Outboard of the timing chain and its die-cast-aluminium cover at the front of the XJ25 twelve was a Holset rubber-in-shear vibration damper and pulleys to four vee-belts for the front-mounted accessories, including the single water pump. Also keyed to the crankshaft, just behind the chain, was a splined sleeve driving a concentric crescent-type oil pump. Then novel, this was the type of pump usually found in automatic transmissions.[4] It neatly exploited space within the forward offset of the left-hand cylinder bank, the same offset as in the twelve's racing forebear. A water/oil heat exchanger bolted to the wet-sump's underside cooled

the oil that was bypassed by the pressure system's relief valve. This left the sump pickup free to deal solely with the oil actually being used by the engine.

Forged of manganese-molybdenum-alloy steel, the XJ25's crankshaft had integral counterweights on its four most central webs and on the pairs of webs at the front and back. Retained by four-bolt iron caps, its seven main bearings remained the same 76.2mm as the racing twelve. The big-end journals were increased in diameter to 58.4mm in sympathy with the bore's enlargement from 87 to 90mm. All the main journals were the same width save the centre and rearmost bearings, which were wider to take higher centrifugal forces at those points. Thanks to the wider centre bearing the cylinder-centre distance at the middle of the block, 107.9mm, was larger than the 105.3mm spacing of the rest. The Jaguar's bottom-end bearings were judged reliable to 8,500rpm.

Baily, Hassan and Mundy made two major changes in the aluminium cylinder block from the racing version of

A cylinder liner, crankshaft, connecting rods and pistons were among the components of the new Jaguar vee-twelve set out for display at its 1971 launch. As Wally Hassan remarked, the twelve was almost certainly Britain's most complex production engine at the time and indeed one of the most intricate in the world.

In an extremely deep crankcase of aluminium, designed for future pressure die-casting, the Jaguar twelve had iron main-bearing caps, each retained by four studs.

their twelve. One was to extend the sides of the block downward some 100mm from the crank centreline to give better sealing, improve engine mounting and attachment to the transmission, and better accommodate the lubrication system. The other was to make it of open-top-deck design – much like Maserati practice – with the aim of making it adaptable to pressure die-casting in the future. Harry Mundy, who would have preferred a more rugged closed-deck block, was overruled.

Only one issue remained: aluminium blocks had a reputation for noisiness, something that could be tolerated in no Jaguar. To resolve this they cast an iron block, using the aluminium patterns. "It proved to be no quieter," smiled Wally Hassan, "though the front of the car went down rather farther." Complete with liners, bearing caps and front cover the aluminium block weighed 161lb.

Measuring 151.3mm from centre to centre, the connecting rods were forged of the same EN 16T steel as the crankshaft. Jaguar tradition was followed by drilling the I-section shank to lubricate the bronze-bushed small end, a measure that had help make its engines quieter in the past. Gudgeon-pin lubrication was aided by internal passages in the piston from its oil-control ring. Two compression rings encircled the Hepworth & Grandage die-cast aluminium pistons with their cutaway skirts to clear the crankshaft's webs.

A shallow circular recess in the piston crown was the XJ25's combustion chamber, plus a narrow gas-squishing ring around the periphery. "The shallower we made the chamber," said Harry Mundy, "the better it was. We could almost have gone to a flat chamber but we had to leave metal in the piston to hold the rings and gudgeon pin." Although development began with a 10.6:1 compression ratio this was progressively reduced to 10.0:1 and finally to 9.0:1 at launch in the interest of lower exhaust emissions. Head sealing was by sandwich-type Cooper's gaskets, helped by six studs spaced around each cylinder, a total of 26 per bank.

To their great disappointment the Browns Lane engineers were unable to introduce their XJ25 with the Brico fuel injection to which they'd devoted immense development time and effort. At the eleventh hour Brico decided it didn't want to pursue that business, leaving Jaguar in the lurch. They had to fall back on the constant-vacuum Zenith Stromberg 175CDSE horizontal carburettor, the only British unit that was able to meet American emissions requirements.

Four carburettors were needed, each feeding a plenum chamber which in turn debouched on ram pipes to a trio of cylinders. Effective ram-pipe lengths in the

water-warmed manifold were 12in to enhance torque between 2,500 and 4,500rpm. As in the racing engine a jackshaft in the central vee drove the ignition distributor, part of a contactless 12-cylinder Lucas Opus Mark 2 system. Its capacity of 800 sparks per second handily exceeded the engine's 600-spark requirement.

Crunch time for the single-cam concept came toward the end of the 1960s when early engines of both types were available for evaluation in cars. The twin-cam version, favoured for image reasons by Heynes and Baily, was a more advanced and lighter design than the racing engine. "Sir William took a neutral – and in my view absolutely correct – view about this," said Wally Hassan, adding that an important aspect would be that "its appearance would maintain an aura of the Jaguar image he had spent so many years building up."

Supplied with detailed reports on both engines, Lyons drove the prototypes. "At a technical board meeting a vote was taken," Hassan said, "and the die was cast in favour of the single-cam type of cylinder heads for production cars."

In spite of this decision, twin-cam versions of the twelve did not go silently into that dark night. Exploiting the Coventry Climax expertise of the Hassan-Mundy team, these had four valves per cylinder and relatively narrow valve vee-angles that resulted from another wave of single-cylinder tests – also including three-valve

An exploded view of the Jaguar XJ25 showed it with the Zenith-Stromberg carburettors that had to be fitted at the eleventh hour when Brico elected not to proceed with its fuel injection. The 5.3-litre Jaguar twelve had an intricate and ingenious system of lubrication and cooling.

variants – in August of 1970. A modestly tuned 48-valve twelve gave 400bhp while a racier version with 10.5:1 compression produced 627bhp "and there was undoubtedly more to come," said a Jaguar engineer. Experience with this engine led to the 3.6-litre 24-valve AJ6 in-line six introduced in the XJ-S in 1983.

In its early configuration and high compression ratio the single-overhead-cam XJ25 developed as much as 380 horsepower. Its gross output at launch in 1971 was constrained to 314bhp at 6,200rpm with 349lb-ft of torque at 3,800rpm. Net, on the DIN standard, the 680lb twelve produced 272bhp at 5,850rpm and 304lb-ft at 3,600rpm. Like other luxury-car V12s the engine's rev range was constrained by the need for compatibility with available automatic transmissions. As initially offered in the Series Three E-Type Jaguar in March 1971 it was paired either with a four-speed manual transmission or a Borg-Warner automatic.

In fact the E-Type had not been the engineers' choice for their engine's launch, but was chosen over their heads, as it were, to give the engine a cautious low-volume introduction.[5] A year later, in June of 1972, it

To give Jaguar's new twelve a gentle introduction to production and hence to the public, it was launched in the Series Three E-Type sports car in March of 1971. It was available with either manual transmission or automatic.

made its saloon appearance in the Jaguar XJ12 and – in a neat historical echo – in its sister, the Daimler Double-Six.

Jaguar's twelve had been slow to market. The first hope had been to have it ready for the XJ6 launch in 1968. At that introduction the press was told to expect new

Developed in the USA, a racing version of the Series Three E-Type was built to compete in the B Production Championship of the Sports Car Club of America. Driven by Bob Tullius, it won the category in 1975.

engines "within two years." It took a year and a half longer than that. In mitigation Wally Hassan pointed out that "at that time it was probably the most complex quantity-production engine to be built in Britain, and was very costly in many ways." That applied to its tooling, which was laid down with transfer lines that could produce 1,000 sets of parts per two-shift week, some 50,000 per year. Facing a total tooling bill of £3million, Sir William asked that the payments be stretched out – another factor delaying production's Job One.

One reason for the costly investment in inflexible tooling for the V12 was that Jaguar hoped to make V8 engines on the same transfer lines as a replacement for the venerable six in its saloons. A number of such eights were made and run in vehicles. "It was a very satisfying engine and was obviously very competitive because it was giving 200bhp ," said a Jaguar engineer. Vibration was mastered, either with engine mounts or secondary balance shafts, but measured against Jaguar's demanding standards its 60° vee with a single-plane crankshaft gave uneven firing intervals which sounded more like a four than an eight. Such an engine was never produced by Jaguar.

Though lively enough with 0–60mph acceleration in 6.4sec and a 146-mph top speed, the vee-twelve Series Three E-Type was short-lived. Production was halted in September 1974. It went out with a bang, winning the SCCA's B Production championship in 1975. Funded by the American Jaguar importer, the racing car was developed entirely in the USA by Group 44 and driven by its chief, Bob Tullius. Externally looking remarkably

standard, Group 44's carburetted engine developed a stimulating 460bhp at 7,000rpm.

On road rather than track, Jaguar's twelve delivered all that could be asked of it. In the E-Type the author found it "still pure essence of Jaguar, claws and all. Unlike the Italian twelves, there's nothing head-turning about its exhaust note. This is a *Jaguar* twelve, smooth, suave and muted like the six but higher-pitched, even more refined. Its mechanical silence is astonishing for a machine with 24 mechanical tappets. Opening the four throttles wide produces some inlet resonance and the whirr of small parts moving fast as the V12 revs up toward its 6,500rpm red-line."

In the XJ12 saloon the XJ25 engine gave sports-car performance with 0–60mph acceleration in 7.7sec – and that in the American version with 8.0:1 compression ratio and automatic transmission. Top speed was just on 140mph. "Moving gently away from rest one hears a slightly busy hum giving away the multiplicity of cylinders," thought *Road & Track*, "but as speed builds this fades into a muted induction sound that could be mistaken for that of a six."

"The XJ12 is the quietest idling car we have yet found in sound-level testing," said *Car and Driver*. "The vibration transmitted to the car is almost below human consciousness. If you tell your unknowing neighbour that the Jaguar XJ12 is turbine-powered, he'll have no reason to doubt your word." *Motor* called it "the only car we know in which the radio can be set at 30mph and doesn't need adjusting right up to 120mph."

The sole fly in the ointment was the big twelve's

Working within the rules established by the SCCA for production sports cars, the Jaguar V12s built to compete in 1975 in America developed as much as 460bhp in spite of their near-standard appearance. The standard sump was replaced by a bespoke unit for competition.

indifferent fuel economy – at its best 10mpg in the USA and 12 in Britain – just in time for the Yom Kippur War and the first Energy Crisis. In 1975 the introduction of fuel injection brought a 17 per cent reduction in fuel consumption with a bolstering of engine performance. Based on Bendix patents, the electronic inlet-port injection was further developed by Bosch and then adapted to the V12 by Lucas and Jaguar. Rated at 285bhp

Jaguar's vee-twelve was finally fuel-injected in 1975. With electronic injectors mounted in its inlet manifolds, as visible at the left, an improvement of 17 per cent in fuel economy was achieved. Also shown is the manner in which the distributor was driven by a jackshaft down the centre of the vee.

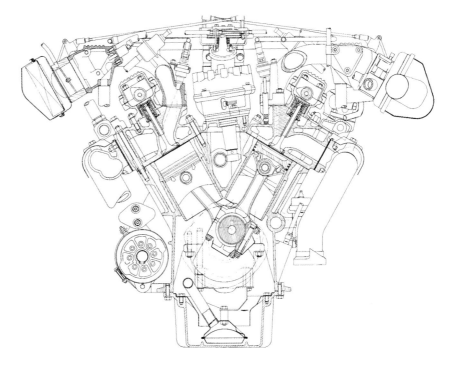

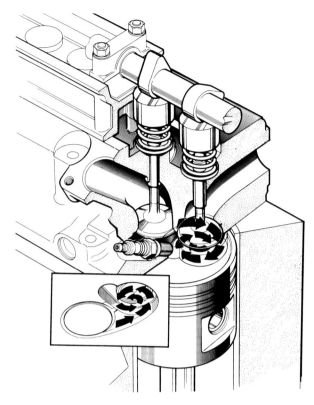

Concentrating the combustion-chamber volume beneath the exhaust valve, where intense swirl was generated during the compression stroke, Michael May's 'Fireball' cylinder head allowed the use of very high compression ratios to improve fuel economy while maintaining good emissions performance. It was adopted for Jaguar's engine in 1981, bringing with it the designation 'HE' for 'High Efficiency'.

Externally the 1981 HE version of Jaguar's twelve looked little different from its predecessors. Adoption of the May 'Fireball' chamber, however, helped secure the engine's long lifetime. It continued to be offered until 1997.

at 5,750rpm, this was the launch engine for the two-plus-two XJ-S in 1975.

Concerns about fuel consumption in the 1970s put paid to any hopes of exploiting another creation of the Jaguar engineers. The V12's crankcase dimensions accommodated a longer stroke, which they exploited to build a 6.4-litre version of their twelve.[6] When these went into test cars their performance bordered on the sensational. At only 1,500rpm the bigger twelve was already delivering 400lb-ft of torque, which endowed the Jaguar saloon with effortless 'oomph'. It easily broke Jaguar's experimental five-speed manual transmission, a Harry Mundy design which regrettably was never released to production.

Instead of going bigger, Jaguar chose new technology to help its twelve make reasonable use of its automated transfer lines. This came in the form of a novel combustion chamber invented by a visionary Swiss engineer, Michael May. A turbocharging pioneer, May was spurred by the Energy Crisis to develop a new type of lean-burn chamber that could consume less fuel at higher compression ratios. In February 1976 Harry Mundy's team prepared a single-cylinder test engine to evaluate May's concept.[7] Results were good enough that a twelve-cylinder version was drawn up by the end of the year.

Fortuitously May's concept, with its chamber concentrated under the exhaust valve where its fresh charge could receive a powerful compression swirl, was eminently adaptable to the Jaguar twelve's vertical valves and flat head. Dubbed the 'Fireball' chamber, it was introduced in 1981 in the twelves of both the XJ12 and the XJ-S, both getting an 'HE' suffix. With the extremely high compression ratio of 12.5:1 it gave 295bhp at 5,500rpm coupled with substantially improved fuel economy. Its introduction was a well-earned *vale* for Harry Mundy, who retired from Jaguar in March 1980. Without his half-million-pound HE update the vee-twelve wouldn't have survived well into the 1990s.

That survival was underpinned by actions taken on the watch of Ford, which acquired Jaguar Cars in November 1989. One was to consummate the marriage of the V12 with the new saloon, the XJ6, which was introduced in 1986 with an in-line six. When the new model gestated as project XJ40 during Jaguar's ownership by British Leyland, the engineers under Bob Knight deliberately made its engine bay too narrow to take the Rover V8 that Leyland threatened to foist upon them. With the car's front damper struts relocated to squeeze in the vee-twelve, the first such installation was made late in 1987.

Development of the new model for production as project XJ81 continued under Ford's aegis. Early tests were not confidence-inspiring, however. Although

Each individual inlet ram pipe had its own butterfly throttle in the racing version of Jaguar's V12 prepared by Ralph Broad's Broadspeed company to compete in the European Touring Car Championship in 1976. The XJ12 coupé's bonnet was made to hinge forwards.

Power as high as 570bhp was extracted from the twelve to help Group 44 win Trans-Am racing titles in the United States in 1977 and '78. The low-lined XJ-S coupé proved a sound develoment basis for racing campaigns both in America and in Europe.

Jaguar's twelve was still nominally rated at 285 horsepower, intensifying emissions demands during the 1980s had emasculated its real output to little better than 260. "We took some prototypes to Nardo in Italy for tests on their high-speed circular track," said Jaguar engineer David King. "One of them was passed on the banking by a Ford Fiesta Turbo!" In charge of Jaguar was a no-nonsense executive, former Ford of Europe production chief Bill Hayden. "This isn't good enough," said Hayden. "What can we do?"

The answer was to ask the help of Tom Walkinshaw's TWR Engineering. For the XJR-S, introduced in 1989 as a Jaguar Sport joint venture with Browns Lane, TWR had already stretched the twelve to six litres. It achieved this by lengthening the stroke to expand displacement to 5,993cc (90 x 78.5mm). The XJR-S's engine was super-tuned to give 333bhp at 5,250rpm and 365lb-ft at 3,650rpm on a compression ratio of 11.2:1.

With compression lowered fractionally to 11.1:1, the twelve as readied for the XJ81 produced 313bhp at 5,400rpm and 341lb-ft at 3,750rpm. "It transformed the car," David King recalled. The new XJ12 was launched early in 1993 and remained available into 1997. With a top speed of 153mph it had little to fear from Fiestas of any description. Its engine bay was also the cleanest of all Jaguar's V12 installations.

Reflecting the expertise of its creators, the Jaguar twelve's racing exploits bordered on the legendary. Its first outing in the 1976 European Touring Car Championship misfired, the coupé version of the XJ12

suffering from oil surging and poor braking. One second-place finish was a poor reward for six pole positions in eight races. The XJ-S proved a better basis, Group 44's winning SCCA Trans-Am titles in America in 1977 and 1978 with 570bhp at 8,000rpm in the latter year from the Weber-carburetted twelve. XJ-Ss from Tom Walkinshaw's stable won the European Touring Car Championship in 1984 in the third year of trying.

Exotic mid-engined sports-racing cars, successors to the XJ13, were also Jaguar-powered. Lee Dykstra built the

Virginia-based Group 44 built special mid-engined sports-racing cars around Jaguar's V12 to compete in the IMSA GTP category from 1984 to '87. In addition to their efforts in North America they raced, as here, in the 24 Hours of Le Mans.

Designed by Tony Southgate, the V12-powered Jaguar XJR-8 of 1987 won the team championship in international Group C racing. In addition, the team's drivers took the first four places in the championship and in 1988 the TWR-run Jaguar team won Le Mans as well.

chassis for Group 44's cars, which used the twelve as part of their structure. They competed in IMSA's GTP category from 1984 to 1987 with only modest success, although from 1986 they were getting 700bhp at 7,000rpm on a compression ratio of 12.8:1 from 6,496cc (94 x 78mm).

Greater success was enjoyed by Tony Southgate's chassis designs for the factory-backed Walkinshaw TWR team, which co-opted the 'XJR' terminology introduced by Group 44. Its XJR-6 of 1986 ran with engines the same size as Group 44's 6.5-litre units, with Zytek engine management to compete under Group C's fuel-consumption rules. Setting up his own engine-development operation, managed by Allan Scott with technical backup by Charles Bamber, Tom Walkinshaw engaged Melling Consultancy Design of Lancashire's Al Melling to design the four-valve twin-cam heads that seemed likely to be needed to develop competitive power.

With the four-valve heads giving development problems, Walkinshaw turned for help to Cosworth, whose Geoff Goddard had helped pump up the power of TWR's XJ-S coupés. Keeping in mind the emphasis on fuel economy imposed by Group C rules, Goddard suggested reworking the single-cam two-valve heads to get the desired result. His attentions to cams, ports, chambers and injection were so successful that they brought the twelve's racing power up from the mid-500s to more than 700bhp for the first time.

The working figure for the 1986 season was 700bhp at 7,000rpm with a flat torque curve from 3,200 to 6,500rpm which, in Goddard's words, "allowed the drivers to stay in high gear and drive around on a wall of torque." This was both fuel-saving and a blessing for the hard-pressed transaxles. Special crankshafts forged of EN40B steel with TWR's own tooling had 53.3mm big-end journals instead of the standard 58.4mm for lighter con-rod weight and reduced friction losses. Cosworth was the source for such vital components as pistons, connecting rods, valve-train parts and the oil-pump assemblies.[8]

TWR's Jaguar's twelve evolved into the 6,995cc (94 x 84mm) XJR-8 which swept the Group C World Championship in 1987. Although with the added half-litre the engine's power was up only slightly to 720bhp, the 7.0-litre twelve was tuned to produce a robust increase in torque at 5,250rpm from 570 to 605lb-ft. As the XJR-9 in 1988, with 745bhp at 7,250rpm, it repeated as World Champion and achieved a long-sought goal for Jaguar: another victory at Le Mans. This was repeated in 1990 by the V12-powered XJR-12 with a one–two finish in the French classic. Into the 21st century Lister's Storm continued to use the Jaguar V12 as the motive force for its sports-racing cars.

TWR used Zytek fuel injection for the 5,993cc Jaguar twelves it fitted to its 1990 XJR-15, a road-car evolution of its 1988 XJR-9. Although conceived for the road, with a 450bhp 5,993cc engine, it was used chiefly for a one-make racing series in 1991. Four fortunate Japanese were the purchasers of final 7-litre versions of the handsome XJR-15, styled by Peter Stevens.

Walkinshaw's XJR-15 was a not-uncontroversial contemporary of Jaguar's own mid-engined supercar, the XJ220, which was revealed at the 1988 British Motor Show with a 6,222cc (92 x 78mm) version of the twelve. The engine in the prototype had twin-cam four-valve cylinder heads of Jaguar's own design. When tested at TWR, however, the new heads failed to deliver the power that the XJ220 needed. Called up for road-car duty were the four-valve heads that TWR had commissioned from independent consultant Al Melling.

Designing new cylinder heads and cam drives to suit the Jaguar block, Melling angled his pairs of valves from the vertical at 14° for the inlets, 16° for the exhausts. He found that the V12's cylinder spacing constrained his ability to fit in four valves per cylinder, with bucket-type tappets, and the cam bearings as well. The latter had to be in individual carriers bolted between the pairs of cam lobes. He used a three-chain camshaft drive not unlike that of the road version of the 1964 four-cam vee-twelve, with one duplex chain from the crankshaft driving two more at the heads. Camshaft sprockets of only 21 teeth minimised the engine's high-level bulk.

Producing more than 500bhp at 7,000rpm in road-car tune, this 6.2-litre engine was intended to be the motivation for the series-production XJ220. Cosworth was assigned the casting of the heads and 100 sets were laid down, but ran into design-related problems that resulted in excessive scrappage. Melling and Walkinshaw fell out over this, with the upshot that the XJ220 was produced in co-operation with TWR with a turbocharged vee-six in place of the magisterial vee-twelve.[9]

Of the six racing versions of these engines made, two were installed in XJR-9 chassis to assess their suitability for Group C racing. Power was not a problem; in racing trim the 48-valve twelve initially produced 800bhp and ultimately 850bhp at 7,000rpm. One was entered for John Watson and Davy Jones at Brands Hatch on 24 July 1988. Virtually untested beforehand, it qualified eighth fastest. Reservations concerned the high placement of the extra 55lb of the four-cam engine atop a twelve that already had a higher centre of gravity than any of its rivals. In the 1,000km race, however, the Watson/Jones Jaguar sat as high as second in the early going before retiring with a sheared ignition rotor. The engine wasn't raced again.

In addition to its Browns Lane duties the versatile Jaguar vee-twelve also powered numerous British one-off specials and limited-production cars. Entrepreneur John Parradine fitted it to his Pegasus V12 of the late 1980s. Designer William Towns used vee-twelve Jaguars as the basis of two of his projects, the Guyson V12 of 1974 and a planned revival of the Railton at the end of the 1990s.

Arthur Wolstenholme fitted twelves to his cycle-winged Ronart W152 and, in 2005, to cars reviving the famed Vanwall racing-car name. Specialists continue to modify and adapt the Jaguar; in 2003 one such, Lynx Engineering, successfully expanded it to 7.3 litres for an engine it quoted as producing 660bhp at only 5,700rpm and 640lb-ft at 4,300rpm.

"It was a very good, very reliable engine," Trevor Crisp, Harry Mundy's successor as Jaguar's power-plant guru, said of the V12. "Michael May's chamber was helpful at part load, though a bit of a handicap at full load. But the twelve hadn't the potential for future development. It was uneconomical in relation to the demands we were facing – fuel economy in particular. And sales were dropping off significantly."

Crisp included a twelve in a proposed new family of Jaguar engines, planned in the late 1980s, that would share the same bore-centre distances among a 60° V6 and V12 and a 90° V8. After Ford bought Jaguar, this plan had to pass the muster of the shrewd and demanding Bill Hayden. "Bill supported the programme," Trevor Crisp recalled, "and we got the V8 running. But then Bill said we'd be lucky to get the money to build one engine, let alone three." It would have to be the eight. Jaguar would not have a new vee-twelve after all.

Were competition to have spurred the building of a new twelve by Jaguar, it would have come from Germany. With its name standing for 'Bavarian Motor Works', Munich's BMW had built many vee-twelves for aircraft, starting in 1918 with a prototype whose development was halted by the end of the war. Work was restarted in 1924 on the 60° twelve of 46.9 litres that became the Type VI production engine in 1926. In 1930 BMW celebrated both the building of the 1,000th Type VI and its powering of the first-ever crossing of the Atlantic from east to west.

After experimenting with front-wheel-drive cars from 1926, BMW started producing automobiles by acquiring, in 1928, a company in Eisenach producing four-cylinder Austin Sevens under licence. It added sixes to its palette before the war and afterward made cars with one, two, four, six and eight cylinders.

An important breakthrough was the introduction in 1968 of BMW's single-overhead-camshaft six, the M06. Its inclined overhead valves, opened by rocker arms, were offset in what BMW called a 'triple-hemi-swirl' chamber to heighten combustion turbulence. Its cylinder centres were spaced at 100mm. Outputs of 150 and 170bhp were delivered by the M06's two versions, one of 2.5 litres (86 x 71.6mm) and the other of 2.8 litres with an 80mm stroke.

With fully counterbalanced crankshafts running in seven main bearings, these sixes were developed by

BMW's tall, distinguished 'engine Pope' Alex von Falkenhausen. They quickly set new standards in the auto industry for their beguiling marriage of performance with smoothness. When Swiss-born executive Robert Anton Lutz left General Motors to become BMW's board member for sales in 1972, this six was one of the Munich company's prime attractions for him. Although trained in business, Lutz had an abiding personal and professional interest in the automotive product.

Discussing the six with Alex von Falkenhausen one day, the equally tall Lutz mused, "Two of those would certainly make a great vee-twelve." Their discussion turned to other matters, but the silver-haired von Falkenhausen, no mean racer in his day, didn't forget the thought. Lutz had, so when a few weeks later von Falkenhausen said he had something to show him, the sales chief had no inkling of what lay in store. It was nothing less than a running vee-twelve based directly on the componentry of the M06 six. It was already on the dynamometer and "it ran beautifully", Lutz recalled.

Here was an initiative that deserved to be pursued, thought von Falkenhausen. As its Type M33, BMW

In 1977 BMW produced another prototype vee-twelve, its M66, in sizes as large as 4.5 litres. It displayed an M66 engine at the 1979 Frankfurt Show, an act that drew the attention of BMW's arch-rivals in Stuttgart.

brought the twelve to fruition in 1974. Although it kept the six's 100mm cylinder centres, the 60° vee engine asked for connecting rods 150mm long instead of the six's 135mm. Using the same cylinder dimensions as the 2.5-litre six gave it 4,991cc, from which it produced 300bhp at 5,700rpm, precisely double the six's output at 6,000rpm. Ingeniously the plenum chambers feeding its induction ram pipes were cast integrally with the camshaft covers on the opposite heads, each fed by its own fuel-injection metering valve. Its right-hand cylinder bank was offset forward and chains drove its overhead cams.

The M33 twelve had moved rapidly – more quickly than BMW was able to provide a suitable car for it. With its iron block the V12 was heavy, 695lb, far heftier than the 470lb of the 3.5-litre sixes that powered its biggest offerings. As well, said Lutz, BMW feared at the time that "doing a twelve would unduly 'provoke Mercedes', such was the underdog mentality at the time." Nevertheless, showing a fine contempt for growing concerns over fuel consumption, von Falkenhausen took a new tack in mid-1974 by basing a fresh twelve-cylinder, his M66, on a new smaller six-cylinder engine, the M60, whose initial design had been prepared by BMW's racers under Paul Rosche.

With its 91mm cylinder centres the smaller six promised a much lighter and more compact twelve. The engineers sought maximum commonality with the M60 by using its cylinder head, valves, valve gear, camshafts, pistons and 135mm connecting rods, though the latter were specially machined. The block was still iron, but to save weight a single enclosed cogged-rubber belt was used to drive both camshafts. Noses of the latter drove the distributors for the M66's electronic ignition. An unusual feature for a road-car engine was dry-sump lubrication.

The M66 was planned in both 3.6- and 4.5-litre versions, the latter measuring 80 x 74mm (4,463cc). Work on it continued into 1977, when it was producing 272bhp at 5,700rpm and torque of 269lb-ft at 4,500rpm with its Bosch L-Jetronic fuel injection, now with a single central air-metering valve. BMW considered this twelve to be a heavy engine at 606lb, however, and with the Energy Crisis still threatening in 1977 the M66 was shelved during that year. To show that it was not overlooking technical opportunities, BMW displayed an M66 twelve at the 1979 Frankfurt Show.

In spite of these frustrating fits and starts, recalled BMW engineer Karlheinz Lange, the V12 "remained a very interesting topic for engine development at BMW." Work on such engines started again at the end of 1982, partly inspired by the M60 in-line six that had entered production in 1977. Redesignated M20 under a new BMW system, this six was produced from 1981 in a new version with its bore enlarged to 84 instead of 80mm. Still with 91mm cylinder centres, this required siamesing of the cylinders in the M20's iron block.[10] Aluminium was experimented with as its block material but not pursued at that time.

Aluminium proved to be the key to the creation of a V12 that met BMW's exacting standards for performance combined with lightness. It traditionally sought a 50/50 front/rear weight distribution in its cars; the earlier iron-block vee-twelves would have far overbalanced the front wheels. By using aluminium for both the block and the heads of its M70 V12, introduced in July 1987, BMW was able to reduce its weight to 530lb.

The closed-deck block was cast of high-silicon aluminium, in which the pistons could run directly against the aluminium bore surface after it had been etched to expose the silicon crystals. As in the Chevrolet Vega and Porsche 928 using the same technology, iron plating of the aluminium piston's skirts gave the required compatibility, especially during running-in.

As in the M20 six that shared 91mm cylinder centres, the M70's dimensions of 84 x 75mm (4,988cc) required siamesing of the outer surfaces of its cylinders. The block extended down past the crankshaft centreline to an aluminium sump casting that had its own small pressed-aluminium oil pan at the front, under the Gerotor-type oil pump driven by a roller chain from the nose of the crank. Both the oil filter and oil cooler were remotely mounted, joined to the right side of the block by braided hoses.

Robust caps for the seven main bearings were retained by two conventional bolts and, uniquely, by two additional bolts aligned with the 60° angles of the cylinder banks. Doubly counterbalanced adjacent to each 44mm rod journal, the forged-steel crankshaft was carried in massive 82.5mm main bearings. A massive vibration damper was bolted to the crank's nose.

Head of engine research and development in Munich since 1975, Karlheinz Lange oversaw the M70's creation. He offset its right cylinder bank forward, accommodating side-by-side 135mm connecting rods made from the same forgings as the M20 six but specially machined at the big ends. Full but short, its piston skirts carried two compression rings and one oil ring. As a weight-saving measure the gudgeon pin was much shorter than the

Above: *It was a case of third-time lucky with BMW's development of its M70 V12, introduced in 1987. The 5.0-litre engine was one of the first in the industry to be equipped with drive-by-wire throttles, one for each cylinder bank.*

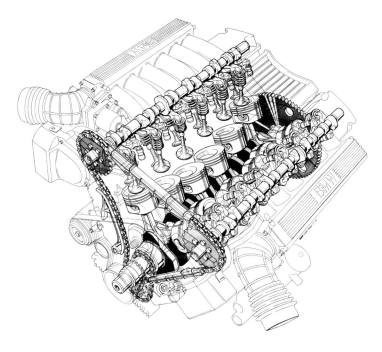

Right: *That the chain driving the M70's two camshafts was only a single roller wide testified to the low power requirement of the engine's valve gear. In a manner that reflected Aurelio Lampredi's designs for Ferrari, the BMW engine had its valves slightly offset in the longitudinal plane to allow the most rigid possible cam-follower design.*

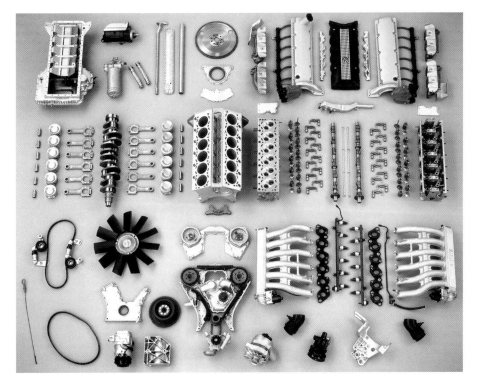

A key feature of the BMW M70 vee-twelve that suited it to the company's car-design philosophy was its aluminium cylinder block, in which the pistons ran directly on cylinder bores of the high-silicon light metal. A single camshaft sat above each cylinder head, both of them driven by a single chain.

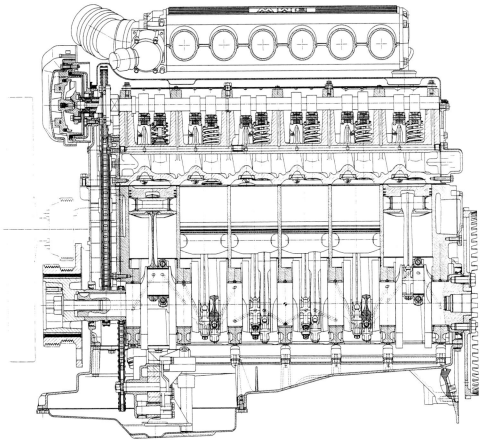

Following the pattern of the six-cylinder M26 which inspired its creation, BMW's M70 had siamesed cylinders in which adjacent bores could hardly have been placed closer. Abbreviated gudgeon pins in short-skirted pistons showed the effort taken with the M70 to achieve smooth high-speed running through low reciprocating masses.

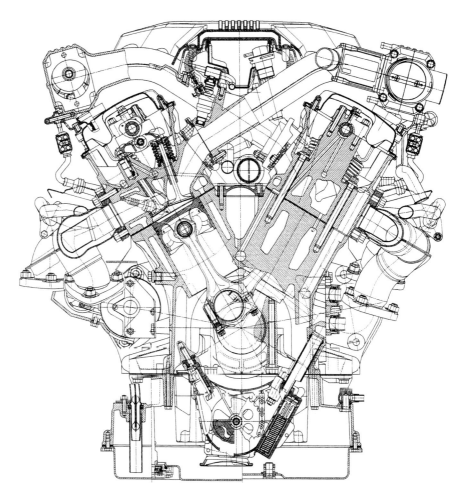

cylinder bore, reflecting an intense design effort to keep reciprocating masses low.

A circular depression in the piston crown matched a shallow combustion chamber in which the two valves were offset longitudinally – in the now-typical BMW manner – to allow the use of straight, short finger-type followers pivoted from spherical fulcrums that hydraulically adjusted valve clearance. Each valve was closed by twin coil springs. Seven bearings integral with the aluminium casting gave rigid support to each cylinder head's single camshaft.

Lange's team designed a single cylinder head that served for both banks of the M70 V12. To make it as compact as possible they adopted the valve layout of BMW's M40 four-cylinder engine, which had the very narrow angle of 14° between its valves – ten for the inlets and four for the exhausts. Both had inserted guides, the latter's nicely encircled by cooling water. One single-roller chain at the front of the block served to drive both camshafts, encased in a two-piece die-cast aluminium housing. Inset at the front was a single water pump driven, like the other accessories, by poly-vee belts.

Criss-crossing above the M70's central vee were long torque-enhancing ram pipes fed by individual plenum chambers, throttles and air-mass measurers. Electric 'drive-by-wire' servos controlled the throttles in response to signals from the third generation of Bosch's Motronic system – one for each bank. The two Motronics also monitored fuel injection and ignition, distributors for which were driven from the camshaft noses. Noise radiated by the engine was reduced by interposing rubber couplings between its manifolds and heads. To the same end the cam-cover pressings were a sandwich of plastic and aluminium.

Shrewdly designed to be economical in operation as well as production, BMW's M70 could run on regular petrol thanks to a compression ratio of 8.8:1 instead of the 9.5:1 of its M33 and M66 predecessors. Nevertheless its power was highly competitive with 300bhp at a moderate 5,200rpm. Maximum torque of 332lb-ft at 4,100rpm was up substantially from that of its developmental antecedents – an impressive engineering achievement.

The M70 was introduced in BMW's 750i, which did indeed achieve 50/50 weight distribution and became

Above: *Powering BMW's 750i, the M70 vee-twelve of 1987 made good use of its 300bhp to be one of the first German saloons to be governed to a 155mph maximum speed. It was thought capable of 170mph without such restraint.*

Right: *BMW's V12 was enlarged to 5.4 litres for introduction as the M73 in 1994. Its bore was increased by 1mm, all that could be tolerated by the closely-packed siamesed cylinders. Visible in its sump was the chain-driven Gerotor-type oil pump.*

one of the first German cars to be governed at a top speed of 155mph, well short of its actual speed potential of almost 170mph. "Torque is no stranger at low rpm," reported *Road & Track*, "and is well in evidence throughout the range." It credited the new twelve with "silky smoothness" even at top speed.

At the 750i's Hamburg launch BMW's chairman, Eberhard von Kuenheim, could state with some accuracy that his new model was "the first twelve-cylinder model from a German manufacturer for almost 50 years." Von Kuenheim forecast that "its aura will reach the most remote markets of the world and make a profound impression on them." It was, he said, "an aspirant for the leading position in the international automobile hierarchy." This was fair comment with its only rival the superannuated Jaguar XJ12, which would not be renewed on the basis of Jaguar's latest platform until 1993.

Soon after the launch General Motors paid BMW the compliment of buying a $69,000 750i in order to get one of its engines to conduct an interesting experiment. "We were looking into ways of achieving ultimate quietness and smoothness," said a Chevrolet engineer, "and one

avenue in that direction was to go with more cylinders to smooth the engine out without losing power." Complete with its four-speed automatic, an M70 twelve was lowered into a 1989 Chevrolet Caprice LS saloon. The "smooth hum" from its exhaust betrayed that its motive power was no banal V8. No Chevrolet V12 resulted, but this Caprice-BMW helped Chevrolet's engineers gain a first experience of the drive-by-wire throttle control that it would later introduce in the C5-generation Corvette.

BMW's next step with its twelve was to increase both bore and stroke to give it 5,379cc (85 x 79mm) for 1994 introduction as the M73. With fuel economy a priority, the use of premium fuel was exploited by a compression-ratio lift to 10.0:1. Because knock sensing was introduced, with four sensors, the V12 would also tolerate lower-octane petrol. Its functions, detecting and adjusting individual cylinders, were performed by a new Siemens EML IIIS management system.

Oil-spray cooling of the pistons was introduced on the M73. Among friction-reduction measures was the use of needle bearinged rollers contacting its cam lobes, which were now individually sintered and shrunk onto steel tubes to create its camshafts. A small increase in weight to 560lb was accompanied by a big power increase to 326bhp at 5,000rpm, with 362lb-ft of torque at 3,900rpm. The lower engine speeds at which these peaks were reached was owed to shorter-duration valve timing, which also allowed a fuel-saving and vibration-reducing lowering of the idle speed.

In 1989 BMW introduced a new family of in-line engines with four valves per cylinder, inclined at an included angle of 39½°. Harking back to Alex von Falkenhausen's first vee-twelve experiment, the engineers could scarcely resist trying two of these six-cylinder heads on a twelve-cylinder block. The result was the M72 of 1988–89, with the same 5.4-litre dimensions as the M73. Hefty at 640lb, it was a formidable package that produced 355bhp at 5,200rpm. It did not, however, "fulfil the comfort demands of the large saloon class in all respects," said Karlheinz Lange, "and, as a result, did not go into production." Only in the 21st Century would BMW power its 7-Series saloons with 48-valve vee-twelves.

Even with only 24 valves the BMW twelve was an attractive engine, and not only in BMWs. In 1991 Italdesign's Giorgetto Giugiaro and his son Fabrizio showed the first of their BMW-powered Nazca sports-car prototypes. These were handsome and practical concept vehicles that showed the potential of the M70 to power a mid-engined sports car. To their regret, this was an opportunity destined to be exploited by McLaren rather than Italdesign.

In 1987 BMW first essayed a 5.4-litre vee-twelve with four valves per cylinder, again basing its design on new 24-valve sixes. The resulting M72 was not short of power at 355bhp but wasn't thought mature enough to be committed to production.

A decade later the automotive world was startled by the emergence of a one-off car created by A:Level of Moscow, a studio dedicated to unique automobiles. Its calling card, a coupé based on the styling lines of a 1957 Volga M21, was crafted on a BMW 8-Series chassis with M70 twelve-cylinder power. The meticulously detailed coupé turned heads at the Geneva Salon in 2003.

"BMW did Mercedes-Benz a favour with its vee-twelves", said Kurt Obländer in retrospect. Balding and twinkling, the Stuttgart company's engine-development chief had long been interested in creating a twelve. Since 1964, with the 6.3-litre engine of its ultra-luxury 600, Mercedes-Benz had relied on vee-eights to power its biggest cars. Daimler-Benz built heavy 1,000-horsepower vee-twelves for industrial uses, but twelves did not power its automobiles.

It could well have been otherwise. Immediately after the war the company abjured the opportunity to proceed with the pre-war and wartime M173 V12 or, indeed, the 6.6-litre successor to it that Rudolf Uhlenhaut suggested. In 1957, however, when the programme to build the 600 was taking shape, envisioned were two engines: a V8 for a model to be the 500 and a V12 to power the ultimate offering in the range, the 750. Under engine-design chief Wolf-Dieter Bensinger, Adolf Wente was assigned to its creation.

Wente's twelve, the M101, was a power unit with which to reckon. Because he derived it from the 5.0-litre

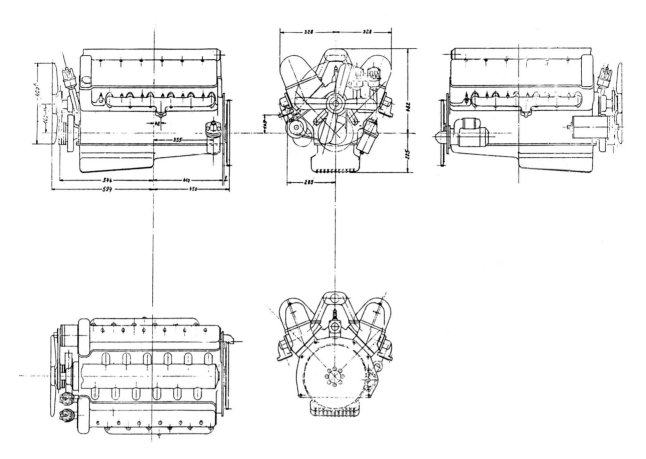

As a possible power unit for the W100, the car that became its 600, Mercedes-Benz planned a 90° V12 of 7.5 litres based on its 5.0-litre V8. Designed by Adolf Wente, the impressive M101 twelve was rendered redundant by progress made with the enlargement of the V8 to 6.3 litres.

V8 being planned for the 500, his M101 shared a 90° bank angle with the eight. Although not ideal from the perspective of balance and uneven firing impulses, this was thought desirable to gain production economies. The twelve's block could be machined on the same transfer line as the eight's. Its dimensions (95 x 88mm) gave it the proud displacement of 7,485cc, fully justifying the planned model's '750' designation.

Each cylinder bank of the M101 was to have a single chain-driven overhead camshaft, opening in-line valves. The timing chains were also to turn a twelve-cylinder Bosch fuel-injection pump mounted in the central vee, underneath a plenum chamber from which ram pipes sloped to the individual cylinders. Twin ignition distributors rose at the front of the engine. Foreseen for the M101 was power in the 380–390bhp range from an engine weighing a hefty 915lb. This counted against it, as did the progress made in the meantime by its sister vee-

eight, which more than met the needs of the new 600 when its capacity was enlarged to 6.3 litres. Adolf Wente's engine was deemed unready for prime time.

The idea of a V12 derived from a V8 refused to die at Untertürkheim. In 1975 rumblings of Munich's work on the M66 prompted development chief Hans Scherenberg to ask his colleagues to consider the creation of V10 and/or V12 engines on the basis of the M117 V8 that had been introduced at the beginning of the 1970s. The M117's biggest version displaced 4,520cc (92 x 85mm) with a single chain-driven overhead cam for each bank, opening in-line valves through finger followers mounted on spherical pivots. Aluminium heads were atop a cast-iron cylinder block which had water jacketing fully surrounding each cylinder. The sides of the block extended down beyond the crank centreline for maximum rigidity. Four bolts retained each of its five main-bearing caps.

A vee-twelve making full use of the M117's dimensions would have displaced a proud 6,781cc, a mighty engine either for the new S-Class under development or for the final years of the regal 600. In January of 1976, however, Scherenberg's engineers delivered a dusty prognosis for a 90° V12 derived from the M117 V8. It would have uneven power impulses, they said, and torsional crankshaft excitation like that of a six.

A year later his team put forward proposals for a twelve derived either from the M117, with offset connecting-rod journals to overcome the uneven-firing problem, or from a 60° V6 then being developed. These thoughts had to be put aside in April 1977 when Scherenberg's board asked him to cease and desist from further thoughts of a twelve on the grounds of lack of engineering capacity.

Two years later, at the prestigious biennial Frankfurt Show, the Daimler-Benz board could not ignore the obvious provocation of BMW's disclosure of a prototype of its M66 V12. Battling back from near-oblivion at the end of the 1950s, BMW was now a feisty rival that Stuttgart could not ignore. "The competition eased the job of pushing through a twelve-cylinder here," said Kurt Obländer about the top management at Daimler-Benz. Were BMW to introduce a V12, managing director Werner Breitschwerdt asked his vehicle-development chief Rudolf Hörnig in September 1983, "could we base a twelve on one of our existing engines? Or should we respond with a four-valve vee-eight?" A meeting of department heads on 11 April 1984 elected to follow the former course.

The new twelve was to be developed as an extension of an experimental late-1970s programme to develop a new engine range that bore fruit in the abovementioned vee-six, first fitted in a 1980 concept car. As a whole the project was known as KOMO for 'kompakt Motor' or 'compact engine', thus targeting the prime objective of the research. In overall charge of the work was Hubertus Christ, with Gwinner the engineer accountable for engines. In his technical team were Hermann Hiereth, Gert Withalm and Roland Merkle.[11]

Their first KOMO V12 ran on the dynamometer on 29 July 1985. Sharing a 60° vee angle with the programme's V6, it had a capacity of 5,209cc (85 x 76.5mm). Cylinders spaced at 101mm were bored in high-silicon aluminium wet liners, which in turn were inserted in an aluminium cylinder block. As in the production BMW V12 the pistons ran directly against the etched surfaces of the aluminium liners. Having experimented with this technology since 1971, Mercedes first used it in a production V8 in 1978. A single head design, also in aluminium, served for both banks, with four valves per cylinder. Twin overhead camshafts on each bank were, unusually for a road-car engine, gear-driven.

Scaling 640lb, the KOMO twelve had separate Bosch injection and ignition systems for each cylinder bank. After measuring its maximum output as 313bhp with 336lb-ft at 4,000rpm, the first such engine was installed in a 560SEL and tested early in 1986 against that car's usual Type M117

V8 of 300bhp. Performing to advantage only over 80mph and showing slightly higher fuel consumption, the twelve was praised for its smoothness and installation compactness. Its best development output was 324bhp at 5,000rpm with the same peak torque as first measured.

Here was an engine with the potential of parity with, if not advantage over, the BMW vee-twelve that Daimler-Benz knew was soon to be introduced. With that in mind, some thought was given to taking it out to six litres, which would have been easy with its bore centres spaced 10mm more generously than BMW's. The project struck the buffers, however, when board member for production Werner Niefer pointed out that it would need a completely new production line that he was unwilling to commission. Final tests of a KOMO twelve were made in March 1986 to assess the effects of different valve timings.

No matter what their superiors decided, the engineers at Daimler-Benz had a knack for keeping programmes moving – off the books if necessary – if they felt that their company might need them one day. The vee-twelve was no exception. It was now Kurt Obländer's turn to be its champion. Its in-house competition was the company's big V8: the Type 117 and, from 1989, its Type 119 version with twin overhead cams and four valves per cylinder. The latter would be no pushover with its 320bhp from five litres, not to mention the AMG version of almost six litres and 391 horsepower.

Kurt Obländer thought there was still room for a vee-twelve. "There's no artistry in making a pile driver of an engine with lots of power and torque," he said. "Especially in a Mercedes-Benz, I'd like to experience torque and power with a certain comfort and culture. Strength and magnificence deserve to be combined, so to speak." Naming Hans Brüggemann as project chief for what was to be – appropriately – the Type M120 engine, Obländer launched work on a twelve at the beginning of 1986. Detailed design work began in March under Ernst Gobien, who was succeeded after his death by Rolf Zeller. Jürgen Willand and Siegfried Lenz assisted Brüggemann in the new engine's design and development.

With weight the obvious enemy of a twelve, the decision to choose an aluminium block for the M120 was self-evident. The technology selected was the same as that of the KOMO V12: an alloy of aluminium with 17 per cent silicon and 4 per cent copper for the block, with iron-plated and zinc-coated aluminium pistons running directly against its bores.

Cast with closed top decks and deeply webbed along its flanks to reduce noise emissions, the cylinder block weighed a moderate 90.4lb. This was all the more impressive in view of the fact that the block extended down to enclose the crankshaft fully, thus ensuring

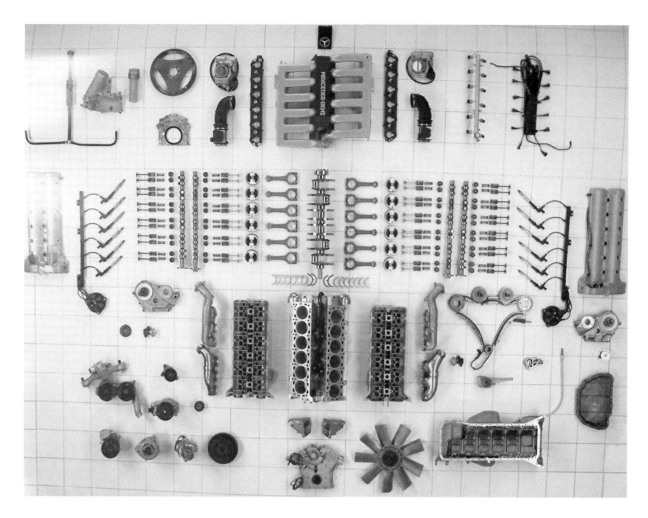

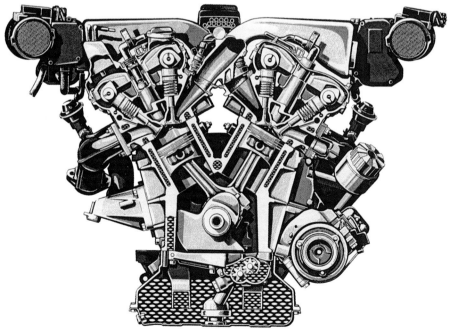

Above: *Like BMW, Mercedes-Benz took advantage of its work on six-cylinder engines to create its first production vee-twelve, the M120 introduced in 1991. Like its Munich counterpart, it had an aluminium cylinder block with liner-free bores.*

Left: *The Mercedes-Benz M120 60° V12 of 1991 shared its right-hand cylinder head with the company's M104 in-line six. This gave the 6.0-litre M120 twin overhead camshafts per bank and four valves per cylinder.*

strong bracing of its seven main bearings and a rigid attachment to the bell housing and transmission. The complete engine's weight would be a wieldy 640lb. Although heavier than BMW's twelve, it would also be much more powerful.

With power production the responsibility of the V12's cylinder heads, Oblända and Brüggemann chose four valves per cylinder operated by twin overhead cams. They didn't have to look far for these. Their M104 in-line six of 3.0 litres (88.5 x 80.2mm) already had just such a cylinder head, with its valves symmetrically inclined at an included angle of 50°. Sliding in bores in the aluminium head were piston-type tappets containing hydraulic lash adjusters, above dual coil springs.

When for 1991 the six's head was modified to accommodate a bore enlarged to 89.9mm, at the same time the detail changes were made that allowed the head, in its entirety, to be used on the right-hand bank of the vee-twelve. The left-hand cylinder head, offset 20mm to the rear, was a new part made as a mirror image of its sister.

For their twelve the engineers kept the stroke of the 3.0-litre version of the six, 80.4mm, and combined it with an 89mm bore to give 5,987cc in a conventional 60° vee. Combustion chambers were pent-roofed with central spark plugs, facing a flat piston top. Although full-skirted the pistons were short and light, carried by I-section rods drilled for pressure oiling of their small ends. No attempt was made to carry over the connecting rods of the six, which were significantly shorter than the twelve's 154mm rods.

In length terms the engine was compact, of course retaining the 97mm cylinder centres of the six, with siamesed cylinder bores. With a dozen large-radius counterweights and induction-hardened journals, the forged-steel crankshaft weighed 64lb. Its main bearings measured 58mm and its rod journals 48mm. A vibration damper was bolted to the crankshaft nose, together with the drive pulley for the poly-vee belt that drove the twelve's accessories. To accommodate steering on either the left or the right side, the starter motor could be mounted on either side of the crankcase.

Although the first engines had individual timing chains for each bank, the final M120 successfully used a single double-roller chain to turn all four camshafts. Sprockets on the inlet camshafts contained hydraulically operated helical ramps that gave automatic control of inlet-valve timing between extremes of 32° of crank rotation. Inlet timing was retarded by the Bosch engine management at idling and low speeds and also above 4,000rpm, and advanced at high loads between those speeds. From the noses of the exhaust camshafts, whose timing didn't vary, the ignition distributors were driven.

A single-roller chain from the crank nose drove a partly submerged oil pump of novel design. It had two paired-gear chambers, one of which was deactivated at low temperatures and, when the oil was warm, at high engine speeds to reduce the pump's power demands. An engine-oil cooler, mounted behind the front bumper of the S-Class, was thermostatically controlled. The sump was made in two parts: primarily an aluminium sand casting

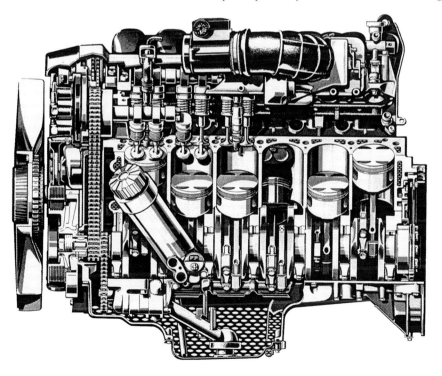

All four camshafts of the Mercedes-Benz M120 were turned by a single double-roller chain, driving inlet-camshaft sprockets that allowed control of valve timing. Its pressure oil pump had two elements, one of which was deactivated at extremes of temperature.

plus a detachable pressed-steel pan under the reservoir proper. A windage tray under the crankshaft guided the oil flung from it and hindered foaming of the lubricant.

Decoupled from the cylinder heads by rubber spacers to reduce vibration transmission, the long ram pipes of the inlet manifold – cast as a single unit – criss-crossed above the central vee. Each bank had its own electrically controlled throttle and metering unit for the Bosch LH Jetronic management system, which used individual solenoid-controlled fuel injectors at each cylinder to match the length of the injection period to the required power demand and to the air supply, which was measured by hot-wire sensors.

Hidden in the M120's central vee were two sensors along each cylinder bank to detect knock and, through the management system, to choose the optimum ignition timing of individual cylinders. This was the first successful fitting of such a system to a twelve-cylinder automobile engine. Exhaust gases reached a 7.1-litre catalyst – the world's largest – through manifolds fabricated of two walls of sheet alloy steel separated by layers of fibres of glass and ceramics as insulation. This not only accelerated the emission system's warming up from cold but also markedly reduced under-hood temperatures.

Now that Kurt Oblander could build his twelve, he wasn't going to drag his feet. Thanks to the fast start given by its existing cylinder heads, work on the M120 could progress with unusual speed. By the end of 1986 the prototype shop was making the first long-lead components, the crankshaft and crankcase, the latter sand-cast instead of the low-pressure die casting used in production. On 30 November 1987 Hans Brüggemann invited Oblander to a test cell to see the first M120 running. It was the project manager's 60th-birthday present to his chief.

Of the first experimental series, some 40 engines were produced. As an expediency these had an older mechanical Bosch KE Jetronic fuel injection – one for each bank – to get testing under way while the LE Jetronic was perfected. Of a second series, circa 70 engines, some were ready to power prototypes of the new S-Class, the Type W140 being developed under Wolfgang Peter, as well as the Type R129, the 600SL, which would also benefit from twelve-cylinder power. Work intensified at this stage on the engine's refinement and silence, including internal ribbing and reshaping of its die-cast magnesium camshaft covers and fine tuning of its running clearances.

In the M120's final perfection before production the 600SL carried a heavier burden than the S-Class, prototypes of which were thinner on the ground. Nevertheless the twelve made its debut at Geneva in March 1991 as the motivation for the 600SE, whose

As installed in the C112 concept car, the M120 vee-twelve showed its individual throttles for each bank and the one-piece inlet manifold whose long ram pipes intermeshed above the engine.

production began in June. The launch of the 600SL took place a year later.

With its 10.0:1 compression ratio the M120 initially produced 408bhp at 5,200rpm, a neat 300 in kilowatt terms, on premium petrol. Its peak torque of 428lb-ft was attained at 3,800rpm, although at 2,000rpm fully 90 per cent of that torque was available. In September 1992, in search of lower fuel consumption through reduced full-load enrichment, the ratings were rolled back to 394bhp and 420lb-ft at the same engine speeds.

Germany's *auto motor und sport* tested the long-wheelbase versions of both the BMW and the Mercedes in 1991. "When it comes to motoring comfort in the broadest sense," it said, "twelve cylinders rate as the *ne plus ultra*. When it comes to uniformity of power delivery there's nothing to equal a twelve. Vibration as well is a stranger to the V12: you can't do better than 100-per-cent balanced masses. There remains only the often-cited silky-silent running. Neither with the BMW nor with the Mercedes is this expectation met. Both are loud when under full load, and with its higher combustion pressures the Mercedes even more markedly than the BMW."

In performance both were fast but the Mercedes was faster: "When it needs to it accelerates easily and notably away from the feebler BMW." While the 4,238lb BMW 750iL motored to 62mph from rest in 8.1 seconds, the 5,030lb 600SEL took two whole seconds less to the same speed, showing that its extra horses were very much on the job. The Munich car had the advantage in fuel consumption at 15.8mpg against 13.6mpg for the Stuttgart twelve. Both were governed to top speeds of

just under 160mph. Wryly, the German magazine noted that for the difference in price – DM138,000 versus DM198,360 – the BMW owner could buy a Mercedes-Benz 300E as a second car.

"This mammoth powerplant hurtles the 600SEL from rest to 60mph in 5.7 seconds," found *Car and Driver*, "and to 150mph in just 42.8 seconds. In the classic V12 idiom, the Benz engine pours out power seamlessly, with a soaring whir its only trail. Its Herculean V12 will stand on its head for you – act like a race car, or purr along daintily with granny behind the multi-adjustable wheel." But the cost was not insignificant: "Add in sales taxes and you need to write a check for about $150,000. That's how much the best costs these days."

The new S-Class courted controversy. To many it seemed extraordinarily large and over-the-top with its double-glazed side windows. Yet its styling was bafflingly banal. It had 'out-everythinged' its twelve-cylinder rival from BMW, proving the validity of the motor-industry watchword, "Last in, best dressed." The Daimler-Benz board director for passenger cars, Jürgen Hubbert, said that it defined "a class of its own". At the very top of that class was the vee-twelve version, a new icon for lovers of the three-pointed star. Up to its replacement by a new 36-valve twelve at the end of 1999, 19,000 were produced.

Though conceived as a luxury-car engine, the M120 twelve was destined to see sporting use as well, an echo of the fate of Jaguar's vee-twelve. Mercedes-Benz chose it as the power for a spectacular GT-style concept car, the C112, which had been a star of 1991's Frankfurt Show. Those developing the C112 had hoped to see it produced; talks to that end were conducted with racing-car builder Sauber in Switzerland, but came to naught.

Nevertheless the M120 did power a sports car. At Affalterbach, north-east of Stuttgart, Hans-Werner

Producing an initial 408bhp at 5,200rpm, the M120 was the premier power unit for the 600SE, the new S-Class from Stuttgart. In spite of its substantial size the new Mercedes-Benz model decisively outperformed its Munich rival.

Aufrecht's AMG was responsible for building small series of special high-performance Mercedes-Benz cars. It also built engines for customers. Among these was Modena's Pagani, headed by Argentine Horacio Raul Pagani. To motivate his mid-engined Pagani Zonda, made at the exclusive rate of a score per year, AMG took the twelve out to 7,291cc (91.5 x 92.4mm), an enlargement that it also offered to Mercedes-Benz owners.

In 2003 trim in Pagani's Zonda the M120 developed 555bhp at 5,900rpm and 553lb-ft of torque at 4,050rpm. Recalling that his compatriot Juan Manuel Fangio raced

In virtually standard form the M120 was chosen to power the C112 concept car introduced by Mercedes-Benz at Frankfurt in 1991. Although designed with production very much in mind, the meticulously detailed C112 failed to be approved for manufacture.

Above: *An M120 vee-twelve under preparation for racing at AMG at Affalterbach showed few deviations from the standard configuration. Visible are its cup-type tappets and seven bearings carrying each camshaft.*

Top left: *Its huge airbox, carrying the two inlet-air restrictors mandatory in GT racing, seemed to overwhelm the M120 as it was modified by AMG to power the CLK-GTR to compete in the FIA's GT Championship in 1997. Displacement of 6.0 litres was chosen after versions with 5.0 and 7.0 litres were tested and rejected.*

Left: *Remarkable coherence between design for racing and for production at the end of the 20th Century is shown by one cylinder head of the Mercedes-Benz M120 V12 being prepared for the CLK-GTR at AMG. Visible are notches in its inlet ports that accommodated the spray pattern of the electronic injection nozzles in the manifold just above.*

Below: *To qualify its CLK-GTR for the GT racing series, AMG produced a small run of cars for road use. This was by any standard one of the most exciting Mercedes-Benz automobiles of all time.*

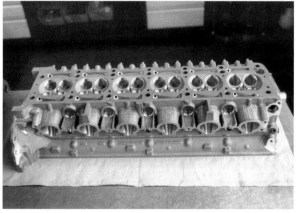

for Mercedes-Benz, Horacio Pagani defended his choice of a German engine for a £330,000 Italian supercar: "This engine is a fabulous unit for several reasons, including its very high torque and lightness compared to an equivalent Italian engine." AMG continued supplying the big twelve to Pagani even after a newer V12 was introduced for Mercedes cars.

Another role for AMG was developing and entering cars with three-pointed stars in saloon and GT series. Looking ahead to the 1997 season, they saw a chance to build a GT car patterned after the recently introduced CLK coupé. To power it AMG chose the M120. With the rules allowing engines of up to 8.0 litres, what size should the GT car's engine be? Taking no chances, AMG built and tested V12s in racing tune with 5-, 6- and 7-litre displacements. The first engine in this series went on the test bench on 21 December 1996. "We revved the five-litre over 10,000", remarked AMG's engine guru Erhard Melcher.

There was a compelling reason to choose the 6-litre version, and it was linked to the fact that AMG had already conducted extensive development for racing on the 2.0-litre M111 four, which was exactly one-third the size of the 6.0-litre V12 and had identical top-end componentry. Tripling their 280bhp suggested 840 horsepower from the twelve, but this reckoned without the air-inlet restrictors that were mandatory in GT racing. In a car weighing less than 999kg, two restrictors would each measure 35.2mm.

The M120 needed surprisingly little modification for its new assignment apart from improvements to the chain drive to its four camshafts, the fitting of racing-profile cams and the use of Kauffman valve springs. Initially the twelves ran with standard crankshafts, rods and even Mahle pistons. The crankshaft was later lightly modified for reliability and ultimately the M120 used Pankl titanium connecting rods, Del West titanium valves and sundry screws and bolts of titanium. With astute dieting the V12 engine's weight was reduced to 507lb, a figure that included a carbon-fibre airbox, fabricated-steel exhaust manifolds and the engine's electronics, but not its cylindrical carbon-fibre oil tank. The new shallow oil pan for its dry-sump lubrication system was cast magnesium.

Individual carbon-fibre inlet trumpets for each cylinder replaced the standard cast-aluminium inlet manifold. Below their butterfly throttles were the fuel injectors, which with the ignition were controlled by a Bosch Motronic 1.2 system. For the racing engine the standard 89mm bore was slightly enlarged, using techniques already familiar to AMG for the V12s it modified to 7.3 litres for its special road-car customers. Final dimensions were 91.0 x 76.7mm for 5,986cc. Power output was quoted as 600bhp at 7,000rpm – 650 may have been nearer the mark – with 516lb-ft of torque available at the moderate speed, for a racing engine, of 3,900rpm.

Installed in the mid-engined CLK-GTR that AMG built to contest the FIA's GT Championship in 1997, the M120 gave yeoman service. In an exciting season it took Bernd Schneider to the drivers' trophy, while among the GT Series teams AMG Mercedes placed first with 110 points. Team BMW Motorsport was second with 85 and Gulf Team Davidoff was third with 37, both racing McLaren F1-GTRs with their BMW V12 engines. Although AMG Mercedes switched to V8 engines for its 1998 racers, its twelves continued to be entered by private teams.

"Smooth and controlled," reported a passenger in one of the 1997 cars, "the CLK seems to flow over the circuit's elevation changes like light-driven mercury. The six-litre twelve has a seamless, quiet sound that just accelerates the car like some inexorable force." That, now and forever, is the distinctive hallmark of the vee-twelve.

Chapter 13 Footnotes

[1] This is not to be confused with the Jaguar XJ6 saloon introduced in 1968, whose internal works code was XJ4.

[2] A crystallised rear magnesium wheel collapsed when the XJ13 was being driven at MIRA on 20 January 1971 by Norman Dewis for a promotional film. Heavily damaged, fortunately without harm to Dewis, it was rebuilt and since 1973 has been a treasured Jaguar promotional icon. Spares for it are in short supply; Jaguar may have been unwise to sell some of the engines, two of which escaped to Brian Wingfield for the making of at least one XJ13 replica.

[3] A man in demand, Hassan kept the title of Technical Director at Coventry Climax, where a new engine family was being developed to power military generator sets.

[4] Other users at the time were Chevrolet, in its Vega four, and Maserati in its V8.

[5] First to get a speeding citation in a V12-powered E-Type was emissions engineer Trevor Crisp, in a prototype on the Pennsylvania Turnpike in mid-August 1970.

[6] Dimensions of 90 x 84mm, still oversquare, give a capacity of 6,413cc.

[7] The link between May and Mundy was made by a German journalist specialising in engine topics, Olaf von Fersen.

[8] So extensively was Cosworth involved in the support of the Jaguar/TWR programme that at one stage it accounted for five per cent of Cosworth's turnover.

[9] The halving of cylinders was a major disappointment for many would-be buyers and an excuse for them to cancel their orders after the crash of October 1987. Only 280 of the planned 350 cars were made.

[10] Siamesing meant that the cylinders were joined together, no water being able to pass between them. Careful design is required to avoid unwanted distortion of siamesed cylinders with heat.

[11] Christ, Hiereth and Withalm would be among those who, later in the 1980s, built successful turbocharged V8s for Peter Sauber's sports-racing prototypes.

Chapter 14

FORMULA TWELVES

Not since the dawn of Grand Prix racing in 1906 had so many different makers of vee-twelve engines been competing in this, the highest category of motor sports. The previous high-water mark had been in 1938, when Auto Union, Alfa Romeo, Delahaye and Mercedes-Benz all fitted twelve-cylinder engines. In 1938's German Grand Prix they fielded the most V12-powered cars ever to leave a starting grid before the war: appropriately enough, a dozen cars.

These totals were rivalled in 1991. In that Formula 1 season seven teams raced with vee-twelve engines made by five companies. The potential was there for fourteen V12-powered cars to take the start. However, in those halcyon days when so many entries were received that pre-qualifying was required, this ideal was never achieved. The norm in 1991 was 10 or 11 twelve-cylinder cars qualified. In 1992, fewer entries succeeded in making more starts. In seven of the season's contests all twelve potential V12 starters took part in the racing. Thus the maximum pre-war field of Grand Prix twelves was matched – but not surpassed – in the early 1990s.

There might have been many, many more. The impetus was a new set of rules for Formula 1. Following Renault's lead, in the 1980s the designers of Grand Prix engines discovered the potential of the 1½-litre supercharged engines that the rules allowed. Taking advantage of turbo-supercharging, their new engines of four, six or eight cylinders quickly outpaced the unblown 3-litre powerplants that had dominated since 1966. To give naturally aspirated engines a chance, their capacity limit was lifted to 3½ litres in 1987, and from 1989 the turbocharged engines were banned.

Many engine designers decided that the enlarged capacity was an engraved invitation for the use of twelve cylinders. A parallel motivation for them, and for the executives who controlled their budgets, was the FIA's decision to change the rules for the big international sports-racing events. In 1989 it allowed 3½-litre unsupercharged cars to run much lighter than the big turbocharged racers that were dominating Group C competition. Nor were they subject to the fuel-consumption limits that governed Group C. In 1991, after a transition period, only 3½-litre cars could race. The change was an all-too-transparent effort to encourage major auto makers to invest in engines that would support both series.

The biggest prize of all would have been General Motors. Neither the American General himself nor any of his divisions, at home or abroad, had ever taken part in modern Grand Prix racing. Any chance of inveigling GM into Formula 1 had to be taken. One of the raciest of its arms was its German subsidiary, Opel, which had fielded Grand Prix cars in 1908, 1913 and 1914. For Opel to enter the GP lists again would be entirely appropriate.

An order to explore possible engine designs was issued from Rüsselsheim, Opel's headquarters near Frankfurt, to Scott Russell Engines in England. There

Opposite: *As in a number of other twelve-cylinder racing engines dating from the early 1960s, Porsche decided to place the gear drive to both camshafts and output shafts at the centre of its Type 3512 V12 of 1991. Extensions of this gearing also powered the pumps along the sides of the 3.5-litre engine.*

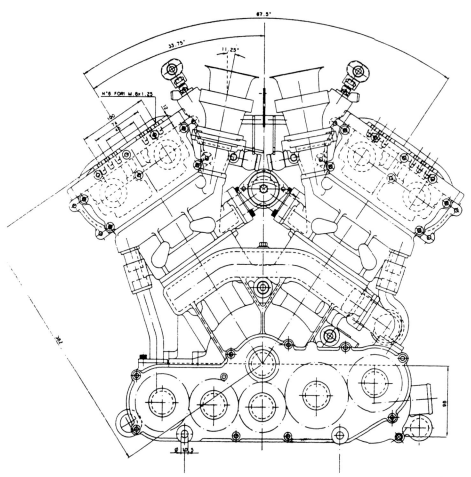

In 1990 Italy's Motori Moderni, led by the ever-creative Carlo Chiti, proposed a 3.5-litre twelve with a 67.5° bank angle for Formula 1 racing. Chiti's mooted V12 had a train of gears driven from the crankshaft nose to power its oil and water pumps.

designer Al Melling prepared layouts of possible engine configurations that favoured twelve cylinders. He shifted the left bank forward, established a cylinder-centre spacing of 93mm and tried various vee angles out to an ultra-wide 168°. Cogged-rubber belts were considered for the camshaft drives, as were five-valve cylinder heads. Main bearings were narrow but large in diameter at 70mm, while connecting-rod big ends were to be 44mm.

In 1989 work was proceeding on Opel's engine, for which Britain's Reynard was to design a chassis. While designed to very fine limits, the Melling layout was capable of being enlarged to 4½ litres with a small increase in its bore and a larger stroke extension. Hopes of an Opel Grand Prix entry were stymied, however, by the much greater interest of Big Daddy GM in a Chevrolet entry at Indianapolis with a V8 built in England by Ilmor Engineering. Opel's ambitions were placed on ice.

Echoes of Al Melling's work at Scott Russell for Opel were audible in an engine he designed around the same time for Motori Moderni, a company set up in Novara, Italy in 1984 to continue the engine-building activity of Carlo Chiti, late of Alfa Romeo's Autodelta and before that Ferrari. The first Melling design for Chiti in 1988 was a

120° vee-twelve of 3½ litres, said to produce 640bhp at 13,000rpm from its five-valve cylinder heads.

When in 1990 Chiti announced an alliance with Subaru, the design was converted into a flat-twelve to suit that Japanese car company's strong brand image as a maker of flat-opposed engines. In 1990 Motori Moderni planned a 67½° vee-twelve of 3,492cc (86 x 50.1mm). Italy's Alba-Tech was a putative customer for its forecast 620-plus horsepower at 13,500rpm, but this initiative wasn't followed through.

As if these multinational alliances weren't exotic enough, another dozen-cylinder initiative came from the heart of the Austrian Alps as a proposal from the motor-mad Pehr brothers. They backed a school chum, Rolf-Peter Marlow, in the design of a 70° vee-twelve of 3,491cc (84 x 52.5mm) and set up the Neotech company in Eisenerz to produce it and lease it to interested teams. In the early 1980s Marlow, once a Porsche engineer, developed a turbocharged in-line six of 1½ litres for Liechtenstein's Max Heideger, a BMW dealer and tuner, whose project was encouraged – but not taken up – by Ron Dennis of McLaren.

Marlow's Neotech twelve had many of the features of

The Neotech 12 designed by Rolf Peter Marlow suffered from the disadvantage that it was not designed to be used as an integral part of the chassis at a time when racing cars were increasingly of that configuration. A feature of the engine, revealed in 1990, was its central gearing both to camshafts and to a power-output shaft.

his six. A prominent characteristic was a central gear train both to the camshafts and to an output shaft that divided the engine into two vee-sixes from a torsional-vibration perspective, recalling designs by Honda and Abarth. He used ultra-thin castings and carbon-fibre camshaft covers to keep his engine's weight to 302lb, which also reflected the fact that Marlow's twelve, like his six, wasn't designed to be used as a structural part of the chassis. With four valves per cylinder and an 11.8:1 compression ratio, the Neotech V12 was said to produce 640bhp at 12,400rpm with an ability to rev to 14,000. Torque was quoted as 355lb-ft at 9,000rpm, a value that is hard to credit.

Work on the engine started in August 1987 and the first tests of a Neotech twelve began in October 1988. When the project was revealed in 1990, one potential customer was Swiss entrepreneur Walter Brun, whose enterprises had ambitions in both Group C and Formula 1. Planned was the production of three more prototypes and then a float of 20 engines for the EuroBrun Grand Prix team, which at the time was using Judd V8s. A test installation of the Neotech was also made in one of Brun's Type 962 sports-racing Porsches. Walter Brun said he was expecting a $50 million injection from an Arabian oil major; its failure to arrive may account for the non-appearance on the circuits of Neotech's V12.

With money no object in Japan's 'bubble economy' of the 1980s, several vee-twelve engine projects bubbled up in that creative nation. One took shape in an advanced research group at the Fujisawa engineering centre of Isuzu, 28 miles south of Tokyo. Though better known for their trucks and diesels, a cadre of Isuzu's engineers struck out boldly with a full-fledged four-cam racing V12 with four valves per cylinder. Carrying its 3½ litres in two banks at 75°, it was badged 'Isuzu Sport'.

In 1989 Lotus Cars announced a new front-drive Elan sports car, powered by a 1.6-litre Isuzu engine.[1] With these links in place it was logical that Isuzu would wonder whether Team Lotus – by then separated from the car-making company – would be interested in its vee-twelve. If good test results could be achieved, the engineers hoped that Isuzu would commit the resources needed to supply engines to a Grand Prix team.

In 1991, under its top-secret Project 799, Team Lotus agreed to modify one of its 102B chassis into a 102C that could take the Japanese twelve for test purposes. "It was a very serious attempt to run an engine and look at its capability with a view to the future," said Peter Collins, manager of Team Lotus, who had carried out the negotiations with Isuzu. "The timing between the first meetings and when we ran the engine was very short," added Collins. Lotus was given only enough information about the engine to allow it to make the installation. "It was such a secret project," said Chris Murphy, who designed the installation, "that I had the Isuzu in my sitting room at home, where I had my drawing board."

Both the test venue and the driver were kept under wraps.[2] "We were very impressed by the job Isuzu did," said Peter Wright, then Team Lotus technical chief. "The engine ran reliably and performance was good." Chris Murphy seconded the motion: "It ran very credibly. We would have

A team of Isuzu engineers produced a 75° V12 of 3.5 litres for which they had high hopes as a Grand Prix engine. Tested in a Lotus chassis in 1991, it showed promising pace. However, the engineers were unable to persuade Isuzu to invest in the fielding of a Formula 1 engine.

considered using it." "Although the engine did show potential, it would certainly not have been the right thing to do in 1992," said Collins. "As to the future, it depends on what the company wants to do with its engine."

In spite of Lotus's positive assessment of the vee-twelve, what Isuzu elected to do with it, ultimately, was nothing. With Isuzu not convincingly profitable, the needed support was not forthcoming. The Isuzu engine's only public appearance was at the Tokyo Auto Show in October 1991, when it was mooted as the mid-engined power of a futuristic concept pickup truck, Isuzu's Como.

The following January in Tokyo saw the unveiling of another twelve-cylinder Japanese contender from HKS, a maker of performance-tuning equipment. While HKS had made major components like five-valve cylinder heads since its founding in 1973 by Hiroyuki Hasegawa, this was its first essay at a complete engine. Although intended chiefly for sports-car racing, the 3½-litre 300E twelve was installed in a Lola T91/50 Formula 3000 open-

Another Japanese vee-twelve with a 75° bank angle was built in 1992 by Tokyo's HKS. Featuring five valves per cylinder, the HKS 300E failed to race after being tested in a Lola chassis.

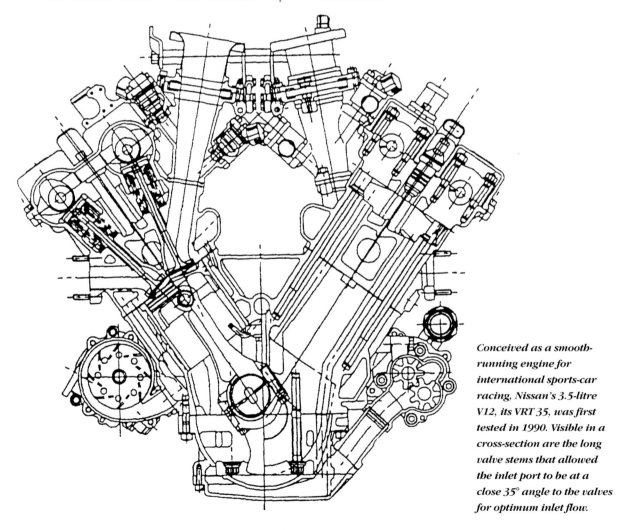

Conceived as a smooth-running engine for international sports-car racing, Nissan's 3.5-litre V12, its VRT 35, was first tested in 1990. Visible in a cross-section are the long valve stems that allowed the inlet port to be at a close 35° angle to the valves for optimum inlet flow.

wheeled chassis for testing at Fuji International Raceway at the end of 1992.

Instead of the ideal 60°, HKS chose a 75° bank angle for its 300E V12 to gain more space in the vee for induction passages. Electronic ignition and injection were by an in-house HKS system. Heads and block were of aluminium with a plating of Mahle's Nikasil – nickel bearing fine silicon-carbide particles – to protect the cylinder bores.

Gearing to the four camshafts was from the clutch end of the nitrided-steel crankshaft. Titanium was used for the three inlet valves and two exhausts per cylinder and for the connecting rods. Nevertheless the 300E was no lightweight at 384lb. Although HKS claimed 650bhp for it at 12,000rpm, this ambitious twelve was never used in anger.

Far more in the way of resources backed the making of another Japanese 3½-litre V12. Since 1985 Nissan had seen a victory at Le Mans as a corporate objective. Making good on this aim would be the responsibility of its own racing team, NISMO (for Nissan Motorsports), for which componentry was made both by a California-based group, Nissan Performance Technology, and by its own factories in Japan.

For its Group C racing cars Nissan relied at first on a turbocharged V8 of its own design, influenced by Cosworth's DFV. Concerned about the chassis-destroying vibrations emitted by the V8, however, Nissan's Yoshimasa Hayashi concluded that a smoother twelve would be by far the better engine for long-distance racing. When the new 3½-litre rules were promulgated in 1989 Hayashi started work on just such an engine at Nissan's Motorsports Engine Development Section in Yokosuka.

Hayashi's team settled on a 70° vee for their VRT35 twelve. They offset its right-hand cylinder bank forward and spaced its cylinders at 94mm. With 3,499.6cc (83 x 53.9mm) its displacement was bang on the limit. Gear drive to its twin overhead camshafts was at the front of the block, where gear trains to the sides powered its water pump, on the right, and oil-scavenging pumps on the left.

Cup-type tappets above twin coil springs opened the Nissan's four valves per cylinder. The latter were symmetrically disposed at a 22½° included angle, with the inlet port closely angled at 35° to the valve stems. Valve diameters were 35mm for the inlets and 29.5mm for the exhausts. For optimum rigidity the camshaft bearings were between the pairs of valves for each cylinder.

Very deep aluminium heads were clamped by long studs to a block of the same material, holding down the collars at the top of wet steel cylinder liners. Nozzles directed cooling oil at the undersides of the Nissan's shallow pistons, with their two compression rings and one oil ring. Connecting rods were 108mm long and ran on 45mm big-end journals. Split at the crankshaft centreline, the bottom of the block was closed by an aluminium casting with which the two-bolt caps for the

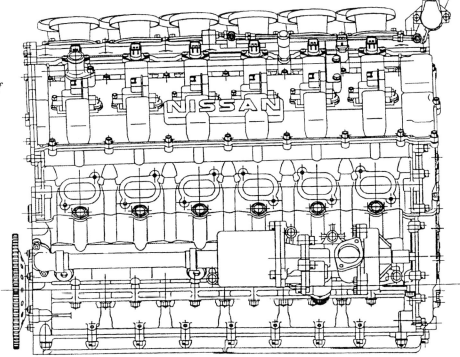

The right-hand side of Nissan's VRT 35 vee-twelve shows its timing-gear housing, at the right, and oval exhaust ports. The water pump is at the side of the crankcase.

52mm main bearings were integrated. Below that a shallow detachable sump collected oil for the twin scavenging pumps. With each cylinder fed by twin fuel injectors below slide throttles, the VRT35 twelve was managed by a system provided by Japanese firm Jecs.

In 1990 the Nissan vee-twelve was ready for its first dynamometer tests. These led to improvements that were incorporated in a second-generation engine. To evaluate its durability in a car, one of these was sent to America to be installed in a redundant Lola Indy-car chassis. Because it wasn't designed to be fully stressed, a tubular frame braced the chassis tub to the rear suspension. In the USA some 600 test miles were covered by the VRT35 in this mule.

One of its American testers was unimpressed, saying, "This doesn't produce as much power as an Indy Lights car." With CART's secondary Lights series using Buick engines producing 425 horsepower, this was a withering assessment. So was the remark of another driver who tested it at Daytona: "There's no power. The engine wants to make power but something's off with the timing." Accustomed as it was to its own turbocharged engines giving more than 1,000 horsepower, Nissan's California contingent was scathing about the Japanese effort. "We were saddled with the world's worst V12 Group C engine," said one of its number. As to the twelve's actual output, he added, "We never had the right from Nissan to put one on the dyno."

Yoshimasa Hayashi went back to his drawing board to produce a third-generation VRT35 to meet these and other criticisms. He shrank the size of its cylinder heads to lower its centre of gravity and reduce its weight to less than 340lb. Power, said Hayashi, was more than 630bhp with in excess of 290lb-ft of torque.

Installed in a provisional sports-racer built by the Californians, the P35, the latest twelve was tested at Daytona, Mid-Ohio and Firebird Raceway in the summer of 1992. Their evaluation, using track data, was that its real power was nearer 500bhp. Tuned more for sprint racing than endurance, the VRT35 first powered its final Japanese-built chassis, the NP35, on 21 October. Eleven days later it raced, with a conservative rev limit, at Mine in the last event of the All Japan Championship. "Plagued with problems throughout the weekend," it qualified slowest and finished last.

NISMO's racers had high hopes of a 1993 Le Mans entry for an evolved version of their car called the R93CP, but these were dashed when Nissan, suffering its first-ever loss-making year in 1992, withdrew its support of racing. After limping through its 1992 season, the 3½-litre formula for endurance-racing cars was terminated after only two years by the FIA. Ironically, Nissan's vee-twelve was one of the entries that had been hoped and prayed for in 1992 to help keep the formula alive.

The withdrawal of another entry had contributed to the 3½-litre Group C's decline in 1992. This was the campaign of Mercedes-Benz, which had fielded its advanced C291 in the 1991 season. Using a chassis built in Switzerland by Peter Sauber, it was powered by the M291, a flat-twelve engine of 3,492cc (86 x 50.1mm). Studies were prepared of a vee-twelve version of the M291 that would be suitable for use in the Formula 1 car that was being designed by a team of engineers at Sauber during 1991. At the end of that year, however, Daimler-Benz announced that it would terminate its Group C effort and would not, for the time being, consider entering Grand Prix racing. There would be no V12 version of the M291.

These feisty motor-sports initiatives from Stuttgart did not escape the attention of arch-rivals BMW in Munich. Over the years from 1982 to 1987 BMW had been hyper-active in Formula 1 with turbocharged engines based on its production four-cylinder iron block. It achieved nine victories and, in a Brabham chassis, took Brazilian Nelson Piquet to the drivers' World Championship in 1983. Thus when Formula 1 was spoken of in Germany, BMW wanted to join the conversation. This held particularly for Paul Rosche, one-time understudy to Alex von Falkenhausen who had succeeded that engineer as the guru of racing engines at BMW.

As soon as the new 3½-litre Grand Prix formula was announced, Paul Rosche's team went to work on a normally aspirated engine. They chose a classical 60° V12 layout, spacing its cylinder centres at 96mm. This gave enough room for an 85mm bore which, with a stroke of 51.3mm, produced a displacement of 3,493cc.

Their aim was to keep their engine as short and light as possible. To achieve this the BMW engineers chose a unique way of driving the overhead camshafts on each cylinder bank. This twelve's right-hand cylinder bank was offset forward, which left gaps to the front of the left-hand cylinder bank and behind the right-hand bank. BMW fitted the cam-drive gear train into these gaps.

The crankshaft had drive gears at both ends. At the front, the gear train rose to drive the cams on the left-hand cylinder bank. At the rear it drove the right-bank camshafts. Take-off gears from these trains drove accessory drives at the sides of the crankcase, the right-hand one (oil scavenge pumps) driven from the rear and the left-hand one (oil pressure pump) from the front. Each side also had its own water pump and manifold feeding cool water to the block.

An attractive feature of the BMW V12's cam-drive concept was that it facilitated the use of a single

Seen in its four-valve version, the 3.5-litre V12 built in 1991 by Paul Rosche's BMW team fitted the gear drives to its camshafts into the gaps left by the offsets between the facing cylinder banks. Producing in excess of 700bhp, the engine was never used in racing but served to keep a team together at BMW to develop Formula 1 engines.

Like its four-valve sister, the five-valve V12 built by Paul Rosche in 1991 was designed to be used as part of the chassis of a Grand Prix car. On its right-hand side, oil and water pumps were driven by a shaft from gearing at the right rear of the cylinder block.

cylinder-head casting to serve on both sides of the engine. Each aluminium cylinder head was topped by a bolted-on magnesium carrier for the camshafts and bucket-type tappets.

Extending down to the crankshaft centreline, the BMW's cylinder block was made of magnesium reinforced by fibres, a highly advanced technique. This helped keep the engine's weight around 320lb. A deep light-alloy sump casting closed the bottom of the block and carried the bearers that allowed the V12 to be used as an integral part of the car's chassis.

Paul Rosche was not satisfied with just one type of cylinder head for his new Grand Prix engine. Better, he and his team thought, to try two different configurations and see which was best. One looked conventional enough with its twin close-spaced camshafts opening four valves per cylinder. It was an advance on the usual layout, however, in that the valves for each cylinder were gently inclined in the fore-and-aft plane to give each chamber a slightly hemispherical form instead of the usual pent-roof shape. To accommodate this the cam lobes were given conical profiles.[3]

The other head design for BMW's V12 was much more radical. Five-valve combustion chambers, with three inlet valves and two exhausts, seemed promising at that time for highest performance. But actuating the three inlet valves was difficult, especially if the designer wanted to give his central valve a different angle to achieve the best combustion chamber shape. Monkey motion in the valve gear was often added to achieve this, but the

consequence could be a reduction in the revs that could be sustained by the valve gear.

Rosche's team came up with a radically different solution. Each head had a single camshaft operating all the exhaust valves as usual, plus *two camshafts* for the inlet valves. One opened the outer pair of inlets while the

In the five-valve version of his Formula 1 engines developed in 1990 and '91 at BMW, Paul Rosche used three camshafts for each cylinder bank to gain the best possible positioning for the three inlet valves. This proved not to be advantageous in terms of weight and power, the four-valve version of the engine being preferred.

other, placed nearer the centre of the engine vee, opened the third central valve. With this solution the valve gear could be simple, rigid and direct – just what was needed to achieve and sustain high engine speeds.[4] The unique drive to the cams was the same as in the four-valve engine.

Not a priority project, the vee-twelves were progressed as and when Rosche's Motorsport team had time and resources. By 1990 they were being assembled and in 1991 they were submitted to the test bed for evaluation. The four-valve was fitted with individual ignition-coil assemblies for each cylinder while the five-valve had a more conventional Bosch Motronic system. Various induction methods were tested, with both slide and rotary throttles and injection both above and below the throttles.

What was the news from the Motorsport dynamometer cells? It was pretty good. Peak output of the two engines was found to be similar: 720bhp at 14,500rpm. BMW had already concluded that of its two versions the four-valve was the more attractive, especially because it was lighter than the five-valve version and crucially so, for the ultra-low modern Grand Prix car, at the top of the engine.

With BMW having introduced a V12 for its road cars, racing a twelve in Formula 1 would have obvious commercial appeal. Instead, BMW committed itself to the very successful exploitation of its M3 in touring-car racing. Paul Rosche dedicated his efforts to some very successful big vee-twelves, described later. And when in the first days of September 1997 BMW decided that it would return to Formula 1 with Williams as its partner, it was aware that a ten, not a twelve, was the best solution. Its experiences with these V12s – and their role in maintaining the skills of the Rosche team – contributed to the later success of the vee-tens from Bavaria.

The third German powerhouse of high-technology motor sports, Porsche, built a vee-twelve to enter Formula 1 in 1991 – and came to regret it. In 1991 Footwork Arrows cars powered by Porsche engines were entered in six Grand Prix races. With a two-car team, that offered 12 starting chances. Half those chances were blown when the cars failed to qualify to start. One was lost when a car was heavily damaged during practice. Of the remaining five opportunities, all were squandered when the cars failed to finish – often with engine failures. And when they were running they were at the back of the field. Well before the end of the 1991 season Porsche withdrew its engines, suffering one of the deepest humiliations the proud company had ever experienced.

Hans Mezger, Paul Rosche's counterpart as the racing-engine authority at Porsche, began thinking about the right layout for a 3½-litre engine in the latter part of 1988.

His choices lay between a V8 and a V12; not until 1989 would Honda and Renault show that a V10 was a valid alternative.[5] Of these he found the V12 the most attractive in terms of its potential for high revs and thus high power. Considering the length of its crankshaft, however, Mezger was apprehensive. Analysis showed that its torsional vibrations could be excessive, especially at the high revs he wanted to reach.

Instead of taking the drive from the end of the crankshaft, Mezger chose a central drive that turned both the camshafts and the output shaft. As in the Abarth, Neotech and Honda twelves with the same feature, he placed the output shaft above the crankshaft so the latter would be as low as possible, reducing the engine's centre of gravity. This layout also allowed Mezger to conceive his new V12 as two of his V6 engines for TAG placed back to back. He used the same 80° cylinder-vee angle, which was adopted after an analysis of both primary and secondary out-of-balance forces showed that this angle gave the best compromise between the two forces.

As in the TAG six, inlet-valve inclination was 14° from vertical and the exhaust angle 15°. In addition the valves were angled away from the bore centreline by $1\frac{1}{2}$° in the fore and aft plane to give the chamber a slightly spherical surface and to improve gas flow. Cylinder dimensions were enlarged from the TAG's 82 x 47.3mm to 86 x 50.2mm to bring the twelve's displacement to 3,499cc. The stroke/bore ratios of both engines rounded to 0.58. With this congruency of concepts, Mezger could start testing a sample engine by the simple means of modifying two of his TAG sixes and coupling them to a central geared power offtake.

Derived from its displacement and cylinder number, the designation of the new engine was Type 3512. Mezger offset the left-hand cylinder bank forward. With its central gearing the twelve needed eight main bearings instead of the usual seven. To keep the engine as short as possible its oil and water pumps were located along the sides and driven from the central gear train. Cylinder-centre distance was 100mm in each of the six-cylinder modules.

Atop the 3512's aluminium block its heads of the same material integrated their cam carriers with the head castings. Wet aluminium cylinder liners were Nikasil-protected and fitted with Mahle pistons. Titanium connecting rods measured 125mm, while bottom-end bearing sizes were 48mm for the mains and 45mm for the rod journals. A particular challenge in designing the block and heads was the requirement that this long engine, with its central gear-train cavity, should take all the stresses as the sole structure of the rear of a racing-car chassis.

Valve sizes were 33.3mm for the inlets and 29.8mm for

After the introduction of the newer and smaller M137, Mercedes's performance arm AMG continued to supply the M120 V12 in 7.3-litre form to power the Zonda produced in Italy by Horacio Raul Pagani, above. In 2005 Morocco's Laraki announced production in Casablanca of its Fulgura, at right, powered by an M137 Mercedes-Benz V12 enlarged by Brabus to 6.2 litres and turbocharged to produce 660bhp and a reported 959lb-ft of torque.

With Maybach having produced Germany's most celebrated twelve of the 1930s, a Maybach for the 21st Century could hardly have had fewer cylinders. Above, Maybach's Type 12, introduced in 2002, is shown next to one of its cost-no-object forebears. Based on Mercedes-Benz's M137 vee-twelve introduced in 1999, the Maybach's engine was twin-turbocharged. Its displacement was reduced to 5.5 litres by smaller bores that gave it greater robustness.

Seen under test on the dynamometer at Mercedes-Benz, where it was known as the M285, the turbocharged Maybach vee-twelve was a power prodigy. Its 550bhp and 664lb-ft of torque encouraged DaimlerChrysler to call it the most powerful engine in any series production car at its 2002 launch. It was not far from producing one horsepower per pound from its 595lb, an extremely impressive achievement for an emissions-controlled road-car engine.

Based on the narrow-angle V6 first introduced in 1991, the VW Group created a W12 to cap its Volkswagen, Audi and Bentley ranges. Above is the dry-sump version for the Audi A8, introduced in 2004 with 450bhp. First used as power for the 550 Maranello in 1996, Ferrari's F133A twelve developed 485bhp from its 5.5 litres. As fitted to 2003's 612 Scaglietti, at left, its 5.7 litres delivered 540 horsepower.

The W12 as used in Audi's A8 combined two 15° V6 engines with their centrelines at a 72° vee. A display engine showed its valve gear and the chain drive to its twin overhead camshafts on each cylinder bank. Unusuallly for a road- *car engine the chain drive was at the flywheel end of the crankshaft. Also cut away are the inlet ram pipes. Owing to the staggered positions of the cylinders in each bank, ram-pipe lengths differed from one cylinder to the next.*

At Geneva in 2004 Maserati unveiled its MC12, a competitor in the FIA's GT championship. Then under the Ferrari corporate umbrella, it used the Enzo's F140 engine, an all-new 65° twelve of 6.0 litres. Its racing version is pictured above, while at left is the engine bay of the road version of the MC12, producing 624bhp at 7,500rpm. In the Maserati tradition, the MC12 was a winner.

The Bologna Show at the
end of 1999 saw the launch
of Lamborghini's Diablo
GTR, above, built in a
series of 30 cars. Its
6.0-litre V12's output was
raised to 590bhp at
7,300rpm, which gave the
GTR a top speed of 214mph.
It accelerated from rest to
62mph in only 3.5 seconds.
First shown as a prototype
at Detroit in 2003, at right,
the roadster version of
Lamborghini's Murciélago
had a tubular stiffening
structure above its 6.2-litre
engine of 580bhp. Four
separate throttle valves
were needed to supply
sufficient air to its twin
plenum chambers.

A king among 21st-Century twelves was the 6.2-litre engine powering Lamborghini's Murciélago, introduced in 2001. New features were variable-volume inlet manifolding and dry-sump lubrication for a lower profile. Maximum power of 580bhp at 7,500rpm was transmitted through four-wheel drive masterfully integrated with the engine, the rear differential protruding from the back of the twelve, underneath its alternator.

the exhausts, opening upon a combustion chamber that provided a 12.8:1 compression ratio. Induction, through short ram pipes, was controlled by slide throttles, while injection and ignition were by Bosch Motronic. At 5:07 p.m. on 6 September 1990 the button was pressed to start the first proper Type 3512 on the dynamometer – thumbed significantly by Ferry Porsche himself. Keenly interested were Porsche engineering director Ulrich Bez, Hans Mezger, project chief engineer Wolfgang Hatz and supporting engineers Claus Brüstle, Gerhard Schuhmann, Staas Gietzen and Manfred Bäumler plus chief mechanic Gerhard Küchle.

Early test-bench running went smoothly, although they soon discovered an expense they hadn't anticipated: the need to upgrade the test cell's soundproofing. The naturally aspirated twelve was more than twice as noisy as its turbocharged predecessors. So smoothly did it go, in fact, that an engine was installed in a car almost at once. "Only six weeks from the first test-stand trials to the first rollout in a car is an extremely short time," said Hans Mezger. "Normally between them there's about six months." Porsche had contracted to supply engines to the Footwork Arrows team, led by Jackie Oliver and newly backed by Japanese transport tycoon Wataru Ohashi. Footwork would pay substantial sums to Porsche for the use of the engine.

From Porsche's side no opportunity was lost to declare 1991 a "test and development year" for its new engine. Not until 1992, emphasised its spokesmen, could any success be expected. This was echoed by Hans Mezger: "In the first year of entries expectations should not be screwed too high." Footwork too was facing challenges, with its new FA12 chassis designed by Alan Jenkins. The designer had to cope with the engine's considerable

As first installed in a Footwork Arrows chassis near the end of 1990, the Type 3512 Porsche twelve was an impressive if lengthy piece of machinery. Disadvantaged by its high weight and major problems with its oiling system, the engine was a disappointment in 1991, the only season in which it competed in Formula 1 racing.

length as well as its weight, which started out at an obese 406lb and was reduced to 396lb by the end of June.

Nor was the 3512's power anything to boast about. The 1991 season began with 650–660bhp at 13,500rpm from an engine that could rev to 14,000. That year Honda and Renault were 'lording it' with their well-developed

Designed by Alan Jenkins, the Footwork Arrows chassis in which the Porsche V12 was installed was a formidable-looking automobile at its early 1991 launch. However, problems with its structure and transmission led to a 'blame culture' between engine supplier and car builder.

V10 engines, Renault's delivering 770bhp at 14,200rpm and Honda's no less powerful. Improvements during the summer raised the Porsche's output to 670–680bhp – still far from competitive. The results, as described earlier, were catastrophic in a year in which many entrants had to pre-qualify for Grands Prix. The Footwork-Porsches were verging on this disgrace when, on 24 June, Porsche announced that it was taking a "pause" from racing to get its engines sorted.

The "pause" became protracted. In a pre-agreed performance test of an improved 3512 against a Cosworth-powered Footwork Arrows at the end of August, Porsche's twelve was still slower than the British-built eight. In the latter part of September Porsche made public its parting with Footwork, but said that it intended to press on with its Formula 1 effort with the aim of finding a new partner. On 17 October it announced a reversal of this decision, on the eve of the most important race for Footwork and Wataru Ohashi, the Japanese Grand Prix. The only vee-twelve in Porsche's car-making history, the 3512 was abandoned as an embarrassing failure.

Porsche wasn't the only engine builder in the 1990s to see the merits of a central gear train to drive the camshafts that divided a vee-twelve into two vee-sixes. This drove the valve gear with greater precision, important in the continuing search for higher revolutions to produce more power. With World Championships for Nigel Mansell in 1992 and Alain Prost in 1993, both in Williams's chassis, Renault had amply proven the effectiveness of the vee-ten as a Grand Prix engine. But its engineers at Viry-Chatillon, led by Bernard Dudot, were disinclined to rest on their laurels.

In 1992 Renault began developing a vee-twelve. Its ten had worked wonders, but the potential of a twelve to attain higher revs reliably couldn't be overlooked. Driving the camshafts from either end of the crank didn't appeal, however, because the valves most remote from the drive would be the most susceptible to torsional fluctuations in their camshafts. Instead, Dudot took the drive from the nose of the crank by a pair of gears that drove a jackshaft down the central vee. At the middle of the engine this in turn drove trains of gears up to the centres of the camshafts. This engine, the EF60, had four valves per cylinder with a pneumatic system, pioneered by Renault, replacing valve springs.

The 3½-litre EF60 had the unusual vee angle of 64°. Careful design meant that the V12 was only two inches longer than Renault's V10 and no more than 13lb heavier at 320lb than the racing ten. Developed at Viry-Chatillon through 1993, its output was a respectable 800bhp at 14,500rpm. Though this development direction wasn't

pursued further, the EF60 served one very important purpose. It impressed Ayrton Senna when he saw it on a visit to Viry in 1993, helping win him over to the Williams-Renault team for 1994. That the Senna-Renault story didn't end more happily wasn't the engine's fault.

In parallel with Renault's efforts, Ford-backed Cosworth Engineering in Britain remained loyal to the vee-eight configuration with which it had revolutionised Grand Prix racing with its DFV in 1967. Such was the growing interest in twelves in 1991, however, that Ford and Cosworth decided that they should have one too. In April 1990 Cosworth had been taken over by industrial conglomerate Vickers, which was keen to ingratiate itself with a customer as important as Ford. That a twelve was on the drawing boards at Cosworth in Northampton was leaked in May of '91 by Ford's racing chief Mike Kranefuss, stealing the thunder of his company's executive vice president, Allan Gilmour. It was Gilmour's assignment to announce the new engine at the Canadian Grand Prix in early June.

With the unusual vee angle of 64°, in 1992 Renault developed a 3.5-litre vee-twelve for Formula 1 racing. Its never-raced EF60 had a central gear drive to its camshafts taken from a jackshaft driven from the nose of its crank.

"The design of the V12 is complete," said the Ford executive, "and prototypes are now being manufactured. Dynamometer running is to start in November and testing of the engine in a car will begin before the end of the year. At some time in the future we could be running at speeds in excess of 16,000rpm, previously unheard of in this size of engine." Kranefuss forecast a race appearance for the twelve by May of 1992.

Internally, however, the new engine was being designed by a project team of relatively junior engineers under racing director Dick Scammell. They were empowered to pursue very tight packaging with thin-wall castings along lines that broke with successful Cosworth principles. Meanwhile, the company's more experienced designers carried on with existing programmes. This was destined to be a flawed approach.

In July 1991 a rendering of the new vee-twelve was released, together with the news that Tom Walkinshaw's TWR was to command the technical side of the Benetton team, for which the twelve was exclusively intended. Not disclosed was that a Benetton vee twelve could have been Jaguar-badged. "At the time we were spending $10 million a year on various sports-car-racing programmes and weren't getting that much benefit from them," said John Grant, then deputy chairman of Jaguar Cars, a Ford property since 1989. "We would have spent all of it on a Grand Prix programme using the Cosworth vee-twelve, which would have fit the Jaguar image perfectly."

Grant, a committed enthusiast for motor sports, led Jaguar's negotiations with Benetton, which were proceeding well. Well, that is, until TWR engineer Ross Brawn assessed the installation problems posed by the lengthy Cosworth twelve. When integrated into a Formula 1 chassis, as it was evolving in both aerodynamic and structural terms, the compact and fuel-economical V8 was found hard to improve upon.

As well, test results from Cosworth for the five engines made were discouraging, one close observer calling the twelve "pathetically unreliable and underpowered". When Grant left Jaguar to take another Ford job the momentum was lost and the idea of a Grand Prix Jaguar dropped – for the time being. Cosworth took another swing at its twelve, designing and building a second derivative with a different basic design that required new castings.

Cosworth and Benetton did prove a strong combination. In 1994 a Benetton-Ford powered Michael Schumacher to the first of his World Championships. But its engine was a vee-eight. After final testing of the 1991–92 twelve confirmed its unreadiness to race, Ford, Cosworth and Benetton persisted with their surprisingly competitive eight. Only in 1996 would Cosworth desert the vee-eight, and then for a vee-ten.

In 1991 Ford published this rendering of the 3.5-litre V12 being built for it by Cosworth. An opportunity to race it as a Jaguar engine was passed over and the unit, neither powerful nor reliable enough, was never to see a race track.

Earlier, Jaguar might have been associated with a bold experiment with an altogether different configuration of the vee-twelve in Formula 1. The broad-arrow or W12 layout, with three banks of four cylinders, continued to beguile. In the form of the Napier Lion, which performed so well both in the air and on land, it proved its merits (see Chapter 4). In the latter years of the 1960s the distinguished engine designer, Harry Mundy, revived the idea of a W12 as a 3-litre Grand Prix power unit. Mundy was by then at Jaguar, but his design, which he called a 'Trident', was created in the context of engine-maker Coventry Climax, where the engineer had helped create championship-winning engines. Climax was then a member of the Jaguar Group of companies.

"At Coventry Climax we are able to make quite spectacular improvements from exhaust tuning," Mundy said, "not only for maximum power but equally important in the shape of the torque curves. These improvements were made on four- and eight-cylinder engines with exhaust pipes in groups of four. This response to exhaust tuning is the main reason for putting forward the proposal for a Trident or broad-arrow layout with its three banks of four cylinders spaced at 60°." Although not so smooth as a vee-twelve, said Mundy, the Trident would have less vibration than a 90°-vee V8 with a single-plane crankshaft, like the Cosworth DFV.

Harry Mundy completed his engine's general layout. With dimensions of 79 x 51mm its capacity was one-eighth of a cubic centimetre less than three litres. He offset its three banks in succession so that three connecting rods could sit side-by-side on each of the flat crank's four journals. Mundy proposed a built-up five-bearing crankshaft to allow the rods to have one-piece big ends with either plain or roller bearings. Like some motorcycle-racing engines and the OSCA V12 the rods were to have elliptical 'sabre' shanks that would reduce losses from windage and oil-churning. Crankcase was to be aluminium with magnesium water jackets for each bank, housing wet steel liners.

For his cylinder heads Mundy foresaw four valves at a 30° included angle surrounding a central 10mm spark plug. He forecast an output of 455–460bhp from his Trident, at revolutions in the 11,500–11,800 range. The W12 would weigh 325lb, he forecast, which would have put it among the lightest engines of the early 3-litre era. As well, it would be even shorter, by up to two inches, than the Cosworth DFV, making it a tidy and rigid contributor to chassis strength. But these promising estimates were never tested. Meritorious though it had the potential to be, Mundy's Trident wasn't able to power either Coventry Climax or Jaguar into Formula 1.

Later, in the heady first years of the 3½-litre Formula 1, two broad-arrow twelves made it off the drawing board, onto the dynamometer and into cars. In France Guy Negré was quick off the mark with an ambitious W12. His engine was

Not content with creating a radical W12 as a 3½-litre Formula 1 engine, France's Guy Negré also fitted it with rotary valves. Although entered at Le Mans in 1990, an MGN-powered car failed to compete. Negré subsequently switched to the development of cars powered by compressed air.

running in 1988 and the following year was tested in an AGS Grand Prix chassis. Acronymically named after Moteurs Guy Negré, the MGN twelve followed the Mundy concept in having its three banks offset so the connecting rods of facing cylinders could share common crankpins. Instead of conventional valves, the MGN had long cylindrical rotary valves topping its combustion chambers.

While a handsome and compact piece of kit, Negré's MGN twelve never matured. Its tests in the AGS came to naught; no MGN-powered car ever started a race. This applied as well to a 1990 installation of the W12 in a Norma sports-racing car. Although entered for Le Mans that year, the Norma-MGN was among the four cars that failed to qualify for the race. Indeed, it never succeeded in leaving the paddock for the track.

Another 3½-litre W12 did indeed make it to the track, in 1991. This was an ambitious effort backed by Ernesto Vita, a young Italian entrepreneur with a hankering for motoring glory. Choosing 'Life Racing Engines' as his banner, Vita used the English translation of his surname because, he said, it was lucky for his businesses and those of his father. He set up offices in Reggio Emilia and well-equipped workshops in Formigine, both in the heart of Italy's motor-racing industry and not far from Modena.

To design his engines, Vita persuaded Franco Rocchi out of retirement. Sixty-four in 1987, when the project started, Rocchi was a legend among racing's insiders. Backing up Mauro Forghieri, Ferrari's mercurial engineering genius (Niki Lauda's description), Rocchi's skills turned Forghieri's engine ideas into metal. After health problems forced his early retirement, the stoop-shouldered Rocchi was concentrating on his oil painting when Vita lured him back to the drawing board.

One of the attractions of the new initiative for Rocchi was that he could pursue an idea he had tested at Ferrari in 1967. At Maranello he had built and tested an engine called the P3C which disposed its three cylinders in a fan-like pattern 80° apart. With two-valve cylinders and dimensions of 65 x 50cc it displaced 498cc. From this odd-looking engine – planned as a module of a potential 18-cylinder broad-arrow engine of three litres – Rocchi extracted 80bhp at 11,000rpm. With 160 horsepower per litre, this promised 480 horses from a full-scale engine. Ferrari didn't proceed with it at the time, but Rocchi never forgot its potential.

A key attribute of Franco Rocchi's P3C was its use of a central master connecting rod from which slave rods extended out to the pistons in the flanking cylinders. The concept was exactly the same as that of the Napier Lion, with the slave rods connected to the upper portion of the master rod's big end by pivot pins similar in size to the gudgeon pins. A signal advantage of this layout over the

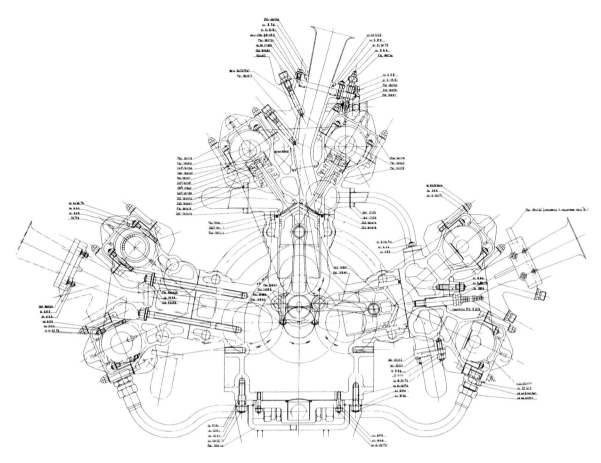

Above: *Back in 1967 Franco Rocchi built and tested a W3 engine module at Ferrari to assess the potential of an 18-cylinder 3.0-litre engine of similar configuration. It developed a highly promising 160bhp per litre.*

Below: *Dubbed the F35 by Life, its producer, this 3.5-litre W12 was launched in December 1988. A design by Franco Rocchi, it had three banks of four cylinders placed at 60° included angles.*

staggered banks proposed by Mundy and used by Negré was that an engine using this design would be significantly shorter – an important advantage in the tight packaging a Grand Prix car required.

Following the P3C's pattern, Rocchi laid out a W12 for Life. It differed in having four valves per cylinder instead of two and angles of 60° instead of 80° between its banks. A single aluminium block with five main bearings was topped by its three cylinder heads, two rows of inlets being in the right-hand vee with a single row atop the left bank. The gear trains to its total of six camshafts were at the drive end of the crankshaft. A Cosworth-like cogged belt at the front of the engine drove its accessories, including the pumps flanking the sump.

On 8 December 1988 Life Racing Engines unveiled Rocchi's brainchild, the F35. It looked ultra-professional, a credit to the Life Racing Engines cadre. As it began its test-bed running in 1989, Enrico Vita's aim was to interest a team and chassis partner in what promised to be an

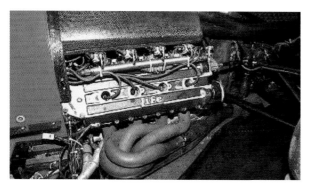

Although the Life W12 engine made a number of appearances during the 1990 Grand Prix season, it failed to pass the pre-qualifying stage at any event. A bold attempt to build a broad-arrow twelve for modern Formula 1 competition had been unsuccessful.

exciting engine. Failing in this, he splashed out on a chassis that had been designed for an Italian team that never made it to the circuits for financial reasons and installed Rocchi's engine to enter a team of his own in the 1990 Grand Prix season.

The Life effort has gone down in history as one of the most conspicuously and comprehensively disastrous in Grand Prix annals. The company's very name became an embarrassing irony as the engines died after only brief efforts on the track. In their first attempt to pre-qualify on the streets of America's Phoenix, the ignition box failed after only four laps. The team had no spare; indeed it was so poorly equipped that it had to borrow a tyre-pressure gauge.

Gary Brabham tried again at Sao Paulo in Brazil, where a connecting rod broke soon after he left the pits. Bruno Giacomelli had no better luck at Imola, making only one slow lap in third gear. At Monaco he completed eight laps, then broke the engine when trying to qualify. Seven laps were the total in Canada, while none of use was completed in Mexico, France or Britain. In Germany, Hungary and Belgium Bruno was far too slow to qualify, while at Monza the engine blew after only two laps. This was the team's final attempt to race their Life F35. They replaced it with a Judd V8 for two pre-qualifying attempts in which – it must be said – Giacomelli was no quicker.[6]

Franco Rocchi had failed in his attempt to make the leap from his 1967 P3C to the Life F35 of 1990. To keep the twelve as compact as possible he had enlarged its bore and shortened its stroke to an extreme.[7] The result was that the slave rods to the side banks of cylinders were severely foreshortened, compromising their geometry. When British consultant Al Melling cast an eye over the engine he concluded that it would be design-limited to 10,200rpm. Indeed, said the Life engineers, that's just the

speed at which it breaks on the dynamometer. Melling also prophesied a horsepower plateau of 500. In the event the F35 was unreliable at much more than 375bhp.

Thus ended the Life Racing Engines adventure and the dream of Ernesto Vita not only to race it but also to build a supercar with a similar engine. Ironically, consultant Melling took the view that in a larger displacement with less congested internals "it would have been a nice sports-car engine". Cutting his losses, Vita sold off the remains of his effort to a Verona industrialist who said he intended to supply racing cars to an engineering company in Leningrad.

The sorry Life saga didn't altogether suppress interest in broad-arrow engines for racing. In 1998 engineers from Ducati Motors and the University of Modena researched the relative merits of V12 and W12 engines for Formula 1, using cylinder dimensions of 89 x 40.1mm (2,994cc) with 96mm connecting rods. They eschewed Rocchi's master-and-slave rod system, adopting instead Harry Mundy's sharing of the rod journals by three big ends. For their analysis they chose a 75° bank angle for the V12 and the differing angles of 60° and 65° for the W12, the wider inclination on one side giving more room for the central cylinder bank's exhaust system.

Estimating both engines' stresses to 18,000rpm, the engineers concluded that the W12 was a "valid alternative" for Formula 1, with the potential for lower friction losses and a more compact and stiff package, set against higher secondary out-of-balance forces. The issue, however, was soon moot. In 1999 the FIA announced new regulations that specified that from 2000 until the end of 2007 expiry of the Concorde Agreement which governed Formula 1, "all engines will have 10 cylinders". This sanctified what had become the status quo.

Toyota was caught on the hop by the FIA's action. At its motor-sports base in Cologne, Toyota was well along in the planning of its Grand Prix campaign in 1999. "We decided that it would be best for Toyota to build a vee-twelve engine," said Norbert Kreyer, who directed its initial engine efforts. Toyota was then planning on a test year in 2000 and its first entry in 2001, but this was cast into disarray by the FIA's edict. Work began on a vee-ten instead. The change of direction meant that the launch of Toyota's campaign had to be put back to 2002.

When Toyota entered Formula 1 another Japanese company, Yamaha, had just departed. Yamaha's last year as an engine supplier to Grand Prix teams was 1997 with Arrows. The Iwata-based manufacturer of motorcycles, marine products and other powered equipment was founded in 1955 to build two-stroke motorbikes. A breakthrough came ten years later when Yamaha became

Toyota's partner in the design and manufacture of the Toyota 2000GT sports car.

To promote its services as an engine supplier to car companies, Yamaha started supplying racing engines in 1984. Its first effort was the OX66, a vee-six with belt-driven overhead cams and a feature that was to become a Yamaha hallmark: five-valve chambers with three inlets and two exhausts. Through an agreement with Cosworth it based its 1987 OX77 six on the DFV bottom end; this took Aguri Suzuki to the 1988 Japanese Formula 3000 championship.

Yamaha's next step was its OX88 V8, which powered the Grand Prix cars of the German Zakspeed team in 1989. Under the leadership of Takehiko Hasegawa, Ryuichi Yamashita headed the engine-development effort. In 1990 Yamaha set up a base in Britain's Milton Keynes for the servicing of its racing engines. After a disastrous season with Zakspeed that saw many engine-related retirements, the Japanese returned to Formula 1 with the Brabham team in 1991 with their latest creation, the OX99 vee-twelve.

Still with five-valve cylinder heads, the 60-valve OX99 had a 70° vee angle. With its right-hand cylinder bank offset forward, it displaced 3,498cc. Its crankshaft nestled into the bottom of a block that was cut off at the crank centreline and enclosed by a sump casting that also carried the main-bearing caps. Side-mounted pumps were driven by a train of gears from the crank nose, while the gears to the camshafts were at the rear, adjacent to the clutch. Though the 308lb OX99 was said to be capable of more than 700bhp, this was not always available in racing as its Yamaha nursemaids, nervous about reliability, were prone to curtail its maximum revs.

Brabham, a shadow of its championship-winning form of a decade earlier, struggled with car problems and chassis failures, demoralising its drivers. Even worse, from Yamaha's standpoint, was that Brabham's meagre sponsorship meant that the Japanese company had to provide cash as well as engines. The season's solitary high was a sixth place for Mark Blundell at Spa that gave Yamaha a first-ever world-championship point. A debilitated Brabham team limped into the 1992 season and then expired.

Cupid in the 1992 marriage between Yamaha and another team, Jordan, was Formula 1's impresario, Bernie Ecclestone. Eddie Jordan's eponymous team had made an impressive Grand Prix debut in 1991 with Ford engines, but the cost of leasing them had put a $5 million hole in the Jordan budget. Ecclestone filled the hole with a loan and introduced Jordan to a company prepared to provide engines for free: Yamaha. Until then Yamaha had been linked with Reynard, which was expected to enter

Formula 1 in 1992 with a car designed by Rory Byrne. When this failed to eventuate, designer Gary Anderson implanted the OX99 in a new Jordan chassis. Forewarned of the vee-twelve's appetite for petrol, Anderson gave his Jordan 192 a 51½-gallon fuel tank – the largest in the field.

Although Jordan had pre-season problems with its new seven-speed transaxle, it was a team with a good chassis that at last could test the OX99. It was found wanting. Early problems with cooling, initially blamed on the radiators, were later traced to faulty water-pump design. Its sump scavenging wasn't up to the high lateral g forces the 192 could generate, said Anderson: "Places like Eau Rouge [at Spa] and the Parabolica [at Monza], the faster you went through the corner, the slower you went down the straight." Bizarrely, the twelves were inconsistent in the orthogonality of their front faces. With this bolted to the monocoque and the engine serving as the rear of the chassis, lack of precision here threw off the chassis alignment. It took the team several months to divine this subtle discrepancy.

The OX99's major drawback was a very peaky power curve. Maximum power was good, but mid-range torque was conspicuous by its absence. "The engine just didn't seem to want to get up and go," Gary Anderson recalled. It was also still susceptible to embarrassing mechanical failures that again prompted Yamaha's motor minders to dial back the rev limit and, with it, performance. Ruefully, Gary Anderson had to conclude that "Yamaha had the basic problem of not really understanding the fundamental needs of a racing engine."

For its part, Yamaha asked John Judd's Engine Developments to assist in sorting its twelve. This was to lead to a long-term relationship in which future V10 Yamahas were based on Judd's designs. Meanwhile, Jordan asked engine builder Brian Hart to take a look at one of the twelve's many problems. When Anderson discovered that Hart had a V10 of his own on the stocks, he jumped at the chance to use it in 1993.

Jordan's four-year relationship with Yamaha ended after one season in which a single solitary championship point was scored by Stefano Modena in the final race at Adelaide. That made a total of two points for the two-year career of the OX99. As a hail and farewell, one of its users called it "too big, too long, too heavy, too complex, too inefficient and too bad to deserve any further time."

Capping the chequered career of the OX99 was its installation in one of the most bizarre supercars ever conceived. Yamaha's Ypsilon Technology in Milton Keynes was assigned the task of building a central-seated road car powered by the vee-twelve. Still revving to more than 10,000rpm, the OX99 was given butterfly instead of slide throttles to improve its driveability for road use. As

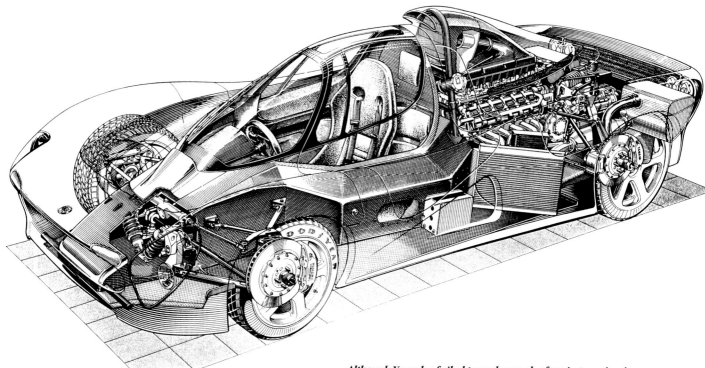

in a Grand Prix car the radiators were athwart the engine, next to a carbon-fibre-clad aluminium honeycomb chassis tub with race-car-style suspension. This, the Yamaha GP SuperCar OX99-11, was an aluminium-bodied coupé with an aircraft-like canopy and a tiny seat behind the driver. Defying the best efforts of Yamaha and Ypsilon, it failed to reach production.

Another Japanese company enjoyed far more success in Formula 1, but even Tokyo's Honda struggled at times to get the best from its vee-twelves. Following a long hiatus

With its high front wing and aeroplane-like canopy, Yamaha's OX99-11 was one of the most unusual cars ever conceived. Built in Britain by Ypsilon Technology, it was aluminium-bodied.

Although Yamaha failed to make much of an impression in Formula 1 racing with its 60-valve OX99 V12 of 3.5 litres, it hoped to recoup some value from its investment by installing it in an extremely unusual road car, the Yamaha GP SuperCar OX99-11 of 1992. It was fashioned very much as a Grand Prix automobile for the road.

Honda returned to car racing in 1980 with vee-sixes in Formula 2 after two years of predevelopment. In 1983 with turbocharged 1½-litre vee-sixes Honda was back in Formula 1, and by 1984 it was winning with Williams.

Honda's return to Formula 1 under the direction of Nobuhiko Kawamoto had the clear aim of achieving an international reputation as one of the 'noble' automotive brands. Noting the participation in GP racing of such great firms as Mercedes-Benz and Alfa Romeo and concluding that taking part at the highest level of motor sports had added great lustre to their names, Honda decided to go and do likewise to enhance its own reputation and that of its new upscale Acura brand in America.

In Honda's racing, at least, it was successful. In partnership with Williams, Honda won the constructors' championship in 1986 and 1987, adding a drivers' trophy for Nelson Piquet in the latter year. The last year for a turbo Honda was 1988, when McLaren became a Honda team. This saw another constructors' championship with a stunning 14 wins in 15 races and a season-long battle between Alain Prost and Ayrton Senna for the drivers' championship in which the latter triumphed.

After such a spectacularly successful year Honda gave serious consideration to withdrawing from Formula 1. Soichiro Honda counselled continuation, however, pointing out that with turbos soon to be banned a new level playing field was being created on which Honda could confirm its superiority. Accordingly it began the new 3½-litre Formula 1 of 1989 with a V10 engine and a continuation of its McLaren partnership, which was to last through 1992.

The V10 was raced in 1989 and '90, bringing two more constructors' cups and driving championships for Prost and Senna. To meet intensifying competition from Ferrari and Renault, Honda decided that a twelve-cylinder engine was required. At the 1989 Tokyo Show it first revealed a vee-twelve, which McLaren tested during 1990 in preparation for 1991. This was the RA121E, which brought McLaren-Honda both championships again with Ayrton Senna the lead driver.

With its left-hand cylinder bank offset forward, the RA121E had a classical 60° vee. All its gearing, to both camshafts and accessories, was at its front end. Very narrow angles separated its four valves per cylinder, above which its camshafts were close-spaced. With its capacity of 3,498cc (86.5 x 49.6mm) Honda's first racing twelve since 1968 weighed 350lb and developed "over 650" horsepower. This was disappointing when several rivals were at and above 700bhp with engines that offered good torque curves as well. As was his style, Brazilian Ayrton Senna made no secret of his dissatisfaction with the twelve's performance when he first drove it in the MP4/6 McLaren at the beginning of 1991.

Strenuous efforts to improve the RA121E during 1991 led to the results mentioned earlier. Overcome were problems with internal oil churning that generated heat and degraded performance, as well as faults in oil distribution that caused main-bearing failures. Output benefited from the mid-season introduction of inlet ram pipes that automatically varied in length, with engine speed, to bolster slumps in the torque curve. Horsepower ultimately penetrated the 700bhp barrier at speeds reaching 14,000rpm.

In parallel with their work on the existing twelve, Kawamoto and company started work on an all-new V12, their RA122E/B, for 1992. The new engine's vee angle was widened to 75° to lower its height and centre of gravity and to make room in the central vee to package the fuel pump and alternator. It was more oversquare than its predecessor at 88.0 x 47.9 (3,496cc) and lighter as well at 340lb.

High-silicon aluminium alloy was used for both its block and its heads. The block terminated at the crankshaft centreline. Bolted to its bottom surface was a large casting of Elektron WE54 magnesium alloy which incorporated the caps for the seven main bearings, the sump and the mountings for the accessory-drive gears across the front of the sump, driven from the crank nose.

Each of the six individual sump chambers, housing a crank throw with its two connecting rods, had a close-fitting circular cross-section. A slot along its lower right-hand side was fitted with guides to collect oil thrown from the crank and channel it to the seven Gerotor-type scavenging pumps on the right. On the left side the gear train drove the water pump and the pressure oil pump. Cast-in galleries for both oil and water ran down the

The state of the art of Formula 1 engines of 1992 was shown by Honda's RA122A/B with its 75° vee angle and strongly oversquare dimensions. The angle between inlet port and valve stem was 35°, commendably low, while the inlet ram-pipe length changed automatically in response to engine speed.

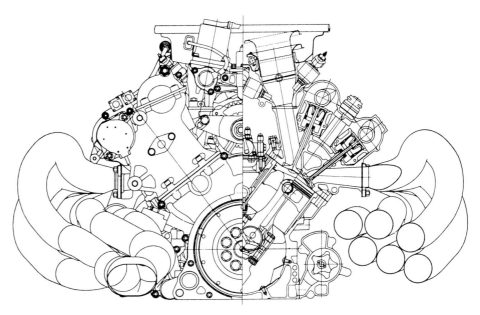

engine's central valley. Included in the oiling system were jets to the undersides of the piston crowns that reduced the temperature of the ring lands by 10–20°C.

Short full-skirted pistons carried two compression rings and a single oil ring in a configuration optimised to reduce blow-by. Their crowns had marked indentations that exactly matched the slightly tulip-shaped contours of the four valve heads. By this close attention to detail Honda could give its RA122E/B the high compression ratio of 12.9:1 in spite of its very large cylinder bore. Surrounding the pistons were aluminium wet liners with a Nikasil running surface, clamped by a top flange into the block. Two O-rings in grooves in the liner completed the bottom seal.

Circlips retained the gudgeon pins. The bushing at the small end of the 111mm connecting rod received splashes of oil through a drilling at its top. Made of titanium, the rods had a robust I-section and massive two-bolt big ends. Each 40mm rod journal was doubly counterweighted in a crankshaft configuration that resulted from tests by Honda of many prototype designs. Drillings in the steel crank cheeks adjacent to the journals helped lighten the throws to reduce the balance mass requirement.

Honda used nitrogen as the medium for the pneumatic valve-closing system of its 1992 RA122E/B. A sectioned view of a tappet shows its movement, together with that of an internal rubber seal, both at rest and at full lift.

Trains of spur gears up the rear of the block drove the V12's four overhead camshafts. Mutually inclined at an included angle of 28°, its 36.5mm inlet valves were made of titanium alloy and the 28.5mm exhaust valves of nickel-alloy steel. The latter were made hollow for lightness and sealed at the head. Cup-type tappets were used instead of Honda's usual fingers, and for a reason. Honda's analysis showed that if a spring force of 236lb were needed to avoid valve bounce at 13,000rpm, a force *half again as great* would be needed at 15,000 and *twice as large* at 15,700rpm. This led it to adopt pneumatic valve closing for the RA122E/B.

Honda chose nitrogen as the system's working gas, the McLaren carrying a reserve supply at 150 atmospheres in two small cylinders mounted on the firewall. Gas was metered at 6 to 8 atmospheres to the volume under each tappet. There the space was sealed by an inverted tulip-shaped titanium cup called a 'piston' by Honda. It was sealed to the valve stem and had a ring seal at its bottom, sliding in the tappet bore. Complete with the required gas passages, bulky tappet-carrying blocks were bolted into each cylinder head. Gas seals were also provided for the inserted valve guides.

The variable-length inlet ram pipes introduced during 1991 were engineered from the start into the new 1992 V12. A hydraulic actuator for each bank of pipes moved the top funnels over a 25mm range. From 8,000 to 15,000rpm an electronic controller operated solenoid valves to raise and lower the funnels three times to help

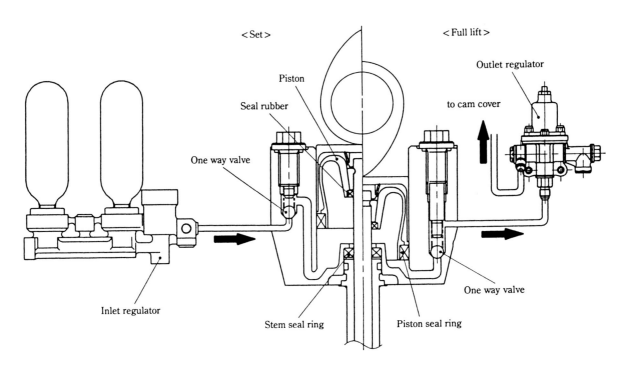

fill in troughs in the power curve. Below the funnels were butterfly-type throttle valves, and below them were two nozzles for the electronically-controlled sequential fuel injection system.

Ayrton Senna and Gerhard Berger had no direct control over their Honda's throttles. Each row of six butterflies was operated by a four-phase electric stepping motor, which was able to position the throttles within 0.1° and move them from closed to open in an eighth of a second. Inputs to the electronic control included engine speed and gears selected as well as throttle position, which dramatically reduced incidents of engine over-speeding – thus making another contribution to reduced valve-to-crown clearance and a high compression ratio.

In the 1992 season these new and complex systems were vulnerable. The failure of a stepping motor cost Senna victory in the Canadian GP, which Berger won. Nor was the high-revving Honda a paragon of fuel economy. McLarens had to start some of the faster races with more than 48 gallons of fuel compared to less than 41 for cars with Cosworth V8 power, a 60lb weight handicap. The RA122E/B began 1992 with 720 horsepower – Senna was complaining again – but by the end of the season its 774bhp at 14,400rpm was highly competitive, as was its torque of 297lb-ft at 12,000rpm.

Although its new MP4/7A chassis was not one of McLaren's best efforts, Ayrton Senna won at Monte Carlo, Hungary and Monza and Gerhard Berger added season-ending Australia to his Canadian win. The two drivers were fourth and fifth in the 1992 World Championship while McLaren-Honda was second in constructors' points. Thereafter Honda took a sabbatical until its return to Grand Prix racing in 2000 – with the then-mandatory V10.

Taking the McLaren MP4/7A to four victories in the 1992 season and second place in constructors' points, the RA122E/B twelve developed 774bhp at season's end. It was Honda's last Formula 1 engine until its return in 2000.

Only two companies – both Italian – succeeded in launching new vee-twelve engines in 1989, the first year of the turbo-free 3½-litre Grand Prix formula. The arrival of one was a distinct surprise. In April 1987 Lamborghini was bought by the Chrysler Corporation. One year later it held a press conference in Modena to show two samples of its new Type 3512 engine, a Formula 1 V12 with its cylinder banks at a wide 80° angle.[8] Present were managing director Emile Novaro, racing director Daniele Audetto and the engine's designer, former Ferrari engineer Mauro Forghieri.

Forghieri's presence was crucial to the credibility of the initiative. Here was the handsome, bespectacled, egotistical and mercurial creative force behind Ferrari's racing cars and engines from the mid-1960s to mid-1980s. He and the tall, patrician Audetto – also a former Ferrari

man – were the prime movers in the establishment of Lamborghini Engineering as a separate entity to build engines and, ultimately, cars as well. The new company set up shop in an industrial estate in Modena, at the very heart of Italy's legendary racing know-how.

The two engines revealed in April had not yet run. The press conferees said they'd sent mock-ups of their new twelve to Lola and March so they could essay installations. The engines looked the business, with both the Chrysler and Lamborghini names on their camshaft covers. Weight was given as 353lb. On 16 September 1988 the Lamborghini 3512 first ran on the test bench. It made its racing debut in Brazil on 26 March 1989, when one engine qualified to race in a hastily adapted chassis and, to its credit, finished – albeit well back in 12th place.

A striking newcomer to the Formula 1 ranks in 1988 was Italy's Lamborghini, offering a new V12 with its cylinder banks at an 80° angle. Its designer was Mauro Forghieri, renowned for his successes at Ferrari.

Chrysler-owned Lamborghini set up a separate facility in Modena to design and build its Formula 1 engines, which first competed in 1989. Lamborghini also designed and built matching transaxles for its customers, among which was Britain's Team Lotus.

Lamborghini's first customer for the 3512 was the French Larrousse Calmels team, which used Lola-built chassis. 'Customer' was the correct term, because Chrysler insisted that Lamborghini Engineering charge for the use of its engines; this was not to be a factory-backed engine-supply effort. *Ergo*, said Mauro Forghieri: "We were serving teams of the fourth category. The teams of the highest standing get their engines free, but we weren't allowed to provide free engines." He did benefit financially from a contract with France's Elf Petroleum for the testing of racing fuels.

Although cylinder heads with both five and four valves were explored for the 3512, four-valve chambers were those used in racing. Cup-type tappets opened the valves, which were at a narrow included angle. The train of gears driving the camshafts was at the rear of the engine. For its 3,496cc capacity the Lamborghini's bore and stroke were 88 x 47.9mm. On an aluminium crankcase, with wet steel cylinder liners, the right-hand cylinder bank was offset forward.

Unlike almost all other Grand Prix twelves, which drove their pumps from the crankshaft nose, the 3512 took the drive from gearing between the first and second pairs of cylinders at the front of the engine. This allowed the engine to be as short as possible – 28.3in – in spite of its large-bore cylinders.

With the block cut off at the crankshaft centreline, a rugged sump with integral main-bearing caps closed the twelve's bottom end. Scavenge pumps were along the left side of the crankcase and pressure and water pumps were on the right. "The Lamborghini

had a very-high-flow-rate oil system," recalled Lotus engineer Chris Murphy. "It had a vicious rate of flow on its output side."

Another novelty was Forghieri's use of only four main bearings. This mirrored his successful use of only four mains for the crankshaft of Ferrari's flat-opposed 312B Grand Prix engine of the early 1970s. He tested engines with both seven and four main bearings, but settled on four as sufficiently strong while demanding less oil and generating lower friction losses.

For the first race Marelli engine management was used, but Lamborghini decided that Marelli was under too much pressure from major customers Ferrari and Renault, so the electronics were switched to Bosch's MP 1.8 Motronic, which with its 15 microprocessors was able to cope with a twelve-cylinder engine running to 16,000rpm.

Such heady revs weren't attempted in 1989. That year Forghieri provided his customers with 620bhp at 13,000rpm; no one was revving any faster. Nevertheless the Franco-Italian team paid the price of a lack of rigorous testing in 1989 with too many engine failures. Fingers were pointed at the Lamborghini's crankcase, which was said to be insufficiently stiff, with the consequence that torsional loadings from the chassis risked its main bearings.

On many occasions only one of the Larrousse Calmels LC89 Lolas qualified; both broke their engines embarrassingly in the French Grand Prix. Finally at Portugal both finished, and then in Spain in the season's penultimate race Philippe Alliot qualified fifth and finished sixth for a single championship point.

Simply as Larrousse in 1990, running a new T90 Lola chassis from the third race, the French team had a bittersweet year. With Eric Bernard as its star driver and the vee-twelve producing 650bhp it accrued the healthy total of 11 points, placing it sixth in the constructors' championship. The following February, however, the FIA struck off the points, saying that Gérard Larrousse's team hadn't identified itself properly because not it but Lola was the maker of its car. In a bizarre compromise with the FIA, the team lost the points but kept its sixth-place standing.

Lamborghini Engineering supplied both engines and transaxles to Larrousse and also to Team Lotus in 1990. The British outfit's new car, its 102 designed by Frank Dernie, needed an early enlargement of its oil tank to meet the needs of the high-revving V12. Forghieri's twelve was also more of a glutton for fuel than the Cosworth and Judd V8s. In a season marred by chassis breakages Lotus scored three points and ranked eighth among constructors.

For 1991 it was all change. Lamborghini finally gained the backing of industrialist Carlo Patrucco for the racing of a car it had completed in 1990 under other auspices. Although the Lambo 291 showed flashes of promise it was unable to score points and the team lasted only one season.

The 3512, now producing 700bhp at 13,800rpm, was also used by the French Ligier team, headed by burly racer Guy Ligier. Reliability was now good but the cars weren't fast enough and Ligier too had a pointless year. An effort by Franz Konrad to field a 3512-powered Group C car, late in 1991, failed to bear fruit.

For 1992 the Minardi Grand Prix team, based in Faenza, became a Lamborghini customer after losing the supply of Ferrari vee-twelves that it enjoyed in 1991. Back in the Lamborghini fold was Gérard Larrousse, now in association with French car-maker Venturi. Neither outfit had a good '92 season, coming away with just a single point apiece. Larrousse stayed with Lamborghini for power in 1993, scoring three points to be ranked equal tenth and last among car makers.

By 1993 the 3512 had been substantially improved, lowered and lightened. It was routinely producing 730bhp and revving to 14,500rpm, meritorious with the continued use of coil valve springs. Its best output seen by Forghieri on his Modena test bench was 754bhp. These were numbers with which to conjure, and no one

For the gearing that drove the twin overhead camshafts on each bank of the Lamborghini Type 3512 Grand Prix engine, Mauro Forghieri chose a location at the rear of the engine adjacent to the clutch. From the gear train a pulley drove an alternator set in the engine's central vee.

Designed to be used as part of the chassis of a Formula 1 car, the Lamborghini vee-twelve was developing 730bhp by the 1993 season. That year Chrysler was deeply disappointed when a planned deal to supply engines to the McLaren team fell through.

knew that better than François Castaing, Chrysler's board member for product development. Castaing had been a key creator of the 1½-litre V6 with which Renault first demonstrated the viability of the turbo engine as a rival to 3-litre unblown engines in Formula 1. Moving to American Motors when Renault owned it, Castaing then became one of the architects of Chrysler's turnaround when that company acquired AMC.

François Castaing was willing to urge a deeper Chrysler and Lamborghini involvement in Grand Prix racing if he could gain the interest of a top team. With this objective in mind he made contact with Ron Dennis, team principal of McLaren International. Suddenly deprived of V12 power after Honda's retirement at the end of 1992, McLaren had fallen back on the leasing of the Cosworth HB V8. Although the Ford-badged eight was capable of 730bhp at 13,500rpm, and with lower fuel consumption, the 3512 from Modena was at least as powerful and offered more development potential, especially if it were converted to pneumatic valves.

"We approached Ron Dennis in the spring of 1993," François Castaing recalled. "We had talks with McLaren about the use of our engine, which was quite powerful." McLaren agreed to test it and produced a special chassis, painted all in white, to evaluate the twelve. "Ayrton Senna

and Mika Häkkinen tested it at Estoril and Silverstone," added Castaing. The results were promising enough to lead to a deal for 1994. At the Frankfurt Auto Show in September Ron Dennis met with Castaing and Chrysler's top brass, chairman Bob Eaton and vice chairman Bob Lutz. "We shook hands on a deal to work for the championship," Castaing said.

This was a big breakthrough for the Chrysler-backed engine. With Lamborghini's owner enjoying better times in America, it would now be in a position to offer free engines to McLaren, in return for the chance to race with a top team. Only six weeks later, however, Castaing received a shock: "Ron called and said, 'I've changed my mind. I've signed with Peugeot, because they give me money as well as engines.'" This was the cynical reality of the world of Grand Prix racing in the 1990s.

McLaren's repudiation of a handshake deal was, recalled François Castaing, "a big wet blanket for Chrysler's efforts." Publicly Ron Dennis played the innocent: "The fact is that we were conducting a technical evaluation of a power plant to provide Chrysler with an indication, rather than making a clear commitment to them." Castaing remembered it differently.

Chrysler was not about to get into a bidding war with Peugeot. Instead, at the end of 1993 Lamborghini Engineering ceased supplying Formula 1 engines and was soon wound up. It was only poetic justice that during McLaren's 1994 season Peugeot's vee-ten was so appalling that the partners fell out well before the end of the year.

It was to the everlasting credit of Chrysler, Lamborghini and Forghieri that they remained in the Grand Prix lists with their twelves for five full years. Only one company used vee-twelves for longer; it was, of course, Ferrari.

Starting with the new Formula 1 in 1989, Ferrari remained true to its V12 traditions through 1995, a total of seven seasons. In the six years of the 3½-litre formula, Ferrari's was not quite the most successful twelve. It clocked up a total of 10 wins and six pole positions against Honda's tally of 13 wins and 11 poles, achieved in just two years. In the first year of the 3-litre formula, 1995, Ferrari added one pole and two more wins to its vee-twelve account.

Ferrari returned to the design of unsupercharged Grand Prix engines after a considerable hiatus. Its last year with its famous flat-twelve 3-litre engine was 1980. Thereafter, from 1981 through to 1987, it joined Renault in competing with turbocharged 1½-litre vee-sixes, at first 120° and later 90°. Never backward where engines were concerned, Ferrari began planning a new unblown vee twelve when, in 1986, word came that such engines would be allowed to displace 3½ litres from 1987.

Conception of the new engine would no longer involve Mauro Forghieri, who stepped down from racing duties at Ferrari in the midst of a turbulent 1984 season. Briton Harvey Postlethwaite managed chassis engineering at Maranello, while from the beginning of 1987 his countryman John Barnard, fresh from a successful career at McLaren, originated new Ferrari Grand-Prix car designs from a base in England. There was little doubt that with Ferrari's traditions the new unblown engine would be a V12, and in this Barnard was in agreement: "We needed to go for the ultimate power option. I was telling them to give me the power and I would package the unit in the best possible way."[9]

Maranello's studies identified the V12 as the optimum where power was concerned. For the eight, ten and twelve they estimated 600, 625 and 645bhp respectively, all other factors being equal. They were aware of advantages in mid-range power for engines of fewer cylinders, but they expected to compensate for this with a completely new semi-automatic seven-speed transmission that would help the driver keep the twelve in its narrower power band.

Work on the new twelve, Type 035, began at the end of 1986 with Giorgio Quattrini as its principal designer and former Renault engineer Jean-Jacques His overseeing development. First thoughts of a 60° vee gave way to a 65° angle to give more room for induction and to allow an oil/water heat exchanger to nestle in the vee. Chosen were dimensions of 84 x 52.8mm (3,498cc) in a cylinder block cast of a special nodular-iron alloy. With the help of

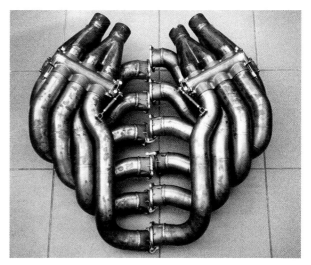

Exhaust manifolds from a 1991 Type 039 Ferrari vee-twelve show the butterfly valves that were controlled by the engine-management system to benefit its torque curve.

Fiat subsidiary Teksid the casting's walls were ultra-thin to minimise any weight penalty over the usual aluminium block. This technique, which allowed compact design by eliminating the need for separate cylinder liners, was used by both Honda and Ferrari in the turbo era.

In its bottom end the 035 carried over a proven attribute of Mauro Forghieri's flat-twelve engines: four instead of seven main bearings. In some engines these would be roller bearings, in others plain bearings. The locations occupied by the missing bearings now carried counterweights, shaped to offer minimum wind resistance. Titanium connecting rods joined to aluminium pistons with two compression rings and one oil ring. Oil and water pumps were ganged along the right side of the 035; the left cylinder bank was offset forward. This left more room in front of the right bank for the piping to the central vee, both for water and for pipes to and from the heat exchanger.

A cogged-rubber belt from the frontal gear train drove the pumps, while a simple belt drove an alternator on the left side to power the electronics. The gears turned two camshafts in each aluminium cylinder head. Through cup-type tappets they opened four valves, in one version of the twelve, and five in another at an included angle of 20°. In the five-valve head the third central inlet valve was tilted to position it better in the combustion chamber, with its single central spark plug. This was the version of the engine finally used, as indicated by its 035/5 designation.

Marelli-Weber electronic fuel injection and ignition managed the Ferrari engine's functions, giving each spark plug its own coil. At the experimental stage the engine had one injector per cylinder but by the beginning of racing in

The 1989 Type 035/5 was redesigned for the 1990 season as the Type 036 by Ferrari. That season brought the team six victories, one for Nigel Mansell and five for Alain Prost.

1989 it had dual injectors. Development began, at the first running of the engine in September 1987, with the moderate compression ratio of 11.5:1. Its output began at 600bhp – matching the best specific power achieved by the 3-litre flat-twelve – and speeds of up to 13,000rpm were explored. Its weight was 311lb.

The plan was to begin racing the engine during 1988, which would have followed a Ferrari tradition. Enzo

As shown in its Type 036 Formula 1 V12 of 1990, Ferrari continued to use cogged-rubber belts to power pumps along the right-hand side of the crankcase. A simpler belt drove an alternator on the left side of the engine. The drive train to the camshafts of the 60-valve engine was at the front.

Ferrari was adept at planning ahead in the power department, as he had shown with his successful four- and six-cylinder engines. However, an early running was ruled out for several reasons. One was that John Barnard's new car was late; the first tests of its initial version, the 639, at Ferrari's own Fiorano track weren't until July of 1988. Another was that the then-current turbo V6 still needed to be brought up to scratch. Yet another reason was that Enzo Ferrari was unwell and died in mid-August. The twelve's first race would not be until 1989.

Although the 035/5 in the final 640 chassis won its debut race in Brazil, the 1989 season brought many disappointments, owed especially to the innovative transmission. Although the twelve proved capable of 640bhp at 12,000rpm, it was retuned for 1989 to a maximum of 600bhp with much-improved torque at 8,000rpm. Having proved inadequate, the oil/water heat exchanger was given up in mid-season and replaced by a separate oil radiator, the drag of which the designers had hoped to avoid. The teething troubles relented enough to see Ferrari score three wins in 1989 and place third in constructors' points behind McLaren and Williams, using Honda and Renault V10s respectively.

Under Jean-Jacques His the Ferrari twelve was updated for the 1990 season as the 036. With a compression ratio raised to 12.5:1 it ultimately produced 680bhp at 12,750rpm. In parallel His began a new programme for a substantially changed V12, the 037. Verging on the quality of steel, its iron block was further refined, as was its crankshaft, even slimmer and lighter. In spite of a 2mm bore increase (86 x 50.2mm, 3,499cc), length and height were reduced and the head lightened as well, with a narrower 19° valve angle and a relocation of its third inlet valve. The result was a Type 037 twelve that was much lighter at 276lb, not including its clutch and exhaust.

Used for qualifying at Imola in May and raced in Hungary in August, the 037 produced 700bhp at 12,800rpm. This marked the attainment of 200 horsepower per litre, a new record for a naturally aspirated car-racing engine. Piloted by the outstanding team of moustachioed Nigel Mansell and crooked-nosed Alain Prost, Ferrari's twelves in John Barnard's last chassis, the 641, won six races in 1990 and placed second among makes with 110 points to McLaren-Honda's 121. With 71 points Prost was second in the drivers' ranking to Ayrton Senna's 78 after the latter crashed into the red Ferrari at the start of the Japanese Grand Prix and terminated any title hopes for the Frenchman.

Promising though it was, 1990 was not a harbinger of future success for Ferrari. It scored no wins at all in 1991 and was again headed by McLaren and Williams in makers' points. At the urging of Fiat chairman Gianni Agnelli, who admired several good finishes by the minnow-sized team of Fiat dealer Giancarlo Minardi, Ferrari also supplied engines to Minardi in 1991. Thanks to two fourth places, Minardi-Ferrari finished seventh in 1991 points. Engine development was now in the hands of former Lancia man Claudio Lombardi.

Ferrari rated its 1991 Type 039 V12 at 725bhp at 14,500rpm from a compression ratio of 13.3:1. A major innovation under Paolo Massai's direction that season was the use of variable geometry for both inlets and exhausts to improve the shape of the 039's torque curve. Triggered electrically, hydraulic cylinders lengthened and shortened the inlet ram pipes, while butterfly valves in the exhausts altered their characteristics. In 1992 – another winless season – the Type 040 twelve produced 740bhp at 15,000rpm, its high speed thanks in part to new dimensions of 88 x 47.95mm (3,499cc). Engines supplied to Scuderia Italia for use in Dallara chassis scored only two points in 1992.

No points at all were scored in 1993 by Ferrari's engine customer that season, BMS Scuderia Italia, which paid $6 million (£4.5 million) for the use of the Maranello twelves. Ferrari itself struggled as well, ranking fourth in constructors' points as it had in 1992 and behind the same three teams: Williams, McLaren and Benetton. Nineteen-ninety-three was the last year for five-valve heads for Ferrari. Thanks to the adoption of pneumatic valve closing its engine's peak revs were now 15,500rpm, still giving well in excess of 700 horsepower.

Responding to customer demand, Ferrari made good use of its 65° vee-twelve, five-valve technology in two sports-car projects in the 1990s. Evolved directly from the Grand Prix engine was the F130B. This was the power unit for the F50 supercar, of which just over 350 were produced. Both the F50 and its 65° vee-twelve were Formula 1-inspired.

The F50's engine had much in common with the 1992–93 Grand Prix Ferrari, sharing the same 94mm cylinder-centre distance and thin-wall cast-iron technology for its cylinder block. Nikasil coating of the bores contributed to quick bedding-in of the piston rings. Studded to the bottom face of the block were individual main-bearing caps, inside a dry sump that curved closely around the crankshaft. Conservatively, its bottom-end bearings were the same sizes as in GT Ferraris, 63mm mains and 43.6mm rod journals. Triple pumps scavenged its sump.

The Formula 1 engine's aluminium cylinder heads translated directly to the F50's F130B twelve. In their five-valve chambers the central inlet valve, set outboard, was inclined at only 4° 34'. The other two inlets sloped at 11° 36' and, as well, 3½° fore and aft to create a shapelier

A crankshaft of the Ferrari 035/5 Formula 1 engine of 1989 shows its streamlined counterweights, to cause the least resistance at high revs, and four roller-type main bearings. It was designed to run to 13,000rpm.

chamber and improve gas flow. In the same manner the exhaust valves had 3½° angles in the longitudinal plane as well as their 10° 17' lateral inclination. Inlet valves measured 26.7mm and exhausts 28.6mm. With twin coils shutting the valves, all that was missing was the Grand Prix engine's pneumatic closing. Clearance adjustment was by shims that also provided the contact faces of the cup-type tappets.

Based on its five-valve Formula 1 technology, Ferrari evolved the F130B to power its F50 supercar. Displacing 4.7 litres, the F130B developed 520bhp at 8,500rpm.

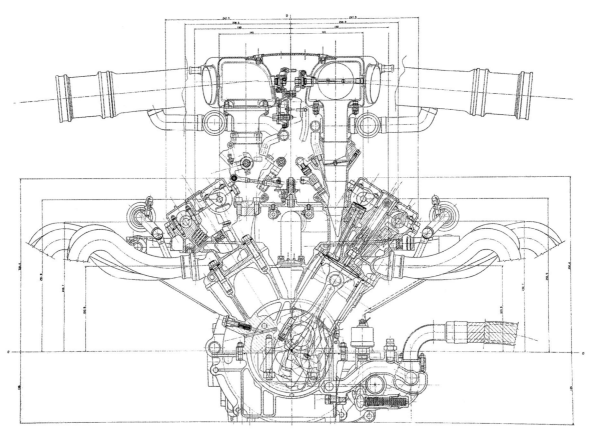

Formula 1 technology was very much to the fore in the internals of the F130B 65° vee-twelve for Ferrari's F50. Achieved was the very narrow angle of 28° between the inlet-valve stems and the centreline of the intake port.

A major change from Formula 1 practice in the design of Ferrari's Type 130B engine for the F50 was the replacement of gears by chains to drive the twin overhead cams on each cylinder bank. Gear drive would have been far too noisy for a road-car application, no matter how exotic.

Pankl provide the H-section titanium connecting rods, 126mm long, and Mahle the forged aluminium pistons for the 85mm bore, conservatively 3mm smaller than the GP engine. With its 69mm stroke, the F130B displaced 4,699cc. Its left-hand cylinder bank was offset forward. Each bank had its own duplex roller chain to turn twin camshafts, driven by individual half-speed gears from the nose of the crankshaft. Large longitudinal plenum chambers fed the vertical inlet ram pipes, with fuel-injection nozzles below their butterfly throttles.

Capable of revving to 10,000rpm, the F50's twelve was rated at 520bhp at 8,500rpm with a compression ratio of 11.3:1. Maximum torque of 347lb-ft was reached at 6,500rpm. Weighing 463lb, this was a thoroughbred engine for the Pininfarina-styled F50, a roadster with hardtop priced at $475,000 in 1995. Weighing 2,712lb, its handling was of sports-racing standard and its top speed just in excess of 200mph.

The F130B engine had in fact made an earlier appearance in 1993 as the motive power for the F333 SP, the first pure sports-racing Ferrari in two decades. Its creation was encouraged by private teams with the favourable intervention of Piero Ferrari, Enzo's son. Fourteen cars were produced by Ferrari, with the help of outside suppliers including Gian Paolo Dallara's company, and another 25 were built by Ferrari tuner Michelotto.

Its engine was a full racing version of the F130B, with its stroke shortened to 58.7mm. This reduced its capacity to 3,997cc to bring it within the 4.0-litre class of IMSA's World Sports Car racing series. Elevating its compression ratio to 13.0:1 and fitting titanium valves fractionally enlarged to 27mm (inlets) and 29mm (exhausts) helped it produce 675bhp at 11,000rpm, with 11,500 imposed by IMSA as the limit for multi-valve vee-twelves. For endurance racing 10,500rpm was a more likely limit. Helping lower the engine's centre of gravity was a Formula-1-type dry-sump casting and scavenge-pump array along the right side of the crankcase.

For many private teams, including that of Momo steering-wheel maker Gianpiero Moretti, who had been a prime mover in its creation, the F333 SP proved a very useful racing car in the IMSA events. Among its laurels were victories in the 12 Hours of Sebring in 1995 and 1997 and wins at Atlanta, Lime Rock and Watkins Glen in 1996.

Meanwhile Ferrari was advancing its Formula 1 engine technology. For its 1994 developments it had the advice of Osamu Goto, a former McLaren-Honda engine specialist, working with Claudio Lombardi. A new wider vee angle of 75° was adopted to lower the twelve's centre of gravity. Otherwise its general configuration, internal dimensions and construction were unchanged. Opposition remained strong, however, and with the sole V12 in the field Ferrari scored only one victory, Gerhard Berger in the German Grand Prix, and was third behind Williams and Benetton in the points.

Major change came in 1995, the first year of 3-litre engines. A new man was in charge. Having joined Ferrari in 1978, Paolo Martinelli looked after its GT-car engines from 1989 through 1994. Starting in 1995 he moved over to the Grand Prix side to work on the engine already laid down by Lombardi. Ferrari's new vee-twelve, its 044, kept the 75° vee of its predecessor and the concept of a ferrous cylinder block. With dimensions of 86 x 43mm (2,997cc) it was 3in shorter and 22lb lighter than its 3½-litre forebear. It was credited with "more than 600 horsepower" at 16,000rpm.

In 1995 Benetton and Williams led in Grand Prix points, with Ferrari third. Two victories, scored in a new John Barnard chassis, hinted at a revival of the famed Scuderia's fortunes. That revival accelerated in 1996 with the engagement of Michael Schumacher plus the historic change to a vee-ten engine. This was the work of Ferrari's own team, although at one stage – clearly in desperation – they had weighed adapting a Brian Hart vee-ten to their cars.

The introduction of a ten was welcomed by car-designer Barnard. "The big thing against more cylinders is that the engines get longer and heavier," he said, "and also they tend to have greater heat rejection so the radiators tend to get bigger, the drag is worse. The twelve was longer," added Barnard, "it was heavier, it used more fuel, it was fundamentally less torsionally stiff, you'd got more exhaust pipes to package – which was no small thing in itself. Your driveability was more difficult to obtain. Everything else apart from the top power was a negative."

This was not, said Paolo Martinelli, a blanket indictment of the twelve, which he saw as a prime power producer, "the very best engine from a dynamometer point of view." For a Grand Prix car, however, a balance had to be struck: "For Formula 1 an engine has to be light and small, with a low centre of gravity and low fuel consumption – and that's why we moved to a V10." Ferrari's men soon got to grips with the more rugged drive-train components needed for the ten, which was significantly rougher than their previous twelves.

Proving Martinelli's point, Ferrari pledged loyalty to the twelve for its ultimate sports and sports-racing cars. In this it has been joined by many others. In fact, where vee-twelves are concerned, it's getting crowded out there.

Chapter 14 Footnotes

[1] An important connection between the two companies was that General Motors was an investor in both, a majority holder of Lotus and a minority investor in Isuzu.

[2] Chris Murphy said it could have been Mika Häkkinen or Johnny Herbert.

[3] This was not a new idea. Porsche had employed it in its turbocharged 1½-litre V6 built under contract for TAG for McLaren to race in the mid-1980s and Mercedes had used it in the 1951 design of its M195 V12.

[4] Although there may have been prior art of a similar kind, so far as the author knows the Rosche/BMW team was the first to try this triple-cam solution in the modern era.

[5] There is some irony in Porsche's failure to identify the V10 alternative. It was the configuration of its never-built sports car of 1938–39, the Type 114 F-Wagen, and of some of its wartime armoured-vehicle engines.

[6] Unable to pay Giacomelli, Life offered him an engine as compensation. He later regretted refusing an artefact that, in its negative way, was as famous as any engine in Grand Prix history.

[7] The author regrets being unable to provide the actual dimensions.

[8] Coincidentally, both Porsche and Lamborghini used the same designation methodology: displacement followed by number of cylinders.

[9] Barnard also said that he "requested that all the pumps should be neatly positioned at the front, just like the Porsche V6." In the event this was not the case.

Chapter 15

AMERICAN AND
GERMAN LUXURY

In the 21st Century daring drivers and builders maintained the glorious tradition of installing ultra-powerful vee-twelves in roadgoing chassis. One such was American comedian and talk-show host Jay Leno, a dyed-in-the-wool car fanatic. Among his rolling stock was a Rolls-Royce Phantom II powered by a Merlin V12, so Leno could hardly refuse when he was offered a hot-rod chassis propelled by an engine from an M47 Patton tank. Displacing 29,366cc and producing 810bhp at 2,800rpm, its air-cooled overhead-cam vee-twelve was a Continental Motors design, Type AV-1790-5B.

Originally built by Randy Grubb and Mike Leeds, Jay Leno's 'Tank Car' roadster needed lots of work to make it road usable. Allison of Indianapolis supplied a six-speed transmission to cope with its 1,560lb-ft of torque, and Rockwell delivered a rugged axle made of what Leno called 'unbreakabillium'. In spite of its 9,500lb weight – 2,100lb of which is engine – the 'Tank Car' was fast, geared at 100mph per 1,000rpm. It could easily overcome its fully applied brakes. And when Leno needed spares he could strip more engines from obsolete Pattons, of which more than 8,500 were made in the 1950s.

Where big twelves weren't available off the shelf, imagineers stepped in to produce them. One such was California's Boyd Coddington, whom to call a 'hot-rodder' would be woefully undervaluing his car-building skills. In 2003 Coddington was planning a sumptuous Talbot-style roadster powered by a V12 that mated two of GM's Vortec straight-six cylinder heads to a block of his own design. With twin chain-driven overhead camshafts operating four valves per cylinder through rollers on finger followers, this sophisticated head would make a formidable twelve – shades of Albert Lory's twin Delahaye heads on a common crankcase for his 1937 Delage. Were Coddington's vee-twelve to use the Vortec's dimensions (93 x 102mm on 103mm bore centres) it would displace 8,315cc and produce more than 500 horsepower.

Others tackled vee-twelve creation from the bottom end. In the 1990s prolific Detroit engine-builder Cyril Batten made in-line fours and sixes from scratch, machining their crankcases from solid billets, and special twin-cam heads for Chevrolet V8s. Using the key bottom-end dimensions of Chevrolet's biggest eight, Batten built what he called his 'Max-12' engine. It had steel cylinder liners in a crankcase of either magnesium or aluminium, and heads with four valves at a 29° included angle opened by twin camshafts, each head having its own half-speed cogged-belt drive.

Batten offered his 60° vee Max-12 in three sizes: 11,143, 12,733 and 16,420cc. Weighing 750lb with a magnesium crankcase, one engine was prepared for drag racing. Unsupercharged but fuel-injected, it produced 1,600lb-ft of torque and in the order of 2,000bhp at 6,800rpm. An awesome engine by any standard, Batten's Max-12 was part of the inventory of Dallas, Texas's Norwood Autocraft in the 21st Century.

Opposite: *A cutaway of Audi's version of the VW Group W12 showed its intersecting inlet-ram passages, which differed in length according to the position of the cylinders they fed.*

Dressed up for display, Ryan Falconer's 9.9-litre 90° V12 was an impressive piece of machinery. Although based on Chevrolet concepts it was a distinctly Falconer engine thanks to its unique aluminium cylinder block and heads.

Roy Gullickson's 1990s effort to revive the Packard brand produced an impressive prototype with styling that was true to the proud Packard tradition. In the same spirit, Gullickson powered his '1999 Packard' with a Falconer vee-twelve.

Chevrolet's vee-eight and its sophisticated cylinder head, with two pushrod-operated valves at shrewdly opposed angles for good breathing, was the inspiration for a vee-twelve conceived by experienced racing-engine builder Ryan Falconer. At the end of the 1980s Falconer's California workshop produced its first vee-twelve, keeping the V8's 90° vee angle but casting its cylinder block in aluminium instead of iron. New cylinder heads were also aluminium, helping keep the engine's weight to 520lb.

Displacing a useful 9,855cc (104.8 x 95.3mm), the Falconer V12 found applications in trucks, cars, hot rods, boats and aircraft. As a dry-sump racing engine it was rated at 1,100bhp at 6,500rpm with as much as 1,600bhp available through pressure induction. For the road Ryan Falconer recommended a wet-sump version giving 650bhp at 5,200rpm and 750lb-ft of torque at 4,500rpm.

In the mid-1990s Falconer produced a special version of his vee-twelve for a man with a dream, Canadian engineer Roy Gullickson. At the beginning of the decade Gullickson, looking for a new challenge after selling his farm-equipment company, decided to resuscitate the moribund Packard brand. With a new base in Phoenix, Arizona he recreated the Packard Motor Car Company and spent $800,000 on a prototype of the 1999 Packard. A handsome four-door saloon, it was powered by an engine that was the cynosure of Packard: a vee-twelve.

Gullickson found the powerplant he needed in Salinas, California *chez* Falconer. The version supplied for his prototype was reduced in size to a still-respectable 7,161cc and fuel-injected to meet emissions requirements. Its output was 460bhp and in terms of torque 520lb-ft, driving through an automatic transmission. On a wheelbase of 119in, a weight of only 3,740lb was claimed. Gullickson's V12 Packard was, in its way, a credible effort to revive a

Under the hood of Roy Gullickson's Packard prototype the Falconer V12 made an appearance entirely consistent with classic Packards. It delivered 460bhp from its 7.1 litres.

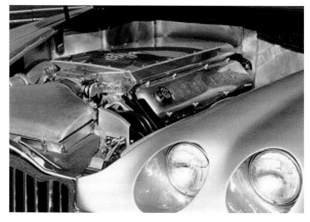

revered marque and to create a luxury brand at the apogee of the American market, selling up to 2,000 cars per year at $160,000 a copy.[1]

Another American luxury brand with vee-twelve associations, Cadillac, opened the new millennium with a twelve it was thinking of producing. Erased from its corporate memory was the ill-fated V-Future of the early 1960s; this was a new initiative – and one that almost had its creator fired. Ned McClurg, engineering vice president of General Motors's powertrain division, was on holiday in Northern Michigan in March 1999 when he perceived a need for Cadillac to have a prestigious twelve at the top end of its range. "Here we were the largest automobile company in the world," he thought, "and we were choosing not to play with the big boys."

Prepared to spend unbudgeted money, McClurg found a willing accomplice in Fritz Indra, GM's German-born executive director of advanced engineering. Indra assembled a German-American design team and asked Britain's Cosworth to help with a four-valve, twin-overhead-cam cylinder-head design. Within twelve months from their first marks on paper in September 1999 the Indra team had a running engine to show McClurg.

A concept rather than a production design, the GMXV-12 – as it was known – had interesting features. With cylinders veed at 60°, its block extended down past the crankshaft centreline. Drives to the camshafts were at the XV-12's flywheel end, a location seen more often on racing engines. Each bank had its own injection system and throttle. From a capacity of 7½ litres its output was "at least 500 horsepower". The twelve's revelation to Cadillac in September 2000 raised calls for McClurg's

Developed in Europe by Opel and Cosworth at the request of GM's Ned McClurg, the GMXV-12 was first shown in running form to its sponsor in September 1999. The sub-rosa project caused a stir – not entirely positive – at GM in 2000.

firing from top executives who were "worried about money," he recalled. "I had two very high-placed people who were very, very angry."

Not so the folks at GM's Cadillac division, who seized on the XV-12 as the motivation for their Cien, a stunning

Claiming 750bhp from its 7½ litres, the GMXV-12 was the power unit for the spectacular Cadillac Cien built to celebrate that GM division's 100th anniversary. In spite of its troubled gestation, Ned McClurg's vee-twelve seemed to have a promising future at General Motors.

concept sports car first shown at California's Pebble Beach Concours in August 2001. Styled by Simon Cox, the Cien was built with the help of Britain's Prodrive. The latter firm was a candidate to put the 750-horsepower Cien into limited production, but any such plans were shelved in August 2002. The XV-12 fitted neatly into Cadillac's big Escalade sport-utility, however, and in October 2002 GM announced that a twelve would be part of a future modular family of vee-type engines. "The vee-twelve could go into a host of things," said Bob Lutz, GM's vice chairman for product.[2]

Also standing by for a fresh injection of vee-twelve technology was a quiescent British marque, Daimler. The property of Ford's Jaguar subsidiary, Daimler vanished from sight early in the 21st Century, producing its last Double-Six in 2001. Jaguar asserted its loyalty to Daimler, saying that "we have never intended to kill off Daimler, which is a brand that has an enormous amount of respect." An open issue was whether Daimler would have access to the vee-twelve that powered the Aston Martins built by another daughter company of Ford.

Japan was the site of a failed effort to use a vee-twelve to jump-start the introduction of a new luxury marque. In addition to launching its upscale Xedos brand in Europe, Hiroshima's ambitious Mazda planned a range badged as 'Amati' for America. A key entry into this segment was to be V12-powered. For this purpose Mazda developed several strains of twelves and was close to launching one when the collapse of its 'bubble economy' put paid to such hubris. "Our engineering and financial resources were pretty thinly stretched by these activities," said a Mazda engineer. The company sought in vain a purchaser for its very promising vee-twelve.[3]

With its awesome resources anything but stretched, dominant Japanese car producer Toyota had no difficulty bringing a vee-twelve to market in April 1997 to power its domestic-market prestige car, the Century. It chose a classical 60° format and virtually square dimensions for its 4,996cc (81 x 80.8mm) V12, its 1GZ-FE. Both cylinder heads and block were of aluminium, carrying the crankshaft in seven main bearings. Chain-driven twin overhead cams on each bank operated four valves per cylinder.

Toyota's 1GZ-FE had electronic fuel injection and ignition, coping with its 10.5:1 compression ratio. Output, remaining unchanged from its launch, was 280bhp at 5,200rpm to suit the Century's four-speed automatic transmission. Torque was a healthy 355lb-ft at 4,000rpm. This was a refined engine for a refined car on a 119.1-inch wheelbase weighing 4,390lb. It was capable of carrying its cosseted corporate passengers at speeds up to 130mph.

In the manner now fashionable among many motor companies, Toyota covered the 5.0-litre V12 of its Century with a styled shield. The twin air-measurement units for its fuel-injection system fed flexible trunking at the front.

Of all the marque-revival exercises none surpassed Maybach. In the Daimler-Benz family since 1961, Maybach lingered solely as a heavy-engine brand of Daimler subsidiary MAN. Yet, possessing a proud if vainglorious tradition as a prestige automobile nameplate, it was well worth resuscitating when BMW successfully bid for the Rolls-Royce brand in 1998. The close competition that characterised German's automobile industry in the 1930s, leading then to an eruption of vee-twelves, was as intense as ever in the 1990s, but now on a European and indeed global scale. Arch-rival Mercedes-Benz had been well aware of the negotiations leading up to BMW's Rolls-Royce coup. This thrust by Munich demanded a parry and counter-thrust from Stuttgart.

A response was already on the stocks. At its advanced styling studios in Japan and America Daimler-Benz was readying a design concept for a new car which would respond to "signals, especially from Asian markets, that people would appreciate a luxury car from our company that would be positioned above the S-Class in the Mercedes-Benz programme with respect to size and status," said Hermann Gaus, who was responsible for the new model's development. "Over many years this limited market has only been served by the two British noble marques, and with cars whose concepts were developed long ago." There were, thought Gaus, some 8,000 people world-wide who were in a position to consider such a car.

First revealed as a Mercedes-Benz Maybach at the 1997 Tokyo Show, the Daimler-Benz concept wasn't based on an outdated platform. Indeed, it was powered by a new-design vee-twelve which it would share with senior Mercedes-Benz models. What Jaguar had hoped to achieve in the late 1980s – the creation of a modular family of closely related V6, V8 and V12 engines – Daimler-Benz managed a decade later. Its new engine family marked its transition away from the in-line sixes that had dominated its production for so long, and from which the cylinder heads of its previous twelve had been borrowed.

In addition to cost reduction, lighter weight and good emissions performance the *Lastenheft* for the new engine – the guidelines for its design – required that it fit into the same space as the existing Mercedes vee-eights. To achieve this its cylinder-centre distances were 90mm, substantially closer than the 97mm of the previous M120 twelve.

A hallmark of all the new vee engines from Stuttgart was their use of a single chain-driven overhead camshaft for each bank opening three valves per cylinder through rocker arms with rollers contacting the cam lobes. This permitted a strong and direct valve gear with three cam lobes in a row serving each cylinder. Built into the tip of each rocker arm was a minuscule hydraulic lash adjuster.

The inlet pair and the exhaust valve were mutually inclined to form the combustion chamber volume; in the naturally aspirated twelve the inlets were 33mm and the single exhaust 34mm in diameter.

By pairing two inlet valves with a single exhaust the Mercedes engineers improved their engines' emissions performance during the critical warm-up phase. Especially for larger engines, it was vital to keep heat inside the exhaust passages to bring the catalyst up to temperature rapidly. By eliminating the heat-dissipating surfaces of a second exhaust valve and port, the single valve kept exhaust temperatures 70°C higher and brought the catalyst up to its working temperature 12sec sooner. This gave a 40 per cent reduction in emissions compared to a four-valve head.

The three-valve layout facilitated another feature of the new engines: dual ignition. Twin spark plugs fitted neatly into niches athwart the exhaust valves. The

In a new V12 that made its debut in an S-Class model in 1999 Mercedes-Benz used the three-valve combustion chambers that it was also introducing in engines of six and eight cylinders. In the M137 twelve, roller-tipped rocker arms opened the valves, two inlets and one exhaust.

Dual ignition was a feature of the M137 vee-twelve introduced by Mercedes-Benz in 1999. Its engine-management system was able to vary the timing of the two spark plugs in each cylinder according to speed and load.

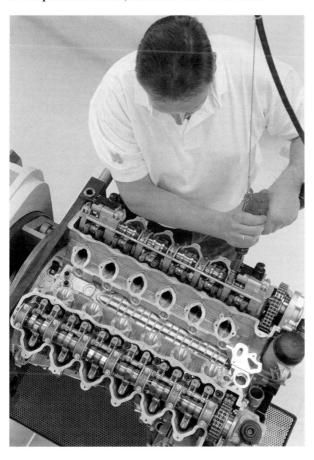

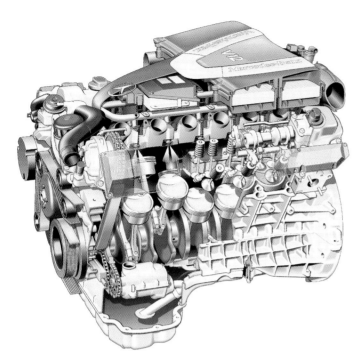

Mercedes-Benz adopted die casting of aluminium for the cylinder block of its 1999 M137 vee-twelve, forming the block around dry cylinder sleeves of high-silicon aluminium. Its wet sump was at the front end of the engine.

Stuttgart engineers found dual ignition helpful in achieving the full combustion needed to keep emissions low and efficiency high. According to speed and load, the engine management adjusted spark timing, if needed, slightly varying the firing of the two plugs in one cylinder in a manner that Mercedes referred to as "phase-

Compared to its M120 predecessor, the Mercedes-Benz M137 V12 was relatively modest in size at 5.8 litres, delivering 367bhp. Nevertheless it provided a robust basis for further development.

shifting". A new feature was the use of the spark plugs as sensors for incipient knocking, telling the engine management to retard the ignition accordingly.

Also under the engine management's control was a system which automatically deactivated half the engine's cylinders below 3,000rpm and at less than half throttle to save fuel. Unlike George Schebler's twelve of 1908, which rested one complete cylinder bank, the affected cylinders were three on each bank, not sharing the same crankpins, to preserve the best balance and firing sequence.

Cylinder deactivation was accomplished by two-piece rocker arms that could be hydraulically decoupled in response to a solenoid valve, closing the valves. Able to respond within a single crankshaft turn, the system shut down by closing the exhaust valve just after a firing so that the cylinder retained hot gases to keep it warm and ready for a return to action. Similarly, when restarting the exhaust valve opened first to dump those waste gases.

A classical 60° vee with its right cylinder bank offset forward, the new Type M137 Mercedes twelve's block was die-cast of aluminium around high-silicon aluminium dry cylinder sleeves dubbed 'Silitec', 2.5mm thick. In what its builders called a "bedplate" design a deeply ribbed lower aluminium casting, united with the block at the crankshaft centreline, held the seven main bearings in iron inserts that ensured consistent clearances around the bearings, reducing the burden on the chain-driven oil pump. The big ends of the forged-steel connecting rods were split by force along fracture lines to give a fit of immaculate precision. Cylinder heads were aluminium with magnesium camshaft covers.

Weighing 503lb and equipped with variable valve timing, the M137 V12 made its debut at Frankfurt in 1999 in the new-series S-Class Mercedes-Benz and in the CL coupé. After the 1998 merger, both were now products of DaimlerChrysler. With a compression ratio of 10.0:1 the twelve's capacity of 5,786cc (84 x 87mm) produced 367bhp at 5,500rpm and maximum torque of 391lb-ft at the relatively high speed of 4,250rpm.

This 5.8-litre version of the Mercedes twelve was initially considered for use in the Maybach, but it was soon evident that a car weighing 6,130lb unladen in its long-wheelbase (150.6in) version would need more punch under its bonnet. Its close cylinder spacing meant that no bore expansion was on the cards. Nor was its three-valve configuration ideal for performance enhancement through better breathing. Turbocharging was the answer, found engine engineer Gerhard Doll. Although Mercedes-Benz had used turbos in racing, this was its first road-car application.

On both sides of the engine KKK-Warner turbochargers were fitted, their turbine housings cast integrally with the exhaust manifolds to save space, conserve heat and allow their bearings to be cooled directly from the engine. En route to an inlet manifold in the central vee, pressure air from the blowers at up to 19psi passed through compact intercoolers. These were refreshed on demand, under the engine management's control, by their own water circuit through a radiator in front of the main coolant core.

To cope with the boosted engine's higher stresses its piston crowns were modified and oil-cooled by jets from below with patterns, volumes and crown under-surfaces tailored to the task. The oil-control rings were narrowed by 2mm to permit the ring lands to be strengthened, while the gudgeon pins were larger with thicker walls. Positioned behind the front apron, an engine-oil cooler was thermostatically controlled.

In a seemingly retrograde step, bore size was reduced by 2mm. This allowed the Silitec liners to be 0.5mm thicker, 3mm, to provide more stable bores under high temperatures and pressures. It also gave more space between the cylinders, which made room for 3mm water passages to pierce the aluminium between the otherwise-siamesed cylinders of the open-deck block. Noise was reduced by adopting a two-stage oil pump and an oil pan that was rubber-isolated from the block.

Top-end changes were implemented as well to create a torque-rich luxury-car engine. In what was the M285 to DaimlerChrysler but known as the Type 12 in the world of Maybach, the chambers were adapted to the smaller bores. To suit the smaller bore size the valve diameters were reduced to 31mm for the inlets and 33mm for the lone exhaust valve. Neither cylinder disablement nor valve-timing variation was required, and valve timing was more conservative with reduced overlap.

The resulting M285 was a V12 of 5,513cc (82 x 87mm) and a compression ratio of 9.0:1 – commendably high in relation to the substantial boost pressure that the engine tolerated. The result was an awesome power unit by any standard, a motive force that left no doubt that the vee-twelve was still a king, even an emperor, among 21st-Century engines. In its era it was as dominant as the 68-bis version of Hispano-Suiza's J12 was in the 1930s.

Right: The Maybach's M285 V12 achieved its high output in spite of a reduction in displacement from the M137 to 5.5 litres in the interest of stronger cylinder bores to handle its turbocharged power. Engines were individually assembled in DaimlerChrysler's factory at Berlin-Marienfelde.

Above: *Developed as the M285 to suit the requirements of the new Maybach range from DaimlerChrysler, the M137 V12 acquired twin turbochargers with water-cooled intercoolers. Many modifications helped the engine cope with its boosted output of 550bhp and 665lb-ft of torque.*

Multiple belts at its front end drove the accessories of the vee-twelve of the new Maybach, an impressive car very much in the tradition of its Zeppelin predecessor of the 1930s. Certainly only a twelve-cylinder engine would have been appropriate for a modern Maybach.

Maybach's Type 12 produced 550bhp at 5,250rpm and 664lb-ft of torque between 2,300 and 3,000rpm, figures that qualified DaimlerChrysler to call it the most powerful engine in any series production car at its 2002 launch. It was not far from producing one horsepower per pound from its 595lb. The twelve's torque curve was unprecedented, showing 458lb-ft at only 1,500rpm and 590 at 1,800. Its 750-odd components were assembled by a team of 30 people in Hall 25 of Daimler's Berlin-Marienfelde factory, erected originally to produce V12 aero engines. In the ultra-clean facility cotton-gloved workers took a day and a half to build each engine.

"Under the fiercest acceleration," wrote Andrew English, "the sensation of that V12 roaring defiance at wind and weight is unlike anything else on the road, more akin to a gigantic locomotive or battleship steaming up to ram speed." "It's near-silent at tickover," found *Autocar*, which timed a Maybach '57' to 62mph in 5.2sec. "It's a figure both believable, given that monstrous torque, yet scarcely credible considering the refinement with which it does it."

Tailored as it was from the start to do, the Type M275 vee-twelve slid easily under the bonnet of the S-Class in the autumn of 2002. Equipment differences, such as only one air-conditioning compressor instead of two, accounted for its lighter weight of 568lb. Although its boost pressure was rolled back to 14½psi, the V12 in Mercedes models produced 500bhp at 5,000rpm and 590lb-ft at 1,800rpm – still respectable numbers. In January 2003 the M275 was announced as power for the SL600 two-seater, deliveries of which began in April.

Those lusting for even more power hadn't long to wait. In 2003 AMG, the Mercedes-Benz house tuner, released its version of the M275 twelve. With a bore slightly enlarged to 82.6mm and a 93mm stroke it displaced 5,980cc. Upgraded pistons, bearings, oil pump and forged crankshaft were mated with inlet valves that were larger with more lift. They admitted boost of up to 22psi from larger turbochargers, pumping through intercoolers whose front-mounted radiator was 70 per cent bigger. Injection nozzles were enlarged as well. To validate the package, AMG completed 5,500 hours' running of 42 test engines.

A hammer of an engine resulted. Over a range from 4,800 to 5,100rpm it produced 450 kilowatts, 612bhp, more than 100bhp per litre, while its peak torque at 4,500rpm, a proud 1,000 Newton-metres, was equivalent to 738lb-ft. In fact during development it had generated 700bhp and 900lb-ft but was detuned to allow existing transmissions to cope with its torque. With this kind of thrust in a CL65 AMG coupé, "Passing is the ultimate in whoosh fulfilment," found *Road & Track*. "Thought is instantly transformed into action." Customers for whom the normal speed limiter setting of 155mph was too tame could have it reset to 185.

With this engine in its cupboard AMG didn't have to look far when, in January of 2003, it had a visit from its former managing director, Wolfgang Bernhard. As chief operating officer of DaimlerChrysler's American arm, Bernhard was set on surprising his rivals at Detroit's 2004 show with a super-performance machine. "We told AMG we need 800 horsepower," said Bernhard about his visit to Affalterbach, "and it should weigh 500lb." Having already seen it produce 700bhp, AMG settled on its version of the M275 V12 for the assignment.

Only one month later the first of four development engines was punishing AMG's dynamometer. Instead of two turbochargers it had four, delivering an intercooled maximum boost of 20psi against a compression ratio of 9.0:1. To lower the engine and improve durability, lubrication was dry-sumped. Although weight came out a bit higher than specified at 525lb, power was higher too at 850bhp at 5,750rpm in an engine that was safe to rev to 6,800. Torque, transmitted through a special Ricardo transaxle, was 850lb-ft between 2,500 and 4,500rpm.

Bernhard got his wish; installed in the aggressive-looking ME Four-Twelve coupé the engine was a sensation at 2004's Detroit show. Chrysler measured a 0–60mph time of 2.92sec for a 3,100lb prototype (production target was 2,880lb) and a quarter-mile time of 10.6sec with a speed at the finish of 136mph. "The sound as the engine climbs toward its 6,200rpm redline is terrific," found Kevin A. Wilson. "Power builds steadily with the familiar turbo sensation." Chrysler developers Dan Knott and Eric Ridenour hoped for a top speed approaching 240mph.

As intended, the ME Four-Twelve was one in the eye for other makers of hyper-sports automobiles. "Whether we build it, and where and how we build it, depends on customer reaction and testing of the prototype," said Chrysler CEO Dieter Zetsche, adding that the maximum annual volume he'd consider would be in the 500–1,000-unit range. Zetsche said that the exotic ME Four-Twelve was consistent both with Chrysler's historic reputation for engineering and innovation and with his goal of "very spirited elegance" for his premier brand. In 2005, however, Chrysler sidelined plans to build the twelve-cylinder supercar.[4]

These provocations by DaimlerChrysler, both in Germany and America, couldn't be ignored by the other builder of sports and luxury cars in southern Germany. BMW's responses took several forms. As usual, Paul Rosche had

not been idle on the sports-engine front. In 1992 his Motorsport group introduced a new twin-cam, 24-valve six to power the latest M3. This, the S50 of 286bhp, was based on a tall-block version of the standard M50 six. Thus it had the same 91mm cylinder-centre distances as the M50, which was the four-valve ($39\frac{1}{2}°$ included angle) version of the M20 six that had provided the starting point for BMW's M70 vee-twelve introduced in 1987.

This evolution assumed added significance in 1990 when, by chance, Paul Rosche met an old colleague, Gordon Murray, at a race meeting. The two were memorable partners in the early 1980s when Murray's Grand Prix Brabhams carried Rosche's turbocharged fours to nine victories and a world championship in 1983 for Nelson Piquet. Now the South African, working in Britain for McLaren, told the German that he was looking for an engine for a new supercar he was designing. "We could do the engine for you," said Rosche in his straightforward way. By February 1991 BMW had agreed to build the power unit for the mid-engined, three-seater car that became McLaren's F1.

Rosche's engine, his S70/2, was based on a special version of the M70 twelve topped, in principle, by twin-cam cylinder heads based on the design of his S50 six. The latter could contribute most directly to the right-hand

At the request of designer Gordon Murray, BMW's Paul Rosche produced the S70/2 V12 to power McLaren's ultimate sports car, its F1. From its 6.1 litres and 604 pounds it produced 601bhp – an impressive achievement.

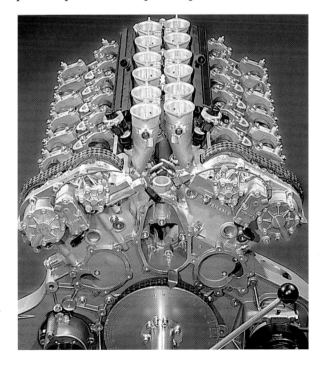

cylinder bank by virtue of its porting and the fact that it was already inclined at 30° to the right for installation in the M3. A new timing chest for the front of the block carried massive bearers for engine mounting, separate duplex roller chains to each bank and the bases of two belt-driven water pumps, each serving one row of cylinders. Lubrication was dry-sump, with four scavenge pumps.

Fractionally undersquare at 86 x 87mm, with 142.6mm connecting rods, the S70/2 displaced 6,064cc. Its compression ratio was a high 11.0:1 and its engine was managed by a TAGtronic system provided by a McLaren business unit. It had twin fuel-injection nozzles for each cylinder to gain more progressive control, infinitely variable inlet-valve timing, individual throttles for each cylinder and an aluminium flywheel. The completed engine weighed 604lb, so with 601bhp at 7,400rpm the S70/2 V-12 was developing near enough one horsepower per pound as well as 99.1bhp per litre – a design stipulation by Gordon Murray. Torque was 480lb-ft at 5,600rpm.

Introduced in 1994, the McLaren F1 was destined to be manufactured in just under 100 examples. Many of these were used for endurance racing in a new GT series. To fit into its six-litre category Paul Rosche shortened the stroke to 85.95mm which, with the 86mm bore, gave a capacity of 5,990cc. Not only the connecting rods but also the crankshafts of these S70/3 twelves were made of light but tough titanium.

Racing rules called for two restrictive orifices for the engine's air inlets, each 39.4mm in diameter. By eliminating the standard catalyst exhausts and remapping the V12's ignition and injection controls its output was recouped to 636bhp at 7,500rpm. This was enough to send McLaren F1s across the 1995 Le Mans finishing line in the first four positions.

For 1996 the S70/3's air restrictors were reduced by 3mm, so Rosche's team fought back with new camshaft profiles, an increase in compression ratio to 12.0:1 and refinements in the induction system, including an air filter in place of the previous screens. Speeds of both the oil and water pumps were lowered, with the racing engine spending more of its time at higher revs, to reduce internal power losses. A reshaping of its dry sump set the engine deeper in the chassis by 0.6in. With reprogrammed TAG engine controls the revised V-12's power output was quoted as 600bhp at 7,300rpm, while torque of 511lb-ft at 4,000rpm was down from the previous 527lb-ft at 4,500rpm.

As the icing on the McLaren F1's cake an added-value model was produced in 1996 for just five well-heeled customers. This, the F1 LM, was built and equipped in honour of the 1995 Le Mans victory. Freed of its inlet-air restrictors, the LM's 6.1-litre engine developed 680bhp at

For racing versions of the McLaren F1, BMW and Paul Rosche produced the S70/3 V12, whose power was constrained by twin mandatory air-inlet restrictors. Nevertheless the F1 proved a competent sports-racing car, winning Le Mans in 1995.

7,800rpm and could rev to 8,500. It delivered 520lb-ft of torque at 4,500rpm.

When, later in the 1990s, BMW got an itch for a Le Mans victory all its own, this twelve provided the propulsion. Air restrictors, on the agenda again, constrained its power to 550bhp in 1998 in a chassis built

Redesignated as the P74, Paul Rosche's twelve was re-tuned to serve as the power unit of a racing sports-prototype. In this form it delivered 550bhp.

by Williams Grand Prix Engineering, the V12 LM. Given the new designation of P74, the twelve was further refined with carbon-fibre covers over individual coils for each spark plug along its cylinder heads. Although unsuccessful in 1998, with a new chassis, the V12 LMR, the P75 engine was victorious in 1999 both at Sebring and Le Mans, its superior fuel economy proving decisive at the latter.

When updating its vee-twelve offering for its road cars, BMW adopted a strategy in diametric opposition to that of its Stuttgart rival. While Mercedes-Benz went for a more compact engine and made up the difference with turbocharging, also for its Maybach, BMW extended its cylinder-bore centres from 91 to 98mm in search of added cubic inches. This was not only for the benefit of the 760i, in which the new N73 twelve was launched in November 2002, but also to accommodate the needs of BMW subsidiary Rolls-Royce, which introduced its new Phantom two months later using the same basic engine but with enlarged bore and stroke. Both twelves were naturally aspirated.

With 98mm cylinder centres BMW brought its N73 twelve into concordance with its N62 family of 90° vee-eight engines. The right-hand cylinder row was offset forward in an open-deck block that was low-pressure-die-cast in Neckarsulm by Kolbenschmidt of high-silicon aluminium alloy. Extending down past the crankshaft centreline, the block was closed by a cast aluminium pan carrying its sump volume at the rear. Three of the seven main-bearing caps were unified by oil passages while the remaining four were individual. In typical BMW style all the crank journals were fully counterweighted. Big ends

BMW raced its P74 vee-twelve in chassis built by Williams Grand Prix Engineering. In 1999 its V12 LMR took first place at Sebring in March, as shown, and went on to win the 24 Hours of Le Mans.

of the forged-steel connecting rods were separated by cracking at a 30° angle to ease maintenance.

From the crank nose a single simplex chain drove all four camshafts, each equipped with a valve-timing variator under the engine management's control. Four valves per cylinder were inclined at 15° for the inlets and 16° for the exhausts, adding up to 31°. Finger followers with hydraulically adjusted pivots and rollers contacting the cam lobes opened the valves, single coils closing them. Interposed between cam lobes and fingers on the inlet side was BMW's unique Valvetronic, an electrically controlled system that varied valve movement from full lift to fully closed. Although in theory Valvetronic eliminated the need for throttles, one of the main sources of inefficiency in an Otto-cycle petrol engine, each of the N73's two inlet plenum chambers did in fact have a drive-by-wire throttle.[5]

Another novelty in BMW's new vee-twelve was its petrol injection, not into its inlet passages but directly into its cylinders. An electrically controlled nozzle sprayed fuel into the chamber at pressures from 30 to 100 atmospheres from its position under the inlet tracts. The fresh fuel's cooling effect in the cylinder was credited with the twelve's ability to tolerate a high compression ratio of 11.3:1. Magnesium inlet-air ram pipes criss-crossed above the central vee.

With dimensions of 89 x 80mm, the 760i's V12 had a capacity of 5,972cc. Weighing 617lb, the N73 produced

In 2003 Rolls-Royce, now owned by BMW, introduced its Phantom powered by an expanded version of BMW's M73 vee-twelve. Both bore and stroke were enlarged to provide 6.7 litres and an impressive 531lb-ft of torque.

BMW's designers gave the engine of their Rolls-Royce Phantom an appearance entirely in keeping with that august marque. Here was a worthy successor to the Phantom III of the 1930s that restored a strong V12 tradition to the annals of Rolls-Royce.

438bhp at 6,000rpm and 443lb-ft of torque at 3,950rpm. Over a range from 1,500 to 6,000rpm its torque was not less than 368lb-ft. Impressive though these numbers were, some felt that Mercedes, with its smaller turbocharged twelve weighing less, had stolen an advantage. The BMW was lacking "the instantaneous punch of the new S600, the direct rival," thought *Autocar*. "The engine feels as if it needs to get up on the cam at around 3,500rpm before it really goes." Some felt that 'V12' emblems in the door sills that glowed red were a frippery too far.

Enlargement of the N73 to propel the 5,580lb Rolls-Royce Phantom emphasised torque over power. Increases in both bore and stroke to 92 x 84.6mm yielded 6,749cc, decisively the largest of the new-wave luxury twelves. It was also agreeably close to the 6,750cc traditionally offered by Rolls-Royce's veteran aluminium pushrod vee-eight. Power was up moderately to 453bhp at a more restrained 5,350rpm, while torque rose a massive 20 per cent to 531lb-ft at 3,500rpm. With more than 400lb-ft available at just over 1,000rpm, the big twelve fulfilled Rolls-Royce's desire for a sense of 'waftability' in the easy acceleration of its new car. Handsome shaping of its plenum chambers and camshaft covers gave the engine a distinctively Rolls-Royce look.

Since 1931 a member of the Rolls-Royce family, in 2003 Bentley found itself in the Volkswagen Group as the result of a deal struck between VW and BMW. As part of the pact Bentley kept the traditional factory base at Crewe in Cheshire while Rolls-Royce set up a new assembly operation in West Sussex at Goodwood.[6] Like Rolls, Bentley would strike out toward a new future with a twelve-cylinder engine – but one strikingly different in concept and execution.

Bentley's twelve, like those of sister marques VW and Audi, traced its origins to an ingenious notion by an engineering team led by Peter Hofbauer, head of power-train development at Wolfsburg. "My team and I carried out a systems analysis," said Hofbauer, "to see how we could get a six-cylinder engine into the Golf. The conventional vee-six was ruled out because it took up too much crush space at the front of the car, so we created a typology of engine configurations that would fit transversely." Of the possibilities that presented themselves, Hofbauer chose one that nested the bores of a six closer together in a narrow vee angle to squeeze six cylinders into little more space than an in-line four. The VW engineers reinvented, for modern application, one of the concepts that made the Lancia engines of the 1920s and 1930s so distinctively efficient.[7]

Like Vincenzo Lancia's vee-twelve of 1919, VW's VR vee-six – as it was called – covered both banks with a single cylinder head.[8] It used an even narrower angle than Lancia, 15° instead of 22½°. If as in a classical vee engine the apex of the angle were at the centre of the crankshaft, interference would occur between the lower ends of adjacent cylinders. For this reason the engineers offset the cylinder centrelines 12½mm outboard of the crank centre, giving a moderate *desaxé* effect. The staggering of its cylinders to left and right meant that with a bore as big as 84mm the centres of successive cylinders could be only 64mm apart.

The crankshaft of the VR engines was akin to that of an in-line six, with four main bearings and individual journals for each connecting rod. Unusually for a road-car engine the chain drive to the VR6's overhead camshafts was taken from the flywheel end of the crank. For two overhead camshafts to be able to operate all the valves – initially two per cylinder – their stems had to differ in length, much as the port lengths inside the head differed as well. Piston crowns were sloped at 15° so they'd match the flat surface of the top of the block.

Volkswagen introduced its VR6 engines in 1991 to considerable surprise and acclaim. The most potent version was the Corrado's, with 2,861cc (82 x 90.3mm) and 190bhp at 5,800rpm. VR engines continued to be mainstays of the VW range, including a VR5 version launched in 1999 and a new VR6 with aluminium for both block and head and four valves per cylinder.

Peter Hofbauer and his team weighed one option for doubling up their V6 to make a twelve-cylinder engine for

At the beginning of the 1990s the VW Group introduced new V6 engines that surprised the automotive world with their remarkable compactness. Two such engines were joined, at a 72° angle, to create a W12 of impressively small size.

One of the concepts for a twelve-cylinder VR-Series engine explored by Peter Hofbauer and his engineers at VW was the marriage of two of their V6s in an engine with twin crankshafts. This concept, the ICV12, would allow the engine to run with either or both units in action according to speed and load demands.

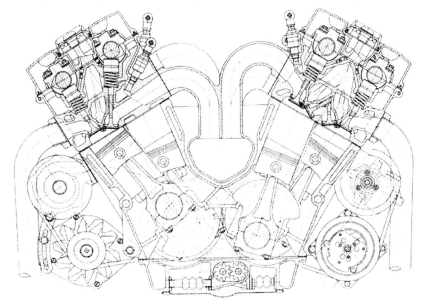

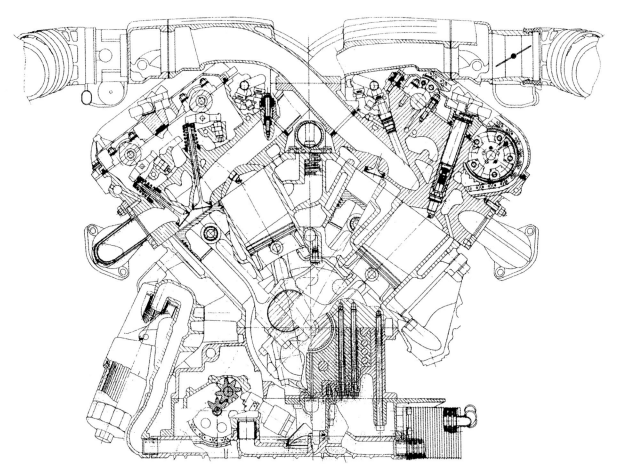

Shown in its dry-sump version as used by Audi, the VW Group's W12 successfully combined two of its VR6 engines on a common crankshaft. Its use of four long studs to retain each main-bearing cap was attributed to excessive conservatism on the part of an outside consultant who designed the engine.

VW's bigger cars. Their concept was to make an engine with twin crankshafts, geared together through a clutching system. "Our idea was to shut down one engine when the power of both wasn't needed," said Hofbauer, "so the unit as a whole could be kept closer to the 'sweet spot' of best performance with best economy." Thanks to improvements in bearing materials they could also see the possibility of building such an engine around a single crankshaft.

Hofbauer's successor at VW was Ferdinand Piëch, the same man whose degree thesis was the design of a Grand Prix vee-twelve. In 1993 this creative and dynamic engineer was charged with management of the VW Group. Piëch's grandfather was Prof Ferdinand Porsche, in whose long and successful engineering career a passenger car powered by a vee-twelve had never

featured. This ironic oversight would be more than rectified by his grandson.

The balding, hawk-faced Piëch, then 56, took over Wolfsburg's top job with twelves very much in his frame as capstones for his product ranges. "I had in mind the offering of a twelve-cylinder as the top of the top," he said. "Even if, for sure, it wouldn't be the best-selling motorisation, the legend of the twelve-cylinder is the locomotive for the entire range." Although Piëch was mainly interested in a twelve for his Volkswagens, he realised that Audi would need one too: "It would have seemed odd if Volkswagen, but not Audi, came out with a twelve-cylinder. The impression could have arisen that the mother company wanted to put the brakes on her daughter."

In fact the daughter, managed at the time by Ferdinand Piëch, had already laid her twelve-cylinder cards on the table. At the Tokyo Show in October 1991 Piëch and his designers unveiled a bombshell of a concept car. Their polished-aluminium Avus was named after a high-speed motorway in Berlin that had also witnessed record-breaking by Auto Unions. Its mid-mounted engine was a classic broad-arrow W12 with three banks of four cylinders, the side banks at 60° to the centre vertical bank.

Cylinder heads of aluminium with chain-driven overhead cams capped an aluminium crankcase in the Audi Avus's W12. Its three cylinder banks were mutually offset so that the three connecting rods of facing cylinders could share a common crankpin on the five-bearing crankshaft. Five valves per cylinder and a capacity of 5,998cc helped the Avus engine produce 509bhp at 5,800rpm.

Elegant and exciting though it was, the Avus's triple-bank twelve didn't represent a way forward for Volkswagen. Instead, Ferdinand Piëch saw a way to combine two VR6s to create a twelve. There was just enough room, he and his engineers found, to allow two of their narrow-angle vee-sixes to share a common crankshaft. The six's shortness meant that it was a tight squeeze indeed, but they cracked it.

"It took six men nine months to advance from a Golf six-cylinder to a rev- and spark-ready twelve-cylinder," recalled Piëch, "in spite of the complications of lubricating this mighty machine." With in-house resources constrained, the engine was designed by an outside contractor, led by a former VW engineer. From the latter's creation of a concept engine Volkswagen insiders Karl-Heinz Neumann and Ulrich Eichhorn were among those who led the development of a production-ready twelve.

Key to the VW twelve's success was establishment of its bank angle and crankshaft layout. The classic 60° angle was foreclosed by the lateral bulk of the VR6 block and head. Also envisioned was a vee-eight using the same concept, marrying two VR4 engines, so an angle was sought that would suit it as well. The final choice was a 72° angle, which is correct for a vee-ten – mid-way between the eight and twelve. The angle was between the centrelines of the two VR6 assemblies.

The job wasn't done yet. Evenly spaced firing impulses were desired, every 60° in the case of the twelve. If the connecting rods of facing cylinders shared a common crankpin, as in conventional twelves, impulses would be unevenly spaced. To remedy this each rod journal was split into two parts, separated by 12° of crank rotation. This gave even firing.[9] Achieving this subdivision of the rod journals in a crankshaft already crowded with seven main bearings and substantial counterbalances was no mean feat of design, analysis and machining. Krupp Gerlach GmbH of Homburg deserved special credit for the steel crankshaft forgings.

So congested were its crank journals and cheeks that only modern bearing and lubrication technology allowed the realisation of Volkswagen's twelve. Its connecting rods were a scant 13mm wide at their big ends, little more than half an inch, matching the 13mm forward shift of the right-hand bank of cylinders. The twelve's aluminium block extended down to the centreline of the crankshaft, which was carried in seven main bearings. Their caps were integral with an aluminium closure for the bottom of the block. Each bearing was snugged by four studs – a conservative solution provided by the outside design consultant. Cast into the caps were iron inserts supporting the bearing shells. These played a crucial role in preventing bearing clearances from increasing excessively when the aluminium engine expanded with heat.

As in the VR6, drive to the overhead camshafts was at the rear of the new VW engine. A duplex chain drove upward to an engine-speed sprocket, from which separate simplex chains turned the two camshaft sprockets in each head. In the final design, as used in passenger cars, both inlet and exhaust camshafts in each head were driven through timing variators. The valves were opened by fingers with rollers in contact with the cam lobes, pivoting from hydraulically adjusted posts. At the front of the engine a roller chain drove its oil pump, on the right side of a two-piece die-cast-aluminium wet sump. An oil/water exchanger extracted heat from the lubricant.

While its new twelve was not strictly of the classical 'W' broad arrow configuration, VW dubbed it the 'W12'.[10] At 90.3mm its stroke was the same as that of the 2.8-litre VR6 while its bore was 84mm, the largest used in the six. This gave 5,998cc in a remarkably compact and light 48-valve twelve: in its first version it weighed only 527lb.

Though it was scheduled for the new luxury Volkswagen that was being developed as the D1 and would launch as the Phaeton, Ferdinand Piëch wanted to establish a sporting pedigree for his new W12, the first and only of its kind. In April 1997 he commissioned Italdesign to create a mid-engined coupé to carry it while his engineers explored its power. They succeeded in extracting 600bhp at 7,000rpm with peak torque at 5,800rpm of 457lb-ft. Simply dubbed the 'W12' to showcase the engine, the racy coupé, with styling echoes of the Passat's greenhouse, was shown at Tokyo in 1997. A roadster version appeared at Geneva in 1998.

Ferdinand Piëch had high hopes of a production run of W12 coupés, perhaps 50 per year. An updated design was shown in Tokyo in 2001, just after a prototype had set nine new class records and two world records on the circular track at Nardo in southern Italy. Included was a 24-hour record at 183.46mph, one of the blue ribbons of the record-breaking world. However VW's chief was "not really enthused" by the result, he said later. With his W12 capable of better than 215mph, even with its power dialled back to 580bhp for endurance, Piëch thought higher record speeds should have been on the agenda.

Although the Volkswagen's W12 sports car failed to reach production, its W12 engine took to the road in VW's

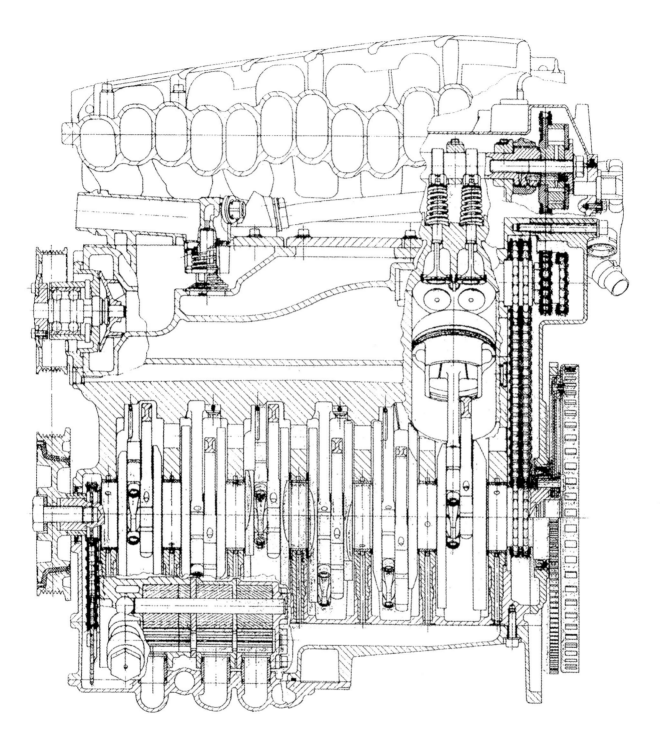

A longitudinal section of a dry-sump version of the VW Group's W12 shows what a challenging task was undertaken in fitting a dozen connecting rods and seven main bearings into a length-constrained bottom end. Roller chains at the clutch end drove the overhead camshafts while another chain at the front powered the oil pressure and scavenge pumps.

2003 Phaeton. As outfitted by Matthias Bach, VW Group's director of twelve-cylinder-engine development, each cylinder bank had its own version of Bosch's ME 7.1.1 Motronic management system, sensing knock at two locations on each bank. Separate throttles fed the crisscrossed ram pipes of its two-piece magnesium inlet manifolding. Owing to the splayed cylinders in each bank,

Above: *In its wet-sump version, the 6.0-litre engine of the VW Phaeton developed 420bhp from a weight of 540lb. Each bank of the W12 had its own Bosch Motronic engine-management system.*

Below: *Although he had originally developed the W12 engine for VW, company chief Ferdinand Piëch realised that Audi would need one as well lest it be seen as a stepchild of the VW brand. As installed in the A8 from 2004 it became the flagship of the Audi range.*

Above: *As used in the Audi A8 of 2004, the W12 engine developed 450bhp at 6,200rpm thanks to tuning that enhanced its higher-revving properties. Dry-sump lubrication reduced power losses from oil churning in its bottom end.*

THE V12 ENGINE

Equipped with twin turbochargers, Bentley's version of the VW Group's W12 retained the Audi's dry-sump lubrication and gave an impressive under-bonnet appearance. Its performance was impressive too, nearly touching 200mph in the Bentley Continental GT.

For its 907, shown at Paris in 2004, Peugeot developed a 6.0-litre V12, giving each connecting-rod big end its own crank journal and taking the gear drives to its camshafts up the centre of the engine. It was an impressive power unit intended to show that Peugeot didn't intend to be left out of the multi-cylinder race.

the effective lengths of the ram pipes differed from one set of three to the other.

Weighing 540lb, the Phaeton's W12 developed 420bhp at 6,000rpm. Its peak torque at 3,000rpm was 406lb-ft from a 10.8:1 compression ratio. This was just the unit to call upon when VW's customers in the Middle East asked for more power for their Touareg sport-utilities. In 2004 its 'VW Individual' department took on the assignment of producing a special series of 300 Sport W12 Touaregs, two-thirds of which went to the oil-rich region and the rest to Europe. Special wheels and decor marked them out from ordinary Touaregs.

These special Touaregs had pepped-up W12s that were shared with the ultimate version of Audi's A8, introduced in 2004. Delivering 450bhp at 6,200rpm, it had freer-flowing throttles and exhausts plus lighter pistons and connecting rods to permit it to rev higher reliably. Between 2,300 and 5,300rpm fully 95 per cent of its peak torque of 428lb-ft (reached at 4,000rpm) was on tap. To cope with its power generation and permit it to be set lower in the chassis, the Audi version had dry-sump lubrication.

"The W12 delivers good throttle response and a wide, flexible torque curve befitting a luxury carmaker's flagship sedan," found *Autoweek* of its test Audi. "Moreover, the revs translate into executive-class thrust. The W12 pulls

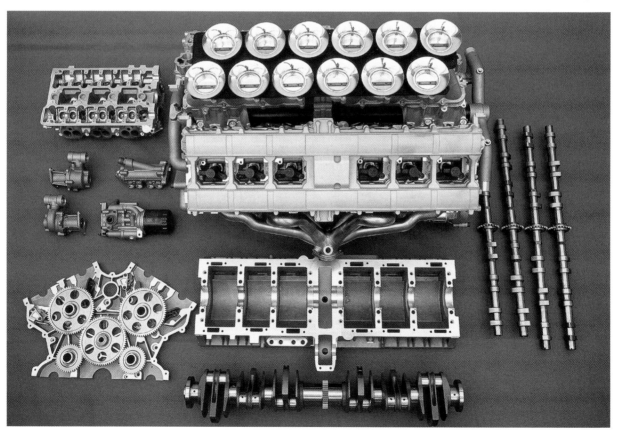

hard up to its 6,200-rpm redline and feels like it still has legs when it hits the limiter." Suspicious of the odd vee pattern, the magazine's testers found "a hint of vibration" in the A8 at high speed, "more than we would anticipate with a conventional V12." The W12's efficient design was reflected in a vehicle dry weight one pound less than the same Audi model with a 90° vee-eight. Its price was another matter: half as much again as the V8 version.

Active in the creation of the W12, Volkswagen's Ulrich Eichhorn was a key architect of its adaptation to the Bentley Continental GT, the first all-new model to emerge from the Crewe factory since its takeover by the VW Group. Driving through all four wheels, as in the Phaeton and A8, the twelve powered a sleek two-door coupé of conventional construction derived from the Phaeton, weighing 5,358lb. To move this kind of mass demanded something special in the way of power, which VW provided by turbocharging its six-litre W12.

Two KKK Warner turbochargers were summoned up for the task. Delivering air through intercoolers at a boost pressure of 10psi, they charged each bank individually through handsome aluminium inlet manifolds. As in the other versions of the W12 the fuel-injection nozzles were in the head, not in the manifolds. The result was output of 551bhp at 6,100rpm and a maximum torque of 479lb-ft available over a generous range from 1,600 to more than 5,000rpm. To accommodate the turbocharging its compression ratio was lowered to 9.5:1, still high for a blown engine. Dry-sump oiling as in the Audi was an aid to durability, validated by an 18,500-mile test at 175mph.

"Winding out the twin-turbo W12 isn't particularly satisfying," found *Car and Driver*. "There are no bad sounds, just the mellow thrum of siamesed VR6s at moderate speeds, replaced by a wheezy rush near redline [6,500rpm] that mimics the sound of an incoming ocean wave just as it crashes over your head." Defying its mass, the Continental GT reached 60mph in 4.9sec. That the aerodynamics were outstanding was confirmed by a top speed timed by *Autocar* at Nardo of 198.4mph. Even when the Bentley was being stretched to its limit its W12 produced only a "distant hum…incredibly quiet". Among its peers the Bentley was not mendaciously priced at £110,000 or $158,000.

As the 21st Century accelerated, yet another volume producer of automobiles realised that it was out of step with its rivals without a twelve-cylinder engine. The French had in fact been lax in this department, failing to honour the proud tradition established by Voisin, Hispano-Suiza, Delage and Delahaye. Only Matra with its racing cars had carried the tricolour for the vee-twelve.

In 1981 and '82 the PSA Peugeot-Citroën group dabbled in the world of twelves by badging Matra's engine as a 'Talbot' to power the Formula 1 Ligiers. The group revived the Talbot marque for the models it acquired when it bought Chrysler's European interests, and this was one of the ways it chose to promote it.[11] When Peugeot made a commitment of its own to sports-car racing, however, with its 3½-litre Type 905 for the 1991 endurance season, it chose a vee-ten instead of a vee-twelve.

For the 2004 Paris Salon Peugeot prepared its 907, billed as showing "Peugeot's view of how the ultimate GT car should look". A front-engined coupé with the obligatory carbon-fibre body, it was powered by a six-litre V12 developing "around 500bhp" delivered through a six-speed transmission. Production of the handsome 907 wasn't on the immediate agenda, but with volume car makers from Ford and Chrysler to Volkswagen and General Motors flaunting their twelves, Peugeot showed that it was more than ready to play with the big boys.

Chapter 15 Footnotes

[1] Although Roy Gullickson never (at this writing) formally abandoned his Packard project, he did attempt to sell it on eBay in 2000. He found no takers.

[2] One car it wouldn't go into was the Cunningham, a planned revival of an American sports car of the 1950s. Bob Lutz personally backed the Cunningham project and hoped that GM's vee-twelve would power it. The effort collapsed after only a mock-up was produced.

[3] Another second-tier Japanese producer, Mitsubishi, experimented with vee-twelves and failed to put them into production.

[4] Abandonment of the ME Four-Twelve was not unrelated to the departure from DaimlerChrysler of its proponent, Wolfgang Bernhard, and his subsequent hiring by the arch-rival VW Group.

[5] Its lack of inlet restriction caused by throttling is an important reason for the diesel engine's high efficiency and fuel economy.

[6] With Derby, production site of the Phantom III, fully occupied with jet-engine production after the war, the manufacture of Rolls-Royce and Bentley cars was moved to Crewe. The decision was taken in 1943.

[7] "We didn't know anything about the Lancia engines!" admitted Hofbauer. "We soon found out about them, however!"

[8] Initially they were called the 'RV' engines, for their combination of *Reihe* – in-line – with vee characteristics. Then when Peter Hofbauer and his chief Ernst Fiala were in California they saw a lot of RVs running around and decided that they'd have to change the name. A simple inversion did the job.

[9] The angle adopted for the W8 version was 18°. Relative to number-one cylinder the twelve's split big-end journal was advanced, while the W8's was retarded.

[10] In German this was in fact highly apt, for 'W' is called '*Doppel-vee*' or 'double-vee', which describes the W12 perfectly.

[11] In 1958 France's Talbot was acquired by Simca, which was later bought by Chrysler. The British arm of Talbot became Sunbeam-Talbot in 1938, since 1935 part of the Rootes Group, another Chrysler acquisition in the 1960s. Thus all the Talbots were united in Peugeot's acquisition.

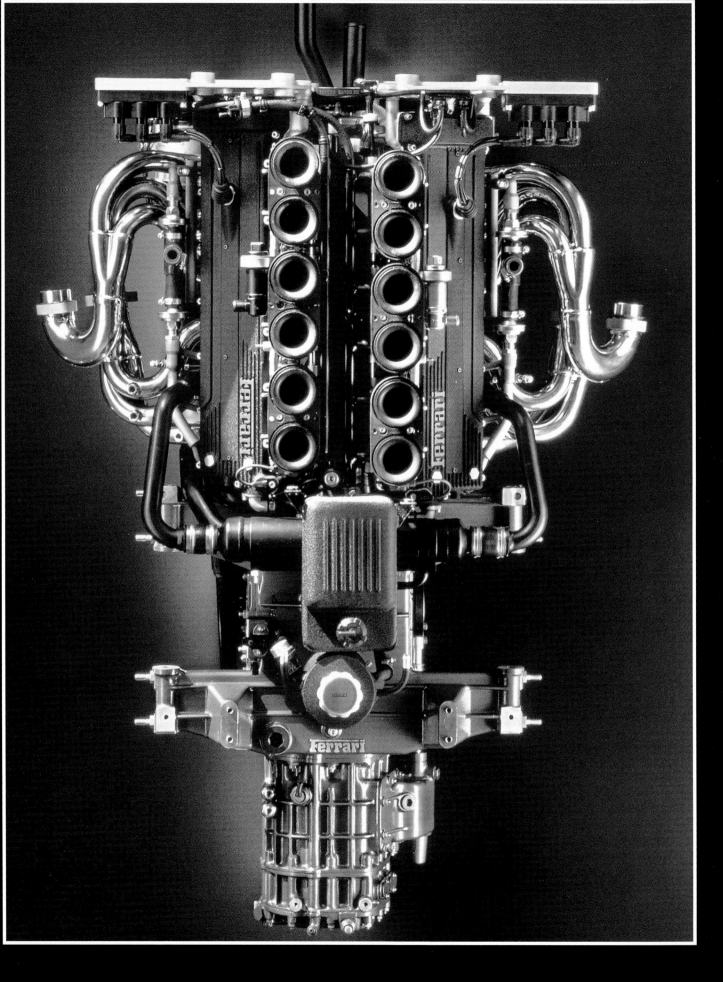

Chapter 16

ULTIMATE SPORTS-CAR POWER

The doomsayers who delight in forecasting the demise of the motorcar must have been dismayed by the way the sports-car industry bounced back in the 1990s with new and exciting offerings – among them twelve-cylinder *bolides* at the zenith of the market. That Ferrari and Lamborghini would build great new twelves was no surprise, but the addition of Bugatti, TVR and Maserati to the list certainly was. So too was the wooing to the cause of Britain's Aston Martin.

After toying disastrously with a twelve for its Lagondas in 1954, Aston Martin settled down with sixes and vee-eights for its sports cars. Acquired by Ford in 1987, Aston introduced its first new model under the blue oval's aegis, the DB7, in 1994. Beneath its styling by Ian Callum were many components from the parts bins of another Ford property, Jaguar, including the underpinnings and in-line six of the XJ-S.

Roots-supercharged though its engine was, "the DB7 was not seen as very credible" in its category, recalled David King, who joined Aston Martin in May 1995. Alternative engine ideas were explored, including a larger version of the Jaguar six and a US-built Ford V8 topped by five-valve cylinder heads made by Britain's Tickford Engineering.

In July of 1995, after a meeting with Aston Martin executives Nick Fry and Tony Batchelor, the search for a more appropriate engine accelerated. David King went to the USA to see what Ford hath wrought. He found an interested party in Jim Clark, head of the Core and Advanced Powertrain Engineering team in Ford's Advanced Vehicle Technology Group. Clark was, King

found, adept at bypassing Ford's convoluted systems to get things done. He was also skilled at exploiting outside suppliers, who were eager to assist his projects in hopes of gaining Ford's business. Most importantly, Clark enjoyed the confidence of Ford chief Jac Nasser, who needed men who were able to work around the huge company's budgetary constraints to generate new products.

Jim Clark brought several projects to a show and tell for Aston Martin. One was an awesome vee-twelve he'd built in 1994 to power Ford's mid-engined GT90 concept supercar. Shown in Detroit at the beginning of 1995, the GT90 was built on a stretched Jaguar XJ220 chassis. To power it Clark made a V12 from two 90° V8s of the new design that was motivating Lincoln's Mark VIII. These were bang up to date with four valves per cylinder and twin chain-driven overhead camshafts.

Clark's team made their twelve by scything off the rear two cylinders of one eight and the front two of another and welding the two cylinder blocks together. All its rotating parts had to be special, including a crankshaft with a stroke reduced from the Lincoln's 90mm to 77.3mm. With the 90.2mm bore this gave 5,927cc. Along the flanks of his twelve Clark arrayed two turbochargers per side. Their boost delivered 660lb-ft of torque at

Opposite: *Its output of 108bhp per litre gave the Ferrari Enzo's F140 vee-twelve the highest specific power of any unsupercharged V12 engine ever produced for road use. Its basic design established a new engine family which is powering Ferraris of the future.*

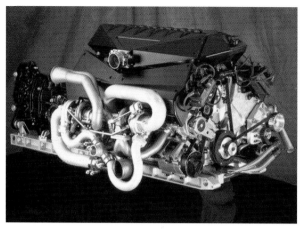

As configured to power Ford's GT90 concept supercar of 1995, Jim Clark's 5.9-litre vee-twelve was equipped with four turbochargers. Its technology was based on that of Ford's four-valve V8 with a 90° vee.

Another experimental Ford vee-twelve from Jim Clark's Advanced Powertrain Engineering was based on Ford's Duratec V6. From its 5.9 litres the 60° twelve developed 435bhp to power the Indigo concept car.

4,750rpm and 720bhp at 6,600rpm – ample thrust for an impressive supercar.

Less fantastical, and of more immediate interest to Aston Martin, was another twelve in the Clark workshops. This time the imaginative engineer used Ford's 3.0-litre 60°

Inspired by the technology of Indianapolis cars, Ford's Indigo concept car of 1996 was a striking show-stopper. Built by Reynard in Britain, it was powered by the experimental Duratech-based 5.9-litre V12.

Duratec vee-six as the basis of his legerdemain. As fitted to the American Ford Taurus and Mercury Sable, this was another of Ford's latest designs, with twin overhead cams and four valves per cylinder in aluminium heads and cylinder block. Keeping the Duratec dimensions of 89 x 79.5mm, Clark gave his twelve economies of scale by carrying over the six's roller-equipped finger-type valve gear, pivoting from hydraulically adjusted fulcrums.

The right-hand cylinder bank of the new 5,935cc twelve was offset forward, the cams in each bank having their own roller-chain drive from the crankshaft nose. To

make his concept engine Jim Clark prototype-machined a sand-cast aluminium block and cut components like cams and crankshaft from billets. He already had an engine running when David King came to call. It was scheduled to power a hyper-exotic concept car that Ford unveiled at Detroit in January 1996. This was the Indigo, inspired as its name suggested by Indy cars. As fitted to this red missile, styled by Claude Lobo and engineered and built in Britain by Reynard, the experimental twelve developed 435bhp at 6,100rpm and 405lb-ft of torque at 5,250rpm.

Here was an engine that looked to have potential for Aston Martin. A preliminary check showed that the 6.0-litre twelve would just fit in the DB7. "It filled the hole completely," said Brian Fitzsimons, Aston's chief power train engineer. But taking it through to production was another matter altogether. Just at this time Ford was running its ruler over the little loss-making British sports-car maker to decide on its future. Should Ford close it? Sell it? Or invest in it? The answer was by no means obvious.

Importantly, Jac Nasser was a fan. In several visits to Aston's factories at Newport Pagnell and Bloxham early in 1996 Nasser expressed his support. For their part, the Aston managers set out their ambitious goals for an overhaul of the DB7. Nasser drew them up short with a warning: "I can only help you if you can do this programme for $20 million." Ford wasn't about to lavish money on a brand which, although 75 years old at the time, had only survived by virtue of a succession of wealthy owners. Paring away their optional extras, the

executives came up with a plan that concentrated on the V12 engine. Finally at the end of 1996 a programme to install it was approved for $24 million.

Included in the $24 million was $11 million for the engine, which Aston Martin people are convinced didn't cover its real cost. "We're sure that Jim Clark tucked some of the cost away somewhere," said David King. "They really wanted to complete the design for production to show what they could do." A ten-strong team under Clark engineered the V12 for production.

Although stateside pressure was strong to produce the engine there, to reward the suppliers whose arms Clark had twisted, Aston Martin counter-argued that its customers would expect an Aston's engine to be made in Britain. Cosworth Technology won the assignment, producing the castings and engines at its Worcester facility. Nevertheless American suppliers did have a look-in, awarded the manifolds, water pump, oil pump, timing-case cover and sundry other parts. With Aston Martin's own engineering staff at the time amounting to only a score of warm bodies, Cosworth also carried out the engine and drive-train calibration. In 2004 V12 assembly was moved to a dedicated Aston facility in Ford's Cologne, Germany factories.

With the help of Cosworth Technology, which made major castings for the engine, Jim Clark's design team in Dearborn engineered a production version of their 5.9-litre V12 for Aston Martin. The first such engine was running in a DB7 in 1997.

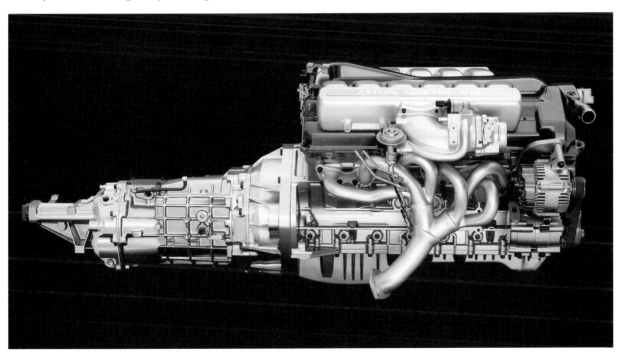

Deriving Aston Martin's new vee-twelve from Ford's Duratech V6 meant that it could depend on proven componentry of a high design standard and, in many cases, low cost through volume production. Chains at its front end drove the four overhead camshafts.

The first DB7 to be vee-twelve-powered was on the road early in 1997. In spite of too-high gearing and rough-and-ready installation of one of Clark's prototypes, David King recalled, "it was a revelation, sporty and characterful. In hindsight, of course, its NVH was shockingly bad." [1]

Although its fit in the DB7 was good, the twelve and the larger radiator it demanded used up much of the frontal crumple zone needed to meet crash standards. The solution was to use a propeller shaft that was rigid, without sliding joints, so that crash energy would be transferred to the differential and its mountings at the rear. [2] Cooling was a challenge too, said Brian Fitzsimons: "You've got a megawatt under your bonnet." The water pump was a high-capacity design and an oil/water heat exchanger was brought on stream.

Carrying over as it did the internal attributes of the Duratec vee-six, Aston's vee-twelve shared its cylinder-centre distance of 102mm. Valve sizes were the same as well, 35mm for the inlets and 30mm for the exhausts, as were valve inclinations at a total of 50°, symmetrically disposed. Pistons, rings and rods could be similar, the latter measuring 138.1mm. They rode on 49.8mm big-end journals on a counterbalanced crankshaft carried in seven 67.5mm main bearings. The mains had individual

caps which were sewed in by four vertical cap screws apiece plus two anchoring the caps to the sides of the block, which extended down past the crank centreline. A die-cast aluminium wet sump closed the bottom of the block, which had dry iron liners protecting its bores.

After a sneak preview with a 'Project Vantage' concept car in 1997, the twelve was launched as the DB7 Vantage at the show that Aston Martin favoured, Geneva, in March 1999. Its rating was 414bhp at 6,000rpm and 398lb-ft at 5,000rpm, only fractionally less than the values of the experimental Indigo for a full emissions-controlled engine. The change to the DB7, said one observer, "radically altered its character and performance and put it into direct competition with Ferrari."

Two years later Aston's new chief Ulrich Bez, formerly engineering boss for Porsche and then Daewoo, had the pleasure of introducing the all-new V12 Vanquish at Geneva. For this new car at the top of its range, Aston's twelve dramatically stretched its legs. While emphasis in the DB7 had been on a strong torque curve, the Vanquish was tuned for power. Without changing lift of 9.8mm, new hollow camshafts were fitted that extended valve timing on the inlet side to give more duration and overlap. Compression ratio went up from 10.3:1 to 10.5:1 by the simple expedient of omitting the previous piston-crown recesses for valve-head clearance. [3] The crankshaft was lightened by reducing the number of counterweights from twelve to eight.

On the emissions side the installation from scratch of the V12 in the Vanquish made room for the catalysts to be closer to the exhaust manifolds, which in turn did away with the DB7's exhaust-gas recirculation (EGR). Aston's engineers rightly took pride in their ability to meet emissions rules by "doing the simple things well" without add-ons such as EGR and variable valve timing. Shorter inlet ram pipes from the twin plenum chambers, fed by a Visteon PTEC engine-management system instead of the DB7's Ford EEC-5, suited higher revs, as did a freed-up exhaust system.

Thus liberated the V12 Vanquish produced 460bhp at 6,500rpm while its torque remained virtually unchanged. Testers raved about its exhaust note, smoothly humming when cruising, not at all disturbing, yet unmistakably authoritative under acceleration. It was an excellent starting point for the new DB9 Aston, introduced as the DB7's replacement in 2004. This called for moderation in power to gain more torque, the latter rising to 420lb-ft at 5,000rpm. Power for the DB9 was 450bhp at 6,000rpm with a redline at 6,800.

Among measures taken to achieve this the inlet ram pipes were lengthened again to 15¼in, exhaust piping amended and a new Visteon engine controller installed. Compression ratio was 10.4:1 in an engine which, with all accessories but no flywheel, weighed 662lb. Its installation in the DB9 could be lower thanks to a redesigned sump with cast-in passages picking up the oil. Also easing manufacture, this was a patentable innovation.

Although Aston's engineers were rightly proud of the DB9's generation of 85 per cent of its peak torque as low as 1,500rpm, it wasn't as thrust-rich at low speed as some of its rivals. "That," said *Car and Driver*, "at least provided an excuse to rev it beyond 4,000rpm, where the engine note changes from moderato to a glorious fortissimo." At Nardo in southern Italy *Autocar* timed the £103,000 DB9 at a top speed of 190.4mph, 0–60 acceleration in 5.0sec and the standing quarter-mile in 13.1sec. This augured well for the performance in 2005 of the DBR9, the racing version of the DB9 prepared for Aston Martin by Britain's Prodrive.

Under pressure from its younger brother, Aston's Vanquish had to raise its game. At 2004's Paris Salon it revealed its riposte. The Vanquish S had a higher compression ratio of 10.8:1, made possible by machining of the combustion chambers to ensure consistency of their contents. Also machined to shape, the inlet ports were fed by altered fuel injectors and a remapped engine management system. Thus unleashed, the 5.9-litre twelve produced 520bhp at 7,000rpm and 425lb-ft of torque at 5,800rpm. Top speed, said Aston Martin, was now in excess of the magic 200mph.

Conceived from the word go for sports-car racing was another British vee-twelve, the work of Blackpool's TVR.

Engineers at Aston Martin proved adept in tuning their new V12 to suit various applications. To power the new DB9, introduced in 2004, its torque was enhanced by means of longer inlet ram pipes.

An authentic maverick among car makers, TVR was founded at the end of the 1940s. It moved up a gear after 1982, when chemical engineer and entrepreneur Peter Wheeler acquired the company. To replace his Rover vee-eight engines, the ambitious Wheeler decided to make his own power units. He turned to Melling Consultancy Design to create a new engine family, a related V8 and V12. Although both were designed, using single overhead camshafts and a 72° vee, only the V8 was produced.

Next TVR commissioned the design of an in-line six from Al Melling's consultancy. This was all-aluminium with twin overhead cams, driven by a two-stage roller chain, and four valves per cylinder opened by high-leverage fingers of distinctive Melling design. Introduced at Britain's motor show in 1996, TVR's AJP6 entered production in 2000. Nineteen ninety-six also saw the revelation of Project 12/7, a spectacular plum-coloured coupé powered by a twelve-cylinder engine of no less than 7.7 litres which the company itself had created. In 1997 it was confirmed in the model range as TVR's Speed Twelve.

Conceived more for GT racing than the road, the Speed Twelve exploited the cylinder heads and bore spacing of the AJP6, albeit with head modifications to suit the 90° vee angle and porting arrangements. Shades of Gabriel Voisin's record-breaker of 1929, the block beneath the heads was a welded fabrication of high-molybdenum EN14T steel. Its crankshaft was of EN40B steel, with nitrided bearing journals, and its connecting rods used EN24B steel. To simplify its construction all the twelve's pumps were driven by electric motors.

TVR's Speed Twelve was a power prodigy. In one state of tune it produced 800bhp at 7,250rpm and 650lb-ft of torque at 5,750rpm. Said to be capable of 880bhp, it was shown in more developed form at Earls Court in 1997. Seen by TVR as an example of quick prototyping, the big vee-twelve was produced in a quantity of four as motivation for both the Speed Twelve and a version of TVR's Cerbera coupé.

Another big British twelve made even less progress toward production. It was conceived in the mid-1990s as the driving force for a GT car to be series-produced, for both road and track, by Lola Cars Limited in Cambridgeshire. Its creation inspired by a new race series for production GT cars, the new model was intended to be a more consistent counterbalance for Lola's traditional business as a maker of racing cars. The assignment to design its engine went to the Melling Consultancy, which penned a handsome 90° vee-twelve.

Measuring 93.5 x 84.9mm, the Lola twelve displaced 6,995cc. Gear-driven at the front of the block, its close-

A most unusual twelve was the 7.0-litre unit designed for Lola in the mid-1990s by the Melling Consultancy. Inlet ports were on the engine's outer flanks, which were to be fed by long passages from inlet-air restrictors mounted well forward. Gear drive to its camshafts was at the front of the 90° engine.

As a potential GT1 competitor Lola designed an extremely attractive sports coupé which would have been produced both as a road car and for racing purposes. Financial problems at Lola forced this exciting project into oblivion.

spaced twin overhead camshafts operated four valves per cylinder through cup-type tappets. Melling splayed its rows of valves equally at a 20° included angle and aligned its inlet ports at a close 38° angle to the valve stems. Valve sizes were 39mm for the inlets and 33mm for the exhausts.

Unusually for a modern engine the Lola GT's wide-angle vee contained the exhaust ports centrally while the oval inlet ports were along the flanks of the engine. This was deliberate to integrate them with the car's design concept, which included two large volutes at the rear to help generate ground-effect downthrust. The inlet-air restrictors required for the GT series would be mounted at the Lola's nose, from which air would flow back through the sills to the rows of inlet ram pipes at each side.

Thin steel wet liners formed the Lola GT's cylinders, which were irregularly spaced: 104.6mm at the centre, then 106.1mm, alternating outward with 104.6mm. Racing-style pistons had gudgeon pins only 57mm long at the top of 140mm I-section connecting rods. Oil pumps were to be gear-driven to the right and left of the Lola twelve's shallow dry sump, meeting the needs of seven 59mm main bearings and 51mm rod journals.

Work on this elegant and attractive engine continued into 1999, with patterns and major sample castings made and assembled to envision its final shape. For his creation Al Melling forecast in excess of 750bhp at 7,000rpm for an engine with a low centre of gravity weighing 365lb without its clutch and exhaust system. A strikingly styled Lola GT was waiting for it, but 1999 found Lola Cars tumbling into

receivership and the promise of this exciting concept fading into disappointment for its supporters. The rights to the vee-twelve reverted to its designer.

Al Melling's studio had already been called upon to design an engine for another GT car, one of history's more enigmatic efforts. Racing driver Fulvio Ballabio was one of the prime movers of a bizarre project to make the principality of Monaco the base for production of an exotic supercar, the mid-engined MCA Centenaire. Although Lamborghini engines were first used in the prototypes, with carbon-fibre chassis, at the end of the 1980s MCA decided to commission its own engines.

Approached for the task was Motori Moderni, Carlo Chiti's engine company in Novara, in co-operation with Melling Consultancy Design. Two different engines resulted. One was a 6,995cc twelve (94 x 84mm) from the Melling office which closely followed the cylinder-head design that it produced in 1988 for TWR's Jaguar vee-twelves, with twin overhead cams and four valves per cylinder. This was a good starting point because the tools for producing the heads had reverted to Melling in the dismantling of his deal with TWR. A suitable aluminium block, much on Jaguar lines, was drawn to support the heads.

The other engine for MCA was a 4.0-litre version of the 3.5-litre vee-twelve that Motori Moderni had schemed for Formula 1 applications. The difference was a longer stroke for 86 x 57mm (3,973cc). Its vee angle was 67½° and its four overhead cams were driven by chains instead of gears as the less noisy solution. Fitted with two turbochargers giving 16psi of boost through an intercooler, the 48-valve engine was credited with 720bhp at 7,000rpm and 538lb-ft of torque.

The 1992 Detroit show was the venue for the introduction of the MCA with the latter engine. After six cars were made the project was sold on to a company in Soviet Georgia that held the rights to the famous MiG aviation name. They had no luck in their effort to relaunch the Centenaire under the MiG brand. One car with the Motori Moderni V12 appeared at Le Mans in 1993, but was far too slow to qualify. In 1996 France's Aixam-Mega took over the effort, and sensibly re-powered it with a Mercedes-Benz vee-twelve. This was not enough to save the supercar, which in this final incarnation returned to its roots with the 'Monte Carlo' brand name.

As a magnificent folly the MCA/MiG saga pales in comparison with the 1991 revival of the Bugatti marque. This was the initiative of genial, white-haired Romano Artioli, who from a garage in Bolzano built up car sales and distribution businesses in the north of Italy and beyond, that turned over $300 million annually. Although

An amazing powerhouse of machinery was under the rear deck of the Bugatti EB110 of 1991. With four turbochargers, Paolo Stanzani extracted 550bhp from its 3.5 litres.

initially only interested in the preservation of the Bugatti brand, Artioli decided to become a car maker as well when Ferrari withdrew his distribution rights in France and Italy.

While a handsome factory was being built at Campogalliano, on the north-western periphery of Modena, Artioli engaged former Lamborghini engineer Paolo Stanzani to design a car worthy of the Bugatti name. In this the fecund Stanzani excelled himself. His creation, the EB110 coupé, was so packed with machinery that its only fault was a lack of interior room and – in the supercar tradition – luggage space. At its core was a 60° all-aluminium turbocharged V12 of 3,499cc (81 x 56.6mm) mounted with its clutch end facing forward to integrate it with a four-wheel-drive system.

Stanzani's twelve had twin chain-driven overhead cams per bank opening three inlet and two exhaust valves per cylinder. Valves were titanium, as were the connecting rods from specialist Pankl in Austria. "Intake pulse effects mean you can't have six cylinders served by the same turbo," said Stanzani of his blower layout, "so we put two per side. It's a solution that also helps acceleration; four small turbos have lower inertia than two large ones." With a 7.5:1 compression ratio and its four IHI turbochargers the boosted Bugatti produced 550bhp at 8,500rpm and 420lb-ft of torque at the remarkably low speed, for a super-sports engine, of 3,800rpm.

In what can only be described as a masterpiece of automotive engineering Paolo Stanzani integrated not only the rear differential but also the six-speed gearbox and the front/rear differential into his engine's cylinder

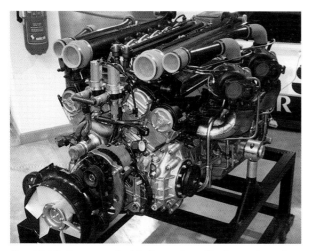

Completely integrated with the twelve-cylinder engine of the Bugatti EB110 were its six-speed gearbox, its drive to the rear wheels and its centre differential sending power to the front wheels. Stanzani had moved on impressively from his accomplishments at Lamborghini.

block, which was split on the crank centreline. The gearbox nestled alongside the right flank of the crankcase, allowing the dry-sump engine to be placed extra-low. A rigid tube around the propeller shaft joined the vee-twelve to the front differential.

Introduced in 1991, the 110th anniversary of Ettore Bugatti's birth, the EB110 entered production late in 1992. By then Paolo Stanzani was a non-person, having

One of the most controversial cars ever manufactured, the Bugatti EB110 was packed with machinery from stem to stern. A tiny aperture in its nosepiece gave a hint of the famed Bugatti horseshoe radiator of yore.

departed from Bugatti after a power struggle with Artioli. Nicola Materazzi led the team charged with making Stanzani's dream a reality. And an impressive reality it was. In its EB110S version, boosted to 611bhp at 8,250rpm, the Bugatti was capable of 217mph at Nardo and from rest to 60mph acceleration in less than 3.6sec, emitting, said one tester, "an incredible cacophony of fizzes and screams". It was, if anything, a bargain at £336,000.

An unsupercharged version of the vee-twelve was also produced with its capacity expanded to 5,995cc (86 x 86mm) to power a front-engined four-door model, the EB112, that was mooted in 1993 as an addition to the range. Before it could be produced, however, Bugatti Automobili SpA collapsed into the hands of the receiver in 1995. To its credit were 154 EB110s, plus a dozen or so cars that were being made at the time of the bankruptcy. Although German racer and entrepreneur Jochen Dauer acquired the plant's main assets at auction in 1997, a car bearing a suspicious resemblance to the Bugatti, the turbocharged 3,760cc V12 Edonis, was on offer from Campogalliano in 2001.

Paolo Stanzani's alma mater, Lamborghini, had not been idle in the meantime. Under the Swiss Mimran brothers and their nominated managing director, Emile Novaro, 'Nuova Lamborghini' battled back to respectability in the 1980s after its several collapses. In 1985, recognising that its Quattrovalvole version stretched the Countach about as far as it could go, Novara issued the command: "Create a Countach successor." Supported now by engineering director Luigi Marmiroli, formerly a racing engineer with Ferrari, general manager Giulio Alfieri was more than equal to the task.

He had an engine already. Since 1977, when it built the rear-engined Cheetah, Lamborghini had been hoping to

generate a parallel money-spinner in light military vehicles. Under the 'LM' appellation it built a series of rugged-looking four-door off-road vehicles, the Hummers of their day. Under the squared-off bonnet of the 1983 LM004 was a brand-new 7.0-litre vee-twelve, the work of Alfieri and Bellentani. No lover of turbocharging, Alfieri was determined to get the power he needed with cubic inches.

Although the gestation of the Diablo, introduced in 1990, was a tortuous and protracted affair, surviving the 1987 acquisition of Lamborghini by Chrysler, there was never doubt that it would be powered by Alfieri's new twelve. At its launch the engine measured 87 x 80mm for 5,707cc, 10½ per cent larger than the biggest-ever Countach, and produced 492bhp at 6,800rpm with a 10.0:1 compression ratio. Torque was up by 16 per cent to 428lb-ft at 5,200rpm. This was serious thrust, also delivered from 1991 through all four wheels by the Diablo VT. For the committed power fanatic the rear-drive Diablo SE offered 520bhp at 7,100rpm from 1993.

Unlike Giotto Bizzarrini's original design, which had block sides extending down to embrace the crankshaft, the new engine's block was cut off at the crank centreline. Also in aluminium, a massive matching casting carried the seven main-bearing caps, each anchored by four studs, and cradled the crankshaft in a curved windage tray through which two slots evacuated the oil from each crank throw. A bottom cover, finned for cooling, closed the wet sump.

Unusually for a limited-production engine, both the block and heads of the Diablo were produced in metal moulds by low-pressure die-casting. The decision to invest in the costly tooling for this dated from the early 1980s, when expectations were high for a big order for the LM004 from Saudi Arabia. When the order failed to materialise, the Diablo's twelve was the beneficiary of this precise casting process. To facilitate it the cylinder banks had open top decks with water passages over the upper quarter of the steel cylinder liners, which were dry the rest of the way down. A light plating of silicon carbide protected the bore surface.

The right-hand cylinder bank was offset forward. Mahle produced the Diablo's slipper-type pistons, which with racing-style design had gudgeon pins only 50mm long. Gently dished from proud rims that gave turbulence-inducing squish areas amounting to 13 per cent of the bore area, the piston crowns had four tiny depressions for valve-head clearance. Although the engine initially had steel connecting rods, Pankl provided titanium rods for its developed version, 138.5mm in length. Big-end journals measured 45.5mm while the mains were 63mm in diameter. All the journals were

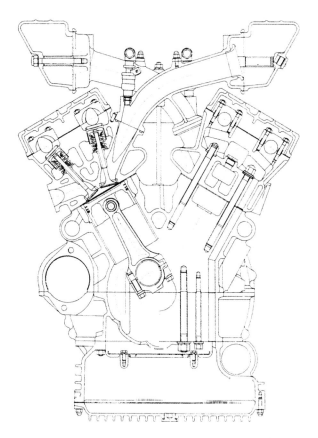

In designing the new V12 engine for their Diablo, Giulio Alfieri and Luigi Marmiroli kept the 95mm distance between cylinders of its predecessor. This required the use of particularly thin steel cylinder liners in its aluminium block.

nitride-hardened on a steel crankshaft that had counterbalances opposite every throw.

As in the Countach, the Diablo's 60° vee-twelve was installed with its clutch facing forward, inputting to a front-mounted gearbox from which the drive to the rear passed along the right side of the sump to a rear differential that was attached to the engine. At the anti-drive end of the engine, the rear as installed, duplex roller chains drove the twin overhead cams on each bank. Hydraulic variators in the sprockets of the inlet camshafts, as originated by Alfa Romeo, gave valve-timing adjustment on the run. Other accessories, including the single water pump with its dual outlets, were also at the anti-drive end.

Set into the tops of the 33mm cup-type tappets were steel valve-clearance shims in the design originated for Fiat by Aurelio Lampredi. Set at a 30° included angle, the Diablo's four valves per cylinder measured 33.5mm for the inlets and 29.5mm for the exhausts. Respective lifts were 9.7 and 7.5mm. Twin coil springs closed each valve. For consistency, both ports and combustion chambers were

Above: *Like its predecessor installation in the Countach, the new Lamborghini twelve in the Diablo was mounted with its drive end forward, right, as shown, to a gearbox and transfer case carrying power to the rear wheels. Thus four-wheel drive was easily accommodated.*

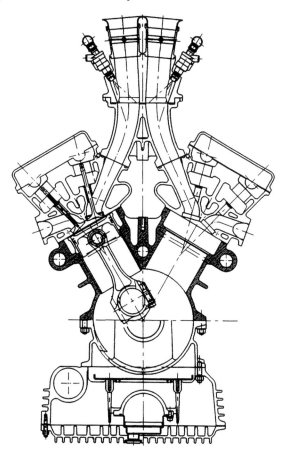

Left: *For the Diablo GT Lamborghini's engineers increased displacement from 5.7 to 6.0 litres and provided downdraft inlet piping. Electronic fuel injectors were mounted high in the ram pipes, below the butterfly throttles.*

fully machined. Inlet porting was in the central vee, with criss-crossed manifolds from plenum chambers fed by two-stage butterfly throttles – one small and one large – to give progressive response. For the first time electronic fuel injection fed a Lamborghini, using the company's own software to control Weber-Marelli hardware.

"Not at all like the high-pitched siren of a Ferrari twelve," found *Road & Track*, "the Lamborghini resonates with a deep brassiness. Think of a dozen trombones." "Demand some real effort from the twelve," said *Car*, "and the roar plunges an octave, drowning the whine with a galvanising hard-edged hammer." Musical analogies apart, the sonorous Diablo lapped Nardo at 202mph and accelerated to 60mph in 4.5sec in spite of its weight of 3,693lb, one-eighth more than the Countach.

This mighty motor stood Lamborghini in good stead. In spite of the turbulence attendant upon an ownership stint from 1994 by an Indonesian group, ending in 1998 when Lamborghini was bought by VW's Audi arm, Diablo improvements rolled on under the technical direction of Massimo Ceccarani. For the racing SVR of 1996 it produced 540bhp at 7,100rpm.

The twelve's first capacity enlargement took place in 1999 for the Diablo GT, which had a 4mm longer stroke (87 x 84mm) for 5,992cc. This automatically brought a compression-ratio increase to 10.7:1. With more radical cam timing and downdraft inlet ram pipes with individual throttles in magnesium inlet piping, the GT version gave 575bhp at 7,300rpm and 465lb-ft of torque at 5,500rpm. Vacuum-operated bypass valves in the exhaust system allowed noise regulations to be met without degrading performance. The mainstream Diablo 6.0, final embodiment of this striking sports car, generated 550bhp at 7,100rpm from its six litres. In all, concluding in 2000, 2,898 Diablos were produced – a more than respectable result.

Under project number L147, Ceccarani oversaw a major overhaul of the vee-twelve for the first new model produced under Audi's aegis, the 2001 Murciélago. One of the most important changes was the adoption of dry-sump lubrication, which allowed the engine's mass to be lowered by two inches. This had the double benefit of sinking the car's centre of gravity for better handling and improving aerodynamics at the rear of the body. A single large scavenge pump with double the pressure pump's capacity was part of the extensively revised oiling system, which included a de-aerator to extract any air and foam from the lubricant.

Another change, under development since 1992 by Massimo Ceccarani and his colleague Rebottini, was a variable-volume inlet manifold. While ram-pipe lengths remained unchanged, vacuum-controlled valves in the plenum chambers altered their volume. Changes in inlet-duct length worked for fours or vee-eights, explained engine-development chief Marco Cassinetti, "because each cylinder in a V8 knows what happened before and after firing. In a V12 or V6, however, the two banks don't 'see' each other, so it's better to use different volumes to modify the torque curve."

Plan A for the L147 had been to continue with the 6.0-litre capacity, but with the better-equipped new model weighing more than its predecessor the decision was taken at the last minute to move to Plan B, an increase in displacement. The stroke was lengthened by 2.8mm (87 x 86.8mm) to raise capacity to 6,192cc. Compression ratio was held at 10.7:1. As reworked the engine was revved higher as well, the limiter kicking in at 7,800rpm – remarkably high for such a big engine.[4] Maximum power of 580bhp was reached at 7,500rpm while peak torque at 5,400rpm was 480lb-ft.[5]

Delivering its massive power through all four wheels, Lamborghini's £168,000 Murciélago was called the "Sant' Agata sledgehammer" by *Autocar*. The British weekly timed its maximum speed on different occasions at 203, 205 and 206mph and its 0–60mph acceleration at 3.7sec. It covered the standing quarter-mile in only 11.8sec. "The big Lambo simply shot off into the distance with little wheelspin," it found, with "aural properties that left the biggest impression on anyone within earshot of Nardo. It

is a menacing but addictive sound that had everyone scrambling toward the pit lane wall every time it howled past on the banking."

The only car that accelerated faster was the Ferrari Enzo – albeit at a price of £425,000 that would purchase a Porsche Turbo as well as His and Hers Lamborghinis. Under its new chief, Luca di Montezemolo, who took charge of Ferrari in 1991, the Maranello sports-car maker consistently raised its game in the last decade of the 20th Century.[6] Elegantly slim and floppy-haired, the patrician, publicity-savvy di Montezemolo led Ferrari away from its big mid-engined Boxers and back to front-engined vee-twelves that were both fast and stylish.

Development of the new F116 engine series was nearly complete when di Montezemolo arrived. Indeed, it had begun well before the death in August 1988 of Enzo Ferrari. He had been the ultimate arbiter of engineering decisions, said Ermanno Bonfiglioli, who had been working on Ferrari engines since the 365GTB Daytona: "We and the Formula 1 designers were in two separate groups, but they were just next door. We would meet to transfer ideas from one side to the other. The ultimate decisions were taken at the very top, because Mr. Ferrari was the only one who could adjudicate between them."

The first edition of the new twelve, the F116A of 1988, was an improved version of the F110A used in the 2+2 412. Its bore and stroke were enlarged by 1 and 2mm respectively (83 x 80mm) to give 5,194cc. Cogged-rubber timing belts drove its four overhead camshafts, and each cylinder bank's ram pipes were cast integrally with the camshaft cover on the opposite side. Though it revved to 7,000 instead of 6,500rpm, however, the F116A could produce only 17 more horsepower than the F110A. Its drawback, the designers found, was that incoming-air density was reduced by the heating it received when flowing through the cam-cover passages.

Deciding that the basic concept of the 412's engine had reached its limits, the engineers went back to Square One. The 83mm bore was the largest possible with the 60° vee angle, because the bores interfered with each other at their bottom ends if they were expanded farther. For this reason, and to allow a lower and more compact block, the vee angle was increased to 65°. This, combined with a 4mm increase in cylinder-centre spacing to 98mm, allowed the bore of the F116B V12 to enlarge to 88mm. With a stroke of 75mm this gave 5,474cc and per-cylinder capacity of 456cc – thus establishing the name of the new model it was to power. No effort was made to split the rod journals to achieve even firing; the twelve easily tolerated its 5° timing differences.

In a reversal of Ferrari tradition, the F116B's left-

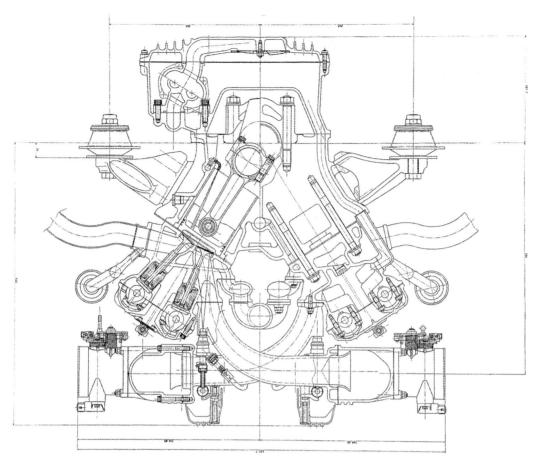

Above: *For their F116B V12 of 1991 Ferrari's engineers increased the vee angle from 60° to 65° to reduce interference between the lower ends of its cylinder bores. Its aluminium block extended only slightly below the centreline of the crankshaft. Clearly shown is the use of an oil jet to cool the underside of its pistons.*

hand cylinder bank was offset forward. The half-speed drive to overhead camshafts was achieved in two stages: firstly by gears at the crank nose and secondly by individual cogged-rubber belts to each head, inside protective shrouds. Two poly-vee belts at the front of the engine turned the single central water pump and accessories from a pulley that did double duty as a vibration damper.

Working through Fiat-style cup-type tappets with top-surface adjusting shims, the cams opened four valves per cylinder splayed at the very narrow angles that were now used in Formula 1: 9° for the inlets and 11½° for the exhausts. With respective head diameters of 30 and 26mm, the valves were closed by twin coils. Inlet ports were at a flow-favourable 33° to the valve stems.

The new twelve's relatively short stroke allowed the use of proportionally stubby I-section steel connecting rods of 131mm. Mini-skirted pistons were cooled by jets of oil from galleries along both sides of the crankcase. Set

Left: *Displayed here minus the plenum chambers and throttle valves that fed its inlet ram pipes, Ferrari's F116B vee-twelve was introduced in 1992 in the 456GT. The drive to its camshafts was by a combination of gears and cogged-rubber belts.*

into the aluminium block, with their top halves exposed to the coolant, were Nikasil-protected aluminium cylinder liners. Cut off 16mm below the crankshaft centreline, the bottom of the block was enclosed by a shallow cast-aluminium sump from which two pumps scavenged the dry-sump system. They and the pressure pump were driven by a simplex chain from the crank nose. Each of the seven main-bearing caps was recessed 16mm into its web across the block and held by two massive studs. Fully counterweighted, the crankshaft preserved the previous bearing diameters of 63 and 43.6mm for mains and rods respectively.

Atop the Ferrari F116B its inlet ram pipes curved up and across to the opposite side in a single casting. Fitted with flared inlets, they sucked air from large plenum chambers, each fed by its own throttle. Ignition and fuel injection – with nozzles set vertically above the inlet ports – were courtesy of a Bosch Motronic 2.7 system. With a 10.6:1 compression ratio the new twelve delivered 436bhp at 6,250rpm and was safe to 1,000rpm more. Torque at 4,500rpm was 406lb-ft. This was a good result for an engine weighing 540lb with its flywheel.

The F116B's installation in the 185-mph 456GT of 1992 marked a new phase of Ferrari's long twelve-cylinder history. With unchanged capacity it served as well to power the 550 Maranello of 1996, although so extensively revised that it deserved a new designation: F133A. Its bottom end received lighter titanium connecting rods and a separate curved windage tray under the crankshaft in place of the previous angular tray, part of the sump. Lightened through slipper-type design, the pistons as well as the rods allowed the crankshaft's balancing masses to be reduced. Still with recesses in their crowns, albeit smaller, the Mahle pistons raised the compression ratio to 10.8:1. Valves were substantially enlarged to 34mm inlets, 29.2mm exhausts.

A major change in the F133A was the adoption of automatic hydraulic valve-clearance adjustment inside the cup-type tappets. Ermanno Bonfiglioli's group had to engage in artful engineering to fit in the adjusters, 15mm long, without changing the location of the camshafts. Five millimetres were gained by recessing the valve-spring bases more deeply into the head, five more by shortening the spring coils and the rest by eliminating the adjusting shims and redesigning the tappets. Welcome by-products were valves 10mm shorter and lighter.

An external sign of change on the F133A was a new chamber running down its centre above the inlet ram pipes. This was a resonant volume joined to each pipe by a butterfly throttle, vacuum-operated by the engine-management system to aid cylinder filling under selected conditions of speed and load. The 550 Maranello's exhaust system had bypass valves as well. Engine control was by Bosch's Motronic 5.2.

Weighing 534lb, Ferrari's F133A produced 420lb-ft of torque at 5,000rpm and revved to 7,000rpm to produce 485bhp. In spite of its hydraulic lifters – usually seen as a

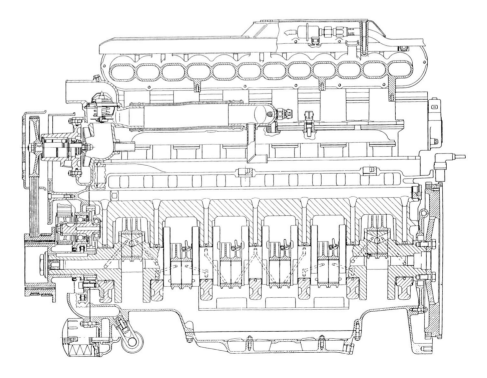

Dry-sump lubrication for the 456GT's F116B V12 allowed it to be set low in the chassis. A rubber insert in the accessory-drive pulley on the nose of the crankshaft allowed it to double in function as a vibration damper.

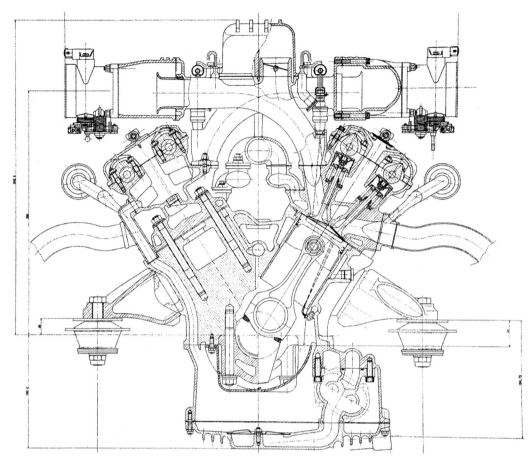

Above: *In 1996 Ferrari's 550 Maranello was powered by a new version of its latest twelve, designated F133A. Tuned for higher-speed running, it had hydraulic lash adjusters inside its tappets and an added central chamber above the ram pipes to help cylinder filling by altering the resonant character of the inlet system.*

barrier to high engine speed – it could rev to 7,700rpm. Even with a bore 1mm larger and stroke 2mm longer (89 x 77mm) it developed its peak power of 515bhp at 7,250rpm in its F133E guise as installed in the 2002 575M Maranello. Its added displacement contributed to a torque increase to 435lb-ft at 5,250rpm.

Torque was little changed when the same engine was tweaked for the 612 Scaglietti of 2003, successor to the 456GT. Freeing up its inlet and exhaust passages and hiking compression to 11.2:1 raised its power output to 540bhp at 7,200rpm. *Car and Driver* praised the Scaglietti's "astonishing engine, equally at ease at 2,000rpm in top gear as it is plundering the 7,600-rpm fuel cut-off. Power builds consistently to the accompaniment of a growing, single-pitch mechanical bellow that is both exhaust and top-end engine noise – all those whirring cams and gears."

Left: *With its Type F133A vee-twelve Ferrari continued its recent tradition of using cogged-rubber belts to drive its overhead camshafts. This was the least appealing feature of the company's engines for its owners, who were faced with high bills for belt changes at fixed maintenance intervals.*

Delivering 540bhp as it was installed in Ferrari's Scaglietti of 2003, the F133A vee-twelve won high praise for its flexibility and broad range of power delivery.

Ferrari's racing experience was clearly visible in the new Type F140 V12 introduced in 2002 to power its Enzo model. Its connecting rods were titanium and its slipper-skirted pistons were deeply indented to provide clearance for four valves per cylinder.

The 612 Scaglietti was a glorious final act for the F116/F133 vee-twelve. Ferrari's next engine family was the F140, first seen as the twelve-cylinder engine introduced in 2002 in its ultra-exotic mid-engined Enzo. Although in this 3,010lb hyper-sports coupé, successor to the F50, the new twelve was equipped to achieve its utmost as a semi-racing engine, it was also tameable for future use in Ferrari's front-engined models. "Today it's not possible to make a special engine for only 360 cars," said Ermanno Bonfiglioli, referring to the Enzo's planned production, "so we decided to make this the basis of a new family of twelves." Work on its creation began during 1999.

Though Ferrari had long committed to ten cylinders for its Grand Prix cars, race-engine developer Paolo Martinelli loyally defended the decision to maintain Maranello's twelve-cylinder tradition for its road cars. "The V10 is a perfect fit for the 3-litre Formula 1 rules," he said. "However, for large-displacement engines the V12 is the best solution, above all with respect to smooth running and coping with the emissions rules." At 5,999cc (92 x 75.2mm) the F140 was twice the size of Martinelli's Formula 1 engines. Its cylinder-centre distance was 104mm, largest at Ferrari since the 108mm of the 1950s Lampredi vee-twelves.

The F140's aluminium cylinder block was as exiguous as modern foundry and design technology could make it. Keeping the 65° vee angle, its open-deck banks accepted wet aluminium liners with Nikasil bores. Left-hand cylinders were offset forward. Cut off on the crank centreline, the block was closed by a one-piece aluminium casting into which the seven main-bearing caps, each

retained by four studs, were integrated. Titanium connecting rods – 134mm long – and slipper-type pistons continued to be worn. Compression ratio was 11.2:1.

The low and tight dry sump, with its right-hand gallery for oil scavenging, side-mounted water pump and quadruple scavenge pumps, showed technology transfer from Formula 1. With capacity three and a half times that of the pressure pump, the scavenge pumps were able to create sub-atmospheric pressure in the bottom end to reduce power loss from windage. Heat was extracted from the oil by the cooling water through an exchanger.

For the ultimate in rigidity, the camshaft bearings of Ferrari's F140 V12 were between the two cam lobes operating the valves of each cylinder. At the left were the control units for the hydraulic variators that changed both inlet and exhaust timing to suit operating requirements.

Above: *Under the airbox of Maserati's MC12, introduced in 2004, was its version of the new F140 twelve from the Ferrari-Maserati Group. In its road version the engine was rated at 624bhp at 7,500rpm.*

Above: *A welcome change in the 2002 Enzo's F140 Ferrari V12 was the adoption of chain drive to its overhead camshafts. From the crank nose a primary chain drove a sprocket from which individual chains went to the respective cylinder heads. Another roller chain drove the engine's oil pumps.*

Below: *Although the MC12 Maserati's main metier was as a competition car, road versions were produced as well. They gave a pleasant echo of the vee-twelves that had so distinguished Maserati's racing offerings of the late 1950s and 1960s.*

Another Formula 1 touch in the aluminium cylinder heads was the placement of the camshaft bearings between the pairs of cam lobes for each four-valve cylinder, instead of between the cylinders. This gave the cams a more rigid and precise attack. The valves were placed at a 29° included angle. To tolerate higher revs and also to reduce engine bulk the drive to the cams was now by chains instead of belts.[7] Continuous valve-timing changes of up to 55° of the crankshaft for the inlets and 50° for the exhausts were provided by hydraulic variators at the nose of each camshaft. A rapid response speed of 500° of crank angle per second was assured by oil pressure of 360psi from pumps at the rear of the inlet camshafts.

For the first time in a Ferrari road-car engine, variation was also introduced for the lengths of the inlet ram pipes, extending vertically into a carbon-fibre airbox. Inside aluminium housings, sliding pipe mouths of the same material were moved over a 3.5-in range by hydraulic rams under Bosch Motronic engine-management control. They were extended to full 16.9in ram-pipe length over the revolutions from 3,000 to 6,500, substantially enhancing torque through the mid-range, and remained at 13.4in above and below those speeds.

Revving to a limit of 8,200rpm, the Enzo's version of the F140 produced 650bhp at 7,800rpm and 485lb-ft of torque at 5,500rpm. This was 108bhp per litre, an outstanding value for an unsupercharged road-car engine, topping the 104bhp per litre of the six in BMW's M3 and the V10 in Porsche's Carrera GT. Its only superior was the 119bhp per litre of Honda's 2.0-litre S2000 sports car. Ferrari capped the Enzo's cylinder heads with covers painted red in the best tradition of the Testarossa racers of the late 1950s.

Light on its 104.3in wheelbase, the £425,000 Ferrari Enzo put all its rivals on their trailers when *Autocar* tested them for top speed at Nardo. "Looking visibly faster than everything else," its maximum was 218.7mph. In 3.6sec it accelerated to 60mph and in 11.4sec it covered the standing quarter-mile. As for the F140 twelve, said *Autocar*, "at high revs, which it craves, it has a hard-edged purpose that wouldn't be out of place half-way down the Mulsanne Straight at Le Mans." Race breeding, it seemed, had its rewards.

First after the Enzo to benefit from F140 power wasn't another Ferrari but, instead, another car from the same stable, Maserati's MC12. Acquired by Fiat in 1993, Maserati came under the protection and ownership of one-time arch-rival Ferrari in 1997.[8] With Ferrari well ensconced in the world of Formula 1, the FIA's GT championship was identified as a competitive venue for Maserati. At Geneva in 2004 Maserati unveiled its GT contender, the Targa-topped MC12. Its power unit was the Enzo's F140 twelve, retuned in the road version of the Maserati to give 624bhp at 7,500rpm.

Priced in the $800,000 bracket, the MC12 was built in a 25-off series to meet the requirements of the GT championship – recalling the rules that led Ferrari to produce its 512S in 1970. Handsomely bodied on a 110.2in wheelbase, the magnificent MC12 was a sonorous echo of the twelve-cylinder racing Maseratis of the 1950s and 1960s. That it was much more than a pretty face was proven at Germany's Oschersleben circuit on 19 September 2004 when an MC12 was driven to victory in an FIA GT Championship race by Mika Salo and Andrea Bertolini. Giorgio Ascanelli was responsible for its preparation.

With Maserati rejoining the club, vee twelves were at the top of their game in the 21st Century. Formula 1's loss was the gain of both luxury cars and the sports cars at the top echelons of the world's production. Outstanding balance and refinement, combined with sheer power and both visual and aural excitement, kept the twelve the engine of choice for those whose aim was to offer the best. In the words of Colonel J.S. Napier, the twelve remains "available for the wealthy faddists of exquisite sensibility".

The twelve's comeback was impressive. After its glory years of the 1930s it seemed unlikely to bounce back after World War II, when vee-eights were all the rage. But Enzo Ferrari's Packard-inspired initiative was the catalyst for new generations of twelves that restored the engine type as the one to have if yours was a no-excuses kind of automobile. The "psychology of numerical appraisal", set out so aptly by Laurence Pomeroy in 1925, still reigns. Nothing on the horizon seems likely to disturb that happy state of affairs.

Chapter 16 Footnotes

[1] NVH = Noise, Vibration and Harshness.

[2] In the DB9 this function was performed by an aluminium housing around its carbon-fibre prop shaft that rigidly united engine and transaxle.

[3] "The valves can make their own dents now," joked Brian Fitzsimons.

[4] The twelve's engine-management system was mapped to 8,000rpm to allow it to cope with inadvertent excursions.

[5] Constrained by inlet-air restrictors and a rev limit of 6,100, the GT-racing Murciélago was less powerful at 550bhp.

[6] We noted his OSCA-owning uncle in Chapter 10.

[7] This also relieved the owners of future Ferraris of the burden of the dreaded cam-belt change, which accounted for much of the $5,800 cost of the 550 Maranello's 30,000-mile service.

[8] In the middle of the first decade of the 21st Century Maserati reverted to ownership by Fiat Auto and forged a new relationship with Alfa Romeo.

V12 FIRING ORDERS

by Dan Whitney

Twelve independent cylinders can be arranged to fire in nearly 20,000,000 different ways. If a requirement is imposed that firing alternates between banks in a V12 this is reduced to *only* 580,400. Finding an acceptable pattern meeting realistic physical and dynamic constraints could be a daunting task!

Fortunately a conventional V12 is in fact two in-line sixes mounted on a common crankshaft. The number of unique firing sequences for an in-line six is 60, reducing to 32 for a V12 firing alternate banks and using a realistically configured crankshaft. This author has found nine firing orders that have been used to one degree or another. Prior to the age of the digital computer analysing even this number still presented a daunting task.

Adding to the design dilemma are considerations of the way the engine breathes, as the type and configuration of the induction system can be very sensitive to firing order. Conventional practice has been to not have adjacent cylinders fire in order, as this can cause excessive mixture velocities in the induction manifold. Likewise, gas-flow and back-pressure considerations in the exhaust manifolds are an issue, unless the engine is to have single-cylinder ejector stacks. In addition, it is usual to fire alternate banks, as this tends to balance the rocking couple induced by the firing events and minimises the forces transmitted to the vehicle.

The realities of a practical six-throw crankshaft require that throws be arranged in three planes 120° from one another. This results in even spacing of firing events, each bank firing six times per 720° as required for a four-stroke engine. From a manufacturing perspective six-throw crankshafts lend themselves to having a mirror-image arrangement of three 120-degree throws reflected about the crankshaft centre. The throws at both ends are in the same plane, as are throws 2-5 and 3-4, with each 120° apart. The only question remaining is whether the number 2 and 3 throws are clockwise or counterclockwise relative to the number 1 throw.

These manufacturing constraints further limit the number of firing-order options available in a given engine. In effect, there are only two practical V12 cranks (1-2-3 or 1-3-2) and the options of having its rotation be either clockwise (CW) or counter-clockwise (CCW). The number of realistic firing orders available for a V12 is eight for each of the two crank-throw options, which may turn either RH or LH, making the total of 32. After discounting the sequences beginning with the number-six cylinder this reduces to sixteen, of which it appears that at least nine have been used at one time or another.

The selected firing order not only determines the pattern of loads on the crankpins but also, significantly, the phase relationship of the higher-order harmonic forces. For example, in an engine with the nominal Liberty V12 firing order the loads on adjacent crankpins are separated by a crank angle of 120°, plus one revolution, making them 480° apart. This results in a vector force that can be viewed as rotating about the axis of the crank. Typically, all of the orders though the 12th are evaluated and have their characteristic angular relationships defined. Changes in firing order directly affect this phase relationship, redefining it for every crankpin, and as a result dramatically affect torsional vibrations throughout the entire power train.

If we are dealing only with the inertial forces of the power train we could easily resolve and balance them using weights properly affixed and located on the rotating elements. Even with such balance, the problems largely come from the dynamic forces that torsionally excite the crank and the power train. In a four-stroke engine the potent power stroke occurs at one-half the speed of the crankshaft and causes what is known as the ½-order excitation. A force occurring at the speed of the crankshaft is a first-order vibration while a second-order vibration occurs twice per revolution.

Very high vibration orders are possible. Fortunately the amplitudes decrease from that of the ½-order and they are typically so high in frequency that they are outside the operating range for the power train. Still it is necessary to consider them all, for there can be surprises due to specifics of design and the resiliency of selected materials.

If we think of the crankshaft as a simple beam or rod of steel, suspended from one end, and strike it with a hammer, the sound we hear will be at its natural frequency and is known as the 'fundamental mode'. If the beam or shaft is properly excited we can also energise and hear the overtones. Effectively, these are the natural frequencies of shorter sections of the shaft, defined by additional locations called nodes. These are the locations where torsional-vibration amplitudes are at their maximum. The second mode has two nodes, one at the drive end of the shaft and the other at the non-drive end. A third mode is also likely; it has three nodes, two like the second mode and a third at the crankshaft centre bearing.

As a beam or rod is shortened so is its wavelength, so the frequency of the vibration will increase proportionally. While we all may have experience with longitudinal vibrations like these, for example in tuning forks, these same phenomena occur in the cross-section of a round rod, or a crankshaft when excited radially. When the vibrations are caused by high-speed variations in the amount of torque being carried, the results are known as torsional vibrations, and they can have a large affect on the crankshaft.

The various harmonic orders important to each of these modes are then used to find the crankshaft speeds where resonance occurs. From this, the amount of vibration energy occurring at the resonance is calculated and the designer determines how to accommodate or resolve it if the magnitude is excessive. As an example, Allison found that in its aviation V12 the first-mode vibrations were mostly damped by internal engine friction, while those remaining, along with all second modes, were damped and stabilised by the inertia of the supercharger acting through the hydraulic vibration damper, located at the rear of the crankshaft.[1] This is an optimum location for a damper as it is the location of one of the primary vibration nodes.

The 'orders', also known as 'harmonics' of the resonance, are not simply mathematical artefacts. Rather, they are driven by things happening in the engine. For example, a four-cycle V12 obviously has first-order vibration forces at the running rpm and the ½-order forces coming from each cylinder as it fires. This ½ order, at half the engine speed, is very powerful as it contains all the combustion-gas energy developed in the cylinder.

Fortunately these primary forces are naturally balanced in a 60-degree-between-the-banks even-firing V12, and are largely damped by internal engine friction. Any such force generated in the engine only presents a problem if the rigidity of the crankshaft is such that the forcing frequencies coincide with the natural frequency of a characteristic crankshaft order.

Most people, author included, look at tabulated V12 firing orders with a degree of confusion and dismay. Not only does it first appear that the 12-cylinder sequence is random, but also the nomenclature often obstructs by introducing numbering schemes and letters such as A, B, L, R, D, G to describe the left and right banks. Also manufacturers use different references as to the location of Number One cylinder. It may be either next to the drive end or the anti-drive end.

In an effort to make V12 firing orders comparable, the author uses a naming convention adapted from the German aero engine V12 manufacturers. Beginning at the propeller, cylinders 1–6 are in the right bank and 7–12 on the left. This applies whether the engine is upright or inverted. With this convention it is also necessary to know the direction of rotation of the crankshaft, either CW or CCW, as viewed from the rear, looking toward the drive end. In aviation engines this resolves the complexity of direct-drive or geared and removes confusion caused by the characteristics of different types of gear systems, such as internal or external spur gears or epicyclic.

Nine different firing orders, used by a number of historically significant V12s, are set out in a table. Those interested in investigating their favourite firing order are invited to check out the additional detail provided on the website of the Aviation Engine Historical Society: www.enginehistory.org.

The following comments are directed toward specific engines and the adopted firing orders.

Liberty-12A

This ubiquitous CW engine uses a firing order that might be considered to be the reference order for all V12s.

(1-8-5-10-3-7-6-11-2-9-4-12) In fact it is being used by V12s being developed in the 21st Century. With this order the bank-firing pattern alternates from front to rear, assuring good mixture flow to each cylinder, as well as a smooth flow of torque by sequencing the banks to load and unload the crank smoothly, though the transient torques reverse direction six times every two revolutions. Most of the early Packard and Curtiss engines used this firing order, as did the Daimler-Benz DB 601 and Allison V-1710.

Rolls-Royce Merlin V-1650

Rolls is somewhat unique in using this firing order (1-12-4-9-2-11-6-7-3-10-5-8). However, it is actually related to the baseline CW Liberty-12 scheme. First, the *Merlin* crank turns in the opposite direction, because of the external spur reduction gear, and the 2-5 and 3-4 throw sequence necessitates firing 1-4-2-6-3-5 rather than 1-5-3-6-2-4. From the perspective of the intake manifolds the breathing will be satisfactory because the pattern for each bank alternates between groups of three cylinders. This engine, like others with the Liberty firing order, enjoys a reputation for emitting a 'smooth' sound when running; a direct result of the even firing pattern. This firing order was also used on the R-R Kestrel, Buzzard and Schneider Cup "R" engines (CCW, 1-3-2), the last two engines having the same capacity as the later Griffon. Rolls-Royce automobiles still use this firing order for their V12-powered luxury models.

Rolls-Royce Griffon

R-R chose a much different firing order (1-10-3-8-5-7-6-9-4-11-2-12) for the powerful Griffon. Here the 'rule' of not firing adjacent cylinders in series is violated, as 2-1-3 and 5-6-4 are fired before the pattern moves to the other end of the bank and fires 5-6-4. We now can see why the Griffon has such a different sound (often described as a 'growl') compared to a Merlin or Allison. All three cylinders at one end of the bank (directed toward an observer) fire before the pattern is repeated at the other end. With the pattern alternating the result is the uneven sound due to the low-frequency switching between ends of the bank. It is hard to rationalise the basis for this firing order. It certainly did not do anything to improve the flow of mixture in the intake manifolds and it resulted in eight, rather than six, reversals of torsional stress in the crank for every two crank rotations.

Daimler-Benz DB 603

For this inverted engine Daimler used a serpentine order similar to that on the Griffon. Both engines use the same crankshaft-throw sequence, only using a 1-2-4-… rather than 2-1-3-… firing pattern. Both fire all three cylinders at one end before going to the other end of the bank, and still have the eight torque reversals in crank loading.

Hispano-Suiza 12Y

These engines were available in both RH and LH turning models, both using the same crankshaft. The RH propeller 12Yfrs (CCW, 1-2-3) firing order is 1-12-4-9-2-11-6-7-3-10-5-8, the same as the Merlin, while the LH propeller 12Ycrs and 12Ydrs models use the Liberty 1-8-5-10-3-7-6-11-2-9-4-12 order (CW, 1-2-3).

Ferrari 456M

The 2001 version of this 65° V12 introduced a new and unique firing order intended to smooth its running. The previous firing order was the same as the Merlin. Because the angle between the banks is not the inherently balanced 60°, some primary and secondary forces are not balanced. This is probably the reason for changing the firing order to one with the same across-bank cylinders fired in series. This also reduces the end-to-end rocking couple created when same-bank cylinders fire at alternate ends of the engine. While this firing order still has the nominal six torque reversals per two-revolution cycle, the loading on the crank journals is sustained for a longer period. However, the peak torque on the common crankpin is not significantly increased.

All V12s do not use the same firing order. Even today the question of the best, or most appropriate, sequence for a given engine and application is still being asked. One of the most important insights should be that picking a firing order is not a simple task, and that the designer has options when selecting the appropriate firing order for an engine.

Note: This is an abridged version of a paper on this subject by Dan Whitney, published by the Aviation Engine Historical Society. The abridgement, by the author, has been approved by Mr Whitney and the AEHS. Their assistance in the presentation of this information is gratefully acknowledged.

---

[1] Other aircraft V12s, such as the *Merlin*, rely on the supercharger, driven through a flexible quill shaft, to provide similar second-mode vibration damping.

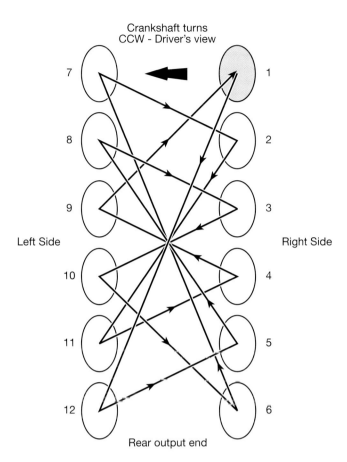

Crankshaft turns
CCW - Driver's view

7

1

8

2

Left Side

9

3

Right Side

10

4

11

5

12

6

Rear output end

Firing Order

1-12-5-8-3-10-6-7-2-11-4-9

This firing pattern is similair to all V-12
engines in automobiles but not in aircraft.
The output shaft is on the opposite end in
tractor-type propeller-driven aircraft
Many various types of firing orders
have been used but the patterns remain
much the same. This is based on the
German DIN 73021 standard.

Table 1 – Single-Bank Firing Order Options

Crank Throw Order	Bank Firing Order	Used by
1-2-3	1-5-3-6-2-4	Liberty, Allison, Curtiss, DB 601/605, Packard, IV-1430-11, Hisso 12Ycrs, Ferrari
1-2-3	1-2-4-6-5-3	DB 603
1-2-3	1-5-4-6-2-3	Not Used
1-2-3	1-2-3-6-5-4	Ford V-1650A
1-3-2	1-4-2-6-3-5	Merlin, RR "R", IV-1430-9, Jumo 210/211, Curtiss C-12, Hisso 12Yfrs, Ranger SGV-770
1-3-2	1-3-2-6-4-5	Not Used
1-3-2	1-4-5-6-3-2	Not Used
1-3-2	1-3-5-6-4-2	Griffon, Jumo 213A Rechlin, Jumo 213E

Both the much-used Liberty and Merlin bank firing orders alternate firings between opposite ends of the crankshaft; their only difference is the throw order. All of the other orders fire all three cylinders at one end of the crank before repeating the pattern at the opposite end. From the perspective of the bank firing order the direction of crankshaft rotation is not a factor. There are actually another eight firing order options, from the perspective of beginning with cylinder number 6. However, these result in repeating the same patterns as above, but shifted by 360°, a trivial case for a single bank.

Table 2 – Tabulation of V12 Firing Orders

Engine	Firing Order as Described by Manufacturer	Standardised Firing Order	Crank Rotation & Throw Sequence
Allison V-1710C & FL	1L-6R-5L-2R-3L-4R-6L-1R-2L-5R-4L-3R	1-8-5-10-3-7-6-11-2-9-4-12	CW, 1-2-3
Curtiss C-12	1-12-4-9-2-11-6-7-3-10-5-8	1-12-4-9-2-11-6-7-3-10-5-8	CCW, 1-3-2
Curtiss D-12 & Conqueror	1L-6R-5L-2R-3L-4R 6L-1R-2L-5R-4L-3R	1-8-5-10-3-7-6-11-2-9-4-12	CW, 1-2-3
DB 601A/E/F/N & DB 605A/B	1-8-5-10-3-7-6-11-2-9-4-12	1-8-5-10-3-7-6-11-2-9-4-12	CCW, 1-2-3
Daimler-Benz DB 603	1-11-2-9-4-7-6-8-5-10-3-12	1-11-2-9-4-7-6-8-5-10-3-12	CCW, 1-2-3
Hispano-Suiza 12Yfrs, RH Prop	1D-6G-4D-3G-2D-5G-6D-1G-3D-4G-5D-2G	1-12-4-9-2-11-6-7-3-10-5-8	CCW, 1-3-2
Hispano-Suiza 12Ycrs & 12Ydrs, LH Prop	1G-6D-5G-2D-3G-4D-6G-1D-2G-5D-4G-3D	1-8-5-10-3-7-6-11-2-9-4-12	CW, 1-2-3
Liberty-12, Upright or Inverted	1L-6R-5L-2R-3L-4R-6L-1R-2L-5R-4L-3R	1-8-5-10-3-7-6-11-2-9-4-12	CW, 1-2-3
Packard A-2025, A-1500, & A-2500	1L-6R-5L-2R-3L-4R-6L-1R-2L-5R-4L-3R	1-8-5-10-3-7-6-11-2-9-4-12	CCW, 1-2-3
Rolls-Royce Merlin	1A-6B-4A-3B-2A-5B-6A-1B-3A-4B-5A-2B	1-12-4-9-2-11-6-7-3-10-5-8	CCW, 1-3-2
Rolls-Royce "R"	1A-6B-4A-3B-2A-5B-6A-1B-3A-4B-5A-2B	1-12-4-9-2-11-6-7-3-10-5-8	CCW, 1-3-2
Rolls-Royce Griffon II/III/IV/-65	1A-4B-3A-2B-5A-1B-6A-3B-4A-5B-2A-6B	1-10-3-8-5-7-6-9-4-11-2-12	CW, 1-3-2
Ferrari 456MGT-Old	1-12-5-8-3-10-6-7-2-11-4-9	1-12-5-8-3-10-6-7-2-11-4-9	CCW, 1-2-3
Ferrari 456MGT-New	1-7-5-11-3-9-6-12-2-8-4-10	1-7-5-11-3-9-6-12-2-8-4-10	CCW, 1-2-3

Source: Dan Whitney, Aviation Engine Historical Society

Table 3 – Angle between Crankpin Vectors

Angle	Harmonic Orders
30 degrees	2-1/2, 3-1/2, 8-1/2, 9-1/2
60 degrees	1, 5, 7, 11
90 degrees	1-1/2, 4-1/2, 7-1/2, 10-1/2
120 degrees	2, 4, 8, 10
150 degrees	1/2, 5-1/2, 6-1/2, 11-1/2
180 degrees	3, 9
360 degrees	6, 12

For CCW "Liberty-12" 1-12-5-8-3-10-6-7-2-11-4-9 firing order

INDEX

General

Abarth, Carlo 249, 251
Achard, Jean 213
Adelaide 359
Ader, Clément-Agnès 14
Agnelli, Giovanni 53, 73, 369
Ahrens, Hermann 157, 168
AIACR 59, 73, 95, 105, 183, 215
Aimini, 67
Alessandria 67
Alfieri, Giulio 239-242, 245-247, 265-267, 301-302, 307, 400-401
All Japan Championship 342
Alliot, Philippe 365
Alpine Rally 172, 289
Altoona board track 93, 105
American Automobile Association (AAA) 93, 95, 171-173
Amon, Chris 192, 255-256, 276-277
Anderson, Gary 359
Andreau, Jean 210
Andretti, Mario 256, 278
Antwerp 198
Arbuthnot, Robert 178-179
Arcangeli, Luigi 184
Arfons, Art 220
Argentine GP 1971 276-277
Arpajon speed trials 63-64, 75
Artioli, Romano 399-400
Ascanelli, Giorgio 409
Ascari, Alberto 186, 225, 230
Ascari, Antonio 33, 220
Ascari, Ennio 245
Ascot, USA 22
Atlanta 371
Auburn Cord Duesenberg Museum 127
Audetto, Daniele 363
Aufrecht, Hans-Werner 333
Australian GP 1992 363

Austrian GP
    1971 270
    1981 277
    1983 278
auto motor und sport magazine 332
Autocar, magazine 66, 79, 94, 131, 137, 141, 148-149, 288, 306-307, 380, 384, 391, 397, 403
Automobile, The magazine 40
Automobile Engineer, The magazine 151
Automobile Racing Club of America 172
Automobile Technical Bureau, Chemnitz 228
Autoweek magazine 306, 390
Avanzo, Baronessa Maria Antonietta 32-33, 49, 220
Aviation Engine Historical Society 10-11, 412
AVUS track 203, 215
Ayto, Frank 139

Bach, Matthias 388
Bailey, Len 271
Baily, Claude W. L. 309, 312-313, 315
Baker, Erwin 'Cannon Ball' 112
Baker, Stanley 243
Baker-Courtenay, John 73
Baldwin, Nick 54
Bamber, Charles 320
Banks, Henry 176, 179
Barbarou, Marius 145
Barcelona 233
Barker, Ronald 149
Barnard, John 367-368, 371
Baruch, Bernard 107
Batchelor, Tony 393
Batten, Cyril 373
Bäumler, Manfred 353
Bazin, François Victor 145

Bazzi, Luigi 220, 230, 300
Becchia, Walter 164, 209-210
Behra, Jean 242
Belgian GP
    1925 67
    1939 197
    1950 230
    1967 269
    1970 270
    1990 358
Bellamy, Ralph 272
Bellentani, Vittorio 307, 401
Bellinger, Edmond 145
Bellini, Giorgio 302
Beltoise, Jean-Pierre 270, 272, 274, 276
Beneš, Edvard 153-154
Benoist, Robert 64, 66-67, 73
Bensinger, Wolf-Dieter 327
Bentley, Walter Owen 138-143, 149, 185, 234, 311
Berger, Arthur 100
Berger, Gerhard 363, 371
Bergere, Cliff 105
Berlin Motor Show
    1921 158
    1938 202-203
Bernard, Eric 365
Bernard, Marius 145
Bernhard, Wolfgang 381, 391
Bernhardt, Julius 158, 169
Berris, Vic 91, 205, 230, 256
Bertarione, Vincenzo 209
Berthon, Peter 267
Bertolini, Andrea 409
Bertram, Oliver 64
Bez, Ulrich 353, 396
Bible, Lee 93
Bira, B. (Prince Birabongse of Siam) 233
Birkigt, Marc 51, 145-149
Bizzarrini, Giotto 300-302, 306-307, 401

Blight, Anthony 142, 181, 210-211, 215
Blundell, Mark 359
Bobbitt, Malcolm 149
Boddy, William 56, 58-59, 148
Bologna Motor Show 1999 351
Bone, Cyril 25
Bonetto, Felice 198
Bonfiglioli, Ermanno 403, 405, 407
Bonnet, René 273
Bonneville Salt Flats 79-80, 99-100, 102-103, 172-174, 179, 202
Bordeaux GP 233
Bordino, Pietro 70-73
Borgeson, Griff 14, 25, 65, 73, 123, 125, 145, 225
BOSS series 273
Boulton & Paul 59
Bowler, Michael 272, 307
Brabham, Gary 358
Brackenbury, 185
Bradley, W. F. 19, 63
Bradshaw, Granville 18
Brands Hatch 321
    Race of Champions 269
Brawn, Ross 355
Brazilian GP 1989 363
Breitschwerdt, Werner 329
Brew, Alec 23, 57
Bridgehampton 243
Brighton Speed Trials 62, 218
British Air Ministry 76
British GP
    1970 271
    1990 358
British Motor Show 1988 321
Broad, Ralph 319
Brooklands 19, 21-23, 25, 34, 56, 58-62, 64, 67, 77-80, 85, 90, 92, 96, 99, 118, 132, 141, 143, 148, 171, 181, 218-219, 288-289
    200-mile race 73

Brough, George 287-288
Brown, David 234-235
Brüggemann, Hans 329, 331-332
Brun, Walter 339
Brundle, Martin 264
Brush, Alanson P. 45, 108
Brussels GP 1946 211
Brüstle, Claus 353
Bryant, Paul 127
Bucci, Clemar 215
Buckley, J. R. 148
Bucknum, Ronnie 249
Buenos Aires 197
    1,000 Kilometres 215, 237
Bugatti, Ettore 213, 291, 400
Bugatti railcar 149
Ballabio, Fulvio 399
Burman, Bob 22, 34
Burns, John 110-111
Burroughs Adding Machine Co. 25
Bussi, Giancarlo 254
Busso, Giuseppe 222, 224-225
Byrne, Rory 359

Caiselli, Franco 33
Callum, Ian 393
Campari, Giuseppe 184
Campbell, Donald 80
Campbell, Sir Malcolm 59-62, 75-77, 79, 91, 93, 95, 98-101, 105
Can-Am series 192, 254-258, 265, 283, 295
Canadian GP
    1981 277
    1990 358
    1992 363
Canestrini, Giovanni 301
Cappa, Giulio Cesare 67-70, 114, 127, 209, 223
Car magazine 402
Car and Driver magazine 304, 317, 333, 391, 397, 406
Caracciola, Rudy 202-203, 206, 213, 213
Carson, Richard Burns 107, 110, 119
CART series 9, 342
Cassinetti, Marco 403
Castaing, François 366
Castrol 105
Cavalli, Carlo 70
Ceccarani, Massimo 402-403
Cevert, François 277
Chanters, Alfred 174
Chassagne, Jean 21-22
Checkpoint film 243
Chevrolet, Louis 31, 113
Chiesa, Adalberto 32
Chicago Auto Show 1930 107
Chicago Speedway 31
Chiti, Carlo 278, 300, 302, 338, 399
Christ, Hubertus 329, 335
Chrysler, Walter 35, 37, 82
Cirio, Nino 72
Clark, Jim (Ford) 260, 393-395
Clutton, Cecil 9, 54, 149
Coatalen, Louis Hervé 19-23, 29-30, 40, 51, 55-58, 60, 75, 93-94, 96-98, 105

Coatalen, Olive 19
Cobb, John 61-62, 64, 78-80, 85, 92, 97, 100, 102-104, 174, 220
Cobb, Price 264
Coddington, Boyd 373
Coffin, Howard 37-38
Cole, Ed 291
Collier, Miles 172
Collier, Samual Carnes 172
Collins, Peter 339-340
Colombo, Gioachino 184, 186, 197, 220-225, 229, 235, 238-239, 243, 250, 291, 295, 299 300
Colucci, Mario 250-252
Comotti, Gianfranco 213
Coppa Acerbo 184, 197, 213
Coppa Ciano 184, 197, 213, 215
Cord, Errett Lobban 29-30, 122-123, 125, 171-172, 174
Corona 22
Cortese, Franco 221-222, 224
Costantini, Meo 68
Cotton Carnival Race 172
Coupe de l'Auto, Dieppe 19
Courteault, Pascal 215
Cowling, William C. 287
Cox, Simon 376
Crisp, Trevor 312, 321, 335
Cunningham, Briggs 127, 141, 242-243
Cutting, Ted 236

Daetwyler, Willy 198
Dai, His Imperial Majesty Bao of Vietnam 232
Daimler, Gottlieb 81
Daimler, Paul 156
Dale-Jones, Graham 273
Dallara, Gian Paolo 302-304, 306, 369-370
Danaher, Sean 73
Daniel, Michael 271
Dauben, Joseph 163-164, 167
Dauer, Jochen 400
Davis, H. 14
Davis, S. C. H. 59, 96
Daytona Beach 34, 59, 75-78, 93, 95, 98-99, 172, 202, 265, 272, 342
de Présalé 182
de Tomaso, Alejandro 294
Deeds, Edward 89
Dees, Mark 28-29, 177, 179
Delage, Louis 62, 64-65, 84, 210
Delaney, L. T. 100
Denly, Bert 10
Dennis, Ron 338, 366
DePalma, Ralph 22, 31-32, 34-35, 49, 113
Depression, The Great 113, 118, 125
Dernie, Frank 365
Detroit 31
Detroit Auto Show
    1992 399
    1995 393
    1996 395
    2003 351
    2004 381

Deutsche Bank 163
Dewar Trophy 14
Dewis, Norman 311, 335
di Montezemelo, Luca Cordero 243, 403
di Montezemolo, Paolo Cordero 243
Diles, Omar J. 122, 127, 172
Dillon, Jim 49
Divo, Albert 61, 63-64, 66-67
Dixon, Freddie 98
Dobson, 185
Dodson, Charlie 79
Doll, Gerhard 378
Doman, Carl T. 110
Domboy, Noël 291
Don, Kaye 61, 96-97, 105
Donington Park 205, 207, 213-214, 229
Donohue, Mark 265
Doster, Bill 179
Drag Racing 220
Dresden Technical University 229
Dreyfus, René 208, 213-214
Dreystadt, Nicholas 110
Dubonnet, André 149
Duckworth, Keith 312
Dudot, Bernard 354
Duerksen, Menno 41
Duesenberg brothers (Augie & Fred) 27-29, 105
Dugdale, John 202, 212
Durant, Billy 35
Duray, Leon 113
Dutry, Raoul 149
Dykstra, Lee 319

Earl, Harley 110
Easter, Eric 139
Eaton, Bob 366
Ecclestone, Bernie 272, 278, 359
Eckener, Hugo 158, 161
Ecurie Bleue 211, 213
Edge, Selwyn F. 13-14
Edwards Air Force base 179
Eichhorn, Ulrich 387, 391
Eldridge, Ernest 59, 75, 99-100
Elkhart Lake 243
Elliot, Albert G. 134-135
Elvington Airfield 73
Endurance races 256, 342, 391
Energy Crisis (1970s) 272, 317-318, 322
Enger, Frank J. 44-45
Erskine, Albert 120-121
Estoril 366
Ethyl Corporation 283
European Touring Car Championship 319
Eves, Edward 281, 304
Eyston, George Edward Thomas 80, 98-102, 104-105, 173, 202

Fairbanks, Douglas 35
Falconer, Ryan 374
Fangio, Juan Manuel 242, 333
Fanoe Island speed trials 32, 59
Farber, Fred 34

Farina, Nino 196-197
Feeley, Frank 142
Fekete, Stephen 37-38
Ferdinand, Archduke Franz 155
Ferrari, Enzo 9, 32, 84, 183, 190, 220-221, 223, 229, 238, 249, 285, 297, 299, 368, 370, 403, 409
Ferrari, Laura 300
Ferrari, Piero 370
FIA 95, 252, 281, 309, 342, 365
    Concorde Agreement 358
    GT Championship 334-335, 409
Fiala, Ernst 391
Fiedler, Fritz 151, 156, 158, 169
Firebird Raceway 342
Firestone, Raymond 297
Fisher, Carl G. 25
Fisher, Prof Irving 107
Fisher, Lawrence P. 107-108, 110
Fitzsimons, Brian 395-396, 409
Flick, Friedrich 162
Fochi, Luciano 222, 250-251, 291
Ford, Edsel 83, 117, 119, 285
Ford, Henry 13, 38, 117, 127, 285
Forghieri, Mauro 221, 254, 356, 363-367
Formula 1 9, 186-188, 225, 228, 231, 233, 240, 247, 252-254, 259, 268, 272, 310, 337, 339, 344, 353, 360-363, 366, 391, 403, 407, 409
    superannuated cars 273
    $1\frac{1}{2}$-litre 278
    3-litre 265, 267, 278, 281, 295, 366
    $3\frac{1}{2}$-litre 262, 343, 356, 366
    10 cylinders 358
Formula 2 186, 224, 228-229, 252, 272, 282-283, 360
Formula 3000 340, 359
Formula Junior 245
Formule Libre 32, 61, 67, 183, 197, 203
Fornaca, Guido 53, 70, 73, 209
Fouré, Ferdinand 145
François, Jean 211-212, 215
Frankfurt Auto Show
    1979 322, 329
    1991 333
    1994 366
Franklin, Herbert H. 110, 112
Fraschetti, Andrea 236-237
French Automobile Club 64
French Bureau of Mines 64
French GP
    1921 270
    1913 67
    1921 65
    1922 64
    1923 64
    1924 66
    1925 67
    1937 210, 212
    1939 205, 207
    1968 283
    1990 358
French Motorcycle Club 63

Frère, Paul 10, 304
Fretter 210
Friderich, Ernst 213
Friderich, Paul 213
Froy, Dudley 61, 67
Fry, Nick 393
Fuji International Raceway 341
Fusi, Luigi 196

Gable, Clark 289
Gaillon hill climb 58, 61, 63, 67
Gallarate speed trials 32
Gallop, Clive 90-91
Ganley, Howard 277
Gardner, Frank 283
Gauntlett, Victor 272
Gaus, Hermann 376
Geneva GP des Nations 243
Geneva Salon
    1932 157
    1966 304
    1991 332
    1998 387
    1999 396
    2003 327
    2004 350, 409
Geneva speed trials 63
George V, HRH King 131, 133-
    134, 149
George Vanderbilt Cup 179, 195
German GP
    1937 195
    1938 197, 213
    1951 226
    1964 246
    1990 358
    1994 371
Gerringong Beach 77
Gethin, Peter 270
Giacomelli, Bruno 358, 371
Gietzen, Staas 353
Gilliland, Stan 127
Gilmour, Allan 354
Ginther, Richie 246, 269, 281
Giro di Sicilia 236
Gitanes 277
Giugiaro, Giorgetto 327
Goddard, Geoff 320
Goering, Hermann 208
Good, Alan P. 138-139, 143, 234
Goodwood 233, 272
Goossen, Leo 36-37, 82, 105, 174
Gordini, Amédée 231-233
Goto, Osamu 371
Gough, Albert 288
Graham, Athol 220
Graham, Zeldine 220
Graham-Paige, 171
Grand Central Palace, New York 115
Grant, John 355
Green, William 62
Group C regulations 273, 320-321,
    339, 341-342, 365
Group 4 sports cars 256-257
Group 6 prototypes 256
Group 7 sports-racers 282-283
Grubb, Randy 373
Guinness Book of World Records
    219, 311

Guinness, Kenelm Lee 58-59
Gulf Oil 272
Gullickson, Roy 374, 391
Gunston, Bill 29
Gurney, Dan 268-270
Guynemer, Georges 145
Gwinner 329

Häkkinen, Mika 366, 371
Hall, Elbert L. 89
Hall, Ira 179
Hampton, Peter 149
Hansgen, Walt 243
Harding, Frank 45
Harding, Warren G. 41, 47
Harkness, Don 78
Harkness, Harry 31
Harrah, Bill 48
Hart, Brian 359, 371
Hasegawa, Hiroyuki 340
Hasegawa, Takehiko 359
Haspel, Wilhelm 169
Hassan, W. T. F. 'Wally' 309-316,
    335
Hatz, Wolfgang 353
Hawker, Harry 58, 73
Hayashi, Yoshimasa 341-342
Hayden, Bill 319, 321
Heal, Anthony 23, 25, 73
Heess, Albert 200
Heidegger, Max 338
Heine, Gustav Otto 48
Heinke, Gottfried 228
Heinkel 100
Henry, Ernest 65
Herbert, Johnny 371
Heron, Sam 55, 283
Hewitt, F. Wyndham 138
Heynes, William 309, 311-312, 315
Hiereth, Hermann 329, 335
Hill, Damon 9
Hill, Graham 267, 277
Hill, Phil 9
Hinnerschitz, Tommy 177, 179
His, Jean-Jacques 367-368
Hitler, Adolf 163, 215
Hives, Ernest 134
Hobbs, David 311
Hofbauer, Peter 384-386, 391
Honda, Soichiro 247, 279, 281,
    283, 360
Hopfinger, K. B. 101
Horch, August 156
Hörnig, Rudolf 329
Horsman, John 271-272
Howe, Earl 141
Hoyle, Terry 273
Hubbard, Tom 127
Hubbert, Jürgen 333
Hughes, Hughie 22
Hungarian GP
    1990 358, 368
    1992 363
Hunt, Ormand E. 38, 40
Hutchison, Ken 288
Hyder, Bill 218

Illustrated London News 40
Imola 265, 358, 368

IMSA 264
    GTP category 319-320
    World Sports Car series 371
Indianapolis Motor Speedway 25,
    31, 35, 42, 49, 176-179, 221,
    243, 338
Indianapolis 500-mile race 32, 49,
    62, 73, 93, 113, 125, 171, 176
Indra, Fritz 375
Inskip, J. S. 137
Interserie 265
IRI 184
Irimaji, Shoichiro 279
Irving, Capt. J. S. 60-61, 76-77, 94,
    95-96
Isle of Man TT 247
Italian GP
    1924 67
    1925 67
    1927 73
    1931 184
    1938 197
    1948 186
    1949 225
    1951 233
    1956 242
    1957 242
    1966 253, 265, 279

Jackson, Robin 64
Jamieson, Paul 218
Jamieson, Murray 211
Jano, Vittorio 70, 183-184, 193,
    195-197, 199, 236-237
Japanese GP
    1969 258, 282
    1990 368
    1991 354
Jaray, Paul 90
Jenkins, Alan 353
Jenkins, David Absolom 'Ab' 104-
    105, 121-122, 127, 172-173, 179
Jenkins, Marvin 105, 179
Jensen, Alan 289
Jensen, Richard 289
Jewell, Lawrence 179
Johnson, Frank 117-118, 127, 285-
    287, 289
Johnson, Geoff 268, 273
Jones, Davy 321
Jones, Ted Lloyd 217-218
Jones, Tom (Jaguar) 309
Jordan, Chuck 307
Jordan, Eddie 359
Joseph, Emperor Franz 155
Joy, Henry 23, 30, 38, 42
Judd, John 359
Justice, James Robertson 243

Kalamazoo dirt track 22,
Kawamoto, Nobuhiko 281, 360-361
Keech, Ray 75, 93, 105
Keydel, Paul 291
Kiekhaefer, Carl 243
Kimberley, Mike 311
Kimes, Beverly Rae 45
Kimmel, Louis 179
King, David 319, 393, 395-396
Kiriloff, Serge 182-183

Kissel, Wilhelm 101, 163-164
Knight, Bob 318
Knight, Charles 129
Knott, Dan 381
Konrad, Franz 365
Kordewahn, Arthur 228
Kranefuss, Mike 354-355
Kreyer, Norbert 358
Kublin, George 127
Küchle, Gerhard 353
Kume, Tadashi 247, 281
Kumera, Vitezslav 154
Kurosawa, Motoharu 283

La Turbie hill climb 289
Labourdette, Jean-Henri 210
Laffite, Jacques 277
Lago, Antony 208-210
Lambert, Percy 21
Lamborghini, Ferruccio 299-303
Lampredi, Aurelio 222-223, 225,
    229-231, 236, 293, 299, 323, 401
Lancia, Vincenzo 51-52, 196, 385
Land Speed Records 58, 60-61, 64,
    75-77, 79-80, 85, 91-92, 99-
    102, 105
Lang, Hermann 204, 213, 228
Lange, Karlheinz 322-323, 325, 327
Langlois, Lucien 211
Langworth, Richard 41
Larrousse, Gérard 276-277, 365
Las Vegas 255
Lauda, Niki 356
Le Mans 272-273
Le Mans 24 Hour race 319, 341
    1925 145
    1926 145
    1933 172
    1939 142-143, 181, 185
    1953 236
    1954 235, 309
    1955 235-236
    1960 10
    1961 243, 265
    1963 239
    1965 310-311
    1966 253
    1972 277, 297
    1973 276-277, 297
    1974 297
    1984 264
    1988 320
    1990 320, 356
    1992 273
    1993 342, 399
    1995 382
    1999 383
    2002 10
Le Mans film 257
Lecointe, Sadi 49
Ledwinka, Hans 151-153
Lee, Tommy 179
Leeds, Mike 373
Lefèbvre, André 145, 181
Leland, Henry M. 14, 90, 117, 285
Leland, Wilfred 14, 117
Leno, Jay 373
Lenz, Siegfried 329
Levavasseur, Léon 15

Liége 198
Ligier, Guy 277, 365
Lime Rock 371
Llewellyn, David 80
Lloyd, Ian 137
Lobo, Claude 395
Lockhart, Frank 60
Lombardi, Claudio 369, 371
London Motor Show
    1919 53
    1935 (Olympia) 135
    1939 (Earls Court) 141
    1997 (Earls Court) 397
Lory, Albert 62, 64-67, 73, 210, 373
Loyer, Roger 211
Lozier, Harry A. 47
Lutz, Robert Anton 322, 366, 376
Lyle, Alastair 272
Lyons 66
Lyons, Sir William 309, 311, 315-316
Lytle, Ed 219
Lytle, Jim 219

Macauley, Alvan 23, 25, 38, 113
Mader, Heini 283
Maglioli, Umberto 250
Magneti Marelli 241
Maina, Joseph 76
Malcolm, Juan 67
Mangoletsi, John 273
Mansell, Nigel 354, 368
Mar del Plata 197
Marchand, César 182
Marco, Pierre 291
Marks, Edward S. 110
Marlow, Rolf-Peter 338-339
Marmiroli, Luigi 401
Marmon, Howard 108, 125-127
Marr, Paul Durant 49
Marr, Walter 35-37, 49, 82
Marston, John 19
Martin, Georges 273, 275, 277
Martin, Percy 130
Martinelli, Paolo 371, 407
Martini 278
Masaryk, Tomáš 153
Maserati brothers (Alfieri, Bindo, Ernesto & Ettore)) 187, 194, 231, 233
Masetti, Giulio 67
Massai, Paolo 369
Massuger, Louis 145
Materazzi, Artioli Nicola 399-400
Matheson, T. A. S. O. 67
May, Dennis 141
May, Michael 318, 321, 335
Maybach, Karl 158-162
Maybach, Wilhelm 13, 15, 81, 158
McCarthy, Mike 142
McClurg, Ned 375
McEwen, Edwin 112, 127
McLaren, Bruce 268, 283
McQueen, Steve 257
Melcher, Erhard 335
Melin, Jan 169
Melling, Al 320-321, 338, 358, 397-399
Merkle, Roland 329

Metternich, Michael Graf Wolff 169
Mexican GP
    1965 246
    1966 265-266, 281
    1967 267
    1968 283
    1990 358
Mexican Road Race 236
Meyer, Lou 105
Mezger, Hans 344, 353
Michelat, Arthur-Louis 62
Mid-Ohio 342
Milan GP 73, 195
Millbrook proving ground 218
Mille Miglia 189, 198, 213, 236-237
Miller, Eddie 171, 173
Miller, Harry 16, 28-29, 31, 171, 174, 177
Millone, Caesare 67
Milton, Tommy 113-114
Mimran brothers (Jean-Claude & Patrick) 307, 400
Minardi, Giancarlo 369
Mine 342
MIRA 311, 335
Miranda Jnr, A. J. 169
Mitchell, Bill 307
Modena GP 195
Modena, Stefano 359
Monaco GP
    1957 241
    1965 248
    1968 274
    1972 270
Monciny, Georges 213, 215
Monte Carlo 363
Montenero 215
Montjuich Park circuit 195
Montlhéry Autodrome 63, 67, 79, 171, 173, 181-183, 210, 212, 215
    million-franc prize 213
    Twelve Hours of Paris race 211
Montreal Auto Show 1970 293
Monza 33, 65, 68-69, 72-73, 90, 184, 197, 207, 230, 233, 253, 265, 270, 281, 283, 359, 363
    Autumnal GP 33
    Race of the Two Worlds 237,242
Moore, Simon 215
Morel, André 66, 182
Moretti, Gianpiero 371
Moretti, Valerio 49
Morley, Peter 80
Moss, Graham 218-219
Moss, R. C. 218
Moss, Stirling 242
Motor Age magazine 25, 33, 40
Motor magazine 80, 118, 149, 317
Motor Sport magazine 288
Mount Washington hill climb 172
Mundy, Harry 310-314, 318, 321, 335, 355-356-358
Muroc Dry Lake 125, 171, 179
Murphy, Chris 339, 365, 371
Murphy, Jimmy 270
Murray, Gordon 272, 278, 381-382
Mussolini, Benito 73, 184

Nacker, Owen Milton 108, 127
Nakamura, Yoshio 247, 249, 279, 281, 283
Nallinger, Fritz 164, 167, 226-227
Nance, James 291
Napier, Col J. S. 55, 409
Napier, Montague 13
Naples 195
Nardo test track 387, 391, 397, 400, 402, 409
Nash, Charles 35
Nasser, Jac 393, 395
National Benzole 79
National Motor Museum 73
Naul, G. Marshall 49
Neal, Robert J. 25, 49, 116
Negré, Guy 356-357
Nesselsdorf Wagon Factory 151
Neubauer, Alfred 101, 203, 226
Neumann, Karl-Heinz 387
New York Auto Show 108
    1902 13
    1916 35, 47
    1930 107
    1932 112, 118
New York World's Fair 215
Newby, Arthur 42
Nibel, Hans 100, 163
Nicolas, Prince of Romania 172
Niefer, Werner 329
Nielson, John 264
Ninety Mile Beach 77-78
Nixon, St John C. 129
Norbye, Jan 42
Novaro, Emile 363
Nürburgring 164, 202, 239, 242, 246
Nuvolari, Tazio 183-184, 195-196, 206-207

Obländer, Kurt 327, 329, 331-332
Offenhauser, Fred 174
O'Gorman, Mervyn 18
Ohashi, Wataru 353-354
Oldfield, Barney 29, 31
Oldham, Wilton 134, 137
Oliver, Jackie 353
Olley, Maurice 55, 134, 137
Olszewski, Stanley 179
Olympia Aero Show 19, 21
Omnia magazine 148
Orange circuit 233
Orsi, Adolfo 239, 246
Orsi, Omer 239-240, 246
Oschersleben circuit 409
Owen, Sir Alfred 268, 273

Pabst, Augie 243
Pace, Harold 243
Pagani, Horacio Raul 333, 335, 345
Pagé, Victor 14
Paige, A. J. 42
Palmer, Brian 141
Pangborne, Clyde 104
Paris-Madrid Race 1903 14
Paris-Rouen Trials 1894 15
Paris Salon
    1919 51, 53
    1921 54
    1929 143

1930 143, 151, 161
1931 146, 148, 154, 157
1932 145
1935 164
1937 210
1938 215
1952 238
1953 236
1966 296
1968 296
2004 391, 397
Parker, Len 288
Parnell, Reg 235
Parradine, John 321
Paton, Clyde 115
Patrucco, Carlo 365
Pau 213
Paul, Cyril 61
Paul, Joseph 210-211
Paul Ricard circuit 272
Pebble Beach Concours 376
Pedrazzi, Oliviero 302
Pehr brothers 338
Pendine Sands 59-60, 76, 90-92, 105
Perkins, W. R. 57, 60
Pescara circuit 184, 195, 242
Pescarolo, Henri 276-277
Peter, Wolfgang 332
Petre, Kay 64
Pfau, Hugo 127
Pichard, Jacques 252-253
Pichetto, Antoine 231-232
Piëch, Ferdinand 245, 386-387, 389
Pierce, George 119
Pierce-Arrow Society 127
Piotti, Luigi 233
Piquet, Nelson 342, 360, 381
Pirelli, Piero 229
Planchon, Charles 62-66, 84
Platt, Maurice 149
Pomeroy, Laurence H. 129-130, 132-135, 149, 40
Pomeroy Jnr, Laurence 9, 195
Porsche, Prof Ferdinand 55, 100-103, 206, 386
Porsche, 'Ferry' 245, 353
Postlethwaite, Harvey 366
Pozzoli, Serge 211
President's Cup race 177
Prince of Wales, HRH The/King Edward VII 129
Prost, Alain 354, 360-361, 368
Providence 31
Purtny, Rex 105

Quanttrini, Giorgio 367

RAC 60
Rader, Bill 31, 34, 42
Rafaela 500-mile race 67
Railton, Reid 62, 77-80, 85, 90, 92, 97, 99, 105, 132
Ramponi, Giulio 223
Rank Organisation 243
'Raph' (Raphaël Béthenod de Las Casas) 213
Rebottini 403

Records
Class A 64
Class B, International 171, 173, 202
Class C 61
Reich Aviation Ministry 100
Reims 204, 213, 241-242
Rempson, Joe 127
Resta, Dario 21
Ridenour, Eric 381
Rindt, Jochen 266
Rishel, William 172
Road & Track magazine 10, 317, 326, 381, 402
Robin, Jean-François 277
Robotham, William A. 135
Robson, Hal 170
Rocchi, Franco 225, 237, 253-254, 356-358
Roche, James 291
Rodriguez, Pedro 266, 270
Roesch, George 164
Rogers, Charles 179
Rogers, John 110-111
Röhr, Hans Gustav 163-164, 167, 169
Rol, Franco 217, 233
Romanelli, Francesco 293-294
Rome 67
Roosevelt Speedway 179
300-mile race 195
Roosevelt, Franklin Delano 119
Rosche, Paul 262, 322, 342-344, 381-382
Rose, Hugh 96-97
Rose-Richards, Tim 79
Rosemeyer, Bernd 206
Rouen 242
Rowledge, Arthur J. 134
Royce, Sir Henry 98-99, 134, 138-139
Royal Flying Corps 56
Rudd, Tony 267, 270, 273-274
Rumpler 158

Sailer, Max 163
St Cloud 213
St Louis 31
Sakurai, Shinichiro 258, 282-283
Salo, Mika 409
Saltburn Sands 21, 59
Salvadori, Roy 265
Salvarani, Walter 225
San Remo 233
San Sebastian 66-67
Sauber, Peter 335, 342
Saunders, Stuart 93
Sayer, Malcolm 311
Scammell, Dick 355
Scarfiotti, Ludovico 253
Schebler, George 10, 24-25, 45, 378
Scheerer, Georg 202
Schell, Laury 211, 213-214
Schell, Lucy O'Reilly 211, 213-214
Scherenberg, Hans 328-329
Schleicher, Rudolf 169
Schlesser, Jo 283
Schlumpf Collection 198
Schmoll, Philip 25

Schneider, Bernd 335
Schneider Trophy Races 75-77, 98-99, 105
Schuhmann, Gerhard 353
Schumacher, Michael 355, 371
Scott, Allan 320
Seaholm, Ernest 108
Seaman, Richard 197
Sebring 239, 383
12-hour race 189, 265, 371
Sedgwick, Michael 73
Segrave, Sir Henry 60-61, 73, 75-77, 91, 93, 95-96, 105, 215
Seboli, Roberto 72
Selsdon, Lord 142, 185
Senna, Ayrton 354, 360-361, 363, 366, 368
Sewell, Charles 139
Shaw, Wilbur 93
Shell 91, 267-269
Sheepshead Bay board track 22, 25, 30-32, 34, 42, 113
Shelsley Walsh hill climb 218
Shoemaker, F. Glen 110-111, 127
Sibley, Hi 40
Sidgreaves, Arthur 137
Siena, Eugenio 197
Siffert, Jo 270
Silcock, Com. Derek 289
Silvani, Eugenio 32
Silverstone 233, 235, 271-273, 312, 366
Simon, André 213
Simpson 132
Skinner, Brad 49
Smith, Brian 149
Smith, Norman 'Wizard' 77-78
Smithsonian Institute 35
Snyder, Ed 220
Sola, Giuseppe 70
Sommer, Raymond 197, 229
South African GP 1967 281
Southgate, Tony 264, 270, 320
Southport Sands 60-61
Spa 67, 242, 253, 270, 359
Spanish GP
1926 67
Sports Car Club of America
B Production Championship 316
Trans-Am series 319
Stanzani, Paolo 302, 306, 399-400
Stark, Leslie 139
Steel, Anthony 243
Stevens, Brooks 127
Stevens, Peter 320
Stevenson, Everett 174, 177
Stewart, Jackie 274
Storey brothers (Edward & Frank) 114
Stout, Richard 286, 290
Straight, Whitney 149
Strauss, Moritz 156
Strickland, W. R. 108
Strobel, Werner 151, 156, 206
Stuck, Hans 100-101, 103-104
Stuckey, Steve 149
Stump 158
Suarez 215
Summers, Bob 75

Surtees, John 253, 265, 281, 283
Susa-Moncenisio hill climb 32
Sutherland, Bob 273
Suzuka circuit 281
Suzuki, Aguri 359
Swedish GP
1957 237
1977 277
Swiss GP
1938 197, 207
1939 206
1949 186
Syracuse 241
Syring, Wilhelm 164, 166-167, 169

Targa Florio 1926 67
Taruffi, Piero 189, 197, 237, 301
Tasman racing 268
Taylor, Admiral 89
Taylor, Norm 220
Teague Jnr, W. Dorwin 127
Ternaire fuel 212
Terry, Len 268-269
Tetzlaff, Teddy 172
Thomas, John Godfrey Parry 90-94, 105, 171
Thomas, René 58-59, 62-64, 66, 75
Thompson, Dick 243
Thomson, Ken 64
Thorne, Maurice 120
Thornycroft 80
Tjaarda, John 285-286
Tokyo Auto Show
1989 361
1991 340, 386
1997 376, 387
2001 387
Torchy, Paul 67
Tours 64-66
Towns, William 321
Träger, Walter 228
Tremoulet, Jean 211
Tresilian, Stewart 139-140
Treue, Wilhelm 162
Treves, Scipione 70
Trevisan, Bruno 193-195, 198-19
Tripoli GP 193, 195, 197
Trossi, Count Carlo Felice 149
Tullius, Bob 316
Turin 195, 233
Turner, Stuart 271
Turnquist, Robert 127

Übelacker, Erich 154
Udet, Ernst 100-101
Ulster Tourist Trophy 233
Uhlenhaut, Rudolf 169, 202, 205, 327
US Aircraft Production Board 89

Vagilenti 70
Vallelunga 272
Valpreda 67
Van Acker, Charles 178-179
Van Ranst, Cornelius Willett 113, 115, 127
Vandervell, Tony 223, 267
Varzi, Achille 183, 197-198
Vermicino-Rocca di Papa hill climb 32

Versois, Odile 243
Vickers Aviation 56, 94
Villa, Leo 59-60, 75
Villa, Pancho 40
Villiers, Amherst 76
Vincent, Charles 33, 37-38, 115
Vincent, Col. Jesse Gurney 22, 25, 27, 30, 32-35, 38, 40-42, 62, 89, 113, 290
Vita, Enrico 357-358
Voelker, Charles 171, 176-179
Voisin, Charles 54
Voisin, Gabriel 54-55, 73, 143-145, 181-182, 397
Volpi, Count 242
von Brauchitsch, Manfred 203, 206
von Eberhorst, Robert Eberan 206-207, 234-235
von Falkenhausen, Alex 322, 327, 342
von Fersen, Olaf 335
von Karajan, Herbert 9
von Kuenheim, Eberhard 326
von Ringhoffer, Baron Hans 151
von Fersen, Hans-Heinrich 154, 157
von Schell Plan 155, 169
von Stauss, Emil Georg 163
von Zeppelin, Graf Ferdinand Adolf August Heinrich 158
Voorhies, Carl 121
Vosper 149

Wagner, Louis 67
Wagner, Max 101, 164
Wakefield, Sir Charles 105
Wakefield Trophy, Sir Charles 105
Waleran 142, 185
Walkinshaw, Tom 320-321, 355
Wall Street Crash 107, 117
Wall, W. Guy 42
Wallace, Bob 302, 304, 306
Walter, Josef 154
Warner, Harold 291
Watkins Glen 276, 371
Watney, Richard 138
Watson, John 321
Watson, William G. J. 'Willie' 139, 234-235
Webb, Louie 179
Weernik, Wim Oude 73
Weidely, George 45-46, 49
Weiffenbach, Charles 211, 214-215
Wellborn, Fred 117
Wente, Adolf 327-328
Werlin, Jakob 163, 203
Werner, William 158
Weslake, Harry 267, 271-272
Wharam, Jack 117
Wheeler, Frank H. 25
Whitaker, Nick 149
White, Derrick 265, 311
White, James M. 75, 92-93
Whitehead, Peter 186
Whitney, Dan 11, 412
Wilcock, F. Michael 217-218
Wilkinson, John 110
Willand, Jürgen 329
Willard Hotel, Washington 89
Williams, Frank 295

Williams, Peggy 211
Wilson, Kevin A. 381
Wimille, Pierre 197
Winkelmann, Otto 169
Wise, Karl M. 120-122, 127
Withalm, Gert 329, 335
Wolf, Werner 228
Wolfe, Maurice 48
Wolstenholme, Arthur 321
Woods, Frank Aubrey 267-270
Wright, Peter 339
Wyer, John 234-236, 271
Wyeth, Nathan 45

Yacco 183
Yamashita, Ryuichi 359
Yom Kippur War 317
Young, Eoin S. 105
Yugoslav GP 1939 206

Zandvoort 274
Zborowski, Count Louis Vorow 90-91
Zehender, Geoffredo 203
Zeller, Rolf 329
Zeppelin 158, 161-162, 169
Zerbi, Tranquillo 70
Zetsche, Dieter 381
Zima, Stefan 162

V12 Cars, engines and teams

Cars, coachbuilders and teams

AAR 270
Abarth 250
    T-140 250-252
Abbott 288
Acura 360
Adlards, George 288
Adler 163
AGS 356
Aixam-Mega 399
A:Level of Moscow 327
Alba-Tech 338
Alfa Corse 196-198
Alfa Romeo 9, 70, 172, 179, 197, 203, 206, 215, 220-222, 243, 300, 337, 360, 409
    P2 183
    P3 62
    Type A 184, 215
    Type B 184
    Type 177 278
    Type 179 278
    6C 1750 Gran Sport 183
    6C 2500 200
    8C 193-195
    8C 2900B Mille Miglia 198
    12C-36 194-195
    12C 193-194
    158 220, 229
    312 197, 220
    412 181
    412S 198
Allard
    Specials 288-289
    Tailwagger I 288
Amati 376

Ambassador 48
AMC 366
American LaFrance 122
AMG 333-335, 345, 380-381
    CLK-GTR 334-335
    CL65 380
Aquila-Italiana 67
Arfons Green Monster 220
Arrows 273, 358
ASA 300
Aston Martin 10, 234, 239, 260, 272, 376
    DB3S 235
    DB7 Vantage 260-261, 393, 395-396
    DB9 Vanquish 260, 396-397, 409
    DBR9 397
Atalanta 288, 307
ATB Type 650 227-229
ATS 300
Auburn 122-123, 125, 127
    Custom Brougham 171
    Model 12-160 123, 125, 171-172
    Speedster 125, 164, 171-172
Auburn Cord Duesenberg Corp 123
Audi 158, 348, 402-403
    Avus 386-387
    A8 348-349, 389-391
Austin Seven 321
Austin (Michigan) 48
Austro-Daimler 101
Auto Union 9, 101, 158, 179, 184, 197, 203, 205-206, 215, 227-228, 337, 386
    D-Type 206
    E-Type 215, 228
AWE 228

Ballot Indianapolis 58
Bean 100
Benetton 355, 369, 371
Benetton-Ford 355
Bentley 10, 138-139, 145, 348, 384, 391
    Continental GT 390-391
Bentley-Napier 80
Benz 34, 156, 202
    Blitzen Benz 22, 35, 101, 172
Bertone 306
Binder 148
Bizzarrini P538 307
Blue Bird 61, 76-77, 80, 91, 95, 99
BMC 311
BMS Scuderia Italia 369
BMW 158, 163, 228, 326, 342, 376, 381
    M3 344, 381, 409
    7-Series 327
    8-Series 327
    600 219
    750i 263, 325-326
    750iL 332
    850Csi 263
    850i 263
BMW Team Motorsport 335
Brabham 259, 272, 342, 359, 381
    BT34 272
    BT39 272

Brabham-Alfa 278
    BT48 278
Brabham-Maserati 283
Brabham-Weslake 272
Briggs 285
British Leyland 318
BRM 267-268, 270-271, 283, 310
    P160 272
    P351 273
Broadspeed 319
Brough 288
Brunn 119, 122
Bucciali TAV12 145
Bugatti 67, 139, 185, 213, 250, 399
    EB110 399-400
    EB110S 400
    EB112 400
    Royale 149
    Type 35A 144
    Type 37A 72
    Type 54 183-184
    Type 57 291
    Type 101 291
    Type 251 291
    Type 252 291
    Type 451 291
Buick 35, 37, 127
    D55 36, 82
Büssing 161

Cadillac 14, 77, 107, 110, 115, 117, 122, 307
    Cien 375-376
    Eldorado 293
    Escalade 376
Chaparral 249
Chapron 148
Charlesworth 288
Chevrolet 110, 326, 338
    Caprice 327
    Corvette C5 327
    Vega 323, 335
Chipstead Group 265
Chiribiri 12/16 72
Christie 34
Chrysler 37, 114, 363-364, 366, 391, 401
Citroën 145
Clement 18
Cooper 245, 265, 268, 283, 311
Cooper-Maserati 265-266, 277, 281
    T81 265
Cord 122, 125, 127
    E-1 122-123, 127
    L29 114, 122-123
    810 125
    812 125
Crossley 218
Cunningham 243, 391
    C-3 243
    C-6R 243

Daewoo 396
Daimler 13, 129, 156, 202
    Stahlradwagen 15, 81
Daimler-Benz (see also Mercedes-Benz) 100-102, 156-157, 162-164, 169, 203, 215, 333, 342, 376

Daimler (UK) 129, 376
    Dingo 217-218
    Double-Six 131, 218
    Double-Six (2001) 316, 376
DaimlerChrysler 163, 347, 379-381, 391
    ME Four-Twelve coupé 381, 391
Dallara 369-370
Datsun 283
De Dion Bouton 19
de Tomaso
    Deauville 294-295
    Pantera 294
Delage 9, 59, 62, 67, 70, 185, 210-211, 221, 243, 373
    DH 63-64, 75, 78
    2LCV 64-67
Delahaye 210, 213, 337
    145 181, 212-213, 215
    148 210-211
    155 181, 213-214
    165 213-215
Dietrich 122
DKW 158
Duesenberg 29, 49, 104-105, 117, 122, 127, 158, 172, 270
    Model J 122, 149

Eagle 270, 281
Edonis 400
EMW 228
ERA 62
Erdman & Rossi 162
EuroBrun GP team 339
Eyston
    Speed of the Wind 99-100
    Thunderbolt 80, 100, 102

Fernandez et Darrin 149
Ferrari 10, 221-222, 224, 249, 256, 277, 307, 361, 363, 365, 367, 400
    Enzo 350, 393, 403, 407, 409
    Scuderia Ferrari 183, 189, 196, 215, 220-221
    F50 369-370
    F333 SP 370-371
    125C 222
    125 F1 225
    125S 221-222
    166 243
    250 Europa 236
    250 Testa Rossa 238
    250GT Berlinetta 238-239, 300
    250GTO 239
    275GTB/4 296
    312B 10
    312F1-66 253
    312F1-67 254
    312P 254
    330GT 239
    330GTC 239
    340 Mexico 236
    365 California 295
    365GT 2+2 295
    365GTB/4 Daytona 297, 403
    365GTC 295
    365GTC/4 297-299
    365GTS 295

365GT4 BB 297
365P 296
375 America 236, 243
375MM 236
400 Superamerica 239, 300
410 Sport 236
412MI 237
456GT 404
512M 257
512P 256
512S 254, 256-257, 265, 409
550 Maranello 348, 405-406, 409
612 Scaglietti 348, 406-407
612P 192, 254, 256
639 368
640 368
Fiat 55, 59, 64, 66-67, 70, 73, 75, 155, 209, 243, 249, 252, 256, 367, 369, 409
501 33
520 'Superfiat' 53-54
806 70-73
Fisher Body 108
Flying Triangle Special 217-218
Footwork Arrows 344, 353-354
FA12 353
Footwork-Porsche 354
Ford 35, 83, 117, 119-120, 219, 249, 253, 260, 271-272, 285, 291, 294, 318-319, 321, 355
Fiesta Turbo 319
GT40 268
GT90 393-394
Indigo 259-260, 394, 396
Taurus 394
Franay 148, 215
Franklin 110, 112, 127
Airman 112
Series 17 112
Super Merrimac replica 127
Frontenac 113

General Motors 35, 107, 110, 117, 307, 322, 326, 337, 371
LeSabre 219
Gläser 157
GMC 219, 285
Golden Arrow 76-78, 96
Gräf & Stift 155
C12 155
SP8 155
Graham City of Salt Lake 220
Graham-Paige 171
Gulf Team Davidoff 335
Gulf-Wyer team 272
Guyson V12 321

H.A.L. Twelve 47
Haynes Light Twelve 48-49
HCM Special 125-127
Heine-Velox 48
Henri Chapron 215
Hispano-Suiza 9, 144, 149, 291
J12 88, 149, 379
H. J. Mulliner 143
Honda 304
Civic 283
RA271 246
RA272E 246

Honda Racing 281
Horch 155, 158, 163, 168, 206
600 156-157
670 86, 156-157
Hudson 14, 25, 33
Humber 19

Isotta Fraschini 225, 231
Isuzu 371
Como 340
Itala 67-70, 223, 231
Italdesign 327

Jackson 45
Jaguar 243, 272, 309, 311, 318, 321, 335, 355-356, 376, 399
E-Type Series Three 315-317, 335
Mark X (XJ5) 309-310
XJ-S 315, 318-320, 393
XJ6 309-311, 316
XJ6 saloon (XJ4) 335
XJ12 316-319, 326
XJ13 311, 335
XJ40 318
XJ81 318-319
XJ220 321, 393
XJR-S 319
XJR-5 264
XJR-6 320
XJR-8 320
XJR-9 320-321
XJR-9LM 264
XJR-12 264, 320
XJR-15 320-321
XK120 309
Jensen 289
H-Type 289, 307
Jordan 259, 359
192 359
J. W. Automotive 271-272

Kellner 149
Kimmel Special 176-177, 179
Kissel 48
Kumpera 155

Lagonda 138, 185, 215, 234, 236, 243, 289
Le Mans 178-179
Rapide 88, 141-142
Lamborghini 10, 296, 299-300, 302-304, 307, 363, 400-401
Cheetah 400
Diablo SE/VT 401-402
Diablo GT/GTR 351, 402
Islero S 306
Lambo 291 365
LM004 401
LP400 Countach 306-307, 400-402
Miura 304, 306-307
Miura S/SV 306
Murciélago 351-352, 403, 409
Quattrovalvole 307, 400
Quattrovalvole Evoluzione 307
350GT 303-304
350GTV 303
400GT 304

Lancefield 143
Lancia 53, 55, 196, 240, 369
Aurelia 291
Laraki Fulgura 345
Larrousse Calmels team 364-365
LC89 Lola 365
LaSalle 287
LeBaron 112, 118, 122, 127
Letourneur 148
Leyland 90, 218
Eight 90
Leyland-Thomas 171
Ligier 365, 391
Ligier-Matra 277
Ligier-Talbot 277-278
Lincoln 83, 117, 119-120, 290
Continental 190, 287, 290, 307
KA 119
KB 83, 117-118
Series L V8 117
Sunshine Special 119
Zephyr 119, 127, 285-287, 290
05L 119
Lister Storm 320
Lola 281, 342, 363-364, 397-398
T70 250, 252
T90 365
T91/50 340
Lorraine/Lorraine-Dietrich 51, 55, 145
Lotus 270, 371
Lotus-Ford 266
Lotus Team 339-340, 364-365
102 365
102B 339
102C 339
Lozier 47
Lynx Engineering 272, 321
D-Type Jaguar replica 272
Lytle
Big Al II 219
Grinder Griper III 220
Quad Al 219

MAB-Liberty 93
March 363
Marion 25
Marmon 107
Model D 127
Sixteen 125
Maserati 10, 224, 247, 304, 307, 335, 409
MC12 350, 408-409
V4 183
4CLT/48 233
63/64 242-243, 265
250F 233, 240
250F T2 242
250P 239
250TR 239
350S 242
450S 189, 240
Matra 277
MS11 274
MS120 276
MS660 277
Matra-Ford 274
Matra Simca 670B 276

Maybach 162, 169, 376, 378, 380, 383
Zeppelin 149, 158, 161-163, 380
12 158-160
Mazda 376
MCA Centenaire 399
McLaren 268, 327, 338, 366-367, 369, 371, 381
F1 262, 381-382
F1 LM 382
F1-GTR 335
McLaren-Chevrolet 192, 256
McLaren-Honda 360-363, 371
MP4/6 361
MP4/7A 363
Mercedes-Benz (see also Daimler-Benz) 9-10, 25, 73, 90, 101, 156, 163, 179, 184, 197, 203, 205, 215, 337, 360, 376, 383
CL coupé 378
C112 332-333
C291 342
Nürburg 163
R129 332
S-Class 328, 331-333, 376-378, 380
SSK 200
W07 163
W07 Grosser 163
W24 226
W25 200-201
W125 202
W140 332
W147 164
W148 600V 167
W150 Grosser 163, 168
W154 179, 213, 215, 226
W157 167-168
W165 208, 226
W195 226-227
300/300S/300SL 169
300SE 333
500 327-328
500K 164
540K 163-164, 167-168
560SEL 329
600 (W100) 327-328
600K 168
600SE 332-333
600SEL 332-333
600SL 332
600V 168
750 327
1901 13
1914 GP 49
Mercedes-Benz Rennabteilung 202
Mercury Sable 394
Meyer 48
Michelotto 371
MiG Centenaire 399
Miller 25, 29, 49, 113, 177
Golden Submarine 31
Miller-Voelker 179
Million-Guiet 148
Minardi 369
Mirage 271
M6 272
Mormon Meteor III 104-105
Moss Thunderbolt 218-219

Napier 14, 25, 134
Napier Mark XIA 78
Napier-Railton 78-80, 85, 100, 220
Napier-Sunbeam 80
Nazca 327
Neri & Bonacini 300
NISMO 341-342
    R93CP 342
Nissan 258, 283
    R381 283
    R382 282-283
    R831 258
Nordyke & Marmon 125
Norma-MGN 356
Norwood Autocraft 373

Oldsmobile Toronado 293
Opel 337
OSCA 231, 243, 409
    Type G 217
OSCA-Maserati 233
Osella 278
Osella-Alfa 278

Packard 9, 22-23, 25, 27, 108, 110,
    113-114, 117, 127, 221, 243,
    290-291, 374, 391
    'M&V' 114-115
    Twelve/Twin Six 115-116
    Twin Six 22-23, 27, 30, 33, 35,
    40-41, 43, 115
    Twin Six Typhoon 42
    120 116, 287
    299 30-33, 42, 49, 62, 84, 113,
    220, 243
    905 33-35, 42, 59-60, 62, 75, 113
    1005 83
Pagani Zonda 333, 335, 354
Panhard 15, 19
Panhard & Levassor 81
Parradine Pegasus V12 321
Pathfinder 45
    Cloverleaf 47
    La Salle 47
Peerless 45
Pegaso 300
Peugeot 15, 252, 391
    905 391
    907 390-391
Pierce 119
    Great Arrow 119
Pierce-Arrow 48, 104-105, 107,
    119, 120-121, 129
    Ab Jenkins Special (Pierce 12
    Special) 173-174, 179
Pininfarina 295-296, 298-299, 370
Pontiac 219
    Tempest 307
Porsche 215, 257, 264, 353, 396
    Carrera GT 409
    Turbo 403
    Type 80 101-104
    Type 114 F-Wagen 371
    908 254
    917 10, 265
    928 323
    962 339
Premier 45, 49
Prodrive 376, 397

PSA Peugeot-Citroën 391
Pullman 168

Railton 321
Railton Special 102, 104, 174
Renault 252, 337, 361, 365
Reynard 338, 359, 394-395
Rolls-Royce 55, 138, 289, 384, 391
    Phantom 191, 384
    Phantom II 134, 373
    Phantom III 9, 135, 391
Rollston 122
Ronart W152 321
Rootes Group 391
Rosche/BMW team 371
Rubery Owen 267-268, 273

Saoutchik 145, 149
Sauber 333, 342
Sauber-Mercedes 264
Schebler 25, 45
Seagrave 122
Serenissima 243
Shadow 277
Simca 231-232, 391
Sindelfingen 167
Singer (New York) 178-179
    Series 20 48
Smith
    Anzac 77-78
    Fred H. Stewart Enterprise 78
Sodomka 153, 155
Spohn 162
Spyker 158
Stearns 127
Steyr 151, 208
Stoewer 156
Studebaker 120-122, 127, 174,
    183
Stutz Black Hawk 60
Sunbeam 9, 23, 25, 29, 60-61, 76,
    78, 95
    Silver Bullet 96-98
    Talbot 61, 63
    Tiger 61-62, 73, 80
    Tigress 61-62, 80, 85
    Toodles IV 20
    Toodles V 19-23, 55-58, 75, 96
    25/30 20
    350hp 57-60, 73, 75-76
    1,000hp 95
Sunbeam-Talbot-Darracq 105, 391
Swandean Flying Saucer 217
Swandean Spitfire Special 217-218

Talbot 21, 229, 391
Tatra 151
    T11 151
    T70 151, 154
    T80 151-154, 156
Thomas Special 'Babs' 90-92, 105
Thomson & Taylor 62, 64, 77-78,
    80, 99, 132
Tom Walkinshaw Racing (TWR)
    264, 319-321, 335, 355, 399
Touring 198, 303
Toyota 258, 283
    Century 376
    2000GT 359

TVR 397
    Cerbera 397
    Speed Twelve (Project 12/7)
    397
Tyrrell-Ford 270

Vandervell 230
    Thinwall Special 267
Vanwall 321
Vauxhall 129
    30/98 217
Venturi 365
Vickers 76, 354
Vignale 198
Voisin 55, 173, 215
    M1/C1 54
    C2 54-55
    C12 181-182
    C16 143, 215
    C18 Diane 143-145, 183
    C19 143-144
    C20 Simoun 143-145
    C21 Mistral 143-145
    C22 143
    V12L 145
Volga M21 327
Volkswagen 348, 384, 391, 402
    Corrado 385
    Golf 384, 387
    Microbus 219
    Passat 387
    Phaeton 387-390
    Sport W12 Touareg 390
    Touareg 390

Weidely 45
White 220
White Triplex ('The Spirit of
    Elkdom') 75, 92-93, 105
Whittingham and Mitchell 289
Williams 344, 354, 360, 368-369,
    371
    V12 LM/LMR 383
Williams-Renault 354
Willys Overland 35
Wolfe Meteor 48

Xedos 376
Xenia 149

Yamaha OX99-11 259-360
Ypsilon Technology 359-360

Zagato 249
Zakspeed 359
Zborowski
    Chitty-Bang-Bangs 90
    Higham Special 90

Engines and engine builders
AAR Eagle V12 9, 271, 283
Abarth 302
    Type 240 V12 250-251, 253,
    279, 339, 344
ABC Motors
    Dragonfly 18-19
    V12 18
Aeromarine 243

Alfa Romeo 401
    A 183-184
    B 193
    S10 V12 198-200
    S10 SS V12 200
    S11 V8 198, 200
    V8 278
    V12 193-198, 212, 223, 278
    two-stroke diesel 223
    158 197, 208, 221, 225
    1260 278
Allison V12 104, 179, 219-220
Antoinette 15, 17
    V8 14
    V16 14
    V24 14
Argus 156
Aston Martin 140
    Project DP1080 V12 272
    V8 272
    V12 393, 395-397
ATB Type 650 V12 228
Auburn
    straight-eight 125
    V12 30, 123-125, 153
Auburn Cord Duesenberg
    V12 108, 122
    V16 108, 122
Audi V12 384
Austin (Michigan) V12 48
Austro-Daimler V12
Auto Union
    D-Type V12 206-208
    E-Type V12 208
    V12 181, 195, 234-235
    V16 206
Autodelta 278, 338
    flat-12 278
    V12 278
Autostar 399
Ballot straight-eight 64
Batten
    in-line four 373
    in-line six 373
    Max-12 V12 373
Bentley 141
    W12 390
Benz 51
    six-cyl 90
BMW 169, 283
    M06 six-cyl 321-322
    M20 six-cyl 322-323
    M26 six-cyl 324
    M33 V12 309, 322, 325
    M40 four-cyl 325
    M50 six-cyl 381
    M60 six-cyl 322
    M66 V12 322, 325, 32-329
    M70 V12 263, 323-327, 381
    M72 327
    M73 V12 326-327, 384
    N62 V8 383
    N73 V12 383-384
    P74 V12 382-383
    P75 V12 383
    S50 381
    S70/2 V12 381-382
    S70/3 V12 262-263, 382
    Type VI V12 321

V6 329
V12 191, 262, 307, 321, 323, 329, 331, 335, 342-344
328 six-cyl 164
Brabus 345
BRM 269, 273-274, 283
H16 267
P101 V12 267-268
P142 V12 268
V8 267-268, 273
V12 9, 271
V16 221
Bugatti 27
straight-eight 64
Type 41 149
V12 27, 250, 291,393, 399-400
Buick 35-36, 342
V6 37
V8 113, 293
V12 36-37, 49, 89, 105, 286

Cadillac 14, 114, 134
Series 370 V12 110
V-Future V12 191, 291-293, 375
V8 14, 108, 110, 292-293
V12 89, 107-110, 123, 127, 154, 191, 210, 291, 293
V16 107-108, 116, 119, 122, 127, 137
Charron 62
Chevrolet 256, 286
V8 45, 283, 373
Chrysler 169
Firepower 'Hemi' V8 164, 166, 169
V8 75, 243, 374
Continental 42
Type AV-1790-5B V12 373
Cosworth 264, 271-272, 275, 295, 320, 335, 354-355, 375
DFV V8 272, 341, 354-356, 359
SCA 283, 312
V8 274, 355, 363, 365
V10 355
V12 355, 395
Coventry Climax 265, 310, 312, 315, 335
CFA 312
W12 Trident 355-356
Craig-Dörwald V12 17, 279
Curtiss 105
Conqueror V12 104-105, 174
D-12 V12 104

Daimler 149
V2 15
V12 55
Daimler-Benz (see also Mercedes-Benz) 100, 158, 167, 200-201
Daimler (UK) 143
Double-Six 130-134, 149
straight-eight 130
six-cyl 129
V8 130
V12 129, 157
25/85 130
de Tomaso 29

Type 102 V12 295
Type 105 V12 294
Delage 73
DH V12 63-64, 73, 149
eight-cyl two-stroke 64
V12 62-67, 84, 181, 210, 212, 391
2LCV 64-66
Delahaye 373
V12 211-214, 231, 391
Delaunay-Belleville 51
V12 51
W24 51
Ducati 358
Duesenberg 27, 115-116
SJ 149
straight-eight 29-30, 64-65, 127, 174
V12 28, 30, 51, 75, 174

Enger V12 44-46, 49
ERA six-cyl 221

Falconer V12 374
Ferrari 197
Dino V6 283
F1-67 V12 254
F101 V12 298-300
F110A V12 299, 403
F116/F116A/F116B V12 403-405, 407
F130B V12 369-371
F133/F133A V12 348, 405-407
F140 V12 350, 393, 407-409
flat-12 249, 367
GP49 V12 225, 229
in-line six 236
P3C W3 356-358
V6 250, 253, 300, 366
V10 371, 407
V12 9, 84, 186, 188, 190, 222, 224-225, 229-231, 234-236, 243, 253, 299, 306, 365-366, 393, 402
035 V12 367
036 (035/5) V12 368
037 368
039 V12 367, 369
040 V12 369
044 V12 371
126 V12 2236
125C V12 240
166 V12 224
226 V12 296
209 V12 239
212 V12 238
243 V12 297
245 V12 295-296
250MM V12 238
250P V12 300
250TR V12 239
251 V12 297
261 V12 192, 254-255
261C 254-257
275F1 230
275GTB V12 303
290MM V12 236-237
312B flat-12 254, 365-366
312S V12 237

315S V12 237-238
330P V12 249
330P2 V12 249
330P3 V12 249, 253
330P4 V12 249
335S V12 237
365 flat-12 297
375F1 V12 230
512 F1 flat-12 283
512M V12 265
Ferro
V8 45
V12 45
Fiat 193, 293
A-12bis six-cyl 75
A-14 V12 53
A-15-R V12 53
Dino V6 283
straight-eight 70
V12 53-54, 136
43 V12 53
120 V12 53
406 U12 70-73
Ford 13, 73, 89, 271, 289, 307, 359
Duratec V6 259, 394, 396
Duratec V12 394
four-cyl 283
V8 149, 190, 249, 268, 286-289, 307, 355, 393
V12 259-260, 393-394
Ford-Cosworth V8 268, 271
HB V8 366
Franklin 110, 113
V12 110-113, 123, 127, 307

Galloway-Atlantic 75
Gasmobile 13
General Motors 108-109, 114, 191, 375
Vortec straight-six 373
V8 86, 156, 290
V12 110
V16 110
XV-12 V12 375-376
GMC Truck and Coach
Twin Six V12 291
V6 285, 291
V12 285, 291
Gnôme-Rhône 62
Gordini 187
Gräf & Stift
straight-eight 155
V12 155
Gurney-Weslake 268
Type 56 V12 269-270, 279

Hall-Scott V12 75
A8 V12 89
Hanomag 169
Harding V12 45
Hart V10 359, 371
Haynes V12 48-49
Hispano-Suiza 145, 149
H6 6-cyl 51, 145
K6 in-line six 149
Type 68 J12 V12 146-149
Type 68-bis 149, 379
V8 51, 57, 67

V12 88, 146, 158-159, 391
HKS 300E V12 340-341
Honda 249-250, 283, 367
K005 V2 247
RA121E V12 361
RA122E/B V12 361-363
RA270E V12 247
RA271E 248, 279-280
RA273E V12 279-281
RA300 281
RA301E 281-282
V6 360
V8 283
V10 344, 353-354, 361, 363, 368
V12 10, 243, 246, 278, 283, 339, 344, 360, 366
Horch
straight-eight 155
V8 157
V12 86, 151, 156-157-158, 164, 169
Hudson 37-38, 288
V8 37
V12 37-38

Ilmor V8 338
Itala
V12 67-69, 114, 157, 209, 240
11/15 V12 67, 70
Isuzu Sport V12 339-340

Jaguar 140, 235
AJ6 in-line six 315, 318
single-cyl 312
V6 321, 376, 393
V8 316, 321, 376
V12 264, 309-310, 312, 316-317, 319-321, 333, 376
XJ25 V12 312-315, 317
XK six-cyl 309
JHS Engines 272-273
BRM 290 V12 273
Judd
V8 339, 358, 365
V10 359

Lago V16 210
Lagonda
DP100 V12 234-236
in-line six 234
V12 88, 129, 138-143, 149, 181, 185, 234-235, 271, 311
Lamb V12 17
Lamborghini
V12 300-302, 304, 306-307, 351-352, 364-366, 393, 401-403
3512 V12 363-366, 371
Lancia 51, 54, 73, 384, 391
V12 51-52, 108, 385
LaSalle 286
Levavasseur 'Antionette'
V32 14
V48 14
Leyland V12 90
Liberty V12 16, 34, 75, 89-91, 93-94, 113, 117, 129

Life F35 W12 10, 356-358, 371
Lincoln
  H V12 190, 286-287, 289, 307
  KA V12 118-119, 286-287
  KB V12 1117-119
  V8 119, 290
  V12 89-90, 108, 117-119, 285-286, 288-291, 307
  Zephyr V12 286-288
Lola V12 397-398
Lorraine-Dietrich/Lorraine 51, 145
  V12 51
  W12 73
Lotus-Ford 310
Lycoming 105, 122, 125, 127
  BA V12 122
  BB V12 123-124
  straight-eight 122
  V12 122, 126, 171
  V16 122, 126

MAN 163, 376
MAP 215
Marmon
  straight-six 125
  V4 25
  V6 25, 125
  V8 25, 125
  V12 125, 127
  V16 107, 122, 125-126
Maserati 302
  four-cyl 221
  V12 9, 239-243, 248, 268, 283, 301, 311, 393
  V16 183
  8 V12 245-246
  9 V12 245, 265-267
  10 V12 266-267
  250F six-cyl 241
  250F T2 V12 240-242
Matra 274
  MS9 V12 273-275, 279
  MS12 V12 274-276
  MS72 V12 277
  MS73 V12 277
  MS76 V12 277
  MS81 V12 277
  V12 9, 273-278, 391
Maybach 158
  DS7 V12 161
  DS8 V12 161
  DSO-8 161
  six-cyl 90, 160
  Type 12 V12 346-347
  V12 149, 158-160, 164, 167, 169, 210
Mazda V12 376
Meadows 6-cyl 138
Melling 397-399
Mercedes-Benz (see also Daimler-Benz) 55, 169
  B-series V8 200
  DAB V12 200-203, 215
  DB600 V12 100
  DB601 V12 100-101, 103
  DB603 V3 V12 102-104
  K-series V12 205
  KOMO V12 329

M25AB 200
M101 V12 327-328
M104 in-line six 330-331
M111 four-cyl 335
M117 V8 328-329
M119 V8 329
M120 V12 329-335, 345, 377-378
M137 V12 345-346, 377-379
M147 V8 164
M148 V12 164, 166-169
M154 V12 181, 204-206, 226
M159 in-line six 169
M163 V12 205, 226
M173 V12 168-169, 327
M186 in-line six 169
M195 226-227
M195 V12 371
M275 V12 380-381
M285 (Maybach Type 12) V12 347, 379-380
Nürburg 8-cyl 168
S600 V12 384
six-cyl 90, 169
straight-eight 163-164
V6 376
V8 164, 208, 226, 376
V12 33, 104, 160, 164, 181, 195, 200, 205, 226, 327-329, 335, 376, 399
Mercury 243
Miller 105
  straight-eight 174
  V12 16, 28-30, 51, 124, 177, 179
Mitsubishi V12 391
Moteur Moderne 252, 274
  V6 252
  V12 252-253, 338
Moteurs Guy Negré MGN W12 356-357
Motori Moderni 399
  V12 399

Napier 13, 91, 93-95, 127
  Lion W12 10, 60, 75-80, 85, 96, 129, 149, 355-356
  V12 75
Nash 289
National 13, 42
  AK Series 43
  Highway Twelve 43
  V12 42-43, 111
Neotech V12 338-339, 344
Nissan 283
  P35 V12 342
  VRT35 V12 340-342
  V8 341
  V12 258, 282-283
Nordyke-Marmon V12 89

Oakland V8 156
Offenhauser 105, 174
  four-cyl 243
Oldsmobile Viking V8 156
Opel GMXV-12 V12 375
Orleans V12 17

OSCA 231, 234
  Type G V12 187-188, 231-233, 356

Packard 35, 51, 89, 409
  straight-eight 290
  V12 22, 27, 30-31, 33, 38-41, 49, 53, 75, 90, 114-116, 119, 127, 130, 153, 157, 307, 374
Panhard 62
  V12 17, 75
Peerless V16 127
Peugeot 62, 366
  V10 366
Pierce-Arrow
  six-cyl 119
  straight-eight 119
  V12 107, 116, 119-122, 127, 149, 167, 172-173, 179
Pipe 164
Pontiac 286
  six-cyl 307
  V8 45
Porsche 338
  V6 243, 371
  V10 371, 409
  3512 V12 337, 344, 353-354, 371
PSA Peugeot-Citroën Talbot V12 391

Reggiane-Caproni 225
Renault 13
  EF60 V12 354
  V6 366
  V8 18
  V10 344, 353-354, 368
  V12 18-19, 75, 354
Rolland-Pilain straight-eight 64
Rolls-Royce 136, 141, 149, 307
  Eagle 77-78
  H-type Buzzard V12 98
  Kestrel V12 99-100, 217-218, 243
  Merlin V12 90, 135, 218-219, 373
  Meteor V12 90, 218
  Phantom PIII V12 86-87, 135-139, 148, 200, 232
  R-type V12 98-100
  six-cyl 134
  V12 17, 33, 60, 75, 79-80, 134-137, 143
  20/25 six-cyl 135
Romanelli V12 293-294
Rover 283
  V8 318
Royal Aircraft Factory V12 18

Salmson 62, 73
Sauda Cappa 18 V12 67
SCAP 62
Schebler V12 25, 38
Spyker 13
Standard 140
Stevens-Duryea 13
Stutz 113
Subaru 338
Sunbeam 13, 19-20, 51, 73, 96

Arab V8 56-57, 75
Cossack V12 94
Gurkha V12 22
Manitou V12 56, 96
Maori 129
Matabele V12 94
Mohawk V12 19, 21-22, 25, 30, 56, 73, 75
Sikh III V12 94
V8 19-20
V12 20, 23, 38, 62, 67, 75, 85, 91, 94, 209

TAG 371
Talbot (France)
  T150 six-cyl 164
  V12 208-209
Talbot (UK) 164
Talbot-Lago V12 231
Tatra
  in-line six 151
  V8 127
  V12 151-153, 167
Toyota
  1GZ-FE V12 376
  V8 283
  V10 358
  V12 358
TVR 393, 397
  AJP6 397
  V8 397
  V12 397

Voelker V12 176, 178-179
Voisin 54
  in-line 12 145
  six-cyl 144
  V12 55, 143-144, 156, 160, 182, 391
Volkswagen 384, 388
  ICV12 V12 385
  VR4 V4 387
  VR5 385
  VR6 V6 385-387
  V6 349, 385
  V8 391
  W12 10, 348-349, 373, 385-391

Walter 154
  Lord 169
  Regent 169
  Royal 154-155, 158
  six-cyl 154
Weidely 45, 48
  V12 45-47
Weslake 267-269, 272, 281, 283
  WRP-190 V12 271-272
Willys 286

Yamaha 358
  OX66 V6 359
  OX77 V6 359
  OX88 V8 359
  OX99 V12 359-360
  V10 359
  V12 259

Zytek 320

Robert.J.Roux